VOLUME **I** TO 1877

AMERICAN
PASSAGES

A HISTORY OF THE UNITED STATES

CANADA

MINNESOTA

Lake Superior

MICHIGAN

Lake Michigan

Lake Huron

WISCONSIN

St. Paul

IOWA

Des Moines

MICHIGAN

Lansing

Madison

Detroit

Dearborn

Flint

Des Plaines

Chicago

Haymarket Square

Tippecanoe

Greenville

Indianapolis

INDIANA

Springfield

ILLINOIS

Westminster College

Alton

St. Louis

Jefferson City

East St. Louis

MISSOURI

White River

Memphis

ARKANSAS

Little Rock

Hope

Shiloh

Scottsboro

MISSISSIPPI

Jackson State University

Jackson

Selma

Montgomery

ALABAMA

Dayton

Mobile

Baton Rouge

New Orleans

LOUISIANA

Pensacola

GEORGIA

Tallahassee

St. Augustine

Cape Canaveral

FLORIDA

Gulf of Mexico

BAHAMAS

Lake Erie

Cleveland

Kent State University

Canton

Gnadenhutten

Columbus

OHIO

Dayton

Frankfort

KENTUCKY

WEST VIRGINIA

Charleston

NORTH CAROLINA

Nashville

TENNESSEE

Raleigh

SOUTH CAROLINA

Columbia

Charleston

Stono

Port Royal

Atlanta

PENNSYLVANIA

Homestead

Pittsburgh

Harrisburg

Harpers Ferry

MARYLAND

Washington, D.C.

VIRGINIA

Richmond

Norfolk

Jamestown

Roanoke Island

Appomattox

Annapolis

DELAWARE

Dover

Three-Mile Island

NEW JERSEY

Philadelphia

Trenton

Princeton

Grovers Mill

Bethlehem

Statue of Liberty

Levittown

New York

Oyster Bay

Newburgh

Hyde Park

Hartford

CONNECTICUT

RHODE ISLAND

Woodstock

NEW YORK

Buffalo

Rochester

Lake Ontario

Seneca Falls

Saratoga

Albany

Brook Farm

MASSACHUSETTS

Lawrence

Lowell

Lexington

Salem

Boston

Plymouth

Pawtucket

NEW HAMPSHIRE

VERMONT

MAINE

ATLANTIC OCEAN

0   150   300 miles

0   150   300 kilometers

■ Important places in American Passages

Vancouver
Island

Strait of Juan de Fuca

Cape
Flattery

Columbia

CASCADE RANGE

COASTAL RANGES

Columbia

Snake

Columbia
Plateau

Sacramento

Central
Valley

SIERRA NEVADA

San Joaquin

Pt. Reyes
San Francisco
Bay

Monterey
Bay

Pt. Conception

Channel
Islands

PACIFIC
OCEAN

GREAT

BASIN

Salmon

Snake

Snake

Snake River Plain

BITTERROOT RANGE

ROCKY

Great
Salt
Lake

Great
Salt
Lake
Desert

Mojave Desert

Colorado

Sonoran

Desert

Gila

Colorado

Missouri

Yellowstone

Little Missouri

Badlands

Black
Hills

GREAT

Great Divide
Basin

MOUNTAINS

Colorado
Plateau

Colorado

Rio Grande

N. Platte

S. Platte

Platte

PLAINS

James

Missouri

Arkansas

Canadian

Llano

Estacado

Red

Pecos

Edwards
Plateau

Brazos

Colorado

Rio Grande

Nueces

MEXICO

Chukchi
Sea

ARCTIC OCEAN

NORTH SLOPE

RUSSIA

Brooks Range

Seward
Peninsula

Yukon

St.
Lawrence
Island

Yukon

Nunivak
Island

Alaska Range

Chugach Mtns.

Mackenzie

CANADA

Bering
Sea

Alaska
Peninsula

Kodiak
Island

Gulf of Alaska

Aleutian
Islands

Queen
Charlotte
Islands

Kauai
Kauai
Channel

Niihau

Oahu

Kaiwi Channel

Molokai

Lanai

Maui

Alenuihaha Channel

PACIFIC
OCEAN

Hawaii

HARCOURT BRACE

soon to become

Harcourt
College Publishers

A Harcourt Higher Learning Company

Soon you will find Harcourt Brace's distinguished innovation, leadership, and support under a different name . . . a new brand that continues our unsurpassed quality, service, and commitment to education.

We are combining the strengths of our college imprints into one worldwide brand: Harcourt Our mission is to make learning accessible to anyone, anywhere, anytime—reinforcing our commitment to lifelong learning.

We'll soon be Harcourt College Publishers. Ask for us by name.

One Company
"Where Learning Comes to Life."

VOLUME **I** TO 1877

AMERICAN
PASSAGES

A HISTORY OF THE UNITED STATES

EDWARD L. AYERS

University of Virginia

LEWIS L. GOULD

University of Texas at Austin

DAVID M. OSHINSKY

Rutgers University

JEAN R. SODERLUND

Lehigh University

HARCOURT COLLEGE PUBLISHERS

Fort Worth   Philadelphia   San Diego   New York   Orlando   Austin   San Antonio
Toronto   Montreal   London   Sydney   Tokyo

Publisher	Earl McPeek
Executive Editor	David Tatom
Market Strategist	Steve Drummond
Project Editor	Laura J. Hanna
Art Director	Linda Beaupré
Production Manager	Diane Gray

Cover image: Winslow Homer, *The Veteran in a New Field.* The Metropolitan Museum of Art, Bequest of Miss Adelaide Milton de Groot (1876–1967), 1967. (67.187.131) Photograph © 1995 The Metropolitan Museum of Art.

ISBN: 0-03-072573-9

Library of Congress Catalog Card Number: 99-65153

Address for Domestic Orders
Harcourt, Inc., 6277 Sea Harbor Drive, Orlando, FL 32887-6777
800-782-4479

Address for International Orders
International Customer Service
Harcourt, Inc., 6277 Sea Harbor Drive, Orlando, FL 32887-6777
407-345-3800
(fax) 407-345-4060
(e-mail) hbintl@harcourtcollege.com

Address for Editorial Correspondence
Harcourt College Publishers, 301 Commerce Street, Suite 3700, Fort Worth, TX 76102

Web Site Address
http://www.harcourtcollege.com

Harcourt College Publishers will provide complimentary supplements or supplement packages to those adopters qualified under our adoption policy. Please contact your sales representative to learn how you qualify. If as an adopter or potential user you receive supplements you do not need, please return them to your sales representative or send them to: Attn: Returns Department, Troy Warehouse, 465 South Lincoln Drive, Troy, MO 63379.

Printed in the United States of America

9 0 1 2 3 4 5 6 7 8 048   9 8 7 6 5 4 3 2 1

Harcourt College Publishers

ABOUT THE AUTHORS

 EDWARD L. AYERS   Edward Ayers is the Hugh P. Kelly Professor of History at the University of Virginia. He was educated at the University of Tennessee and Yale University, where he received his Ph.D. in American Studies. He has written and edited five books. *The Promise of the New South: Life After Reconstruction* (1992) won prizes for the best book on the history of American race relations and on the history of the American South. It was a finalist for both the National Book Award and the Pulitzer Prize. He is the co-editor of *The Oxford Book of the American South* (1997) and *All Over the Map: Rethinking American Regions* (1996). Ayers has won a number of teaching awards, including the Outstanding Faculty Award from the State Council of Higher Education and the Distinguished Young Teacher Award from the Alumni Board of Trustees.

Ayers' current work is "The Valley of the Shadow: Two Communities in the American Civil War." The World Wide Web version of the project has been ranked as one of the top forty education sites in the world by the *Encyclopedia Britannica* and named as the best Civil War site by Yahoo! Ayers is Executive Director of the Center for Digital History, an institute at the University of Virginia dedicated to crafting and teaching history in new media. Ayers is the author of Chapters 9–15.

 LEWIS L. GOULD   Lewis Gould is the Eugene C. Barker Centennial Professor Emeritus at the University of Texas at Austin. After receiving his Ph.D. from Yale University, he began a teaching career in which he had more than ten thousand students. He was recognized for outstanding undergraduate teaching in large lecture sections of the American History survey and for his excellent graduate teaching. He remains active in teaching correspondence and distance learning courses at The University of Texas at Austin in Texas History, Women's History, and American Diplomatic History.

Gould is a nationally recognized authority on First Ladies and the presidency. His comments have appeared in numerous press accounts about presidential wives, including *The New York Times, The Washington Post,* and *The Los Angeles Times.* He has appeared on C-Span, The CBS Morning News, Nightline, the ABC Evening News, and a large number of nationally syndicated radio programs. He also participated in the PBS program on Lyndon Johnson and the A&E biography of Lady Bird Johnson. Among his important publications are *American First Ladies: Their Lives and Their Legacy* (1996); *1968: The Election That Changed America* (1993); *The Presidency of Theodore Roosevelt* (1991); *Lady Bird Johnson and the Environment* (1988); and *The Presidency of William McKinley* (1980). Gould is the author of Chapters 16–24, 31, and 32.

 DAVID M. OSHINSKY   David Oshinsky received his undergraduate degree from Cornell University and his doctorate from Brandeis. He has taught history for the past 26 years at Rutgers University, where he holds the Board of Governors Chair and is presently chairman of the History Department. Oshinsky is the author of four books, including *A Conspiracy So Immense: The World of Joe McCarthy* (1983), which was voted one of the year's "best books" by the "New York Sunday Times Book Review," and won the Hardeman Prize for the best work about the U.S. Congress. His latest book, *"Worse than Slavery": Parchman Farm and the Ordeal of Jim Crow Justice* (1996), won both the Robert Kennedy Book Award for the year's most distinguished contribution to the field of human rights, and the American Bar Association's Scribes Award for distinguished legal writing.

Oshinsky is a regular contributor to scholarly journals, to the "Washington Post Book World," "New York Sunday Times Book Review," "New York Times Op-Ed Page," and "New York Times Sunday Magazine." He has been awarded a senior fellowship by the National Endowment for the Humanities and will spend 1999–2000 as a Phi Beta Kappa Visiting Scholar. Oshinsky is the author of Chapters 25–30.

 JEAN R. SODERLUND   Jean Soderlund is Professor and Chair of the Department of History at Lehigh University and Co-Director of the Lawrence Henry Gipson Institute for Eighteenth-Century Studies. She received her Ph.D. from Temple University and was a post-doctoral fellow at the Philadelphia Center for Early American Studies at the University of Pennsylvania. Her book, *Quakers and Slavery: A Divided Spirit,* won the Alfred E. Driscoll Publication Prize of the New Jersey Historical Commission. Soderlund was an editor of three volumes of the Papers of William Penn (1981–1983) and co-authored *Freedom by Degrees: Emancipation in Pennsylvania and Its Aftermath* (1991).

She has written articles and chapters in books on the history of women, African Americans, Native Americans, Quakers, and the development of abolition in the British North American colonies and early United States. She is currently working on a study of race and cultural identity in early New Jersey and Pennsylvania. She is a council member of the Philadelphia Center for Early American Studies, the Pennsylvania Historical Association, and the David Library of the American Revolution, and served as a committee chair for the American Historical Association. Soderlund is the author of Chapters 1–8.

IT'S ABOUT TIME

Everyone who writes about history faces the same problem: how do we get the past to stay still long enough to see it clearly? Textbooks on the history of the United States typically pursue one topic at a time. They devote chapters to a particular part of the country, such as the slave South or the Old West, or focus on broad topics such as immigration, urbanization, or industrialization. They place certain groups or individuals in special boxes or on specially colored pages. They set aside politics or diplomacy for long periods while they describe social or cultural life. Such ways of organizing textbooks have obvious costs—loss of continuity, context, and narrative force—but these strategies have seemed necessary bargains with the complexity of the past.

This book follows a different strategy. Rather than isolating people and topics it integrates them into the flow of time. Rather than sorting topics into tidily organized chapters, we show the complicated and subtle ways that strands of history interact. Each chapter is devoted to a particular sequence of years, carefully following the contours of events, weaving politics, economics, and culture into an interrelated pattern. As a result, foreign policy and domestic life connect and influence one another. The history of blacks and whites, men and women, emerge as parts of the same stories. Authors and artists speak of their particular times. Political battles continually punctuate the story. Depressions and panics disrupt the lives of people in every class. Technological innovations do not merely happen but emerge as solutions to felt problems.

Students who read *American Passages* come to understand that history is often about the unexpected. No one, after all, could have predicted figures such as Thomas Paine, Harriet Beecher Stowe, Henry Ford, or Martin Luther King, Jr. Nor could Americans have foreseen events such as Bacon's Rebellion, John Brown's Raid, the Haymarket Riot, or the Watergate break-in. While long-term processes are fully treated in this book, it also strives to show that history often turns around unique events, unintended outcomes, and singular individuals. *American Passages* calls our attention to the twists and turns of history, to the way various facets of history are connected.

Not only does the thoroughly chronological organization of this book make for a good story, we believe, but it helps history make sense. In our own lives, after all, things happen simultaneously. Every newspaper and news show reminds us of the way that events abroad touch on events at home, the way that politics and economics entangle, the pervasiveness of a particular book or film in a certain season. We are used to the idea that our lives are defined by a mixture of major and minor events, by the interplay between the momentary and the momentous. The past was like that as well.

American Passages offers several tools to help us see the past as a whole. Its timelines and "Passages" sections provide broad overviews that connect across chapters. Its illustrations and graphs are tightly woven into the narrative. Its rich Web site amplifies the themes and materials of the book, offering hundreds of documents, maps, illustrations, and multimedia selections carefully attuned to the time in which they were produced. We hope that such a story will help convey the excitement, drama, and importance of this nation's past.

ANCILLARY ITEMS

Test Manual, Volume I: To 1877; Volume II: From 1863

Marlette Rebhorn, Austin Community College

This test manual provides the instructor with a variety of question styles which emphasize critical thinking skills for the student. In addition to multiple choice questions, there are identification questions, essay questions, and book report questions. This item is free to instructors.

Computerized Test Banks

The EXAMaster + system simplifies test generation and allows instructors the flexibility to add or edit questions. It includes all test items from both volumes of the printed Test Bank and is free to instructors.
Available in the following formats: CD-ROM for MS Windows™ and Macintosh®, 3.5″ disks in both MS Windows™ and Macintosh®.

Instructor's Manual, Volume I: To 1877; Volume II: From 1863

Barbara Stites, Los Angeles City College

This guide is designed to support the instructor in preparing lectures and developing discussion questions and assignments. This manual contains objectives for each chapter; a "Making it Real" section which provides recommendations for assignments, lecture topic suggestions, and a "Futher Resources" part which lists additional readings and audio and visual resources.

Overhead Transparency Acetates

Burt Rieff, University of North Alabama

This full color OHT package contains over 180 transparencies comprising most of the outstanding maps, charts, and graphs from *American Passages*. Also included are a number of carefully selected images from the text. Provided for each acetate are teaching notes which provide the instructor with a brief explanation of each acetate, features to note, and questions to facilitate classroom discussion.

American Passages: A History of the United States Online Resources

This innovative *American Passages* Web site provides access to many online resources for both instructors and students. On this site can be found the following:

- Chapters: All items are organized according to the same thirty-two chapters contained in the *American Passages* text. Within each chapter, the primary source materials are presented in modules organized around a particular event, place, time, or theme within the chapter's chronological structure.
- Exercises: Study questions, with answers, encourage students to think more deeply about the primary source materials, the issues and themes to which they connect, and the relevant parts of *American Passages* to which they relate. The exercises follow a variety of strategies: some focus on a particular document; others concentrate on several documents within one chapter, still others address themes and issues which connect items in different chapters and across time periods.
- Links: An annotated list of links directs students outside the *American Passages* Web site to especially useful and relevant content-rich sites on the Internet. The list is organized by chapter and is designed to complement material presented both in the Web site and in the text.
- Maps: Dynamic and animated interactive maps dramatically illustrate major developments and changes occurring over a period of time.
- Index: Several indices provide an archive of all primary source materials in the site. The indices point to summaries of the documents and to the documents themselves. Students may browse by subject, chapter, date, and type of item.

American Passages Web site Manual

It's about time . . . for an American history textbook and its Web site to be fully integrated; for the narrative of the text and the primary materials of the Web site to work together to heighten students' understanding of the past; and for both components to be organized chronologically so as to remain true to the flow of history.

Study Guide, Volume I: To 1877; Volume II: From 1863

Richard McMillan, Los Angeles Pierce College

This Student Resource Guide is organized to assist the student in his or her comprehension of the material found in each chapter. It contains not only a thorough chapter outline, but also includes essay questions, identification questions, and objective questions which provide aid in the student's understanding of the text. At the end of each chapter are map exercises, which reinforce the student's geographical knowledge as well.

Computerized Student Tutorial

Available to students, at an affordable price, are a variety of interactive exercises taken directly from the Student Manual.

American Passages Historical Geography Guide, Volume I: To 1877; Volume II: From 1863

Marlette Rebhorn, Austin Community College
This mapping workbook provides students with challenging and engaging exercises designed to test their geographical knowledge. In addition to labeling exercises there are also fill-in questions to reinforce the student's comprehension.

United States History Documents Collection, Volume I: To 1877; Volume II: From 1863

Robert Weise, Eastern Kentucky University
This outstanding collection of documents includes over 100 primary source readings with introductory notes for each selection. This is available free to instructors and may be purchased by the student.

PowerPoint Slide Archive for U.S. History Presentation CD-ROM

Prepared by Raymond M. Hyser and J. Christopher Arndt, James Madison University
This electronic archive is intended to enhance lectures by providing historical photos, cartoons, posters, maps, charts and graphs as well as lecture outlines, which can be used as framework for the material. The 1642 slides (including 669 photos and 143 maps) are organized in chronological units. The professor has flexibility to edit, add, delete, and rearrange slides into customized presentations. The CD-ROM includes separate indexes of the images, maps, and charts/graphs for ease in locating specific illustrations, as well as PowerPoint viewers for both Mac and PC platforms.

The American History CD-ROM

The American History CD-ROM is an interactive learning tool that provides a vast library of pictures, film clips, sound recordings, and maps. It is indexed and organized in a unique, flexible format that makes it easy to explore U.S. history from ancient times through the 1990s. Features include: Overviews, narrated by Charles Kuralt; thousands of captioned illustrations; 68 motion pictures; dozens of brief sound bites; a quiz that offers students several levels and options for self-assessment;

and *The Histriopix Game,* a challenging test of students' recall for key concepts and information that is conveyed through the images. In addition to independent study, students and professors can create lessons, lesson plans, and presentations. Adoption requirements apply.

Second World War Photo CD-ROM

The Second World War CD-ROM is a three-disc set that features selections from the National Archives. It includes more than 900 black and white images taken during the war that are accompanied by historically accurate captions. Adoption requirements apply.

Zane Publishing's Home Library CD-ROM Package for U.S. History

The home library includes a 10-disc CD-ROM package that covers major subject areas in U.S. history, ranging from the 1700s to the present. Topics include Jacksonian Democracy, the Civil War, Reconstruction, the American West, the Great Depression, U.S. Government, U.S. Foreign Policy from 1788 to 1933 and 1933 to 1963, and the Social Reform movement. Adoption requirements apply.

U.S. History Videos/*Films for the Humanities*

Contact your local Harcourt sales representative for a complete listing of the many videos that are available from the extensive *Films for the Humanities* catalog. Adoption requirements apply.

U.S. History Videos/*Arts and Entertainment*

Many outstanding U.S. history selections are available from the *Arts and Entertainment* video library. Choose from "American Revolution," "Civil War Journal," "The Real West," "Mike Wallace's Twentieth Century," and selections from *A & E*'s extensive *Biography* series collection. Adoption requirements apply.

Twentieth-Century American History Video Disk

The history of the American 20th century comes alive in a one-hour videodisk produced expressly for Harcourt by Fountain Communications. It addresses the pressing issues that Americans have faced in this century: immigration, the Great Depression, the Second World War, the Cold War, the United States in the 1950s, the civil rights movement, the Vietnam War, and the women's movement. Adoption requirements apply.

ACKNOWLEDGMENTS

I would like to thank my students and colleagues at the University of Virginia, who have helped me struggle with the tough questions of American history. I am grateful, too, to the diligent Harcourt editors David Tatom, Kristie Kelly, and Laura Hanna for their patience, good will, and good advice in the creation of this book. Thanks also go to Linda Beaupré, designer; Diane Gray, production manager; and Lili Weiner, photo researcher. Finally, I am very appreciative of my co-authors, who have been engaged scholars, thoughtful critics, devoted teachers, and good friends throughout the years it took us to write *American Passages*.

EDWARD L. AYERS

I would like to acknowledge the help of the following former students who contributed in constructive ways to the completion of the textbook: Martin Ansell, Christie Bourgeois, Thomas Clarkin, Stacy Cordery, Debbie Cottrell, Patrick Cox, Scott Harris, Byron Hulsey, Jonathan Lee, John Leffler, Mark Young, and Nancy Beck Young. Karen Gould gave indispensable support and encouragement throughout the process of writing the text. I am grateful as well to the readers of my chapters who made so many useful and timely criticisms.

LEWIS L. GOULD

I would like to thank my colleagues and students at Rutgers for allowing me to test out an endless stream of ideas and issues relating to modern American history, and also for their thoughts on how a good college textbook should "read" and what it should contain. As always, the support and love of my family—Matt, Efrem, Ari, and Jane—was unshakable. Above all, I must commend my co-authors and my editors at Harcourt for their remarkable patience and professionalism during this long collaborative process.

DAVID M. OSHINSKY

I am grateful to my husband, Rudolf Soderlund, and my family for their support throughout this project. My mother, Joyce Ruth, went well beyond the limits of parental duty by reading and critiquing each chapter. Many scholars in the colonial and early national periods shared their ideas verbally and through publications. I received very helpful comments from James S. Saeger, Roger D. Simon, Marianne S. Wokeck, my co-authors of this text, and the anonymous readers for the press.

JEAN R. SODERLUND

LIST OF REVIEWERS

Joseph Adams — St. Louis Community College, Meramec Campus

Charles Allbee — Burlington Community College

Julius Amin — University of Dayton

Melodie Andrews — Mankato State

Robert Becker — Louisiana State University

Peter Bergstrom — Illinois State

John Brooke — Tufts University

Neil Brooks — Essex Community College

Colin Calloway — Dartmouth

Milton Cantor — University of Massachusetts

Kay Carr — Southern Illinois University

Paul Chardoul — Grand Rapids Junior College

Myles Clowers — San Diego City College

William Cobb — Utah Valley State College

David Coon — Washington State University

Stacey Cordery — Monmouth College

Debbie Cottrell — Smith College

David Cullen — Collin County Community College

Christine Daniels — Michigan State University

Ronnie Day — East Tennessee State University

Matthew Dennis — University of Oregon

Robert Downtain — Tarrant County Junior College — Northeast Campus

Robert Elam — Modesto Junior College

Linda Foutch — Walter State Community College

Robert G. Fricke — West Valley College

David Hamilton — University of Kentucky

Beatriz Hardy — Coastal Carolina University

Peter M. G. Harris — Temple University

Thomas Hartshorne — Cleveland State University

Ron Hatzenbuehler — Idaho State

Robert Hawkes — George Mason University

James Houston — Oklahoma State University

Raymond Hyser — James Madison University

Lillian Jones — Santa Monica College

Jim Kluger — Pima Community College

James Lacy — Contra Costa College

Alton Lee — University of South Dakota

Liston Leyendecker — Colorado State University

Robert Marcom — San Antonio College

Greg Massey — Freed-Hardeman

Michael Mayer — University of Montana

Elsa Nystrom — Kennesaw State

David O'Neill — Rutgers University

Betty Owens — Greenville Technical College

Mark Parillo — Kansas State University

J'Nell Pate — Tarrant County Junior College, Northeast Campus

Louis Potts — University of Missouri at Kansas City

Noel Pugach — University of New Mexico

Alice Reagan — Northern Virginia Community College

Marlette Rebhorn — Austin Community College, Rio Grande Campus

David Reimers — New York University

Hal Rothman — Wichita State University

Ralph Shaffer — California Polytechnic University

Kenneth Smemo — Moorhead State University

Jack Smith — Great Basin College

Thaddeus Smith — Middle Tennessee State University

Phillip E. Stebbins — Pennsylvania State University

Marshall Stevenson — Ohio State University

William Stockton — Johnson County Community College

Frank Towers — Clarion University

Daniel Usner — Cornell University

Daniel Vogt — Jackson State University

Stephen Webre — Louisiana Technical College

John C. Willis — University of the South

Harold Wilson — Old Dominion University

Nan Woodruff — Pennsylvania State University

Bertram Wyatt-Brown — University of Florida

Sherri Yeager — Chabot College

Robert Zeidel — University of Wisconsin

LIST OF DOCUMENTS

LIST OF MAPS

LIST OF TABLES

LIST OF CHARTS AND GRAPHS

BRIEF TABLE OF CONTENTS

Detailed Table of Contents

PASSAGES
1764 TO 1814 144

VOLUME I TO 1877

AMERICAN
PASSAGES

A HISTORY OF THE UNITED STATES

PASSAGES

And so we journeyed for seventeen days, at the end of which we crossed the river [Rio Grande] and traveled for seventeen more. At sunset, on plains between some very tall mountains, we found some people who eat nothing but powdered straw for a third of the year. Since it was that season of the year, we had to eat it too. At the end of our journey we found a permanent settlement where there was abundant corn. The people gave us a large quantity of it and of cornmeal, squash, beans and cotton blankets. . . . From here we traveled [to where people] gave me five emeralds made into arrowheads. . . . Since they seemed very fine to me, I asked them where they had gotten them. They told me that they brought them from some very high mountains to the North.

—CABEZA DE VACA, 1542*

FROM 1534 TO 1536, the Spanish explorer, Álvar Núñez Cabeza de Vaca, and three others, including a black man, Esteban, traveled through Texas and northern Mexico, trying to reach Mexico City. They had been part of an expedition to Florida that ran afoul of Apalachee Indians, escaped across the Gulf of Mexico in makeshift boats, then were enslaved in Texas by Karankawa Indians. In his *Relación,* Cabeza de Vaca described their adventures, including the harrowing passage across the gulf, long journeys without food, and sojourns among Texas Indians.

Warpaths, ocean voyages, hunting trails, trade routes, death, communication and exchange among people—creating societies in America embodied passages of every kind. Asians moved across the Bering land bridge more than 14,000 years ago, settling throughout North and South America. Over time, they created distinct cultures in every part of the hemisphere, from the empire-building Aztecs of Mexico to the peaceful Lenape, whom the English called Delawares, of eastern North America. Over thousands of years, American civilizations rose and fell, as empires built pyramids and temple mounds, developed cities and cultures, and competed for territory and trade.

In the fifteenth century A.D., Western Europeans came to America to fish, trade, and establish colonies, bringing new technology, lust for wealth, and destructive microbes that spelled death for millions of Native Americans. The Europeans adapted their traditions and goals to exploit the abundant, yet often unfamiliar, resources of the New World. The Spanish struck it rich with the Potosí and Zacatecas silver mines that financed their religious wars in Europe and became the envy of other nations. Privateers from France, England, and the Netherlands attacked the Spanish silver fleets, while explorers searched unsuccessfully for mines in North America. Instead, they found treasures in furs, sugar, tobacco, and rice.

To reap fortunes from the earth, the colonizers first exploited Native Americans, who died in such numbers from disease and harsh treatment that Europeans turned to another continent, Africa, for laborers. Portugal had developed the Atlantic slave trade during the fifteenth century, initially buying slaves to toil on sugar islands near Africa. With the development of sugar, and later tobacco and rice, in America, the Portuguese and other Europeans purchased millions of people from African merchants for transport across the Atlantic. For more than 350 years, the cultures, sweat, and blood of enslaved Africans enriched the New World societies.

From the sixteenth century on, Europeans battled for North America with Native Americans and among themselves. The French settled Canada and the Mississippi Valley, primarily for furs. Spain held Florida, Texas, and New Mexico as outposts to protect its silver mines and fleets. The English founded colonies in New England, the Chesapeake, and Carolinas for economic opportunity and religious freedom. In 1664, they pushed the Dutch out of New Netherland, thus connecting their chain of colonies along the Atlantic. Throughout America, Europeans hoped for a new chance in the New World.

The thirteen mainland British colonies had various beginnings, charters, provincial governments, economic bases, peoples, and religions. Yet they all had ties with England, in language, imperial government and laws, culture, and commerce. During the eighteenth century, the colonies forged closer bonds with the English—with greater participation in imperial wars, increased trade, and better communication. At the same time, the British provinces also became more distinctly American, as people from Africa,

Legend:
- Settled areas (non-Indian)
- Forests
- Non-forested open land

Population Growth of the Thirteen British Mainland Colonies, 1630–1760

1630	1640	1650	1660	1670	1680	1690
4,646	26,634	50,368	75,058	111,935	151,507	210,372

Ireland, and the European continent diversified the population and its culture. With natural population growth and swelling immigration, the British colonies expanded across the continent.

Native Americans responded to depopulation, defeat, and white expansion by creating new worlds of their own. Despite some military successes, they ultimately reshaped their communities and cultures, as disease worked its tragic course and European-American societies grew. The surviving members of Indian nations often merged to forge new ethnic identities, or lived together in multi-ethnic communities, often with whites and escaped slaves. Some retained remnants of their land within white settlements, while the majority moved to the frontier for political autonomy.

Three centuries passed from the time Western European fishermen first camped on North American shores until Great Britain and its colonies expelled France from the continent with the French and Indian War. By 1763, the land and people of America had permanently changed.

* Martin A. Favata and José B. Fernandez, *The Account: Álvar Núñez Cabeza de Vaca's Relación* (1993), p.103.

1700	1710	1720	1730	1740	1750	1760
50,888	331,711	466,185	629,445	905,563	1,170,760	1,593,625

	38,000 BC	1000 AD	1300	1400	1500
POLITICS & DIPLOMACY	**38,000-12,000 BC:** Ancient hunters migrate to America **300-1600 AD:** Ghana, Mali, and Songhay empires in West Africa **700-1450 AD:** Cahokia and other Mississippian centers in North America	**c. 1000 AD:** Leif Eriksson's colony on Newfoundland **c. 1300 AD:** Aztecs settle in Valley of Mexico			**1420:** Prince Henry of Portugal begins exploration **1492:** Christopher Columbus crosses Atlantic Ocean **1513:** Juan Ponce de León explores Florida for Spain **1519:** Magellan's expedition to circumnavigate world **1521:** Hernán Cortés conquers Aztecs **1528:** Cabeza de Vaca to Florida and Texas **1540:** Coronado explores American Southwest
SOCIAL & CULTURAL EVENTS			**1324:** Gonga-Mussa's pilgrimage to Mecca		**1507:** Martin Waldseemüller names New World after Amerigo Vespucci **1517:** Martin Luther challenges the Church of Rome **1534:** English Act of Supremacy **1536:** John Calvin's *Institutes of the Christian Religion* **1542:** Bartolomé de las Casas's *A Short Account of the Destruction of the Indies*
ECONOMICS & TECHNOLOGY	**Pre-2500 BC:** Corn developed as staple crop in central Mexico **c. 1200 BC:** Corn produced in American southwest				**1440s:** Portuguese mariners take Africans as slaves **c. 1450:** European fishermen at Grand Banks off Newfoundland **c. 1452:** Portugal begins sugar production on Madeira **c. 1460:** European improvements in navigation and ships **1478:** Abraham Zacuto calculates latitude using sun **1502:** Enslaved Africans imported in Spanish America **1503:** Spanish Casa de Contratación to supervise trade **1540s:** Silver mines at Zacatecas and Potosí

c. 1550: Iroquois form confederacy

1565: Spanish found St. Augustine, Florida

1585: English colony at Roanoke Island

1599: Spanish destroy Ácoma

1607: English colony at Jamestown

1608: French establish Quebec

1620: Separatists found Plymouth

1630: Puritans establish Massachusetts Bay Colony

1634: The *Ark* and the *Dove* arrive in Maryland

1642: English Civil War begins

1643: New England Confederation

1663: Carolina proprietors receive charter

1664: English forces conquer New Netherland

1675: Metacom's War
Bacon's Rebellion

1680: Popé's Rebellion

1681: William Penn receives Pennsylvania charter

1688: Glorious Revolution in England

1689: Massachusetts, New York, and Maryland revolutions

1691: Salem witchcraft hysteria

1699: French establish Louisiana

1712: Slave revolt in New York City

1732: Founding of Georgia

1739: Stono Uprising in South Carolina

1754: Albany Congress

1754-1763: French and Indian War

1763: Pan-Indian war in Ohio Valley and Great Lakes

1585: John White's drawings of Roanoke

1590: Theodor de Bry's *America*

1636: Harvard College established
Roger Williams's exile to Rhode Island

1637: Anne Hutchinson tried for heresy

1638: First printing press in the English colonies

1639: French establish first hospital in North America

1647: Massachusetts requires town schools

1649: Maryland's act for religious toleration

1650: Anne Bradstreet's *The Tenth Muse Lately Sprung Up in America*

c.1661: Henri Couturier's portrait of Peter Stuyvesant

1662: Halfway Covenant

1663: John Eliot's Bible in Massachusetts Indian language

c.1674: *Mrs. Freake with Baby Mary* by unknown artist

1682: Publication of *The Narrative of the Captivity and Restoration of Mrs. Mary Rowlandson*

1687: *Isaac Newton's Principia Mathematica*

1688: Germantown, PA, Quakers issue antislavery protest

1690: John Locke's *Essay concerning Human Understanding*

1693: College of William and Mary founded

1695: Jews worship openly in New York

1704: First regular newspaper in Anglo-America, *The Boston News-Letter*

1716: Theater built in Wiliamsburg, Virginia

1720: Theodore Jacob Frelinghuysen's revivals in New Jersey

1721: Smallpox inoculation in Boston

1731: Benjamin Franklin's circulating library in Philadelphia

1739: George Whitefield tours northern colonies

1751: Benjamin Franklin's reports on electricity

1752: Adoption of Gregorian Calendar in Anglo-America

1761: John Winthrop observes the transit of Venus

1763: Rise of Delaware prophet Neolin

1562: John Hawkins interlopes in slave trade

c. 1585: Growth of Amsterdam as mercantile center

1602: Dutch East India Company

1617: Tobacco successful staple crop in Virginia

c. 1619: Africans arrive in Virginia

1621: Dutch West India Company

1640s: Sugar production in English West Indies

1642: French found Montreal for fur trade

1651: First English Navigation Act

1672: Royal African Company

1673: Regular postal route between Boston and New York

1670s: Shift to slaves in Chesapeake

1698: Royal African Company loses slave trade monopoly

1699: Woolen Act

1700s: Adoption of rice in South Carolina

1720s: Expansion of German and Scots-Irish immigration

1732: Hat Act

1733: Molasses Act

1740s: Eliza Pinckney cultivates indigo in South Carolina

1750: Iron Act
Georgia legalizes slavery

1750s: British colonial trade expands with Southern Europe
"Consumer revolution" in British colonies

early 1760s: Economic slump in British colonies

CHRISTOPHER COLUMBUS

Christopher Columbus, an Italian mariner, was convinced he could find a direct route to Asia by sailing west. He was wrong, and instead opened the Western Hemisphere to European conquest and settlement.

Chapter 1

Contact, Conflict, and Exchange in the Atlantic World to 1590

ON OCTOBER 12, 1492, the *Santa Maria, Pinta,* and *Niña,* under command of the Italian navigator Christopher Columbus, sighted an island in the Caribbean Sea he called San Salvador. The expedition took much preparation and bravery, for no one had followed this route before. A seasoned sailor, Columbus had gained a taste for exploration on an earlier trip to Iceland. He spent years trying to obtain support from the rulers of England, France, Portugal, and Spain for a voyage westward across the Atlantic Ocean to find Asia. Finally he convinced Isabella and Ferdinand of Spain to provide funds. If he found a transatlantic route to Asia, Columbus argued, Spain would have the competitive edge in eastern markets over Portugal, which had not yet reached India.

Sailing from one Caribbean island to another, Columbus met many Native Americans, whom he described as "very well formed, with handsome bodies and good faces." He called them "*Indios,*" or Indians, because he thought he had reached islands in the Far East. For the rest of his life, until his death in 1506, Columbus believed he had found Asia. What he actually had done was initiate the conquest and settlement of two continents—the Americas—whose vast extent and riches were previously unknown to Europeans.

Columbus's arrival had momentous consequences for the peoples of America, Europe, and Africa. For Native Americans, whose ancestors had arrived from Asia thousands of years earlier, white men and sailing ships spelled demographic catastrophe. Within 150 years, the pre-contact Indian population was reduced by 90 percent, their cities conquered and destroyed, and, for many, their lands appropriated for farming and grazing livestock. For Europeans, Columbus's unexpected "discovery" represented new challenges and opportunities, some of many they experienced as they explored the far reaches of the globe. For sub-Saharan Africans, the navigator's landfall half a world away signaled the burgeoning slave trade, which over the next four centuries transported at least 10 million Africans across the Atlantic to work and die on plantations and in mines. To exploit the riches of America, Europeans used the labor of both Native Americans and Africans.

Yet contact among Native Americans, Europeans, and Africans involved more than conquest, enslavement, and death. Together the three major cultural groups created new traditions and societies in the New World. While the Europeans must be declared winners in the contest for power, the American colonies were shaped by exchange of knowledge, culture, and work among all participants. Contact introduced new crops and technology to inhabitants of both the Old and New Worlds. Three major cultural traditions came together in the Western Hemisphere. The patterns of

CHRONOLOGY

38,000–12,000 B.C. Migration of ancient hunters to the Americas

300–900 A.D. Height of Mayan civilization in Yucatan

300–1600 A.D. Succession of empires, Ghana, Mali, and Songhay, in West Africa

700–1450 A.D. Mississippian people build Cahokia and other urban centers in North America

c. 1000 A.D. Leif Eriksson establishes Viking colony on Newfoundland

c. 1300 A.D. Aztecs settle in Valley of Mexico

1420 Prince Henry of Portugal initiates search for ocean route to Asia

1440s Portuguese mariners take Africans as slaves

c. 1452 Portugal begins sugar production on Madeira

c. 1460–1500 European improvements in navigation and ships

1487 Bartholomeu Dias of Portugal rounds Cape of Good Hope

1492 Christopher Columbus crosses Atlantic Ocean

1494 Treaty of Tordesillas establishes Line of Demarcation

1497–1498 Vasco da Gama reaches India for Portugal

1517 Martin Luther challenges the Church of Rome

1519–1521 Hernán Cortés conquers the Aztecs

1519–1522 Magellan's expedition circumnavigates the world

1528–1536 Cabeza de Vaca's adventures in Florida and Texas

1534 Act of Supremacy separates England from the Church of Rome

1539–1542 Hernando de Soto explores the region from Florida to the Mississippi River

1540–1542 Coronado explores the American Southwest

1541 Cartier establishes Charlesbourg-Royal in Canada

1556 Philip II of Spain takes the throne

1558 Elizabeth I becomes queen of England

1564 French Huguenots build Fort Caroline in northern Florida

1577–1580 Francis Drake circumnavigates the globe

1585 English attempt colonization at Roanoke Island

1588 English defeat the Spanish Armada

---

annihilation, exploitation, resistance, accommodation, and trade created new cultures and social systems throughout the hemisphere.

THE FIRST AMERICANS

In 1492, an estimated 70 million Native Americans lived in North and South America. They possessed widely divergent cultures, ranging from the Inuit who hunted seal and walrus along the shores of the Arctic Ocean, to the Aztecs of central Mexico and Incas of the Peruvian Andes who lived in state-level agricultural societies. In the geographic area that now encompasses the United States, they included mound-building farmers of the Mississippi valley, the pueblo-dwelling Hopi and Zuñi Indians and nomadic Apaches of the southwest, and the Iroquois and Algonquians of the eastern woodlands.

Native American Societies Before Contact

These diverse peoples were descendants of small bands of hunters who crossed the Bering land bridge from Siberia to Alaska some time between 40,000 and 14,000 years ago. When the glacier covering much of Canada receded, they followed big game south from Alaska, through western Canada, to the Great Plains. Among the earliest evidence of their arrival, dating from about 12,000 B.C., are sites containing human remains and the skeletons of animals with the stone spearheads used to slay them. As the climate of North America became warmer with the end of the Ice Age,

MAP 1.1 | AMERICA BEFORE COLUMBUS

and perhaps as a result of overhunting, several species of large animals disappeared, including mammoths, horses, steppe bison, camels, and mastodons. Buffalo remained plentiful on the Great Plains, but elsewhere Indians hunted smaller game, fished, and collected berries, seeds, and nuts. As groups migrated throughout North and South America and adapted to their environments, their cultures and languages diverged.

When ancient Americans began cultivating crops, they laid the foundation for more densely populated societies. Agriculture evolved first in Central America and somewhat later in Peru. Of greatest importance to Indians of North America was the development of maize, or Indian corn, probably from the grass *teosinte,* which grew in dry areas of Mexico and Guatemala. Through a process of selective planting, over hundreds of years, farmers enlarged the size of the cob and seeds, thus increasing the amount of food per cob. Even so, the earliest known corncobs are only slightly longer than one inch. In addition to maize, early Mexicans domesticated beans, squash, chili peppers, and avocado. Agriculture proved revolutionary for some ancient American societies, as higher yields spurred population growth and a greater division of labor.

Between 1500 B.C. and Columbus's arrival, civilizations rose and declined throughout the Americas—just as the ancestral cultures of the Europeans developed in ancient Egypt, Greece, and Rome. Ancient Americans built empires, much like their counterparts in the Mediterranean, with cities, extensive trade networks, systems of religion and knowledge, art, architecture, and hierarchical social classes. Two of the best-known civilizations of pre-contact America were the Mayan, located on the Yucatan peninsula, and the Mexican. The Maya, at their height from 300 to 900 A.D., built cities of stone pyramids, temples, and palaces, with populations ranging to more than 60,000. Mayan kings, considered divine, extended their empire to over fifty different states and maintained trade with distant peoples. Stone and wood carving, jade jewelry, wall painting, and pottery revealed Mayan artistry. They had a numeral system based on units of twenty, hieroglyphics, a knowledge of astronomy, and several calendars—one of 365 days and another of 260 days, which correlated approximately with human fertility (an average pregnancy lasts 266 days) and the agricultural growing season.

The Mexicans, who lived in the Valley of Mexico, built the city of Teotihuacán east of Lake Texcoco. Its population of about 200,000 depended on intensive farming of nearby irrigated lands. The grid-patterned Teotihuacán, which Mexicans considered the place where time began, held at its core the Pyramid of the Sun and the Pyramid of the Moon. Even after the city's decline it retained religious significance for later Mexicans and became a place of pilgrimage.

The Aztecs settled in the Valley of Mexico in the fourteenth century, building their capital, Tenochtitlán, on the only vacant land available, an island in

A Mayan jade death mask, c. 700 AD.

Lake Texcoco which they connected to the shore by causeways. They cultivated intensively the marshlands surrounding their island and built a militaristic state. By the time the Spanish *conquistadores* arrived in 1519, the Aztecs controlled territory from the Pacific to the Gulf Coast. One Spaniard described Tenochtitlán as they approached: "And when we saw all those towns and villages built in the water, and other great towns on dry land, and that straight and narrow causeway leading to Mexico, we were astounded. These great towns . . . and buildings rising from the water, all made of stone, seemed like an enchanted vision." The Aztecs required tribute from the people they conquered—gold, feathers, turquoise, food, cotton, and human beings for sacrifice. The Aztecs believed that every day they had to feed human hearts to the sun god, Huitzilpochtli, to prevent the world from coming to an end.

To the north of the Valley of Mexico, Indians also developed distinctive cultures. The Hohokam occupied desert lands in Arizona and northern Sonora, where, with irrigation, they cultivated Indian corn,

The Pyramid of the Sun, located in the center of Teotihuacán, the ancient Mexican capital.

cotton, squash, and beans. Their canals, up to ten miles long, diverted water from nearby rivers. When Athabaskan raiders from the north attacked Hohokam towns, they tried to protect themselves by building high adobe walls, then after 1400 A.D. simply abandoned many of their villages.

Enemy attacks and crop failures from lack of rain forced other Indians of the southwest to leave their towns. The Anasazi farmers of northern Arizona and New Mexico, Colorado, and Utah relied on rain and floods to water their crops. One of their settlements was Pueblo Bonito in Chaco Canyon, which housed perhaps 1,000 people in 800 rooms surrounded by high walls; another was the complex of rock dwellings built high in the canyon cliffs at Mesa Verde. While both were deserted during the fourteenth century, descendants of the Anasazi—the Hopi and Zuñi Indians—witnessed Spanish exploration. The Spanish called them "Pueblo" Indians for the adobe villages with large apartment dwellings in which they lived.

Farther east, in a large area drained by the Mississippi River, by 1000 B.C. early Americans developed civilizations characterized by large earthen burial mounds, some sixty feet high. These mounds entombed corpses and such grave goods as tobacco pipes, copper beads and spoons, bracelets, and beads made from seashells. The Great Serpent Mound, located near Cincinnati, Ohio, is the most famous of their earthworks. These Mississippian people lived in small villages along rivers, hunted game, fished, and raised squash, Indian corn, sunflowers, and gourds. As evidenced by the grave goods, their trading network extended from the Gulf Coast (shells) to Lake Superior (copper). By 700 A.D., the Mississippian people constructed large towns, such as Cahokia, which was located near the confluence of the Mississippi, Illinois, and Missouri rivers. At the center of these towns were large rectangular mounds topped by temples and mortuaries in which members of the upper class were buried. Around 1200 A.D., Cahokia and its environs

Hohokam pottery decorated with bird motif, c. 700–900 AD, found at Snaketown, Arizona.

Secotan village, 1585, by the Englishman John White, who journeyed to North America with the Roanoke expedition. His watercolor drawings depict Algonquians of the North Carolina coast.

had about 40,000 residents but by 1450, the region's population declined, perhaps as a result of illness spread by urban crowding.

People of the Eastern Woodlands

Along the Atlantic seaboard extending inland to the Appalachian Mountains, where the English, French, and Dutch later colonized, lived Native Americans of two major language groups, the Algonquian and the Iroquois. The eastern woodlands incorporated a wide variety of habitats, from beach to highlands. In most parts, decent soil and moderate rainfall and temperatures supported agriculture and many kinds of game, fish, and wild plants. Algonquian-speaking people dominated the Atlantic coast from Canada to Florida; they included the Pokanokets, Narragansetts, and Pequots in New England; the Delawares of the middle Atlantic region; and members of the Powhatan confederacy in what became Virginia. Many of the Iroquois lived in the Finger Lakes area of central New York. They belonged to five tribes: the Mohawks, Oneidas, Onondagas, Cayugas, and Senecas, from east to west, who banded together in the Iroquois confed-

eracy to unite against their enemies and stop feuding among themselves. Iroquoian people who were not part of the confederacy included the Hurons of the eastern Great Lakes and the Susquehannocks of central Pennsylvania and Maryland.

While important cultural differences existed between the two language groups and even among bands within each group, Indians of the eastern woodlands had much in common. They held land cooperatively, without private ownership. The tribe as a whole claimed ownership rights, not individual members or families. Except in far northern New England, where the growing season was too short to plant corn, Indians had a mixed economy of agriculture, gathering,

Woman and girl of Pomeioc, another watercolor by John White, 1585. Algonquian women cared for children and raised crops, including corn and tobacco.

fishing, and hunting. Women were responsible for raising corn, squash, beans, and (where possible) to-bacco. They also gathered nuts and fruit, built houses, made clothing, took care of the children, and prepared meals, while men cleared land, hunted, fished, and protected the village from enemies. Because this division of labor between the sexes was quite different from that of England and the Continent, Europeans believed that Indian women worked too hard. One Englishman said, "Their wives are their slaves, and do all the work; the men will do nothing but kill beasts,

fish, etc." The combination of corn, squash, and beans enriched the soil, providing high yields from small plots of land; eaten together these foods were high in protein. The Native Americans cleared land by girdling the large trees (removing a strip of bark around the trees about three feet from the ground), thus killing them. When the trees died, the Indians removed them, burned the underbrush, and sowed crops among the stumps. Eastern woodlands people used nets and weirs to catch fish and, to assure good hunting, they periodically burned underbrush from sections of forest, thus giving ecological advantages to species of trees such as pines and oaks, which were resistant to fire. The burning stimulated the growth of lush grass, providing fodder for deer and other game. The fires allowed some sunlight to penetrate the forest, promoting the growth of strawberries, raspberries, and blackberries, and creating an environment very much like a park.

Indian religions, though widely diverse in many ways, incorporated a common worldview. The people of the eastern woodlands believed that the earth and sky formed a spiritual realm of which they were a part, not the masters. They made no distinction between the secular, or nonreligious, and the sacred. They feared the power of nature, recognizing its control over crops, the availability of game, and the weather. Spirits inhabited the earth and could be found in plants, animals, rocks, or clouds. Each spirit, or *manitou,* could become the guardian of a young Indian man (less often a young woman), who, in search of a manitou, went into the woods alone, without eating or sleeping perhaps for days. If the spirit made itself known, it would provide help and counsel to the individual for the rest of his life. These Native Americans also believed in a Master Spirit or Creator, who was all-powerful and all-knowing, but whose presence was rarely felt. Religious leaders were *shamans,* who performed rituals, such as making sacrifices of food, tobacco, furs, or weapons, to influence weather conditions or ward off danger. They were usually men, but in some communities were women. Indians believed that shamans, through religious ritual, could cure illness, interpret dreams, bring good weather, and predict the future.

The kinship group, or extended family, formed the basis of Native American society and government. The heads of kinship groups chose the band's chief leaders, called *sachems,* who with advice assigned fields for planting, decided where and when to hunt, managed trade and diplomacy with other Indians and

Man with Body Paint *by John White, 1585. Men were the political leaders, warriors, and hunters in Algonquian society.*

cils or serve as sachems, but they chose these political leaders and advised them on such matters as waging war.

Thus, in 1492, at the time Columbus crossed the Atlantic, highly complex and differentiated societies existed in North and South America. The Americas were not a vacant land, a wilderness waiting to be tapped. Dense populations inhabited parts of South, Central, and North America, sustaining elaborate networks of empire and trade. Throughout the hemisphere, Indian people had distinctive cultures tied to the resources of their environment. Despite this wide variety of languages and cultures, as different from one another as those of European countries, most Europeans adopted the single name that Columbus mistakenly employed—Indians. An alternative the colonists used was "savages," the term the French preferred. The view of many Europeans, that Native Americans had undifferentiated, uncivilized societies, justified conquest and expropriation of their lands.

BEGINNING OF EUROPEAN OVERSEAS EXPANSION

The Europeans who invaded the Americas after 1492 had more in common with Native Americans than they liked to admit; nevertheless, in important ways, their cultures were distinct. Europeans spent most of their energy producing or gathering food: They farmed, raised livestock, and gathered nuts and berries. In the south and west of England, for example, where the land was fertile, farmers engaged in intensive cultivation of wheat, rye, and other crops. In most of England and Wales, however, where the land was hilly and less fertile, farmers planted just an acre or two and spent more time gathering. In contrast to Native Americans, Europeans believed in private property, that individuals could own land and thus had the right to sell, fence, plant, erect buildings, hunt, cut lumber, and exclude others from use.

The societies from which most colonizers came, particularly Spain, France, and England, were patriarchal, meaning that descent followed the father's line and political power was nearly always in the hands of men. Men dominated their wives and children, and by extension dominated society. Though women occasionally took the throne, for instance, Isabella of Spain

Europeans, and judged whether or not to go to war. Among Algonquian-speaking natives, the heads of extended families were men, as were the sachems they chose. But in Iroquois culture women served as clan leaders, taking a share of political power. Iroquois society was matrilineal, with family membership passing from mother to children; and matrilocal, as the husband left his family to live with his wife's. A woman divorced her husband by setting his possessions outside the door; a man could divorce his wife by removing his belongings from her family's longhouse. Women elders could not speak publicly at tribal coun-

MAP 1.2 | EUROPE AND WEST AFRICA IN THE 15TH CENTURY

and Elizabeth I of England, men controlled government, the church, and the military. Married women were considered subordinate to their husbands and under most circumstances could hold no personal property or real estate, a significant handicap in a society based on private property. For example, under English common law—the legal system that had evolved by custom and court precedent over centuries—a married woman was a *feme covert,* or covered woman, who could not own or manage property, make a contract, write a will, take custody of her children, own a business, or sue in court, without her husband's permission. An unmarried woman or widow, in legal terms a *feme sole,* was not subject to these restrictions.

In the fifteenth century, as Europeans began exploring the reaches of the "Ocean Sea," as they called the Atlantic, the pope headed a united Christian church in western and central Europe. At the same time, monarchs consolidated power in Portugal, Spain, France, and England, providing financial support and a greater sense of national identity to fuel European expansion. In turn, wealth from distant empires and trade funded wars among these emerging nations.

Trade with the East

When Columbus sailed out into the Atlantic Ocean in 1492, he expected to establish a new trade route with Asia, not discover and colonize a New World. He was unaware of the voyages of the Viking Leif Eriksson and his family, who established a short-lived colony in Newfoundland around 1000 A.D. In the fifteenth century, eastern trade was a chief source of riches, for affluent Europeans wanted black pepper, cinnamon, cloves, mace, nutmeg, and ginger for preserving and flavoring their food. The spices would not grow in Europe, so merchants commanded high prices for transporting them from India, the East Indies, and other parts of East Asia. Imports also included silk, cotton cloth, rugs, perfumes, rubies, sapphires, and emeralds.

Before 1500, Arab and Italian merchants dominated the eastern trade. Arabs controlled eastern trading centers and carried goods across the Arabian Sea in *dhows*—boats with lateen, or triangular, sails—to the Red Sea and Persian Gulf. From there caravans took cargoes to Mediterranean ports for purchase by Italian merchants, particularly traders from Venice and Genoa. The Italians then distributed the spices

and luxuries throughout Europe by way of pack train and coastal shipping. European cities developed to handle the exchange of valued eastern products in return for silver, gold, woolen and linen cloth, furs, and leather. Centers of trade and banking included Paris, Lyons, Amsterdam, London, Hamburg, Danzig, Barcelona, Cadiz, and Lisbon, in addition to Venice and Genoa. The rise of great cities accompanied the growth of unified political states. Merchants provided funding for kings to consolidate small feudal states into nations. In Portugal, Spain, France, and England, commercial interests supported unification to obtain social order, monopolistic privileges, and standardized codes of law.

Portugal Explores the West African Coast

Early in the fifteenth century, Prince Henry of Portugal, called "the Navigator," decided to challenge the Arab and Italian hold on eastern commerce. The son of King John I, Henry brought together men interested in overseas trade and exploration at his court on Cape St. Vincent, overlooking the Atlantic Ocean. Many were Italian navigators, whose experience came from the Mediterranean trade. Beginning in 1420, Prince Henry sent ships down the western coast of Africa into parts unknown. He had four goals: to increase the power of Portugal by adding territorial possessions; to benefit economically from commerce with the African coast; to reach Asia and take a share of that trade; and to spread Christianity, and thereby combat the expansion of Islam in Africa. The Portuguese knew West Africans through the centuries-long exchange across the Sahara of African rubber, ivory, slaves, and gold, for European fruit, wheat, and sugar.

Headway down the African coast was slow, despite the lure of trade, because European sailors knew nothing of the ocean beyond Cape Bojador. Their sea charts were guesses, and their navigational instruments rudimentary. In 1420, cartographers knew a great deal about the Mediterranean Sea and constructed highly accurate charts, called *portolano,* of its shorelines and harbors. Such maps did not exist for the West African coast, so one task of Prince Henry's explorers was to chart their progress. Seamen had heard that monsters, and perhaps even Satan, dwelled in the waters beyond Cape Bojador, while other stories told that the ocean boiled at the equator. In fact, strong south-

Prince Henry the Navigator, of Portugal, who sponsored exploration down the west coast of Africa to find a sea route to Asia. From a painting by Nuno Gonçalves.

tuguese navigators tried not to lose sight of land. Compasses had been in use since at least the thirteenth century, but not until about 1460 did Europeans develop the means of determining latitude (distance north or south from the equator). In the Northern Hemisphere, sea captains calculated the height of the Pole Star from the horizon to determine their latitude. The Pole Star cannot be seen south of the equator, however, so navigators there measured the altitude of the sun at midday. In making these calculations, they used the astrolabe or the quadrant to determine the angle of the sun from the horizon, then consulted astronomical tables that Abraham Zacuto, a Jewish astronomer, compiled in 1478. A method for determining longitude remained unknown until the eighteenth century.

Improvements in ships and gunnery during the fifteenth century also aided exploration and conquest. By 1400 it had become clear that Mediterranean galleys, powered by oarsmen, were impractical in the high waves of the Atlantic. The first European ocean-going ships were square-rigged. Their broad sails could power large vessels, but they required a favorable tailwind to proceed from one point to another. The square-rigged ships could not explore ragged coastlines. To increase maneuverability, Portuguese seafarers designed the caravel with lateen rigging, which the Arabs originated on their dhows. The most successful Portuguese ship for long voyages was the *caravela redondo,* the square-rigged caravel, developed late in the fifteenth century and adopted by other European nations. This ship combined the speed of square rigging with the more responsive handling of lateen sails. For protection from privateers and in time of war, the Portuguese mounted artillery on the caravels and by 1500 introduced the practice of broadside fire. They changed nautical warfare by sinking enemy vessels with gunfire instead of boarding them with foot soldiers.

Despite these improvements in the design of ships, they remained uncomfortable places in which to live on voyages of months and years. Except for senior officers, none of the seamen had regular sleeping quarters—they slept on deck, or below in bad weather. Their shipmates included rats and cockroaches. When it rained, everything got wet, including the cooking fire built in a sandbox on deck. The mariners ate ship's hardtack, beans, and salt pork and beef, and drank mostly wine, since their casked water quickly became foul.

ward ocean currents facilitated outbound progress, but made return to the Mediterranean difficult. From ancient mathematicians and geographers, most notably Ptolemy, mapmakers knew that the world was round, but they also adopted Ptolemy's belief that a southern continent joined Africa to China, thus eliminating the possibility of a sea route from the Atlantic to the Indian Ocean. Prince Henry challenged current wisdom by sending ships down Africa's coast to find a route to the east.

New Technology

In the early and mid-fifteenth century, the lack of adequate instruments hampered navigation. The first Por-

Engraving by Stradunuse of an early sixteenth-century cosmographer working in his study with contemporary instruments, including dividers, rule, compass, quadrant, and sand glass.

AFRICA AND THE ATLANTIC SLAVE TRADE

Despite their fears and limited technology, the Portuguese explorers ventured farther and farther down the West African coast. In 1434, Gil Eannes sailed past Cape Bojador. Subsequent voyages established a lucrative coastal trade in slaves, gold, and malaguetta pepper in the Senegal region and farther south and east to the Gold Coast and Benin. Merchants now began investing in expeditions, seeing the profits to be made. Up to that point, Prince Henry had financed the voyages himself. Between the 1440s and 1505, Portuguese traders transported 40,000 Africans to perform domestic labor in Portugal and Spain, and to work on the sugar plantations of the Azores, Madeira, and Canary Islands in the Atlantic.

West African Cultures

Several great empires had risen and fallen in the area bounded by the Mediterranean Sea, the Gulf of Guinea, and the Atlantic Ocean. From before 300 A.D. to 1600, a succession of empires—Ghana, Mali, and Songhay—dominated the area. They had large armies, collected tribute over vast distances, and traded with Europeans and Arabs. Like Native Americans and Europeans, West Africans were predominantly agricultural people. Ghana declined by 1100 as a result of droughts that dried up several rivers. Mali then took control, as its monarchs, with access to the rich gold mines of Bure, regulated the gold trade. The Mali kings were followers of Islam: One of the most famous, Gonga-Mussa, made a pilgrimage to Mecca in 1324 to fulfill his religious duty as a Muslim. His caravan is said to have included 60,000 people and 80 camels carrying over 24,000 pounds of gold.

This 1375 European map of northwest Africa shows an Arab trader approaching Mansa Musa of Mali, who is holding a large nugget of gold.

A bronze relief of Benin, a powerful kingdom when the Portuguese began trading along the African coast in the late fifteenth century.

Mali provided stable government over a wide area until the fifteenth century, when Songhay successfully challenged its dominance. Songhay was centered at Gao and had been subordinate to Mali in the time of Gonga-Mussa. Under Sonni Ali, who ruled from 1468 to 1492—as the Atlantic slave trade developed—Songhay captured Timbuktu, an important trading and cultural center of Mali, consolidating power over a large part of West Africa. Askia Mohammed, who ruled from 1493 to 1528, expanded the empire even farther. In waging wars, the Songhay armies, like those of other African states, captured and enslaved their enemies. Askia Mohammed strengthened ties with other Muslims and reformed government, banking, and education. He introduced a uniform system of weights and measures, adopted Islamic law, and encouraged intellectual growth at Timbuktu and Gao, drawing scholars from throughout West Africa, Asia, and Europe. After Askia Mohammed's reign, Songhay declined; Moroccans conquered Timbuktu in 1593.

Beyond these empires, along the West African coast lay smaller states with highly developed cultures. While influenced by Islam, they retained much of their traditional religions, including some belief in witchcraft and the power of charms. Divine kings governed many of the coastal states as the sacred, physical symbols of their realms. Like Native Americans and Europeans, the people of Africa kept religion central to their lives and endowed their leaders with both political and religious authority.

Most important in traditional African religions was a single all-powerful God, the Creator. Africans generally believed, however, that God was "too high exalted above us, and too great to condescend so much as to trouble himself or think of Mankind." Thus, the Creator provided lesser gods, including gods of rain, thunder, and lightning; of rivers and lakes; of animals, trees, and hills. These gods could be benevolent or harmful, so people had to seek positive relationships through rituals, sacrifice, and prayer. Africans also believed that their ancestors watched over the extended family, with power over fertility, health, even life. When the eldest father, or patriarch, of a kinship group died, his spirit became a god. Elaborate funeral rites demonstrated the importance of the dead to the living. All family members paid respect to the deceased, whose internments were delayed until distant relatives could arrive. Before his death, the patriarch had been the extended family's priest; he communicated with its ancestors through prayer and the sacrifice of animals such as chickens and sheep. The patriarch also served as political leader. Thus in many African societies, the state, religion, and family united under a single hierarchical structure.

Kinship in West Africa varied from one culture to another, as extended families could be either patrilineal or matrilineal. In all cases, however, a child belonged to only one kin group, that of the father or the mother. If the system was patrilineal, then descent and paternal responsibility flowed from father to child. If it was matrilineal, descent proceeded from mother to child, but the mother's brother, not the mother, assumed responsibility and control. When a woman married, she remained a member of her own kin group, but usually went to live with her husband's family. The intended husband compensated her family for the loss of her services with a payment called bridewealth, which did not represent purchase of the woman herself. *Polygyny,* or having more than one wife, was legal in African societies, but generally reserved to men of high status. Kinship groups paid the bridewealth for the services of the first wife, not a second, and few men could meet the expenses for marrying another. When men had more than one wife, each woman lived with her children in a separate house.

The extended family formed the basis of economic organization, holding land in common and assigning plots to individual families. Women and men worked in fields growing crops such as rice, cassava, wheat, millet, cotton, fruits, and vegetables. They had live-stock, including cattle, sheep, goats, and chickens. Families produced food for their own use and for the market, where women were the primary traders. Artisans were skilled in textile weaving, pottery, basketry, and woodwork. They also made tools and art objects of copper, bronze, iron, silver, and gold. As in the case of Native Americans, West Africans had experienced the rise and fall of empires and possessed diverse, complex cultures at the time Europeans arrived on their shores in the mid-fifteenth century.

The Atlantic Slave Trade Begins

Over the course of four centuries, West Africa lost to the Atlantic slave trade at least 20 million people, of whom 10 million actually survived to toil in American fields. Slavery had existed in Africa and throughout the Mediterranean for centuries before the Portuguese arrived on the West African coast. African slavery was different, however, from the institution that developed in America. In comparison with plantation areas of the New World, a small percentage of African people were in bonds. Most African slaves were prisoners of war; others had committed some offense that caused their kinfolk to banish them. All were considered "outsiders." While most bond-

A Fula town in West Africa, drawn by a European. West Africans, like Europeans but not Native Americans, kept domestic livestock. Note that this village is raising Indian corn, a Native American crop.

men and women did menial work, the primary function of slavery in West Africa was social rather than economic—to provide a place in society for people cut off from their families. Trans-Saharan traders transported some African slaves for sale to wealthy European households where they served as domestic workers and artisans. Because this trade was limited, most slaves remained in West Africa, where they lived under the protection of law, achieved status as a member of a household, married, and had children. Enslaved Africans could be transferred from one owner to another at will, but their children could not be sold and were frequently emancipated. Traditionally, slavery had a quite different meaning in Africa than what developed in the New World.

The plantation slave system that became dominant in America began near Africa, however, before Columbus crossed the Ocean Sea. Portugal began growing sugar as early as 1452 on the island of Madeira, off West Africa. Sugar cane, which originated in South Asia, required large amounts of menial, unpleasant labor in a hot climate; thus workers were generally coerced. To supply Madeira, Portuguese merchants purchased black slaves from Muslim trans-Saharan traders and from Africans along the coast. When sugar production could expand no farther in Madeira for lack of land, the Portuguese colonized the small islands in the Gulf of Guinea: São Tomé, Príncipe, and Fernando Po. Sugar production was successful, but mortality was high and the demand for laborers great, spurring growth of the slave trade on the Gold Coast. By the end of the fifteenth century, before European settlement in America, Portugal developed both the plantation system that consumed large numbers of African slaves and the commercial mechanism for purchasing human beings from African traders. The growth of slavery and the slave trade in America after 1500 represented an expansion of these earlier developments, not innovations.

SPAIN AND PORTUGAL DIVIDE THE GLOBE

Once Portugal had established trade on the West African coast, Spanish merchants tried to participate. Prince Henry appealed to the pope, who in 1455 gave Portugal sole possession of lands to the south and east toward India. Mariners and merchants from other nations who attempted to trade in Africa were to be thrown into the ocean. In an age when the line between religious and secular authority was blurred, the pope's decision gave Portugal a monopoly on the Atlantic slave trade, and in effect sanctioned that commerce in return for efforts to Christianize the "heathen." Spain and Portugal affirmed the decision with the Treaty of Alcaçovas (1479), in which Spain recognized Portugal's sphere of interest in Africa, and Portugal acknowledged Spain's claim to the Canary Islands.

As the Portuguese sailed south, they came to recognize the vastness of the African continent. They made rapid progress only after 1482, when King John II of Portugal, a geographer himself, stepped up the program of discovery. In 1483, Diogo Cão reached the Congo River and in 1487 Bartholomeu Dias rounded the Cape of Good Hope. The Portuguese now knew that a sea route to India existed, yet the enormity of the enterprise discouraged them from immediately sending out ships.

Columbus Sails West

Because the Spanish recognized Portugal's claim to Africa and the eastern sea route, they had to find

Columbus's arrival in America, by Theodor de Bry.

MAP 1.3   EUROPEAN EXPLORATIONS, 1492-1542

another course if they were going to trade with the Far East. Thus, Isabella and Ferdinand funded Columbus, despite their skepticism of his calculation of the distance to Asia, which turned out to be a serious underestimate. In August 1492, Columbus sailed west from the Canaries, taking advantage of the favorable current and trade winds that flow westward north of the equator then circle clockwise in the Gulf of Mexico to emerge as the Gulf Stream. The ships reached San Salvador in October, but Columbus thought they had located the East Indies. Hoping to establish trade, Columbus sailed southward to Cuba, then touched Hispaniola, where Native Americans offered gold in return for the trade goods he brought. When the Spanish lost their flagship *Santa Maria* on a coral reef, they built a small fort with its timbers.

Leaving behind a small contingent of men, Columbus set out for home in January 1493, again found favorable winds, but encountered a violent storm and sought shelter in Portugal. King John II, whose explorers had not yet reached India by sailing around Africa, refused to believe that Columbus located Asia. The lands he had found, the king claimed, lay within Portugal's sphere.

Spanish and Portuguese "Spheres"

Isabella and Ferdinand rejected Portugal's argument, petitioning Pope Alexander VI, who was Spanish, to grant them dominion over the newly discovered lands. After negotiations with John II, the pope established a Line of Demarcation, giving all lands "discovered or to be discovered" west of the line to Spain and all lands east of the line to Portugal. The Treaty of Tordesillas, which finalized the negotiations in 1494 and located the line 370 leagues (about 1,000 miles) west of the Azores, expanded the principle of "spheres of influence" by which European nations sought to dominate most of the world. Portugal retained its rights to the Atlantic slave trade and the sea route around Africa to India. Spain received permission to explore, conquer, and Christianize all lands and people to the west. The question of where Portuguese and Spanish spheres should be divided in the Far East was left unresolved until 1529, when the Treaty of Saragossa established a line seventeen degrees to the east of the Moluccas (Spice Islands), thus placing most of Asia within Portugal's sphere.

Between 1494 and 1529, Portugal and Spain sent out expeditions to explore the reaches of their spheres and to find the sea routes to the East. Columbus made three more voyages to the west: In November 1493 he sailed with seventeen ships to the Lesser Antilles, Puerto Rico, and Hispaniola, where he reestablished the colony, which Native Americans had destroyed in the interim. Later he explored the shores of South and Central America. Meanwhile, Columbus's claim that he had found a passage to the East by sailing west prodded the Portuguese to complete their efforts to reach India. In 1497–1498, Vasco da Gama rounded the Cape of Good Hope, sailed across the Indian Ocean, returning to Portugal with a cargo of pepper and cinnamon. The voyage to India was much more difficult than Columbus's Atlantic crossing. During the two-year journey that included at least 300 days at sea, more than one-third of the sailors died. In 1500, Portugal instructed Pedro Álvares Cabral to find the Cape of Good Hope by sailing west. Instead, he touched the coast of Brazil, further convincing the Portuguese that this was not Asia, but lands previously unknown. On the basis of Cabral's expedition and because a section of Brazil lay east of the Line of Demarcation, Portugal claimed that part of South America. Amerigo Vespucci, a native of Florence, made two separate voyages, in 1499 and 1501, for Spain and Portugal respectively. He explored much of the Atlantic coast of South America, demonstrating that it was a huge land mass that had to be circumnavigated to reach Asia. In reward for his insights, many Europeans associated his name—not that of Columbus—with the newly "discovered" continents.

An Expanding World

Despite the promise of riches in America, Europeans continued to search for a western sea route to Asia. Ferdinand Magellan convinced King Charles I of Spain that he could sail around the cape of South America and claim the Molucca Islands, which he believed lay within Spain's sphere. Magellan was Portuguese but his country gave him no support for his plan since they already had a profitable sea route to the East. With five ships, in 1519 Magellan set out on an expedition that would take three years. The voyagers experienced shipwreck, a harrowing passage through the straits subsequently named for Magellan, and starvation: The Pacific was so much wider than anticipated that the mariners had to eat ship rats and leather to survive. When inhabitants of the Philippines killed Magellan, Sebastian del Cano took command, returning to Spain with one surviving ship, laden with cloves. Together, Magellan and del Cano commanded the first circumnavigation of the globe. In doing so, however, they demonstrated that the southwest passage through the Straits of Magellan and across the Pacific Ocean was much more difficult than envisioned.

England and France also wanted a part of the eastern trade, so they ignored the pope's division of the world between Spain and Portugal. With their more northerly location and some knowledge of the coast of North America, they sought a northwest passage to the East. During the fifteenth century (before Columbus's landfall), seafarers from England and France had

Admiral Christopher Columbus's Diary Account of Reaching America, October 12, 1492

This document is from an abstract of Columbus's diary made by the Spanish missionary Bartolomé de las Casas. The Admiral's original diary no longer exists. This selection begins as the Europeans sight land and describes their first contact with the Native Americans. Because Columbus thought his expedition had reached the East Indies, he called the people Indians.

At two hours after midnight the land appeared, from which they were about two leagues distant. They hauled down all the sails . . . passing time until daylight Friday, when they reached an islet of the Lucayas, which was called Guanahani in the language of the Indians. Soon they saw naked people; and the Admiral [Columbus] went ashore in the armed launch, and Martín Alonso Pinzón and his brother Vicente Anes, who was captain of the *Niña*. The Admiral brought out the royal banner and the captains' two flags with the green cross, which the Admiral carried on all the ships as a standard, with an F and a Y, and over each letter a crown, one on one side of the ✝ and the other on the other. Thus put ashore they saw very green trees and many ponds and fruits of various kinds. The Admiral called to the two captains and to the others who had jumped ashore and to Rodrigo Descobedo, the recorder of the whole fleet, and to Rodrigo Sánchez de Segovia; and he said that they should be witnesses that, in the presence of all, he would take, as in fact he did take, possession of the said island for the king and for the queen his lords, making the declarations that were required, and which at more length are contained in the testimonials made there in writing. Soon many people of the island gathered there. What follows are the very words of the Admiral in his book about his first voyage to, and discovery of, these Indies. I, he says, in order that they would be friendly to us—because I recognized that they were people who would be better freed [from error] and converted to our Holy Faith by love than by force—to some of them I gave red caps, and glass beads which they put on their chests, and many other things of small value, in which they took so

caught tuna, cod, mackerel, and other fish that teemed in the Newfoundland Banks. Some sailors had camped ashore, where they dried their catch and traded with Native Americans. When King Henry VII of England sent John Cabot, an Italian whose name was really Giovanni Caboto, in search of a northwest passage in 1497, the expedition reached Newfoundland. Cabot sailed again the next year, but most of his ships were lost and he died at sea. While the English were discouraged by Cabot's failure to find a passage or bring back valuable goods, nevertheless, his efforts supported England's later claim to land in North America.

A generation after Cabot, the French entered the search for a route to Asia. In 1524, King Francis I sent another Italian, Giovanni da Verrazano, to look for the elusive passage. Landing at Cape Fear (now North Carolina), Verrazano sailed north along the Atlantic seaboard to Newfoundland, finding no evidence of a waterway through the continent. In expeditions dating 1534 and 1535, Jacques Cartier hoped to find the route by way of the gulf and river of St. Lawrence. He mapped the river and in 1541 established a short-lived colony named Charlesbourg-Royal near the future site of Quebec. While neither Verrazano nor Cartier found much pleasure and became so much our friends that it was a marvel. Later they came swimming to the ships' launches where we were and brought us parrots and cotton thread in balls and javelins and many other things, and they traded them to us for other things which we gave them, such as small glass beads and bells. In sum, they took everything and gave of what they had very willingly. But it seemed to me that they were a people very poor in everything. All of them go around as naked as their mothers bore them; and the women also, although I did not see more than one quite young girl. And all those that I saw were young people, for none did I see of more than 30 years of age. They are very well formed, with handsome bodies and good faces. Their hair [is] coarse—almost like the tail of a horse—and short. They wear their hair down over their eyebrows except for a little in the back which they wear long and never cut. Some of them paint themselves with black, and they are of the color of the Canarians, neither black nor white; and some of them paint themselves with white, and some of them with red, and some of them with whatever they find. And some of them paint their faces, and some of them the whole body, and some of them only the eyes, and some of them only the nose. They do not carry arms nor are they acquainted with them, because I showed them swords and they took them by the edge and through ignorance cut themselves. They have no iron. Their javelins are shafts without iron and some of them have at the end a fish tooth and others of other things. All of them alike are of good-sized stature and carry themselves well. I saw some who had marks of wounds on their bodies and I made signs to them asking what they were; and they showed me how people from other islands nearby came there and tried to take them, and how they defended themselves; and I believed and believe that they come here from *tierra firme* to take them captive. They should be good and intelligent servants, for I see that they say very quickly everything that is said to them; and I believe that they would become Christians very easily, for it seemed to me that they had no religion. Our Lord pleasing, at the time of my departure I will take six of them from here to Your Highnesses in order that they may learn to speak. No animal of any kind did I see on this island except parrots. All are the Admiral's words.

a northwest passage, they supplemented European knowledge of North America and supported France's claim to part of the continent.

THE SPANISH EMPIRE IN AMERICA

Because England and France showed only occasional interest in America before 1560, and Portugal focused on the eastern trade and Brazil, the Spanish had little interference from other Europeans in exploring and settling the rest of the New World. By 1543, their colonies extended south to Chile and north through Mexico; they had explored from Florida to California in what is now the United States. From Columbus's first colony, on the island of Hispaniola, Spanish conquistadores advanced from island to island in the West Indies, then moved to conquer the people of Mexico and Central America. Lured by stories of cities of gold, they ascended the Andes and crossed deserts. The conquistadores expected to make their fortune in America and retire to Spain. Their chief objective was to get rich. In contrast, the Spanish Crown had a more complicated set of goals in colonizing America: to enhance its power among European nations by dominating huge territories in the west; to exploit the wealth of these lands, especially gold and silver; and to convert the conquered Americans to Christianity. While in many ways the goals of the Spanish monarchy and its settlers overlapped, sometimes their interests diverged, especially when it came to the welfare of Native Americans. Often, when they wished, the colonists could subvert the will of the government because its gears worked so slowly and its center of power rested in far-off Spain.

Spanish Conquest

From Hispaniola, the Spanish conquered nearby islands and then wealthier and more powerful peoples on the mainland. When they found little gold on Hispaniola, the conquerors exploited the remaining resources of the island: the labor of its inhabitants and the land. The natives died when the Spanish enslaved them to work on plantations and tend livestock. European diseases took their toll, as did cruel treatment and the psychological effects of bondage. As a result, the colonists sent slave-raiding parties to other islands and to the mainland. The conquistadores who first explored Cuba in 1508 were seeking slaves and gold. For the same reasons they colonized Puerto Rico in 1509. Juan Ponce de León, known for his search in 1513 for the legendary "fountain of youth" in Florida and Yucatan, sought Indian slaves. The same year Vasco Núñez de Balboa led explorers across the Isthmus of Panama, becoming the first Europeans to see the Pacific Ocean.

As the Spanish explorers became aware of the vastness of the Americas and the potential for riches, they organized militarily to subdue the Americans. Despite the small size of their armies, the Spanish prevailed over large empires, in part because of superior technology, including metal weaponry and the use of horses and ships, and in part because they made alliances with the enemies of the Indian emperors. They also had help from disease. The conquistadores, in their quest for wealth and glory, competed with one another to conquer the Native Americans. The most famous of these conquerors is Hernán Cortés who, in 1519, launched an expedition against the Aztecs, who them-

Portrait medal of Hernán Cortés, who conquered the Aztecs, produced when he visited Spain in 1529.

selves had recently consolidated their Mexican empire. With an army of only 500 troops, Cortés persuaded the Totonacs of Cempoala, who were dominated by the Aztecs, to join him. Then defeating the Tlaxcalans and gaining their support as well, he marched to Tenochtitlán, the Aztec capital. The Spanish and their Indian allies entered the city without opposition and seized Moctezuma, the emperor. When Cortés outlawed human sacrifice, denied the primacy of Aztec gods, and made incessant demands for gold, Aztec priests and people rebelled. In the heat of battle, they killed Moctezuma and forced the Spanish and their allies to retreat, slaying many as they tried to escape across the causeways linking Tenochtitlán with the shore of Lake Texcoco. Cortés was not finished, however, and in 1521 with reinforcements advanced methodically on the Aztec capital. This time the Spanish built small ships to cross Lake Texcoco, took control of all causeways, and destroyed Tenochtitlán building by building. A smallpox epidemic killed many Aztecs. The conquerors rebuilt the city as Mexico City, the Spanish capital of Mexico, which they called New Spain.

After 1521, the Spanish extended their conquest through Mexico, Central and South America. Having defeated the Aztecs, Cortés sent troops to take

Guatemala; in 1524 rival conquistadores took control of Honduras. Then they advanced to the south, as Francisco Pizarro vanquished the Incas of Peru in 1531–1534, and others expanded into Argentina and Chile. The Spanish also explored the lands north of Mexico, in the area that is now the United States. Alonso Álvarez de Pineda in 1519–1520 sailed the coastline of the Gulf of Mexico from Florida to Mexico, demonstrating the existence of a continent of North America, not just islands.

Exploration of Florida and the American Southwest

In 1528, the Spanish conquistador Pánfilo de Narváez led an expedition to Florida in quest of cities of gold. Though his venture failed, it led to later exploration of territories that became the southern United States. Narváez and his men landed at Tampa Bay where they met Native Americans who immediately warned them to return to the sea. When the Europeans refused, and spoke of their search for silver and gold, the Indians directed them to the north, to a place called "Apalachen," near the present site of Tallahassee. The Spanish left their ships and most of their supplies, marching northward through insect- and snake-infested terrain. Soon discouraged, they made the mistake of kidnapping a chief of the Apalachees, who had initially been friendly. Highly skilled archers, the Indians attacked, convincing the Spanish to return to New Spain immediately. The soldiers constructed barges, with sails made from their shirts, to carry them across the Gulf of Mexico. When storms separated the craft, most of the explorers, including Narváez, were lost at sea.

Two barges crossed the gulf intact, beaching their occupants on the Texas coast, probably at Galveston Island. The native Karankawas enslaved the survivors, who were nearly starved and lacked weapons or horses. After several years, one of the Spaniards, Álvar Núñez Cabeza de Vaca, who had become an Indian priest and healer, escaped with three others, Alonso del Castillo, Andrés Dorantes, and Esteban, a black slave. They hoped to reach New Spain, but lacked maps or instruments to find their way. For several years they sojourned with a series of Native American peoples, learning their languages and customs. The Spanish earned the Indians' friendship and respect with seemingly miraculous cures. When they finally reached Mexico City in 1536, Cabeza de Vaca told the Spanish viceroy about their journey and tales that they had heard of treasures in the north.

Cabeza de Vaca's report, which he later published, excited interest in exploring lands north of Mexico. When Cabeza de Vaca refused to head an expedition, the viceroy sent the enslaved man, Esteban, with a Franciscan monk, Fray Marcos de Niza, along with several Indians, to scout for the "Seven Cities of Cibola." When Esteban was killed by Zuñis, Fray Marcos returned to Mexico City with extravagant claims that the seven cities existed, that the land flowed with riches.

In 1540, an army of 336 Spanish and about 1,000 Indians marched north under command of Francisco Vásquez de Coronado, with Fray Marcos as their guide. The explorers intended to conquer the cities of gold, claiming the wealth for themselves and the king of Spain. Like Narváez in Florida, they were disappointed. The "golden" city that Fray Marcos had spotted was actually a Zuñi Indian pueblo, Hawikúh, made of adobe, not gold. Coronado sent the monk back to Mexico City with the complaint, "He has not told the truth in a single thing that he said, but everything is the opposite of what he related, except the name of the cities and the large stone houses." The Zuñis resisted the intruders, but were conquered, then informed the Spanish that the Seven Cities lay to the west. Another Indian, whom the Spanish named "El Turco" (the Turk), told stories about great wealth in the country to the east. Over the next year, Coronado's troops explored in both directions. They encountered the Hopi of northeastern Arizona and buffalo-hunting Indians of the Great Plains, saw the Grand Canyon, and traveled as far east as Kansas. They found no gold or silver but left descriptions of a substantial part of the American Southwest.

To reinforce Coronado's army, the viceroy in 1540 sent Hernando de Alarcón by ship up the western coast of Mexico. Though the two explorers failed to make contact, Alarcón sailed into the Colorado River, investigating its banks for several weeks. Two years later, Juan Rodríguez Cabrillo sailed with two ships up the coast of Baja California, past San Diego Bay. They were the first Europeans to visit what is now California. After Cabrillo died in January 1543, his deputy Bartolomé Ferrelo sailed almost as far north as Oregon, passing San Francisco Bay without actually seeing it because of fog.

Unknown to Coronado, an expedition led by Hernando de Soto, governor of Cuba, came within a few

AN AZTEC REPORT OF THE FALL OF TENOCHTITLÁN 1521

The Aztecs fought the Spanish and their Indian allies for months before the invaders, led by Hernán Cortés, prevailed. This document gives an Aztec view of the surrender and shows the immediate impact of the conquest on ordinary men, women, and children.

And when night had fallen, then it rained and sprinkled at intervals. Late at night the flame became visible; just so was it seen, just so it emerged as if it came from the heavens. Like a whirlwind it went spinning around and revolving; it was as if embers burst out of it—some very large, some very small, some like sparks. Like a coppery wind it arose, crackling, snapping, and exploding loudly. Then it circled the dike and traveled toward Coyonacazco; then it went into the middle of the lake there to be lost.

None shouted; none spoke aloud.

And on the next day, nothing more happened. All remained quiet, and also our foes [so] remained.

But the Captain [Cortés] was watching from a roof-top at Amaxac—from the roof-top of [the house of] Aztauatzin—under a canopy. It was a many-colored canopy. He looked toward [us] common folk; the Spaniards crowded about him and took counsel among themselves.

And [on our side] were Quauhtemoc and the other noblemen—the vice ruler Tlacotzin, the lords' judge Petlauhtzin, the captain of the armies Motelchiuhtzin; the constable of Mexico; and the lord priest; and also the noblemen of Tlatilulco—the general Coyoueuetzin; the commanding general Temilotzin; the army commander Topantemoctzin; the chief justice Auelitoctzin; the captain of the armies Uitziliuitzin; and the courier Uitzitzin. All of these noblemen were assembled at Tolmayecan; they appeared to consult among themselves how to do that which we were to undertake and how we should yield to [the Spaniards].

Thereafter only two [men] took Quauhtemoc in a boat. The two who took him and went with him were the seasoned warrior Teputzitoloc, and Yaztachimal, Quauhtemoc's page. And the one who poled [the boat] was named Cenyaotl.

And when they carried Quauhtemoc off, then there was weeping among all the common folk. They said: "Now goeth the young lord Quauhtemoc; now he goeth to deliver himself to the gods, the Spaniards!"

And when they had betaken themselves to bring and disembark him thereupon all the Spaniards came to see. They drew him along; the Spaniards took him by the hand. After

---

hundred miles of his own company at about the same time. In 1539, De Soto and about 600 troops landed in Tampa Bay. Over the next three years, with aid in translating from a survivor of the Narváez disaster who was living with the Indians, they trekked through the southeast, exploring lands hitherto unknown to the Spanish but finding no gold. The Spanish plundered the populous, thriving towns of the Apalachees and other Florida Indians who were part of the Mississippian cultures, with temple mounds and long-range trading networks. Stealing food, taking Indians as slaves, cutting off limbs, and killing those who re-that they took him up to the roof-top, where they went to stand him before the Captain, the war leader. And when they had proceeded to stand him before [Cortés], they looked at Quauhtemoc, made much of him, and stroked his hair. Then they seated him with [Cortés] and fired the guns. They hit no one with them, but only made them go off above, [so that] they passed over the heads of the common folk. Then [some Mexicans] only fled. With this the war reached its end.

Then there was shouting; they said: "Enough! Let it end! Eat greens!" When they heard this, the common folk thereupon issued forth. On this, they went, even into the lagoon.

And as they departed, leaving by the great road, once more they there slew some, wherefore the Spaniards were wroth that still some again had taken up their obsidian-bladed swords and their shields. Those who dwelt in house clusters went straightway to Amaxac; they went direct to where the ways divide. There the common folk separated. So many went toward Tepeyacac, so many toward Xoxouiltitlan, so many toward Nonoalco. But toward Xolloco and toward Macatzintamal no one went.

And all who lived in boats and [in houses] on poles, and those at Tolmayecan, went into the water. On some, the water reached to the stomach; some, to the chest; and on some it reached to the neck. And some were all submerged, there in the deeps. Little children were carried on the backs [of their elders]; cries of weeping arose. Some went on happy and rejoicing as they traveled crowding on the road. And those who owned boats, all the boatmen, left by night, and even [continued to] leave all day. It was as if they pushed and crowded one another as they set out.

And everywhere the Spaniards were seizing and robbing the people. They sought gold; as nothing did they value the green stone, quetzal feathers and turquoise [which] was everywhere in the bosoms or in the skirts of the women. And as for us men, it was everywhere in [our] breech clouts and in [our] mouths.

And [the Spaniards] seized and set apart the pretty women—those of light bodies, the fair[-skinned] ones. And some women, when they were robbed, covered their face with mud and put on old, mended shirts and rags for their shifts. They put all rags on themselves.

And also some of us men were singled out—those who were strong, grown to manhood, and next the young boys, of whom they would make messengers, who would be their runners, and who were known as their servers. And on some they burned [brand marks] on their cheeks; on some they put paint on their cheeks; on some they put paint on their lips.

And when the shield was laid down, when we gave way, it was the year count Three House and the day count was One Serpent.

sisted, De Soto's men marched north from the Florida peninsula, through central Georgia to the Carolinas, then west across the Appalachians into the Tennessee River valley. They followed the river south into Alabama, then traveled west toward the Mississippi, which the Native Americans called the "Father of Waters." Still intent on finding the Seven Cities of Cibola, despite heavy losses when Chickasaws burned their camp and supplies, De Soto crossed into Arkansas. After he died of a fever in 1542 and was buried in the Mississippi, the 300 survivors of his expedition safely reached New Spain by boat.

The failure of Coronado and De Soto to find the Seven Cities ended exploration of the region north of Mexico for forty years. Indeed, in 1542, the initial period of Spanish expansion came to a close throughout America. They had sufficient land for agriculture, so, without discovery of precious metals, they had little immediate reason to push farther into North America. During the half century since Columbus sailed west, monumental changes had taken place in the New World. Contact and exchange among Native Americans, Europeans, and Africans created new political and social systems. While the Spanish expected to conquer the people of America and create a society much like the one at home, the results of colonization proved different than planned.

Spanish Patterns of Colonization

As conquest of the Americas progressed, Spain established a colonial government that, in theory, was supposed to be uniform throughout the empire. Its purposes were to convert Native Americans and bring them under control of the Spanish monarchy, and to exploit their labor and the wealth of the New World. In reality, the Spanish were only partly successful in imposing their rule over the Indians. The colonial government was most effective in central Mexico and the Andes, where the Europeans substituted their own imperial rule for that of the Aztecs and Incas. Ordinary families now paid tribute to the Spanish instead of Indian emperors. Native Americans in northern Mexico, Florida, Arizona, New Mexico, and central Chile, who had never been subject to empires, evaded Spanish rule, in some cases for centuries. Many in the fringe areas, such as Apaches, avoided Spanish domination altogether because their bands were highly mobile and autonomous.

The Spanish colonial administration was hierarchical and tied closely to Spain. Sovereignty, or supreme political power, rested in the monarch who had the last word in all decisions. The Spanish, like other Europeans at the time, believed that God vested such power in the Crown. Neither Spanish colonists nor Indians had much say in making and enforcing laws. The right of subjects to appeal official decisions to the king, however, along with delays in decision making caused by distance, corruption, and bureaucratic inefficiency, introduced flexibility into the rigid governmental structure.

Directly below the monarch in colonial matters was the Council of the Indies, located in Spain and composed of men who knew little about conditions in the New World. The council's power over the settlements was all-encompassing: It regulated trade, appointed officials, made laws, and determined who should be allowed to emigrate. The highest officials residing in America were the viceroys, who ruled "in the place of the king." They held court in their palaces with ceremonies and etiquette similar to the king's. In the sixteenth and seventeenth centuries the Spanish empire consisted of two viceroyalties: New Spain, with its capital in Mexico City, and Peru, with its capital in Lima. The viceroyalties were divided into provinces, ruled by governors and *audiencias,* which advised the governors and functioned as courts to settle disputes and judge criminal cases. The audiencias could appeal all decisions to the king, thus limiting the wide powers of the viceroys and governors. So did, at least in theory, the *residencia,* which investigated these officials at the end of their terms and reported any corruption to Spain.

In central Mexico and Peru, the Spanish viceroys, governors, and audiencias took the place of the ruling native elite. At the local level, native leaders often retained their positions or were replaced by Indian rivals to act as intermediaries between the Native Americans and Spanish officials. These native leaders, called *caciques,* headed the Indian towns, collected tribute from every household, and recruited forced laborers upon the demand of the colonial authorities. The caciques received a portion of the tribute they collected.

Spanish Mercantilism

The Crown regulated commerce in the colonial empire through the *Casa de la Contratación,* a trading house founded in 1503 in Seville. Thus Spain elaborated its economic policy of mercantilism, which held that nations had monopolistic rights to trade with their colonies. With tight governmental control, the primary goal of economic activity under mercantilism was to achieve a favorable balance of trade. Colonies were expected to serve as markets for goods from the home country and provide raw materials, gold, and silver to increase its wealth. All merchants desiring to send ships to Spanish America needed permission from the Casa, as did anyone wishing to emigrate. The Casa denied leave to persons of Jewish ancestry, for example, though in fact many found passage to America without official permission. To the monarch, a crucial function of the Casa was registration of precious metals, because the king received one-fifth, called the "royal fifth," of all silver and gold. The Spanish monarch claimed sovereignty over all the land and people of his empire. Colonists had to obtain permission to build plantations and mines. In return they paid taxes to the king and, if they found precious metals, the royal fifth.

When Columbus, on his first voyage, obtained gold from the inhabitants of Hispaniola, he raised expectations of great wealth. Beyond the pearl fisheries off the coast of Venezuela and some gold ornaments, however, the explorers at first met disappointment. Even the Aztecs failed to satisfy the Spanish thirst for gold, so most colonists turned to agriculture, especially sugar and livestock production, to make their fortunes. Then, in the 1540s, the Europeans located two immensely rich silver mines, one at Potosí in present-day Bolivia and the other at Zacatecas in Mexico. These mines yielded huge amounts of silver. Between 1500 and 1650 about 181 tons of gold and 16,000 tons of silver officially reached Europe from America; probably much more was smuggled. The gold was more important before the 1540s and the silver after. Production of silver expanded greatly in the 1570s with the introduction of mercury to the refining process.

The Spanish organized their silver trade to outwit privateers of other nations, especially France and England. In 1565, the Spanish founded St. Augustine in Florida as a base to fight the buccaneers and to rescue crews and cargo from ships wrecked in hurricanes and on shoals. Sea captains hugged the Florida coast to help navigate as they caught the Gulf Stream home. St. Augustine, the first permanent European settlement in what is now the United States, also reinforced Spain's claim to North America (as discussed later in this chapter). The Spanish devised a convoy system to protect their fleets. Two convoys left Seville each year carrying goods such as wine, swords, books, oil, grain, clothing, and other luxuries: One left in May headed for Mexico, and the other departed in August for the Isthmus of Panama, from which mules carried the goods to Peru. Both convoys stayed the winter with the intention of meeting in Cuba by early summer so they could return to Spain before the onset of hurricanes. The Panama fleet sometimes ran into trouble when the mule train carrying Potosí silver arrived late. The silver could be delayed by as much as two months

in Bolivia because of lack of rain, which was needed to refine the ore.

For the Spanish monarchy, the discovery of rich mines fulfilled their dreams in the New World. The king used the bullion to pay for his European wars—60 percent of the precious metals left Spain immediately. American silver and gold helped to create what has been called a "price revolution," or inflation, throughout Europe. With the immense supply of the metals their value declined and the prices of other goods increased. Merchants depended on the bullion to pay for luxuries from the East. Goods worth about one-half the value of the metals were returned to the colonies in subsequent fleets.

New World Societies

While the Spanish colonists changed America significantly, the new societies were not exactly what they had planned. If some European settlers hoped to duplicate Spanish society and culture, and have millions of Christianized Indian workers do their bidding, they were disappointed. For a number of reasons, including the lack of women among Spanish immigrants, the catastrophic level of native deaths, and the resistance of Indians to conversion, the developing New World societies diverged from what both the Spanish and Native Americans had previously known.

Despite continuing emigration from Spain and rapid demographic decline among the Native Americans, the Spanish colonists remained a small percentage of the population. In 1550 about 100,000 whites lived in the Spanish colonies. By comparison, the population of the Aztec empire before the conquest had been an estimated 25 million; of Peru, 9 million. With the devastating effects of diseases that Europeans brought to the Western Hemisphere, by 1570 the number of natives in central Mexico was only 2.6 million and in Peru 1.3 million.

In conquering the Native Americans, the chief ally of the Spanish was disease, of which smallpox was most lethal. Other Old World killers included measles, chicken pox, influenza, whooping cough, diphtheria, malaria, amoebic dysentery, and bubonic plague. The Indians had no immunity to these diseases because the microbes were new to the Western Hemisphere. Disease spread from one native population to another, infecting the people of North

Sixteenth-century drawings of Aztecs suffering from smallpox when the Spanish invaded.

America even before the English and French established colonies along the Atlantic coast. Some regions of the continent seemed uninhabited to European latecomers because of prior contact with disease. As the native population of the Americas declined by an estimated 90 percent, whole tribes were eliminated and others weakened severely.

Nevertheless, most surviving Native Americans resisted assimilation to Spanish culture: They retained their languages, clothing, housing, agricultural methods, and, to a considerable extent, religion. The degree to which they blocked acculturation depended largely on class. The Spanish focused much attention on the caciques and their sons, with whom they interacted more frequently than with ordinary Indians. Many caciques learned to speak Spanish, converted to Christianity, and adopted Hispanic clothing, housing, and furniture. Their sons attended schools where they learned Latin and other advanced subjects. The common Indians avoided some Spanish ways of living and accepted others. They raised and ate chickens, but grew wheat primarily to pay as tribute. They abhorred cattle, which trampled their crops, but groups like the Apache quickly accepted the horse. Natives favored their digging-sticks over the European plow, which would have required the use of draft animals and alteration in the assignment of fields.

The "Columbian exchange," as the transfer of culture among Americans, Europeans, and Africans has been called, did not proceed in just one direction.

While the Europeans introduced deadly diseases, livestock, European wheat, the wheel, firearms, and Christianity to the Indians, the Native Americans in turn provided crops that had a major impact on the growth of world populations. The white potato of South America became a major staple in northern Europe; the sweet potato, cassava, and Indian corn are important throughout the world. Native Americans also helped Europeans adapt to the New World environment, for example, by showing them how to raise Indian corn, catch fish using weirs, and build canoes.

The complexity of interaction between the Spanish and Native Americans can be seen most vividly in religion. The Europeans had a mandate from the pope to convert the "pagans" of America to Christianity. The missionaries believed their goal was just, that it was an act of humanity to introduce the Indians to Catholicism, which they understood to be the only true religion. The Spanish eliminated human sacrifice and destroyed temples and relics, but for the most part avoided forced conversion. At first, the missionaries expected most Native Americans to accept Spanish religious practice without change, as many Indians consented to baptism and voluntarily built churches in every town. But most Indians merged the European faith with rituals and beliefs of their traditional religions, resulting in *syncretism,* the blending of two faiths. For example, some natives added the Christian God to their polytheistic system; others focused on the saints or the Trinity rather than the supreme God. In some churches, idols stood behind Catholic altars. Indians organized *cofradías,* which were societies to raise money for church functions and festivals. The natives controlled the cofradías and at times asserted independence from the Spanish church authority.

The retention of native beliefs and practices disappointed many Spanish priests, who would accept nothing less than complete submission to their form of Catholicism. Nevertheless, missionaries worked for humane treatment of Indians, challenging other Spaniards who denied that natives were human. Colonists often justified enslaving Indians because they had "inferior" cultures and religion. A number of priests, of whom Bartolomé de las Casas is best known, condemned the cruelty and enslavement. In his *Short Account of the Destruction of the Indies,* written in 1542 for the Crown, Las Casas argued for more enlightened policies. Describing atrocities and slaughter in one colony after another, he informed the king of "the excesses which this New World has witnessed, all of them surpassing anything that men hitherto have imagined even in their wildest dreams."

Forced Labor Systems

Because the Spanish colonists were few in number and had no intention of working in mines or fields, they adopted ways to compel Native Americans to work. When the first explorers on Hispaniola tried to consign the native Arawaks to slavery, most of the Indians died. In 1500, the Spanish Crown ruled that only Indians captured in a "just war" could be forced into perpetual bondage. This judgment had little impact because conquistadores could define as hostile any natives who resisted capture, thus rationalizing slavery. In 1513, the government drew up a document called the *Requerimiento* (or Requirement), which explorers read when they entered an Indian town for the first time. The requerimiento informed the natives that they must accept the sovereignty of the Catholic church and the Spanish monarchy. If they did, they would become

Spanish subjects in peace; if they did not, the soldiers would "make war against you . . . take you and your wives and your children and . . . make slaves of them . . . and shall do to you all the harm and damage that we can." By the time the king outlawed most Native American slavery in 1542, the Arawaks of the West Indies had been destroyed. The Spanish had expropriated their lands for sugar plantations, replacing the Indians with enslaved Africans. On the mainland, the Spanish government established two forms of forced Indian labor. In neither type were the natives actually enslaved, but they could be required to perform service. With the *encomienda*, Indians living on specified lands had to pay tribute to individual colonists and sometimes provide labor for which they received minimal wages. At first, the encomienda system included no transfer of land to the colonists, but as the numbers of Native Americans declined and Spanish increased, the colonists took Indian property for farms and ranches. By the seventeenth century, grazing livestock—sheep, horses, mules, goats—replaced Indian farms on vast stretches of Spanish America.

An exterior view of Potosí, the Spanish silver mine in what is now Bolivia. The mine yielded immense wealth, but with a dreadful toll as laborers worked in harsh conditions deep underground.

In 1600, about 1 million Indians survived in central Mexico, down from 25 million a century before. This severe decline was obviously catastrophic for the natives, but also caused problems for the Spanish who depended upon them for food and labor. Thus, the government devised the *repartimiento* system, which rationed labor for both public and private projects. Indians could be forced to work in mines, agriculture, or public works for several weeks, months, or even a year. For example, natives labored for yearlong stints at the Potosí silver mines in Bolivia, where they were paid and provided subsistence, but had to travel long distances from their homes (often for several weeks) to reach the mines. They experienced harsh conditions and, as a result, many died. At Potosí, workers assigned as carriers climbed some 600 feet through tunnels about as wide as a man's body with heavy loads of silver ore on their backs. Those who worked in refining were exposed to mercury poisoning because part of the process involved walking with bare legs through the slurry of mercury, water, and ore. As the Indian population declined, in consequence of disease and these conditions, the Spanish had difficulty in finding enough workers. When they attempted to increase the length and frequency of work periods, Indians resisted the changes, sometimes successfully.

As early as 1502, on West Indies plantations, the Spanish turned to the people of Africa because they knew that Native Americans could not meet their insatiable labor demands. The Spanish took this step easily because they had already purchased Africans from Portuguese traders to work in Spain and on the sugar plantations of the Canary Islands. The government set up a system of licenses, or *asientos,* for merchants to supply certain numbers of slaves. During the sixteenth century, ships transported approximately 75,000 Africans to Spanish America, with perhaps an equal number dying en route, either in Africa or at sea. Compare this number of enslaved Africans with the estimate of 100,000 Spanish colonists in America in 1550. The Spanish imported Africans to work on sugar plantations in the West Indies and coastal areas of the mainland where most Native Americans had died. Severe work regimes and rampant disease also resulted in high death rates among imported blacks. Slavery in New Spain—and indeed in all of the New World colonies—was harsher than what bondpeople had experienced in Africa.

PROTESTANT NORTHERN EUROPEANS CHALLENGE CATHOLIC SPAIN

Until 1560, French and English activity in America remained much more tentative and sporadic than Spain's. While fishing expeditions regularly visited the North American coast, setting up summer camps, trading with Native Americans, and undoubtedly spreading disease, initiatives for permanent colonies gained little support. But significantly, religious and political change in Northern Europe in the sixteenth century provided the impetus to test Spain's domination of the New World. In the age of Reformation and religious wars, America became both a refuge for religious dissidents and a battlefield on which European nations fought for wealth, glory, and national sovereignty.

The Protestant Reformation

When the German priest Martin Luther in 1517 circulated his ninety-five theses against the sale of indulgences, the Church of Rome was the sovereign faith of western and central Europe. Luther challenged the unity of western Christianity because he believed the church was corrupt. The sale of indulgences, which were supposed to reduce the amount of time a deceased person spent in purgatory, was an example of its waywardness. Luther believed that people received salvation as a gift from God in return for faith ("justification by faith") rather than for good works. They could not earn salvation from eternal hellfire by taking pilgrimages, giving money to the church, hearing masses, or going on crusades against the Muslims. Luther also challenged the authority of priests, arguing for a "priesthood of all believers." Christians should seek the word of God in the Bible, which he translated into German to make more available to laypeople. He believed that he had found the way to salvation by reading scripture and suggested that others do the same. Luther contended that the Bible recognized only two sacraments, baptism and communion, not the seven authorized by the Catholic church. He opposed the requirement of celibacy for priests, marrying Katharina von Bora, a former nun.

Luther's teachings led to many divisions in western Christianity, as common people and princes alike adopted his beliefs. In Germany, which was composed of many individual states, some princes accepted Lutheranism and others remained Catholic. They expected their subjects to follow their example. Lutheranism spread through northern Germany and into Scandinavia. Luther inspired other critics of Catholicism to offer variant Protestant doctrines, including the Mennonites, Hutterites, and Swiss Brethren, all called Anabaptists because they required adult baptism as the sign of membership in their community of believers.

The most influential of the systems of belief that Lutheranism spawned was that of John Calvin, a native of France, who attempted to create a model society at Geneva, Switzerland. Followers of Calvin established churches in the Reformed tradition: They were known variously as French Huguenots, English Puritans, Scottish Presbyterians, and Dutch and German Reformed. Calvin agreed with Luther in challenging many Catholic teachings, but went further, arguing that humans were totally depraved and could do nothing to save themselves. This concept of predestination meant that God alone determined who would be saved (the "elect") and who would go to hell. Through communion with God, the elect learned that they were saved; they strove to live blamelessly to reflect their status.

Calvin and his followers convinced the city council and churches of Geneva to adopt many Reformed doctrines, stripping the churches of decoration, images, and colorful rituals. The Bible, as interpreted by Calvin, became the basis for law. The civil government punished moral offenders and nonbelievers identified by the church elders. The Calvinists disciplined individuals for dancing, charging high medical fees, wearing fancy clothes, and insubordination. They forced one man to walk through the city wearing only a shirt because he criticized Calvin, and burned another at the stake for heresy. While Calvin failed to obtain all of his demands from the Geneva council, he came close to establishing a theocracy, in which the church fathers ruled in the name of God. His Puritan successors in New England in the next century found much to emulate in Calvin's Geneva.

Protestant ideas spread to France and England quickly. In France, Calvin attracted many adherents, called Huguenots, among the nobles and prosperous commoners, though relatively few peasants adopted the faith. The French monarchy considered Protestants a threat to its monopoly of power and the established Catholic church. Even after the Edict of Nantes of 1598, which offered freedom to worship, Huguenots faced serious discrimination.

In England, years before Luther, opposition had existed to the Catholic hierarchy, its taxes, monasteries, and the use of images in church. Thus Henry VIII found sympathy for his break with Rome when the pope refused to allow an annulment of his marriage to Catherine of Aragon. Henry wanted to marry Anne Boleyn, who he hoped would provide a male heir. Parliament passed the Act of Supremacy (1534), mandating that the king be "taken, accepted, and reputed the only supreme head on earth of the Church of England." The Crown dissolved the monasteries and confiscated their property. Henry was no Lutheran, however, for the Six Articles (1539) that formed the theological basis of Anglicanism confirmed Catholic beliefs on priestly celibacy, the mass, confession, and sacraments. But because the Six Articles were ambiguous on many points, the Church of England from its inception allowed a fairly wide range of doctrine. In 1552, the revised Anglican prayer book incorporated many Protestant beliefs. Soon after, Henry's daughter Mary I attempted to force England back to the Church of Rome. Her persecution of Protestants earned her the name "Bloody Mary"; her marriage to the staunch Catholic Philip II of Spain inspired an English nationalism that fused loyalty to church and state. When Mary died in 1558, her half-sister, Elizabeth I, became queen, ending the immediate threat that England would return to Catholicism. The new English monarch and a large proportion of her subjects identified Spain as a threat to their national church, now Protestant, and their independence as a nation.

Under Elizabeth, the English confronted Spain on a number of fronts, leading to a showdown against invasion in 1588. In the religious struggles of the late sixteenth century, England became a dominant Protestant power, supported the Dutch revolt against Philip II, and challenged Spain's monopolistic claims to the New World. Though pragmatic and more interested in power than theology, Elizabeth confirmed England's break with the pope and approved earlier moderate Protestant reforms. The Act of Uniformity (1559) required adherence to the Anglican Book of Prayer. The queen suppressed resistance from both Calvinists, who

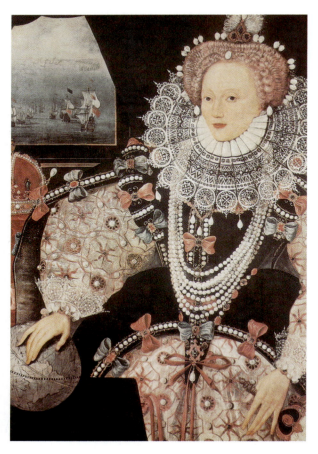

Queen Elizabeth I at the time of England's defeat of the Spanish Armada. With the globe, the artist suggests Elizabeth's interest in exploration, resting her hand on North America.

The Dutch rebelled against this persecution, foreign control, and high taxes. In 1581, the northern part of the Netherlands, composed of seven provinces, including Holland, declared its independence as the United Provinces. The southern region, called the Spanish Netherlands (now Belgium), remained under Philip's control. When Elizabeth sent aid to the United Provinces in 1585, she in effect declared a war on Spain that lasted until her death in 1603. The most important battle occurred in 1588, when Philip sent his mighty Armada of 130 ships and 30,000 men to invade England. The English defeated the Armada, despite the heavy odds against them, thus preserving their national sovereignty and religion.

French Huguenots and English Sea Dogs

In France, in the mid-sixteenth century, persecution led some Protestant Huguenots to look to America as a refuge, as well as a source of wealth. Though the French monarchy had not followed up Jacques Cartier's unsuccessful effort to colonize Canada, in 1555, a group of wealthy Frenchmen sent Huguenot settlers to Brazil. When disputes occurred among the colonists, some returned to France; the Portuguese, who claimed Brazil, killed or enslaved the majority who remained. In 1562, Huguenots tried again, establishing Charlesfort on the South Carolina coast, in part to attack the Spanish silver fleet as it headed home. When the Spaniards moved against the small French colony in 1564, they found it already abandoned. But the Huguenots attempted another settlement that year, this one at Fort Caroline on the St. Johns River in northern Florida. The Spanish quickly destroyed it, murdering most of the settlers and establishing their own outpost at St. Augustine. They sent missionaries as far north as the Chesapeake Bay, but withdrew to Florida in the face of strong resistance from Native Americans.

The English "sea dogs," the adventurers who propelled their nation into competition for America and preyed on Spanish treasure ships, learned a great deal about the New World from the Huguenots. With Elizabeth I's ascension to the throne in 1558, seafarers and colonizers like John Hawkins, Francis Drake, Humphrey Gilbert, and Walter Raleigh gained favor and support. Hawkins visited Fort Caroline in 1565, before the Spanish destroyed it; other Englishmen gained knowledge of the North American coast from

wanted further reforms, and the supporters of Rome. She withstood opposition from Catholics most firmly. Some Catholics turned to Elizabeth's cousin, Mary, Queen of Scots, a Roman Catholic and heir to the English throne. In 1587, after several unsuccessful plots on Elizabeth's life, Mary was tried as a conspirator and beheaded.

One of Mary, Queen of Scot's most fervent supporters was Spain's Philip II, who considered himself the champion of Catholicism. Throughout Europe he strove to wipe out the Protestant heresy. He considered Elizabeth a dangerous foe, not least for her support of the revolt in the Netherlands, a part of his vast domains. When many Dutch adopted Calvinism, Philip retaliated with his Inquisition, executing thousands.

the French. The English also acquired a taste for conquest in Ireland, where their brutal subjugation of the native Irish presaged later actions against the Indians.

The English took their time before attempting an American colony. As the slaughter of Fort Caroline Huguenots made clear, the Spanish remained a serious threat. Thus for two decades, until the 1580s, English adventurers sought wealth by sea—by interloping in the slave trade and as privateers. In 1562, the sea captain John Hawkins violated Spanish mercantilist regulations by taking 300 Africans to Hispaniola without a license. The local Spanish officials, contrary to government policy, allowed him to exchange the slaves for sugar and hides because the colony needed labor. Hawkins made a second voyage, earning another handsome profit, this time mostly in silver. When the Spanish authorities protested, Elizabeth forbade further expeditions, but reversed her decision in 1567, with dire results. On his third voyage, Hawkins was conducting business in the harbor of San Juan de Ulúa, Mexico, when the annual fleet arrived from Spain several weeks early, destroying three of his ships. Hawkins and his cousin Francis Drake escaped with two badly damaged vessels; they returned to England, their crews nearly starved.

Hawkins stopped interloping in Spanish trade, but other English privateers followed, preying on Spanish ships and settlements. The most famous was Francis Drake, who in 1572, with the help of Native Americans and runaway African slaves, intercepted the mule train carrying Potosí silver across Panama. Five years later he set out to circumnavigate the globe. Following Magellan's route through the straits, he attacked Spanish towns along the Pacific coast, captured Peruvian silver, explored the North American coast for evidence of a northwest passage, and returned to England in 1580 by way of Asia and the Cape of Good Hope. Six years later, when England and Spain were formally at war, Drake attacked Spanish ports in America, including St. Augustine in Florida, which he looted and burned.

While Drake was making his fortune, and that of his queen, through piracy, other Elizabethan sea dogs hoped to make their mark by starting colonies. With experience in Ireland, they decided to ignore Spain's claim to North America. On the basis of Cabot's voyage of 1497, Elizabeth granted a charter to Humphrey Gilbert, who sailed to Newfoundland in 1583. He assumed ownership for the English Crown, collecting dues from fishermen. Nothing came of Gilbert's colony, however, as he was lost at sea on his return to England.

Walter Raleigh then attempted a settlement farther south, in the land named for the "virgin" Queen Elizabeth. This effort ended tragically. In 1585, after looting in the Spanish West Indies along the way, the first group of settlers arrived at Roanoke Island in a part of Virginia that later became North Carolina. Their goals were to solidify England's claims in North America and search for silver and gold. After their ships returned home leaving them with short supplies, the colonists tried to force neighboring Indians to provide food. Quickly a pattern of hostility emerged between the English and Native Americans. Francis Drake saved the Roanoke colonists from starvation, carrying them home in 1586. A year later, Raleigh sent out another expedition which also suffered from lack of provisions. This time the war with Spain prevented ships from returning to Roanoke until 1590, when all that was left of the colony was the word "Croatoan" carved on a tree. The colonists may have moved to nearby Croatoan Island, or farther inland to live with Native Americans, but the fate of the "Lost Colony" has never been determined. The most enduring legacy of Roanoke was the introduction of tobacco and the potato in Ireland and England. The English did not colonize successfully in North America until the founding of Jamestown in 1607.

CONCLUSION

By 1590, the Spanish had created an empire that extended from South America through the West Indies and Mexico. They funded their European wars to extinguish Protestantism with American silver and gold. The Portuguese, united under the Spanish Crown in 1580, had developed the Atlantic slave trading system that sent enslaved Africans to Brazil and New Spain. The irony of colonization in America was that European nations at war over religion and national influence in the Old World emulated one another in the New. The Spanish and Portuguese provided the model for later colonizers in expropriating land and labor from Indians and Africans. With superior weaponry and the will to conquer, Europeans justified their behavior toward the people of America and Africa by emphasizing religious and cultural differences, ignoring much that they had in common. While European nations organized colonization in various ways, all sought mercantilistic ends. In the early seventeenth century, when the English, French, and Dutch settled in North America, their goals were very similar to those of Spain. They hoped to locate precious metals, find the elusive northwest passage, exploit Indian labor, extend Christianity to America, and expand the power of the state.

RECOMMENDED READINGS

Bethell, Leslie, ed. *Colonial Spanish America* (1987). Essays provide useful syntheses on the development of the Spanish colonies.

Casas, Bartolomé de las. *A Short Account of the Destruction of the Indies.* Ed. and trans., Nigel Griffin (1992). A priest's sharp denunciation of Spanish colonization, written in 1542.

Davidson, Basil. *The Search for Africa: History, Culture, Politics* (1994). A recent, readable history by a veteran historian of the continent.

Kupperman, Karen Ordahl. *Roanoke: The Abandoned Colony* (1984). A lively account of the early English attempt to settle in North America.

Meinig, D. W. *The Shaping of America: A Geographical Perspective on 500 Years of History, Vol. 1: Atlantic America, 1492–1800* (1986). Provides a broad cultural view of European expansion.

Nash, Gary B. *Red, White, and Black: The Peoples of Early North America,* 3d ed. (1992). An excellent introduction to the meeting of cultures in the New World.

Parry, J. H. *The Establishment of the European Hegemony, 1415–1715: Trade and Exploration in the Age of the Renaissance,* 3d ed. (1966). A short, interesting introduction to the European explorations.

Quinn, David B. *North America from Earliest Discovery to First Settlements: The Norse Voyages to 1612* (1977). A comprehensive source on early European explorations.

Weber, David J. *The Spanish Frontier in North America* (1992). The best synthesis on Spanish exploration and colonization north of Mexico.

Native American Cultures Before 1492
Dowd, Gregory Evans. *A Spirited Resistance: The North American Indian Struggle for Unity, 1745–1815* (1992).

Driver, Harold E. *Indians of North America,* 2d ed. (1969).

Fagan, Brian M. *Kingdoms of Gold, Kingdoms of Jade: The Americas Before Columbus* (1991).

Josephy, Alvin M., Jr. *America in 1492: The World of the Indian Peoples Before the Arrival of Columbus* (1991).

Josephy, Alvin M., Jr. *500 Nations: An Illustrated History of North American Indians* (1994).

Kehoe, Alice B. *North American Indians: A Comprehensive Account* (1981).

Ortiz, Alfonso, ed. *Handbook of North American Indians,* vols. 9, 10: *The Southwest* (1979, 1983).

Early Contact Between Native Americans and Europeans
Crosby, Alfred W., Jr. *The Columbian Exchange: Biological and Cultural Consequences of 1492* (1972).

Kupperman, Karen Ordahl. *Settling with the Indians: The Meeting of English and Indian Cultures in America, 1580–1640* (1980).

Salisbury, Neal. *Manitou and Providence: Indians, Europeans, and the Making of New England, 1500–1643* (1982).

Seed, Patricia. *Ceremonies of Possession in Europe's Conquest of the New World, 1492–1640* (1995).

Thornton, Russell. *American Indian Holocaust and Survival: A Population History Since 1492* (1987).

Africa and the Atlantic Slave Trade
Curtin, Philip D. *The Atlantic Slave Trade: A Census* (1969).

Curtin, Philip D. *The Rise and Fall of the Plantation Complex: Essays in Atlantic History* (1990).

Davidson, Basil. *The African Slave Trade: Precolonial History, 1450–1850,* rev. ed. (1980).

Fage, J. D. *A History of West Africa: An Introductory Survey,* 4th ed. (1969).

Lovejoy, Paul E., "The Volume of the Atlantic Slave Trade: A Synthesis." *Journal of African History* 23 (1982): 473–501.

Miller, Joseph C. *The Way of Death: Merchant Capitalism and the Angolan Slave Trade, 1730–1830* (1988).

Oliver, Roland, ed. *The Cambridge History of Africa, Vol. 3: From c. 1050 to c. 1600* (1977).

Raboteau, Albert J. *Slave Religion: The "Invisible Institution" in the Antebellum South* (1978).

Solow, Barbara L., ed. *Slavery and the Rise of the Atlantic System* (1991).

Thornton, John. *Africa and Africans in the Making of the Atlantic World, 1400–1680* (1992).

European Explorations
Cipolla, Carlo M. *Guns, Sails, and Empires: Technological Innovation and the Early Phases of European Expansion, 1400–1700* (1965).

Dunn, Oliver, and Kelley, James E., Jr., eds. *The Diario of Christopher Columbus's First Voyage to America, 1492–1493* (1989).

Favata, Martin A., and Fernández, José B., trans. *The Account: Álvar Núñez Cabeza de Vaca's Relación* (1993).

Parry, J. H. *The Age of Reconnaissance* (1963).

Phillips, William D., Jr., and Phillips, Carla Rahn. *The Worlds of Christopher Columbus* (1992).

Scammell, G. V. *The First Imperial Age: European Overseas Expansion, c. 1400–1715* (1989).

Spanish Empire

Bethell, Leslie, ed., *The Cambridge History of Latin America,* vols. 1 and 2 (1984).

Burkholder, Mark A., and Johnson, Lyman L. *Colonial Latin America* (1990).

Elliott, J. H. *Imperial Spain, 1469–1716* (1963).

Gibson, Charles. *Spain in America* (1966).

Lockhart, James, and Schwartz, Stuart B. *Early Latin America: A Short History of Colonial Spanish America and Brazil* (1983).

Lynch, John. *Spain Under the Hapsburgs,* 2 vols. (1964, 1969).

McAlister, Lyle N. *Spain and Portugal in the New World, 1492–1700* (1984).

Pagden, Anthony. *Lords of All the World: Ideologies of Empire in Spain, Britain and France c. 1500–c. 1800* (1995).

Parry, J. H. *The Spanish Seaborne Empire* (1966).

Super, John C. *Food, Conquest, and Colonization in Sixteenth-Century Spanish America* (1988).

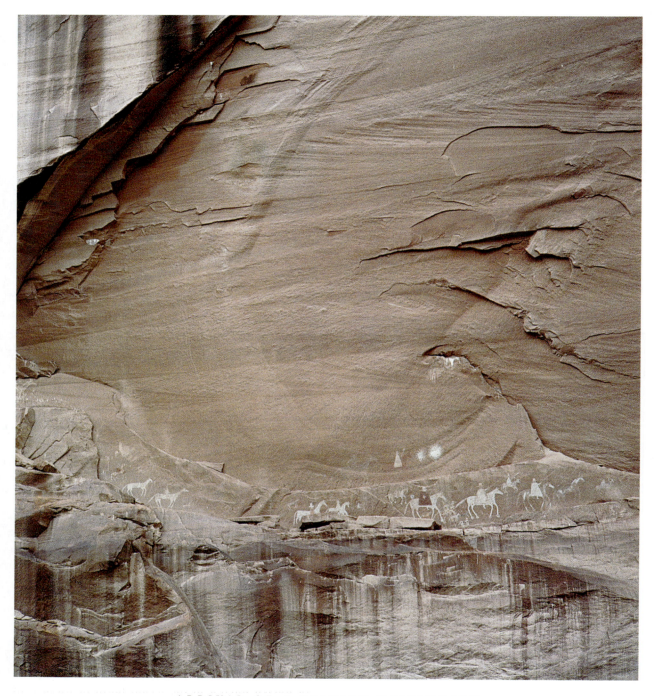

ARRIVAL OF A SPANISH MISSIONARY

Navajo wall art in the Canyon del Muerto, Arizona, showing the arrival of a Spanish missionary and soldiers in the late sixteenth or early seventeenth century.

Chapter 2

COLONIZATION OF NORTH AMERICA,
1590–1675

IN 1590, THE only permanent European settlement in what is now the United States was St. Augustine, the struggling Spanish town in Florida that the English privateer Francis Drake had burned four years earlier. Spain was much more concerned with its silver mines and West Indies plantations than in colonizing along the Atlantic coast, yet wanted to prevent intrusion by other nations, for good reason. In the late sixteenth century, buccaneers from France and England thought the best way to get rich was by looting the Spanish silver fleet and ports. Their countrymen had tried to settle in North America and find a northwest route to Asia without success.

By 1675, however, the major European nations had planted colonies in America. The West Indies became a magnet, with colonizers vying for tiny islands as sugar boomed. In North America, the Spanish held Florida and New Mexico, the French occupied Canada, and the English had a string of settlements along the Atlantic coast. Unlike the highly centralized Spanish empire, English colonization proceeded with little regulation from the Crown, resulting in a variety of social, economic, and political structures. The English government even helped to create the diversity by granting different kinds of charters to individuals and groups.

The expansion of European settlement, particularly in the Chesapeake Bay area and New England, changed the countryside forever. Cheap, even free land and developing commerce offered opportunity to men and women of all economic classes who were willing to risk their lives by crossing the Atlantic. Their farms eliminated Indian hunting lands, altering the ecological balance of plants and animals. Though many Native Americans resisted the European invasions, disease seriously undermined their power, modifying and sometimes destroying their cultures. The fur trade also changed the cultural values of many Indians, drawing them into Atlantic commerce and tempting them to overhunt. For Native Americans from New Mexico to Canada, European colonization was a disaster.

THE SPANISH IN NORTH AMERICA

After Coronado and De Soto in the early 1540s failed to locate cities of gold, Spain abandoned further exploration in North America. Then, Francis Drake's voyage along the Pacific coast during his circumnavigation of the earth in 1577–1580 raised alarms of foreign interest in the region north of Mexico. In 1581, the viceroy of New Spain gave Franciscan priests permission to establish missions among the Pueblo

CHRONOLOGY

1598	Spanish expedition into New Mexico
1599	Destruction of Ácoma by the Spanish
1603	James I takes the English throne
1605	French establish Port Royal
1607	English found colony at Jamestown
1608	French establish Quebec
1609	Henry Hudson explores for the Dutch East India Company
1609–1614	Anglo-Powhatan War in Virginia
1616–1618	Plague epidemic decimates eastern New England natives
1619	Africans arrive in Virginia
	Virginia Company establishes a representative assembly
1620	Separatists found the Plymouth colony
1622	Native Americans attack the Virginia colony
1624	Virginia Company loses charter; Virginia becomes a royal colony
	Dutch West India Company establishes New Netherland
1625	Charles I becomes king of England
1630	Massachusetts Bay Colony founded by Puritans
1634	The *Ark* and the *Dove* arrive in Maryland
1636	Founding of Connecticut and Rhode Island
1637	Massachusetts and Connecticut troops destroy the Pequots
	Anne Hutchinson is tried for heresy
1642–1648	English Civil War
1649	Charles I of England is beheaded
1651	English Parliament passes first Navigation Act
1660	Charles II of England becomes king
1663	Carolina proprietors receive charter
1664	English forces conquer New Netherland; New York and New Jersey are founded
1673	Dutch recapture New York, then return the colony to England with the Treaty of Westminster (1674)

Indians of the Rio Grande Valley. The friars named the area San Felipe del Nuevo México, sending reports to the viceroy of legendary riches. The missionaries described the Pueblos, who raised corn and lived in towns with apartment-style houses, as friendly and numerous: Thousands could be made Christian and forced to labor for Hispanic colonists. But by the time a party arrived in 1582 to escort the Franciscans back to Mexico, the missionaries had been killed by the Native Americans they sought to convert and control.

Settlement of New Mexico

Despite this setback, Spaniards remained interested in the region. Conquistadores needed permission from

the Crown to invade new lands, however, for the king had issued Orders for New Discoveries (1573), which more strictly regulated colonization, in part to protect Native Americans from the atrocities Bartolomé de las Casas had described decades earlier. When one would-be conqueror led an illegal expedition into New Mexico in 1590, he was arrested and returned to Mexico City in chains.

The Spanish government delayed appointing a governor of New Mexico until 1595, when the viceroy authorized Juan de Oñate to undertake settlement with his own funds. Oñate, a native of Mexico whose father had helped discover the Zacatecas silver mines, inherited great wealth and obtained even more by marrying Isabel Tolosa Cortés Moctezuma, a descendant of both Cortés and the Aztec emperor. The expedition proved expensive as delays increased costs. Finally, in 1598, 129 soldiers, their families, servants, and slaves, eighty-three baggage wagons, and 7,000 head of livestock headed north, all subsidized by Governor Oñate. Ten Franciscan missionaries accompanied the colonists. Oñate expected his investment to yield an empire. As he wrote King Philip II, "I shall give your majesty a new world, greater than New Spain." The governor envisioned mines of silver and gold and a water passage through the continent. He believed his province would extend from the Atlantic to the Pacific.

Upon arrival in New Mexico, Oñate declared Spanish sovereignty over Pueblo lands. In a ritual complete with trumpets and High Mass, he promised peace and prosperity to those who cooperated. According to the Spanish, the Pueblos acquiesced "of their own accord": Previous experience with Coronado and more recent explorers probably convinced them they had little choice. The Franciscans founded missions in the largest pueblos and supervised construction of a church in the Tewa pueblo, Yungé, which the Spanish designated as their capital, San Gabriel.

For some months, the Spanish and the Indians coexisted without serious incident. The colonists moved into the Pueblos' apartments in Yungé, now San Gabriel, forcing the inhabitants to depart. Soon the Indians tired of providing food, which they had intended as gifts but the Spanish considered tribute. The soldiers resorted to murder and rape to obtain supplies. The crisis came in December 1598, when a Spanish troop demanded provisions from the people of Ácoma, a pueblo high atop a mesa west of the Rio Grande. One of Coronado's party had described Ácoma as "the greatest stronghold ever seen in the world." The Pueblos refused to give flour to the soldiers and killed eleven men, including Oñate's nephew, when they attempted to take the food by force. Oñate swiftly punished the village so others would not join in revolt. His small army laid siege to Ácoma with several cannon; men and women defended the town with arrows and stones. The Spanish killed approximately 500 men and 300 women and children; they captured the survivors, including eighty men and 500 women and children. The town was leveled. Everyone was sentenced to servitude, and each man over age twenty-five had one foot cut off. The Ácomas would not rebuild their town until the late 1640s.

With this harsh action, Oñate only temporarily prevented further resistance among the Pueblos, for another town rebelled the following year. The colonists also complained of food shortages and the governor's mismanagement; many returned to Mexico.

The Pueblo stronghold at Ácoma, which revolted against the Spanish in 1598.

Oñate's long absences from the capital to explore for gold and silver—unsuccessfully—added to this discontent. The Franciscans charged that his cruelty to the Indians made conversion difficult. Bankrupt, Oñate was removed as governor, tried, and found guilty of mistreating the Native Americans and some of his settlers. He was banished from New Mexico, but renewed his wealth at the Zacatecas mines, sailed to Spain, where he received a knighthood and position as the Crown's chief inspector of mines.

After Juan de Oñate's departure, New Mexico became a royal province, but developed slowly. Pedro de Peralta, the next governor, established a new capital at Santa Fe in 1610. While the Franciscans maintained their missions among the Pueblos, as late as 1670 only 2,800 Spanish colonists lived in the Rio Grande valley. The Hispanics lived on farms and ranches along the river, exploiting the Pueblos' labor through the encomienda system (see Chapter 1) to produce hides, blankets, sheep, wool, and pinenuts for sale in Mexico.

Spanish Missions in New Mexico and Florida

The Franciscan missionaries, who assumed a major role in colonizing the Spanish borderlands during the seventeenth century, were members of the Catholic religious order that Francis Bernardone of Assisi had founded (in Italy) in 1209. The friars vowed not to engage in sexual relations or acquire property, living on the gifts of others. Unlike other religious brotherhoods, which remained in seclusion, the Franciscans operated in the world among ordinary Christians; with exploration of the Americas, they sought to convert a hemisphere, even if that meant martyrdom by hostile Indians. The Orders for New Discoveries of 1573 gave primary responsibility to the monks for "pacifying" the Indians of New Mexico and Florida.

During the first part of the seventeenth century, many Pueblos of New Mexico seemed to accept the Franciscans' message. The friars arrived in villages offering gifts of food, metal tools, beads, and clothing. Placing some confidence in the priests, the natives agreed to build convents and churches, using their traditional methods of construction. Women built the

walls, while men did carpentry. The priests decorated the sanctuaries with paintings, statues, and silver chalices, attempting to capture the Indians' devotion through sacred rituals and music. The Franciscans created missions by imposing their influence over existing Indian towns, backed by threat of military force. In both New Mexico and Florida, the missionaries were most successful among Native Americans who lived in villages before contact. In New Mexico, the Spanish started more than fifty churches by 1629; in Florida, missions extended west from St. Augustine to the Gulf Coast and north into Georgia (or Guale, as the region was called).

The Native Americans who came under Spanish control could, in theory, choose whether or not to accept Christian baptism, but all recognized that soldiers supported the priests. The Franciscans expected the natives to learn the catechism and enough of the Castilian (Spanish) language to communicate, and to adopt European dress, food, and farming methods. The friars understood conversion to mean acceptance of Spanish customs as well as Christianity. Many Indians embraced Catholicism—the Franciscans claimed that 35,000 Pueblos had accepted baptism by 1626—but in doing so, modified the religion. The Indians held on to ancient rituals and beliefs despite the friars' efforts to eradicate them. Even in the twentieth century, the Pueblos preserved both native and Catholic religious practices. Christian Indians in Florida continued to play a ball game during the 1600s until the missionaries realized it had religious significance and abolished the game, calling the pole used as a target, the "ballpost of the devil."

In merging Indian gods with the Christian trinity and adding Catholic holidays to native celebrations, Native Americans altered Spanish Catholicism. With the "Lady in Blue," they created a religious tradition that both the Indians and Spaniards accepted. In the 1620s, Plains Indians reported that a nun appeared to them, telling them in their language to become Christians. Though the woman remained invisible to the missionaries, they believed the stories, which persisted for generations. On a trip to Spain, one priest discovered that a Franciscan nun, María de Jesús de Agreda, claimed to have made flights to America with the help of angels, though she later denied most of her tale. Despite this denial, María de Agreda's initial claims and the Indians' visions together created the resilient legend of the Lady in Blue.

THE ENGLISH INVADE VIRGINIA

New Mexico and Florida remained marginal outposts in the Spanish empire, places where small Hispanic populations dominated some Indians through forced labor and missions. Spanish control was tenuous because their military forces were small and cultural influence weak. In the aftermath of the Spanish Armada's failure to conquer England, Philip II's government proved incapable of preventing other European nations from settling in North America, albeit well north of St. Augustine. During the first decade of the seventeenth century, the English, French, and Dutch stepped up activity; they sent expeditions to fish, search for a northern passage to the East, trade for furs, and establish colonies.

English Context of Colonization

Seventeenth-century England was an intensely hierarchical society, in which the king claimed divine right, or God-given authority, and the nobility and gentry dominated Parliament. But it was a society undergoing turmoil and change. Elizabeth I's successor was her cousin, James I, who governed from 1603 until 1625, when he died and his son, Charles I, took the throne. Both James and Charles had strife-torn reigns marked by power struggles with Parliament, culminating in Charles's loss of the English Civil War and his beheading in 1649. Parliament was composed of two houses: the House of Lords, made up of nobles and high church officials; and the House of Commons, who were elected representatives from the counties and boroughs. The Commons normally comprised country gentry, government officials, and lawyers; the electorate included male landowners, or an estimated 15 to 30 percent of all Englishmen. By imposing levies without Parliament's consent, James I and Charles I challenged its prerogative to approve or reject new taxes. For their part, the legislators tried to whittle away at royal powers, claiming the right to initiate legislation rather than wait for the king and his councillors to submit bills for consideration. The fundamental issue concerning how the powers of the king versus property holders, as represented in Parliament, should

James I of England, who chartered the Virginia and Plymouth companies to colonize North America. Portrait by Daniel Mytens, 1621.

be balanced remained unsettled until the Glorious Revolution of 1688.

Economic developments loosened English society, giving individuals greater opportunity to change from one social class or occupation to another, though traditional class distinctions remained in place. Many found it necessary to move geographically, as the woolen industry expanded in England, causing landowners to raise more sheep to meet the demand for wool. In what has been called the "enclosure movement," landlords ended leases for tenant farmers living on their lands, confiscating common fields that peasant communities had shared for grazing their livestock and raising crops. The landowners enclosed the commons with fences and hedges. In 1500, peasants had farmed 70 percent of arable land in England, but by 1650, they farmed only 50 percent. Thus many tenants were forced from the land. Some went to London, where the population expanded from 55,000 in 1520 to 475,000 in 1670. Others were among the colonists who signed for America.

A developing economy meant dislocation and uncertainty for poor English tenants; it spelled opportunity for merchants. They found it first in the woolen trade with Antwerp, in what is now Belgium. When this trade declined after 1550, English merchants looked for alternative investments, which they found as war with Spain brought demand for coal, lead, glass, ships, salt, iron, and steel. Investors formed joint-stock companies to explore trade routes, establish new markets, and attract settlers to Ireland. The companies obtained capital by selling stocks, which were expected to earn a profit within a few years. These investments were risky, for shareholders were liable for all company debts. The stocks could also be im-

mensely profitable, as in the case of Francis Drake's circumnavigation of the globe, which brought a 4,600 percent profit. Other joint-stock ventures included the Guinea, Muscovy, and East India companies, created respectively to trade with Africa, Russia, and Asia.

Joint-stock companies also provided capital for the first permanent English colonies in America, at Jamestown, Plymouth, and Massachusetts Bay. Unlike the Spanish monarchy, the English Crown had little role in funding, or even governing, its first New World settlements. In 1606, James I granted a charter to the Virginia Company with rights to settle colonies in North America. The Virginia Company included two groups, one in London and the other in Plymouth, in the west of England. The groups received overlapping claims, with the Plymouth group obtaining lands from what is now Maine to Virginia and the London group receiving Connecticut to the Carolinas. Either could settle in the overlapping area, but initial colonies had to be at least one hundred miles apart.

London in 1616, a magnet for people from rural England. London Bridge, in the center right, crosses the Thames River.

In this conjectural view of Jamestown c. 1614, the fortified wall shows concerns for defense against the Spanish and the Powhatan confederacy.

Jamestown

In 1607, the Virginia Company of London funded the first permanent English colony at Jamestown, retaining control until the Crown revoked its charter in 1624. When the first 104 settlers arrived in Virginia in May 1607, they had endured a long winter crossing. The native inhabitants watched the invaders select a site on the James River, chosen for safety from Spanish attack, but—unknown to the English—next to malarial swamps. The Native Americans called their territory Tsenacommacah, or "densely inhabited land." They were Algonquian-speaking Indians; most belonged to a confederacy that Powhatan, head sachem of the Pamunkey tribe, had forged in eastern Virginia. Before the arrival of the English, the chief unifying force among the bands of the Powhatan confederacy was the threat from powerful enemies, the Manahoacs and the Monacans, who controlled lands to the west,

in the Virginia piedmont. The leaders of tribes subject to Powhatan were supposed to follow his direction, pay tribute, and provide military assistance, but they sometimes refused.

One of Powhatan's brothers, in line for the head sachem's position, was Opechancanough, described as having "large Stature, noble Presence, and extraordinary Parts" and "perfectly skill'd in the Art of Governing." Historical evidence suggests that Opechancanough was born around 1544 and, at about age sixteen, was taken by a Spanish ship to Spain, where he received instruction in the Castilian language and Christianity. He adopted the name Don Luis de Velasco, after the viceroy of New Spain. The new Don Luis stayed with the Spanish, in Spain and America, until 1570, when he accompanied several missionaries to his homeland on Chesapeake Bay. He broke with the priests when they criticized him for taking several wives, and murdered them the next year. If

Opechancanough and Don Luis were the same man, as seems likely, he was well prepared with knowledge of the Europeans when the Jamestown settlers arrived.

The English colony's first decade was a struggle, as the Virginia Company and the settlers made one mistake after another. From the outset, the company ran Virginia as a business enterprise, keeping control of government, land, and trade. Settlers were company employees, not landholders. To satisfy investors, the company instructed the colonists to search for gold and silver mines, find a passage to Asia, and establish industries and trade that would offer handsome returns. The company had chosen individuals for these purposes, not people who were willing to grow crops. Among the first Jamestown settlers were many gentlemen, who by definition avoided manual labor. They were adventurers who expected to strike it rich and return to England. The rest of the first colonists, who were nearly all men, included the gentlemen's personal servants, a jeweler, goldsmith, perfumer, carpenters, blacksmiths, and some laborers. No one described himself as a farmer.

When the colonists failed to locate mines or a passage to the East, their lives became aimless. Rather than plant crops or even hunt and fish in their bountiful environment, they expected the Virginia Company and neighboring Indians to provide food. When sufficient provisions failed to arrive, the settlers starved. One of the leaders, a young officer named John Smith, took control in 1608, stabilizing the colony briefly by making everyone work. When criticism of his strict discipline reached company officials the next year, they removed him from command. During the particularly bitter winter of 1609–1610, one man killed his pregnant wife and chopped her up, planning to eat her body. Others dug up graves to eat the corpses. By spring 1610, only sixty colonists remained of at least 600 who had come to Jamestown in three years. Though some had returned to England or escaped to live with the Indians, the majority died of starvation and disease, most likely dysentery and malaria. The death rate during these early years is estimated at about 50 percent.

The Virginia Company took several steps to make its venture profitable. It continued to send settlers and supplies, though the former died at a high rate and the latter were insufficient. In 1609, without gold mines or a trade route to Asia, the Virginia Company hoped to salvage its investment by exploiting the land. It recognized that profits had to come from a staple crop. To recruit farmers, the company offered each emigrant one share of stock and a parcel of land after seven years of service. The settlers remained employees of the company in the meantime, with assigned tasks and the obligation to buy all supplies and ship all products through the company store.

Still, the Jamestown settlers lacked discipline and refused to work. When Sir Thomas Dale arrived as governor in May 1611, he found nothing but a few gardens planted and the inhabitants at "their daily and usual work, bowling in the streets." Thus, he established his *Laws Divine, Morall and Martiall*, which were mostly martial. The men received military ranks, were divided into work gangs, and proceeded from home to work—and to church twice daily—at the beat of a drum. Laws prescribed death for a variety of crimes, including rape, adultery, theft, lying, slander against the company, blasphemy, killing any domestic animal including a chicken without permission, and stealing an ear of corn. For taking two or three pints of oatmeal, one man had a large needle thrust through his tongue, then was chained to a tree until he starved. For the first offense of failing to work regular hours, an idler was tied neck to heels all night. The punishment for a second offense was whipping and for a third offense, death. Though the required hours of work were reasonable—five to eight hours per day in the summer and three to six in the winter—the punishments specified in "Dale's Laws" became a scandal in England, discouraging prospective emigrants. In the words of John Smith, "no man will go from [England] to have less liberty there."

The Struggle for Virginia

In searching for gold and silver, the Jamestown adventurers had imitated Spain. They expected to put the Indians to work in mines and fields, as in Mexico, but the inhabitants proved too few in number for an adequate workforce, yet too powerful for the wretched gang of English settlers to conquer. During the early years at Jamestown, the English seemed irrational in their dealings with the Native Americans. To many colonists, despite their desperate need for provisions, the natives were barbarians with savage customs and a heathen religion. While some settlers attempted to trade for food, others burned Indian villages and crops. They stole corn and killed.

In 1608–1609, Captain John Smith tried to force the sachems to provide food. His life had been spared by the Indians several times, including one occasion

John Smith threatening Opechancanough in 1608, with images in the background of skirmishes between colonists and Indians that took place at other times, not on this occasion. From Smith's Generall Historie of Virginia.

when Powhatan's daughter Pocahontas intervened on his behalf. Nevertheless, he kidnapped two men, obligating Opechancanough to beg for their release. Next, he entered the Pamunkey village with soldiers demanding food, which the Indians refused to give, and again humiliated the tall sachem: In Smith's words, he did "take this murdering Opechancanough . . . by the long lock of his head; and with my pistol at his breast, I led him [out of his house] amongst his greatest forces, and before we parted made him [agree to] fill our bark with twenty tuns of corn." Otherwise, Smith warned, he would load the ship with their "dead carkases."

Opechancanough probably never forgot this scene. Between 1609 and 1614, full-scale war existed between the Virginia colonists and the Powhatan confederacy. The English, who received reinforcements of experienced soldiers and arms from the Virginia Company, defeated Powhatan, taking control of the

James River. Powhatan faced another disappointment when Pocahontas married John Rolfe, accompanying him to England, where she died. The colonists had less success against Opechancanough, who began consolidating his power among the Virginia natives.

In contrast to Spain, the English Crown failed to take responsibility for protecting any rights of Native Americans and, over the entire colonial period, English churches showed little interest in converting them. When colonists had sufficient power, they enslaved Indians, sending them away from their homelands to prevent escape. The English justified expropriation of native lands with several doctrines. One was the belief that the king of England, as the Christian monarch, received sovereignty over North America from God. Thus, the Virginia Company, and later other groups and individuals, obtained rights to land from the Crown, not the Indians. The other basis for taking native territory was the legal concept, *vacuum domicilium,* which meant that lands not occupied could be taken. To the English, "occupation" meant improving the land with buildings, fences, and crops; they did not recognize Indian sovereignty over the vast stretches of hunting lands that extended beyond small villages and fields. Even when the English purchased land from the Indians, their contrasting concepts of ownership caused grave misunderstanding. While the colonists believed in private property, the natives had no such concept of exclusive ownership, but rather thought they were selling the rights to use lands for hunting, fishing, and communal farming. They expected to continue using the territory they had "sold" for these purposes. Conflicts resulted when, for example, a settler's cattle trampled Indian crops, or when a native killed a colonist's cow, mistaking it for a deer. Ultimately, as disease ravaged the Native American population, white settlers dispossessed the Indian survivors of their lands.

Tobacco Boom

Demand for land became paramount in Virginia after 1617, when the colonists discovered tobacco as a staple crop. Though James I called smoking "a custom loathsome to the eye, hateful to the nose, harmful to the brain, dangerous to the lungs, and in the black stinking fumes thereof, nearest resembling the horrible stygian smoke of the pit that is bottomless," the habit consumed England. The mercantilist advantages were clear. With production in Virginia, the English could

Earliest known illustration of an American tobacco factory, c. 1670.

acquire tobacco from its own colony, rather than pay premium prices to foreign countries, and could generate an industry to process the leaves for domestic use and export. For Virginians, the tobacco trade meant capital to develop the colony, attract settlers, and purchase manufactures from home. Tobacco became the first staple crop in England's colonial mercantilist system, followed by sugar, after 1640, in the West Indies.

In 1619, the Virginia Company made several changes to encourage the colony's growth. It updated the land policy, granting "headrights" of one hundred acres of land to those who came before 1616 and fifty acres to those who came after. Settlers who paid their own way received land immediately; those who immigrated at the company's expense received land after seven years of service. Virginia settlers thus fell into two categories: freeholders who paid for their own transportation; and servants, whose way the Virginia Company or someone else financed, and who received a headright only after their time expired. Recipients of headrights did not pay for the land, but owed quitrents, annual payments to the company, of one shilling per year for each fifty acres. The company hoped these charges would ensure a steady income. Also in 1619, the Virginia Company relaxed its hold on the government of Virginia by establishing an assembly of elected delegates. The governor, who was

appointed by the company, retained the right to veto all laws; the company's General Court in London could also disallow any decision. The Virginia Company also adopted English common law to replace the martial law under which the colony had operated.

While the revised land policy and the assembly gave settlers a greater stake in society, the adoption of tobacco assured Virginia's ultimate success. Finally, the colonists had found a way to wealth: During the 1620s, tobacco drew high prices, as much as three shillings per pound. Virginia became the first North American "boom town," as settlers threw all of their energies into growing tobacco. Between 1617 and 1623, approximately 5,000 new immigrants arrived. Because the amount of the crop a planter could grow depended largely on the number of workers, those with capital eagerly paid for transporting servants. The Virginia Company imported workers too, but still failed to show a profit, partly because company officials diverted many servants to their own plantations.

Africans in Early Virginia

To strike it rich from tobacco, Virginia planters also purchased Africans, probably even before 1619 when a Dutch ship brought about twenty blacks. Though some of these Africans became servants, with terms shorter than lifetime bondage, others probably were slaves. Little is known of their status during the early decades. While, over the years, slave traders brought more Africans to Virginia, English servants provided most of the labor in the colony until late in the seventeenth century. In 1625, Africans numbered twenty-three of 1,200 Virginia colonists. Fifteen were the property of two men: Abraham Peirsey, the wealthiest man in the colony, and George Yeardley, who had served as governor. In 1660, about 900 blacks and 24,000 Europeans lived in the Chesapeake Bay area.

In contrast, by that same year, Africans outnumbered whites in Barbados, the richest of the English West Indies. Founded in 1627, Barbados quickly turned to sugar production, importing Africans to raise and process the crop. The white islanders created a harsh slave regime to prevent organized rebellion and force the rapidly growing black population to perform hard, repetitive labor.

Until the 1660s, conditions for Africans remained less rigid in Virginia than in the West Indies, for no law codifying slavery existed. Some Virginia blacks achieved freedom, married, and a few acquired land. For example, by the 1650s, free blacks Anthony and Mary Johnson owned a 250-acre plantation on Virginia's eastern shore and, like neighboring whites, protected their property by going to court. Even so, other Africans remained in bondage, as Virginians adopted the practice by example from the Portuguese, Spanish, and Dutch. In purchasing people from slave traders, the white colonists bought into the Atlantic slave system.

Early Virginia documents distinguished consistently between white servants and blacks, always with the suggestion that Africans were subordinate. In a 1627 will, Governor Yeardley bequeathed his "goode debts, chattels, servants, negars, cattle or any other thing" to his heirs. Censuses of the 1620s also point to the lower regard for Africans: English settlers were listed with full names while most Africans were enumerated simply with a first name or designated as "negar" or "Negro." For example, Anthony and Mary Johnson were called "Antonio a Negro" and "Mary a Negro Woman" in early records. The Virginia tax law of 1643 further demonstrated that the colonists viewed Africans as different from themselves. Everyone who worked in the field was to be taxed—all men and black women. White women apparently were not expected to tend tobacco. Virginia also excepted blacks, but not white servants, from the obligation to bear arms.

The Colony Expands

The colonists had found the way to success—by growing tobacco—but Virginia experienced difficulty for many years. Because mortality remained high and settlers had few children, the population grew slowly despite immigration that averaged about 1,000 people per year. From 1619 to 1640, the population rose from 700 to about 8,000, though approximately 20,000 immigrants had arrived during that time. Dysentery, typhoid fever, and malaria took their toll on new settlers who suffered a period of "seasoning" after their arrival in Virginia. A 1625 census indicated that more than three-quarters of the Virginia colonists were male and less than one-fifth were children, statistics that reflected high immigration in these early years. Men were much more likely to migrate to the colonies than women. Many people came as servants, which meant that they could not legally marry and have children for years, until their terms expired. The census also provided ample evidence of mortality and disrupted families, as many of the married couples were childless, in part because of high infant and childhood mortality. And with short life expectancy for adults, more than one-half of the colony's children had lost one parent, and one-fifth apparently had no relatives in Virginia at all. The census revealed the misery of living in early Virginia despite the prospect of getting rich. Young men and women who left England to become servants in Virginia gambled with their lives to obtain land, which they could not gain at home. Many thought the risk worth taking: Between 1607 and 1680, about 65,000 Europeans immigrated to Virginia.

By 1621, Opechancanough and a prophet Nemattanew, whom the colonists called "Jack of the Feathers" because he wore clothes covered with plumes, recognized the threat of increased immigration. Now that the English had tobacco, they were not going to leave. Nemattanew inspired a nativist religious revival among the Powhatans, rejecting Christianity and European customs. Opechancanough organized a military offensive to push the English back into the sea. At the same time, he used diplomacy to convince the settlers to lower their guard. He even told them that they were welcome to take unoccupied lands. When several whites killed Nemattanew in 1622, Opechancanough rallied his troops, slaying one-fourth of the settlers before the colony could react. A ten-year war followed, in which each side tried to annihilate the other, but failed, and in 1632 agreed to peace.

Though the bankrupt Virginia Company lost its charter in 1624, in the wake of the 1622 massacre,

**RICHARD FRETHORNE,
A VIRGINIA COLONIST,
WRITES HOME, 1623**

Conditions in Virginia remained terrible for immigrants in the 1620s, as Richard Frethorne tells his parents at home in England. A year after the 1622 massacre by the Powhatan confederacy, the Englishman reports ongoing hostilities and the settlers' constant fear of "the enemy."

Loving and kind father and mother:

My most humble duty remembered to you, hoping in God of your good health, as I myself am at the making hereof. This is to let you understand that I your child am in a most heavy case by reason of the nature of the country, [which] is such that it causeth much sickness, [such] as the scurvy and the bloody flux and diverse other diseases, which maketh the body very poor and weak. And when we are sick there is nothing to comfort us, for since I came out of the ship I never ate anything but peas, and loblollie (that is, water gruel). As for deer or venison I never saw any since I came into this land. There is indeed some fowl, but we are not allowed to go and get it, but must work hard both early and late for a mess of water gruel and a mouthful of bread and beef. A mouthful of bread, for a penny loaf must serve for four men which is most pitiful. [You would be grieved] if you did know as much as I [do], when people cry out day and night—Oh! that they were in England without their limbs—and would not care to lose any limb to be in England again, yea, though they beg from door to door. For we live in fear of the enemy every hour, yet we have had a combat with them on the Sunday before Shrovetide, and we took two alive and made slaves of them. But it was by policy, for we are in great danger, for our plantation is very weak by reason of the death and sickness of our company. For we came but twenty for the merchants, and they are half dead just; and we look every hour when two more should go. Yet there came some four other men yet to live with us, of which there is but one alive; and our Lieutenant is dead, and [also] his father and his brother. And there was some five or six of the last year's twenty, of which there is but three left, so that we are fain to get other men to plant with us; and yet we

immigration to the colony continued. Its economic promise helped convince the English Crown to claim it as a royal colony. Desire for new tobacco lands placed constant pressure on the Powhatans, so in 1644, Opechancanough launched another attack. This time the Indians killed 500 settlers, a much smaller proportion than in 1622. After two years of war, the Powhatans submitted and Opechancanough, now "so decrepit that he was not able to walk alone," was captured and murdered by a guard. The 1646 treaty required the Native Americans to live on lands north of the York River and, to symbolize their subordination, pay an annual tribute of twenty beaver skins.

Colonists expanded rapidly north and south of the James River and to the eastern shore, having defeated their most dangerous opponents.

FISHING, FURS, AND SETTLEMENTS IN THE NORTH

While settlers and Native Americans struggled for Virginia during the first decades of the seventeenth are but 32 to fight against 3000 if they should come. And the nighest help that we have is ten miles of us, and when the rogues overcame this place [the] last [time] they slew 80 persons. How then shall we do, for we lie even in their teeth? They may easily take us, but [for the fact] that God is merciful and can save with few as well as with many, as he showed to Gilead. And like Gilead's soldiers, if they lapped water, we drink water which is but weak.

And I have nothing to comfort me, nor there is nothing to be gotten here but sickness and death, except [in the event] that one had money to lay out in some things for profit. But I have nothing at all—no, not a shirt to my back but two rags (2), nor no clothes but one poor suit, nor but one pair of shoes, but one pair of stockings, but one cap, [and] but two bands. My cloak is stolen by one of my own fellows, and to his dying hour [he] would not tell me what he did with it; but some of my fellows saw him have butter and beef out of a ship, which my cloak, I doubt [not], paid for. So that I have not a penny, nor a penny worth, to help me to either spice or sugar or strong waters, without the which one cannot live here. For as strong beer in England doth fatten and strengthen them, so water here doth wash and weaken these here [and] only keeps [their] life and soul together. But I am not half [of] a quarter so strong as I was in England, and all is for want of victuals; for I do protest unto you that I have eaten more in [one] day at home than I have allowed me here for a week. . . .

Good father, do not forget me, but have mercy and pity my miserable case. I know if you did but see me, you would weep to see me; for I have but one suit. (But [though] it is a strange one, it is very well guarded.) Wherefore, for God's sake, pity me. I pray you to remember my love to all my friends and kindred. I hope all my brothers and sisters are in good health, and as for my part I have set down my resolution that certainly will be; that is, that the answer of this letter will be life or death to me. Therefore, good father, send as soon as you can; and if you send me any thing let this be the mark. ROT

Richard Frethorne,
Martin's Hundred

century, French, Dutch, and English adventurers explored and colonized the region to the north. French and English sailors had fished the Newfoundland Banks since the fifteenth century. By 1600, groups monopolized specific waters, such as the French who caught walrus in the Gulf of St. Lawrence. The beaver furs that Europeans obtained in petty trade with Native Americans became popular in Europe for making felt hats, exciting merchants in France, the Netherlands, and England to seek more permanent arrangements. All three nations claimed the northern territories as their own, ignoring, of course, the prior ownership of the Indians.

New France

In North America, French traders focused on furs, for Europeans prized the thick animal pelts of frigid Canada. When a ship sent to North America in 1582 returned to France with a cargo of furs earning a 1,500 percent profit, merchants enthusiastically organized more voyages and considered colonies to facilitate trade. Samuel de Champlain established the first successful French colony in the New World. Working for Pierre du Gua de Monts, who had received a charter from the French king, in 1605 Champlain planted a temporary base at Port Royal on the Bay of Fundy in

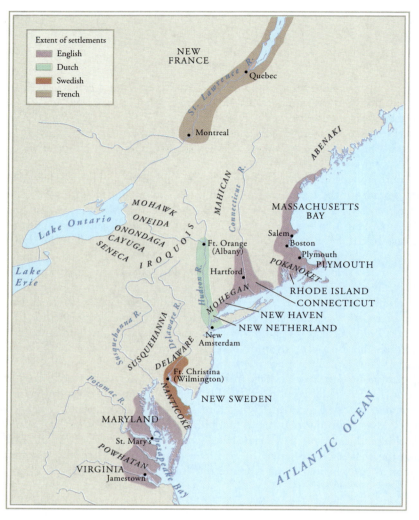

Map 2.1 French, English, Dutch, and Swedish Colonies in Eastern North America, 1650

alliances with several groups: the Montagnais, who lived in the region north of the St. Lawrence River and like the Algonquins and Micmacs spoke Algonquian languages; and the Hurons, who were Iroquoian and lived north of Lake Ontario, a location that enabled them to link the French outposts with the interior, the source of the most valuable furs. In 1609, to demonstrate allegiance to his allies, Champlain helped them fight a group of Iroquois from what is now New York, thus making the Five Nations enemies of New France. He also explored the watershed of the St. Lawrence River and lands as far west as Lake Huron, thereby establishing France's claim to the interior of North America.

In 1627, Quebec was still essentially a trading post with about 100 French inhabitants, including few women. Cardinal Richelieu, who for all practical purposes ruled France, organized the Company of One Hundred Associates to spur colonization. The company received a charter for territory from the Arctic Circle to Florida and from the Atlantic to the Pacific, with a monopoly on the fur trade and power to establish a feudal system of land tenure. The company also pledged to send missionaries to the Indians, to bring them "to the knowledge of the true God" and grant them the status of "natural French" when they were baptized. In fact, the French missionaries, like the Spanish, took seriously their mandate to convert Native Americans. They established missions in Indian villages and learned their languages, looking for similarities between the two cultures in an effort to make the Indians part of French society.

Because the company focused on the fur trade and considered transporting settlers too expensive, in 1663 just 3,000 French settlers lived in the colony. The Crown revoked the company's charter, making New France a royal province. Nevertheless, population

Canada. He sailed south to Cape Cod looking for a permanent site, but decided in 1608 to retain Port Royal and establish a main settlement on the St. Lawrence River. The French chose Quebec, which meant "the place where the river narrows" in Algonquian, an ideal location for controlling the Canadian interior.

For two decades, both Port Royal and Quebec remained little more than trading posts. The French had already traded with the Micmacs of the coastal region and Algonquins of the St. Lawrence Valley. Champlain strengthened these ties, and made new growth remained slow. From the beginning, the government refused to allow Protestants, who were the most likely immigrants, to settle there; it wanted to maintain control of the society through the Catholic church. Further, New France developed under feudal land tenure, in which wealthy lords received large manors, or *seigniories,* along the St. Lawrence River. Ordinary settlers on these manors became tenants rather than independent farmers. Lacking the opportunity to improve their status in the New World, French peasants were reluctant to make the dangerous transatlantic voyage.

The fur trade and small population made French relations with the Native Americans different from those of New Spain and Virginia, where labor demands and white expansion put greater pressure on the Indians. The most efficient way to obtain furs was to offer desirable products from Europe, including textiles, metal tools, guns, pots, and alcohol, not drive trading partners from the land or exploit their labor. One French priest reported that, at least for a while, the Montagnais thought they were getting the better deal: "I heard my [Indian] host say one day, jokingly, *Missi picoutau amiscou,* 'The Beaver does everything perfectly well, it makes kettles, hatchets, swords, knives, bread; and in short, it makes everything.' He was making sport of us Europeans . . . [and said], showing me a beautiful knife, 'The English have no sense; they give us twenty knives like this for one Beaver skin'."

Nevertheless, the French arrival had tragic effects for the Indians of Canada, who succumbed to disease in large numbers. The demand for furs altered cultural attitudes and intensified hostility among nations, as with the Hurons and the Iroquois of New York. In keeping with their religion, Indians had taken only what they needed from nature and little more; they generally used entire animals, the meat as well as the skins. With the fur trade, natives killed animals just for their furs and in numbers far greater than before. As a result, the balance of nature that the Native Americans had maintained was broken. They had to reach farther and farther back into the continent as they exterminated the deer, beaver, and other fur-bearing animals.

New Netherland

In the first decade of the seventeenth century, the Dutch, too, challenged the dominance of Spain in the New World. The seven northern United Provinces had declared independence from Spain in 1581 and remained at war until 1609, when they signed a twelve-year truce. With its expiration, the war resumed and continued as part of the Thirty Years' War, which ended in 1648 with the Treaty of Münster, recognizing Dutch independence. The revolt failed in the southern Netherlands, forcing Calvinists to flee north.

Despite this ongoing struggle, Dutch commerce flourished. The migration of Protestants from Antwerp, which had been the thriving business center of the southern provinces, to Amsterdam transferred capital and commercial know-how to the north. As Antwerp foundered, Amsterdam tripled in size between 1585 and 1622, with a mercantile community eager to start new ventures. Because land was scarce and high priced in the Netherlands, and agriculture insufficient, affluent individuals put their capital into trade. They formed joint-stock companies to challenge the dominance of Portugal and Spain (which Philip II united in 1580) in Asia, Africa, and the West Indies. In 1602, merchants formed the United East India Company, which six years later had 160 ships around the globe. In 1609, the company sent out Henry Hudson, an Englishman, to search for the long-sought northwest passage through North America. He sailed up the river that later bore his name, trading for furs with the Native Americans. The pelts brought a good return in Holland, so the company dispatched traders who set up a post near the present site of Albany and explored Long Island Sound and the Connecticut River. In 1621, the Dutch government chartered another group, the West India Company, to establish commerce and colonies in America. Like the East India Company, it received broad powers, including the rights to make war and sign treaties. During the seventeenth century, the Dutch muscled their way to control a large part of international commerce, including the Atlantic slave trade and routes to Asia. They wrested the African slave trading fort of El Mina and Brazil sugar plantations from the Portuguese, changed the fishing industry off Newfoundland by sending "sack" ships to purchase fish rather than catch them, and captured the Spanish silver fleet off Cuba in 1628.

To provide a base for trade in the Hudson River region, in 1624 the Dutch West India Company appointed Cornelius Jacobsen May to found New Netherland; the first colonists were mostly Protestant refugees from the Spanish Netherlands. They

The Seal of the Province of New Netherland, 1623, with an image of a beaver in center, evokes the Dutch focus on trade.

established their primary settlement, called New Amsterdam, on Manhattan Island, and maintained trading posts at Fort Orange (near Albany), and on the Delaware and Connecticut rivers. As in Jamestown, the first settlers were employees of the company who received no land of their own. The company paid for their transportation, tools, livestock, and two years' worth of supplies, assigning them company land on which to plant. The colonists were expected to trade only with the company. The government consisted of appointed company officers headed by a director-general, or governor, with wide powers. The colonists could not elect an assembly or any of their officials.

With good soil on Manhattan Island and in the upper Hudson Valley, the lucrative fur trade, and lumbering, the colony prospered economically, though its population grew slowly. Brewing became the second most important industry; in 1638, New Amsterdam residents complained that they were losing sleep from the singing of drunken sailors. People of many nationalities and religions arrived to take advantage of the Dutch policy of religious freedom, but few Dutch could be convinced to emigrate. In 1629, the company attempted to spur population growth by offering huge manors, called patroonships, to any member of the company who transported fifty persons to work his land. On the Hudson River, each patroonship extended for miles along one bank or both banks, as far back into the countryside as the lord, or patroon, wanted — or the Native Americans allowed. Similar to New France, the settlers were tenants of the manor, owing feudal dues to the lord. This arrangement attracted few settlers: In fact it discouraged immigration because the manors tied up large tracts that might otherwise go to small farmers. The only patroonship to succeed was Rensselaerswyck, on the upper Hudson River, which had Fort Orange at its center.

At first, New Netherland had good relations with the Indians because the colony grew slowly and depended on the fur trade. In the famous 1626 purchase, Director-general Peter Minuit exchanged goods worth about 60 guilders for Manhattan Island. Upriver, the Dutch bought furs from the Iroquois, the enemies of the Algonquians and Hurons who supplied the French, thus contributing to the devastating warfare among tribes. When game near the Hudson River quickly gave out, Dutch merchants encouraged the Mohawks, the easternmost of the Five Nations, to take control of the Huron supply routes from the interior of Canada. By the late 1640s, the Iroquois, with help from epidemics, destroyed the Hurons, a nation of about 20,000 people. At the same time, constant warfare and disease seriously debilitated the Iroquois as well.

In the region surrounding New Amsterdam, relations deteriorated between the whites and the Indians after 1638. As with the English, the Dutch and natives had different conceptions of land ownership. While the Indians understood that they had sold rights to share the land and intended to continue using it themselves, the Dutch believed they had bought exclusive rights. Violence erupted as the settlers' cattle trampled the Indians' corn, and dogs belonging to Native Americans attacked Dutch livestock. The Dutch also had trouble distinguishing among friendly and hostile Indians: for example, after some Hackensacks killed two settlers in 1642, eighty Dutch soldiers attacked two villages of Wecquaesgeeks, allies of the New Netherland government. Beginning in 1640, the Dutch and Indians of the lower Hudson Valley fought a series of damaging wars that ended only in 1664, when the English took control of New Netherland and made peace with the Native Americans.

New England Before the Pilgrims

Along the coast of New England, relations between the Indians and English were rocky from the start. Before the Pilgrims established Plymouth in 1620, a number of expeditions explored the region, traded,

Theodor de Bry's illustration emphasizes friendly exchange rather than hostility between Bartholomew Gosnold and the Indians of Martha's Vineyard. De Bry also suggests a larger fleet than Gosnold's single ship, the Concord.

and tried to colonize. In 1602, Bartholomew Gosnold and thirty-two men sailed the *Concord* to Maine, expecting to establish a colony. They continued south to Martha's Vineyard, where they stayed five weeks, trading for furs. When they alienated the natives and one of their men was wounded, Gosnold and his crew returned to England. In 1607, the Plymouth group of the Virginia Company sent an expedition to the Kennebec River in Maine, but the colony lasted only one year. The company abandoned efforts to establish a permanent base, instead funding voyages for fish and furs. The English immediately came up against the French at Port Royal and Quebec, and traded with their enemies among the Indians. Like the Dutch and French, the English set up commercial networks with tribes who had contested land and resources before the Europeans arrived, thereby intensifying these rivalries with competition for furs and European goods.

Even before the founding of Plymouth, then, the natives of New England had considerable experience with the English. Sadly, this contact had catastrophic effects on the Indian population and foretold future relations. A plague epidemic brought by Europeans swept eastern New England during 1616–1618, killing thousands. Large areas along the coast were depopulated, opening them for English settlement in the 1620s and 1630s. The Massachusetts natives were initially friendly and interested in trade, but good relations proved elusive. The English shot some Native Americans and set dogs on others. A few they kidnapped, then expected them to serve as diplomats to their people. The English also made trade agreements, then failed to honor them. By the time the Pilgrims arrived in 1620, the surviving Indians along the coast had been severely weakened by disease and were understandably wary of the newcomers.

RELIGIOUS EXILES FROM ENGLAND

While the colonizers of Virginia, New France, and New Netherland had primarily economic motives, the English founders of Plymouth, Massachusetts Bay, and

Maryland sought a place where they could practice their religion free from persecution and at the same time earn a decent living. Like other European nations, seventeenth-century England was rife with religious controversy, as Protestant and Catholic dissidents challenged the monopoly of the Church of England. The government required attendance at Anglican worship and financial support of ministers. When dissenters refused to obey, holding separate services, they could be imprisoned and fined. Roman Catholics could also be stripped of their property and jailed for life if they refused to take the oath of supremacy to the king, which denied the authority of the pope. The search for freedom of worship, which the king permitted in America but not at home, became a major impetus for crossing the Atlantic.

English Calvinists

By 1603, when James I took the throne, two strains of English Calvinism, or Puritanism, had developed. One group included the Separatists, or Pilgrims, who founded Plymouth in 1620; the others, known as Puritans, established the Massachusetts Bay colony ten years later. Both groups charged that the Anglican church retained too much Catholicism, that it needed to be "purified" of its rituals, vestments, statues, and bishops. They rejected the church hierarchy, believing each congregation should govern itself. The Separatists started their own congregations, abandoning all hope that the church could be reformed. The Pilgrims' decision to begin a colony in America, away from European corruption, was the ultimate expression of this separatism. The Puritans, on the other hand, were non-separating congregationalists who hoped to reform the Church of England from within. Their purpose in founding Massachusetts Bay was to build a society to serve as a model for corrupt England and other English colonies. In coming to America, the Puritans were separating themselves geographically, but would use their isolation to develop a moral government which they hoped the people of England would someday make their own.

The Plymouth Colony

The Pilgrims were a small band who had originated in Scrooby, England, where they established a separate congregation. In 1607, when some were jailed as nonconformists, they decided to leave England for the Netherlands, which offered freedom of worship. The Pilgrims settled in Leyden, but were unhappy there, too. They found Dutch society corrupt and feared for their children's souls. With difficulty locating work and a preference for English government, the Pilgrims made an agreement with a group of London merchants who obtained a patent for land from the Virginia Company. In exchange for funding to go to America, the Pilgrims promised to send back fish, furs, and lumber for seven years. James I offered the Pilgrims freedom to worship in their colony.

Thirty-five of the Leyden congregation, a minority, chose to emigrate. Sailing first to England, they joined sixty-seven others, of whom many were not Separatists. In September 1620, the *Mayflower* departed Plymouth, England, crowded with 102 passengers, about twenty crew members, and assorted pigs, chickens, and goats. Headed for Virginia, the ship reached Cape Cod on November 9th. In shallow waters, fearing shipwreck, the exhausted travelers built their colony at Plymouth, even though they were outside the jurisdiction of the Virginia Company. Their decision entailed risks because they now lacked a legal basis for governing themselves or for claiming land. The first problem was most urgent because some of the colonists questioned the authority of the Pilgrim leaders. The group avoided a revolt by drafting and signing the "Mayflower Compact," a social compact by which they agreed to form a government and obey its laws. The London merchants eventually solved the second problem by obtaining title to the land.

Plymouth's first years were difficult, though the settlers found unused supplies of corn left by Indians struck recently by an epidemic, and chose the site of a deserted Patuxet village with relatively clear fields. Over the first winter they built houses, but one-half of the colonists died of disease and exposure to the cold. In the spring of 1621, they planted corn with the help of Squanto, perhaps the lone surviving Patuxet, and other crops.

The natives helped the Plymouth Colony, despite earlier problems with Englishmen. In 1614, Squanto and about twenty other Patuxets had been kidnapped by an English sea captain, who intended to sell them as slaves in Spain. Saved from bondage by Spanish priests, Squanto made his way to England, where he learned the language, then to Newfoundland, and finally back to Patuxet in 1619. There he found

THE MAYFLOWER COMPACT, 1620

When the *Mayflower* reached land at Cape Cod (in what is now Massachusetts) and the colonists decided to settle there instead of prolonging their difficult journey, they lacked the legal basis (a charter) to establish a government. Thus, the adult males of the colony signed a mutual agreement for ordering their society, what John Locke called, decades later, a "social compact."

In the name of God Amen. We whose names are underwriten, the loyall subjects of our dread soveraigne Lord King James by the grace of God, of great Britaine, Franc, & Ireland king, defender of the faith, &c.

Haveing undertaken, for the glorie of God, and advancements of the Christian faith and honour of our king & countrie, a voyage to plant the first colonie in the Northerne parts of Virginia, doe by these presents solemnly & mutualy in the presence of God, and one of another, covenant & combine our selves togeather into a civill body politick; for our better ordering, & preservation & furtherance of the ends aforesaid; and by vertue hearof to enacte, constitute, and frame shuch just & equall lawes, ordinances, Acts, constitutions, & offices, from time to time, as shall be thought most meete & convenient for the generall good of the Colonie: unto which we promise all due submission and obedience.

In witnes whereof we have hereunder subscribed our names at Cap-Codd the · 11 · of November, in the year the raigne of our soveraigne Lord King James of England, France, & Ireland the eighteenth and of Scotland the fiftie fourth. An°: Dom. 1620.

John Carver	John Turner
William Bradford	Francis Eaton
Edward Winslow	James Chilton
William Brewster	John Crakston
Isaac Allerton	John Billington
Myles Standish	Moses Fletcher
John Alden	John Goodman
Samuel Fuller	Degory Priest
Christopher Martin	Thomas Williams
William Mullins	Gilbert Winslow
William White	Edmund Margeson
Richard Warren	Peter Brown
John Howland	Richard Britterige
Stephen Hopkins	George Soule
Edward Tilley	Richard Clarke
John Tilley	Richard Gardiner
Francis Cooke	John Allerton
Thomas Rogers	Thomas English
Thomas Tinker	Edward Doty
John Rigdale	Edward Leister
Edward Fuller	

unburied bodies of many of his people who had perished in the epidemic. One Englishman described the scene: "[T]heir bones and skulls made such a spectacle. . . . it seemed to me a new found Golgotha."

At harvest in 1621, the Indians and colonists celebrated together for three days. The future seemed bright for the fifty-one surviving colonists, but soon after their feast, the ship *Fortune* arrived with thirty-five new settlers, for whom no food was available until the next year's crop. When the colonists filled the *Fortune* with furs and lumber in hopes of starting to repay their debt to the London merchants, the French captured the ship.

By 1623, though, the Plymouth Colony was well established and growing, as new immigrants arrived. The community solved the problem of food supply by assigning individual plots to families, making them responsible for their own food. Still, the hard-working colonists had trouble fulfilling their bargain with the merchants, as all of their efforts came to naught. During a trading voyage, the crew mutinied. On one fishing trip, the ship sank; when it was raised and sent out again, the Spanish captured it. The London merchants gave up, ended the partnership, and in 1626 agreed to sell the land to the colonists for a large sum, which they paid by 1645, receiving a patent of ownership. While Plymouth's economic fortunes improved, the colony remained small and self-consciously separate from the larger group of English dissenters who streamed into New England.

Reconstructed village at Plymouth, with fences to protect gardens from roaming livestock.

The seal of the Massachusetts Bay Company, 1629, shows an Indian calling to the English, "Come over and help us."

The Great Puritan Migration

The Puritan migration to Massachusetts Bay was much larger and more tightly organized than Plymouth. During 1630, the first year, 700 women, men, and children arrived in eleven ships. Though at least 200 died during the first winter because of lack of food and bitter weather, the colony grew quickly. The Massachusetts Bay Company, made up primarily of Puritans, organized the "great migration" of about 12,000 people who came to Massachusetts during the 1630s. From King Charles I, the company obtained a charter specifying its government and the colony's boundaries. When most of the company officials emigrated, taking the charter with them, they greatly enhanced the colony's independence from the Crown and the Anglican church.

Thus the Massachusetts Bay colonists, unlike the first settlers of Jamestown and Plymouth, had their own charter and did not answer to London merchants who expected handsome profits. The Puritans themselves financed colonization; they included wealthy investors as well as many middling families who could pay their own way. As a result, the founders devoted much of their energy to creating a model society, a godly commonwealth. In the words of leader John Winthrop, the colony would be "as a Citty upon a Hill, the Eyes of all people are upon us; soe that if

Unlike most English colonists, John Winthrop came from a well-to-do background. He helped finance the Massachusetts Bay colony and served as governor.

wee shall deale falsely with our god in this worke wee have undertaken and soe cause him to withdrawe this present help from us, wee shall be made a story and a by-word through the world." The Puritans believed that in addition to their charter from the king, which set up their secular government, they had a covenant with God that bound them to create a moral community. The Puritans, as Calvinists, held that individuals were saved from eternal damnation by faith, rather than by good works. Men and women could seek to avoid sin, work hard, and help their neighbors throughout their lives, but unless they were among God's chosen, or the "elect," they would go to hell. Under the covenant, the elect were responsible for the behavior of unsaved members of their households and the community at large. The Puritan leaders were responsible to God. They thought that if they maintained a moral society, the Lord would help it prosper.

In Massachusetts, the Puritans restructured the company government to create their version of a godly commonwealth. According to the Massachusetts Bay charter, the company officials included a governor, deputy governor, and executive board of eighteen "assistants," to be elected by "freemen" (stockholders) who would meet in a general assembly, called the General Court. These officers, as long as they did nothing in violation of the laws of England, could make laws and regulations, appoint lower officials, grant lands, and punish lawbreakers. The colony's leaders changed the rules to allow all male church members (the male elect), not just stockholders in the company, to become freemen. In theory, every freeman would be a member of the General Court, or colonial legislature. But as the population grew and towns formed quickly, freemen voted in town meetings for representatives to the assembly.

With the governor and assistants, the General Court drew up a law code for the colony, which after several revisions was published as the *Laws and Liberties of Massachusetts* (1648). The code was a combination of biblical law, English common law, and statutes tailored specifically to colonial needs. It protected the liberties of individuals by upholding trial by jury and due process of law, including the rights of the accused to a prompt, public trial and to call witnesses. It also prohibited feudal tenure of lands and outlawed slavery, "unless it be lawfull captives, taken in just warrs, and such strangers as willingly sell themselves or are solde to us." This provision limited the possibility that whites would be enslaved, but had little effect on black bondage. The *Laws and Liberties* prescribed the death penalty for many fewer crimes than in England, but included as capital offenses blasphemy and adultery (in cases where the woman was married), which under the English common law were lesser crimes. Children could be put to death for failing to respect their parents, while fornicators were required to marry and be whipped or fined. The code enabled judges to extend the terms of negligent servants and send back to England any married persons who arrived in Massachusetts without their spouses. While these terms may seem harsh, the colony did not actually impose the death penalty for blasphemy or abuse of parents by children, and executed only two people for adultery. The magistrates evidently wanted to instill fear in the hearts of potential offenders rather than exact harsh punishments. With trial by jury and due process, Massachusetts preserved important civil liberties.

The Puritans attempted to create a theocracy, a government operated according to God's will, as determined by the colony's patriarchs. They were sure that their religion was the only one God ordained. The Puritan government was composed of members of the elect; ministers advised the magistrates but could not serve officially. The government required all inhabitants to attend Puritan churches whether or not they accepted the faith. Persons who disagreed with orthodox doctrines, and made their position known, could be expelled, whipped, fined, and even executed. The church was the center of each town, with all property owners paying taxes for its support. Though the Puritans had suffered persecution for their beliefs in England, they refused to allow freedom of worship in Massachusetts. Instead, they replaced one established church for another.

Massachusetts Society

Unlike the Jamestown settlers, a large proportion of Puritan immigrants came in families. Many originated from Norfolk, Suffolk, and Essex (together called East Anglia), Kent, London, and the West Country. Fewer came from the north of England. East Anglia, located directly across the North Sea from the Netherlands, was the center of both the wool trade and Puritanism. By 1630, its residents had kept contact with European Calvinists for almost a century. Entire congregations and their ministers, ostensibly part of the Church of England, adopted Puritan ways. They conducted services without the Book of Common Prayer and tore down communion rails. For decades they had worshipped freely, protected by the local Puritan gentry. Then during the 1620s and 1630s, the Puritans faced a series of hardships, including a depressed market for woolen cloth, poor harvests, and bubonic plague. Charles I and the Anglican church hierarchy, most notably Archbishop William Laud, enforced laws against nonconformists, removing Puritan ministers from their pulpits. Many families—grandparents, parents, children, and servants—migrated to Massachusetts, where they could make a new start under a congenial government. Some entire communities accompanied their ministers.

In Massachusetts, the migrants created towns that often resembled the ones they had left. When a group arrived, its leaders petitioned the General Court for a

The Fairbanks House in Dedham, Massachusetts, was originally built c. 1637 and later expanded, as shown in this 1880 photograph.

place to settle and permission to establish a church and town government. The town meeting, composed in some places of male church members only and in others of all male landowners, elected a board of selectmen who administered town business, including road building, maintenance of schools, and law enforcement. The town meeting also divided the town lands. The amount of land a family received depended upon its wealth and social status. Typically, a town followed one of two patterns of land distribution, according to the kind of land tenure its founders knew in England. Emigrants from East Anglia generally chose the *closed field* system, in which families received individual farms, with house lot and land for planting, grazing livestock, and cutting lumber. These settlers also created commercial towns, such as Ipswich, that quickly entered the West Indies trade. In contrast, emigrants from Yorkshire, in northern England, chose the *open field* system, designating town lands for different purposes—house lots lined up in compact rows, fields, meadows, and wood lots. In Rowley, Massachusetts, for example, families received strips in the fields, where they grew crops in cooperation with their neighbors. Together they made many decisions, including which fields to plant and which to leave fallow. Families also received "stinting rights," or permission to pasture animals on common lands. The number of cattle and sheep a family could pasture depended upon the size of their lands.

The Puritan notion of an ideal community defined the ways in which they acted toward one another and toward outsiders. If the model society were to succeed, everyone had to have a place, in the family, church, and commonwealth. Like other English, the Puritans kept a hierarchical social order. In the family, the husband was superior to the wife, but together they ruled the children and servants. In the church, the minister and elders dominated the congregation. In the commonwealth, the officials led the people. Ideally, this hierarchy required little coercion, when people saw themselves as part of the community and worked for the common good, or "weal" (hence "commonwealth"), rather than for their own benefit. They understood that all humans were equal spiritually—because everyone had the possibility of being saved—but accepted social inequality as the will of God.

Most Puritan women accepted a subordinate place in their society without complaint. They viewed themselves as part of a community and a family, with duties determined by their sex and age, not as individuals with equal rights. Official records often listed wives without their given names, as in the case of "John Brown his wife." Women raised children; kept the house and garden; preserved fruits and vegetables; made beer, cider, cheese, and butter; tended livestock and poultry; spun and wove cloth; sewed clothing, cared for the sick, and supervised the training of daughters and servants. Women often specialized in certain trades, such as spinning, weaving, poultry-raising, or medicine; they conducted trade among themselves, separate from the commercial networks of their husbands. Men had responsibility for raising grain such as wheat, Indian corn, and rye; cutting firewood; and maintaining the fences, buildings, and fields. In addition to farming, many followed a trade or profession such as fishing, carpentry, shopkeeping, overseas trade, medicine, or the ministry. Only men could vote in church and town meetings, serve as government officials, or become ministers. They were the heads of household, representing their wives and children in public affairs. Only when a man became incapacitated, or was away from home, was his wife expected to take his place at work or to represent the family in legal matters or disputes. She temporarily as-

Mrs. Elizabeth Freake and Baby Mary, *painted c. 1674 by an unknown artist, illustrates one of the many roles of seventeenth-century women, that of mother. The wife and child of a successful merchant, their clothing depicts the family's wealth.*

sumed the role of "deputy husband," then yielded it when he became well or returned. Puritans recognized women's ability in public matters, but expected them normally to confine themselves to accepted women's tasks.

The role of Puritan women in the church was indicative of their place in society. On the one hand, women were the spiritual equals of men, held responsibility for the religious education of their children, and formed one-half (and as time went on a greater proportion) of church members. On the other hand, the Puritans emphasized the inheritance of Eve, who they believed led Adam to sin in the Garden of Eden. Women were expected to keep quiet in the church. They could not preach or vote on church business, though they could exert informal influence on their husbands. The Puritans, like other Christians of the time, embraced Saint Paul's instruction to the Corinthians: "Let your women keep silence in the

Churches. . . . And if they will learn anything, let them ask their husbands at home." The Puritans believed that by nature women, as daughters of Eve, were morally and intellectually weak. They had to submit to their husbands for guidance. The pain of childbirth was God's punishment of all women for Eve's seduction of Adam. Although a few rebelled against the injunction to keep quiet, and some were consequently tried as heretics or witches, most Puritan women and girls accepted their subordination to men.

In this patriarchal society, children deferred to their fathers, assuming a subservient role until they were able to establish households of their own. Though some New England colonists held servants and a few owned enslaved Africans, sons and daughters comprised the majority of the workforce. Families on average had five children who reached adulthood. They worked for their parents until marriage—longer in the case of sons who inherited the family farm. Unlike seventeenth-century Virginia, living conditions in Massachusetts promoted patriarchy, for life expectancy was long. Persons who survived childhood diseases often lived past age sixty or even seventy. Thus, eldest sons could be middle-aged before their fathers died and willed them control of the family homestead. On the other hand, younger sons who had little hope of receiving the farm often moved away from their parents, settling in the new towns that developed throughout New England. Parents usually attempted to give all of their children a start in life, with a farm, apprenticeship, money, or college tuition to sons, and personal property or cash to daughters.

Connecticut and New Haven

An early destination for emigrants looking for good land was Connecticut. The first Puritans went there to trade with Native Americans, but when news of attractive land in the Connecticut Valley arrived in Massachusetts, many settlers decided to move. The Earl of Warwick owned the rights to the land at the mouth of the Connecticut River, which he ceded to a group of Puritan noblemen. To build a trading post and settlement they sent John Winthrop, Jr., who convinced Thomas Hooker, the minister of Newtown, Massachu-

setts, to lead some of his congregation there. Another group left from Dorchester. They founded Connecticut in 1636, followed by families who could not obtain suitable land in the old settlements and established towns up the Connecticut River and on Long Island. Though they had no charter from the king, the founders agreed upon the *Fundamental Orders of Connecticut,* which created a General Assembly of representatives from each town. In most respects, the Connecticut government resembled that of Massachusetts, with the exception that freemen, or voters, did not have to be church members. The assembly elected a governor, who could serve only one year at a time, and a group of magistrates who functioned as the upper house of the assembly. As in Massachusetts, Puritanism was the only recognized religion and received tax support.

As white settlement expanded, relations between the Puritans and Native Americans deteriorated. Like other English, the Puritans believed that the Indians worshipped the devil and had barbarous customs. The settlers justified expropriation of native lands on the basis of *vacuum domicilium.* Even more, the Puritans considered the Indians "strangers," who could have no role in building the model society. They were dispensable and dangerous, presenting a dual threat because their customs could corrupt the holy commonwealth and they resented their loss of lands.

The 1637 war against the Pequots of eastern Connecticut showed the lengths to which the New England settlers could go. The Pequots, a powerful tribe, attempted to unite New England Indians against the English. They traded with the Dutch, thus encouraging Dutch claims to Connecticut. In May 1637, troops from Massachusetts and Connecticut, with their Indian allies, the Narragansetts, attacked a Pequot village on the Mystic River before dawn, killing hundreds of sleeping women, children, and old men. The Pequots who escaped this massacre, mostly young men absent from the town, were later executed or enslaved. The Treaty of Hartford (1638) declared their nation dissolved.

Shortly after the Pequot War, in 1638, a group of staunch Puritans established New Haven, on the Long Island Sound west of the Connecticut colony. Persecuted in England, Reverend John Davenport took his flock first to Boston, but decided to move on. They had no charter for New Haven, so the freemen made the Bible their law, eliminating trial by jury, for example, because it had no scriptural basis. Only male church members could vote. The colony grew, despite its lack of legal authority, as the settlers built towns farther west along the sound and on Long Island. Together, the towns agreed upon a government comprised of a governor, magistrates, and a representative assembly.

Exiles to Rhode Island

The founding of Rhode Island resulted from another kind of emigration from Massachusetts, that of persons who refused to subordinate their own beliefs to those of the Puritan magistrates. The first was Roger Williams, a likeable but stubborn, independent-minded minister, who challenged Massachusetts Bay's policy toward the Indians and its theocratic laws. Williams had studied divinity at Cambridge University, where he became a vocal Separatist, rejecting the Anglican church altogether. He immigrated to Massachusetts Bay in 1631, arousing the colony when he refused the pulpit in Boston church because its members had not renounced the Church of England. He explained, "I durst not officiate to an unseparated people, as upon examination and conference I found them to be."

Williams then accused Massachusetts of holding fraudulent title to its territory because the king had no authority to give away Indian lands. The king's grant depended upon "a solemn public lie." The colony should send the charter back to the king for correction; the settlers should return to England if they could not obtain rights from the true owners of the land. Williams raised a troublesome issue that the Puritan officials refused to recognize, so they ordered him to be still. He would not be quiet, soon broaching the issues of religious freedom and separation of church and state. "Forced worship stinks in God's nostrils," he proclaimed. "There is no other prudent, Christian way of preserving peace in the world, but by permission of differing consciences." He attacked the laws requiring church attendance and tax support of Puritan churches. Williams feared that government would pollute the church, not that giving legal preference to one religion was unfair. He opposed laws regulating religion to protect the church from state interference.

The General Court banished Williams from Massachusetts for challenging the government; in 1636 he went to Narragansett Bay. There he purchased land from the Narragansett Indians, establishing Providence Plantation at the Great Salt River. With the sympathizers who joined him, he created a society based on religious toleration, separation of church and state, and participation in government by all male property owners. Church membership was not a requirement to vote. In fact, Williams welcomed people of all religions to Providence Plantation, as long as they accepted the right of others to worship freely. Williams himself became wealthy through trade with the Native Americans and the Dutch. In 1638, he transferred ownership of Providence to a group of thirteen associates, of whom he was one. This board had responsibilities much like the selectmen of Massachusetts towns.

Another exile from Massachusetts was Anne Hutchinson, a midwife and nurse, who in 1634 arrived in Boston with her husband, merchant William Hutchinson, and children. She had given birth to fourteen sons and daughters, of whom three died before the family left England; she had one more child in 1636. As Hutchinson assisted women in childbirth and sickness, she became convinced that Bostonians placed too much emphasis on good works and not enough on faith. She was a follower of one of Boston's ministers, the influential John Cotton, who stressed the importance of the individual's relationship with God over the obligation to obey laws. Hutchinson went further than Cotton, nearly saying that if a person were saved it did not matter how she or he behaved, a belief known as the Antinomian heresy.

To the orthodox Puritan faction led by Governor John Winthrop, Hutchinson was a threat for several reasons. She emphasized individual judgment over the community's, thus questioning the authority of the colony's leaders. She told the Puritan patriarchs that God spoke to her directly, that she did not need the assistance of magistrates and ministers in interpreting God's will. They feared that the community would disintegrate if everyone heeded her words. Further, Hutchinson went outside the accepted role of women by taking a public stand on religion. But most seriously, she became the standard bearer for a group who contested power with the Winthrop faction. In 1637, Winthrop's government put Hutchinson on trial for defaming ministers and exiled her from the colony. With her family and supporters she founded a colony at Portsmouth on Narragansett Bay. When she later had a miscarriage, Winthrop pronounced the "monstrous birth" God's judgment upon her. Even more fitting, the Puritans thought, was her death in 1643 at the hands of Native Americans, after she moved to New Netherland.

Following the settlement of Williams and Hutchinson on Narragansett Bay, several other dissenters established colonies there. William Coddington, a supporter of Hutchinson, started the town of Newport; and Samuel Gorton, who had first migrated to Massachusetts because he thought they practiced religious freedom, founded Warwick. The four leaders had trouble cooperating, but knew they needed a charter from the English government to avoid annexation by Massachusetts. Roger Williams went to England for that purpose, in the midst of the Civil War. The 1644 Rhode Island charter, which Parliament granted, united the four settlements under one representative assembly, which could pass statutes consistent with the laws of England. The Rhode Island colonists based their government on Williams's principles of freedom of worship, separation of church and state, and wide participation in government.

The Proprietary Colony of Maryland

In 1632, Charles I granted a charter for Maryland, the first successful proprietary colony in his domains. George Calvert, the first Lord Baltimore, had served in high office until he converted to Catholicism. Forced to resign, but still a royal favorite, Calvert requested a grant in America to build a haven for Catholics. He also expected to support his family by selling the land. He died before obtaining the charter, so his son, Cecilius Calvert, the second Lord Baltimore, became lord proprietor of Maryland. The colony was carved out of the northern part of Virginia, much to the dismay of its residents. Calvert received ownership of the soil and was sovereign in government, subject only to the king. His dues to the Crown were a token tribute of two Indian arrowheads each year.

Calvert soon discovered that the cost of colonization was great. He spent £40,000 for two ships, the

Cecilius Calvert, the second Lord Baltimore, with his grandson and an enslaved African. Calvert was proprietor of Maryland until 1675 when he died and the boy's father, Charles, succeeded him.

Ark and the *Dove,* with supplies to send the first 150 settlers, who arrived in Maryland in 1634. The proprietor planned a feudal system in which manorial lords held large tracts, which they rented to tenants. For example, a person who transported five laborers at a total cost of £20 received a manor of 2,000 acres. Among his manorial rights, the lord could establish a court for trying cases among his tenants.

Though Maryland settlers suffered no "starving time" as in Virginia and had a cash crop in tobacco, the colony grew slowly. Mortality was high and immigration sluggish. By 1642, Calvert had granted rights for only sixteen manors, mostly to wealthy Catholic friends. These manors comprised 31,000 acres, or more than 80 percent of the patented land. To improve his income, Calvert distributed farms to more ordinary immigrants, who had to pay annual quitrents. Over the seventeenth century, rich investors acquired sixty manors but by far most settlers were small landowners.

The extension of land ownership beyond Calvert's circle of loyal supporters created problems for the lord proprietor. Under the charter, he was obligated to call together an assembly of freemen, or landowners, to enact laws. Calvert interpreted this to mean that they should approve legislation he prepared, while the freemen, meeting first in 1635, claimed the right to draft the code of laws. Calvert refused to accept their draft, so for three years the colony operated without a code. In 1638, they reached a compromise, with the proprietor and assembly each drafting some of the bills. The colony finally had a legal basis for governing and punishing crime.

But the struggle for power between the proprietor and freemen continued, intensifying on account of religion. The ordinary planters, who formed the majority of freemen and were mostly Protestant, resented the power of the Catholic elite. They were strongly prejudiced against Catholics and had little sympathy for Calvert's vision of a society in which all Christians could worship freely. Religious and political strife became most acute in Maryland during the English Civil War and the Puritan Commonwealth, from 1642 to 1660.

Impact of the English Civil War

For two decades, the English Civil War altered the political situation in England, with unsettling effects on the colonies. The war—or more accurately, the revolution—resulted from a contest for power between Parliament and Charles I, who claimed absolute power and attempted to raise taxes without approval of the legislature. Charles imprisoned opponents without due process, and launched a crusade, carried out by Archbishop Laud, to force all his subjects, even those in Presbyterian Scotland and Catholic Ireland, to conform to the Anglican church. In 1642, war broke out between the "Cavaliers," or royalists, and the "Roundheads," or parliamentary forces, of whom many were

Puritans. Oliver Cromwell led the Roundheads to victory in 1648; the following year they beheaded the king.

The revolutionaries attempted to rule through an elected Parliament, but conflicting factions of Puritans and radical sects undermined their plans. Some radical theorists wanted an entire restructuring of society—in the words of one contemporary, "a world turned upside down." They called for extension of the vote to all men and redistribution of land. The gentry and wealthy merchants who had led Parliament to victory considered these ideas anathema. In 1653, to reestablish control, they named Cromwell the Lord Protector of the Commonwealth of England, Scotland, and Ireland. Cromwell ruled alone, backed by the army, until his death in 1658. An attempt failed to make his son Richard the successor, and two years later, the monarchy was restored. The accession of Charles II did not mean a complete reversal to the time of his father. Most important, the king confirmed Parliament's right to approve taxes and abolished the royal courts that had punished opponents of the Crown. But the Restoration brought the Cavaliers back into power, making the Anglican church the state religion once again.

The struggle for power during the Civil War and its aftermath had repercussions in the colonies. Initially, the rebellion of English Puritans against the king raised hopes among New Englanders that English society would be reformed. Some colonists returned to join the battle. Most stayed in America, however, convinced that English society would not be purified. Of more practical importance to the New England colonies was the lack of military protection from England. Plymouth, Massachusetts, Connecticut, and New Haven counted among their enemies the French, Dutch, Native Americans, and Rhode Island. In 1643, they joined together to form the New England Confederation. Rhode Island also requested membership but was refused. The confederation agreed to share the cost of war, provide soldiers in proportion to population, and make no treaties without each colony's consent. They also mutually promised to return fugitives and arbitrate disputes among themselves. The New England Confederation was the first league of colonies in English North America and the only successful one before the Revolutionary War. In assuming power to conduct war and make treaties, it went beyond colonial rights. The English government, in

Charles II, who became king upon the restoration of the English monarchy in 1660, fostered colonization in North America, in part, to pay his debts.

stricted the right of Catholics to worship, and created a Puritan code of behavior, including laws against swearing, drunkenness, and breaking the sabbath. Calvert appealed to Oliver Cromwell, who confirmed his proprietorship, but Lord Baltimore regained control of the colony only in 1657, after a period of local civil war.

ENGLISH COLONIZATION AFTER 1660

The accession of Charles II in 1660 initiated a new phase of colonization, in which the English government, at least in fits and starts, paid more attention to its colonies than it had before the Civil War. In 1662, the Crown granted Connecticut a charter that included New Haven, and the following year confirmed the charter Rhode Island had received from Parliament. To end the Dutch trade that had flourished with the English colonies during the 1640s and 1650s and to tighten colonial administration, the king and Parliament approved a series of navigation acts that formed the basis of a mercantilist colonial policy.

Navigation Acts

The English Commonwealth, recognizing the growing economic value of the colonies, had passed the Navigation Act of 1651. The law required that goods brought to England or its colonies from Asia, Africa, or America be carried on English ships (including those of its colonies). Goods from European nations had to be transported on either English ships or those of the country of origin. The chief purposes of the act were to encourage growth of England's merchant marine and to challenge Dutch ascendancy on the seas and in colonial ports. The Commonwealth went further in 1652–1654, with the first Anglo-Dutch War, by attacking Dutch vessels in the English Channel and North Sea. The English took more than one thousand Dutch ships, greatly expanding their merchant fleet.

the midst of Civil War, was too preoccupied to react.

In the Chesapeake colonies, whose governments had close ties to the king, the Civil War and its aftermath were more disruptive. In 1652, after some delay, the English Commonwealth removed the royalist Virginia governor, William Berkeley, because he had proclaimed Charles II the king upon his father's execution. In Maryland, the parliamentary revolt weakened the position of Lord Baltimore, whose authority came directly from the king. Protestants, especially Puritans, constituted an antiproprietary force. Ironically, the proprietor had encouraged Puritans to migrate from Virginia, where they had suffered Governor Berkeley's persecution. Calvert approved the "Act Concerning Religion" (1649), which guaranteed freedom of religion to all Christians. Nevertheless, in 1654, the Maryland Puritans established a commonwealth. Their assembly deposed the proprietor's government, re-

The Navigation Acts of 1660, 1663, and 1673 confirmed the 1651 restrictions on transport and created a list of "enumerated articles"—major colonial products including tobacco, sugar, indigo, cotton, ginger, and dyewoods—which could be shipped only to England or another English colony. The colonists could not sell these goods directly to other nations. The "articles" first went to England, where they were taxed and reexported by English merchants, who benefited from the business. Conversely, with some exceptions including salt, horses, and wines, all goods shipped from other nations to the English colonies had to go to England first. The colonists considered these laws detrimental because English middlemen added charges to products going in both directions. The English government created a colonial administration to enforce the acts, but the results were complicated and inefficient. Colonial governors, required to ban foreign ships from their ports, lacked the resources (and in many cases the will) to eliminate smuggling.

Carolina

Charles II was penniless when he ascended the throne and owed substantial debts to his supporters. Expansion of the colonial empire permitted him to repay these creditors with land and offices, and at the same time advance England's commerce and national power. Carolina, named for the king, was the first post-Restoration colony on the North American mainland. In 1663, the area between Virginia and Spanish Florida was unoccupied by Europeans, but Spain had better title to the land than England. Nevertheless, the English proceeded with plans to establish a colony and, with the Treaty of Madrid (1670), obtained Spain's concession of lands north of present-day Charleston. The chief promoters of Carolina were Anthony Ashley Cooper, Governor William Berkeley of Virginia, and John Colleton, a West Indies planter. They obtained help from five men who were close to the king; together the eight associates became proprietors of Carolina. They obtained a charter like Maryland's, permitting them to make laws with the consent of the freemen. The proprietors received wide latitude in matters of religion, with the power to build churches and offer freedom of worship. They drew up the "Fundamental Constitutions of Carolina," creating

a complicated feudal society with nobles and lords, a scheme the ordinary settlers of Carolina refused to accept. As in Maryland and elsewhere, immigrants wanted land ownership, not tenancy. And freemen who owned property demanded a voice in government.

Two colonies developed in Carolina. Small planters from Virginia built the first, which later became North Carolina. As early as 1653, people had settled on the shores of Albemarle Sound, where they raised tobacco, corn, and livestock. In 1664, William Berkeley, governor of Virginia and one of the Carolina proprietors, sent William Drummond to organize a council and assembly. The Albemarle settlement remained poor, a haven for pirates, and difficult to govern. In 1691, the Carolina proprietors effectively established North Carolina by appointing a separate governor.

The second Carolina colony, which the proprietors actually planned, was located at Charles Town, in the future South Carolina. After two unsuccessful attempts, Anthony Ashley Cooper in 1670 organized a permanent settlement. South Carolina has been called "the colony of a colony" because so many of its early settlers came from the West Indies island of Barbados, which had run out of vacant land. The Barbadian planters had money to develop plantations in Carolina and owned African slaves to do the work. The proprietors partially abandoned their feudal land scheme, offering generous acreages to household heads for each person brought to the colony. A planter, with his own family and several enslaved blacks, could qualify for hundreds of acres. From the colony's founding, a large proportion of South Carolinians were African slaves, comprising between one-fourth and one-third of the settlers during the earliest years. They produced food, livestock, firewood, and barrel staves for Barbados, where sugar was the dominant crop.

New York and New Jersey

To control North America, the English next had to seize New Netherland. With a series of outposts, the Dutch held the region between Connecticut and Maryland, including lands on the Delaware River that Sweden settled in 1638 and the Dutch took in 1655. The English justified their attack in 1664 against New

Netherland on several grounds, including John Cabot's 1497 voyage to the region and Dutch illegal trade with English colonies. Settlers from New England living under Dutch jurisdiction complained that Governor Peter Stuyvesant ruled as a dictator. They reported to the English that Dutch military defenses could not withstand attack. James, the duke of York, Lord High Admiral of the Navy, urged his brother, Charles II, to send a fleet. The king granted James a proprietary charter for lands between the Connecticut and Delaware rivers, as well as Long Island, Nantucket, Martha's Vineyard, and part of present-day Maine. The charter gave the duke wide governmental powers, even dispensing with an assembly, which the Maryland and Carolina charters required. The duke could write his own legal code as long as it conformed to the laws of England; inhabitants had no role in making laws, but could appeal court judgments to the king.

With charter in hand, James forced out the Dutch. In 1664, his deputy governor, Richard Nicolls, with

Governor Peter Stuyvesant in 1664 surrendered New Amsterdam to the English without a fight. This portrait, painted c. 1661, is attributed to Henri Couturier.

four ships and 400 soldiers, took New Amsterdam without a fight—the Dutch defenses were indeed inadequate. The second Anglo-Dutch War (1665–1667) in part resulted from this action. Assuming ownership, James called his colony New York, but granted the land between the Delaware and lower Hudson rivers to John Lord Berkeley and Sir George Carteret, who named the area New Jersey. Though not mentioned in his charter, James also claimed the region west of the Delaware River, later Pennsylvania and Delaware, which he administered though New York.

Despite his extensive powers, as granted in the charter, James realized that he had to make New York attractive to inhabitants and future settlers if his colony was to prosper. He gave residents the choice of keeping their Dutch citizenship or becoming naturalized as English subjects. In 1665, he issued a legal code, called the "Duke's Laws," which guaranteed freedom of religion, recognized preexisting titles to land, and allowed New Englanders living in towns on Long Island to choose selectmen. The New York government consisted of a governor and council appointed by the duke, but no legislature.

When England and the Netherlands continued their rivalry in the third Anglo-Dutch War (1672–1674), the Dutch easily recaptured New York. After sixteen months they returned the colony to England as part of the Treaty of Westminster (1674). Receiving a new charter, James resumed possession of New York and reconfirmed his grants to New Jersey. Since 1664, that proprietorship had undergone several changes. A line drawn diagonally from the Delaware River to the Atlantic Ocean divided the territory into two colonies, West New Jersey and East New Jersey. Berkeley had sold West Jersey to a Quaker, Edward Byllinge, who then transferred title to a group of co-religionists, including William Penn. The duke confirmed Carteret's right to East Jersey immediately, but waited until 1680 to approve the Quaker proprietorship of West Jersey.

◆ CONCLUSION ◆

During the first three-quarters of the seventeenth century, the English, French, and Dutch ended Spain's mastery of the New World. By 1675, in North America, the English held colonies along the Atlantic coast from New England to the Carolinas. The French controlled Canada, where its settlements grew slowly, and had explored the Great Lakes and the upper Mississippi Valley. The Dutch established, but lost, New Netherland, just as their commercial empire expanded, then faced serious threats. The Spanish, though more vulnerable than a century earlier, retained its borderland outposts in New Mexico and Florida. Everywhere the Europeans colonized, the Indians died from epidemic disease. Their relations with the white invaders depended a great deal on the numbers of Europeans who arrived, their attitudes, and goals of settlement.

From the beginning, the English colonies were diverse—in their form of government, degree of stability, relations with Native Americans, and economic base. The Crown fostered this variety by granting charters to an assortment of companies and individuals, including Puritan and Catholic opponents of the established church. Virginia and Maryland prospered from tobacco, but battled persistent high mortality. Still, in the mid-seventeenth century, the Chesapeake was "the best poor man's country" for English people willing to take risks. Most New Englanders came primarily to start a model society based on their Calvinist beliefs. They enjoyed a healthier climate than the people of the Chesapeake, but inferior soil. They supported themselves modestly by fishing and mixed farming, developing trade with the West Indies to pay for English imports. In New Mexico, Hispanic colonists exploited the Pueblos' labor to support their trade with Mexico, while Catholic missionaries tried to claim the Indians' souls. In all three areas—New England, the Chesapeake, and New Mexico—pressures between Europeans and Native Americans, and within the colonial societies, would soon erupt in war.

RECOMMENDED READINGS

Anderson, Virginia D. *New England's Generation: The Great Migration and the Formation of Society and Culture in the Seventeenth Century* (1991). Compares the motivations and experiences of Puritan settlers with succeeding generations.

Berkin, Carol. *First Generations: Women in Colonial America* (1996). A balanced survey of women of different backgrounds.

Breen, T. H., and Innes, Stephen. *"Myne Owne Ground": Race and Freedom on Virginia's Eastern Shore, 1640–1676* (1980). Focuses on opportunities of free blacks before the onslaught of rigid racial slavery.

Cronon, William. *Changes in the Land: Indians, Colonists, and the Ecology of New England* (1983). Contrasts Native American and settler use of the environment.

Dunn, Richard S. *Sugar and Slaves: The Rise of the Planter Class in the English West Indies, 1624–1713* (1972). An insightful history of the creation of slave regimes in the English Caribbean.

Greene, Jack P. *Pursuits of Happiness: The Social Development of Early Modern British Colonies and the Formation of American Culture* (1988). Provides a useful framework for understanding the various ways in which British settlements evolved.

Gutiérrez, Ramón A. *When Jesus Came, the Corn Mothers Went Away: Marriage, Sexuality, and Power in New Mexico, 1500–1846* (1991). Provocative evaluation of Spanish settlement, focusing particularly on women's status.

Morgan, Edmund S. *American Slavery, American Freedom: The Ordeal of Colonial Virginia* (1975). A detailed, stimulating account of English settlement and the transition to slavery.

Ulrich, Laurel Thatcher. *Good Wives: Image and Reality in the Lives of Women in Northern New England, 1650–1750* (1982). Considers the various roles of colonial women.

Wood, Peter H. *Black Majority: Negroes in Colonial South Carolina from 1670 Through the Stono Rebellion* (1974). Demonstrates the impact of rice culture on blacks in the Lower South.

Native Americans and Indian-European Relations

Axtell, James. *The Invasion Within: The Contest of Cultures in Colonial North America* (1985).

Bridenbaugh, Carl. *Early Americans* (1981).

Delage, Denys. *Bitter Feast: Amerindians and Europeans in Northeastern North America, 1600–64* (1993).

Lurie, Nancy O. "Indian Cultural Adjustment to European Civilization," in James M. Smith, ed., *Seventeenth-Century America: Essays in Colonial History* (1959).

Merrell, James H. *The Indians' New World: Catawbas and Their Neighbors from European Contact Through the Era of Removal* (1989).

Nash, Gary B. *Red, White, and Black: The Peoples of Early North America*, 3d ed. (1992).

Richter, Daniel K. *The Ordeal of the Longhouse: The Peoples of the Iroquois League in the Era of European Colonization* (1992).

Richter, Daniel K. and Merrell, James H., eds. *Beyond the Covenant Chain: The Iroquois and Their Neighbors in Indian North America, 1600–1800* (1987).

Salisbury, Neal. *Manitou and Providence: Indians, Europeans, and the Making of New England, 1500–1643* (1982).

Sweet, David G., and Nash, Gary B., eds. *Struggle and Survival in Colonial America* (1981).

Trigger, Bruce G. *Handbook of North American Indians,* Vol. 15: *The Northeast* (1978).

Wood, Peter H., Waselkov, Gregory A., and Hatley, M. Thomas., eds. *Powhatan's Mantle: Indians in the Colonial Southeast* (1989).

New France

Eccles, W. J. *The Canadian Frontier, 1534–1760,* rev. ed. (1983).

Eccles, W. J. *France in America* (1972).

Harris, R. Cole, ed. *Historical Atlas of Canada, Vol. 1: Origins to 1800* (1987).

Jaenen, Cornelius J. *Friend and Foe: Aspects of French-Amerindian Cultural Contact in the Sixteenth and Seventeenth Centuries* (1976).

Trigger, Bruce G. *Natives and Newcomers: Canada's "Heroic Age" Reconsidered* (1985).

New Netherland and the English Conquest

Condon, Thomas J. *New York Beginnings: The Commercial Origins of New Netherland* (1968).

Goodfriend, Joyce D. *Before the Melting Pot: Society and Culture in Colonial New York City, 1664–1730* (1992).

Kammen, Michael. *Colonial New York: A History* (1975).

Merwick, Donna. *Possessing Albany, 1630–1710: The Dutch and English Experiences* (1990).

Rink, Oliver A. *Holland on the Hudson: An Economic and Social History of Dutch New York* (1986).

Ritchie, Robert C. *The Duke's Province: A Study of New York's Politics and Society, 1664–1691* (1977).

Seventeenth-Century England

Campbell, Mildred. *The English Yeoman Under Elizabeth and the Early Stuarts* (1942).

Clark, Peter, and Slack, Paul, eds. *Crisis and Order in English Towns, 1500–1700: Essays in Urban History* (1972).

Hill, Christopher. *The World Turned Upside Down: Radical Ideas During the English Revolution* (1972).

Notestein, Wallace. *The English People on the Eve of Colonization, 1603–1630* (1954).

Wrightson, Keith. *English Society, 1580–1680* (1982).

Chesapeake and South Carolina

Billings, Warren M., Selby, John E., and Tate, Thad W. *Colonial Virginia* (1986).

Carr, Lois Green, Menard, Russell R., and Walsh, Lorena S. *Robert Cole's World: Agriculture and Society in Early Maryland* (1991).

Carr, Lois Green, Morgan, Philip D., and Russo, Jean B., eds. *Colonial Chesapeake Society* (1988).

Craven, Wesley Frank. *White, Red, and Black: The Seventeenth-Century Virginian* (1971).

Land, Aubrey C. *Colonial Maryland: A History* (1981).

Main, Gloria L. *Tobacco Colony: Life in Early Maryland, 1650–1720* (1982).

Norton, Mary Beth. *Founding Mothers and Fathers: Gendered Power and the Forming of American Society* (1996).

Salmon, Marylynn. *Women and the Law of Property in Early America* (1986).

Silver, Timothy. *A New Face on the Countryside: Indians, Colonists, and Slaves in South Atlantic Forests, 1500–1800* (1990).

Sirmans, M. Eugene. *Colonial South Carolina: A Political History, 1663–1763* (1966).

Tate, Thad W., and Ammerman, David L., eds. *The Chesapeake in the Seventeenth Century: Essays on Anglo-American Society and Politics* (1979).

Weir, Robert M. *Colonial South Carolina: A History* (1983).

New England

Allen, David Grayson. *In English Ways: The Movement of Societies and the Transferal of English Local Law and Custom to Massachusetts Bay in the Seventeenth Century* (1981).

Bailyn, Bernard. *The New England Merchants in the Seventeenth Century* (1955).

Dayton, Cornelia Hughes. *Women Before the Bar: Gender, Law, and Society in Connecticut, 1639–1789* (1995).

Demos, John. *A Little Commonwealth: Family Life in Plymouth Colony* (1970).

Foster, Stephen. *The Long Argument: English Puritanism and the Shaping of New England Culture, 1570–1700* (1991).

Greven, Philip J., Jr. *Four Generations: Population, Land, and Family in Colonial Andover, Massachusetts* (1970).

Hall, David D. *Worlds of Wonder, Days of Judgment: Popular Religious Belief in Early New England* (1989).

Hall, David D., Murrin, John M., and Tate, Thad W., eds. *Saints and Revolutionaries: Essays on Early American History* (1984).

James, Sydney V. *Colonial Rhode Island: A History* (1975).

Martin, John Frederick. *Profits in the Wilderness: Entrepreneurship and the Founding of New England Towns in the Seventeenth Century* (1991).

Morgan, Edmund S. *The Puritan Family: Religion and Domestic Relations in Seventeenth-Century New England,* rev. ed. (1966).

Morgan, Edmund S. *The Puritan Dilemma: The Story of John Winthrop* (1958).

Morgan, Edmund S. *Visible Saints: The History of a Puritan Idea* (1963).

Vickers, Daniel. *Farmers and Fishermen: Two Centuries of Work in Essex County, Massachusetts, 1630–1850* (1994).

METACOM

Metacom, the Wampanoag leader, who in 1676 tried to drive the New England settlers back "into the Sea."

Chapter 3

CRISIS AND CHANGE,

1675–1720

IN FEBRUARY 1676, Narragansett Indians burned Lancaster, Massachusetts, killing many of the English settlers and taking others prisoner, including Mary White Rowlandson, a minister's wife, and her three children. The Narragansetts had joined the Wampanoags and other New England Algonquians the preceding June, under leadership of the Wampanoag sachem, Metacom, to destroy the European settlements. In the Indians' words, according to Rowlandson, "they would knock all the Rogues in the head, or drive them into the Sea, or make them flie the Country."

In a published narrative of her captivity, Rowlandson described her eleven-week ordeal, during which she traveled more than 150 miles, mostly on foot, as the Narragansetts attacked towns and fought the colonial forces. Though Rowlandson began her captivity with hatred toward the Indians, whom she called "Barbarous Creatures," she came to respect some as individuals and to appreciate aspects of their culture. She was most impressed, she said, that while the Algonquians had little corn, "I did not see (all the time I was among them) one Man, or Woman, or Child, die with Hunger." They ate "Ground-nuts . . . also Nuts and Acorns, Hartychoaks, Lilly-roots, Ground-beans, and several other weeds and roots that I know

not." Desperately hungry, Rowlandson ate unfamiliar foods too, surviving to rejoin her husband in Boston. Though she credited God for keeping her alive, clearly her adaptability helped pull her through.

Metacom's War was just one of the crises that afflicted colonial America in the years 1675 to 1680. In fact, the last quarter of the seventeenth century was generally a period of turmoil and change. In the Chesapeake, at the time of Metacom's War, a comparatively minor skirmish between Indians and whites escalated into serious warfare, resulting in Bacon's Rebellion, a civil war among the English settlers of Virginia. In 1680, the Pueblos expelled their Spanish taskmasters from New Mexico for thirteen years. During the 1680s, an unstable English government disrupted politics in the colonies. Charles II died just a few years after granting a charter for Pennsylvania. His brother, James II, a Roman Catholic, succeeded him and attempted to make sweeping changes in both the home and colonial governments, including consolidation of many colonies under the Dominion of New England. James's efforts met strong resistance: The Glorious Revolution of 1688 in England quickly ended his reign. The following year, settlers in Massachusetts, New York, and Maryland overthrew his provincial governments, declaring allegiance to the new king and

CHRONOLOGY

1675	Appointment of English Lords of Trade
1675–1676	Metacom's War
	Bacon's Rebellion
1678	Charles II demands renegotiation of Massachusetts charter
1680	Popé's Rebellion
1681	William Penn receives Pennsylvania charter
1682	La Salle claims the Mississippi Valley for France
1683	Iroquois of New York defeat New France
1684	Revocation of Massachusetts charter
1685	James II becomes king of England
	Dominion of New England created
1688–1689	Glorious Revolution in England
	William and Mary ascend throne
1689	Revolutions in Massachusetts, New York, and Maryland
1689–1697	King William's War
1690	Spanish settlements in Texas
1691	Massachusetts receives its new charter
1691–1692	Salem witchcraft hysteria
1693	Spanish regain control of New Mexico
1696	Board of Trade and Plantations replaces Lords of Trade
1698	Royal African Company loses slave trade monopoly
1699	French establish Louisiana
1701	Iroquois treaty of neutrality
1702–1713	Queen Anne's War
1704	South Carolina defeats Spanish Florida
1712	Slave revolt in New York City
1715	Calverts regain Maryland government
	Yamasee War in South Carolina

queen, William and Mary. In Massachusetts, the impact of years of political uncertainty helped spread witchcraft hysteria from Salem to other towns.

From 1689 to 1713, European wars spilled into North America, fueling conflicts in Florida and Canada among Native Americans, English, French, and Spanish. The French moved south through the Mississippi Valley and founded Louisiana, while the English pushed south into Florida, west across the Appalachian Mountains, and north into Maine. As the English colonies expanded and matured, their economies and labor systems diverged, particularly with the entrenchment of slavery in the south. While slave traders imported Africans into all of the English provinces by 1700, by far the largest proportion worked in fields of tobacco and rice. Even with so much conflict during the late seventeenth century, planters built successful staple crop economies in the southern colonies, while northerners profited from networks of trade with England, Europe, and the slave regimes of the Caribbean, Carolina, and the Chesapeake.

REBELLIONS AND WAR

The wars of 1675 to 1680 in New England, Virginia, and New Mexico resulted from pressures that had been building for decades. In Massachusetts, the spread of settlement as second and third generations of colonists came of age forced Native Americans to defend their homes. In Virginia, demands of ex-servants for good land precipitated a civil war, while in New Mexico, severe droughts deepened opposition to forced labor and religious persecution, impelling the Pueblos to rid themselves of Spanish overlords. After the upheavals, elites in each settlement made changes that avoided further serious revolt.

Decline of New England Orthodoxy

In 1675, with the prospect of a major Indian war, Massachusetts seemed to have lost sight of the goals of

The Hingham, Massachusetts, church was originally built in 1681, when ship carpenters framed the interior of the roof as a ship's keel in reverse (left). The exterior view (right) reflects renovations completed in the eighteenth century.

its first settlers. When the Indians attacked, Puritan ministers warned the sons and daughters of the founding generation that God was punishing them for their faithlessness and sin, for their departure from the godly commonwealth.

In fact, Puritan church membership had declined since 1650, especially among men, who were less successful than women in reaching God, of being saved. After mid-century, women became a large proportion of the "elect," comprising 60 percent, and in some congregations 75 percent, of newly admitted members. The ministers believed that men were becoming more worldly, thus undermining the church's social and political authority. A related problem was that the children of nonchurch members could not be baptized. In 1662, the clergy devised an alternative to full church membership, the Half-Way Covenant, to keep influential citizens within the religious community. The covenant permitted adults who had been baptized but who were not yet saved to be "half-way" members. In congregations that accepted this innovation (not all churches did), people could assume partial status by showing that they understood Christian principles and would strive to obey God. As unconverted members,

they were not entitled to take communion, but could have their children baptized.

The growth of competing religions in New England also proved to Puritan ministers that the model society had failed. Believing theirs to be the only true religion, Puritans rooted out dissent, as with Roger Williams and Anne Hutchinson in the 1630s. After 1650, though, the Quakers and Baptists threatened religious unity. The Society of Friends, or Quakers, was a radical Protestant sect born in the turmoil of the English Civil War. Like the Puritans, they were reformers who believed that the Church of England was corrupt and should be purified of its rituals, decorations, and hierarchy. But the Quakers went even further. They claimed that the Puritans also practiced false doctrine by paying ministers to preach, relying too much on the Bible as the word of God, and retaining the sacraments of baptism and communion. The Friends believed that God communicated directly with individuals, through the "Spirit" or "Light." They worshipped by gathering in plain meetinghouses (or in the early years, in fields and private houses) to "wait upon the Lord." In worship services, they had no Bible reading, prepared sermon, music, or ritual.

Statue of Mary Dyer, the Quaker missionary hanged in Massachusetts in 1660.

Rather, they waited in silence for the Spirit to inspire one or several of the congregation to communicate God's message. Those to whom the Spirit manifested itself regularly were ministers, including women as well as men. They required no advanced learning because their words were supposed to come straight from God, not a prepared text.

Appalled by these Quaker teachings, Puritan leaders tried to prevent their spread by deporting the traveling English missionaries who arrived on their shores. The ministers were stubborn, however, repeatedly returning to Massachusetts. They interrupted Puritan church services, preached in the streets, and made some converts among the people. The Puritan magistrates arrested and whipped them, even cropping their ears. In 1658, the General Court prescribed the death penalty for Quakers who returned after banishment. Several missionaries were hanged, including Mary Dyer in 1660, who had determined to "look their bloody laws in the face."

The hangings proved a turning point in the history of New England, for they caused consternation on both sides of the Atlantic. When Charles II demanded an explanation, the Puritans—fearing the loss of their charter—ended the executions. The magistrates continued to persecute nonconformers, but over the decades following 1660 realized that their policy of intolerance had failed. Rhode Island, a haven for people of all religions, served as a base for Quaker missionaries to evangelize in the Puritan colonies, further supporting its reputation among Puritans as "the sewer of New England." The Baptists, whose objection to infant baptism was their chief disagreement with orthodox Puritans, increased in numbers after approval of the Half-Way Covenant, which they vehemently opposed. They believed that a church should include only the saved, indeed that only the saved should be baptized. Despite persecution, dissenters successfully formed congregations throughout New England.

Metacom's War

Despite the Puritan ministers' plaintive cries, increasing worldliness and religious diversity did not cause Metacom's War. Rather, the unceasing expansion of white settlers into the frontier destroyed the relative peace between the Algonquians and the settlers of New England. By 1675, more than 50,000 whites inhabited the region. With a healthful environment, the colonists had successfully heeded the biblical injunction "to be fruitful and multiply." They had large families of sons and daughters who desired farms of their own. These settlers occupied more and more of the hunting, fishing, and agricultural lands of the Indians who, decimated by European diseases and outnumbered by the whites, recognized the threat to their ways of life.

Since the massacre of the Pequots in 1637, the Puritans and Native Americans of New England had managed an uneasy peace. The colonists traded for furs with local nations and with the Mohawks, the closest nation of Iroquois in New York. Some Puritan ministers, of whom John Eliot is best known, convinced several local tribes who were greatly diminished by disease and loss of lands to dwell in "praying towns." In these villages, adjacent to but separate from the towns of white settlers, the Indians were supposed to adopt English customs and learn the fundamentals of Puritan religion. By 1674, Eliot had organized four-

MAP 3.1 NEW ENGLAND AT THE TIME OF METACOM'S WAR, 1675–1676

teen praying towns of Native Americans who took the first steps toward giving up their traditional ways.

Many New England Indians kept their autonomy, however, including the Wampanoags of Plymouth and Mohegans of Connecticut. Even so, they remained allies of the Puritan governments for many years. Trouble began in 1671, when the Plymouth government attempted to subordinate the Wampanoags by forcing them to surrender their firearms and obtain permission to sell land. Metacom, whom the colonists called King Philip as an insult, built a league with neighboring

tribes. When John Sassamon, an Indian educated at Harvard College, informed the Plymouth government of impending attack and was murdered, the white authorities hanged three Wampanoags for the deed.

Metacom mobilized Algonquians throughout New England, attacking fifty-two of ninety English towns within the region, including some within twenty miles of the coast. White refugees fled to Boston. But by the end of summer 1676, with the help of the Mohawks, the colonial governments turned back the attack, as disease, hunger, and a weapons shortage weakened

Metacom's war club, inlaid with wampum beads. This club was stolen in 1970 from the Fruitlands Museum in Harvard, Massachusetts.

Metacom's troops. The war took a heavy toll on both sides, for the Algonquians destroyed twelve towns and killed many colonists. White frontier settlement would not reach its 1675 limits for another forty years.

For the Indians of southern New England, the war was calamitous. Thousands died and many others were enslaved. Even bands who supported the English lost autonomy. At the outbreak of war, the colonists had forced residents of the praying towns, who were allies of the white governments, to live on desolate Deer Island in Boston Harbor, where they suffered from lack of food and shelter. Some of the Indian men later fought in the colonial militia against Metacom, but when the war was over, all Native Americans in southern New England had to live in praying towns, now essentially reservations, where they worked as servants or tenant farmers for neighboring whites. Metacom was killed, his head paraded before the white settlements, and kept on a pole in Plymouth for twenty years; his wife and son were sold as slaves.

War in the Chesapeake

Just as New England struggled over land in Metacom's War, Virginia faced a similar crisis in Bacon's Rebellion. The Chesapeake uprising was more complicated, for it involved civil war among the English as well as Indian-white conflict. But at its root, the chief issue was land: How could the competing interests of landless immigrants and dispossessed natives be resolved? Since the 1640s, the white population of Virginia and

Maryland had grown quickly with the arrival of immigrants—both wealthy and poor—who sought to increase their fortunes in America. By 1670, approximately 40,000 colonists lived in the Chesapeake, including native-born sons and daughters of early settlers as well as the more recent arrivals. Among the new immigrants were servants who expected to obtain land upon completing their terms.

In the 1670s, however, many Virginians discovered that the combination of low tobacco prices and high land prices blocked their dream of obtaining plantations. They received headrights, but could find no good vacant tobacco land to claim. Part of the problem, these landless freemen believed, was that the Indians held too much territory. Specifically, the 1646 treaty between the Virginia government and the Powhatans designated the area north of the York River for Native Americans. This agreement had been acceptable to whites in the 1640s when space south of the York seemed ample, but was unsatisfactory thirty years later, when white settlement was pushing north. It was also true, many freemen recognized, that wealthy planters, powerful in government, speculated in large acreages that they left empty while others starved for land.

The first flames of war occurred in July 1675, when some Doeg Indians attempted to take hogs as payment for a settler's unpaid debt. After people on both sides were killed, the Susquehannocks, who were allies of both the Doegs and the Virginia government, got involved. When the Susquehannocks attacked frontier settlements, a thousand-man army of Virginia and Maryland colonists marched against their village on the Potomac River. Vastly outnumbered, several sachems agreed to negotiate, but when they left their stockade, the colonists murdered them. During the winter of 1675–1676, the Susquehannocks retaliated, raising fears that Metacom's War had spread south. Discontented and vengeful colonists responded indiscriminately, killing friendly neighboring Indians rather than those who were actually attacking the frontier.

The landless freemen found a leader in Nathaniel Bacon, also a newcomer but of a different class. Only twenty-nine years old, Bacon belonged to a wealthy family and had come to Virginia with enough money to purchase a large plantation. Governor Berkeley nominated him to the Virginia council, despite his youth, giving him other privileges as well. Nevertheless, Bacon evidently saw his opportunity to challenge Berkeley for leadership of the colony by mobilizing freemen and small planters against the Indians. While Berkeley wanted peace with the Susquehannocks, Bacon's forces intended to annihilate all of the natives, whether friends or foes, because they viewed all Indians as obstacles to white control of the land. The settlers knew that the natives were weak, with just a fraction of their pre-1607 population. Bacon's supporters

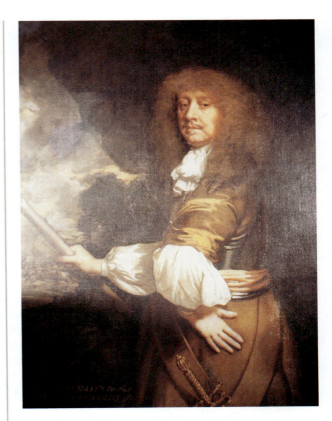

Sir William Berkeley was governor of Virginia for more than a quarter century. He alienated landless Virginians by ignoring their grievances and attempting to keep peace with the Indians.

A reconstruction of a typical Chesapeake colonist's house at the Godiah Spray tobacco plantation at historic St. Mary's City, Maryland.

also demanded a greater voice in the Virginia government, for they believed that the large planters who dominated the Assembly were out for their own profit, while ignoring the needs of ordinary settlers.

Governor Berkeley declared Bacon a traitor, sent troops to end his forays against the Indians, and requested reinforcements from England. The governor also called new elections that brought many Bacon supporters into the House of Burgesses. The delegates passed measures to stop the political abuses of the elite: They extended suffrage to landless freemen, taxed provincial councilors, required the election of local representatives for assessing taxes, and placed limits on the terms and fees of local officials. These efforts failed to end the rebellion, as Bacon's army burned Jamestown. For months, Virginians plundered the plantations of neighbors who took the other side. Few

MARY ROWLANDSON'S NARRATIVE OF HER CAPTURE BY NARRAGANSETT INDIANS, 1676

Mary Rowlandson was the wife of the minister of Lancaster, Massachusetts, which the Narragansetts assaulted in 1676 during Metacom's War. The following account of the attack, taken from the published narrative of her captivity, illustrates the religious framework in which she cast her experiences.

At length they came and beset our own House, and quickly it was the dolefullest day that ever mine eyes saw. The House stood upon the edge of a Hill; some of the *Indians* got behind the Hill, others into the Barn, and others behind any thing that would shelter them; from all which Places they shot against the House, so that the Bullets seemed to fly like Hail; and quickly they wounded one Man among us, then another, and then a third. About two Hours (according to my observation in that amazing time) they had been about the House before they could prevail to fire it. . . . They fired it once, and one ventured out and quenched it; but they quickly fired it again, and that took. Now is that dreadful Hour come that I have often heard of, (in the time of the War, as it was the Case of others,) but now mine Eyes see it. Some in our House were fighting for their Lives, others wallowing in their Blood; the House on fire over our Heads, and the bloody Heathen ready to knock us on the Head if we stirred out. Now might we hear Mothers and Children crying out for themselves and one another, *Lord, what shall we do?* Then I took my Children (and one of my Sisters, hers) to go forth and leave the House; but as soon as we came to the Door and appeared, the *Indians* shot so thick that the Bullets rattled against the House as if one had taken an handful of Stones and threw them; so that we were fain to give back. We had six stout Dogs belonging to our Garrison, but none of them would stir, though another time, if an *Indian* had come to the Door, they were ready to fly upon him, and tear him down. The Lord hereby would make us the more to acknowledge his Hand, and to see that our Help is always in him. But out we must go, the Fire increasing and coming along behind us roaring, and the *Indians* gaping before us with their Guns, Spears, and Hatchets to devour us. No sooner were we out of the House but my Brother-in-Law (being before wounded, in defending the House, in or near the Throat) fell down dead, whereat the *Indians* scornfully shouted

white fatalities resulted from this depredation, however, as rebels vented most of their frustration by killing Indians, not fellow colonists. The rebellion finally ceased with Bacon's death, probably of dysentery, in October 1676. The war marked a serious defeat for the Indians of the Chesapeake, who lost the protection of the 1646 treaty and gradually surrendered their lands.

Bacon's Rebellion awakened the Virginia elites to the dangers of a large class of landless freemen, but resulted in no substantive political change. A new assembly in 1677 reversed the reform acts of the 1676 House of Burgesses, including the law extending the vote to landless freemen. A commission appointed by the Crown to end the rebellion also opposed expanding popular power, stating that to grant suffrage to unpropertied men was "repugnant to the Lawes of England and to the Lawes and Peace of the Colony." The commission did call for taxing "the great Ingrossers of Lands" who caused "misery and mischiefs" by "occa-

and hallowed, and were presently upon him, stripping off his Clothes. The Bullets flying thick, one went thorow my side, and the same (as would seem) thorow the Bowels and Hand of my dear Child in my Arms. One of my eldest Sister's Children (named William) had then his Leg broken, which the *Indians* perceiving, they knock'd him on the head. Thus were we butchered by those merciless Heathen, standing amazed, with the Blood running down to our Heels. My elder sister, being yet in the House, and seeing those woful Sights, the Infidels hauling Mothers one way and Children another, and some wallowing in their Blood, and her elder son telling her that (her Son) William was dead, and myself was wounded; she said, *And, Lord, let me die with them!* which was no sooner said but she was struck with a Bullet, and fell down dead over the Threshold. I hope she is reaping the Fruit of her good Labours, being faithful to the Service of God in her Place. In her younger years she lay under much trouble upon Spiritual accounts, till it pleased God to make that precious Scripture take hold of her Heart, *2 Cor. xii. 9, And he said unto me, My grace is sufficient for thee.* More than twenty years after, I have heard her tell how sweet and comfortable that Place was to her. But to return: the *Indians* laid hold of us, pulling me one way and the Children another, and said, *Come, go along with us.* I told them they would kill me. They answered, *If I were willing to go along with them, they would not hurt me.*

O the doleful Sight that now was to behold at this House! *Come, behold the works of the Lord, what desolation he has made in the earth.* Of thirty seven Persons who were in this one House, none escaped either present Death or a bitter Captivity, save only one, who might say as he, *Job i. 15, And I only am escaped alone to tell the news.* There were twelve killed, some shot, some stabb'd with their Spears, some knock'd down with their Hatchets. . . . It was a solemn Sight to see so many Christians lying in their Blood, some here and some there, like a company of Sheep torn by Wolves; all of them stript naked by a company of hell-hounds, roaring, singing, ranting, and insulting, as if they would have torn our very hearts out; yet the Lord, by his Almighty power, preserved a number of us from death, for there were twenty-four of us taken alive; and carried Captive.

I had often before this said, that if the *Indians* should come, I should chuse rather to be killed by them than taken alive; but when it came to the trial my mind changed; their glittering Weapons so daunted my Spirit, that I chose rather to go along with those (as I may say) ravenous Bears, than that moment to end my daies.

sioning the Planters to stragle to such remote distances when they cannot find land neerer to seat themselves but by being Tenants which in a Continent they think hard." Nothing was done, however, to remedy that situation. Rather than create a society in which power and wealth were distributed more evenly, in which Virginia once again would offer opportunity to poor Englishmen, the planter elite began importing more enslaved Africans. Bound for life and restricted by laws, black slaves could not demand farms or a voice in government. With settlement in New Jersey, Carolina, and Pennsylvania during the 1670s and 1680s, immigrants had better options than Virginia.

Popé's Rebellion

Four years after Bacon's Rebellion, across the continent in New Mexico, the Pueblos drove out the Spanish—and kept them out for thirteen years. The

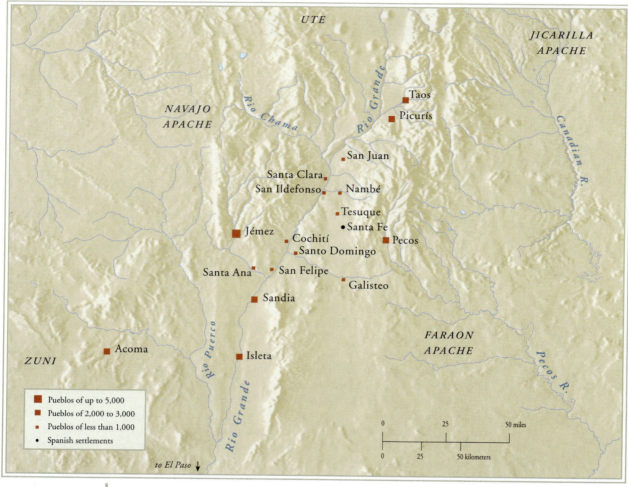

MAP 3.2 | NEW MEXICO, CA. 1680

Pueblos had the advantage of a much smaller white population in New Mexico—2,800—than in New England or the Chesapeake. The Spanish hold over the missions was tenuous, for native fighting men greatly outnumbered Spanish troops. Nevertheless, the Hispanic settlers and priests demanded forced labor and strict adherence to Christianity from the Pueblos. A number of Indian towns had rebelled during the previous half century, but most failed to win autonomy because they fought the Spanish individually instead of combining with other villages.

The Pueblos became more desperate and enraged during the 1670s, when New Mexico endured severe drought. As famine persisted, Apaches and Navajos attacked the Pueblos. According to one missionary, "a great many Indians perished of hunger, lying dead along the roads, in the ravines, and in their huts." The Pueblos became convinced that the root of their troubles lay in their rejection of ancient gods, the *katsina*. To bring rain and renewed prosperity, some presented gifts to the katsina and performed dances that the Spanish had outlawed. When punished for abandoning Catholicism—as in 1675, when the Spanish government executed three Pueblo priests and whipped 43 others—the Indians felt even greater resentment, leading to revolt.

The leader of the 1680 rebellion was Popé, a medicine man of the village of San Juan, north of Santa Fe. When the katsina told him that the Spanish must be driven from the land, he organized a general insurrection, sending knotted ropes to allied villages, indicating when the uprising should start. On August 10, 1680, a day earlier than planned because the Spanish governor, General Antonio de Otermín, had been warned of the impending revolt, the Pueblos launched a full-scale attack, killing 400 colonists and twenty-one priests. Strategically, the Indians confiscated or destroyed the settlers' chief means of transportation, their horses and mules. When Santa Fe fell to the rebels on September 21, the whites escaped south, settling in the area of present-day Ciudad Juárez, Mexico. Some Spaniards explained the revolt as God's punishment for their sins (much as the Puritans had understood Metacom's War), while others blamed the harsh labor and efforts to repress native religions. As Popé supervised, the Pueblos destroyed churches, broke up church bells, and burned images of Christ and the saints. According to one witness, "in order to take away their baptismal names, the water, and the holy oils, [the Indians] were to plunge into the rivers and wash themselves."

Several times during the next few years, the Spanish attempted without success to retake New Mexico. The rebellion spread south into northern Mexico, where Native Americans demolished settlements and missions. But by 1692, as famine continued, the Pueblo alliance fell into disarray, with resulting war over scarce supplies of corn. The new Spanish governor of New Mexico, Don Diego de Vargas, marched north to Santa Fe with 160 troops. Though many Indians resisted, the Spanish reestablished control over the province. In December 1693, after a three-day siege, Vargas's troops took Santa Fe, killing all of the Indian men and making slaves of the women and children. The Spanish subsequently retained a foothold in New Mexico, but not without further struggle. The Pueblos rejected the Franciscan missionaries, revolting once again in 1696, killing five priests and destroying churches. Some Pueblos fled from New Mexico while others submitted as Vargas systematically conquered the Indian towns once again. After 1696, the Spanish and Pueblos lived together in relative peace, but only because the Hispanics eased requirements for tribute, forced labor, and adherence to Christianity.

WILLIAM PENN'S "HOLY EXPERIMENT"

In England, in the same year as Popé's Rebellion, the Quaker leader William Penn approached Charles II with a petition to establish a new colony in America, one that would avoid bloodshed by dealing justly with the Indians. While the Pueblos had not yet driven out the Spanish, Penn knew of Metacom's War and Bacon's Rebellion. He was determined to do things differently in Pennsylvania, to create a model society, but one that was distinct from the Puritan "city upon a hill."

Plans for Pennsylvania

William Penn had inherited a £16,000 debt owed to his father by the king, but had little hope for repayment in cash, so he requested a colony on the west bank of the Delaware River. Charles's brother James, the duke of York, governed the territory, which was inhabited by a small number of Dutch, Swedes, and Delaware Indians. The king approved Penn's request in 1681, granting him a charter for Pennsylvania which was more restrictive than either Lord Baltimore's or the duke of York's, in part because the English government was attempting to assert greater control over its colonies, in part because Penn was a Quaker. The new proprietor received the right to enact laws and impose taxes with the consent of the freemen, but was required to submit all laws for approval to the home government within five years of passage. And to protect the status of the Church of England, the charter stipulated that twenty Anglican inhabitants could request a minister from the bishop of London.

In establishing Pennsylvania, Penn hoped to provide a haven for Quakers where they could practice their religion and raise their families without harassment. Like New England Quakers, those in England confronted persecution as an outlaw sect. English Friends refused to pay tithes for church support or

William Penn was a wealthy Quaker who sought to create a model, peaceful society in Pennsylvania.

and colonists to resolve conflicts peacefully. He paid the Delawares a much lower price than he in turn charged the settlers, however, and failed to consider ways in which the Indians might be incorporated into Pennsylvania society. As in other colonies, the Pennsylvanians assumed the Indians would leave after they sold their land.

Like Lord Baltimore, Penn intended to make a fortune from Pennsylvania, summing up his goals: "the service of God first, the honor and advantage of the king, with our own profit." Despite Penn's strong Quaker convictions, which for some suggested a simple life, he appreciated fine food, drink, and accommodations. He was a gentleman who was chronically in debt. He possessed large landholdings in southern England and Ireland, retained many servants, and enjoyed such delicacies as salmon, partridges, saffron, and chocolate. Urgently needing money, he thought the sale of millions of acres in America would solve his financial problems.

attend Anglican services, and instead held their own meetings, which the government considered illegal "conventicles." Even more, Quakers refused to give oaths, arguing that one should always tell the truth, so they could not legally pledge allegiance to the king. They adopted pacifism as one of their central beliefs. Friends also professed to live according to the doctrine that all were equal in the eyes of God; they refused to follow certain customs, such as removing one's hat in the presence of superiors. For practicing their faith, they were jailed and fined, and when they refused to pay, local English officials took their property.

William Penn conceived of his colony as a "holy experiment," a place where Quakers could exercise their beliefs without interference, where everyone would live in harmony, and the government would operate like a Quaker meeting, acting in unison as it followed God's will. Penn also intended to reverse the pattern of Anglo-Indian relations in North America by consistently paying the Delaware Indians for tracts of land and setting up arbitration panels of Native Americans

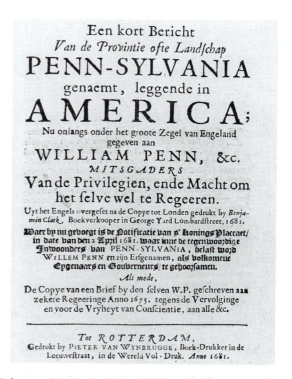

Een kort Bericht
Van de Provintie ofte Landschap
PENN-SYLVANIA
genaemt, leggende in
AMERICA;
Nu onlangs onder het groote Zegel van Engeland gegeven aan
WILLIAM PENN, &c.
MITSGADERS
Van de Privilegien, ende Macht om
het selve wel te Regeeren.

Uyt het Engels overgeset na de Copye tot Londen gedrukt by *Benjamin Clark*, Boekverkooper in George Yard Lombardstreet, 1681.
Waer by nu gevoegt is de Notificatie van s' Konings Placcaet/ in date van den 2 April 1681. waar inne de tegenwoordige Inwoonders van PENN-SYLVANIA, belast word WILLEM PENN en zijn Erfgenamen, als volkomene Eygenaars en Gouberneurs/ te gehoorsamen.
Als mede,
De Copye van een Brief by den selven W.P. geschreven aan zekere Regeeringe Anno 1675. tegens de Vervolginge en voor de Vryheyt van Conscientie, aan alle &c.

Tot ROTTERDAM,
Gedrukt by PIETER VAN WYNBRUGGE, Boek-Drukker in de Leeuwestraat, in de Wereld Vol-Druk. Anno 1681.

Title page of the Dutch edition of William Penn's promotional pamphlet, Some Account of the Province of Pennsylvania.

William Penn's plan of Philadelphia, which his surveyor-general Thomas Holme rendered in 1683 as A Portraiture of the City of Philadelphia. *During the colonial period, the city developed along the Delaware River (to the right), not on the Schuylkill River (to the left).*

Penn spent a great deal of time planning the colony. His scheme of government was quite progressive for its time, for it established an assembly with two houses, both elected by the freemen. In some colonies, such as Virginia, members of the upper house, or council, were appointed by the governor. Freemen included adult males who owned at least fifty acres of land or paid taxes on other property. During the early decades, when servants received fifty acres at the end of their terms, nearly every man in Pennsylvania could vote. Penn did not extend that right to women, even to those who owned property, nor did he alter the common law restrictions on married women. Though women Friends took an active role in their meetings as ministers, missionaries, and supervisors of discipline, their legal status in the Quaker commonwealth was similar to that in other colonies. Penn's laws stood out in another respect, however, requiring capital punishment for just two offenses, treason and murder, whereas other governments prescribed the death penalty for many more crimes.

The proprietor's planning went beyond politics, for he also drew up specifications for his capital city and the division of lands. In designing Philadelphia, in taking on the role of city planner, Penn was unique among early English colonizers. He conceived the city as a large "green country town," with wide streets in a grid pattern, public parks, ample lots, and brick houses, to avoid the conditions that had contributed to the London fire of 1666. He failed to fulfill his plan completely because he could not obtain enough acreage to build Philadelphia as he wanted. Dutch and Swedish residents already owned the land along the Delaware River, so Penn decided to buy a site of just 1,200 acres between the Delaware and Schuylkill rivers. His plan remained orderly, with the grid design and parks, but with lots of one-half to one acre instead of one hundred acres for those who purchased "proprietary shares" of 5,000 acres, which Penn was most eager to sell. Like the proprietors of other colonies, Penn discovered that buyers of large acreages were scarce, so he sold much smaller tracts. To maintain a constant income from the colony, landowners would pay annual quitrents.

A Diverse Society

Penn used his Quaker connections in England, Scotland, Ireland, and Holland to promote the colony, but

Wampum belt, which according to legend the Lenape gave to William Penn in 1682. It has become a symbol of Penn's efforts to preserve peace with the Indians of Pennsylvania.

did not restrict recruitment to Friends. He sold land briskly, as 600 people bought 700,000 acres within four years. Most of the buyers were Quaker farmers, merchants, artisans, and shopkeepers from England, though many also originated from Scotland, Ireland, Wales, Europe, the West Indies, Maryland, and New York. Their goals were both religious and economic: They wanted freedom to worship as well as opportunity to succeed in farming or trade.

Penn's settlers had a number of advantages, for they moved into an area inhabited by the Delaware, or Lenape, Indians, who were peaceful, sedentary Algonquians, and by Swedes, Finns, and Dutch, who served as intermediaries with the Indians. Both groups gave advice on adjusting to the new environment. The Delawares, who farmed, hunted, and fished, had welcomed trade with the Dutch as early as 1610 and yielded land to the whites. Because Dutch and Swedish settlements remained small, relatively few violent incidents occurred. By the time Penn arrived with thousands of colonists, the Lenape had declined significantly from disease, so they had little choice but to sell their lands and move away if they wanted to remain autonomous. In deeds negotiated between 1682 and 1684, the Delaware sachems sold tracts along the Delaware River from Christiana Creek in northern Delaware to the falls of the river in Bucks County, Pennsylvania. They received wampum, blankets, guns, ammunition, tools, rum, and other goods in return for their land.

By contrast, the European "old residents" integrated with the new arrivals, though not without friction. Some earned money by selling land and provisions, or serving as guides and interpreters. One local Swede, Captain Lasse Cock, in 1682 translated for the Indians and English, arranged food, drink, and trade goods for the Delawares during negotiations, and traveled to the Susquehanna and Lehigh rivers as Penn's emissary. The Swedish, Dutch, and Finns continued to worship in their own congregations, but became naturalized as English subjects and some served in the assembly and local government. The old residents made up a large part of the population in the Lower Counties (later Delaware), leading to conflict as the different interests of the Lower Counties and Pennsylvania became clear. In 1704, after two decades of wrangling over the appointment of judges and the distance Lower County legislators had to travel to meetings, the three southern counties obtained their own separate Delaware assembly.

Pennsylvania got a boost from its late arrival on the colonial scene because its merchants could tap existing networks in the Atlantic economy. Substantial traders came from New York, the Chesapeake, and the West Indies, bringing their connections and capital to build breweries, tanneries, warehouses, wharves, and ships. Farmers found a market for wheat, livestock, and lumber in the West Indies trade. The Pennsylvanians faced nothing like the "starving times" or bloody conflict that had occurred in early Virginia, Plymouth, and Massachusetts. By 1700, Philadelphia became a thriving port town, with 700 houses and more than 3,000 people.

But for William Penn, his colony was deeply disappointing, as land sales reaped smaller profits than he had hoped and the costs of administering the colony soared. When purchasers refused to send him quitrents, he went more seriously into debt, even spending time in debtors' prison. Penn traveled to his colony twice, but stayed a total of only four years, in part because he had to defend his charter at Court. While the province became prosperous and quite successful as a tolerant, diverse society, he reckoned it a failure.

THE GLORIOUS REVOLUTION AND ITS AFTERMATH

The founding of Pennsylvania coincided with the English government's effort to tighten colonial administration and enforce the Navigation Acts. Since the Restoration in 1660, Charles II's advisors, English merchants, and especially the king's brother James, the duke of York, pressed for greater control over the American colonies. They recognized the economic value of West Indian sugar, Chesapeake tobacco, and a burgeoning colonial population that promised a welcome market for manufactured goods. Compared to the Spanish empire, with its colonial government centralized under the Council of the Indies, English administration was a hodgepodge. The Privy Council at first appointed temporary committees to address colonial concerns, then in 1675 formed a permanent committee, the Lords of Trade, which met sporadically. Even after 1696, when the more formalized Board of Trade and Plantations was established, this body could gather information and give advice, but lacked authority to appoint colonial officials or enforce laws. These powers belonged to a host of governmental offices, including the secretary of state, the Treasury, and the War Office.

Dominion of New England

While experimenting with these committees, the Crown made other efforts to rein in the colonies. Most vulnerable was the Massachusetts Bay Colony, both for its unrestrictive charter and the perceived intransigence of Puritan leaders. Metacom's War proved to be only the first of a series of trials for the holy commonwealth. In 1678, Charles II required Massachusetts to send agents empowered to renegotiate the

charter. He specifically wanted the New Englanders to comply with the Navigation Acts and apologize for having coined their own money. The colonists delayed action, though they sent regrets for having passed laws contrary to the laws of England. They offered to renounce any "except such as the repealling whereof will make us to renounce the professed cause of our first coming hither." Half a century after settlement, Massachusetts leaders jealously guarded their autonomy and the mission of the founders.

Impressed by neither the Puritans' arguments nor the speed of their response, the English government brought legal proceedings against the Massachusetts Bay Company for "usurping to be a body Politick," and revoked the charter in 1684. The colony's assembly, the General Court, was prohibited from meeting. In February 1685, before a royal governor could be appointed, Charles died and the duke of York became king. James II quickly took advantage of events to move toward centralizing the colonies. With the Privy Council's consent, in 1685, he combined Massachusetts, New Hampshire, and Maine under the Dominion of New England, added Plymouth, Rhode Island, and Connecticut in 1686, and New York and New Jersey in 1688. Apparently, James's plan for the colonies was to create two large dominions, one north of the fortieth degree of latitude (the approximate location of Philadelphia) and one to the south. These dominions would supersede colonial charters, eliminating the confusing diversity of laws and political structures. Representative government would end. Before the Glorious Revolution of 1688, which removed James from the throne, he established the northern dominion, but not the southern.

For Massachusetts Puritans, who felt the force of James's scheme most harshly, the Dominion of New England was a disaster. James's governor-general, Sir Edmund Andros, made sweeping changes that undercut the Puritan notion of a covenanted community. He levied taxes without the approval of a representative assembly, restricted the power of town meetings, mandated religious toleration (a positive change by modern standards but not to the Puritans), and confiscated a Boston church for use by Anglicans. Andros enforced the Navigation Acts, favored his own cronies over the Puritan elite in distributing patronage, required landowners to obtain new land titles from the Crown, demanded payment of quitrents, and took control of common lands, portioning some to his

James II at the time of his accession in 1685, by Godfrey Kneller. An opponent of representative government, James was quickly deposed in the Glorious Revolution of 1688.

A nineteenth-century rendering of Sir Edmund Andros's unpopularity in Boston, by Howard Pyle. Through Andros, James II disbanded colonial governments in New England and New York, creating his Dominion of New England.

friends. A number of colonists rebelled, refusing to pay taxes without a voice in their passage, but were jailed and fined.

Revolutions of 1689

Governor Andros managed to avoid serious revolt until the spring of 1689, when news of James's removal from the throne reached Massachusetts. The king's rule had been as heavy-handed in England as in the colonies. A Roman Catholic, he installed his friends in office and defied Parliament. Protestants feared James would make England a Catholic nation under authoritarian rule. Thus, parliamentary leaders forced him into exile in France, inviting his Protestant daughter Mary and her husband William of Orange, the leader of the Dutch, to take the throne. The Glorious Revolution, though bloodless, had long-lasting results in England: It permanently limited the king's power by establishing parliamentary control of taxation, supremacy of law, and autonomy of the courts.

In the morning of April 18, 1689, many of Boston's populace left their homes, armed, and formed companies with the militia. The rebels, who included several Puritan ministers and some wealthy merchants, arrested Andros and his supporters. Numbering more than one thousand by afternoon, the insurgents deposed the dominion government. They interpreted the revocation of the charter and James's illegal taxation and expropriation of lands as part of a "popish plot" that Protestant New England must help destroy.

With the dominion gone, Plymouth, Rhode Island, and Connecticut reactivated their charters, but Massachusetts, which had lost its charter under Charles II, had to negotiate a new one. The colonists' arguments for the charter were based less on the old covenant theory than on the fundamentals of the Glorious Revolution, especially the right of English people to representative government. The resulting 1691 Massachusetts charter, which annexed Plymouth to the Bay Colony, established a royal province with an elected assembly and a governor appointed by the king. The charter required freedom of worship and forbade religious restrictions on voting. Massachusetts Bay thus lost the constitutional basis for the theocracy of the founders, which had limited political participation to God's "elect."

Revolutions also took place in New York and Maryland in the wake of James II's fall. New York, which had been James's proprietary colony and part of the Dominion of New England, fell into turmoil with news of William and Mary's ascent to the throne in England and Andros's arrest in Boston. The reports unleashed opposition to Lieutenant Governor Francis Nicholson, who headed the dominion's government in New York. Residents of the colony, especially New England Puritans who had established towns on Long Island, had chafed for decades under the duke of York's arbitrary rule. They too defined the struggle in religious terms, as a crusade to destroy the "papist" threat.

In the city of New York, insurgents included merchants and artisans who had been denied economic privileges to trade and mill flour under James's government. In 1689, with Jacob Leisler, a German-born merchant and militia captain in the lead, they forced Nicholson back to England and elected a Committee of Safety to replace James's council. When Henry Sloughter, the new governor appointed by William and Mary, arrived in 1691, however, he reinstalled James's councilors, executing Leisler for treason. Despite Leisler's early proclamation of the new monarchs in 1689, his enemies had better connections in London.

In Maryland, simmering resentment of Protestants against the Roman Catholic proprietor erupted in the summer of 1689. Charles, Lord Baltimore, had

Charles Calvert, third Lord Baltimore, by Sir Godfrey Kneller. A Roman Catholic, Calvert lost control of the Maryland government in the wake of the Glorious Revolution.

departed the province in 1684 to defend at Court his northern boundary against William Penn. Baltimore's troubles intensified when his nephew, George Talbot, president of the provincial council, murdered the king's customs collector "with a dagger newly prepared and sharpened" aboard a royal ship. This event rocked the colony, so Baltimore sent a man he thought would provide strong leadership as governor, William Joseph, a Roman Catholic and adherent of James II. Upon arriving in 1688, Joseph proceeded to alienate Maryland's assemblymen, calling them adulterers and drunks. When he required them to renew their oaths of fidelity to the proprietor, they refused.

In July 1689, when Lord Baltimore still had not proclaimed the new monarchs, a handful of Maryland

THE TRIAL OF BRIDGET BISHOP, AN ACCUSED WITCH, SALEM, 1692

This report of Bridget Bishop's trial, published by Cotton Mather in *Wonders of the Invisible World*, shows the grounds on which Massachusetts courts convicted women and men of practicing witchcraft, including spectral evidence. In Goody Bishop's case, her accusers said her "shape" had attacked them. They also testified that Bishop's specter had tried to compel them to sign the devil's "book."

I. She was indicted for bewitching of several persons in the neighborhood, the indictment being drawn up, according to the form in such cases usual. And pleading, not guilty, there were brought in several persons, who had long undergone many kinds of miseries, which were preternaturally inflicted, and generally ascribed unto a horrible witchcraft. There was little occasion to prove the witchcraft; it being evident and notorious to all beholders. Now to fix the witchcraft on the prisoner at the bar, the first thing used was, the testimony of the bewitched; whereof, several testified, that the shape of the prisoner did oftentimes very grievously pinch them, choke them, bite them, and afflict them; urging them to write their names in a book, which the said specter called, ours. One of them did further testify, that it was the shape of this prisoner, with another, which one day took her from her wheel, and carrying her to the riverside, threatened there to drown her, if she did not sign to the book mentioned; which yet she refused. Others of them did also testify, that the said shape, did in her threats, brag to them, that she had been the death of sundry

leaders formed the Protestant Association. Aroused by rumors that Catholics were plotting with the Indians to destroy the Protestants, the Association raised troops, defeating the proprietary government without a shot. The rebels obtained articles of surrender that banned Catholics from provincial offices; sent a message to William and Mary informing them of the takeover and requesting a Protestant government; and elected an assembly—the "Associators' Convention"—which ruled Maryland for the next two and one-half years. Baltimore desperately tried to retain the colony. Though he kept proprietary rights to the soil and quitrents, in 1690 he lost the privilege to govern. The Calverts regained Maryland's government only in 1715, after Benedict Leonard, Charles's son, became an Anglican.

The three provincial revolutions of 1689, in Massachusetts, New York, and Maryland, had similarities to England's Glorious Revolution in the relative absence of bloodshed and the recurring theme of "popish plots." They failed, however, to bring about permanent change in the constitutional relationship between England and its colonies. The provincials, lacking delegates in Parliament, continued to endure taxation and mercantilist regulation without their assent. The colonial revolts of 1689 resembled Bacon's Rebellion of 1676, as they mobilized out-of-power elites, and their less affluent confederates, against those who controlled the colonial governments. In 1676, in Virginia, the insurgents had manipulated landless discontents by appealing to hatred against Native Americans as well as grievances against Berkeley's government. In persons, then by her named; that she had ridden a man, then likewise named. Another testified, the apparition of ghosts unto the specter of Bishop, crying out, you murdered us! About the truth whereof, there was in the matter of fact, but too much suspicion.

II. It was testified, that at the examination of the prisoner, before the magistrates, the bewitched were extremely tortured. If she did but cast her eyes on them, they were presently struck down; and this in such a manner as there could be no collusion in the business. But upon the touch of her hand upon them, when they lay in their swoons, they would immediately revive; and not upon the touch of anyone's else. Moreover, upon some special actions of her body, as the shaking of her head, or the turning of her eyes, they presently and painfully fell into the like postures. And many of the like accidents now fell out, while she was at the bar. One at the same time testifying, that she said, she could not be troubled to see the afflicted thus tormented.

III. There was testimony likewise brought in, that a man striking once at the place, where a bewitched person said, the shape of this Bishop stood, the bewitched cried out, that he had tore her coat, in the place then particularly specified; and the woman's coat, was found to be torn in that very place.

IV. One Deliverance Hobbs, who had confessed her being a witch, was now tormented by the specters, for her confession. And she now testified, that this Bishop, tempted her to sign the book again, and to deny what she had confessed. She affirmed, that it was the shape of this prisoner, which whipped her with iron rods, to compel her thereunto. And she affirmed, that this Bishop was at a general meeting of the witches, in a field at Salem Village and there partook of a diabolical sacrament, in bread and wine then administered!

1689, the leading rebels employed the twin specters of authoritarianism and Catholicism, with rumors of impending French and Indian attack, to gain support from the populace.

Witchcraft in New England

In May 1692, Governor William Phips arrived in Boston harbor with the new Massachusetts charter in hand. He found the colony in disarray after three years without stable government. Symptomatic of the Massachusetts state of affairs was the witchcraft hysteria that had erupted months earlier in Salem Village, a farming community north of Boston. Since 1675, the Bay Colony had one crisis after another—Metacom's War, loss of the charter, Andros's dominion, the Revolution of 1689, and the long period of uncertainty awaiting the new charter. Accompanying this turmoil were structural changes in the society, as traditional, religious authority yielded to elites whose power rested on mercantile wealth and imperial connections. The Salem witch mania was a tragic holdover from a passing culture. Its fury was aggravated by the psychological reaction of traditionally-minded folk to the new, more commercial, secular society of turn-of-century New England.

Belief in witchcraft was embedded in European and Anglo-American culture, though, ironically, it was losing force by the time of the outbreak in Salem. The colonists, like their contemporaries in the Old World, believed that both God and Satan influenced everyday events. When something bad happened that they could not explain, people turned to supernatural explanations, including the possibility that an individual had compacted with the Devil to do evil deeds. In England, witchcraft had been a capital offense since the time of Henry VIII in the early sixteenth century, with many prosecutions; colonial governments followed suit in condemning those who gave "entertainment to Satan." Over the seventeenth century, the Puritan governments charged many more men and women with witchcraft than did other English colonies: Three hundred and fifty New Englanders were accused during the years 1620 to 1725. Of this number, the Salem episode accounted for almost 200. The southern and middle colonies tried few accused witches and executed none.

The witchcraft cases of Salem in 1691–1692 at first resembled those in other places and times. Several girls experimented with magic, aided by a slave woman Tituba and her husband John, who together baked a "witch cake" of rye meal and urine, feeding it to a dog. The girls, who included nine-year-old Betty Parris, the daughter of Salem Village's minister, started having fits, presumably caused by witches. According to one report, the girls began "getting into holes, and creeping under chairs and stools, and to use sundry odd postures and antic gestures, uttering foolish, ridiculous speeches, which neither they themselves nor any others could make sense of." Possession spread to other village girls, leading to the arrest of three women as witches—Tituba; a poor beggar, Sarah Good; and an ailing elderly woman, Sarah Osborne.

These three alleged witches were the sort of people traditionally prosecuted for the crime. Generally, in witchcraft cases, the accused were women past menopause, who in various ways deviated from expected roles. They had fewer children than the average woman their age. Lacking sons, a significant number were heirs or potential heirs of estates, with greater economic autonomy than most New England women. Some accused witches claimed the power of a "cunning woman" to heal and foretell the future; many had been convicted of assaultive speech at a higher rate than women not accused of witchcraft; and they often were involved in conflict within their families and neighborhoods. Revealingly, men of the same age group and troublesome character were much less likely to be identified as witches. These assertive old women went beyond the accepted bounds of female behavior. As a result, they became vulnerable to prosecution as witches.

Hanging of witches in England c. 1650. No similar image exists of the Salem hangings.

While the Salem craze commenced in the time-worn pattern, it soon engulfed people of all social levels, though still many more women than men. Accusations descended upon prosperous church members, a minister, a wealthy shipowner, and several town officials. Hysteria spread from Salem throughout Essex County. Over three-quarters of the alleged witches were women; half of the accused men were their relations. Of those executed, fourteen women and five men were hanged on "Witches Hill" and another man was crushed to death with stones. Only one of the dead was of high status—the Puritan minister George Burroughs. Governor Phips, supported by influential clergymen, had allowed the prosecutions to proceed after his arrival, but put a stop to them when the accusers pointed to people at the highest levels of society, most significantly, to his own wife, Mary Phips. It had become clear, to many besides the governor, that the situation was out of control, that the evidence presented by the possessed was unreliable and quite likely the work of the Devil. After Salem, witchcraft no longer assumed its earlier importance in colonial society.

WARS AND RIVALRY FOR NORTH AMERICA

From 1680 to 1713, the Spanish, English, French, and many Indian nations battled for control of territory in

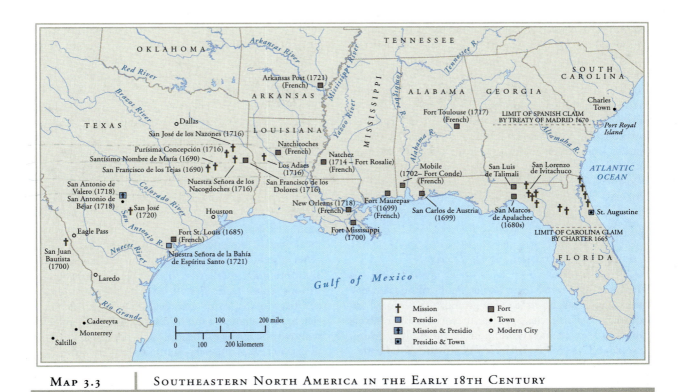

MAP 3.3 | SOUTHEASTERN NORTH AMERICA IN THE EARLY 18TH CENTURY

North America. Despite the political and social turmoil of the 1680s and early 1690s, the English settlements, stretching from New England to South Carolina, were the largest and most dynamic European colonies on the continent. By the mid-1680s, New France had approximately 10,000 settlers, compared with more than 70,000 in New England alone. Spanish Florida was comprised chiefly of missions, run by forty Franciscan priests, and the fortified town of St. Augustine, which held about 1,400 Hispanic, African, and Indian residents. Despite declining populations, many Native American peoples remained powerful in eastern North America, in particular the Five Nations of the Iroquois in New York. To defend their territory and control the fur trade, Indian tribes fought one another as well as the invading whites.

In the late seventeenth century, the three primary areas of dispute on the continent were Florida and Guale (later Georgia), Louisiana and Texas, and Canada. Conflict occurred against the backdrop of two long European wars, the War of the League of Augsburg, 1689–1697, and the War of the Spanish Succession, 1702–1713 (respectively known as King William's War and Queen Anne's War to the English colonists).

Florida and Guale

Beginning in 1680, the English colonists of South Carolina decided to take advantage of smoldering unrest among the mission Indians of Guale and Florida to attack the Spanish colony. The Native Americans had rebelled against forced labor and efforts to stamp out their traditional religions. They killed Spanish missionaries and destroyed property, but had not closed the missions altogether. The Carolinians raided Guale and Florida from no humanitarian motives to assist the Indians. In fact, a chief reason for attacking the Spanish missions was to capture Native Americans to sell as slaves in the West Indies. The English also wanted to control the deerskin trade in the southeast.

By 1686, the Carolinians thrust the missionaries out of Guale. Then in 1704, during Queen Anne's

War, an army under former Carolina governor James Moore crushed the missions in Apalachee, killing and enslaving hundreds, if not thousands, of Indian men, women, and children. The Carolinians obtained help from their trading partners, the Yamassees, and from many of the mission Indians, who resented Spanish oppression. Moore's troops inflicted brutal torture, burning people alive. The surviving Apalachees dispersed, losing their identity as a nation. The Spanish retained St. Augustine and a fort they built at Pensacola in 1698, but lost control of Guale and most of Florida.

Louisiana and Texas

The Spanish erected their fort at Pensacola Bay in response to French efforts to establish a colony in Louisiana. At risk, the Spanish knew, were their silver mines in Mexico and domination of the Gulf of Mexico. In 1682, René Robert Cavelier, Sieur de La Salle, had explored the Mississippi River from New France to the gulf, claiming its entire watershed and naming the territory Louisiana in honor of King Louis XIV. La Salle sailed to France, then returned to set up a colony from which to attack New Spain. His expedition was an utter failure, as he miscalculated the location of the Mississippi, instead building Fort St. Louis in Texas, near Matagorda Bay. The colony quickly dissolved from disease, loss of ships, and attacks by Karankawa Indians; in 1687, La Salle was murdered by his men.

Despite its quick and grisly end, the French incursion in the Gulf of Mexico inspired the Spanish to expand its settlements in the borderlands. Reconquest of New Mexico from the Pueblos was part of this effort. The Spanish in 1690 founded missions among the Caddo people of eastern Texas and western Louisiana, from whom they took the Caddo word, Tejas or Texas, meaning "friends." Three years later, when the Caddos blamed the friars for bringing smallpox, they escaped, burying their church bells. The Spaniards abandoned Texas until the French once again entered the area.

In 1699, Pierre LeMoyne, Sieur d'Iberville resumed the French search for an opening to the Mississippi River, which was difficult to locate in the muddy Mississippi Delta. Iberville found the river's mouth by accident, then built forts at Biloxi Bay and on the Mississippi to establish French possession. Spain might have forced the French out of Louisiana with quick action, but in 1700, the grandson of French King Louis XIV took the Spanish throne; the two nations became allies against the English, Dutch, and Austrians in the War of the Spanish Succession. In fact, the French helped the Spanish defend St. Augustine and Pensacola against the English and they jointly tried but failed to conquer Charleston.

Although the French-Spanish alliance gave Louisiana a chance to develop without interference from New Spain, the colony grew slowly for lack of immigrants. In 1708, about one hundred white soldiers and settlers lived in Louisiana. They obtained food, deerskins, and the right to occupy the land from local Native Americans by exchanging firearms and other goods. Relations between the French and Indians were not trouble-free, however, as rivalries among various tribes, the Carolinians, and French created conflict. In 1715, for example, after Natchez Indians killed four French traders, the colonists literally demanded the assassins' heads. When the Natchez failed to execute all of the perpetrators, the French murdered Indian hostages and required the Natchez to accept a fortified trading post on their land. The Louisiana settlers also established trade with Caddo Indians in western Louisiana, prompting the Spanish to renew their missions in Texas and build a presidio (or fort) at San Antonio.

Canada

Conflict developed in the north when the Iroquois confederation attacked New France to stop French fur trading in the Ohio Valley and Illinois. The Iroquois defeated New France in 1683, but war continued as the English, French, and Native Americans struggled over trade routes and territory. The outbreak of King William's War in 1689 fueled the contest, as the Five Nations attacked settlements in Canada, while the French and their Indian allies destroyed English frontier outposts from New York to Maine. New England troops, under Sir William Phips, took Port Royal in Acadia, but failed to conquer Quebec. In the Atlantic, the war interrupted trade, as French privateers harassed English fleets carrying tobacco and sugar. Though the European belligerents agreed in the Peace of Ryswick (1697) to return to prewar status in North

America, the Canadians won an important victory over the Iroquois and their English allies. The Five Nations, badly beaten, decimated by disease, and their fur trade disrupted, signed a neutrality treaty in 1701. Frustrated by New York's failure to provide reinforcements, they ended their alliance with the English. New France then developed trade, religious missions, and agricultural settlements in the Great Lakes and Illinois Territory.

The renewal of hostilities between the English and French in 1702, with Queen Anne's War, again brought raids on the New England frontier. In 1704, the Canadians and Native Americans attacked Deerfield, Massachusetts, burning houses and barns, killing inhabitants, and taking many captives. The English once again took Port Royal, after several unsuccessful tries, but called off an attack on Quebec when they lost 900 men in storms on the St. Lawrence River. This time, however, the peace treaty gave the victory to England (which had joined with Scotland in 1707 to form Great Britain). In North America, the Treaty of Utrecht (1713) ceded Nova Scotia (formerly Acadia), Newfoundland, and control of the Hudson Bay territory to the British. Yet they had failed to oust France from North America. What can be called the Second Hundred Years' War between France and England, from 1689 to 1815, resumed a generation later in the 1740s.

THE ENTRENCHMENT OF SLAVERY IN BRITISH AMERICA

Despite wars, rebellions, and witch hysteria, the most significant development in British North America during the late seventeenth and early eighteenth century was large-scale investment in enslaved Africans. The decisions of thousands of individual colonists to purchase men, women, and children who had been seized from their homelands in Africa left an indelible imprint on American society and culture. The slave buyers could not foretell the monumental effects of their actions. They responded to economic conditions: their need for workers, the declining availability of white servants, and the developing Atlantic slave trade.

Adopting Slavery

How could people who increasingly prized their own freedom—who had braved a treacherous ocean voyage to find opportunity in a new land—deprive other human beings of liberty, and often life itself? The answer lies in traditional English culture and the colonists' perceived economic needs.

The English, like other Europeans, believed that hierarchies existed in human society and, indeed, all of nature. Humans were superior to animals; Christians superior to "heathens." English language and culture also differentiated sharply between white and black, with whiteness suggesting purity and good, blackness imbued with filth and sin. The English compared their light skin with the Africans' darker brown color, judging the latter to be inferior. In African religion, social customs, dress, and political organization, the Europeans found serious deficiencies, just as they had found deficiencies among Native Americans. The people of sub-Saharan Africa, the English thought, were lower on the scale of humanity and could justifiably be enslaved. The example of the Portuguese, Spanish, and—most recently—the Dutch, who had fabricated the Atlantic slave trade over the previous two centuries, made the decision to buy Africans seem natural. The mainland English colonists could also look to their countrymen in the West Indies, where thousands of African slaves toiled in sugar fields, outnumbering whites.

Despite this cultural context, colonists viewed their investment in slaves as an economic decision. In Virginia and Maryland, planters purchased Africans because they needed large numbers of workers to grow tobacco. Chesapeake settlers had learned that Native Americans, who easily escaped enslavement and died in catastrophic numbers, would not fill their labor needs. White servants filled the gap until about 1675. Many young Englishmen, and fewer women, willingly signed up to work for three or more years in return for passage and rights to fifty acres of land. In the last quarter of the century, however, the supply of English servants declined in Maryland and Virginia. Economic conditions improved in England, while good tobacco land became scarce. Bacon's Rebellion taught Chesapeake elites the danger of importing thousands of white servants under these circumstances. With the founding of the Carolinas, New Jersey, and Pennsylvania, where land was plentiful, servants had a wider range of options.

Chesapeake planters searching for an alternative labor supply turned to African slaves. Population figures for Virginia and Maryland demonstrate graphically the result of individual decisions. In 1660, only 900 blacks resided in the Chesapeake, some of whom had come as servants and were free. Two decades later, their number had grown to 4,300; by 1720, blacks comprised one-fifth of the population. A similar increase occurred in the Carolinas (primarily South Carolina), where 38 percent of the residents in 1720 were African slaves. The situation was different in New England, where only 2 percent of the population was enslaved, and in the Middle Colonies (New York, New Jersey, Pennsylvania, and Delaware), where about one resident in ten suffered perpetual bondage.

The Slave Trade

English entry into the Atlantic slave trade helped spur the transition to an African workforce. Though smugglers like John Hawkins had interloped earlier in the Spanish trade, England officially became involved in selling human beings in 1663. Charles II granted a monopoly to supply captives to the English colonies first to the Company of Royal Adventurers, then in 1672 to the Royal African Company. When the companies could not meet the demand of labor-hungry colonists, smugglers got involved, so in 1698, the Crown abandoned the monopoly, opening the slave trade to any English merchant who wanted to participate. As a result, the supply of Africans in the English colonies soared and slave prices declined, thus encouraging colonists to invest in even more black labor.

The experience of enslavement and transport across the Atlantic Ocean was dehumanizing and perilous. Probably one-half of the persons sold into slavery died before reaching the New World. Approximately three-quarters of those taken to English North America came from the area of West Africa between Senegambia and the Bight of Biafra, with the remainder coming mostly from Angola. Slaves were "black gold"—prisoners of war and kidnapped children and young adults—whom African merchants collected for sale. As European sea captains made successive trips to the coast, African traders had to reach farther and farther into the continent to find enough people to enslave. Some captives marched 500 miles or more to the sea in "coffles," the term given to the files of shackled pris-

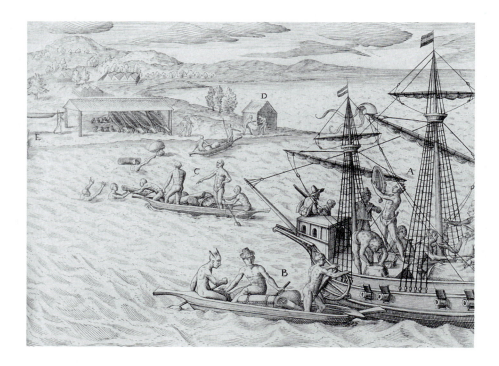

Theodor de Bry's illustration of a Dutch ship trading on the coast of West Africa. The people in the canoe, indicated with "B," represent African merchants who traded human beings to the Europeans for goods such as cloth, rum, and firearms.

Diagram showing the tight packing of enslaved Africans during the "middle passage."

oners. On the coast, they were confined in enclosures called barracoons, often exposed for long periods to the sun without adequate food and drink. When a ship arrived, according to a Dutch trader, Willem Bosman, in 1700, the Africans were lined up on shore,

> where, by our surgeons . . . they are thoroughly examined, even to the smallest member, and that naked both men and women, without the least distinction or modesty. Those that are approved as good, are set on one side; and the lame or faulty are set by as invalids, which are here called *mackrons:* these are such as are above five and thirty years old, or are maimed in the arms, legs or feet; have lost a tooth, are grey-haired, or have films over their eyes; as well as all those which are affected with any venereal distemper, or several other diseases.

The Africans were treated like any other commodity offered for sale, at best as livestock sold at auction. The process of enslavement, of turning autonomous people into property, required nothing less.

For the Africans chosen for transport, the horror had only begun. The Europeans branded them with the insignia of the company—for example, slaves of the Royal African Company had their skins burned with the letters "DY," for James, duke of York. Then followed the voyage across the Atlantic, called the "middle passage," which could take from three weeks to more than three months, depending upon the weather and destination. Ships normally carried rations for three months, so bad storms could mean starvation. Weather permitting, the captives spent their days on deck, the men in chains, the women and children unrestrained. At night, and around the clock if weather was bad, slaves occupied spaces about the size of coffins in the hold of the ship, where sanitation and ventilation were poor. Temperatures could reach extremely high levels. Disease was often rampant, the experience altogether dehumanizing. Some slaves attempted suicide by jumping overboard or refusing to eat: The latter was so common that traders invested in a tool called the *speculum oris* to force open a person's mouth.

Africans also rebelled violently, attacking the white captain and crew, occasionally taking over the ship. Because they were unfamiliar with ocean navigation, mutineers had the best hope for success when the ship was still in African waters and large numbers could carry out the revolt, escaping to shore. When rebels failed, punishment was swift and brutal. The slave trader Bosman described an incident when a sea captain placed an extra anchor in the ship's hold. The enslaved Africans,

> unknown to any of the ship's crew, possessed themselves of a hammer, with which, in a short time they broke all their fetters in pieces upon the anchor: After this, they came above deck, and fell upon our men, some of whom they grievously

wounded, and would certainly have mastered the ship, if a French and English ship had not very fortunately happened to lie by us; who perceiving by our firing a distressed-gun, that something was in disorder on board, immediately came to our assistance with shallops and men, and drove the slaves under deck: notwithstanding which, before all was appeased, about twenty of them were killed. The Portuguese have been more unlucky in this particular than we; for in four years they lost four ships in this manner.

Upon arrival in America, the Africans faced the ordeal of sale by auction or prearranged contract. They were stripped naked once again and examined for disease and physical defects. Because the greatest need was for strong field hands who would provide years of labor, plantation owners paid the highest prices for healthy young men in their prime. Buyers paid less for women, children, and older men, from whom they expected less production. For both the Africans and their owners, who had just invested a large sum, the year following debarkation was most critical. During this period of seasoning, Africans endured serious illness and high mortality from the new disease environment.

Systems of Slavery in British North America

As more and more Africans arrived, colonial assemblies instituted black codes to define slavery and control the black population. The result was legal entrenchment of the institution. Before 1660, Maryland had officially sanctioned perpetual bondage, but Virginia moved more slowly. While its assembly forbade Africans from bearing arms, it remained silent on the subject of slavery. Enough flexibility existed in Virginia society to allow black servants to gain freedom, earn their livelihoods, and in some cases acquire land. In the 1660s, however, Virginia joined Maryland in enacting laws that recognized differences in the terms of white servants and African slaves. By law, slavery lasted a person's entire lifetime, descended from mother to child, and was the normal status of blacks, but never whites.

In the late seventeenth and early eighteenth century, both Virginia and Maryland created clearly articulated caste systems based on perceptions of race. A person's skin color denoted status: all Africans and their descendants encountered severe discrimination, whether enslaved or free. The Virginia assembly ruled

that any master who killed a slave during punishment was not guilty of a felony. Conversely, no black person, slave or free, could strike a white, even a bound servant—even in self-defense. Virginia lawmakers made emancipation difficult to obtain, specifying that conversion to Christianity would not free a slave. Evolving black codes banned interracial marriage, forbade owners from releasing their slaves except in special cases, and restricted enslaved blacks from traveling without permission, marrying legally, holding property, testifying against whites, or congregating in groups. Over the course of the eighteenth century, other British colonies passed similar codes that ranged from fairly moderate New England laws to a harsh regime in Carolina, keyed in large part to the density of the black population.

In the life of an African slave, these laws had force, but more direct was the power of the master over work and family. To be a slave meant that someone else possessed your body and could command your daily activities. The owner chose your job; he or she decided whether your children would stay with you or be sold away. During off-hours, Africans generally maintained autonomy in religion, social customs, and family life, but the law and the master's will remained dominant.

The work Africans and native-born African Americans performed varied from one region to another. In the Chesapeake and the Carolinas, with labor-intensive staple crops, most slaves spent long hours planting, weeding, and harvesting tobacco, corn, and rice. A farm's production depended largely upon the number of workers tending the crop. Masters apparently felt no concern about requiring black women to do hard physical labor in the fields, for it was there that they would yield the greatest return. Over time, as the southern black population increased naturally and importation continued, the supply of labor became more plentiful. Plantation owners assigned slaves to different tasks, though most still raised the staple crop. Some men became drivers and artisans; some women served as nurses, cooks, and spinners. Both women and men performed domestic service. At the same time, female slaves were responsible for the household needs of their own families, including food preparation, laundry, and sewing.

Agricultural production in the middle colonies and New England centered on grains and livestock, which demanded less labor than tobacco or rice, so most parts of the northern countryside had relatively few slaves. Exceptions included New York and neighboring eastern New Jersey, which had difficulty attracting European immigrants; thus, well-to-do farmers purchased large numbers of Africans to work their land. The largest slaveholder in New Jersey was probably Colonel Lewis Morris of Shrewsbury, who employed more than sixty slaves at his plantation and ironworks. In Rhode Island's Narragansett region, some plantation owners held as many as fifty blacks. Most northern slaves lived in the port towns, however, where women worked as cooks and household servants, and men labored at crafts, domestic service, and as shipbuilders and sailors. Boston, New York, and Philadelphia merchants imported Africans as part of the West Indies trade. In New York City, blacks were about one-fifth of the population; in Boston and Philadelphia they comprised about one-tenth.

A source of comfort to slaves who had lost their African homelands and kin was to establish new families in America. Slaves achieved some autonomy from their masters by creating families and kinship networks. All knew, however, that owners could destroy loving relationships by selling away spouses, children, brothers, and sisters. The ability of blacks to form families changed over time and varied from one region to another. High mortality and a skewed sex ratio prevented many African-born men from marrying and having children. In the disease-ridden West Indies and northern cities like Philadelphia, mortality was so high that colonists had to keep importing Africans to avoid population decline. In the Chesapeake colonies, however, natural population growth began with the first generation of native-born slaves. African American women had more children than their African mothers, creating communities of slaves on large plantations. Whereas most of the first Africans dwelled in white households with just a few blacks, their offspring, known as "country-born" slaves, lived with parents, brothers, and sisters. The third generation lived with grandparents and cousins as well. After 1720, in the Chesapeake, almost one-half of slaves resided on plantations with more than twenty blacks.

Resistance and Rebellion

While for many slaves family and kin helped to reduce their feelings of despair, for others nothing relieved the pain of lifetime bondage. Many resisted their masters'

power by staging slowdowns, pretending illness, destroying crops and tools, committing theft, arson, assault, and murder. Newly arrived Africans were especially likely to rebel against their new status, often running away, sometimes to live with Native Americans. Slaves who were sold away from their families frequently escaped to join them once again. Men ran away in greater numbers than women, who, as mothers, found it difficult to escape with children in tow. If motivated by the threat of punishment or rape to absent themselves from the plantation, women became truants, hiding in nearby woods.

While slaves in the English West Indies often rebelled, blacks in the mainland colonies rarely took the ultimate step of armed insurgency, primarily because they were so outnumbered by whites. Before 1713, West Indian blacks staged seven full-scale revolts; their large population made success seem possible. In Barbados, in 1675, for example, conspirators planned to take over the island, installing an elderly slave Cuffee as king. When whites got wind of the plot, they burned alive or beheaded thirty-five blacks. On the mainland, just one slave revolt occurred by the early 1700s. In New York City, in 1712, about twenty slaves set fire to a building, attacking the white men who came to extinguish it. Nine whites were killed; terror spread up and down the Atlantic coast. As in the case of later slave revolts and conspiracies, the revenge wreaked upon the black community surpassed any violence the rebels had committed. White authorities did not care whether everyone they punished had actually been involved. In the wake of the New York revolt, thirteen slaves were hanged, three burned at the stake, one tortured on the wheel (an instrument used to stretch and disjoint its victims), and another starved to death in chains; six committed suicide to avoid such treatment. The town fathers expected, with these barbarous punishments, to prevent further insurrection.

Early Abolitionists

As slavery became entrenched in the American colonies, a few white colonists questioned its morality. They feared slave rebellions and abhorred the violence needed to enslave Africans, transport them to the colonies, and keep them in bondage. Slavery was morally repugnant, they believed, because all humans are equal in the eyes of God. One of the American opponents of perpetual bondage was Samuel Sewall, a

Boston judge, who wrote in 1700, "It is most certain that all Men, as they are the Sons of Adam . . . have equal Right unto Liberty, and all other outward Comforts of Life."

Quakers also spoke out publicly against the institution. Certainly not all Friends were abolitionists—in Pennsylvania and New Jersey before 1720 a large proportion of the Quaker elite owned slaves—but a few interpreted Quaker ideals to mean that human bondage reeked with sin. According to John Hepburn of New Jersey, for example, slavery violated the Golden Rule to do unto others as you wish others to do unto you. He abhorred slavekeeping. While owners got rich without physical labor, wore fine-powdered wigs and greatcoats, and their wives and children similarly lived well, slaves endured beatings, wore rags, and slept in the ashes of the fire. In the context of rising importation throughout the colonies, however, the protests of Sewall, Hepburn, and a few other critics had little effect.

ECONOMIC DEVELOPMENT IN THE BRITISH COLONIES

While the southern colonies employed slave labor much more extensively than the north, every British province was implicated in the institution. Despite differences in agriculture, labor, and commerce from one region to another, the mainland colonies were all part of the Atlantic economy, dominated by the staple crops, sugar, tobacco, and rice. The developing mercantile economies of New England and the mid-Atlantic region depended heavily upon the slave system, because their chief market was providing food for the multitudes of blacks laboring on West Indies sugar plantations.

Northern Economies

Family farms and dependence on the sea characterized New England's economy. When its agriculture failed to provide a lucrative staple crop, traders turned to fishing and shipping to earn credits to buy imports. With rocky, generally poor soil and a cool climate, the region could not grow a profitable commercial crop like tobacco or sugar, so rural New England families raised livestock, wheat, rye, Indian corn, peas, other vegetables, and fruit. They ate most of what they produced—a fairly monotonous diet of brown bread, boiled or baked peas, boiled meat and vegetables, and dark beer or apple cider—within their families and communities.

Fishing and shipping developed as important industries during the seventeenth century. The New Englanders replaced English fishermen who had come to the Grand Banks for cod since the 1400s. The New England fishers initially sold their catch, in return for manufactured goods such as shoes, textiles, glass, and metal products, to London merchants, who sent the fish to Spain, Portugal, and the Wine Islands, off the coast of Africa.

The fishing industry spurred the growth of maritime trade, as New England merchants recognized even greater profits to be made by trading directly with the Wine Islands and the West Indies. They formed partnerships among themselves and with English merchants, encouraging a local shipbuilding industry. The New Englanders exported fish, barrels, and other wood products to the islands. They imported wine, fruit, and salt from the Wine Islands, and rum, molasses, sugar, dyes, and other goods from the Caribbean. Soon, aided by the Navigation Acts, they were the chief carriers of goods along the North American coast, exchanging enslaved Africans and rum distilled from West Indies molasses for Pennsylvania wheat and livestock, Chesapeake tobacco, North Carolina tar and turpentine, and South Carolina rice. The credits they earned in shipping were as significant as the value of New England products sold in the trade.

The economy of the Middle Colonies resembled New England's in a number of ways, but was much more prosperous agriculturally. With plenty of good land, farmers raised wheat and livestock commercially, purchasing servants and some slaves to supplement family labor. The region had two ports: one at New York City, which served New York, western Connecticut, and eastern New Jersey; and the other at Philadelphia, which served Pennsylvania, western New Jersey, Delaware, and northern Maryland. Though neither city matched Boston in population or commercial importance before 1750, both quickly surpassed the Massachusetts seaport after that date. New York merchants maintained links with Amsterdam, the Dutch West Indies, and New Spain even after the English takeover in 1664. Philadelphia Quakers exploited their connections with Friends in other ports, especially in England and the West Indies. Before 1750, Philadelphia primarily exported food, livestock, and barrel staves to the Caribbean for credits to buy English manufactures.

Life in the Seaports

Maritime trade encouraged the development of port cities in the British provinces: Boston, New York, Philadelphia, and Charleston. Until 1750, merchants of Boston and other seaport towns in Massachusetts (Salem, Marblehead, and Newbury) and Rhode Island (Newport and Providence), dominated colonial trade. The ports thrived because they forged commercial links between farmers and external dealers, housing the markets through which imports and exports flowed. The maritime industry itself created demand for shipbuilders, suppliers of provisions, rope and sailmakers, carters, dockworkers, and sailors.

Commercial growth brought social change, distinguishing an urban lifestyle from the countryside. Some merchants became fabulously wealthy from transat-lantic and coastal trade. They spent their income conspicuously, building costly mansions, purchasing enslaved Africans as household servants, and wearing expensive clothes. They lived comfortably, with servants and slaves to do their menial chores. Other city dwellers were much less fortunate, because they earned minimal wages or lacked employment. Port cities stimulated both affluence and dire poverty. A much wider range of wealth developed there than in rural areas of the north, where most families owned farms of moderate size. The seaport cities attracted many people who hoped to make their fortunes, or at least a decent living, but died with little more than the clothes on their backs. Maritime commerce frequently suffered disruption from war, bad weather, and economic downturns. Seamen and artisans, dependent on overseas trade, could expect little work during the winter, when few ships sailed. City folk were also at greater risk of death than those who lived in the country, as some arriving ships spread smallpox and other diseases to the dense urban populations. The towns lacked adequate sanitation facilities, so garbage and waste cluttered streets, polluting the water supply. With insufficient food and firewood, the poor endured the highest rates of illness and death, but no one was immune to the fevers and dysentery that repeatedly afflicted urban residents.

As trade expanded, sailors became an important segment of the labor force. They were a varied lot. Some men, particularly those who lived along the coast, went to sea only part-time, to supplement the income of their farms. Others chose seafaring as a career, joining a fraternity who divided their time between shipboard and the taverns and boardinghouses of port towns throughout the Atlantic world. Some had no choice in the matter at all, for they were enslaved Africans whose masters purchased them to man the ships. Sailors led a difficult and dangerous life. Crews on ordinary merchant ships were small, so seamen worked long hours loading and unloading the ship, maintaining the rigging and sails, and pumping water from the bilge, an especially backbreaking job. The organization of labor on board was hierarchical, with power descending from the captain to mate, to specialists like ship carpenter and surgeon, to seamen. Discipline could be harsh. The crewmen had little hope of moving up through the ranks, for captains were generally from affluent families, often merchants and part-owners of their ships. Instead, the more common fate of an ordinary "Jack Tar" was early death or disability from shipwreck, combat with enemies or

Cod fishing was an early industry of Europeans in the North Atlantic. This illustration depicts a dry fishery on the Newfoundland coast in which cod were lightly salted and dried for sale in southern Europe.

pirates, and such occupational hazards as falling over-board, broken bones, scurvy, rheumatism, and hernia, or the "bursted belly" as they called it.

When conditions on ship became insufferable, the seamen rebelled, sometimes refusing to work until their grievances were redressed, sometimes deserting the ship at the next port. Most radically, men mutinied and, if successful, sometimes became pirates, or robbers at sea. They plundered merchant vessels and port towns, sharing the proceeds evenly among themselves, electing officers, and recruiting much larger crews than could be found on merchant ships. With eighty or more men on a pirate ship of average size, compared with fifteen on a comparable merchant vessel, each had much less work to do. One pirate, Joseph Mansfield, admitted in 1722 that "the love of Drink and a Lazy Life" were "Stronger Motives with him than Gold."

Plantation Economies in the Chesapeake and South Carolina

From 1675 to 1720, tobacco remained king in Maryland and Virginia, as planters increasingly purchased enslaved Africans instead of white servants. The wealth of plantation owners grew with each child born to a slave mother. At the same time, the richest planters bought up the land of small farmers who found it difficult to compete with the slaveholders. The wealthiest man in early eighteenth-century Virginia was Robert Carter of Lancaster County, called "King" Carter. As a slave trader and land speculator, he parlayed his inheritance of £1,000 and 1,000 acres into an estate of £10,000 in cash, 300,000 acres of land, and over 700 slaves. Carter, with his relatives and friends, formed a tightly knit group of Chesapeake gentry, who consolidated their wealth in land, commerce, and slaves.

In 1720, and throughout the eighteenth century, Chesapeake society was hierarchical. At the bottom of the social structure were African and country-born slaves, who owned no property and had little hope for freedom. Above them were the non-landholding whites, perhaps 40 to 50 percent of white families, whose living conditions were rough. They rented land, owned a horse or two, some cows, a few pigs, tools, and some household goods, but rarely held bound servants or slaves. They lived in shanties and ate from wooden dishes rather than pottery. Their incomes from tobacco were so meager that they had trouble paying taxes and rent. Often they were in debt to the local merchant-planter for needed manufactured goods, such as ammunition, fabric, shoes, and tools. Next higher were small landholders whose incomes allowed them to live more comfortably, with pottery, more furniture, and nicer (though still quite small) homes. If they owned several slaves, which few did before 1720, they worked alongside them in the fields and house.

In the upper 5 percent were the gentry, who owned many slaves, large acreages, and usually acted as merchants as well. They served as intermediaries for smaller planters, selling tobacco abroad and importing manufactured goods. As such, they became creditors of their poorer neighbors, who often owed them substantial debts. In Maryland and Virginia, the merchant-planters conducted trade without the development of port cities. Ships docked at their plantations along the many tributaries of the Chesapeake Bay to load casks of tobacco and unload imported goods. Tobacco required little processing: planters dried the leaves in sheds and packed them in casks made by local coopers. Merchant-planters and rural artisans, including slaves, provided goods and services for the community without centralizing their activities in towns. Even the two capitals, Williamsburg and Annapolis, remained small throughout the colonial period.

Situated in a semi-tropical climate, South Carolina developed a plantation economy that was linked to, and in many ways resembled, the West Indies. Most early settlers, both black and white, came from the English colony of Barbados, where land was in short supply and almost entirely devoted to sugar cultivation. White planters claimed Carolina headrights, then sold corn, salt beef, salt pork, barrel staves, firewood, and Native American slaves to the islands. South Carolinians enslaved the Indians they captured in raids throughout the American southeast and also obtained them in exchange for guns, ammunition, and cloth from native traders. Native Americans also supplied deerskins, which found a ready market in England, though they were not valued quite so highly as Canadian furs.

As with the northern fur trade between Europeans and Indians, the Carolinians used English trade goods to establish alliances with native groups. However, such major trading partners as the Yamassees quickly discovered that white merchants used theft, violence, rum, and false weights to gain unfair advantage. In 1715, in league with the Creeks, the Yamassees attacked white settlements, nearly destroying the colony.

The whites saved themselves by getting help from the Cherokees, who at first vacillated but then accepted the promise of continued European trade. The Yamassees and Creeks were defeated, their people killed, enslaved, or forced to migrate from the coastal area. White South Carolinians then expropriated their lands.

The settlers wanted the new territory because they had found an export that became much more lucrative than provisions, enslaved Indians, or deerskins. Planters had experimented with a variety of crops—tobacco, cotton, sugar, silk, wine grapes, and ginger—but rice proved most successful in the wet lowlands of the Carolina coast. Also significant were the skills in rice production that many Africans brought to America. Rice exports expanded rapidly in South Carolina, reaching 1.5 million pounds per year by 1710 and nearly 20 million pounds by 1730. The chief markets for rice were Europe and the West Indies. Carolinians first sent their crop directly to Portugal, but in 1705 Parliament added rice to the list of enumerated products that had to be shipped to England first, taxes paid, and then reexported to Europe. The colonists argued that, in the case of southern Europe, this detour made their crop arrive too late for Lent, when much of it was consumed. In response, Parliament allowed South Carolina after 1731 to trade directly with Spain, Portugal, and Mediterranean Europe, but the larger share of the rice crop, which went to northern Europe, still required transit through Britain.

The conversion to rice transformed South Carolina society, affecting the black population with special force. Before planters adopted full-scale rice production, slaves had performed a variety of jobs in crafts, timber, livestock, and agriculture. Their workloads were moderate, especially in comparison with the West Indies; with the first generation of African Americans, natural increase of the population had begun. Rice monoculture changed this situation altogether, as planters imported thousands of Africans. In the coastal areas north and south of Charleston, blacks reached 70 percent of the population in the 1720s (38 percent of the Carolinas overall). With high importation and harsher working conditions, death rates surged. As in the Chesapeake, wealthy planters bought up neighboring farms while investing heavily in slaves. They created large rice plantations, worked by growing numbers of African slaves, not unlike the sugar regime of Barbados. Small planters moved to the periphery, where they raised grain and livestock for the rice dis-

trict and the Caribbean. The rice planters found the Carolina lowlands isolated and unhealthy, so they left their plantations part of the year to make social contacts and escape the oppressive heat and disease. However, the Carolinians supervised their plantations directly—unlike British West Indian sugar planters who fled to England, leaving management in the care of overseers.

Charleston, where the rice planters spent at least several weeks each year, was the fourth largest city in the British colonies. The port channeled the trade in provisions, deerskins, rice, slaves, and English manufactures. Charleston remained smaller than Boston, Philadelphia, and New York because British and New England shippers controlled its trade. Without a strong merchant community, the South Carolina seaport lacked the impetus for shipbuilding and associated crafts.

CONCLUSION

Between 1675 and 1720, the people of North America shed their blood over territory, trade, and political autonomy. As English, French, and Spanish settlers expanded into new regions, they established commerce, but also spread smallpox and fostered conflict among the Indians. Despite ardent defense of homelands and the temporary successes of the Pueblos and the Iroquois, Native Americans throughout the continent, weakened by disease and war, yielded to the Europeans.

By the turn of the eighteenth century, the Spanish reconquered New Mexico and infiltrated Texas, France had started Louisiana, and the English were pushing out in many directions. To develop their economies, the British colonists imported Africans in large numbers, creating rigorous slave regimes to control their new, rebellious laborers. With the growth of plantation slave economies in the South and maritime commerce in the North, British North America developed distinctive regional characteristics. Yet in 1720, the Atlantic seaboard colonies had much in common: their settlement by enterprising men and women, regard for English rights of property and representation, and governance within the British imperial system. During the next half century, the importance of these commonalities, as well as the contradictions that emerged from them, would become clear.

RECOMMENDED READINGS

Many of the sources listed for Chapter 2 are useful for the period from 1675 to 1720 as well.

Demos, John. *The Unredeemed Captive: A Family Story from Early America* (1994). The evocative tale of a Puritan minister's daughter who was held captive by the Mohawks and refused to return home.

Dunn, Mary Maples, et al., eds. *The Papers of William Penn,* 5 vols. (1981–1987). Basic documents, with scholarly introductions, on the founding and early development of Pennsylvania.

Innes, Stephen, ed. *Work and Labor in Early America* (1988). Insightful essays that demonstrate the range of labor systems and working conditions in the British colonies.

Jordan, Winthrop D. *White over Black: American Attitudes Toward the Negro, 1550–1812* (1968). Basic source on the construction of ideas about race in Anglo-America.

Karlsen, Carol F. *The Devil in the Shape of a Woman: Witchcraft in Colonial New England* (1987). Convincing argument about the significance of gender in witchcraft trials.

Lovejoy, David S. *The Glorious Revolution in America* (1972) The best introduction to the colonial revolutions of 1689.

McCusker, John J., and Menard, Russell R. *The Economy of British America, 1607–1789, With Supplementary Bibliography* (1991). An excellent survey of economic and demographic development.

Pestana, Carla Gardina. *Quakers and Baptists in Colonial Massachusetts* (1991). Contrasts the experience of two persecuted sects in early New England.

Usner, Daniel H., Jr. *Indians, Settlers, and Slaves in a Frontier Exchange Economy: The Lower Mississippi Valley Before 1783* (1992). A history of colonial Louisiana and West Florida, focusing on relations between Europeans and Native Americans.

Religious Change and Witchcraft in New England

Ahlstrom, Sydney E. *A Religious History of the American People* (1972).

Bonomi, Patricia U. *Under the Cope of Heaven: Religion, Society, and Politics in Colonial America* (1986).

Boyer, Paul and Nissenbaum, Steven. *Salem Possessed: The Social Origins of Witchcraft* (1974).

Demos, John Putnam. *Entertaining Satan: Witchcraft and the Culture of Early New England* (1982).

Hall, David D., ed. *Witch-Hunting in Seventeenth-Century New England: A Documentary History, 1638–1692* (1991).

Pope, Robert. *The Half-Way Covenant: Church Membership in Puritan New England* (1969).

Worrall, Arthur J. *Quakers in the Colonial Northeast* (1980).

Founding of Pennsylvania

Dunn, Richard S., and Dunn, Mary Maples, eds. *The World of William Penn* (1986).

Lemon, James T. *The Best Poor Man's Country: A Geographical Study of Early Southeastern Pennsylvania* (1972).

Nash, Gary B. *Quakers and Politics: Pennsylvania, 1681–1726* (1968).

Schwartz, Sally. *"A Mixed Multitude": The Struggle for Toleration in Colonial Pennsylvania* (1987).

Soderlund, Jean R., et al., eds. *William Penn and the Founding of Pennsylvania, 1680–1684: A Documentary History* (1983).

Weslager, C. A. *The Delaware Indians: A History* (1972).

Imperial Relations and the Revolutions of 1689

Archdeacon, Thomas J. *New York City, 1664–1710: Conquest and Change* (1976).

Carr, Lois Green, and Jordan, David William. *Maryland's Revolution of Government, 1689–1692* (1974).

Hall, Michael Garibaldi. *Edward Randolph and the American Colonies, 1676–1703* (1960).

Olson, Alison Gilbert. *Anglo-American Politics, 1660–1775: The Relationship Between Parties in England and Colonial America* (1973).

Webb, Stephen Saunders. *The Governors-General: The English Army and the Definition of the Empire, 1569–1681* (1979).

Entrenchment of Slavery

Davis, David Brion. *The Problem of Slavery in Western Culture* (1966).

Higginbotham, A. Leon, Jr. *In the Matter of Color: Race and the American Legal Process, the Colonial Period* (1978).

Kulikoff, Allan. *Tobacco and Slaves: The Development of Southern Cultures in the Chesapeake, 1680–1800* (1986).

Littlefield, Daniel C. *Rice and Slaves: Ethnicity and the Slave Trade in Colonial South Carolina* (1981).

Soderlund, Jean R. *Quakers and Slavery: A Divided Spirit* (1985).

Walvin, James. *Black Ivory: A History of British Slavery* (1993).

Regional Development

Bushman, Richard L. *From Puritan to Yankee: Character and the Social Order in Connecticut, 1690–1765* (1967).

Clemens, Paul G. E. *The Atlantic Economy and Colonial Maryland's Eastern Shore: From Tobacco to Grain* (1980).

Hann, John H. *Apalachee: The Land Between the Rivers* (1988).

Heyrman, Christine Leigh. *Commerce and Culture: The Maritime Communities of Colonial Massachusetts, 1690–1750* (1984).

Kross, Jessica. *The Evolution of an American Town: Newtown, New York, 1642–1775* (1983).

Landsman, Ned C. *Scotland and Its First American Colony, 1683–1765* (1985).

Nash, Gary B. *The Urban Crucible: Social Change, Political Consciousness, and the Origins of the American Revolution* (1979).

Rediker, Marcus. *Between the Devil and the Deep Blue Sea: Merchant Seamen, Pirates, and the Anglo-American Maritime World, 1700–1750* (1987).

Shammas, Carole. *The Pre-Industrial Consumer in England and America* (1990).

Wacker, Peter O. *Land and People: A Cultural Geography of Preindustrial New Jersey: Origins and Settlement Patterns* (1975).

Weber, David J. *The Spanish Frontier in North America* (1992).

BENJAMIN FRANKLIN AND LIGHTNING

Benjamin Franklin Drawing Electricity from the Sky, *by Benjamin West, c. 1805. Franklin's kite experiment demonstrating the electrical nature of lightning, along with his various activities promoting social welfare, placed him in the forefront of the American Enlightenment.*

Chapter 4

THE EXPANSION OF COLONIAL BRITISH AMERICA,

1720—1763

IN 1721, SMALLPOX hit Boston viciously, infecting about 6,000 residents and killing 844. Business stopped for several months, as almost every family battled the contagion. In many respects, this epidemic was unremarkable in the British American colonies: Settlers and Native Americans alike had previously experienced the ravages of disease. But this time, one Puritan minister took an unprecedented step. Cotton Mather, who thirty years earlier had helped aggravate the Salem witch hysteria, encouraged a Boston doctor, Zabdiel Boylston, to test inoculation. Mather had learned from Onesimus, his African slave, and from English scientific papers that inoculation was used in Africa and Turkey to prevent smallpox epidemics. An experiment would be risky, for the procedure involved introducing the smallpox virus into the body, thereby giving the person what was usually (but not always) a mild case of the disease. Many doctors, as well as much of Boston's populace, condemned the proposal, fearing further contamination. Nevertheless, Dr. Boylston inoculated about 250 persons over the course of a year. Those who submitted to the procedure had a much lower death rate than Bostonians who contracted the disease naturally.

Cotton Mather was far ahead of his time in advancing the theory that disease was caused by an invasion of the body by viruses, which he called invisible "worms." Significantly, it was a minister, rather than a physician or scientist, who advanced this hypothesis. During the eighteenth century, science lacked the rigid boundaries of complexity and specialization that would later separate it from other fields of intellectual endeavor. American theologians and philosophers, as well as doctors, naturalists, and astronomers, read the latest scientific literature from England and Europe. The great divide between science and religion did not yet exist, in either university training or intellectual pursuits. Like many other theologians, Mather understood epidemics as God's punishment for sin. But he also believed inoculation was a divine gift, that people should use any means available to combat disease.

Mather's support for inoculation has been called the greatest contribution to medicine by an American during the colonial period. Certainly it represented change, as the Enlightenment, a new intellectual movement, spread from Britain to the colonies. During the years 1720 to 1763, the British provinces experienced intellectual, religious, and social ferment as they continued to expand through North America. As new knowledge, beliefs, and consumer goods arrived from Europe, colonists from Maine to Georgia (founded in 1732) increasingly lived within a

CHRONOLOGY

1720 Theodore Jacob Frelinghuysen begins revivals in New Jersey	**1745** New Englanders conquer Louisbourg
1721–1722 Smallpox inoculation in Boston	**1747** Boston riot against impressment
1732 Founding of Georgia	**1750** Iron Act
Hat Act	**1754** Defeat of Virginia militia at Fort Necessity
1733 Molasses Act	Albany Congress proposes plan for colonial unity
1734 Jonathan Edwards starts revivals in Northampton, Massachusetts	**1754–1763** French and Indian War
1737 Walking Purchase in eastern Pennsylvania	**1755** Braddock's defeat near Fort Duquesne
1739 Stono Uprising in South Carolina	**1758** British capture Louisbourg
1739–1740 George Whitefield tours northern colonies	**1760** British conquer Montreal, seizing control of Canada
1739–1744 War of Jenkins's Ear	**1763** Pan-Indian war begins in Ohio Valley and Great Lakes region
1740 James Oglethorpe leads invasion of Florida	Proclamation of 1763 outlaws white settlement west of the Appalachians
1741 British attack on Cartagena	Paxton Boys revolt in Pennsylvania
1744–1748 King George's War	

common cultural framework. With rising wealth, colonial elites supported colleges, and purchased books and luxury goods. This common culture had important ties to England, yet was not altogether English, for immigrants from Scotland, Ireland, and the continent of Europe, and slaves from Africa brought ideas and practices from their native lands.

Immigration into the British colonies also promoted regional diversity, as the newcomers from Europe settled on the frontier from Pennsylvania to Georgia, and the numbers of enslaved Africans grew to 40 percent of the southern population. The Europeans came looking for land: When they set up farms in contested territory, they provoked conflicts with the Native Americans, French, and Spanish, resulting in a series of wars that lasted a quarter century. When the French and Indian War ended in 1763, the British colonies took a great deal of pride in their contribution to the victory, offering it as evidence of their economic and political maturity within the empire.

INTELLECTUAL TRENDS IN THE EIGHTEENTH CENTURY

The willingness of Mather and Boylston to try inoculation showed important changes in the way people viewed their world. The Puritan clergyman's personal journey from witch hunter in 1692 to medical investigator in 1721 reflected the growing inclination to find natural rather than supernatural causes for unexplained events. The Enlightenment blossomed first in Europe and then in America, encompassing political theory and philosophy as well as science. Though primarily intellectual, the Enlightenment had far-reaching effects, inspiring new technology as well as concepts of human freedom. For Americans, its greatest significance lay in the acceptance of natural rights philosophy, which paved the way for independence and republican government.

Newton and Locke

In the late seventeenth century, two English theorists, Sir Isaac Newton and John Locke, had challenged traditional notions that humans had no role in determining their fate, that they could only trust in God to rule the universe, even if divine will seemed inscrutable. They confronted this older view without denying the existence of God. Newton discovered universal laws that predictably govern the motion of planets, moons, and comets, the motion of falling bodies on earth (gravity), and the ebb and flow of tides. His work demonstrated that the universe operated according to fixed principles, which humans are capable of detecting and understanding. Locke built upon Newton's breakthrough in his extraordinarily influential *Essay Concerning Human Understanding* (1690). Locke argued against the accepted belief in innate knowledge, that infants are born with ideas implanted by God in their minds. He contended that all knowledge is gained by experience, not preordained at birth. Humans are born with the ability to learn, to use their acquired knowledge to benefit society.

Locke, and the Enlightenment thinkers he inspired, believed in freedom and the possibility of human progress, in the right of people to improve the conditions in which they live. Science, of course, was an important means of such improvement. The English philosopher also had a major impact upon eighteenth-century politics, in particular providing a theoretical basis for the American Revolution and the Constitution. In *Two Treatises on Civil Government* (1690), published to justify the Glorious Revolution in England, he argued that humans, according to natural law, had rights to life, liberty, and property. By social contract, they formed governments to guarantee those rights. If a state failed in its obligation, the people had the duty to rebel and establish a new government.

Education in the British Colonies

Throughout British North America, formal education beyond basic reading, writing, and arithmetic was rare, so few read the works of Locke and Newton directly. After 1720, however, as newspapers became more available and reprinted articles from London, provincial readers gained greater familiarity with Enlightenment thought. Many colonists learned to read, though boys and girls spent much of their time in apprenticeships, or with their parents, learning the occupations they would pursue as adults. Daughters learned housewifery and spinning, while sons mastered husbandry (farming) or a craft such as carpentry or printing. The availability of formal schooling varied widely by region, class, and gender. Nowhere did a system of

The New England Primer, *first published in the 1680s, taught children moral lessons along with their alphabet and spelling.*

universal, free, public education exist, though New England had some tax-supported schools. Everywhere, schools emphasized moral behavior and used religious texts.

New England made the greatest effort of the British colonies to educate its populace. In 1642, the Massachusetts legislature required parents and ministers to teach all children to read so they could obtain direct understanding of the Bible and the colony's laws. In 1647, the assemblymen took another step, ordering towns with at least fifty families to establish petty (elementary) schools, and those with one hundred families to maintain Latin grammar (secondary) schools. Connecticut and Plymouth passed similar legislation. Towns financed the schools in a variety of ways, through taxes, donations, bequests, and tuition. Though some towns ignored the laws, most New England children learned to read, whether from their parents, at the town school, or at dame schools, where women in their homes taught young girls and boys for a fee. Writing was considered a separate skill, less crucial for girls to learn. The percentage of New England females who could write and do arithmetic was significantly lower than for males, especially in rural districts. Girls, on the other hand, commonly learned sewing and knitting. Boys who planned to enter college attended grammar school from about age seven to

In colonial America, children—especially girls—were less likely to learn to write than to read. Many people could not write their signatures so they made a mark on legal documents, then someone else wrote their name next to the mark.

fourteen, studying Latin, elementary Greek, and sometimes Hebrew. Latin was necessary for the professions, including law, medicine, and the ministry, and to be considered a gentleman.

South of New England, the colonies lacked the common religious and educational values that impelled the Puritans to require town schools. In the Middle Colonies, churches and private teachers offered instruction. Affluent Quaker and Anglican boys were most likely to obtain formal education, though after 1750 girls and poor boys, including African Americans, had better access to schools. As in Massachusetts, females were much less likely to learn to write than males, especially if they lived outside New York and Philadelphia. In the Chesapeake, with dispersed settlement, neither Maryland nor Virginia had many schools. Upper-class boys and girls had private tutors, while middling families in some localities pooled their resources to establish schools. Overall, sons received much more instruction than daughters, and large numbers of poor whites obtained no education at all. Very few slaves learned to read and write, for owners thought these skills would breed discontent and enable them to forge passes, facilitating escape.

New England also surpassed other regions in higher education, as the Puritans established Harvard College in Massachusetts in 1636, and Yale College in Connecticut in 1701. William and Mary, founded in Virginia in 1693, was the only other college in the British colonies before the 1740s. None of the colonial colleges admitted women. The Puritans intended Harvard to preserve classical learning and civilization in what they considered a wilderness, provide liberal education to the region's male elite, and ensure a supply of well-educated ministers. Its faculty would transfer from England the goals and ideals of higher education, perpetuating them from one generation to the next. Harvard offered a curriculum of ethics, religion, logic, mathematics, Greek, Hebrew, rhetoric, and natural history (biology and geology). Most early graduates became clergymen, while others went into medicine, public service, teaching, commerce, and agriculture.

Harvard alumni in Connecticut established Yale to provide advanced education closer to home. Yale had a tentative beginning, but gained more stability by 1720, after receiving funds from Elihu Yale and about 800 volumes for its library, including the books of Locke, Newton, and other Enlightenment figures. The College of William and Mary in Virginia also struggled at first. Chartered by the Crown to train Anglican

The College of William and Mary in Virginia, designed by Christopher Wren.

clergy, educate young men in religion, and convert Native Americans, the school failed to offer college-level courses until the 1720s. Many elite families in the southern provinces continued to depend upon private tutors, trips to Britain, and northern colleges to educate their sons. No college existed in the Middle Colonies until the mid-eighteenth century, when the Great Awakening stimulated a surge in college founding (discussed later in this chapter).

The Growth of Science

After 1720, influenced by Scottish universities that quickly absorbed Enlightenment thinking into their curricula, American colleges expanded their coursework to include French, English literature, philosophy, and science. They offered mathematics and what was then called natural philosophy—astronomy, physics, and chemistry. The colleges hired some of their faculty from Scotland and purchased scientific apparatus, including telescopes, sextants, clocks, and orreries, which demonstrate the motion of planets and moons within the solar system.

American professors of natural philosophy were part of a larger community of scholars centered in the prestigious Royal Society of London, which published a journal, *Philosophical Transactions,* of the latest scientific ideas and knowledge. This transatlantic community included academics like John Winthrop of Harvard College, a descendant of the early Massachusetts governor, as well as largely self-taught men like Benjamin Franklin and John Bartram. More than thirty colonists belonged to the Royal Society. Scientists took from the Enlightenment a commitment to experiment and observe natural phenomena to obtain information that would lead to human progress. The Royal Society's goals for members were to "impart their knowledge to one another, and contribute what they can to the Grand design of improving Natural knowledge, and perfecting all Philosophical Arts, and Sciences. All for the Glory of God, the Honour and Advantage of these Kingdoms, and the Universal Good of Mankind." John Winthrop was the most renowned professor of natural philosophy in British America, with research interests in such wide-ranging subjects as sunspots, mathematics, earthquakes, and the weather. A member of the Royal Society, he published numerous papers in *Philosophical Transactions.* In the 1760s, Winthrop participated in an important international scientific effort to calculate the distance between the earth and sun, made possible by the transit of the planet Venus across the face of the sun. Venus had last crossed the sun in 1639, when no useful measurements had been made. In 1761, Winthrop was the only American scientist to participate, as he journeyed to Newfoundland to observe the transit. His data, combined with observations from the Cape of Good Hope, were inexact, but eight years later, scientists—including Winthrop—had another chance. This time, at least part of the transit could be viewed in the mainland British colonies. The stakes were high, as observers set up telescopes in Massachusetts, Pennsylvania, and elsewhere, because another transit would not occur for 105 years. The data were again imprecise, but when combined with measurements from around the globe, yielded results very close to the accepted

BENJAMIN FRANKLIN DESCRIBES HIS EXPERIMENTS ON ELECTRICITY 1755

In this letter, Franklin answers some queries from John Lining of Charleston, South Carolina, a physician who had published his own scientific work. Franklin's description of his experiments and explanation of how he came to the conclusion that lightning was electrical exemplify the scientific method. His use of men as guinea pigs in one experiment, however, is shocking in more ways than one.

Sir,   Philadelphia, March 18, 1755

I send you enclosed a paper containing some new experiments I have made, in pursuance of those by Mr. Canton that are printed with my last letters. I hope these, with my explanation of them, will afford you some entertainment.

In answer to your several enquiries. The tubes and globes we use here, are chiefly made here. The glass has a greenish cast, but is clear and hard, and, I think, better for electrical experiments than the white glass of London, which is not so hard. There are certainly great differences in glass. A white globe I had made here some years since, would never, by any means, be excited. Two of my friends tried it, as well as myself, without success. At length, putting it on an electric stand, a chain from the prime-conductor being in contact with it, I found it had the properties of a non-electric; for I could draw sparks from any part of it, though it was very clean and dry. . . .

As to the difference of conductors, there is not only this, that some will conduct Electricity in small quantities, and yet do not conduct it fast enough to produce the shock; but even among those that will conduct a shock, there are some that do it better than others. Mr. Kinnersley has found, by a very good experiment, that when the charge of a bottle hath an opportunity of passing two ways, i.e. strait through a trough of water ten feet long, and six inches square; or round about through twenty feet of wire, it passes through the wire, and not through the water, though that is the shortest course; the wire being the better conductor. When the wire is taken away, it passes through the water, as may be felt by a hand plunged in the water; but it cannot be felt in the water when the wire is used at the same time. Thus, though a small vial containing water will give a smart shock, one containing the same quantity of mercury will give one much stronger, the mercury being the better conductor; while one containing oil only, will scarce give any shock at all.

distance of 93 million miles between the earth and sun.

Other colonists, with less formal education, contributed to understanding the physical world. Though Benjamin Franklin never attended college, he performed important experiments in electricity. Perhaps best known for his diplomacy and political leadership during the Revolutionary era, he has become a symbol of the American Enlightenment for his efforts to improve society through science, inventions, and civic organizations. Franklin was born in Boston, ran away at age seventeen from an apprenticeship with his older brother, and arrived in Philadelphia nearly penniless. He built a highly successful printing business, publishing a newspaper, books, and *Poor Richard's Almanack,* which gained a readership throughout the colonies. He became wealthy

Your question, how I came first to think of proposing the experiment of drawing down the lightning, in order to ascertain its sameness with the electric fluid, I cannot answer better than by giving you an extract from the minutes I used to keep of the experiments I made. . . . By this extract you will see that the thought was not so much "an out-of-the-way one," but that it might have occurred to any electrician.

"Nov. 7, 1749. Electrical fluid agrees with lightning in these particulars: 1. Giving light. 2. Colour of the light. 3. Crooked direction. 4. Swift motion. 5. Being conducted by metals. 6. Crack or noise in exploding. 7. Subsisting in water or ice. 8. Rending bodies it passes through. 9. Destroying animals. 10. Melting metals. 11. Firing inflammable substances. 12. Sulphureous smell. The electric fluid is attracted by points. We do not know whether this property is in lightning. But since they agree in all the particulars wherein we can already compare them, is it not probable they agree likewise in this? Let the experiment be made." . . .

The knocking down of the six men was performed with two of my large jarrs not fully charged. I laid one end of my discharging rod upon the head of the first; he laid his hand on the head of the second; the second his hand on the head of the third, and so to the last, who held, in his hand, the chain that was connected with the outside of the jarrs. When they were thus placed, I applied the other end of my rod to the prime-conductor, and they all dropt together. When they got up, they all declared they had not felt any stroke, and wondered how they came to fall; nor did any of them either hear the crack, or see the light of it. You suppose it a dangerous experiment; but I had once suffered the same myself, receiving, by accident, an equal stroke through my head, that struck me down, without hurting me: And I had seen a young woman that was about to be electrified through the feet, (for some indisposition) receive a greater charge through the head, by inadvertently stooping forward to look at the placing of her feet, till her forehead (as she was very tall) came too near my prime-conductor: She dropt, but instantly got up again, complaining of nothing. A person so struck, sinks down doubled, or folded together as it were, the joints losing their strength and stiffness at once, so that he drops on the spot where he stood, instantly, and there is no previous staggering, nor does he ever fall lengthwise. Too great a charge might, indeed, kill a man, but I have not yet seen any hurt done by it. It would certainly, as you observe, be the easiest of all deaths. . . .

I am, &c. B.F.

enough to retire from his print shop at age forty-two. Throughout his life, Franklin put the Enlightenment ideal of human progress into action. He founded a debating club to discuss politics, morals, and natural philosophy, and helped establish the first American lending library, a hospital, and the College of Philadelphia. Franklin's experiments in electricity yielded information about its properties, including the basic concepts of "plus" and "minus." His inventions, which applied scientific principles to improving daily life, included bifocal eyeglasses, the lightning rod, and an iron stove that was more efficient than colonial fireplaces.

John Bartram, also of Pennsylvania, was the most energetic of American naturalists, whose chief contribution to science was collecting specimens of New World plant life. In return for a yearly pension from the king and payment for seeds he sent to wealthy collectors in England, Bartram traveled all over the eastern seaboard searching for new plants and animals. His efforts greatly expanded botanical knowledge of the Western Hemisphere, for he sent specimens to such scholars as Carl Linnaeus, the Swedish author of the modern classification system.

Another prominent American naturalist was Cadwallader Colden, a Scot who immigrated to the colonies after receiving his medical degree. Like many well-educated doctors, Colden had broad interests in science. While serving as surveyor-general and lieutenant-governor of New York, he collected and classified plants in the neighborhood of his estate. He corresponded with European botanists, sending them specimens and descriptions. As their demands became overwhelming, Colden taught his daughter, Jane, how to classify according to Linnaeus' scheme. Her accurate descriptions and drawings earned high praise from Linnaeus, Bartram, and other naturalists. Cadwallader Colden also ventured into the field of physics, publishing a pamphlet in which he attempted unsuccessfully to explain the causes of gravity.

Changes in Medical Practice

Just as Colden and other university-trained doctors were interested in many scientific fields, the practice of medicine itself attracted people of widely different backgrounds. Medicine was beginning to develop as a profession. During the colonial period, men with formal medical education comprised a small proportion of the people who provided care for disease, physical injury, and childbirth. Having completed formal coursework abroad—the first medical school in the British colonies, located in Philadelphia, did not open until 1766—educated physicians were at the top of their profession, and charged the highest fees. Consequently, they practiced primarily in the cities, with a wealthy clientele. Below them were men who learned their craft as apprentices; though they assumed the title of doctor in the colonies, they were actually akin to the surgeon-apothecaries of Great Britain. As surgeons, they performed emergency procedures such as setting bones, amputating limbs, and removing superficial tumors, but no major surgery. As apothecaries, they prepared and prescribed drugs for a variety of illnesses.

Female midwives traditionally attended childbirth, treated the ill, and prescribed herbal remedies. Having learned their skills through informal apprenticeships and from witnessing the childbirths of neighbors and relatives, they received payment for their services. During the colonial period, childbirth was the province of women. As an expectant mother's labor began, she called together a group of women, presided over by the midwife, who assisted in the birth. In the early stages of her labor, the woman provided special refreshments, called "groaning beer" and "groaning cakes." The attendants helped her walk around and offered herbal teas or liquor to relieve the pain. In normal deliveries, the mother squatted on a "midwife's stool" or remained standing while supported by several women. If complications occurred, the midwife manipulated the infant manually, but would not perform a Caesarean section. In the worst cases, the midwife had to kill the child; sometimes the mother died. Without modern antibiotics, women constantly faced the threat of infection during pregnancy and in the weeks following delivery.

In the last half of the eighteenth century, the practice of obstetrics changed. In 1762, Dr. William Shippen, Jr., returned from studying medicine in England and Scotland to give lectures in anatomy to Philadelphia midwives and doctors. Soon he accepted only male students; physicians in Boston and New York followed his example. Shippen established an obstetrical practice of his own, quickly attracting well-to-do patients who expected, in return for his higher fee, a more elevated level of care than they received from midwives. Affluent urban women were convinced that the male physicians offered a better chance for a safe, less painful delivery. The doctors' obstetrical training, their use of opiates and instruments such as forceps, spelled progress to these women, inducing them to abandon the traditional woman-dominated rituals of childbirth. That the new obstetrics brought improvement is doubtful. The male doctors, faced with taboos against observing the private parts of ladies, attended their clients in darkened rooms, with the woman lying in bed under covers. The physicians also lacked the means to prevent infection; their use of blood-letting and opium could impede safe delivery. Success still depended primarily upon the skill and experience of the practitioner, whether midwife or physician. In any case, midwives continued to attend the great majority of women, those who lived in rural areas and the poor who could not afford the doctors' fees.

THE GREAT AWAKENING

As Enlightenment ideas gained sway among British colonial elites and in the colleges by 1720, many Protestant ministers embraced Christian rationalism, a theology influenced by Locke and other theorists. Stressing moral, rational behavior and the free will of individuals to lead their lives and achieve salvation, they argued that one could "follow God and obey Reason" at the same time. Some rationalists spoke of an impersonal God who had long ago created the universe to operate according to natural laws, rather than a loving or angry God who controlled a person's daily life. For many, the rationalist religion was comforting, because it included in the church all who tried to live decent Christian lives, not just those who believed they were saved. To others, however, Christian rationalism was heretical, for it rejected the Calvinist belief that salvation came from grace, as the gift of God, and that people must be saved to be full members of the church.

From the 1720s to the 1760s, ministers from various denominations called for the renewal of these beliefs in a series of revivals, known as the Great Awakening. Several of the most important Awakeners brought the impetus for revival from Europe and Great Britain. Religious ferment convulsed British North America, spreading from the churches to threaten social and political authority.

Religious Diversity Before the Great Awakening

In 1720, the British provinces varied widely in religious and ethnic makeup. New England was the most homogeneous, for Massachusetts, New Hampshire, and Connecticut remained predominantly Puritan and of English descent. The established Puritan churches received tax support, but Anglicans, Baptists, and Quakers could also worship freely. Rhode Island, which still embraced the principles of religious liberty and separation of church and state, was home to various denominations, including Quakers, Baptists, and Separatists.

From their founding, the Middle Colonies offered an open door to people of various backgrounds, as both the Dutch West India Company and the duke of York tried to attract settlers. In the late seventeenth century, according to one report, residents of New York City spoke eighteen different languages, including Dutch, Swedish, various African languages, English, German, and French. In eastern New Jersey, Scottish Presbyterians, Dutch Reformed, New England Puritans, Baptists, and Quakers settled towns and plantations, and farther south, on both sides of the Delaware River, Native Americans, Dutch, Swedes, and Finns met the Quakers who accompanied William Penn. Philadelphia and its environs in the 1720s boasted organized meetings of Swedish Lutherans, Quakers, Mennonites, Baptists, Anglicans, Presbyterians, Dunkards, German Reformed, Dutch Reformed, German Lutherans, and Roman Catholics. Though disputes occasionally arose between churches, the Quaker government upheld liberty of conscience throughout the colonial period.

With few towns in the Chesapeake, the Anglican church, which had been established in Virginia since 1607 and in Maryland since 1702, suffered from southern rural conditions. With large parishes, ministers in Virginia faced serious obstacles in meeting the spiritual needs of their scattered congregations. Only half of the Anglican churches had regular preachers. Few planters were interested in converting their African slaves, who kept—and passed on to their children—many traditional African beliefs. The colony's laws against nonconformity prevented most dissent, so only a few Presbyterians and Quakers worshipped openly. In Maryland, many Quakers and Roman Catholics retained their faith, but suffered legal disabilities.

The established Church of England in South Carolina was in better condition than in Virginia; some prosperous parishes could pay adequately their dedicated, well-trained clergy. Even so, Presbyterians, Baptists, Huguenots, and Quakers worshiped freely, for the proprietors had actively recruited dissenters from England, Scotland, and France to increase population and obtain their political support.

The Great Awakening shattered the existing church structure of the colonies, as congregations wakened to the teachings and vigorous preaching style of revivalist, or New Light, ministers. Religious diversity grew in provinces where established churches, with government support, dominated religious life—especially Puritan churches in Connecticut and Massachusetts, and the Anglican establishment in Virginia. As a result of the revivals, these colonies became more like Rhode

Island, New York, New Jersey, Pennsylvania, and South Carolina, where many denominations already flourished.

Early Revivals in the Middle Colonies and New England

In 1720, New Jersey felt the first stirrings of the Great Awakening, when Theodore Jacob Frelinghuysen emigrated from Holland to serve four churches in the Raritan Valley. He had been educated in Dutch Reformed pietism, which emphasized the importance of conversion and personal religious experience (or piety). Using an emotional, revivalist preaching style, he led many people to experience salvation. But Frelinghuysen offended members of his congregations by refusing communion and baptism of their children to the unconverted. He created a split in the Dutch Reformed churches of New Jersey between his followers, who believed a person must experience God's saving grace before participating in church sacraments, and his opponents, who thought that a commitment to living a godly life was sufficient. This was the fundamental conflict between those who supported and opposed the Great Awakening.

Next, revivals engulfed Presbyterian churches in New Jersey, as they adopted doctrines preached by Gilbert and John Tennent, the sons of William Tennent, a Scots-Irish immigrant and Presbyterian minister. The younger Tennents, convinced by their father of the importance of religious piety and conversion, took pulpits in New Brunswick and Freehold, close to Frelinghuysen's congregations. Impressed by the Dutch Reformed pastor's style of preaching, they inspired revivals of their own. Meanwhile, in Neshaminy, Pennsylvania, the elder Tennent established a seminary, called the "Log College" by his critics, where many New Light ministers received training.

In New England, revivals began in 1734, when minister Jonathan Edwards of Northampton, in the Connecticut River valley of western Massachusetts, preached a series of sermons on salvation, inclining many of his parishioners to believe they were saved. They went through the process of self-judgment— first feeling despair as sinners who were damned to hell, then rejoicing in the conviction that God rescued them from this fate. Edwards wrote to a colleague that "this town never was so full of Love, nor so full of Joy,

Reverend Gilbert Tennent, son of the founder of the "Log College," was an avid New Light minister during the Great Awakening.

nor so full of distress as it has lately been." Over the next few years, the revival spread to other towns along the Connecticut River.

Revivalism Takes Fire

Beginning in 1739, the Great Awakening spread throughout the British mainland colonies after a young Anglican minister, George Whitefield, arrived from England to tour the Middle Colonies. Called the Grand Itinerant, he had a magnificent voice, ranging from a whisper to a roar, that could be heard by large crowds in fields and city streets. Benjamin Franklin described one of these occasions in Philadelphia, as Whitefield

> had a loud and clear voice, and articulated his words and sentences so perfectly that he might be heard and understood at a great distance, especially as his auditories, how-

George Whitefield, the itinerant English evangelist, had a spellbinding effect on his listeners, as portrayed here by John Wollaston.

large as 8,000 in Boston. Other New Light ministers followed, including Gilbert Tennent and James Davenport, a Puritan preacher of Southold, Long Island. Davenport took the Awakening to extremes, harshly attacking other pastors as "unconverted." In 1743, he instigated the burning of books written by well-known clergymen; a year later he repented this excess.

The full force of the Awakening hit the south later than New England and the Middle Atlantic. During the 1740s, Presbyterian missionaries—men who received their education at Tennent's Log College—worked successfully among Scots-Irish immigrants to set up churches on the southern frontier. The new settlements were a fertile field for the revivalists because few regular clergy had migrated west. The more explosive Baptist revivals began a decade later, in the 1750s, when itinerants traveled through Virginia and North Carolina making converts and forming churches. The Baptists believed in adult baptism—that individuals should be saved before they are baptized. With their emotional religious style and challenge to the Anglican establishment in Virginia, they appealed particularly to ordinary white farmers and enslaved African Americans. Followers called each other "Sister" and "Brother," whether slave or free, affluent or poor. They refused to attend their local parish services and condemned many aspects of gentry culture, including horseracing, cockfights, elegant dress, and entertaining on Sunday. Lacking formal churches, Baptists met in fields and homes. The ministry was open to all, even women and slaves, with no requirement for college training.

The Awakening's Impact

The revivals proved to be socially divisive, as many communities split into two groups, the "New Lights" and the "Old Lights." The style of most New Light preachers was to give impassioned, extemporaneous sermons that contrasted dramatically with the closely reasoned sermons of their opponents, the rationalist Old Light ministers. New Lights believed that salvation was more important than religious training; they required a "saved" ministry, with a dynamic preaching style that helped to demonstrate one's conversion. Congregations responded by fainting, shrieking, and shedding tears. Old Light clergymen, who defended their advanced education in theology, Greek, Hebrew,

ever numerous, observed the most exact silence. He preached one evening from the top of the courthouse steps, which are in the middle of Market Street and on the west side of Second Street, which crosses it at right angles. Both streets were filled with his hearers to a considerable distance.

Franklin calculated that 25,000 people could easily hear the spectacular preacher at one time.

Whitefield told enthusiastic audiences that they must change their ways and seek God. He found adherents across denominational lines and among native-born Americans and immigrants alike—English, Scots-Irish, African Americans, Dutch, Germans, and Welsh. In 1740, Jonathan Edwards invited Whitefield to Northampton, prompting the itinerant to travel through New England, where he attracted crowds as

NATHAN COLE DESCRIBES GOING TO HEAR REVEREND GEORGE WHITEFIELD, 1740

This Connecticut farmer's account of Reverend George Whitefield's visit to Middletown vividly portrays how people throughout the countryside heard of the New Light evangelist's arrival and flocked to hear him preach. Cole's last sentence shows the effectiveness of Whitefield's message that salvation came from God, not from an individual's good works.

Now it pleased God to send Mr. Whitefield into this land; and my hearing of his preaching at Philadelphia, like one of the old apostles, and many thousands flocking to hear him preach the Gospel, and great numbers were converted to Christ, I felt the Spirit of God drawing me by conviction; I longed to see and hear him and wished he would come this way. I heard he was come to New York and the Jerseys and great multitudes flocking after him under great concern for their souls which brought on my concern more and more, hoping soon to see him; but next I heard he was at Long Island, then at Boston, and next at Northampton. Then on a sudden, in the morning about 8 or 9 of the clock there came a messenger and said Mr. Whitefield preached at Hartford and Wethersfield yesterday and is to preach at Middletown this morning at ten of the clock. I was in my field at work. I dropped my tool that I had in my hand and ran home to my wife, telling her to make ready quickly to go and hear Mr. Whitefield preach at Middletown, then ran to my pasture for my horse with all my might, fearing that I should be too late. Having my horse, I with my wife soon mounted the horse and went forward as fast as I thought the horse could bear; and when my horse got much out of breath, I would get down and put my wife on the saddle and bid her ride as fast as she could and not stop or slack for me except I bade her, and so I would run until I was much out of breath and then mount my horse again, and so I did several times to favour my horse. We improved every moment to get along as if we were fleeing for our lives, all the while fearing we should be too late to hear the sermon, for we had twelve miles to ride double in little more than an hour and we went round by the upper housen parish. And when we came within about half a

and ethics, resented accusations that they were unsaved. In turn, they charged the revivalists with being unlearned.

As congregations broke apart, bitter disputes ensued over church property and tax support, spilling what had begun as a religious controversy into the courts and politics. Where strong established churches existed—as in Massachusetts, Connecticut, and Virginia—the New Lights challenged political as well as religious authority. In response, the Connecticut As-

sembly, for example, passed an Anti-Itinerancy Act, which made it illegal for a clergyman to preach in another's parish without his permission and repealed the 1708 law permitting religious dissent. While this heavy-handed approach prevailed in the short run, it generated long-term support for freedom of worship.

Higher education in the British colonies also felt the flames of revivalistic fervor. Yale College was at the center of the intense religious and political battles in Connecticut, as George Whitefield, Gilbert Tennent, mile or a mile of the road that comes down from Hartford, Wethersfield, and Stepney to Middletown, on high land I saw before me a cloud of fog arising. I first thought it came from the great river, but as I came nearer the road I heard a noise of horses' feet coming down the road, and this cloud was a cloud of dust made by the horses' feet. It arose some rods into the air over the tops of hills and trees; and when I came within about 20 rods of the road, I could see men and horses slipping along in the cloud like shadows, and as I drew nearer it seemed like a steady stream of horses and their riders, scarcely a horse more than his length behind another, all of a lather and foam with sweat, their breath rolling out of their nostrils every jump. Every horse seemed to go with all his might to carry his rider to hear news from heaven for the saving of souls. It made me tremble to see the sight, how the world was in a struggle. I found a vacancy between two horses to slip in mine and my wife said "Law, our clothes will be all spoiled, see how they look," for they were so covered with dust that they looked almost all of a colour, coats, hats, shirts, and horse. We went down in the stream but heard no man speak a word all the way for 3 miles but every one pressing forward in great haste; and when we got to Middletown old meeting house, there was a great multitude, it was said to be 3 or 4,000 of people, assembled together. We dismounted and shook off our dust, and the ministers were then coming to the meeting house. I turned and looked towards the Great River and saw the ferry boats running swift backward and forward bringing over loads of people, and the oars rowed nimble and quick. Everything, men, horses, and boats seemed to be struggling for life. The land and banks over the river looked black with people and horses; all along the 12 miles I saw no man at work in his field, but all seemed to be gone. When I saw Mr. Whitefield come upon the scaffold, he looked almost angelical; a young, slim, slender youth, before some thousands of people with a bold undaunted countenance. And my hearing how God was with him everywhere as he came along, it solemnized my mind and put me into a trembling fear before he began to preach; for he looked as if he was clothed with authority from the Great God, and a sweet solemn solemnity sat upon his brow, and my hearing him preach gave me a heart wound. By God's blessing, my old foundation was broken up, and I saw that my righteousness would not save me.

Jonathan Edwards, and James Davenport all stopped at New Haven on their preaching tours. When the New Haven church separated, a large number of students, many of them studying for the ministry, followed the New Lights. They skipped classes to attend revivals, challenged Yale's curriculum, and questioned whether their teachers were saved. To suppress the student rebellion, Thomas Clap, head of the college, obtained permission from the Connecticut Assembly to expel any student who attended New Light services.

Clap's opposition to the Awakening was not permanent, however, for by 1753 he himself had become a New Light. In 1764, George Whitefield preached in the college chapel. As in many congregations, people eventually found ways to heal the bitterness and division that the Great Awakening had caused.

A more lasting effect of the revivals was the founding of new colleges. Until the mid-1740s, only Harvard, William and Mary, and Yale—all with ties to established churches—existed in the British colonies.

The revivals created a need for ministerial training, for despite their emphasis on a converted ministry, most New Lights believed that preachers should have advanced education. Between 1746 and 1769, the revivalists founded the College of New Jersey (now Princeton), the College of Rhode Island (Brown), Queen's College (Rutgers) in New Jersey, and Dartmouth College in New Hampshire. Anglicans established King's College (Columbia) in New York City, while a group of civic leaders, headed by Benjamin Franklin, started the College of Philadelphia (University of Pennsylvania) on a nonsectarian basis. Though each of these new schools except the College of Philadelphia was tied to a specific religious denomination, they all accepted young men of various faiths. These new colleges taught traditional subjects, including classical languages, but also adopted the new curricula in mathematics, science, and modern languages.

IMMIGRATION AND EXPANSION

Between 1720 and 1760, the population of British North America grew by more than 1 million people, from 472,000 to 1,600,000. Much of this growth came from natural increase, as the creole (or native-born) sons and daughters of white immigrants and enslaved Africans married younger and had more children than their parents. But new arrivals also spurred population growth, as thousands of Germans and Scots-Irish immigrated, and slave traders continued to import blacks.

The newcomers brought ideas, religious beliefs, skills, and ways of life that significantly altered the cultural mix of the British colonies. Some played important roles in spreading the Enlightenment, while others started the Great Awakening. The immigrants from the European continent and the British Isles sought a new beginning in "the best poor man's country": Many disembarked in the Middle Colonies, traveling west to settle the backcountry from Pennsylvania south through the Shenandoah Valley to the Carolinas. Others went directly to Georgia, which reformers started in 1732 as a haven for the poor. The population explosion and demand for new lands brought the British colonists face to face with the Spanish in

Florida, the French in Canada and the Ohio Valley, and Native Americans all along the frontier. The result was war—a series of struggles lasting over twenty years.

German and Scots-Irish Immigrants

More than 100,000 Germans left their homelands for America during the century after 1683; most of them immigrated between 1727 and 1756. Some were forced out by religious persecution, oppressive regulations, and the devastation of war; others pulled up stakes to find economic opportunity. Promoters called "newlanders" told Germans of cheap fertile land and mild government in the British colonies. Many immigrants paid their own passage. Those who could not signed on as "redemptioners," the equivalent of indentured servants, whose labor would be sold for a number of years upon arrival, often to Germans already living in the colonies. Immigrants went to ports from New York to Georgia, with most entering the Delaware Valley. Some Germans remained in Philadelphia, but the majority headed for the Pennsylvania hinterland and south through the backcountry of Maryland, Virginia, and the Carolinas. By 1775, Germans comprised one-third of the population of Pennsylvania and one-tenth of the people of the mainland British colonies.

German-speaking immigrants found the freedom they sought in North America, congregating in distinct communities, building separate churches and schools, and maintaining German language and culture. Pennsylvania was the heart of German America, as the colony's religious freedom allowed a multitude of sects and churches to flourish—the Mennonites, Amish, Brethren, Moravians, Schwenkfelders, Lutheran, and Reformed.

Cultural exchange between the Germans and English enriched American society. German churches introduced the sophisticated choral music of their homelands, installing organs in Philadelphia, Germantown, and Lancaster, Pennsylvania. The printer Christopher Saur reprinted German hymnals along with his German-language newspaper and almanac. Congregations founded schools in which children learned both German and English. Immigrants retained the old tongue in their churches and homes, but used English in business, the courts, and politics. In material culture, they transported Old World traditions, then created new forms of expression as they responded to British culture and the new environment. German American decorative arts proliferated by the 1740s, in house ornaments, furniture, and elaborately illustrated documents, such as marriage certificates, with gothic *Fraktur* lettering.

German farm women did much heavier fieldwork than most English wives, but otherwise played a similar role in maintaining domestic culture. Germans favored the more efficient European stoves over English fireplaces, and pewter over tinware. In diet, they ate relatively little meat, and preferred coffee to tea. But like their English neighbors, German women served as midwives and dispensed herbal remedies.

Though some German immigrants engaged in politics and law, most remained uninvolved in government before the Revolution. The majority of Germans lived many miles from the provincial capitals located near the seaboard, making political participation difficult. As non-British immigrants with little wealth, they needed time to become naturalized, learn the language and political culture, and establish themselves economically. As exiles from persecution, high taxes, and war, Germans were grateful for the high degree of freedom that they found in the new land.

Large numbers of Scots, Scots-Irish, and Irish Catholics also came during the eighteenth century, settling in New York, Pennsylvania, Delaware, western Maryland, and the southern backcountry. Most were Ulster Scots (or Scots-Irish as they were called in America), Presbyterians whose families had migrated during the 1600s from Scotland to northern Ireland in search of economic opportunity. There they had combined tenant farming and weaving until the early eighteenth century, when their leases expired. Because landlords raised rents exorbitantly, many Ulster Scots left with

MAP 4.1   GERMAN AND SCOTS-IRISH SETTLEMENTS IN COLONIAL BRITISH AMERICA, CA. 1760

their families for the colonies. The first large wave of immigrants departed during 1717–1718; poor harvests and downturns in the linen industry impelled successive groups toward America. Smaller numbers of Irish Catholics, mostly single young men, migrated from southern Ireland throughout the pre-Revolutionary period.

The baptismal certificate is an example of German-American "fraktur," or documents illustrated with color designs and drawings.

In the colonies, the Scots-Irish achieved a reputation as tough defenders of the frontier. As relatively late arrivals, they had to stake out farms on the edges of existing white settlements to obtain enough good land to raise grain, livestock, and the flax they needed to weave linen cloth. The combination of agriculture and linen manufacture was a distinctive contribution of the Ulster Scots to the colonial economy. As frontier inhabitants, the Scots-Irish came into frequent contact with Native Americans, often with tragic results. Like the English colonists of seventeenth-century New England and Virginia, the new settlers often marked out their farms on Indian hunting lands without negotiating a sale. One Pennsylvania frontiersman, not recognizing the Indians' rights, echoed the early Puritans when he argued that it was contrary to "the laws of God and nature, that so much land should be idle, while so many Christians wanted it to labor on, and to raise their bread."

The Founding of Georgia

The last of the British mainland colonies, Georgia (named for King George II, who governed from 1727 to 1760), lured many German and Scots-Irish immigrants, as well as Scots and English. Animated by Enlightenment ideals of human progress and freedom,

James Oglethorpe and John Viscount Percival, members of the Associates of the Late Doctor Bray, a philanthropic society, sought a charter for the colony. After studying the deplorable conditions of debtors' prisons in England, they were convinced that something had to be done to help the poor. They also argued that the settlement could serve as a buffer between Spanish Florida and South Carolina. The English had craved the region since the late seventeenth century when Carolinians destroyed the Spanish missions of Guale. George II granted the charter, placing control of the colony in the hands of trustees, or proprietors, who could neither receive financial benefits from the province nor own land within its bounds.

The double function of Georgia as a haven for the poor and military outpost shaped the terms under which settlers immigrated. The trustees intended to create a peaceful, moral society of small farmers in which everyone, except indentured servants, worked for themselves. The proprietors wanted to avoid duplicating lowland South Carolina where large plantation owners lived off the toil of their slaves. The Georgia Trustees, led by Oglethorpe, set three significant policies: They prohibited importation of hard liquor, banned slaveholding, and limited land ownership to 500 acres or less. Each free male immigrant was granted land at no charge, but no one could buy or sell real estate, and only men could inherit land. The trustees hoped to keep Georgia as a refuge for small farmers who, coincidentally, would defend the southern frontier. The rule that only men could inherit land, a carryover from the Middle Ages called "tail-male," meant that each farm must be owned by a man who, at least ideally, could fight.

The settlement of Georgia held promise, for in February 1733, the ship *Anne* with approximately one hundred passengers arrived at a site on the Savannah River. Here they built the first town, Savannah, on a high bluff overlooking the river. Oglethorpe purchased land from the Native Americans and pledged to prevent price gouging in trade, a significant complaint of the Indians against South Carolina merchants. He established alliances with Lower Creeks, Cherokees, and Chickasaws against Spanish Florida, not least because English traders offered better merchandise than their rivals. The congenial negotiations boded well for the new colony.

But many settlers in Georgia believed that the prohibitions on liquor, land sales, and slavery were unrea-

A view of Savannah as it stood on the 29th of March 1734.

sonable. They could do little to change the colony's direction because they lacked an elective assembly. The colonists knew that the embargo on rum, a major Caribbean commodity, prevented expansion of trade with the West Indies, a ready market for their abundant lumber. The bans on slavery and large landholdings were also unpopular with many settlers, who coveted the grander lifestyle of planters north of the Savannah River, in South Carolina.

In consequence, Georgia grew slowly, as some settlers left almost immediately. Of an estimated 5,000 people who arrived in Georgia before 1751, fewer than one-half remained. The trustees gradually recognized their failure, allowing the importation of rum in 1742, and land sales and slavery in 1750. Preparing to turn the colony over to the Crown, in 1751 they called together Georgia's first elected assembly, which obtained legislative powers three years later when the royal government took control. The Georgia population swelled as South Carolinians migrated across the Savannah River, transforming Georgia into a slave society. By 1773, the province had 33,000 inhabitants, of whom 45 percent were enslaved blacks.

Despite its halting start before 1750, Georgia attracted settlers of a variety of nationalities and reli-gions. The colony tapped the eighteenth-century flow of European immigrants, including a group of Spanish and German Jews who settled in Savannah, and German-speaking Lutherans who founded Ebenezer and other farming communities. One of the Lutheran ministers described their satisfaction with the new land: "Every year God gives them what they need. And since they have been able to earn something apart from agriculture, through the mills which have been built and in many other ways, they have managed rather well with God's blessing, and have led a calm and quiet life of blessedness and honesty." Another group of German Protestants, the Moravians, were less content in Georgia, where they hoped to convert the Native Americans. Led by Count Nikolaus Ludwig von Zinzendorf, they arrived in 1735 and were gone five years later, because as pacifists, Moravian men could not serve in the militia. When the threat of Spanish invasion intensified in the late 1730s, most of the Moravians departed for Pennsylvania, which required no military service. In contrast were the Scottish Highlanders, whom the trustees recruited in 1735 for their reputation as rugged soldiers. They agreed to settle at an outpost on the Altamaha River to provide defense against Spanish Florida.

MAP 4.2   AFRICAN-AMERICAN POPULATION IN
COLONIAL BRITISH AMERICA, CA. 1760

Nowhere—not even in Quaker Pennsylvania—did significant abolitionism exist before 1750. Like the Germans and Scots-Irish, Africans helped diversify the American population and shape its culture. Though the number of African Americans grew naturally in many places, especially in the Chesapeake, slave traders imported over 200,000 people between 1720 and the Revolution, most from West and Central Africa, from Senegambia to Angola. In 1750, blacks comprised one-fifth of the population of the mainland colonies, including about 40 percent in the Chesapeake and the Lower South. In comparison, enslaved Africans were 90 percent in the British West Indies, where much larger numbers were imported each year to replace people who died from harsh working conditions and a lethal disease environment.

As the number of African Americans increased and slave societies matured on the mainland, blacks created patterns of community, work, and culture. Extended kinship networks structured community life on large plantations, and even in places where slaves lived in small numbers, such as in northern urban households, family ties remained paramount. Blacks were most successful in perpetuating African language and customs in regions where they were most numerous, particularly the South Carolina low country and, later, Georgia. Because they came from hundreds of societies in Africa, with many different cultural attributes, they had difficulty keeping traditional ways intact. They melded African and European forms together, and in the process, influenced evolving mainstream cultures, especially in the south.

The opportunity of slaves to engage in independent activities varied with the amount of time they had to spend working for their master. In South Carolina, blacks labored by the task; each slave received a certain

The Growth of the African American Population

The failure of the trustees to create a free society in Georgia was symptomatic of the entrenchment of slavery in America, as Africans labored throughout the British mainland colonies in perpetual bondage.

This vivid painting, The Old Plantation, *by an unknown artist, portrays social life among enslaved Africans on a southern plantation. The banjo is just one of the African instruments that became incorporated into American music.*

amount of work to perform each day—a field to hoe, thread to spin, a fence to build. Those who completed their assignments quickly had time to raise their own crops and livestock. Consequently, Carolina slaves participated in trade, selling their production at the "Negro market" in Charleston on Sundays. As in Africa, women were responsible for marketing the family's goods. In the Chesapeake, most slaves on plantations labored for a specified number of hours rather than by the task. They planted, weeded, or harvested in gangs until the overseer told them to stop. As a result, they had little time to work for themselves.

The persistence of African culture, and its influence on white Americans, was conspicuous in language, food, music, dance, and religion. Some newly arrived Africans knew Dutch, Spanish, Portuguese, French, or English from former contacts in Africa or the West Indies, but to communicate with other slaves and with Europeans, most adopted creole speech, a combination of English and African languages. In the Lower South, for instance, the creole tongue known as Gullah evolved from English and various languages from southern Nigeria, the Gold Coast, Angola, and Senegambia. African Americans retained black dialect from creole, contributing to a group identity separate from their masters. For example, most blacks used the word *buckra,* from the African word meaning "he who governs," to refer to white men. Africans also influenced white speech patterns, when white children and immigrants sometimes adopted African American dialect. One British traveler complained that plantation owners allowed "their children . . . to prowl amongst the young Negroes, which insensibly causes them to imbibe their manners and broken speech." Some African words became part of American vocabulary, including cola, yam, goober (peanut), and toting (carrying) a package.

Blacks contributed to the food and material culture of British America, popularizing new foods such as okra, melons, and bananas. They made clay pipes, pottery, and baskets with African designs, and carved eating utensils, chairs, and other useful objects from wood. They built houses on African models rather than European. In music, they introduced the use of percussion instruments—cymbals, tambourines, and drums—to British military bands. While masters discouraged Africans from drumming because of the potential to call others to revolt, whites enjoyed the music of black fiddlers. Slaves helped create the Virginia "jig," a fusion of African and European elements, accompanied by banjos and fiddles.

Along with whites, during the Great Awakening, Africans shaped the forms of worship in southern Baptist churches, as they responded with enthusiasm to traveling missionaries. Blacks retained traditional African concepts of the hereafter, where the deceased reunited with ancestors, combining these beliefs with European views of heaven. Funerals remained important to African Americans throughout the colonies, as mourners buried the dead facing Africa, with traditional rituals, music, and dance. In Philadelphia, for example, the blacks' burial ground was the focus of community activities where they gathered on Sundays and holidays, "dancing after the manner of their several nations in Africa, and speaking and singing in their native dialects." Blacks also passed down African medical practice, a combination of physical and psychological treatment including magic. More women than men were African American doctors, practicing midwifery as well as nursing and providing cures.

Despite cultural exchange and indications of human understanding, the antagonism and economic exploitation inherent in slavery poisoned relationships among whites and blacks. Whites believed that African Americans were an inferior race; masters used their power in the slave system to control their human property with harsh punishments. Nevertheless, blacks refused to accept their subordinate position, as increasing numbers ran away or were truant for weeks at a time.

Some enslaved Africans took more violent means, killing their masters or setting fire to fields and homes. In 1739, a group of more than fifty bondmen mounted an armed revolt near the Stono River in South Carolina. For most of a day, they marched with drums and banners from one plantation to another, killing about twenty whites. When armed planters defeated the rebels in battle, some of the slaves regrouped and headed for St. Augustine, Florida. But the South Carolina militia pursued the insurgents, putting to death everyone suspected of being involved. By one account, they placed the heads of the revolu-

Colonial newspapers regularly published advertisements of enslaved Africans for sale and notices of escaped servants and slaves. These advertisements often provide detailed information about the skills, health, and living conditions of African Americans.

tionaries on mileposts as a warning to other slaves contemplating rebellion. The Stono Uprising sent shock waves throughout the American colonies. The South Carolina legislature enacted a harsh slave code in an effort to prevent future revolts and limited slave importation for a decade. Most of the core group who planned the Stono Rebellion were African-born slaves, who hoped to escape to Florida, where Spanish authorities offered them religious sanctuary and freedom as a way to bolster the colony's population and undermine stability in the English settlements. By 1740, about one hundred former Carolina slaves had built the village of Gracia Real de Santa Teresa de Mose, called Mose, two miles north of St. Augustine.

During the eighteenth century, newly arrived Africans, often called "salt-water Negroes," were more likely to rebel or run away than creole, or "country-born" slaves. Predominantly male, imported Africans often lacked wives and children to root them to a plantation. Finding slavery intolerable, some fled as soon as they arrived. With Native Americans and runaway white servants, escaped slaves created maroon societies in frontier areas of Virginia, the Carolinas, and Georgia. They farmed, raised livestock, hunted, and fished. In the Great Dismal Swamp, on the North Carolina-Virginia border, communities numbering perhaps 2,000 people took refuge from colonial authorities. The Dismal Swamp settlements grew from small groups of Native Americans who survived the seventeenth-century English invasion of Virginia to include Indians and whites from the Carolinas, and increasing numbers of escaped Africans. Outlaw maroon communities on the southern frontier remained hostile to outside whites, often raiding nearby plantations for supplies.

WARS FOR EMPIRE

The Spanish offer of refuge and the Stono rebels' goal to reach Florida were part of the ongoing conflict between Britain and Spain in the southeast. The War of Jenkins's Ear (1739–1744) heralded a quarter century of hostilities among Europeans and Native Americans for domination of North America. The War of Jenkins's Ear, King George's War (1744–1748), the French and Indian War (1754–1763), and the Indian war for autonomy in the Ohio Valley (1763–1765) required British colonists to participate more actively in defending the empire, bringing them into greater contact with the British imperial government and armed forces.

The Southern Frontier

The colonies along the southern tier—from east to west, British South Carolina and Georgia, Spanish Florida, French Louisiana, and Spanish Texas and New Mexico—competed for trade with Native Americans and control of territory. Except for war between Georgia and Florida in the early 1740s, the most important battles along the southern rim were commercial, a competition the British traders often won because they had more plentiful and cheaper goods. They exchanged tools, clothing, scissors, guns, ammunition, and rum, in return for slaves, deerskins, and furs from the Indians, who allied militarily with the British to sustain this commerce. In comparison with the English provinces, the Spanish and French colonies remained small and badly supplied by their parent nations. In 1760, Florida had approximately 3,000 Hispanic settlers, Texas had 1,200, and New Mexico

about 9,000, while Louisiana counted 4,000 whites and 5,000 enslaved Africans. In contrast, in the same year, South Carolina and Georgia had a population of about 45,000 whites and 59,000 black slaves.

Governor James Oglethorpe of Georgia tried to use the outbreak of the War of Jenkins's Ear, which developed from trade disputes, to eject the Spanish from Florida. As part of the 1713 Treaty of Utrecht, Britain had obtained the right to sell a specified number of African slaves and commodities to the Spanish provinces. This opening led to British smuggling, which the Spanish, zealously protecting their mercantilist hold on colonial trade, countered with heavy-handed searches of British ships. Accounts of Spanish brutality inflamed the British public, especially when Captain Robert Jenkins displayed one of his ears, which he claimed the Spanish cut off when they caught him smuggling. In 1740, Oglethorpe attacked Florida with seven ships and 2,000 troops, including regiments from Georgia and South Carolina and Native American allies. They captured several Spanish forts and Mose, the village of escaped Carolina blacks, but failed to conquer Fort San Marcos, where the residents of St. Augustine and Mose took cover. Though the European population of Florida was small, a large percentage were soldiers, since the main purpose of the colony was to guard Atlantic shipping lanes. When Hispanic and black soldiers slipped out of the fort and recaptured Mose, and then the fort was resupplied by Cuba, Oglethorpe retreated.

In 1741, a force of 3,600 colonists participated in the British expedition against the Spanish fort at Cartagena, in what is now Colombia. The campaign, the largest British effort of the war, ended bitterly, with heavy losses from battle and smallpox. One-half of the provincial soldiers died, a fact the British colonists long remembered. The following year, the Spanish took revenge for the invasion of Florida by attacking St. Simon's Island, Georgia, but withdrew before conquering it. After some minor skirmishes, both sides gave up, bringing calm to the Georgia-Florida border.

King George's War

The British avoided further conflict with Florida because in 1744, they began hostilities with France in the War of the Austrian Succession, known to the colonists as King George's War. Thus the hundred-year struggle between these two European powers continued.

The war began in Europe, but spilled into North America when, provoked by French attacks on Nova Scotia, Governor William Shirley of Massachusetts organized an offensive against the French fort at Louisbourg, which controlled access to the St. Lawrence River. New Englanders rallied to the cause, intending to drive Catholic France from the continent, while Pennsylvania and New York contributed £11,000. In April 1745, untrained in formal warfare but supported by the British navy, 4,000 New England farmers and fishermen assaulted Louisbourg. The French garrison held out against the badly organized offensive until June, then surrendered. New Englanders considered Louisbourg a great victory, even after many of their troops succumbed to disease and the war degenerated into a series of debilitating border raids. The Canadians and their Indian allies ravaged Saratoga, New York, and northern New England. In spring 1746, a fleet of seventy-six ships left France to retake Louisbourg, but after fighting disease and Atlantic storms for three months, with a loss of 3,000 men, they returned to France empty-handed.

Despite this reprieve, New Englanders had little to celebrate, for they faced another threat—from their own imperial navy. During the war, Parliament permitted naval officers to impress sailors without the permission of colonial authorities. The Royal Navy used impressment, or involuntary recruitment, because many seamen fled the harsh conditions on naval vessels. Indeed, the brutality could make impressment the equivalent of a death sentence. In 1747, several thousand Bostonians protested when a British press gang from the fleet of Admiral Charles Knowles swept up men along the waterfront. The crowd demanded release of the sailors, taking hostage several British officers. The mob surrounded the governor's house and burned a British barge in his courtyard. When the governor called up the militia, the troops refused to move. Knowles threatened to shell the town, but after negotiations lasting several days, he released the impressed men instead.

Though crowd action occurred at other times in Anglo-America, as in the 1750s and 1760s when impressment continued, Bostonians particularly resented Knowles's press gang in view of their sacrifice at Louisbourg. But as the colonists became more involved in imperial politics, they learned that their interests held little sway. To their shock, the British government restored Louisbourg to the French in the Treaty of Aix-la-Chapelle (1748), as the combatants agreed to return all North American territories seized during the war.

Despite heavy human and financial costs, the war brought no change in the power balance between Great Britain and France in North America.

Native American Worlds in the Mid-Eighteenth Century

The conflict ended in 1748 for neither the European colonists nor the Native Americans who contested the continent. With bulging population growth and immigration, the British settlements pushed into the Appalachians, forcing Native Americans once again to rearrange their lives.

Some Indian survivors of earlier struggles remained within the British provinces, called by white Americans, "Settlement Indians," "domestic Indians," or "little Tribes." They worked as servants, slaves, day laborers, artisans, and tenant farmers, assimilating some parts of English culture, but rejecting others. Some continued to hunt, peddling venison and turkeys to the colonists. Dr. Alexander Hamilton, a recent immigrant from Scotland, recorded many encounters with Indians in 1744 as he traveled through the settlements from Maryland to Maine. The Native Americans he met varied greatly in status, from an Indian sachem who had established himself as a wealthy planter, to those on the margins, who tried to hold on to native traditions within an alien culture. In Rhode Island, he approached the large plantation of

> an Indian King named George . . . upon which he has many tennants and has, of his own, a good stock of horses and other cattle. The King lives after the English mode. His subjects have lost their own government policy and laws and are servants or vassals to the English here. His queen goes in a high modish dress in her silks, hoops, stays, and dresses like an English woman. He educates his children to the belles letters and is himself a very complaisant mannerly man. We pay'd him a visit, and he treated us with a glass of good wine.

During worship in a Boston church, Hamilton sat near several Native Americans. But he also met natives who retained at least some of their customs, like the Indian at Princeton who saluted him with "How' s't ni tap." In New York, Hamilton watched "about ten Indians fishing for oysters . . . stark naked" near his tavern. While most Indians who stayed in white settled areas had given up political autonomy, they had not surrendered all of their traditions. Many spoke English in addition to their native language, but did not learn to read and write. One Rhode Island woman knew only one English word, "broom." The Great Awakening converted many settlement Indians who had long resisted Christianity. The dynamic preaching of New Light ministers, who welcomed enthusiastic response from their listeners, was attractive to Native Americans who had retained traditional rituals and dance.

Many Indians tried to preserve their political independence by moving west, a strategy that worked temporarily. From 1660 to the 1740s, for example, Iroquois, Shawnees, and Delawares moved into the eastern part of the Ohio Valley, from the Allegheny River in western Pennsylvania to west-central Ohio. Wyandots inhabited the lands to the west, at Sandusky and near the French fort at Detroit. Some Iroquois migrated from western New York, while Delawares and Shawnees moved from eastern Pennsylvania under pressure from white settlers. Some of the Delawares left the east as a result of the "Walking Purchase" of 1737, when two of William Penn's sons, the proprietors, used an alleged 1686 deed to cheat the Indians out of their last stronghold on the Pennsylvania side of the Delaware River. The deed, of which only a copy survived, ceded lands as far as a man could walk in one and a half days. Coerced by an alliance between the Penns and the Iroquois, the Delawares agreed to comply. The Penns sent runners in relay to cover almost sixty miles of land in a day and a half, a deception the Delawares could not fail to remember; with the outbreak of war in 1754, they sought revenge.

The Ohio Valley became the focus of conflict in the 1740s as the British and French competed for trade. Following the Delawares and Shawnees west, some Pennsylvania traders took up residence in the multi-ethnic towns such as Chiningue (or Logstown), where Iroquois, Delawares, Shawnees, Ottawas, and other Indians lived. The Ohio Valley, as one Indian leader said, was "a country in between" the English and the French, unfortunately a country that the Europeans craved. From 1754 to 1814, the Native Americans fought the British and Americans to keep their lands and native religions, forging pan-Indian alliances to meet the Anglo threat.

The French and Indian War

During King George's War, the British and Iroquois had evicted French traders from the Ohio Valley. The Canadians returned, however, backed by a government that was determined to force out the British. The French built forts to stop the incursion of Anglo-American traders and to block Virginia's claim to the territory, which dated from its charter. In 1754, after the British government granted half a million acres to the Ohio Company, the Virginia governor sent a young militia officer, George Washington, with 160 troops to expel the French. The Virginians were defeated at Fort Necessity by a superior force of French and Indians.

Recognizing that war was imminent, seven colonies sent delegates to a congress at Albany, New York, where they negotiated unsuccessfully with the Iroquois for an alliance against the French. The Albany Congress also supported a plan devised by Benjamin Franklin to unite the colonies for common defense. When the delegates returned home with the proposal for an inter-colonial government empowered to tax, pass laws, and supervise military defense, not one of the assemblies approved. The provincial elites were unready to surrender their political power, even in the face of a dangerous war. Nor did the imperial government approve unification by its provinces.

Instead, the British decided to destroy French forts in what they considered their territory, even before a formal declaration of war. In early 1755, Major General Edward Braddock landed in the colonies with two British regiments. Joined by hundreds of provincial soldiers, the army of 1,400 marched through the Virginia backcountry to capture Fort Duquesne, the French outpost near the site of present-day Pittsburgh. The British troops were unprepared

Benjamin Franklin published his "Snake Device" just before the Albany Congress in 1754. Considered the first political cartoon in the colonies, it later became an important symbol of American resistance to Britain.

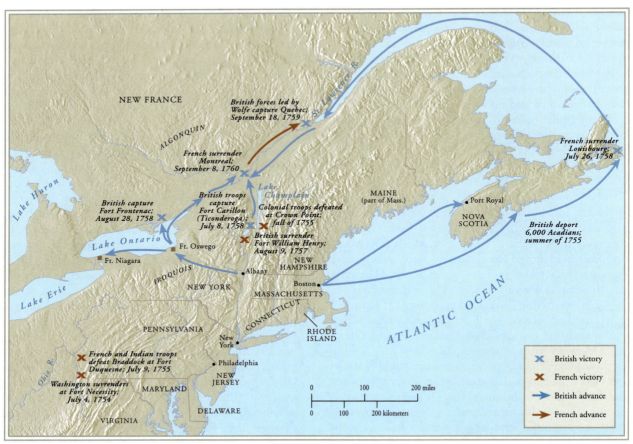

MAP 4.3   SEVEN YEARS' WAR IN NORTH AMERICA

for frontier fighting, but thought their mission was easy because the garrison had only 250 French troops. Ten miles short of Fort Duquesne, however, the French and allied Indians ambushed Braddock's army, killing or wounding two-thirds of the British force. The general himself lay dead. George Washington, his uniform ripped by bullets, led the retreat.

The 650 Native Americans who fought with the French included their traditional allies and some Delawares and Iroquois of the Ohio Valley who had previously supported the British. By 1754, some Ohio Indians were convinced that Britain and its colonies posed the greatest threat to their lands; with the defeat of Braddock, many more joined the French. Between 1755 and 1757, Delawares, Shawnees, Iroquois, and many others attacked the white frontier from Pennsyl-

vania to Virginia, burning settlements and killing or capturing thousands of colonists. The settlers streamed eastward, seeking military help. After seventy years of relative peace, Quaker Pennsylvania was at war with Native Americans.

But help for the westerners was slow in coming. In 1756, the struggle in North America became part of the larger European conflict known as the Seven Years' War, in which Great Britain supported Prussia against Austria, Russia, and France. Through 1757 and half of 1758, in America, the British and provincials lost one battle after another. They tried but failed to take Louisbourg and the French forts on Lake Ontario. Even worse, the French penetrated into New York, seizing Fort William Henry and 2,000 soldiers at Lake George. The tide changed after the British statesman

William Pitt took command of the war effort. He poured money and men into the American theater, expecting colonial legislatures to do the same. The new generals Jeffery Amherst and James Wolfe, with an army of almost 10,000 men, captured Louisbourg in July 1758. The French then pulled their troops out of the Ohio Valley to protect Quebec and Montreal, allowing the British to take control of the west. Without French supplies and devastated by smallpox, the Native Americans ended their war on the frontier, entering negotiations with the Pennsylvania government for peace.

In 1759, the British and provincial armies had even greater success, leading some of the Iroquois of New York to abandon neutrality to join their side. The British reestablished control of New York, while from Louisbourg, General Wolfe sailed up the St. Lawrence to Quebec, where after several months he finally pierced the defenses of the well-fortified city. The next year, Amherst's army seized Montreal, thus ending French control of Canada.

While the defeat of Canada marked the end of the French and Indian War in North America, the Seven Years' War continued off the coast of France, in India, and in the West Indies. The British military took a number of French sugar islands, including the richest, Guadeloupe. When Spain entered the war as France's ally in 1762 in return for the promise of lands west of the Mississippi River, the British captured Manila in the Philippines and Havana, Cuba. Provincial troops participated in the campaign against Cuba, but, reminiscent of the siege of Cartagena twenty years before, approximately one-half died from disease.

The victory at Quebec came with the loss of one of the commanders who helped win the war in North America for the British. The Death of General Wolfe *by Benjamin West.*

During the French and Indian War, thousands of colonists joined the harshly disciplined British army, and many more served in the provincial forces. The experience brought ordinary settlers into close contact with the imperial authorities—and many loathed the experience. The British army contained professional soldiers drilled rigorously in military tactics, cleanliness, and order. Small numbers of women served in the field, generally soldiers' wives who cooked, washed, and nursed. British officers, from the upper classes, maintained discipline with punishments of death for major offenses such as desertion, and up to 1,000 lashes—which could also kill—for lesser crimes. The British officers disdained the colonial units, which submitted to much lighter discipline and sometimes elected their superiors. Because the provincials failed to keep their camps and clothing clean, many died from disease. Many also deserted, confident that they would be protected from military justice in their communities. For their part, the colonial soldiers thought the British regulars were immoral, profane men who needed to be controlled with brutal discipline. On both sides, this disrespect later contributed to the worsening relationship between Great Britain and its North American colonies.

In the short run, however, the British colonists welcomed the Treaty of Paris in 1763, which finally ended the war. They benefited to a much greater extent than the parent country from the peace terms, which granted lands east of the Mississippi River to Great Britain. Under the treaty, France lost all of its territory in North America, but retrieved the valuable sugar islands of Guadeloupe and Martinique. Spain relinquished Florida to get back Cuba and the Philippines and, because the British lacked interest in the region, acquired French territory west of the Mississippi and New Orleans, located on the east side of the river. The Treaty of Paris gave the British colonists security from France and Spain, while the home government received two unprofitable colonies, Canada and Florida. The provincials celebrated the victory with patriotic fervor, as New York City raised a statue of George III, who had taken the throne in 1760 at age twenty-two. Many colonists, especially New England ministers, had interpreted the war as a fight against Catholicism and tyranny. They viewed the victory as a sign that God favored Britain and its colonies. One Massachusetts clergyman preached,

Safe from the Enemy of the Wilderness, safe from the griping Hand of arbitrary Sway and cruel Superstition; Here shall be the late founded Seat of Peace and Freedom. Here shall our indulgent Mother [Britain], who has most generously rescued and protected us, be served and honoured by growing Numbers, with all Duty, Love and Gratitude, till Time shall be no more.

The Indians Renew War in the Ohio Valley

For Native Americans, the Treaty of Paris was a disaster that failed to resolve the struggle for eastern North America. The agreement ended the conflict among European powers, but not for them. Indeed, the defeat of France worsened the situation of tribes in the Ohio Valley, for they could no longer play one European nation off the other. East of the Mississippi, the British alone supplied European goods, so they could set prices and the terms of trade. They ended the custom of giving annual presents, charged high prices, stopped selling rum, and reduced the amount of ammunition sold. Further, with the end of the French and Indian War, white settlers streamed west into Indian lands, as wealthy land speculators and poor squatters alike ignored treaties that colonial governments had made with the Native Americans.

The altered British trade policies, refusal to offer gifts, and land grabbing drove many Delawares, Shawnees, Iroquois, and others to renew the fighting. They gained spiritual unity from the Delaware prophet Neolin, one of a line of spiritual leaders among the Delawares and Shawnees, who preached that Indians must reject Christianity and European goods, particularly rum. They should revitalize their ancient culture, asserting autonomy and resistance. Neolin called on Native Americans to drive the Europeans out, demanding: "Whereupon do you suffer the whites to dwell upon your lands? Drive them away; wage war against them. I love them not." He warned his followers, "if you suffer the English among you, you are dead men. Sickness, smallpox, and their poison will destroy you entirely."

Many Indians throughout the Ohio Valley adopted Neolin's strategy, boycotting the fur trade by hunting only for their own food and personal needs. The Delaware councils called for a gradual return to mili-

Chief Pontiac, *by Jerry Farnsworth. When whites streamed west at the end of the Seven Years' War, Indians allied under Pontiac's leadership to attack British forts and settlements in the Ohio Valley and Great Lakes region.*

tary skills with bow and arrow and adopted a ritual tea, which caused vomiting, to cleanse themselves of the "White people's ways and Nature." In 1763, Indians from western Pennsylvania through the Great Lakes region launched a pan-Indian assault on British garrisons, often called Pontiac's War. A follower of Neolin and leader of the Ottawas, Pontiac laid siege unsuccessfully to the British fort at Detroit. Other Indians defeated thirteen British outposts, though not Forts Niagara or Pittsburgh. While the British army established military dominance in the Ohio Valley by the end of 1763, after the Native Americans ran short

of ammunition and succumbed to smallpox, fighting continued for two more years.

In addition to armed force, the British government tried to end the war by keeping white settlers out of the Ohio Valley. The king issued the Proclamation of 1763, which drew a line along the crest of the Appalachian Mountains from Maine to Georgia, requiring colonists to move east of the line. Colonial governors were instructed to prohibit surveys or land grants west of the Proclamation line; only authorized agents of the Crown could buy lands from the Indians. The proclamation failed in its purpose, however, as land speculators continued their operations and immigrants demanded farms. The British government, weighed down by debt from the Seven Years' War, failed to supply manpower to enforce the law. The government withdrew troops from the Ohio Valley and Great Lakes region, while provincial governments, dominated by speculators, ignored encroachment on Indian lands.

THE BRITISH PROVINCES IN 1763

The end of the French and Indian War brought pivotal changes in British North America. For over a century and a half, Europeans had crossed the ocean to trade with the Native Americans, build farms and businesses, and develop networks of Atlantic commerce. The colonies had dealt with crises, from economic slumps to rebellions, becoming ever more confident of their position as semi-independent societies. During the last quarter century, with greater involvement in imperial affairs and rising importation of consumer goods, the provincials felt more a part of the British empire—more English—even as they created a separate identity as Americans. Most importantly, they believed that they were equal to the residents of Great Britain, that they possessed the rights of English people.

The Economy

In 1763, the mainland provinces still operated within the system of British mercantilism, which consisted of

MAP 4.4 | COLONIAL OVERSEAS TRADE

regulations on colonial trade and manufactures. For mercantilism to work to Britain's benefit, the colonies had to produce raw materials and agricultural staples needed by the home economy and serve as a market for its manufactured goods. Such colonial products as sugar, molasses, tobacco, cotton, certain wood products, copper, and furs were "enumerated," meaning that they could be shipped only to Britain or British colonial ports, not to foreign countries such as France and Spain. The basic laws establishing the British mercantilist system were the seventeenth-century Naviga-

tion Acts, which Parliament supplemented from time to time. Though most colonial trade conformed to the law by the eighteenth century, smuggling occurred often enough to prompt demands within the British government for strict enforcement. In particular, colonial shippers bribed customs officials to ignore the Molasses Act (1733), which levied prohibitive duties on foreign sugar products, including a tax of sixpence per gallon on molasses. The British West Indies planters had pushed for the act to create a monopoly for themselves, lowering the cost of provisions and raising the price of their exports. If the Molasses Act had been enforced, it would have severely damaged the economies of New England and the Middle Colonies, who traded with the French, Spanish, and Dutch West Indies as well as the British islands. The mainland colonies exported food and lumber in return for sugar and molasses, from which distillers produced rum.

Other laws passed by Parliament prior to 1763 had a significant but uneven impact on colonial economic growth. British legislation, combined with lack of investment capital, limited the development of most manufactures. The Woolen Act (1699) and the Hat Act (1732) banned the export of American-produced woolen products and hats from one colony to another. Other laws prohibited the export of machinery and the migration of skilled craftsmen from Britain to America. The Iron Act (1750) allowed duty-free import of colonial bar iron into Britain, but forbade fabrication of iron goods in the colonies. Nevertheless, crude iron production received substantial investment, as did shipbuilding and rum distilling. Unhampered by mercantilist regulation, North American shipbuilders produced nearly 40 percent of vessels in the British-owned merchant fleet.

Despite these laws, the wealth of the British colonies increased between the 1720s and 1760, as trade flourished with the West Indies and, after 1750, with southern Europe, where crop failures and population growth swelled demand for wheat and flour. The Middle Colonies, already expanding with German and Irish immigration, were well situated to supply new markets. Philadelphia became the largest city in the British colonies: Its wealthy merchants invested in ships, built mansions, purchased coaches and other luxuries, and speculated in western lands from the profits of trade. Artisans, shopkeepers, and farmers prospered from the European and West Indies markets and from demand during the Seven Years' War for ships, clothing, boots, food, rum, and other supplies. To the south, large planters in the Chesapeake and Carolinas accumulated great estates, while ordinary farmers more modestly improved their standard of living. All along the eastern seaboard, after 1750, white families indulged in what has been called a "consumer revolution." Not only could they purchase cloth, clothing, carpets, paper, gloves, mirrors, clocks, silverware, china tea sets, pottery, and books, but they had more choices in the specific kind of cloth or paper or gloves they could buy. In New York City in the 1750s,

for instance, merchants advertised gloves of various colors—purple, orange, white, and flowered—as well as different sizes and materials, including chamois, silk, "Maid's Lamb Gloves," and "Men's Dog Skin Gloves." This is just one example of the wide variety of consumer goods that became available in mid-century.

The colonies became major markets for textiles, metalware, and other items, which under the Navigation Acts they could import only from Britain. The consumer revolution made the British more attentive to their North American provinces, while at the same time, the imports helped to create in America a more standardized English culture. Affluent colonists became aware of the latest fashions in England, and complained when they received out-of-date merchandise. The young George Washington groused in 1760, for example, "that instead of getting things good and fashionable in their several kinds we often have Articles sent Us that coud only have been usd by our Forefathers in the days of yore."

The economic upswing of the 1750s gave way to a depression after 1760, as the Seven Years' War moved to the Caribbean and military spending dropped. The seaport towns, having attracted workers during the wartime boom, faced deepening poverty and rising demands for relief. With depressed wages and long periods of unemployment, families found survival difficult. The resumption of immigration from Europe after the war intensified economic hardships and contributed to unrest on the frontier.

Politics

In late 1763, after months of Indian attacks in the Ohio country, a band of western Scots-Irish Pennsylvanians used violence to force the Quaker-dominated assembly to provide military protection. The "Paxton Boys" of Lancaster County murdered a number of Christian Indians at Conestoga, then marched on Philadelphia. By the time the rebels reached the capital, the legislature had passed a bill raising 1,000 troops to defend the frontier. The westerners returned home without attacking the city. At the heart of their revolt was the belief that they were poorly represented in the provincial government. As the backcountry population exploded, eastern politicians in Pennsylvania and other colonies guarded their power by

Grey's Inn Creek Shipyard, *by an unknown artist, c. 1760. Shipbuilding, at this Maryland shipyard as well as in northern seaports, was a major industry in the British colonies.*

allotting fewer assembly seats to outlying counties than they deserved. Unfair representation stimulated a series of uprisings from the North Carolina Regulator movement in the 1760s to the Whiskey Rebellion three decades later.

The Paxton Boys revolt signaled the end of an era of political stability as both the western farmers and imperial government put pressure on colonial elites. Since the late 1720s, the British mainland provinces had enjoyed relative peace in their capitals, if not

The Paxton Expedition, *by Henry Dawkins, depicts the threat by western "Paxton Boys" against Philadelphia, demanding frontier defense during Pontiac's War.*

along their frontiers. The period of stability contrasted markedly with earlier decades, before 1720, when Bacon's Rebellion, the revolutions of 1689, and constant strife between governors and assemblies, and among factions of assemblymen, characterized politics.

As part of Britain's empire, the eighteenth-century colonists believed themselves among the most fortunate people on earth. The Glorious Revolution of 1688–1689, which removed James II, had ended the long, bitter contest between king and Parliament. The monarch's power was subsequently limited by the national legislature, comprised of the House of Lords, which represented the aristocracy, and the House of Commons, which in theory represented everyone else. As a result of the 1689 settlement, Parliament's consent was necessary for taxes, new courts, raising an army in peacetime, and foreign invasions. It gained control over its own meetings and, after 1707, the Crown lost veto power over legislation. The balance of powers, political theorists argued, prevented domination by a single segment of society, the monarch, aristocracy, or common people. Thus, the British avoided forms of government considered destructive of liberty: rule by a single despot (tyranny); corrupt and self-serving rule by a group of aristocrats (oligarchy); and uncontrolled rule by the mob (democracy). In their provincial governments, the British

colonists expected to find a similar balance, one that would protect their rights. Indeed, the prevailing structure of governor, appointed council, and elected lower house of assembly reflected the English model. The British provinces were the only European settlements in North America where ordinary people had representative legislatures. Further, an estimated 50 to 75 percent of white men were qualified to vote in the British colonies, the result of much broader property ownership than in England, where about 15 to 30 percent of adult males had the franchise. According to English political theory, a person needed a "stake in society," a certain amount of property, to vote or hold office. Servants, slaves, children, and unpropertied men were beholden to someone else, so could not make independent decisions. Giving them suffrage would award their owner, father, or employer another vote, the theorists claimed, especially in many places where people voted orally, in public. By tradition, women also lacked the franchise, whether or not they owned property or were married. Though part of the reason was the dependency theory that wives would follow the lead of their husbands, not all women had spouses. Denial of the vote to all females arose from the general belief that they were intellectually and morally inferior to men and thus should have no formal role in government.

King George III, *at the time of his coronation in 1760, by Allan Ramsay.*

houses of prostitution, and stop the British navy from impressing men into the king's service, as with the 1747 Knowles riot in Boston.

The most important and sustained political development in British America during the first half of the eighteenth century was the rise of the elected lower houses of assembly. The legislatures acquired greater power and assumed more functions, most significantly, the right to initiate bills to raise taxes and disburse public funds—the "power of the purse." They also gained the authority to initiate other legislation, choose their own leadership, and settle disputed elections.

The political stability and rise of the assemblies that marked the mid-eighteenth century resulted from a number of factors, including the long period of economic growth that began in the 1720s. Prosper-

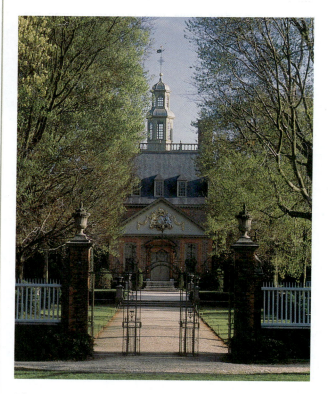

The Governor's Palace at Williamsburg, Virginia, built in the early eighteenth century. At a time when most Virginians lived in rough-hewn, one-room dwellings, the elegant mansion symbolized the king's authority in America.

The colonists often required their legislators to live in the area from which they were elected and to advocate the interests of their constituents, unlike England, where members of the House of Commons did not have to reside in their electoral districts. The British believed that Parliament represented all of the people of the empire whether they elected delegates or not, a concept known as virtual representation.

Beyond suffrage, English political theory also recognized the right of common people to resort to crowd action to withstand tyranny and require authorities to protect them from harm. The people had this right, theoretically, as long as violence was limited—directed at property rather than persons. At various times, colonial mobs protested to prevent grain from being exported when food was in short supply, destroy ity supported the formation of cohesive, politically adept elites—mostly second, third, and fourth generation Americans with inherited wealth and large estates, enslaved Africans or servants to meet their domestic needs, and (consequently) sufficient leisure time for politics. They formed a class of skilled politicians, men who learned from their fathers how to govern, then elaborated the art. Many studied the law: The growth of the colonial bar accompanied the professionalization of politics. Economic prosperity inclined ordinary whites to defer to the elites as long as opportunity was good and they had crops to tend or other work to do. Their deference to social and economic superiors became most visible after 1725, when participation at the polls declined among eligible voters, and incumbent assemblymen won reelection year after year.

The provincial elites also benefited after 1720 from the British decision to administer the colonies with a light touch, allowing royal governors to accommodate the assemblies. And while riots occurred during the 1740s and 1750s over land claims and impressment, none threatened social disorder on the level of the seventeenth-century rebellions. Indeed, most ordinary whites feared attacks by Native Americans and slave revolts more than misuse of governmental power by elites.

CONCLUSION

By the end of 1763, the British colonists of North America had reason to be optimistic about their future, despite the pan-Indian assaults in the Ohio Valley and postwar economic downturn. The British army had withstood the worst attacks in the west and colonists could expect a return to prosperity. After a quarter century of war, they celebrated the withdrawal of Spain and France east of the Mississippi, and looked forward to peace and semi-autonomy within the empire. Free colonists appreciated the benefits of being British—their liberties and right to participate in government as well as access to advanced learning and consumer goods. At the same time, the Americans were creating societies quite different from the English, with greater ethnic and religious diversity, dependence on enslaved labor, and wider opportunity to acquire land (even if it meant pushing out the Indians). After 1763, the London

government shocked the American colonists with its effort to rein in the empire, to make them surrender some of their accumulated rights. In turn, the British were unprepared for the coordinated fury with which the thirteen mainland provinces greeted their "reforms."

RECOMMENDED READINGS

Anderson, Fred. *A People's Army: Massachusetts Soldiers and Society in the Seven Years' War* (1984). An influential study of the origins and motives of ordinary soldiers.

Bailyn, Bernard, and Morgan, Philip D., eds. *Strangers Within the Realm: Cultural Margins of the First British Empire* (1991). Important essays on specific groups, including Native Americans, Scots-Irish, African Americans, Germans, and Dutch.

Carson, Cary, et al., eds. *Of Consuming Interests: The Style of Life in the Eighteenth Century* (1994). Excellent essays on topics ranging from housing and art to consumer behavior.

Isaac, Rhys. *The Transformation of Virginia, 1740–1790* (1982). Uses anthropological methods to explore cultural and political change in eighteenth-century Virginia.

Jedrey, Christopher M. *The World of John Cleaveland: Family and Community in Eighteenth-Century New England* (1979). Shows continuity of family strategies over the colonial period.

Merrell, James H. *The Indians' New World: Catawbas and Their Neighbors from European Contact Through the Era of Removal* (1989). Shows how South Carolina Indians created a new nation and identity in the wake of European settlement.

Morgan, Philip D. *Slave Counterpoint: Black Culture in the Eighteenth-Century Chesapeake and Lowcountry* (1998). A comprehensive study of African-American work and culture in the South.

Steele, Ian K. *Warpaths: Invasions of North America* (1994). Examines the Seven Years' War as one of a series of European invasions of Indian territory during the colonial period.

Ulrich, Laurel Thatcher. *A Midwife's Tale: The Life of Martha Ballard, Based on Her Diary, 1785–1812* (1990). The prize-winning account of a Maine midwife within the context of eighteenth-century society.

Enlightenment, Science, and Medicine
Bailyn, Bernard. *Education in the Forming of American Society* (1960).

Cassedy, James H. *Medicine in America: A Short History* (1991).

Cremin, Lawrence A. *American Education: The Colonial Experience, 1607–1783* (1970).

Hindle, Brooke. *The Pursuit of Science in Revolutionary America, 1735–1789* (1956).

Leavitt, Judith Walzer. *Brought to Bed: Child-Bearing in America, 1750 to 1950* (1986).

Leavitt, Judith Walzer, and Numbers, Ronald L., eds. *Sickness and Health in America: Readings in the History of Medicine and Public Health* (1978).

May, Henry F. *The Enlightenment in America* (1976).

Scholten, Catherine M. *Childbearing in American Society: 1650–1850* (1985).

Shryock, Richard Harrison. *Medicine and Society in America 1660–1860* (1960).

Ulrich, Laurel Thatcher. *Good Wives: Image and Reality in the Lives of Women in Northern New England, 1650–1750* (1982).

Great Awakening

Ahlstrom, Sydney E. *A Religious History of the American People* (1972).

Bonomi, Patricia U. *Under the Cope of Heaven: Religion, Society, and Politics in Colonial Amerca* (1986).

Gaustad, Edwin Scott. *The Great Awakening in New England* (1957).

Goen, Clarence C. *Revivalism and Separatism in New England, 1740–1800: Strict Congregationalists and Separate Baptists in the Great Awakening* (1962).

Lovejoy, David S. *Religious Enthusiasm in the New World: Heresy to Revolution* (1985).

Stout, Harry S. *The Divine Dramatist: George Whitefield and the Rise of Modern Evangelicalism* (1991).

Westerkamp, Marilyn J. *Triumph of the Laity: Scots-Irish Piety and the Great Awakening, 1625–1760* (1988).

Immigration and Cultural Diversity in British Colonies

Berlin, Ira. "Time, Space, and the Evolution of Afro-American Society in British Mainland North America," *American Historical Review* 85 (1980):44–78.

Fogleman, Aaron Spencer. *Hopeful Journeys: German Immigration, Settlement, and Political Culture in Colonial America, 1717–1775* (1996).

Herskovits, Melville J. *The Myth of the Negro Past* (1958).

Hoffman, Ronald, et al., eds. *Through a Glass Darkly: Reflections on Personal Identity in Early America* (1997).

Klepp, Susan E., ed. *The Demographic History of the Philadelphia Region, 1600–1860* (1989).

Klepp, Susan E., and Smith, Billy G., eds. *The Infortunate: The Voyage and Adventures of William Moraley, an Indentured Servant* (1992).

Lemon, James T. *The Best Poor Man's Country: A Geographical Study of Early Southeastern Pennsylvania* (1972).

Piersen, William D. *Black Yankees: The Development of an Afro-American Subculture in Eighteenth-Century New England* (1988).

Roeber, A. G. *Palatines, Liberty, and Property: German Lutherans in Colonial British America* (1993).

Schwartz, Sally. *"A Mixed Multitude": The Struggle for Toleration in Colonial Pennsylvania* (1988).

Sobel, Mechal. *The World They Made Together: Black and White Values in Eighteenth-Century Virginia* (1987).

Wolf, Stephanie Grauman. *As Various as Their Land: The Everyday Lives of Eighteenth-Century Americans* (1993).

Wood, Peter H. *Black Majority: Negroes in Colonial South Carolina from 1670 Through the Stono Rebellion* (1974).

Southern Frontiers

Bannon, John Francis. *The Spanish Borderlands Frontier, 1513–1821* (1970).

Davis, Harold E. *The Fledgling Province: Social and Cultural Life in Colonial Georgia, 1733–1776* (1976).

Landers, Jane. "Gracia Real de Santa Teresa de Mose: A Free Black Town in Spanish Colonial Florida," *American Historical Review* 95 (1990): 9–30.

Usner, Daniel H., Jr. *Indians, Settlers, and Slaves in a Frontier Exchange Economy: The Lower Mississippi Valley Before 1783* (1992).

Weber, David J., ed. *New Spain's Far Northern Frontier: Essays on Spain in the American West, 1540–1821* (1979).

Weber, David J. *The Spanish Frontier in North America* (1992).

Economy and Politics in the British Colonies

Bailyn, Bernard. *The Origins of American Politics* (1968).

Doerflinger, Thomas M. *A Vigorous Spirit of Enterprise: Merchants and Economic Development in Revolutionary Philadelphia* (1986).

Gilje, Paul A. *The Road to Mobocracy: Popular Disorder in New York City, 1763–1834* (1987).

Greene, Jack P. *The Quest for Power: The Lower Houses of Assembly in the Southern Royal Colonies, 1689–1776* (1963).

Maier, Pauline. *From Resistance to Revolution: Colonial Radicals and the Development of American Opposition to Britain, 1765–1776* (1972).

McCusker, John J., and Menard, Russell R. *The Economy of British America, 1607–1789, With Supplementary Bibliography* (1991).

Nash, Gary B. *The Urban Crucible: Social Change, Political Consciousness, and the Origins of the American Revolution* (1979).

Olson, Alison Gilbert. *Making the Empire Work: London and American Interest Groups, 1690–1790* (1992).

Shy, John. *Toward Lexington: The Role of the British Army in the Coming of the American Revolution* (1965).

— 1764 TO 1814 —

During the American Revolution, sixteen-year-old Dicey Langston of the South Carolina frontier left home in the middle of the night, by herself, to warn her brother's unit about tory troop movements. As a historian later described Langston's journey,

Many miles were to be traversed, and the road lay through woods, and crossed marshes and creeks where the conveniences of bridges and foot-logs were wanting.

She walked rapidly on, heedless of slight difficulties; but her heart almost failed her when she came to the banks of the Tyger—a deep and rapid stream, rendered more dangerous by the rains that had lately fallen. . . . But the energy of a resolute will, under the care of Providence, sustained her.*

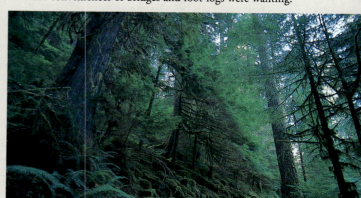

PASSAGES

POPULATION OF THE UNITED STATES AND OF EACH STATE OR TERRITORY ENUMERATED IN 1790: 1790 TO 1900.

State or Territory	1790	1800	1810	1820	1880	1840	1850	1860	1870	1880	1890	1900
United States	3,929,625	5,308,483	7,239,881	9,638,453	12,866,020	17,069,453	23,191,876	31,443,321	38,558,371	50,189,209	62,979,766	76,303,387
Area enumerated in 1790	3,929,625	5,247,355	6,779,308	8,293,869	10,240,232	11,781,231	14,569,584	17,326,157	19,687,504	23,925,639	28,188,321	33,553,630
New England	1,009,206	1,233,011	1,471,973	1,660,071	1,954,717	2,234,822	2,728,116	3,135,283	3,487,924	4,010,529	4,700,749	5,592,017
Maine	96,643	151,719	228,705	298,335	399,455	501,793	583,169	628,279	626,915	648,936	661,086	694,466
New Hampshire .	141,899	183,858	214,460	244,161	269,328	284,574	317,976	326,073	318,300	346,991	376,530	411,588
Vermont	85,341	154,465	217,895	235,981	280,652	291,948	314,120	315,098	330,551	332,286	332,422	343,641
Massachusetts ..	378,556	422,845	472,040	523,287	610,408	737,699	994,514	1,231,066	1,457,351	1,783,085	2,238,947	2,805,346
Rhode Island ...	69,112	69,122	76,931	83,059	97,199	108,830	147,545	174,620	217,353	276,531	345,506	428,556
Connecticut ...	237,655	251,002	261,942	275,248	297,675	309,978	370,792	460,147	537,454	622,700	746,258	908,420
Middle states	1,017,087	1,466,838	2,087,376	2,772,594	3,664,412	4,604,345	5,990,267	7,571,201	8,935,821	10,643,486	12,874,713	15,639,413
New York	340,241	589,051	959,049	1,372,812	1,918,608	2,428,921	3,097,394	3,880,735	4,382,759	5,082,871	6,003,174	7,268,894
New Jersey	184,139	211,149	245,562	277,575	320,823	373,306	489,555	672,035	906,096	1,131,116	1,444,933	1,883,669
Pennsylvania ...	433,611	602,365	810,091	1,049,458	1,348,233	1,724,033	2,311,786	2,906,215	3,521,951	4,282,891	5,258,113	6,302,115
Delaware	59,096	64,273	72,674	72,749	76,748	78,085	91,532	112,216	125,015	146,608	168,493	184,735
Southern states ...	1,903,332	2,547,506	3,219,959	3,861,204	4,621,103	4,942,064	5,851,201	6,619,673	7,263,759	9,271,624	10,612,859	12,322,200
Maryland and District of Columbia	319,728	355,641	404,569	440,389	486,874	513,731	634,721	762,129	912,594	1,112,567	1,272,782	1,466,762
Virginia and West Virginia ..	747,610	880,200	974,600	1,065,366	1,211,405	1,239,797	1,421,661	1,596,318	1,667,177	2,131,022	2,418,774	2,812,984
North Carolina .	395,005	478,103	555,500	638,829	737,987	753,419	869,039	992,622	1,071,361	1,399,750	1,617,949	1,893,810
South Carolina .	249,073	345,591	415,115	502,741	581,185	594,398	668,507	703,708	705,606	995,577	1,151,149	1,340,316
Georgia	82,548	161,414	201,937	226,739	233,831	231,681	272,151	299,411	327,490	441,659	526,052	640,538
Kentucky	73,677	220,955	406,511	564,317	687,917	779,828	982,405	1,155,684	1,321,011	1,648,690	1,858,635	2,147,174
Tennessee	35,691	105,602	261,727	422,823	681,904	829,210	1,002,717	1,109,801	1,258,520	1,542,359	1,767,518	2,020,616
Added area	....	61,128	460,573	1,344,584	2,625,788	5,288,222	8,622,292	14,117,164	18,870,867	26,263,570	34,791,445	42,749,757

*Map labels:*

UNEXPLORED

Hudson Bay

CREE

OJIBWA

BLACKFEET

ATSINA

SALISH
NEZ PERCÉ

CROW

MANDAN

TETON SIOUX

SANTEE SIOUX

KLAMATH
MODOC

SHOSHONE

NORTHERN PAIUTE

CHEYENNE

MAJDU

WASHO

OGLALA SIOUX

PAWNEE

IOWA

POMO

UTE

ARAPAHO

OTO

KANSA

MISSOURI

COSTANOAN

SALINAN

HOPI

NAVAJO

PUEBLO

KIOWA

OSAGE

MOHAVE

SERRANO

APACHE

COMANCHE

WICHITA

CHUMASH

PIMA

MESCALERO

OPATA

Taos
Santa Fe
Albuquerque

El Paso

San Antonio

Chihuahua

Monterrey

Saltillo

Durango

Rio Grande

ALGONQUIN
OTTAWA

Lake Superior

MENOMINEE

Lake Huron

SAUK
FOX
LeBaye
KICKAPOO

Lake Michigan

Fort Michilimackinac

Fort Frontenac

L. Ontario

Fort Niagara

IROQUOIS

Fort Detroit

L. Erie

DELAWARE

MIAMI

ILLINOIS

St. Joseph

Vincennes

Ohio R.

SHAWNEE

St. Louis
Ste. Genevieve
Kaskaskia

CHICKASAW

CHEROKEE

CATAWBA

Arkansas Post

CREEK

CHOCTAW

Fort Toulouse

Natchitoches

Natchez

Mobile
Pensacola

New Orleans

SEMINOLE

Quebec

Montreal

St. Lawrence R.

Falmouth
Portsmouth

Boston
Plymouth
Providence

Hartford

New Haven

New York

Philadelphia
Wilmington

Baltimore
Annapolis

Richmond
Williamsburg
Norfolk

Edenton

New Bern

Columbia

Wilmington

Charleston

Savannah

St. Augustine

Mississippi R.

PACIFIC OCEAN

ATLANTIC OCEAN

Gulf of Mexico

Legend:
- English
- Spanish
- Russian
- Proclamation Line of 1763

Dicey Langston's effort, like those of thousands of Americans, was emblematic of her country's passage from a collection of British provinces in 1764, to a stable republic with some international standing a half century later. The thirteen mainland colonies, proud of their contribution to victory in the French and Indian War, were stunned by Britain's program to curtail their rights. Stretching from the mountains of northern New England to the rice fields of coastal Georgia, diverse in economics, religion, ethnicity, and politics, they mustered enough unity to organize a revolutionary Congress, stop British imports, raise an army, obtain help from France, and win the war.

The states refused to create a unified nation, however, and instead established, under the Articles of Confederation, thirteen separate republics joined loosely by a representative Congress. Without power to tax or raise troops, the Congress faced severe postwar problems in demobilizing the army, paying the war debt, protecting the frontiers, and unifying a populace divided by war. In the wake of bankruptcy and insurrection, nationalists called together in 1787 a constitutional convention. Through a series of compromises, the framers drafted the new Constitution, which gave more authority to the central government yet retained considerable power in the states. Americans ratified the document with the understanding that amendments to protect individual liberties and states' rights would be forthcoming.

After the first national elections, the Constitution's proponents, the Federalists, controlled the new government, with George Washington as president, John Adams as vice president, Alexander Hamilton as secretary of the treasury, and Thomas Jefferson as secretary of state. Having agreed upon the frame of government, they were unprepared for the bitter factionalism that forged political parties in the 1790s. Nor were they ready for the foreign entanglements that resulted from two decades of war between Great Britain and post-revolutionary France. Only after the United States declared war on the British in 1812 and held its own as the conflict ended in stalemate, did the nation finally demonstrate its independence. By 1814, most of the men who led the American Revolution had passed from power—though James Madison would remain president for several years—and a new generation was taking control.

The heroic story of the young nation surmounting difficulties— two wars against Great Britain, a constitutional crisis, several internal rebellions, an undeclared conflict with France, and constant fighting on the frontier—masks other narratives, those of women, African Americans, and Native Americans, who failed to achieve autonomy. Though Dicey Langston was just one of thousands of sisters, mothers, and wives who risked their lives during the Revolution, they gained little as a result of their efforts. In the new republic, women still lacked basic legal and political rights to hold property after marriage, vote, and take part in government. And while Revolutionary rhetoric against slavery resulted in abolition in the north and many private manumissions in the Chesapeake region, most African Americans remained enslaved, a condition perpetuated by the new Constitution and development of cotton. Even most free blacks had little opportunity to acquire property and were denied suffrage and participation in government.

For Native Americans, the success and growth of the new nation meant their decline. Despite revitalization movements to restore traditional cultures led by Neolin, Handsome Lake, Tenskwatawa, and many others, and destructive wars to defend their homelands in Alabama, Tennessee, Kentucky, and Ohio, by 1814 the United States dominated most of the territory east of the Mississippi River. Native Americans tried various routes to survive and retain as much of their autonomy as possible—adoption of white culture, cession of some lands for the promise they could keep others, alliances with Great Britain and Spain, raids on white settlements, and pan-Indian war. In the face of unremitting westward movement of new settlers and the continuing effects of disease, the Indian peoples of eastern North America became remnants of formerly powerful nations.

* Elizabeth F. Ellet, *Domestic History of the American Revolution* (1850), p. 234.

	1764	1775	1780	1785	1790

POLITICS & DIPLOMACY

1765: Stamp Act protest
1766-1771: Regulator movements in North and South Carolina
1767: John Dickinson's "Farmer" letters against Townshend Act
1768: Non-importation movement
1769: Spanish colonize California
1770: Boston Massacre
1772: Committees of Correspondence
1773: Boston Tea Party
1774: Coercive Acts; port of Boston closed
First Continental Congress
1775: Battles of Lexington and Concord
Lord Dunmore's proclamation to servants and slaves

1776: Thomas Paine's *Common Sense*
Declaration of Independence
1777: Burgoyne surrenders to Americans at Saratoga
1778: Alliance with France
Iroquois attacks in New York and Pennsylvania
1780: Pennsylvania law for gradual abolition of slavery
1781: Articles of Confederation ratified
Surrender of Cornwallis at Yorktown
1783: Treaty of Paris

1787: Shaysites attack Springfield, MA, arsenal
Northwest Ordinance
Constitution sent to states for ratification
1789: Inauguration of President George Washington
1791: Bill of Rights ratified

SOCIAL & CULTURAL EVENTS

1765: First American medical school
1766: Queens College (Rutgers)
New Southwark Theatre in Philadelphia
1769: *The American Magazine* (Philadelphia) published
Benjamin West's *Death of General Wolfe*
American scientists observe transit of Venus
1770: Equestrian statue of George III installed in New York
1771: Benjamin Franklin starts *Autobiography*
c. 1772: John Singleton Copley's portrait of Samuel Adams
1773: Phillis Wheatley's *Poems on Various Subjects, Religious and Moral*

1776: Jemima Wilkinson becomes Public Universal Friend
1779: John Murray's American Universalist Church
1780s: Northern black separate churches and societies
1783: Noah Webster's American spelling book
First daily newspaper, *Pennsylvania Evening Post*
1784: Judith Sargent Murray begins essays on women's status

1786: Virginia statute for religious liberty
Gilbert Stuart's portrait of Joseph Brant
1791: Charles Willson Peale's *Thomas Jefferson*
c.1793: Mary Wollstonecraft's *Vindication of the Rights of Women* circulates in the U.S.

ECONOMICS & TECHNOLOGY

1760s: British American traders cross Mississippi River
1764: Sugar and Currency Acts
1776: Adam Smith's *An Inquiry into the Nature and Causes of the Wealth of Nations*
1778: Captain James Cook explores the Pacific Northwest
1779: Continental money becomes nearly worthless

1780s: Rapid settlement of Kentucky and Tennessee
Oliver Evans automates grist mills
1781: Bank of North America in Philadelphia
1783: Great Britain closes West Indies to American ships
1784: Spain closes port of New Orleans to Americans
1784: Debt crisis spurs protests in U.S.

1788: Pennsylvania Society for the Encouragement of Manufactures and the Useful Arts introduces spinning jennies
1790: Samuel Slater builds first U.S. water-powered textile mill
Congress passes patent law
1791: Bank of the United States
Excise tax on whiskey
Alexander Hamilton's plan for promoting manufactures
1793: British blockade of French West Indies
Eli Whitney's cotton gin

1794: Whiskey Rebellion
1795: Jay Treaty
1798: Alien and Sedition Acts
Quasi-war with France
1799: Fries Rebellion

1800: Washington, D.C., becomes national capital
Gabriel's Rebellion
Jefferson elected President
1803: *Marbury v. Madison* case
Louisiana Purchase
1804: Lewis and Clark expedition

1809: Tecumseh organizes pan-Indian confederacy
1812: U.S. war with Great Britain
1814: Treaty of Ghent

1795: Philadelphia Quaker women establish first female benevolent society in U.S.
1797: Second Great Awakening begins in New England
1799: Rise of Handsome Lake as Seneca prophet
Charles Brockden Brown's *Wieland*

1800s: Tenskwatawa, the Shawnee Prophet, inspires following
1800: Library of Congress
1801: Cane Ridge, Kentucky, camp meeting
1805: Pennsylvania Academy of Fine Arts

1795: Great Britain opens West Indies to U.S. trade
1796: Spain opens navigation on Mississippi River
Alexander Hamilton's industrial town in New Jersey fails
1798: Eli Whitney attempts to manufacture guns with interchangeable parts
1790s: U.S. international trade soars with European conflict
Cotton expands Southern slavery
Northern cities become magnets for African Americans

1802: Oliver Evans's high pressure steam engine
1806: Non-Importation Act
1807: Embargo Act
1808: Federal ban on international slave trade
1809: Giles's Enforcement Act
Embargo repealed; replaced with Non-Intercourse Act

1811: Charter of national bank expires

BURNING THE GASPÉE

Burning of Gaspée, *by Charles De Wolf Brownell. The seizure and burning of the British customs ship* Gaspée *by Rhode Island merchants in June 1772 moved the colonies closer to revolution.*

Chapter 5

WARS FOR INDEPENDENCE,

1764–1783

THE TREATY OF 1763 forced Spain and Great Britain to reassess their North American colonies. Both nations had new kings, as Charles III took Spain's throne in 1759 and George III became the British monarch in 1760. For the Spanish, the borderlands in North America were of secondary importance, serving as a buffer to protect the Mexican silver mines. For Britain, however, the mainland provinces had become increasingly significant as a source of revenue and market for consumer goods. The Seven Years' War marked Britain's ascendancy to world power, but resulted in a national debt of £130 million. Annual interest payments alone amounted to £4.5 million, equal to more than half of the government's yearly expenditures prior to the war.

When Parliament imposed levies on the American colonies to help pay expenses, the colonists protested vehemently that they should not be taxed without their consent. They complained that they had no representatives in Parliament, that only their elected provincial assemblies could constitutionally tax them. Beginning in 1764, the Americans petitioned, rioted, boycotted British goods, destroyed tea, and ultimately defied George III and parliamentary leaders when they sent troops. The colonists' belief that they possessed the same rights as the English was something for which many were willing to fight.

Nevertheless, the consensus to declare independence did not come quickly, nor was the war to defend independence easily won. Americans who disagreed that the British actions warranted insurrection remained loyal to the king. These loyalists, also called tories after the pro-monarchy faction in England, tried to subvert the revolutionary governments and formed loyalist militia units to fight alongside British troops. They found allies in many Indians and African Americans who conducted wars of independence of their own. Other colonists remained neutral, whether from principled opposition to violence or from sheer indifference. The Revolution touched everyone, Native Americans, women, and enslaved blacks, as well as the white men who served as military and civilian leaders and comprised most of the armed forces. The cause of the patriots—or whigs, as the American revolutionaries called themselves after the English party that had led opposition to the Crown—depended upon the efforts of many people, those who supplied and supported the troops, as well as those who fought.

CHRONOLOGY

1764	Sugar and Currency Acts		**1776**	Thomas Paine publishes *Common Sense*
	St. Louis founded			British evacuation of Boston
1765	Stamp Act provokes widespread colonial protest			Declaration of Independence
	Stamp Act Congress			Cherokee War on the southern frontier
1766	Parliament repeals Stamp Act, passes Declaratory Act			Americans defeated on Long Island; British occupation of New York City
	Spanish governor arrives in Louisiana			Battle of Trenton
1766–1771	North Carolina Regulator movement		**1777**	Battle of Princeton
1767	Passage of Townshend Act			British occupy Philadelphia after defeating Washington at Brandywine
	John Dickinson publishes "Farmer" letters			Battle of Germantown
1767–1769	South Carolina Regulator movement			Burgoyne surrenders to Americans at Saratoga
1768	Massachusetts assembly sends "circular letter"			Congress approves Articles of Confederation; sends document to states for ratification
	Non-importation movement against Townshend duties		**1778**	Alliance with France
	British troops stationed in Boston			Iroquois and loyalist attacks in New York and Pennsylvania
	Louisianans expel Spanish governor			British withdraw from Philadelphia
1769	Spanish reestablish control of Louisiana			Whig frontiersmen take settlements in the Illinois country
1770	Boston Massacre			British invade Georgia
	Partial repeal of Townshend Act		**1780**	Americans surrender at Charleston
1772	Burning of *Gaspée*			Battle of Camden
1772–1773	Committees of Correspondence established		**1781**	Battle of Cowpens
1773	Boston Tea Party			Articles of Confederation ratified
1774	Passage of Coercive Acts; port of Boston closed			Battle of Guilford Courthouse
	Quebec Act			Southern army reconquers most of South Carolina and Georgia
	First Continental Congress			Surrender of Cornwallis at Yorktown
	Congress organizes Continental Association		**1782**	Massacre at Gnadenhutten
1775	Battles of Lexington and Concord		**1783**	Signing of Treaty of Paris
	Second Continental Congress			
	Battle of Bunker Hill			
	Congress authorizes invasion of Canada			
	Lord Dunmore's proclamation to servants and slaves			

REALIGNMENTS IN THE SPANISH BORDERLANDS

The peace of 1763 required Spain to withdraw from Florida, assume the government of Louisiana, and rethink its defenses in Texas and New Mexico. With Britain's enhanced power, especially in light of its recent victories in Cuba and the Philippines, safeguarding the Mexican silver mines took high priority. The Spanish also considered the soaring population of the British colonies a dangerous, if future, threat to their American empire.

Florida and Louisiana

Spain ordered all of its subjects to leave Florida when Britain took control. Though the British promised religious freedom to the Catholic Floridians, some 200 Christian Indians, 79 free African Americans, 350 slaves, and nearly all of the 3,000 Hispanics departed from St. Augustine to Cuba, and from Pensacola to Mexico. Most of the Spanish colonists served in the military or were dependent on government funds, so they had little choice but to leave. They sold their property at a loss to British bargain hunters. The free blacks of Mose, near St. Augustine, could expect enslavement by the English, so took Spain's offer of homesteads in Cuba. They received some tools and money from the government, but faced hard times because they never received adequate compensation for their property in Florida. The British, who would hold the province for only twenty years, created two administrative districts, East and West Florida.

Acquisition of Louisiana, including all French territory west of the Mississippi River and New Orleans, on the east bank, gave Spain an extensive region to administer. Spain needed to win the loyalties of French inhabitants and Native Americans, and hoped to keep the British colonists out. The concern about British expansion became all too real as interlopers spanned the Mississippi River to trade with Indians on the Great Plains. The Spanish feared that the traders would lay the basis for a British takeover of Louisiana, increasing the vulnerability of the Mexican mines. British colonists moved quickly to the Gulf Coast and

eastern shore of the Mississippi (West Florida), where, within a decade, 4,000 whites and 1,500 African American slaves were living.

The more immediate challenge for Spanish authorities in Louisiana, however, was asserting political control of the province. Unlike the Floridians, most settlers stayed in Louisiana, hoping that the French government would return. In fact, for several years, French government remained; even after the first Spanish governor, Antonio de Ulloa, arrived in 1766, he tried to govern jointly with the last French governor. Adhering to Charles III's instructions, Ulloa left the French administration and legal system intact, even allowing the French flag to fly over the capital.

Ulloa did not extend this leniency to commerce, however, for his mission was to pull Louisiana under Spanish mercantilism. He tried to stop business with France and Great Britain and restricted the Native American trade to certain dealers. New Orleans merchants, who had enjoyed little regulation under the French, feared loss of markets and lower prices for their tobacco, indigo, sugar, deerskins, and lumber. Like the thirteen British provinces on the Atlantic coast, at about the same time, the merchants protested the new restrictions, then in October 1768 issued a declaration of loyalty to the king of France. With few Spanish troops at his disposal, Governor Ulloa left for Cuba. When the French refused to intervene, the colony became independent, but only for a year.

The Spanish regained Louisiana when General Alexander O'Reilly arrived in 1769 with more than 2,000 soldiers. An Irishman with a successful career in the Spanish army, O'Reilly arrested the rebels, put five of them to death, but pardoned most who had participated in the uprising. He raised the Spanish flag and within a year ended French government, changed the legal system, made Castilian the official language, and outlawed trade with other nations. Despite the merchants' fears, the economy flourished as smuggling continued with Britain, and Spanish markets welcomed their goods. St. Louis, established in 1764, became the thriving center of trade for beaver, buffalo, and deerskins with Native Americans of the Illinois and Missouri countries. Louisiana remained culturally French, as the numbers of French settlers far surpassed the Spanish. During the 1760s, some French moved into Louisiana from the east bank of the Mississippi, and at least 1,000 Acadians, who had been forced out of Nova Scotia by Britain, settled in the colony.

Fortifying the Southwest

With ownership of Louisiana, the Spanish could alter their defenses along the frontier in Texas and New Mexico. They removed several forts from East Texas. By the 1760s, the most immediate danger in the southwest came from the Apaches and Comanches, who defended their freedom from Hispanic slave catchers and attempted to drive the Spanish back into Mexico. Skillfully adopting the European horse and gun, they refused to submit to Spanish rule or Christianity. Spain gave up trying to convert them through missions, emphasizing military defense instead. The Apaches and Comanches raided settlements and pack trains, stole horses, mules, cattle, and supplies, killing Pueblos and white settlers alike.

During the 1760s and 1770s, in the face of constant Indian assaults that killed hundreds of settlers in New Mexico and Texas, Spain—like Great Britain in its colonies—tried to reform administration and improve defense. From 1766 to 1768, the Marqués de Rubí, a high-level military official from Spain, inspected the fortifications and missions of the southwest. He discovered badly located presidios (or forts) and soldiers suffering from lack of food and clothes because of their commanders' greed. At one Texas presidio, Rubí found sixty troops without shoes or uniforms and, among them, only two muskets that worked. He recommended building new presidios and relocating others to create an orderly cordon of military bases situated about a hundred miles apart. The presidios would extend from the Gulf of California to the Gulf of Mexico, along a line that was close to the present boundary between the United States and Mexico. The purpose of the cordon was to protect Mexico. Small numbers of Spanish troops would hold garrisons at Santa Fe and San Antonio, north of the cordon, to help defend Hispanics and allied Indians in New Mexico and Texas. The borderlands officials also received more autonomy to deal with local problems, but lacked sufficient troops to conquer the Apaches and Comanches. The settlements remained open to attack with such long distances between presidios.

THE BRITISH COLONIES RESIST IMPERIAL REFORM

In Britain's colonies, which experienced few restrictions before 1763, trouble began when George III appointed George Grenville as first minister, with responsibility for solving the debt crisis. Grenville decided that Americans should pay more taxes because they benefited from the Seven Years' War and continued to drain the government's budget for administrative and military costs. Because the British at home were highly taxed, Grenville's plan to make the colonies pay their way seemed reasonable to many. The Americans saw it differently, however, because they were proud of their role in the war and expected better treatment, so moved quickly to the brink of revolt.

The Sugar and Currency Acts

Grenville began his program in 1764 with the Sugar Act, which initiated a new policy of charging duties primarily to raise revenue rather than to regulate trade. It reduced the duty on foreign molasses from sixpence (under the Molasses Act of 1733) to threepence per gallon, which was further reduced to one penny in 1766. Grenville assumed merchants would pay the lower tariff rather than go to the risk of smuggling and bribery. The law also added timber, iron, and hides to the list of enumerated goods. To make smuggling more hazardous, the act gave increased powers to the vice-admiralty courts, which had been established earlier to hear maritime cases. Because these courts lacked juries, the government expected easy convictions for smuggling. In addition, the law expanded the use of writs of assistance (search warrants), empowered the Royal Navy to inspect ships, and required endless bureaucratic paperwork from colonial shippers. Parliament also passed the Currency Act (1764), which had the potential to cause further hardship by forbidding colonies from issuing paper money, thus creating a shortage of currency.

Coming in the midst of an economic depression, this legislation stirred up colonial protest. Provincial assemblies sent petitions to England requesting relief.

Most urgently, merchants feared that if imports of foreign molasses were cut off, their provision trade to the Spanish and French West Indies would be lost and the rum industry destroyed. Without foreign credits, they could not pay for British manufactures. The Americans slowed down their orders from Britain and encouraged home industry, arousing opposition to Grenville's policies from English businessmen. One colonial merchant wrote to associates in England that if the government deprived Americans of paper currency, "we shall not be able to export Provisions &c. in the same Degree as formerly, and if we are not on any Terms allow'd a Trade to get Money from abroad, we shall have none to pay you for Goods, and then unless you will send them Gratis our Dealings must end."

The Stamp Act

Passed by Parliament in 1765, the Stamp Act provoked an even greater storm of protest. The law departed entirely from the confines of mercantilist policy, for its purpose was to raise an internal revenue, which would be used to pay troops in the colonies. The act required individuals to purchase stamps for official documents and published papers, including deeds, liquor licenses, bills of lading, court documents, wills, passports, playing cards, newspapers, and pamphlets. All publications and official transactions were to be subject to this special tax, which increased with the value of a land sale or the size of a pamphlet. The tax could be paid only in specie, an onerous requirement because colonists generally used paper money and credit instead of the scarce gold and silver. The vice-admiralty courts would enforce the act, confiscating any land or property involved in transactions conducted without the stamps.

Colonists of all walks of life found the Stamp Act offensive. Everyone who engaged in public business, whether to buy a newspaper or sell property, would have to pay the tax. Because Parliament, not their provincial assemblies, passed the act, Americans considered it a violation of their rights as British subjects. As they understood the British constitution, the people must consent to taxes through their representatives. The provinces could not send delegates to Parliament, so that body should not tax them to raise revenue. As one Philadelphia merchant said succinctly, "the point in dispute is a very Important one,

Paul Revere's engraving of the hanging in effigy of an American-born member of Parliament, John Huske, an alleged Stamp Act supporter.

if the Americans are to be taxed by a Parliament where they are not nor can be Represented, they are no longer Englishmen but Slaves." Only tariffs to regulate trade such as the 1733 duty on molasses, many colonists believed, were constitutionally valid.

Recognizing Parliament's attack on their powers, provincial assemblies protested the Stamp Act. In the Virginia House of Burgesses, the newly elected Patrick Henry, only twenty-nine years old, introduced fourteen resolves against the tax. The Virginia assembly refused to accept all of Henry's proposals, for members considered some too radical, but in June 1765, approved the more moderate resolutions that defended the colonists' right to tax themselves.

When newspapers spread word of Virginia's action, other provinces responded. Rhode Island instructed its officials to ignore the stamp tax; Massachusetts,

Connecticut, New York, New Jersey, Pennsylvania, Maryland, and South Carolina passed resolves similar to Virginia's. In October 1765, representatives from nine colonies traveled to New York City to attend the Stamp Act Congress. In resolutions and petitions to Parliament, the congress upheld the power of representative assemblies, not Parliament, to tax the colonists. Further, the congress defended trial by jury, which the expanded authority of the vice-admiralty courts threatened. By issuing resolves and organizing the Stamp Act Congress, the colonial elite challenged British efforts to assert control. The wealthy merchants and planters who sat in provincial assemblies condemned Grenville's assault on their political and economic power.

Ordinary colonists recognized the threat as well. They drew upon the tradition of the mob to protest what they considered tyranny, just as residents of port cities had earlier resisted naval impressment. Crowds in the seaport towns were at the heart of the swelling revolutionary movement, as they blocked implementation of the odious law. The anti-Stamp Act riots began in Boston on August 14, 1765, when a group who called themselves the Loyal Nine organized a demonstration to hang in effigy the appointed stamp collector for Massachusetts, Andrew Oliver. The crowd destroyed a partially constructed building they thought he intended as his stamp office, then damaged his home. Oliver resigned his commission. Twelve days later, a Boston mob attacked the houses of several other officials, gutting the mansion of Lieutenant Governor Thomas Hutchinson.

Protesters all along the Atlantic seaboard mobilized to prevent stamp distribution, scheduled to begin November 1. News of Oliver's resignation prompted anti-Stamp Act mobs in other cities to demand the same from their appointed stampmen. The strategy seemed sensible: if the distributors quit, the stamps could not be sold. In some colonies, rioters forced stamp officials to relinquish their commissions. In others, just the threat of disorder was effective. By the end of 1765, distributors in every colony except Georgia had resigned.

The men who led the crowds called themselves Sons of Liberty, at first informally, then in organized resistance groups. They were mostly propertied men—small merchants, shopkeepers, and craftsmen—from neither the wealthiest nor the most destitute rungs of society. The activists were people who needed documents to conduct business, who would regularly feel the pinch of the stamp tax. The Sons of Liberty also established networks to organize boycotts of British goods. Merchants and retailers in New York City, Philadelphia, and Boston signed pacts to stop imports until Parliament repealed the act. By early 1766, the Sons of Liberty coerced customs officials and judges to open the ports and resume court business without stamps. To Thomas Hutchinson, it appeared "the authority of every colony is in the hands of the sons of liberty." In truth, the American resistance aimed to expunge the stamp tax, not end British authority. The movement achieved success in 1766, when Parliament repealed the Stamp Act, after British businessmen from more than twenty cities petitioned for relief. Suffering from postwar economic depression and unemployment, the British textile industry faced even worse times with an American boycott. They clearly understood the growing significance of the colonial market.

Protest Widens in the Lower South

In the Carolinas, the Stamp Act resistance spawned revolts against colonial elites, who in the eyes of African American slaves and many backcountry whites were more serious oppressors than Great Britain. To blacks, the radicals' oft-spoken argument that the English government intended to deprive white Americans of freedom—to make them slaves—seemed ironic. Yet such statements also gave hope, for the revolutionary movement spotlighted the institution of slavery and its immorality and injustice. While African Americans did not need the imperial crisis to know that slavery was wrong, they gained confidence from the political unrest. In January 1766, in Charleston, 1,400 seamen and a group of black slaves threatened serious disorder. The sailors became restless because the customs agents refused to release ships from port without stamped documents. The people of Charleston were even more concerned, however, when a group of enslaved men marched through the town shouting "Liberty!" The city armed itself against a slave revolt, while the South Carolina assembly became so frightened that it restricted slave imports for three years.

The North Carolina Regulator movement also began in 1766, inspired by the uproar against the Stamp Act, but targeted the colonial elite, not Britain. Six thousand western farmers demanded confirmation of land titles and the end of speculators' monopoly of the

VIRGINIA RESOLVES AGAINST THE STAMP ACT, 1765

When news arrived in 1765 that Parliament had passed the Stamp Act, the colonists protested the internal tax. In the Virginia assembly, Patrick Henry introduced resolutions defending the right of "taxation of the people by themselves, or by persons chosen by themselves to represent them" and accusing Parliament of attempting to destroy "American freedom." Newspapers published seven resolutions, of which the Virginia legislators passed the first four listed below, which were more moderate than the rest.

Resolved, That the first adventurers and settlers of this His Majesty's Colony and Dominion of Virginia brought with them, and transmitted to their posterity, and all other of His Majesty's subjects since inhabiting this His Majesty's said Colony, all the liberties, privileges, franchises, and immunities, that have at any time been held, enjoyed, and possessed, by the people of Great Britain.

Resolved, That by two royal charters, granted by King James the First, the colonists aforesaid are declared entitled to all liberties, privileges, and immunities of denizens and natural subjects, to all intents and purposes, as if they had been abiding and born within the realm of England.

Resolved, That the taxation of the people by themselves, or by persons chosen by themselves to represent them, who can only know what taxes the people are able to bear, or the easiest method of raising them, and must themselves be affected by every tax laid on the people, is the only security against a burthensome taxation, and the distinguishing characteristick of British freedom, without which the ancient constitution cannot exist.

Resolved, That His Majesty's liege people of this his most ancient and loyal Colony have without interruption enjoyed the inestimable right of being governed by such laws, respecting their internal polity and taxation, as are derived from their own consent, with the approbation of their sovereign, or his substitute; and that the same hath never been forfeited or yielded up, but hath been constantly recognized by the kings and people of Great Britain.

Resolved therefore, That the General Assembly of this Colony have the only and sole exclusive right and power to lay taxes and impositions upon the inhabitants of this Colony, and that every attempt to vest such power in any person or persons whatsoever other than the General Assembly aforesaid has a manifest tendency to destroy British as well as American freedom.

Resolved, That His Majesty's liege people, the inhabitants of this Colony are not bound to yield obedience to any law or ordinance whatever, designed to impose any taxation whatsoever upon them other than the laws or ordinances of the General Assembly aforesaid.

Resolved, That any person who shall, by speaking or writing, assert or maintain that any person or persons other than the General Assembly of this Colony, have any right or power to impose or lay any taxation on the people here, shall be deemed an enemy to His Majesty's Colony.

best land. The Regulators also protested corrupt local officials, excessive court fees and taxes, and lack of adequate representation for ordinary backcountry farmers in the North Carolina legislature. They called for a secret ballot to reduce the influence of wealthy planters in assembly elections. The North Carolina Regulators refused to pay taxes and closed several courts. In 1771, when the government sent the eastern militia, 2,000 Regulators met them at Alamance Creek but were dispersed.

Most of the grievances of the South Carolina Regulators were different, except that they too lacked fair representation in the provincial government. As in Pennsylvania (with the Paxton Boys revolt) and North Carolina, representation in the assembly had not kept pace with western settlement. In South Carolina, however, the Regulators were planters who wanted to bring order, "to regulate" the backcountry. The legislature had failed to create local government for the westerners, so they had no courts or jails. Everyone had to travel to Charleston to conduct legal business, but even worse, bandits roamed freely, stealing horses and cattle, destroying property, and sometimes torturing and killing their victims. The frontier robbers were mostly propertyless whites and some free blacks and escaped slaves; one report in the *South-Carolina Gazette* noted "a Gang of Banditti, consisting of Mulattoes—Free Negroes, and notorious Harbourers of run away Slaves." The Regulators resorted to vigilante "justice," capturing and whipping suspected felons, taking some to jail in Charleston, and evicting others from the colony. They finally ceased their activities in 1769 when the legislature established a circuit court system for the entire province.

The Townshend Revenue Act

In other British mainland colonies, attention focused on imperial tensions rather than regional disputes. The British government and American radicals emerged from the Stamp Act crisis with conflicting views: While the Americans celebrated the Stamp Act's repeal, convinced that they had won, the British yielded no authority. In the Declaratory Act, passed with the repeal in March 1766, Parliament affirmed its power to tax the colonies, indeed "to make laws and statutes of sufficient force and validity to bind the colonies and people of America, subjects of the crown of Great

Britain, in all cases whatsoever." The act generated little response in the colonies, but should have, for it laid the basis for subsequent restrictions. The government had withdrawn the offensive Stamp Act, but still argued that the colonies must support the army and Crown officials in America.

Thus, in June 1767, Parliament passed three more laws affecting the Americans: an act establishing the American Board of Customs Commissioners to enforce legislation against illegal trade, the New York Restraining Act, and the Townshend Revenue Act. The Restraining Act would have dissolved the New York Assembly for refusing adequate supplies to British soldiers stationed in the province. Instead, the New York legislators gave in, pledging additional funds for the troops. The Townshend Revenue Act was conceived by Charles Townshend, the British chancellor of the exchequer, who wanted the Americans to contribute, over time, an increasing percentage of imperial expenses in North America. The Townshend Act, which placed duties on tea, glass, paper, and paint would be just the beginning, for they would raise about £40,000 per year, less than one-tenth of the colonial administrative and military costs. The revenues would pay the salaries of governors and judges, thus removing their dependence upon the provincial legislatures. The act also required colonial courts to provide customs officials with writs of assistance to search houses and businesses for smuggled merchandise.

To American whigs, the Townshend Act was dangerous for two reasons: It raised revenue without the approval of colonial assemblies and it removed royal officials from the lawmakers' control. If the king rather than the legislatures paid provincial governors, the colonies lost a powerful negotiating tool for obtaining consent to the laws they wanted. While the British saw the Townshend Act as an appropriate way to force the Americans to begin paying their share, the colonists believed it was a step towards tyranny—towards the loss of traditional English rights.

At first, colonial reaction to the Townshend Act was restrained, largely because the impact of the new law seemed limited. Then, in December 1767, a few weeks after the Townshend Act went into effect, John Dickinson, a Philadelphia lawyer and owner of a Delaware plantation, began publishing a series of twelve letters signed "A Farmer." Soon reprinted by newspapers throughout the thirteen colonies and published in pamphlet form as *Letters from a Farmer in Pennsylvania*

John Dickinson inspired opposition to the Townshend Act with his Letters from a Farmer in Pennsylvania. *This engraving shows the right arm of Dickinson's "Patriotic American Farmer" resting on the English Magna Charta.*

(1768), Dickinson's arguments galvanized opposition to the Townshend duties. He warned that the colonies must work together; for lack of support from the other provinces, New York had little choice but to cave in and supply the British troops. He rejected the position that the colonists should accept external taxes (duties) but not internal taxes (like the stamp tax), stating that only elected representatives could legally impose *any* revenue tax. He believed that Parliament could collect duties in the colonies if the purpose was to regulate trade (as with the Molasses Act of 1733), but not to raise revenue. Further, the purpose of the funds collected under the Townshend Act was oppressive, for it eliminated the power of the colonial legislatures over Crown officials. Dickinson predicted that if the Americans failed to have this act repealed, harsher measures would be forthcoming: "If we can find no relief from this infamous situation . . . we may bow down our necks, with all the stupid serenity of servitude, to any

drudgery which our lords and masters shall please to command." Dickinson urged the thirteen colonies to petition for repeal; if that failed, they should once again boycott British goods.

Massachusetts responded first and most enthusiastically to Dickinson's call to action. In early 1768, its assembly petitioned George III for redress, then dispatched a "circular letter" to the other twelve colonies suggesting they do the same. The new English secretary of state for the colonies, Lord Hillsborough, realized that the circular letter was a call to unified resistance. He took his job—to bring colonial affairs in America under control—most seriously. In doing so, he fanned rebellion. Denouncing Dickinson's pamphlet as "extremely wild," he targeted the Massachusetts assemblymen as troublemakers, ordering them to rescind their circular letter. They refused. When he ordered colonial governors to dissolve assemblies that responded to the letter, most legislatures sent petitions and were disbanded. Simultaneously, Hillsborough reassigned military units from the Ohio Valley to Florida, Nova Scotia, Quebec, and the mid-Atlantic region where they could be called upon to control the defiant provinces.

In June 1768, when Massachusetts remained unbowed and the customs commissioners demanded protection against rioters, Hillsborough sent British regiments to Boston. The colonial secretary wanted even more drastic measures to punish the colony—to quarter soldiers in private homes and install a provincial government more sympathetic to the Crown—but failed to convince his colleagues that these steps were necessary. Unrest in Ireland and rumors of Spanish expansion in the American west probably made them unwilling to risk revolt. When troops disembarked in Boston in October 1768, they heard cries of protest but met no armed resistance. As months passed, however, the presence of the redcoats created tensions that would eventually erupt in bloodshed.

Between the time Lord Hillsborough ordered the regiments to Boston and their arrival four months later, city residents had signed a non-importation agreement against the Townshend Act. Most Boston merchants pledged to stop importing goods from Great Britain after January 1, 1769, unless the Townshend duties were repealed. The non-importation movement soon spread to New York City, where artisans supported the merchants by agreeing to boycott any retailer who imported British goods. Traders in

The Occupation of Boston, *1768, engraving by Paul Revere(?), illustrates the arrival of British troops on the Long Wharf (center).*

Philadelphia, New Haven, and other northern ports delayed action, however, because they would face economic loss. They waited until 1769 for the imperial government to respond to their petitions, then approved non-importation. In Virginia, George Washington kindled the boycott. He wrote, "At a time when our lordly masters in Great Britain will be satisfied with nothing less than the deprivation of American freedom, it seems highly necessary that some thing should be done to avert the stroke and maintain the liberty which we have derived from our Ancestors."

The boycotts, which were unofficial agreements without the force of law, met uneven success as colonists disagreed over whether to join. Between 1768 and 1769, American imports from England declined fairly substantially, by 38 percent. As the months passed, however, importers wavered as their incomes fell. In contrast, craftsmen—beyond their concern for liberty—often benefited from the boycott because it created a demand for their products. Some artisans organized into street groups to threaten merchants and customs officials who tried to undermine the non-importation pacts.

Women participated both as purchasers of goods and as producers. Many "Daughters of Liberty" gave up imported tea and clothing, signing agreements to avoid the banned goods. The *Boston News-Letter* reported that "a large circle of very agreeable ladies in this town . . . unanimously agreed" not to purchase ribbons and other imports. Instead, throughout New England, women organized spinning bees to produce woolen yarn. In Boston, some impoverished women profited from the temporary demand for American-made cloth, when William Molineaux, a merchant and radical whig, contracted with local artisans to build 400 spinning wheels, which he distributed to women to spin yarn in their homes. With this "putting-out" system, Molineaux and the spinners responded to both their patriotism and economic needs.

Crisis in Boston

During the years 1769 to 1775, while opposition to British policies grew throughout the colonies, Boston became the powder keg of the Revolution. Violence broke out in the summer of 1769 between the Bostonians and British redcoats, as the heavily armed strangers imposed themselves upon a populace hostile to standing armies. The chief responsibilities of the troops were to protect the despised customs commissioners and help them collect duties. The soldiers became even more unpopular when they took jobs at low pay during their off-duty hours, thus throwing city laborers out of work.

The first serious incident occurred in July 1769, when a redcoat, John Riley, was jailed for hitting a local butcher who had insulted him. A near riot followed as twenty of Riley's comrades tried to rescue him from jail. The soldier's commander said that the butcher had gotten what he deserved. Such episodes continued into early 1770, as each side assaulted the other. On March 2, the violence escalated when soldiers seeking revenge for an insult attacked workers at John Gray's ropeworks. Street fights intensified over the next few days, as townspeople and soldiers exchanged angry words and blows. On March 5, the bloodiest incident occurred, the so-called Boston Massacre. A young apprentice taunted the British sentry at the Customs House, who hit the boy with his gun. When a crowd gathered, shouting at the sentry, "Kill him, kill him, knock him down," Captain Thomas Preston led seven soldiers to assist him. The crowd grew larger, throwing snowballs, ice, and sticks at the soldiers, threatening them with clubs, and calling them "bloody backs," lobsters, and cowards. Then someone hit a redcoat with a club, knocking the gun out of his hands. Preston's men fired, killing five townspeople and wounding six. The dead became martyrs, with March 5 commemorated as "Massacre Day" in the years ahead. The incident crystallized the colonists' opposition to standing armies. Nevertheless, when Captain Preston and six soldiers were tried for murder, the jury found two soldiers guilty of manslaughter and cleared the others. The radical whig lawyer John Adams defended them, saying that all Englishmen should have a fair trial.

Just as the crisis in Boston reached its head in spring 1770, the British government decided on partial repeal of the Townshend Act. The duties had raised under £21,000 in revenues, but cost hundreds of thousands of pounds sterling in trade as a result of the non-importation movement. Lord North, the new British leader, recommended removing the Townshend duties on paint, paper, and glass, but keeping the duty on tea. North wanted to help British merchants who had suffered from the American boycott "without giving up that just right which I shall ever wish the mother country to possess, the right of taxing the Americans." So, as in the case of the Stamp Act, British officials backed away from a specific revenue measure without abandoning their right to levy taxes. Following Parliament's action, merchants in New York City and other colonial ports, eager to resume trade, cancelled their boycotts except on tea. Imports into the thirteen colonies from England rebounded over the next several years, increasing from £1.3 million in 1769 to £4.2 million in 1771, which was twice the value of imports before the boycotts.

The Gaspée Incident

For two years, the conflict between Great Britain and the colonies abated, then flared again in 1772. Trouble began this time in Rhode Island, when more than one hundred men burned the British schooner Gaspée, wounding its commander, William Dudingston. Avidly enforcing the Sugar Act, the Gaspée had harassed merchant vessels sailing through Narragansett Bay. The Crown named a Commission of Inquiry to locate the perpetrators and send them to England to be tried for high treason. Though the Commission identified none of the Gaspée's attackers, colonists viewed the policy of taking defendants to England for trial as a serious threat to their constitutional rights.

In response, the Virginia assembly reignited the resistance movement by appointing a Committee of Correspondence to monitor British policy and facilitate communication among the provinces. The Virginians recommended to other colonies that they do the same. Within a year, Committees of Correspondence in all thirteen provinces coordinated opposition to Britain's restraints.

The Boston Tea Party

The final showdown began in 1773, when Parliament passed the Tea Act to bail out the nearly bankrupt East India Company. Though some colonists purchased British tea, the boycott on the product was still in effect and many purchased cheaper, smuggled Dutch tea. To sell the company's huge surplus, the government dropped a heavy import duty into England on tea headed for America, but retained the Townshend duty, which Lord North insisted on keeping to uphold Parliament's power to tax. Indeed, he viewed the Tea Act as a way to induce Americans to accept parliamentary authority, since the price of tea would fall. The company also received a monopoly in the colonies, with the right to choose certain provincial merchants as agents. The company selected consignees in the ports of Charleston, Philadelphia, New York, and Boston, to whom it promptly dispatched nearly 600,000 pounds of tea.

The Tea Act was doubly offensive to American whigs as it renewed opposition to the duty and caused outrage over favoritism and privilege. One radical called the act "a dirty trick" and accused Lord North of "low cunning" for trying to break American resistance by reducing the price of tea. Before the tea ships arrived in Charleston, Philadelphia, and New York, militants convinced the East India Company's agents to resign. The Charleston tea was stored in a customs warehouse, while the ships headed toward Philadelphia and New York turned back to England with their cargo. In Boston, the consignees, two of them sons of pro-British Governor Thomas Hutchinson, declined to quit. When three ships arrived, members of the Boston Committee of Correspondence, led by Samuel Adams, prevented them from unloading. Adams, the cousin of John, had been the chief agitator in Boston since the Stamp Act. A skilled politician and writer, though

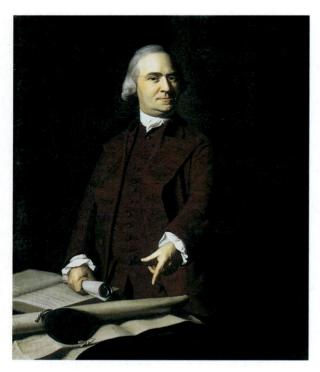

Samuel Adams, *portrait by John Singleton Copley. Sam Adams helped make Boston the center of colonial radical resistance from the Stamp Act to the Boston Tea Party and its aftermath.*

failed businessman, he kept the pot simmering against British policies and Governor Hutchinson. Now, with the Boston committee, he brought matters to a head: In a series of meetings, thousands of residents of Boston and surrounding towns met to refuse the tea. On December 16, 1773, when customs officials and Hutchinson denied the ships clearance to leave port, radicals ill-disguised as Mohawks boarded the ships, broke open the tea chests, and dumped them overboard. The destruction cost nearly £10,000.

For the British, the Boston Tea Party required stern action, for once again the Bostonians had defied them. London decided that steps must "be taken to secure the Dependence of the Colonies," and in particular, "to mark out Boston and separate that Town from the rest of the Delinquents." George III believed that the Americans must be forced to submit, because they increasingly assumed the "independency which one state has of another, but which is quite subversive of the obedience which a colony owes to its Mother Country." In 1774, Parliament passed four Coercive Acts that closed the port of Boston until residents of the city paid for the destroyed tea; altered the provincial charter to limit the power of town meetings and make the council the appointees of the Crown instead of elected officials; expanded the governor's control over the courts; provided that trials of royal officials could be moved to England or to another colony; and permitted quartering of troops in private buildings if a colony failed to provide suitable barracks. The Crown appointed General Thomas Gage, commander of the British army in North America, as Massachusetts governor, thus threatening the colonists with military force.

Americans called these the Intolerable Acts and believed that the Quebec Act (1774) was another, though London did not intend it to punish the Bostonians. The Quebec Act provided that an appointed council not an elected assembly make laws, confirmed religious freedom to Roman Catholics in Canada, allowing them to hold public office, and gave control of the Ohio Valley to the Quebec government. The law boded ill for representative government in the colonies. The New Englanders abhorred the act because it extended rights to "papists," while speculators in other colonies bemoaned the loss of western lands.

The First Continental Congress

Though the British government expected the Coercive Acts to isolate Boston and convince other provinces to

Cartoon showing the Americans providing food to Bostonians "caged" by the Boston Port Act, one of the Coercive Acts.

recognize the rights of Americans, but was not ready to declare independence. Some of its leadership, notably Galloway (who later became a loyalist), argued for a moderate course, but the Congress was committed to action. It confirmed the Suffolk County Resolves forwarded to Philadelphia by a local Massachusetts convention. The Resolves blasted the Coercive Acts as "gross infractions of those rights to which we are justly entitled by the laws of nature, the British constitution and the charter of this province." The laws should "be rejected as the attempts of a wicked administration to enslave America." Everyone qualified to fight should learn "the art of war as soon as possible, and . . . appear under arms at least once a week." By endorsing these Resolves, the Congress took a militant stance.

Further, the Continental Congress passed non-importation, non-exportation, and non-consumption resolutions, ending all trade with Great Britain and Ireland, and exports to the West Indies. It also banned importation of slaves. If the British had hoped to divide the colonies by closing Boston, expecting other cities to pick up its trade, the plan backfired when all of the colonies closed their ports. The boycott would

be obedient, the policies actually pushed Americans toward more unified resistance. After the port of Boston closed, residents faced severe unemployment and food shortages. Neighboring towns provided supplies and harbored refugees looking for work. When Sam Adams and the Boston Committee of Correspondence requested an immediate boycott of British trade, instead the other provinces favored a Continental Congress to consider what action to take. The Massachusetts assembly proposed a meeting in Philadelphia on September 1, 1774, to which all of the thirteen colonies except Georgia sent delegates. The fifty-five representatives included Richard Henry Lee, Patrick Henry, and George Washington of Virginia; Sam and John Adams of Massachusetts; and John Dickinson and Joseph Galloway of Pennsylvania.

The primary purpose of the First Continental Congress was to obtain repeal of the Coercive Acts and other restrictions. The Congress wanted Parliament to

A British cartoon mocking American women who joined the boycott on tea, titled "A Society of Patriotic Ladies at Edenton in N.C."

continue until repeal of the Coercive Acts. Congress set up the Continental Association to enforce the ban on trade through elected local committees, called Committees of Observation and Inspection, or Committees of Safety. The groups would expose violators of the boycott as "enemies of American liberty," publicizing their names and interrupting their business. Almost every town and county in the thirteen colonies elected these committees, which soon took on other functions of local government, including raising militias and collecting taxes. This transfer of authority from colonial governments to the Committees of Observation was revolutionary, for Americans were vesting sovereignty in themselves rather than in Parliament. For its part, the Continental Congress agreed to meet again in May 1775 if the British failed to repeal the acts, thus confirming its role in coordinating the opposition.

RESISTANCE BECOMES A WAR FOR INDEPENDENCE

Over the winter of 1774–1775, the rift widened between the thirteen colonies and Great Britain. George III and his ministers considered the colonies in rebellion, yet the colonists themselves were unprepared to declare independence, a step they delayed for more than a year after hostilities began in April 1775.

Lexington and Concord

The British wanted to quell the revolt quickly, so instructed General Gage to take forceful action. Headquartered in Boston, he decided to seize the patriots'

MAP 5.1   BATTLES IN EASTERN MASSACHUSETTS

Battle of Lexington, *engraving by C. Tiebout after the drawing by E. Tisdale. The artist evokes the confusion and shock of the first battle of the Revolution.*

stores of food and ammunition at Concord, which he had learned about from an informer. Militant Bostonians discovered Gage's plan from their own spies, so were ready to spread the alarm on the night of April 18, 1775, when 700 redcoats mustered on Boston Common. Paul Revere and William Dawes escaped the city to raise the colonial militia and alert leaders Sam Adams and John Hancock, who were staying at Lexington, on the route to Concord. The Massachusetts Provincial Council, just a few weeks before, had resolved to resist any advance by Gage's troops.

As the British marched the sixteen miles to Concord, they heard church bells and saw lights in windows. Soon after sunrise on April 19th they reached Lexington, where they met about seventy armed militia, nearly half of the town's adult males. The Lexington company, led by Captain John Parker, had formed only a few weeks earlier, so their training was incomplete. But they were willing to defend, in the words of their town meeting, their "natural, constitutional and chartered rights." In the face of six companies of British infantry, Captain Parker attempted to disperse his troops. The British officer, Major John Pitcairn, wanted to disarm the Americans, not engage in battle. As the British advanced, a shot rang out, then several shots, and a British volley. Pitcairn tried to stop his troops, but the carnage continued for fifteen to twenty

minutes, leaving eight Lexington men dead and ten wounded. Only one British soldier was wounded and none killed. With the Battle of Lexington, which both commanders tried to avoid, the American war for independence began.

The British reached Concord at about eight o'clock in the morning, long after the patriots had hidden most of their military stores. Following a brief skirmish in which the Americans inflicted more casualties than the British, the redcoats headed back to Boston. The march became a harrowing escape for their lives. Hundreds of colonial militia from throughout the Massachusetts countryside rushed to battle. These farmers ignored standard eighteenth-century European military order of shooting and firing from fixed field positions. Instead, they used guerrila tactics, shooting from behind trees, walls, rocks, and buildings. The British countered the guerrilas by sending advance parties to clear houses along the route. Using their famed skills with the bayonet, the redcoats killed the occupants and set fire to the homes. By the end of the day, British losses totaled seventy-three dead and 200 wounded or missing, while Massachusetts counted forty-nine killed and forty-three wounded and missing.

In the days that followed the battles of April 19, New England went to arms. Over 20,000 volunteers streamed to Cambridge from as far away as a hundred miles. A large proportion of these soldiers soon returned home, but many stayed, expecting their wives, mothers, and sisters to work the family farms and defend the towns. One group of thirty to forty women of Pepperell and Groton guarded a bridge on the route British reinforcements might travel from Canada. Dressed in men's clothes and armed with muskets and pitchforks, they met no military action but arrested a tory spy. As Abigail Adams, the wife of John Adams, later wrote, "We are in no wise dispirited here. If our men are all drawn off and we should be attacked, you would find a race of Amazons in America."

Troops from throughout New England besieged Gage's redcoats in Boston. Nathanael Greene, a young ex-Quaker who later demonstrated his brilliance as a military strategist in the southern campaign, led 1,500 troops from Rhode Island. Connecticut promised 6,000 men and New Hampshire sent 2,000. From these earliest days of conflict, African American men served in the militia units. Without a unified army, each colony separately raised troops, selected officers, and secured provisions. By May 1775, the New England forces surrounding Boston numbered about 17,000, as the patriots considered themselves at war. Ethan Allen and his Green Mountain Boys of Vermont captured Fort Ticonderoga, the British garrison on Lake Champlain in northern New York. They commandeered the fort's heavy artillery, with plans to draw by sled the cannon east to Boston when snow fell the next winter.

George Washington, *by James Peale. In choosing Washington as commander-in-chief, the Continental Congress selected a revolutionary dedicated to republican government. His perseverance and leadership kept the army together despite battlefield reverses and lack of supplies.*

The Second Continental Congress

On May 10, 1775, the day after Allen's victory at Ticonderoga, the Second Continental Congress met in Philadelphia. While the delegates remained unwilling to support independence, they were disappointed by Parliament's refusal to change its course. They faced the prospect of executing a war already in progress, convinced that British troops had fired the first shots and committed atrocities. Congress moved slowly to ensure that all of the colonies backed the war, that it was America's effort, not just New England's. The delegates also wanted Congress to control the military, so to serve both purposes, they appointed George Washington of Virginia as commander-in-chief of the Continental army. Designating a southerner to head the military, which in June 1775 consisted of New England-

landers, broadened the appeal of the Massachusetts cause. At the same time, Washington was himself a delegate to Congress and steadfastly committed to civilian control of the armed forces. Despite his limited military experience, and early failures in the field, Washington proved to be an excellent choice. Indeed, for many he became the symbol of the American cause. His military bearing, determination, dignity, physical stamina, and ability to learn from his mistakes suited his role as commander-in-chief.

To serve under Washington, Congress appointed thirteen generals. Its four major generals were Artemas Ward of Massachusetts, the less than energetic commander of the troops surrounding Boston; Philip Schuyler of New York; Israel Putnam of Connecticut; and Charles Lee, a veteran officer of the British army and recent immigrant to Virginia. The adjutant general was Horatio Gates, also a veteran British officer and Virginia planter. The brigadier generals included seven New Englanders and one New Yorker, reflecting the regional origins of men in arms at that time.

"An Open and Avowed Rebellion"

Before Washington could arrive in Massachusetts, his troops engaged in the Battle of Bunker Hill. Learning that the British planned to seize the hills overlooking Boston, a detachment of the patriot army began to fortify the Charlestown heights. By mistake, the men built defenses on Breed's Hill rather than on the higher and less exposed Bunker Hill. This lapse might

Battle of Bunker Hill *(1786) by John Trumbull of Connecticut, who had fought for American independence. This is one of a series of paintings by Trumbull on the Revolution.*

have isolated the detachment from the rest of the army had the British moved more quickly. Instead of attacking immediately, however, General Gage and the man who would soon replace him as commander of British forces, William Howe, foolishly allowed the Americans to complete their fortifications and obtain reinforcements. The British regulars lined up in proper European formation to storm Breed's Hill. Boston residents climbed to their roofs to watch. While the redcoats shot as they advanced up the hill—to little effect—the patriots waited until the enemy was within range of their guns. The Americans refused to engage the British in standard European warfare. The redcoats failed on their first two assaults, losing many officers and troops, then with reinforcements took the hill when the Americans' ammunition gave out. The patriots retreated, pounded by artillery from British ships. While the British won the battle, their losses were staggering, as over 40 percent of their combatants were killed or wounded.

During the year following Bunker Hill, while the British and American governments moved toward the ultimate break, many colonists became whigs. The lives lost on battlefields in eastern Massachusetts undercut advocates of restraint. Still, given opposition from many delegates, the Continental Congress could not declare independence. During the summer of 1775, Congress pursued two strategies: It asked the king for peace while preparing for war. In July, it approved a petition to George III, called the Olive Branch Petition, asking that he resolve their dispute with Parliament. Upon receipt of the petition in August, outraged by the colonists' armed resistance, the king proclaimed the thirteen provinces in "an open and avowed rebellion." In December, Parliament cut off all trade with the colonies, making American ships and any vessels engaging in commerce with the mutinous provinces subject to confiscation. For many Americans, these actions proved that the British government meant to crush the colonies militarily and economically. For militant whigs, there was no turning back.

The Continental Congress further alienated the British by ordering General Philip Schuyler to invade Canada. The congressmen hoped to make Canada the fourteenth British colony in rebellion. They expected to obtain help from French Canadians and perhaps even France itself, but even more, they wanted to prevent a northern attack. The American invasion of Canada was a failure from the start. Schuyler, suffering from illness and indecision, assembled troops and provisions too slowly, wasting valuable summer days. In September, much too late, Brigadier General Richard Montgomery took charge and moved the army north via Lake Champlain, but as Montgomery said, a "winter Campaign in Canada! Posterity won't believe it!" Compounding this mistake, the enlistments of many of the soldiers would expire at the end of the year.

Concurrently, Washington dispatched a small army under Benedict Arnold and Daniel Morgan, two talented officers, over a rugged route through Maine. Their march took so much longer than predicted that the men had to eat their dogs and soap. When the combined American forces finally attacked Quebec in a blinding December snowstorm, they were defeated with heavy casualties, including Montgomery dead and Arnold wounded. The army remained in Canada until May 1776 when British reinforcements arrived, pushing the patriots back into New York. For Congress, the campaign was a tragic error. The thirteen colonies lost 5,000 troops to battle, desertion, and disease and an enormous amount of supplies, which would prove difficult to replace in coming months.

Taking Sides

The deepening conflict forced colonists to decide whether or not to support the revolutionary whigs. Some people remained neutral, either because they cared little about the issues involved or because, like the pacifist Quakers, they were opposed to violence on religious grounds. Loyalists rejected the Revolution for a variety of motives. Some, out of principle, believed that the king and Parliament were right, or at least had reason to expect the colonists to pay their share toward imperial administration. During the course of the war, about 80,000 loyalists departed for Britain or other British colonies. Many more, numbering perhaps several hundred thousand, continued to live among their patriot neighbors. Tories included Crown officials, Anglican clergy, and merchants with close ties to Britain. Some of the best known loyalists were wealthy gentlemen and officeholders: Governor Thomas Hutchinson and Chief Justice Peter Oliver of Massachusetts; Joseph Galloway, speaker of the Pennsylvania Assembly; and Frederick Philipse, landlord of a 50,000-acre manor in New York, whose tenants reported him as a tory to the whig authorities.

Many tories were not rich or intimately tied to Great Britain, for the Revolution became a power struggle within American society, not just one between the colonies and London. The tenants of New York manors, for example, took the opposite side of their landlords. Thus, residents of Frederick Philipse's manors became whigs, while tenants of the patriot Livingstons and Schuylers supported the British. In Maryland, the loyalists gained widespread backing in Eastern Shore counties where farmers, suffering from economic decline and lack of political power, regarded the patriot elite as their enemies. The South Carolina backcountry divided along lines drawn during the 1760s, with the more affluent former Regulators supporting the whigs, and their opponents, the "lower sort," casting their lot with the British.

Of considerable concern to white Americans, especially those living in the south, were the loyalties of enslaved African Americans. Of the 2.5 million people in the thirteen colonies in 1775, about 500,000 were blacks, most living in the Chesapeake and Lower South. As the rhetoric of revolution reached African American slaves, increasing numbers escaped. On Maryland's Eastern Shore, loyalist whites made common cause with the bondpeople of whig planters: In fall 1775, a Dorchester County committee reported that "the insolence of the Negroes in this county is come to such a height, that we are under a necessity of disarming them which we effected on Saturday last. We took about eighty guns, some bayonets, swords, etc. The malicious and imprudent speeches of some among the lower classes of whites have induced them to believe that their freedom depended on the success of the King's troops."

A chief source of unrest, the patriots believed, was the November 1775 proclamation of Lord Dunmore, royal governor of Virginia, declaring "all indented [sic] servants, Negroes, or others [owned by rebels] free, that are able and willing to bear arms, they joining His Majesty's Troops." Whigs considered this proclamation foul play, an attempt to start an insurrection. They increased slave patrols, tried to convince blacks that the British would sell them to West Indies planters, and warned of harsh punishments to those who ran away or took up arms against their masters. The penalty for slave rebellion, of course, was death. Nevertheless, African Americans aided the British by joining the army and employing their firsthand knowledge of Chesapeake Bay. Some served as pilots along its tribu-

Baron Ludwig von Closen's sketch of American army uniforms reflects the military role of African Americans.

taries, while others delivered fresh provisions to the British ships by foraging plantations at night.

African Americans also supported the Revolution, but received little welcome from the whigs. As the Americans created an army from volunteer forces besieging Boston, they excluded slaves and even free blacks from participating. From 1775 through much of 1776, when white enlistments seemed adequate, the patriot leaders, many of them slaveowners, were unwilling to exchange freedom for military service. Whites feared the results of arming slaves. By 1777, however, when recruiters found it difficult to fill their quotas, the states north of Virginia began accepting free blacks and slaves. Officially, Virginia took only free African Americans, but some masters sent slaves as substitutes for themselves. An estimated 5,000 African Americans served in the Continental army and state militias or at sea on American privateers. They fought side by side with whites, not in segregated units. At the end of their service, many but not all of the enslaved African Americans who fought for indepen-

dence received freedom. Some masters who had pledged liberty to their slaves if they served as substitutes broke the promises after the war.

Estimates of the total number of Americans who joined the whig forces range from 100,000 to 250,000. Because most signed up for tours of duty lasting several months or a year, not for the duration of the war, the exact number of troops is impossible to determine. An ardent Boston patriot, for example, a poor shoemaker named George Robert Twelves Hewes, served at least six different stints for a total of twenty months. Ordinary people like Hewes did their best to support both the patriotic cause and their families. Thus, Washington and his generals constantly faced the problem of expiring enlistments, a condition that severely hampered execution of the war. The inability of Congress to pay soldiers adequately also hindered recruitment and retention of troops. As time went on, the American troops became more professional, better trained, and disciplined, but originated from less privileged rungs of society. By 1778, most of

Deborah Sampson, *by Joseph Stone, 1797. After the Revolution, Sampson gave public lectures about how she disguised herself as a man and enlisted in the Continental Army.*

the states had to adopt conscription to fill their quotas. Men were drafted by lottery, but could pay a fine or hire a substitute, loopholes that contributed to disproportionate service by the poor.

Women took part in the American war effort by operating farms and businesses in their husbands' absence, defending their homes and families against marauding enemy soldiers, supplying food and clothing for the troops, and joining the army. Perhaps several hundred women put on uniforms to become soldiers. These troops included Deborah Sampson of Massachusetts, who enlisted under the name Robert Shurtleff. She fought in battle, but was discovered when she received a wound; after the war she collected an army pension. Another took the name of Samuel Gay, attained the rank of corporal, then according to the record was "discharged, being a woman, dressed in men's clothes. August 1777." Others performed unofficial short-term service as spies. The most substantial contribution of women to the American military was that of the Women of the Army, as George Washing-

ton called them. Numbering perhaps 20,000 over the course of the war, they served as nurses, cooks, laundresses, and water carriers. They were regular members of the army who drew rations and were subject to military discipline. Some saw action in battle, particularly women in artillery crews who carried water to swab out the cannon after each firing. The story of "Molly Pitcher" evolved from women like Mary Hayes of Carlisle, Pennsylvania, who took the place of fallen soldiers.

Independence and Confederation

During the winter and spring of 1776, fighting continued between Great Britain and the thirteen colonies. Though the Canada campaign was a disaster, the Americans gained success in their siege of Boston. They sledged the heavy guns from Fort Ticonderoga about 300 miles, installing them in March 1776 on the Dorchester Heights. Instead of storming the artillery, the British withdrew from the city, sailing to Nova Scotia in preparation for an invasion of New York City, which General William Howe considered a more central location for defeating the rebels. About a thousand tories left Boston with Howe's troops, a pattern that was repeated in British evacuations throughout the war.

In 1776, London undertook a huge effort to put down the revolt. It sent across the Atlantic Ocean 370 transports with supplies and 32,000 troops, of whom many were German mercenaries (called Hessians because the largest proportion came from the principality of Hesse-Cassel). The British intended these soldiers to join William Howe's 10,000 troops from Nova Scotia, take New York City, and destroy Washington's army. The British navy, with seventy-three warships and 13,000 sailors in American waters, would bombard seaports and play havoc on colonial shipping. The British expected considerable assistance from the loyalists.

As the British military descended upon New York in midsummer 1776, the Continental Congress finally declared independence. The force of events propelled most moderate delegates to cast their vote for a complete break. In January 1776, Thomas Paine, a recent immigrant from England, had published *Common Sense.* Though his arguments were familiar to Congress and readers of political tracts, Paine convinced the American public of the need for independence.

Thomas Paine, *by John Wesley Jarvis. A superb propagandist, the recent English immigrant convinced many Americans, "'tis time to part"—to declare independence.*

Common Sense sold over 100,000 copies within a few months, reaching hundreds of thousands of people as copies changed hands and nonreaders listened to Paine's words read aloud. An equivalent press run in the United States today would be over 12 million copies. In Philadelphia, according to a report, the tract was "read to all ranks." Paine used language that appealed to ordinary Protestant Americans, employing biblical arguments that churchgoing farmers and craftspeople could appreciate, and avoiding Latin phrases and classical references known only to well-educated elites. He wanted to demonstrate that the time for compromise had passed, that the proper course was to shed the British monarchy and aristocracy to create an American republic. "We have it in our power to begin the world over again . . . ," he wrote, "the birthday of a new world is at hand." The bloodshed that began at Lexington justified rejection of the king: "No man was a warmer wisher for a reconciliation than myself, before the fatal nineteenth of

April, 1775, but the moment the event of that day was made known, I rejected the hardened, sullen-tempered Pharaoh of England for ever; and disdain the wretch, that with the pretended title of Father of his People can unfeelingly hear of their slaughter, and composedly sleep with their blood upon his soul." Pragmatically, Paine argued that the colonists must break their ties with London if they expected aid from France and Spain. He pointed out the importance of American exports, which "will always have a market while eating is the custom in Europe." He exclaimed, "'TIS TIME TO PART . . . there is something very absurd, in supposing a continent to be perpetually governed by an island."

Through the spring of 1776, sentiment for independence increased. News that the British had engaged German mercenaries heated the debate. The provincial assemblies of Georgia, South Carolina, and North Carolina gave their delegates in Congress permission to support the break, while Rhode Island declared independence on its own. Virginia proposed that Congress separate from Britain, taking measures "for forming foreign alliances and a confederation of the colonies." But in June, the New York, Pennsylvania, Delaware, and Maryland assemblies, controlled by moderate factions that feared a radicalization of politics, were still not ready to condone a split. Nevertheless, Congress appointed a committee to draft the Declaration of Independence, of which Thomas Jefferson, a wealthy thirty-three-year-old Virginia planter and lawyer, was the principal author. A graduate of the College of William and Mary and a serious intellectual, he had been an active opponent of British policies since first elected to the Virginia assembly in 1769.

The Declaration set forth Congress's reasons for separating from the government of George III; the revolutionaries focused on the king's offenses because they had already denied the sovereignty of Parliament. It held "these truths to be self-evident: That all men are created equal; that they are endowed by their Creator with certain unalienable rights; that among these are life, liberty, and the pursuit of happiness." (See the Appendix for full text.) Employing the philosophy of John Locke and other Enlightenment writers, Jefferson continued, "that, to secure these rights, governments are instituted among men, deriving their just powers from the consent of the governed; that whenever any form of government becomes destructive of these ends, it is the right of the people to alter or to

In this painting, The Declaration of Independence *by John Trumbull, the drafting committee stands at center: from left to right, John Adams, Roger Sherman, Robert Livingston, Thomas Jefferson, and Benjamin Franklin.*

abolish it, and to institute new government." Congress placed the blame for the breach on the king, on his attempt to establish "an absolute tyranny" over the colonies. It listed his misdeeds: refusing to approve necessary laws passed by the colonial assemblies, dissolving legislatures and courts, stationing a standing army, interrupting trade, and imposing taxes without colonial consent. Most recently, Congress announced to the world, George III had declared "us out of his protection and wag[ed] war against us. He has plundered our seas, ravaged our coasts, burned our towns, and destroyed the lives of our people. He is at this time transporting large armies of foreign mercenaries to complete the works of death, desolation, and tyranny already begun." In reference to Lord Dunmore's proclamation, the congressmen accused the king of exciting "domestic insurrection among us." For these reasons and more, Congress declared the thirteen colonies, now to be called the United States of America, "free and independent states" having "full power to levy war, conclude peace, contract alliances, establish commerce, and do all other acts and things which independent states may of right do."

On July 2, 1776, all delegations to Congress approved independence except New York's, which had not received new instructions so was forced to abstain. Completing revisions two days later, Congress adopted the Declaration. For many Americans, independence ended the problem of fighting a government that they continued to recognize as sovereign. When the Continental troops heard the Declaration read on July 9, they cheered, as did civilians throughout the states. However, the battles to defend this independence still lay ahead. General Washington cautioned "every officer and soldier . . . that now the peace and safety of his Country depends (under God) solely on the success of our arms."

To mount sufficient military force to win the war, the states needed unity. In mid-July 1776, Congress began debating the Articles of Confederation, a plan for permanent union, which it approved and sent to the states for ratification over a year later. The chief disagreement among the congressmen was one that remained central to American politics for two centuries, the power of the national government versus that of individual states. The Articles permitted less centralized authority than would the Constitution, which was drafted a decade later. Under the Articles, Congress had responsibility to conduct foreign affairs, make war and peace, deal with Native Americans residing outside the states, coin and borrow money, supervise the post office, and negotiate boundary disputes between states. The "United States" meant thirteen sovereign states joined together by a Congress with specific functions. Article 1 established the "confederacy" to be called the United States of America, not a sovereign nation. Article 2 held that "each State retains its sovereignty, freedom and independence, and every power, jurisdiction, and right, which is not by this confederation expressly delegated to the United States, in Congress assembled." The Congress could neither tax nor raise troops, but could only assess quotas on the states, a serious disadvantage in time of war. Even so, the Articles failed ratification until 1781, when the last of the thirteen states finally approved. Conflict over state claims on western lands held up ratification. In the meantime, Congress attempted to govern within the limits of the unratified Articles, but its inability to raise revenue and draft troops obstructed the American war effort, creating huge shortages of supplies and men.

WAR IN THE NORTH, 1776–1779

For the American patriots, the Revolution was a defensive war. It lasted eight years, from 1775 to 1783, longer than any other in United States history until the Vietnam War. The Continental army was often outmatched, for it remained smaller than General Washington wanted; his troops constantly needed training as veterans left and new recruits arrived. But as the theater of war moved from one region to another, American generals obtained reinforcements from state militias and local volunteers, as men rose to defend their territory. The British, despite considerable assistance from tories, lacked enough reserves to subdue the rebellious North American seaboard. The sheer expanse of the thirteen states and the 3,000-mile distance from England made the British army's task extremely difficult, despite its formal training and Britain's larger population and wealth.

Invasions of New York

To conquer New York, and thus divide New England from the rest of the states, in July 1776, British troops landed on Staten Island. In August, they attacked Washington's army at Brooklyn Heights. The redcoats defeated the Americans badly, pushing them back to Manhattan Island, and then to White Plains. Still, in this series of advances, General William Howe and his brother, Admiral Richard Howe, missed one opportunity after another to deal the blow that might have won the war in 1776. They failed to take advantage of Washington's mistakes, which could have allowed them to surround his troops. In November, however, the British did hand Washington a humiliating defeat by capturing the 2,900 defenders of Manhattan's Fort Washington.

The Continental army retreated across New Jersey with the British and German allies at its heels. The patriots crossed the Delaware River into Pennsylvania, allowing the British to occupy New Jersey towns. The Howes gathered tory support by offering a pardon to anyone who would take a loyalty oath within sixty days. For the whigs, as Thomas Paine wrote, these were "times that try men's souls." The army was in retreat, the New Jersey government had dispersed, and citizens who were skeptical of Washington's abilities rallied to the British. Even Congress, afraid that Howe could easily take the capital, fled Philadelphia for Baltimore.

Before the end of the year, however, fortunes changed. British and Hessian plundering across New Jersey turned indifferent farmers into radical whigs, who became guerrilas, ambushing the enemy and stealing supplies. Meanwhile, Washington devised a plan that bought him time, acting before the enlistments of a large proportion of his army would expire on December 31. He attacked 1,400 Hessians at Trenton on Christmas night, in the midst of a winter storm. Taking the enemy by surprise, the Americans captured more than 900 men. In early January, Washington took the offensive once again, having convinced many of his soldiers to extend their terms for six weeks. Pennsylvania and New Jersey militia, inspired by the victory at Trenton, reinforced his troops. Washington eluded a superior British army under Lord Cornwallis, then defeated a smaller force at Princeton. General Howe withdrew most of his army to New York, leaving troops in just two eastern New Jersey towns. Though Washington's army shrank as

Map 5.2 | Northern Campaigns, 1776–1778

Battle of Princeton, *1777,* *painted by William Mercer* *ten years later. The battles at* *Trenton and Princeton, New* *Jersey, renewed hope for the* *Patriot cause.*

militia units returned home and enlistments of Continental soldiers expired, it had demonstrated its ability to win. In the words of one British officer, the Americans had "become a formidable enemy."

In 1777, as the British made plans to suppress the rebellion once and for all, their strategy for the upcoming campaign became confused. William Howe intended to take Philadelphia, not by crossing New Jersey, but by means of his brother's fleet. At the same time, London organized an invasion from Canada, to win back Fort Ticonderoga and divide the states. The campaigns were not coordinated and neither commenced before June, when British General "Gentleman Johnny" Burgoyne led his force of over 7,000 British regulars, German mercenaries, Native Americans, and Canadians by boat down Lake Champlain. True to his reputation, Burgoyne overburdened his troops with baggage, including thirty cartloads of personal clothing and champagne. Burgoyne easily took Fort Ticonderoga, then headed for Albany. The American forces under Philip Schuyler felled trees and rolled boulders into the path of Burgoyne's heavy column. Covering twenty-three miles of terrain that was difficult even without American sabotage took the British army twenty-four days. Short on supplies and

horses, Burgoyne sent 800 troops to Bennington, Vermont, where General John Stark and his militia ambushed them by pretending to be tories. Reinforcements under British officer Barry St. Leger returned to Canada when they heard that Benedict Arnold was headed west to intercept them. The rebel forces, on the other hand, burgeoned with volunteers as British soldiers pillaged the countryside. In September, near Saratoga, Burgoyne encountered the American army under General Horatio Gates, who had replaced Schuyler. The Americans surrounded the enemy, firing upon them day and night. Burgoyne sent for help from New York City, but Howe had long since sailed with most of his troops to Philadelphia. Burgoyne's 5,800-man army thus surrendered at Saratoga on October 17, 1777.

The British Occupy Philadelphia

As Burgoyne marched toward disaster in New York, General Howe more successfully reached Philadelphia. Still, his campaign fell short of triumph. In July, his 13,000 soldiers departed from New York City aboard a fleet of 260 ships, but instead of disembarking within a week along the Delaware River, they sailed south to the Virginia capes then up the Chesapeake Bay to Head of Elk. Their voyage lasted over a month, costing Howe valuable time that might have permitted him to assist Burgoyne. Washington tried unsuccessfully, with an army of 11,000 at Brandywine, to block Howe's advance through southeastern Pennsylvania. The British occupied Philadelphia, dividing their forces between Germantown and the capital. On October 4, 1777, Washington attacked the British encampment at Germantown, inflicting serious damage though he was once again defeated. Elizabeth Drinker, a Quaker resident of Philadelphia, in her diary reported significant losses on both sides. She wrote, "this has been a sorrowful day at Philadelphia and much more so at Germantown and thereabouts." She recorded news of the Continental army's movements, fearing that the troops would carry the battle to her city. "The apprehensions of their entering," she believed, "will render this night grievous to many." Washington did not attack Philadelphia, so the enemy retained control of the capital until they withdrew the next June.

Even so, in 1777, the British had failed to put down the American rebellion during yet another season of war. Upon hearing that Burgoyne's army had surrendered, the Howe brothers resigned. General Henry Clinton, who had repeatedly advocated a more forceful execution of the war, became the new commander of British forces in North America. The redcoats wintered in relative comfort at Philadelphia while Washington's troops nearly starved and froze to death at Valley Forge, to the west of the city. In February 1778, Continental soldiers lacked adequate clothing and received just three pounds of bread and three ounces of meat to last a week. Some ate only "fire cakes," baked from a paste of flour and water. Nevertheless, they became a disciplined army at Valley Forge, under the Prussian officer Baron von Steuben, who rigorously trained the Americans in the European art of war.

Alliance with France

While February 1778 brought despair to the Americans, it also brought hope—in the form of an alliance with France. Already supporting the United States with economic and military assistance, the French government hoped to recoup the international status it

had lost during the Seven Years' War. Convinced by the victory at Saratoga that the former colonies could win the war, the French signed two pacts with the United States. The first was the Treaty of Amity and Commerce, in which France recognized American independence and both nations pledged "a firm, inviolable and universal peace" and most-favored-nation status in each other's ports. The second was the military Treaty of Alliance, in which they agreed to fight Great Britain jointly until the Americans had won independence, pledged not to negotiate a separate peace, and confirmed their defensive alliance "forever." France renounced claims to its former colonies in North America, but could retain any of the British West Indies that it conquered.

In supporting the Americans, the French renewed their long struggle with Great Britain that had been suspended in 1763. France's entry widened the war, placing greater focus on the West Indies, whose sugar production made them more valuable than the North American mainland to the British. The following year, Spain allied with France, but refused to recognize or assist the American insurgents beyond providing limited financial aid. Unlike France, which denied interest in North America, the Spanish viewed the Americans as potentially dangerous competitors.

The Wartime Economy

Despite France's economic assistance of over $8 million and Spain's smaller contribution of about $600,000, the United States had grave economic problems during the war. The loss of British markets devastated farmers, merchants, and fishermen, as the embargo closed crucial ports in the West Indies and British Isles. The Royal Navy attempted to prevent colonial trade with other nations; it attacked and blockaded American harbors and ravaged ships at sea. On land, the armies laid waste to farms and towns, confiscating livestock, crops, and supplies.

For Congress, the chief economic problem was paying for the war. Without the power to tax, it printed money, a total of almost $200 million in paper bills by 1779. The states printed a similar amount, despite their ability to tax, primarily because printing money was easier than trying to collect revenues from a financially strapped populace. Unfortunately, as the war continued year after year, the demand for military equipment, food, medical supplies, clothing, and sol-

Continental currency depreciated in value as Congress attempted to fund the war with paper money.

diers' wages persisted. This extraordinary demand for provisions coupled with the continuing emission of paper money sent prices soaring. By 1779, the paper money was nearly worthless, inspiring the slogan "not worth a Continental." Pennsylvania and neighboring states were hardest hit by inflation because most military activity took place there from 1776 to 1779.

The depreciation of currency resulted in popular unrest in the American capital, as a group of Philadelphia militia in 1779 demanded a more equitable military draft and regulation of food prices. They were angry that the burden of militia service fell disproportionately on the poor because others could pay fines to avoid the draft. At the same time, the prices of food and firewood skyrocketed. In just two months, August and September 1779, the price of beef, flour, and molasses rose by more than 80 percent. The protesters, according to one broadside posted along the streets, blamed "a few overbearing Merchants, a swarm of Monopolizers and Speculators, an infernal gang of Tories" for the spiraling costs.

In what has been called the "Fort Wilson Incident," armed members of the Philadelphia militia met at Burns's Tavern on October 4, planning to capture and exile from the city four suspected tories. Several hundred militiamen marched their prisoners through the streets to the fife and drum of the Rogue's March, ordinarily played by the military when a soldier was discharged dishonorably. The militia was ridiculing the reputed tories, all four of them wealthy citizens. When rumors raced through the capital that the militia planned to arrest others, about thirty gentlemen who thought they might be targets armed themselves and gathered at the house of lawyer James Wilson. Though a member of Congress, Wilson, like other conservative whig leaders, was suspect because he opposed price regulation. The militia marched past "Fort Wilson," gave three cheers, then shots rang out. Though it is unknown who shot first, both sides subsequently exchanged fire. After cavalry broke up the battle, six people lay dead and seventeen wounded, the majority of them militia.

The Fort Wilson Incident terrified many people because lower-class patriots had directed armed force against the whig elite, protesting the policies of their own government. Henry Laurens, a wealthy South Carolina merchant and member of the Continental Congress, thought the events of October 4 were ominous. He wrote, "we are at this moment on a precipice, and what I have long dreaded and often intimated to my friends, seems to be breaking forth—a convulsion among the people."

THE WAR MOVES WEST AND SOUTH

The failure of the British army to defeat Washington's troops and entry of France into the war led the imperial government to rethink its military strategy. Protection of Caribbean sugar islands from the French navy gained top priority. With redeployment of forces to the West Indies, British General Clinton had to consolidate his army, so in June 1778, he pulled his occupation forces out of Philadelphia, marching across New Jersey toward New York. Washington's army caught up with Clinton at Monmouth Courthouse, where the battle, fought in traditional European style, was indecisive. The British escaped to New York.

The Frontier War

In the west, from New York to Georgia, fighting devastated the backcountry. The Native Americans had not expected the conflict between the American provinces and Great Britain since, as recently as 1774, the whites had cooperated to defeat, in Lord

Dunmore's War, a coalition of militant Delawares, Shawnees, and Iroquois for Kentucky. When the Revolution broke out, many Indians supported the British, who still held garrisons in the west and had more gunpowder and provisions than the patriots. Yet Native Americans responded in various ways to "this dispute between two brothers," as neutral Iroquois called the Revolution in 1775. "The quarrel seems to be unnatural," they said; "you are two brothers of one blood." Just as colonists divided among radical whigs, tories, and neutrals, so did the Native Americans, even within some tribes, separate into factions who favored the British or the Americans, or wanted to avoid any involvement. The militant Indians who sided with Great Britain considered the threat of white settlers crossing the Appalachians as most dangerous to their future. Many attempted to form pan-Indian alliances to fight their own wars of independence against land grabbers from the east. Over the course of the Revolution, the pro-British factions garnered strength from the neutral camp, the result of murders of noncombatants by white frontiersmen and Congress's failure to provide supplies.

Beginning in 1776, Indians attacked Anglo-Americans from the Georgia frontier to the Great Lakes. The Cherokees raided the southern backcountry and planned a major assault on Tennessee, but ran short of gunpowder and were defeated by whig militia in fall 1776. Many Cherokees, Choctaws, Creeks, Shawnees, Iroquois, and others did not give up, however, but rather planned in 1779 "a general invasion of the Frontiers" coordinated by Henry Hamilton, the British lieutenant governor of the Illinois country. George Rogers Clark, a surveyor, who the year before with about 175 frontier soldiers had captured Kaskaskia and Cahokia from the British, heard of plans for the Indian and British offensive. To Patrick Henry, he wrote, "the Case is Desperate but Sir we must Either Quit the Country or attack Mr. Hamilton." In 1779, with a small force, Clark assaulted Fort Vincennes, obtained the British surrender, captured supplies intended for the Indians, and sent Hamilton to a Virginia jail, thus ending the pan-Indian campaign.

Despite Clark's victory at Vincennes, the Kentucky-Ohio frontier remained embattled throughout the war. The same was true of Pennsylvania and New York, where after 1777 most Iroquois and Delawares abandoned their neutrality to ally with the British. In 1778 and 1779, Major John Butler, his son Captain Walter

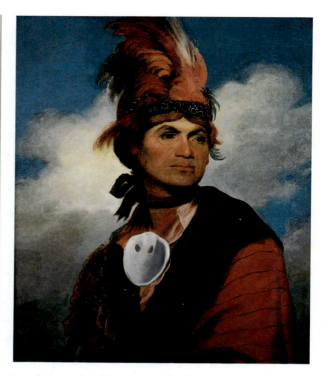

Joseph Brant, *by Gilbert Stuart. The Mohawk leader, who was educated among whites and traveled to Great Britain in 1775, convinced many Iroquois to ally with the British.*

Butler, and the Mohawk leader Theyendanegea, also known as Joseph Brant, led tory and Native American forces against white settlements. Theyendanegea had visited England and believed that British help was needed to keep white Americans out of Indian lands. The loyalists and Iroquois burned houses, barns, fields, and orchards, ran off livestock, and killed or captured settlers over a swath of frontier ranging from fifty to a hundred miles wide. In summer 1779, General Washington sent General John Sullivan with 4,000 troops, who retaliated by burning Iroquois villages, orchards, and fields of corn. At Newtown, New York, in the one battle of the campaign, Sullivan defeated a contingent of about 700 loyalists and Indians. His scorched-earth policy seriously damaged most of the Iroquois towns; displaced Indians suffered through the winter of 1779–1780 on short rations. But the next spring, they renewed their raids, as the frontier remained aflame until the end of the war and after.

Because many Anglo-Americans had trouble distinguishing between Indian friends and foes, Native

Americans who allied with the United States or remained neutral throughout the war fared little better with the whigs than those who sided with the British. By 1781, for example, killings by Americans and loss of lands had driven most of the Coshocton Delawares of Ohio into the arms of the British. Then in March 1782, frontier militia massacred ninety-six pacifist Indian men, women, and children at the Moravian mission of Gnadenhutten, near Coshocton. More successful, the 500 surviving Catawbas of South Carolina, who lived on a reservation adjacent to white settlements, performed extensive service for the patriots. They searched for loyalists and escaped slaves, supplied food to the rebels, fought the Cherokees in 1776, and battled the British, who destroyed their village in retaliation. After the war, the South Carolina assembly compensated the Catawbas for their loyalty and livestock, refusing to abet the governor's plan to lease out their reservation. The Mahicans of Stockbridge in western Massachusetts were less fortunate after fighting in the American army, for they returned home to find that whites had taken over their town.

The Southern Campaigns

While the Revolution ravaged the frontier, the main theater of war remained east of the Appalachians, where in 1778, the British inaugurated a new strategy. Retaining troops in New York City, they invaded the south, counting on loyalist support in Georgia, the Carolinas, and Virginia to restore colonial governments to the Crown. The British also expected the large numbers of enslaved African Americans in the south to weaken the patriots' defenses. In November 1778, General Clinton sent 3,500 troops under Lieutenant Colonel

MAP 5.3 | SOUTHERN CAMPAIGNS, 1778-1781

Archibald Campbell to Georgia, where they joined 2,000 soldiers from Florida. They captured Savannah and Augusta, but had trouble conquering the backcountry. Then, with 10,000 troops, the British turned to Charleston, where in May 1780 they compelled the American general Benjamin Lincoln to surrender 5,500 men, the most serious U.S. loss during the Revolution. The British fanned out through South Carolina, as many residents pledged their loyalty to the

THE NARRATIVE OF
MARY JEMISON,
1775–1779

Mary Jemison was a white woman who had been captured by Indians and spent most of her life among the Senecas. Her journal provides the view of an Iroquois woman, as her adopted people tried to maintain neutrality during the Revolution. But they became embroiled in the war and lost their villages and stocks of food when the American general John Sullivan conducted his scorched earth policy.

Thus, at peace amongst themselves, and with the neighboring whites, though there were none at that time very near, our Indians lived quietly and peaceably at home, till a little before the breaking out of the revolutionary war, when they were sent for, together with the Chiefs and members of the Six Nations generally, by the people of the States, to go to the German Flats, and there hold a general council, in order that the people of the states might ascertain, in good season, who they should esteem and treat as enemies, and who as friends, in the great war which was then upon the point of breaking out between them and the King of England.

Our Indians obeyed the call, and the council was holden, at which the pipe of peace was smoked, and a treaty made, in which the Six Nations solemnly agreed that if a war should eventually break out, they would not take up arms on either side; but that they would observe a strict neutrality. . . .

About a year passed off, and we, as usual, were enjoying ourselves in the employments of peaceable times, when a messenger arrived from the British Commissioners, requesting all the Indians of our tribe to attend a general council which was soon to be held at Oswego. The council convened, and being opened, the British Commissioners informed the Chiefs that the object of calling a council of the Six Nations, was, to engage their assistance in subduing the rebels, the people of the states, . . .

The Chiefs then arose, and informed the Commissioners of the nature and extent of the treaty which they had entered into with the people of the states, the year before, and that they should not violate it by taking up the hatchet against them.

The Commissioners continued their entreaties without success, till they addressed their avarice, by telling our people that the people of the states were few in number, and easily subdued; and that on the account of their disobedience to the King, they justly merited all the punishment that it was possible for white men and Indians to inflict upon them; and added, that the King was rich and powerful, both in money and subjects: That his rum was as plenty as the water in lake Ontario: that his men were as numerous as the sands upon the lake shore:—and that the Indians, if they would assist in the war, and persevere in their friendship to the King, till it was closed, should never want for money or goods. Upon this the Chiefs concluded a treaty with the British Commissioners, in which they agreed to take up arms against the rebels, and continue in the service of his Majesty till they were subdued, in consideration of certain conditions which were stipulated in the treaty to be performed by the British government and its agents.

As soon as the treaty was finished, the Commissioners made a present to each Indian of a suit of clothes, a brass kettle, a gun and tomahawk, a scalping knife, a quantity of powder and lead, a piece of gold, and promised a bounty on every scalp that should be brought in. Thus richly clad and equipped, they returned home, after an absence of about two weeks, full of the fire of war, and anxious to encounter their enemies. Many of the kettles which the Indians received at that time are now in use on the Genesee Flats. . . .

Previous to the battle at Fort Stanwix, the British sent for the Indians to come and see them whip the rebels; and, at the same time stated that they did not wish to have them fight, but wanted to have them just sit down, smoke their pipes, and look on. Our Indians went, to a man; but contrary to their expectation, instead of smoking and looking on, they were obliged to fight for their lives, and in the end of the battle were completely beaten, with a great loss in killed and wounded. Our Indians alone had thirty-six killed, and a great number wounded. Our town exhibited a scene of real sorrow and distress, when our warriors returned and recounted their misfortunes, and stated the real loss they had sustained in the engagement. The mourning was excessive, and was expressed by the most doleful yells, shrieks, and howlings, and by inimitable gesticulations. . . .

In one or two days after the skirmish at Connissius lake, Sullivan and his army arrived at Genesee river, where they destroyed every article of the food kind that they could lay their hands on. A part of our corn they burnt, and threw the remainder into the river. They burnt our houses, killed what few cattle and horses they could find, destroyed our fruit trees, and left nothing but the bare soil and timber. But the Indians had eloped and were not to be found.

Having crossed and recrossed the river, and finished the work of destruction, the army marched off to the east. Our Indians saw them move off, but suspecting that it was Sullivan's intention to watch our return, and then to take us by surprize, resolved that the main body of our tribe should hunt where we then were, till Sullivan had gone so far that there would be no danger of his returning to molest us. . . .

The weather by this time had become cold and stormy; and as we were destitute of houses and food too, I immediately resolved to take my children and look out for myself, without delay. With this intention I took two of my little ones on my back, bade the other three follow, and the same night arrived on the Gardow flats, where I have ever since resided. . . .

. . . The snow fell about five feet deep, and remained so for a long time, and the weather was extremely cold; so much so indeed, that almost all the game upon which the Indians depended for subsistence, perished, and reduced them almost to a state of starvation through that and three or four succeeding years.

king. In July 1780, General Horatio Gates arrived to build a new southern army. Disaster struck once again, when Gates placed too much responsibility on untrained militia in action against Lord Cornwallis at Camden. The battle was a rout, because even the regular Continentals were dispersed, and Gates—the hero of Saratoga—was disgraced.

The tide turned after General Nathanael Greene, the ex-Quaker from Rhode Island who had joined the American cause immediately after Concord, replaced Gates as commander of the southern army. The British contributed to the turnaround, as they became more insistent in demanding oaths of allegiance from Carolinians who preferred to keep out of the fray. This provoked a backlash, particularly because the British army stretched itself so thin that it withdrew protection from the people who took the oaths, thus exposing them to punishment by the whigs. The redcoats and tories also plundered, outraging many southerners

Nathanael Greene, *by Charles Willson Peale. A former Quaker, Greene used both guerrila tactics and formal military methods to wage his successful southern campaign.*

and pushing them into the American camp. Most notorious was Banastre Tarleton's Tory Legion, which executed prisoners of war and destroyed houses and fields, leaving many families homeless. "Bloody" Tarleton created new revolutionaries, who joined Greene's army or the smaller irregular brigades led by Thomas "The Gamecock" Sumter, Colonel Andrew Pickens, and Francis Marion, "the Swamp Fox." During 1780 and 1781, Greene rebuilt the southern army using both traditional and guerrila forces.

While not welcome as soldiers in South Carolina and Georgia, African American slaves, who comprised about 40 percent of the population, played an important role in the southern campaigns. Knowledgeable of the terrain, they acted as spies and counterspies for each side. One man, Antigua, received freedom by act of the South Carolina assembly for himself, his wife Hagar, and child in reward for "procuring information of the enemy's movements and designs." Throughout the south, African Americans provided much of the supporting labor for both armies, as they built fortifications, worked in lead mines, constructed and repaired roads, produced arms and ammunition, and drove wagons. American officers complained about the chronic shortage of black laborers, because whig slaveowners jealously guarded their strongest and most talented slaves to work on their plantations. Further, thousands of African Americans took advantage of General Clinton's 1779 proclamation offering freedom to those who joined the king's service. The slaves of loyalists, while subject to confiscation by the whig governments, were often taken by their masters behind British lines.

One practice of rebel leaders that highlighted their ability to dissociate their own fight for liberty from the plight of enslaved African Americans was to offer recruits enlistment "bounties" in slaves, much as other states promised bounties in land. In South Carolina, Thomas Sumter offered one African American bondman or woman to each private who would enlist for ten months. A colonel would receive three mature blacks and one child. The practice was adopted by Andrew Pickens as well, and supported by General Greene, who expected to pay the bounties from slaves confiscated from loyalist estates. Because sufficient numbers of African Americans owned by tories were lacking, regiments reported "pay" in arrears, some with grotesque precision. One payroll noted a deficit of 93 3/4 mature slaves and "Three Quarters of a Small Negro."

In fall 1780, Lord Cornwallis decided to head north, for while the British had destroyed two American armies and taken control of South Carolina and Georgia, the time had come to conquer the entire south. As his forces marched toward North Carolina, however, they met heavy resistance. In several battles, the conflict became a civil war, as Americans fought on both sides. In October 1780, just to the south of the state line at King's Mountain, whig frontier units defeated an enemy force, of which only Patrick Ferguson, the commander of the loyalists, was British. In January 1781, at Cowpens, an area where Carolinians grazed their cattle, General Daniel Morgan crushed Tarleton's Tory Legion by making the most of his sharpshooting frontiersmen. Morgan lined up the riflemen in front of his disciplined Continentals. The sharpshooters, who were untrained for sustained combat, fired several volleys at Tarleton's troops then withdrew to back up the regulars, who took the brunt of the fighting.

When Cornwallis learned that Tarleton's legion was lost, he chased the Americans into North Carolina, abandoning most of his equipment and supplies to move quickly. In March, Cornwallis met Greene at Guilford Courthouse, where the American general used Morgan's Cowpens tactics, though less effectively because his successive lines of irregulars and Continentals were spread too far apart. Though the battle ended indecisively, one-fourth of Cornwallis's troops lay wounded or dead. Having discarded tents, medical equipment, and food—and cut off from his base in South Carolina—the British general withdrew to the North Carolina coast where he sought naval support.

Meanwhile, Greene moved south to reconquer South Carolina and Georgia, where the British still had 8,000 men in arms. Because these troops were spread out in numerous towns and forts, Greene's 1,500 Continental soldiers and the guerrila brigades of Sumter, Pickens, and Marion could pick off the garrisons one by one. Greene wrote to Washington in May 1781 that if the enemy "divide their force, they will fall by detachments, and if they operate collectively, they cannot command the country." By July, the Americans had pushed the redcoats and tories back to a narrow strip of territory between Charleston and Savannah, which the British held until their evacuation the next year. Despite initial disastrous defeats, the whigs prevailed in the Carolinas and Georgia by recruiting irregular forces and employing them strategically. The great sweep of territory controlled by the former thirteen colonies proved impossible for the British army to subdue.

Surrender of Lord Cornwallis, *by John Trumbull. Their loss at the Battle of Yorktown convinced the British that retaining the thirteen rebellious colonies was not worth the cost.*

Preliminary Peace Negotiations with Great Britain, *by Benjamin West. This unfinished portrait of the American diplomats includes, from left to right, John Jay, John Adams, Benjamin Franklin, Temple Franklin (Franklin's grandson who served as the commission's secretary), and Henry Laurens (who was not present to sign the final treaty).*

The surrender of Cornwallis at Yorktown in October 1781 effectively ended the war. The general had moved into Virginia, replacing Benedict Arnold as commander of the British forces there. Arnold, the former American officer, had turned traitor, joined the British army, and most recently captured Richmond. With an army of about 8,000 men, Cornwallis intended to concentrate British military efforts in Virginia, so requested more troops from New York. General Clinton refused. Their squabbling and delay allowed the Americans and French to surround by land and sea Cornwallis's camp on the Virginia peninsula. Several times before, the French forces had collaborated with the Americans, but their joint efforts had resulted in failure. This time, soldiers under the Comte de Rochambeau and French fleets commanded by the Comte de Grasse and Comte de Barras played a decisive role in defeating Cornwallis. Washington's army marched south from New York to join American and French troops assembled in Virginia. The operation was a marvel of military cooperation for the eigh-

teenth century; it included even the construction of bake ovens outside New York City to camouflage Washington's departure. With 17,000 men and heavy artillery, the American and French forces won the British surrender, finally placing the seal on American independence.

The Peace Settlement

In negotiating the peace, the United States had to reckon with both its adversary Great Britain and its ally France, which in turn was beholden to Spain. American peace commissioners Benjamin Franklin, John Jay, and John Adams, whom Adams called "militia diplomats," shrewdly worked one European nation against the other to obtain a desirable settlement. They ignored Congress's instructions to take advice from France because they understood that French and Spanish goals were different from their own. France

Gundersen, Joan R. *To Be Useful in the World: Women in Revolutionary America, 1740–1790* (1996).

Hatley, Tom. *The Dividing Paths: Cherokees and South Carolinians Through the Era of Revolution* (1993).

Kerber, Linda K. *Women of the Republic: Intellect and Ideology in Revolutionary America* (1980).

Nash, Gary B. *Race and Revolution* (1990).

Norton, Mary Beth. *Liberty's Daughters: The Revolutionary Experience of American Women, 1750–1800* (1980).

Trigger, Bruce G., ed. *Handbook of North American Indians* Vol. 15: *Northeast* (1978).

Wallace, Anthony F. C. *The Death and Rebirth of the Seneca* (1970).

GREAT SEAL OF THE U.S.

The Great Seal of the United States, adopted by Congress in 1782, incorporated as symbols of the new nation: the thirteen stars and stripes,
the eagle with the olive branch of peace and arrows of war, and the motto E Pluribus Unum, *Latin for "Out of Many, One."*

Chapter 6

TOWARD A MORE PERFECT UNION,

1783–1788

THE AMERICAN PATRIOTS had won victory on the battlefield and, at least on paper, in negotiating the peace. The new country soon discovered, though, that independence brought severe challenges as well as opportunities. In 1786, Benjamin Rush of Philadelphia, a physician, whig, and promoter of female education and the abolition of slavery, summarized in a pamphlet the tasks facing the United States:

> There is nothing more common than to confound the terms of *the American revolution* with those of *the late American war*. The American war is over: but this is far from being the case with the American revolution. On the contrary, nothing but the first act of the great drama is closed. It remains yet to establish and perfect our forms of government; and to prepare the principles, morals, and manners of our citizens, for those forms of government. . . .

Having fought for liberty and self-government, Americans now had to create an effective political framework to protect those rights. Their first government was a confederation of small republics in which property-holding white men, the minority of the population defined as having a "stake in society," elected representatives. But questions remained about how to avoid the opposite evils of tyranny and anarchy, questions that inspired fiery debates and even rebellion during the 1780s. Indeed, Rush's pamphlet was part of that dispute, as he argued for a stronger national government.

American leaders had understood since 1776 that the task of creating a workable government lay before them. They were less prepared for other problems that arose soon after the peace. With limited powers under the Articles of Confederation, the Congress faced challenges in demobilizing the army, conducting trade outside the confines of British mercantilism, paying the war debt, finding a way to coexist with the neighboring Spanish colonies in Louisiana and Florida, dealing with Native Americans, and supervising white settlement in the west. Despite Congress's competent action on some of these issues, the need for a more powerful central government became clear. Just four years after the conclusion of peace, delegates from the states met in Philadelphia to draft the new Constitution, which became law upon ratification in 1788. Though the product of political maneuvering as well as high-minded theory, this Constitution has endured, with relatively few amendments, for over two centuries.

THE LIMITS OF REVOLUTIONARY CHANGE

In contrasting "the American revolution" with "the late American war," Rush made a distinction that

CHRONOLOGY

1783	Protest of Continental Army officers at Newburgh, New York		Country Party takes control of Rhode Island assembly
	Great Britain closes British West Indies to American ships		Virginia statute for religious liberty
			Annapolis Convention fails
	Massachusetts Supreme Court finds slavery unconstitutional		Western Confederacy rejects treaties ceding lands in the Northwest Territory
1784	Rhode Island and Connecticut pass gradual abolition laws		Massachusetts farmers close county courts
	Spain closes port of New Orleans to Americans	**1787**	Shaysites attack the federal arsenal at Springfield, Massachusetts
	Spain signs treaty of alliance with the Creeks		Constitutional Convention meets in Philadelphia
	United States forces Iroquois to cede rights in Northwest Territory with Treaty of Fort Stanwix		Congress passes Northwest Ordinance
1785	Native Americans yield lands in Ohio with Treaty of Fort McIntosh		Constitution signed and sent to the states for ratification
	Congress passes land ordinance for the Northwest Territory	**1787–1788**	Publication of *The Federalist* essays
1786	Shawnees sign Treaty of Fort Finney		Ratification of the Constitution by eleven states

many people have debated since the 1780s. Rush thought the revolution had to continue because the government was not yet "perfect"—the states had too much power, leading to disunity and inertia. Others have framed the question in a different way: To what extent did the War of Independence bring about basic changes in politics and society? Though Americans won the right to rule themselves from the British and incorporated in their state constitutions many of the English liberties they had fought for, the definition of the electorate remained the same. The war was revolutionary for propertied white men, but less so for women, African Americans, religious minorities, and the poor.

Republican Politics

Under the Articles of Confederation, ratified in 1781, the United States consisted of thirteen sovereign states

rather than one nation. In framing the Confederation, representatives from the states had refused to transfer sovereignty to a central government. Only state assemblies, elected by the voters, could impose taxes; the central government, or Congress, would be an agent of the states. This decision was based on republican theory, that only in a small republic could representatives act according to the will of its citizens. If the territory was large, the interests and desires of the people would be too diverse, making harmony impossible. The states feared that a too-powerful national government would be dominated by factions whose interests conflicted with their own. And local leaders cherished their power. Thus, the Articles formed a confederacy of sovereign states, with a weak Congress as the only organ of national government. Comprised of delegates from each of the states, "appointed in such manner as the legislature of each State shall direct," Congress had responsibility to conduct foreign affairs, declare war and peace, and coin money, but could not levy taxes or raise troops. Each state had an equal vote in Congress. During the 1780s, its dependence on the states for funds brought the Confederation to a standstill. For years, Congress sought an amendment of the Articles to permit a national tax, but failed to obtain the required unanimous agreement of the states.

The structure of the state governments, where sovereignty lay, reflected their framers' concept of republicanism. Most of the state constitutions resembled the old colonial governments, but incorporated changes that made them more responsible to the people. Most had two-house legislatures and a governor, but gave the largest share of power to the lower house of assembly, elected annually by the voters. The radical Pennsylvania constitution of 1776, more democratic than others, dropped the office of governor and the upper house of assembly, or senate, which was designed to represent the wealthier segment of society. Georgia also excluded the upper house and denied its governor any power. Fearing executive power, given their experience with George III, even states that retained the governor prevented him from appointing many officials or dissolving the assembly. They eliminated the governor's veto over legislation or allowed the assembly to override with a two-thirds vote. All of the states produced written constitutions as a protection against the kind of changes they believed the British had made in their unwritten constitution before the Revolution.

During the late 1770s and 1780s, as Americans formulated and revised state constitutions, they also developed the method by which frames of government were written and approved, the constitutional convention. Pennsylvania radicals called the first state convention in 1776, explaining that its members would be "invested with powers to form a plan of government only, and not to execute it after it is framed; for nothing can be a greater violation of reason and natural rights, than for men to give authority to themselves." Then, in 1780, Massachusetts voters demanded a convention to write a new constitution rather than accept a document that assemblymen had prepared. The constitution was ratified by the people (voters), who thus claimed to be sovereign—the ultimate source of political power—because the frame of government originated with them. Within a few years, other states adopted the same process, recognizing that a constitution should not be written by a governmental body—the legislature—that the constitution created. As one theorist argued, "Conven-

tions . . . are the only proper bodies to form a Constitution, and Assemblies are the proper bodies to make Laws agreeable to that Constitution." Remarkably, in Massachusetts in 1780, every free man, even those without property, could vote for or against the new constitution. The document they approved limited suffrage to propertied men, despite opposition from the western counties.

State constitutions also provided some protection for the liberties many Americans had defended in the Revolution. Virginia included a model Declaration of Rights that other states copied loosely. Most state constitutions offered freedom of worship, required search warrants, and banned excessive fines and quartering of troops in private dwellings. Only some of the states, however, guaranteed trial by jury and the rights of free speech, press, and assembly. A few opposed monopolies and imprisonment for debt, and New England, Pennsylvania, North Carolina, and Georgia promised public support for schools.

While the state constitutions were radical in the context of eighteenth-century politics, because they vested power in the voters and lower houses of assembly, the definition of who was qualified to cast ballots and hold office remained traditional. John Adams spoke for most politicians of his time when he wrote that only property holders should be counted among the sovereign people who could choose and serve as magistrates because the purpose of government was to safeguard property. "It is dangerous," Adams wrote,

> . . . to alter the qualifications of voters. There will be no end to it. New claims will arise. Women will demand a vote. Lads from 12 to 21 will think their rights not enough attended to, and every man, who has not a farthing, will demand an equal voice. . . . It tends to confound and destroy all distinctions, and prostrate all ranks, to one common level.

Voters, according to republican theory, must have a stake in society. Wives, slaves, servants, and unpropertied laboring men were dependent on others and thus unqualified for suffrage. Yet in most places, women and free African Americans who owned property were also barred from voting, by law or by informal pressure. One exception was New Jersey, where the 1776 state constitution extended the vote to "all free inhabitants" who held sufficient property; in 1807, the legislature fell into line with other states by disenfranchising all women and blacks.

"Keep Within Compass," published during the era of the new republic (c. 1785–1805), warned young women to remain within traditional female roles despite the revolutionary change in government.

Women's Rights

Republican politics brought little change to women's lives. Not only were women excluded from government, but their legal and economic status failed to improve. A married woman was still subject to the English common law that gave control of her property and earnings to her husband and denied her the right, without his permission, to make a will, sign contracts, sue in court, or act as a guardian. Despite independence, the American lawmakers refused to cast off this English tradition. Women were also barred, by custom and insufficient education and capital, from positions of high status. They could serve as ministers among Quakers and some Baptists but in no other churches; they taught school only at the primary level. None were lawyers or wealthy merchants, though some became successful shopkeepers. Women also lost ground in medicine, where they had long played important

roles as midwives. As medical courses at the college level became available to men, doctors with formal training displaced lay practitioners, including some midwives. Change occurred most noticeably in Boston, New York, and Philadelphia, where affluent clients demanded the new college-trained obstetricians.

In the post-Revolutionary years, increased support for female education marked the most positive alteration in women's lives. This change accompanied the more general perception that a republic needed an educated people. Though women were denied entrance to all colleges, including Harvard, Yale, and William

Girl in Green, by an unknown artist, c. 1790. While women's status remained circumscribed in many areas after the Revolution, their access to education improved, as suggested in this rare image of a girl reading a book.

Judith Sargent, *by John Singleton Copley, before her marriage to John Murray. She became a proponent of advanced education for women.*

and Mary, a number of academies opened their doors to provide secondary-level education to well-to-do girls. The school curricula included the three R's, English composition and grammar, geography, music, dancing, and needlework. The young women did not receive instruction in Latin, Greek, and advanced science and mathematics, the courses that their brothers took to prepare for college.

Discussion of the need for better female education became intertwined with ideas about women's roles in the new nation. Beginning in 1784, Massachusetts writer Judith Sargent Murray published a series of essays, later compiled in a book titled *The Gleaner,* in which she argued that young women should prepare to support themselves in case they found no suitable husband or their spouse died. "Our girls," she wrote, "are bred up with one particular view: . . . an establishment by marriage. . . . *An old maid,* they are from infancy taught, at least indirectly, to consider as a contemptible being; and they have no other means of advancing themselves but in the matrimonial line." Murray believed that young women should learn a vocation for independence, but also justified advanced female education on the grounds that girls with developed minds would become better wives and mothers. Dr. Benjamin Rush pointed out that improved school-

ing would help women fulfill their duties in running households and preparing sons to be virtuous, wise leaders of the republic. Carefully avoiding the suggestion that women should participate in politics, he wrote: "The equal share that every citizen has in the liberty and the possible share he may have in the government of our country make it necessary that our ladies should be qualified to a certain degree, by a peculiar and suitable education, to concur in instructing their sons in the principles of liberty and government." Nurturing incorruptible future leaders, or "republican motherhood," was women's principal responsibility under the new government, not voting or holding office.

The Question of Abolishing Slavery

The revolutionary rhetoric of freedom and self-determination unleashed a public debate over the legitimacy of slavery. African Americans fueled the discussion by escaping to the British and serving in the American army. Many took opportunities opened by the Revolution to grasp their own personal liberty. In doing so, African Americans made whites more aware of the hypocrisy of fighting a war of independence while they kept other human beings in chains. In petitions, Massachusetts blacks made the connection explicit during the war, writing that as long as whigs failed to emancipate slaves, they were "chargeable with the inconsistency of acting . . . the part which they condemn & oppose in others. . . . [E]very principle from which America has acted in the course of her difficulties with Great-Britain, pleads stronger than a thousand arguments from your Petitioners."

In the north, the first significant opposition to slavery had developed among Pennsylvania and New Jersey Quakers well before the Revolution. Since the seventeenth century, individual members of the Society of Friends had argued that black bondage violated basic Christian concepts, particularly the belief that all humans are equal in the eyes of God. For decades, these Quaker abolitionists failed to convince their meetings that slavery was wrong because many wealthy, powerful Friends held slaves. But after 1750, the Society of Friends became the first American religion to denounce perpetual bondage as a sin and to prohibit members from holding slaves. The Quakers then spearheaded an emancipation movement that gained strength among other whites in the 1770s and

One of the goals of the Pennsylvania Abolition Society was to end the international slave trade. The text of this 1789 tract states that enslaved Africans on slave ships were "packed, side by side, almost like herrings in a barrel, and reduced to the state of being buried alive."

1780s, contributing, along with escapes by African Americans, to the growth of free black communities in Philadelphia, New York, and other northern towns. In addition, by the 1780s, slavery was less important economically in northern states than in the south, thus the combination of religious conviction, natural rights concepts of liberty and equality, and pressure by African Americans could undercut its viability. Prospective owners, already sensitized by guilt, grew wary of purchasing slaves, who were likely to demand emancipation or run away. Instead, northern employers hired workers from among the growing numbers of free laborers in cities and commercial agricultural areas, including many African Americans.

In Pennsylvania and New England, state governments acted against slavery by the mid-1780s. The Pennsylvania assembly passed the first abolition law in 1780, its preamble reflecting the ideas that inspired many abolitionists of the revolutionary era:

> When we contemplate our abhorrence of that condition to which the arms and tyranny of Great Britain were exerted to reduce us, when we look back on the variety of dangers to which we have been exposed, [we are grateful for] the manifold blessings which we have undeservedly received. . . . We conceive that it is our duty, and we rejoice that it is in our power, to extend a portion of that freedom to others.

The act was less comprehensive than its heartiest supporters wished, including radical George Bryan, who probably wrote the initial draft, and Anthony Benezet, the aged Quaker schoolteacher and abolitionist who lobbied every assemblyman for the law. As a result of compromises required for passage, the Pennsylvania act abolished slavery gradually—so gradually that under its provisions no black Pennsylvanian would achieve freedom until 1808. The law provided that children born to slave mothers after March 1780 would be freed when they reached the age of twenty-eight. Slaves who had been born before that date would remain in bondage.

Nevertheless, the Pennsylvania act was more effective than expected, as many enslaved blacks, exasperated that the law failed to free them, escaped their masters, and hundreds of slaveholders conformed to the spirit of the law by manumitting their slaves, regardless of birth date, at about age twenty-eight. Though these owners benefited from the labor of African Americans during their prime years, still, the manumissions helped to bring about the early end of slavery in the state. Also significant was the work of the Pennsylvania Abolition Society, which tested the limits of the 1780 abolition act by providing legal counsel to African Americans to defend their liberty. The PAS, which was dominated by Quaker artisans but also included such luminaries as Benjamin Franklin and Benjamin Rush, kept a record of manumission papers in the event freed men and women were kidnapped into slavery. The number of slaves in Pennsylvania declined from almost 7,000 in 1780, to 3,700 in 1790, and 795 in 1810.

Elsewhere in the north, the Massachusetts supreme court in 1783 decided that slavery was incompatible with the state's 1780 constitution, which said all men are free and equal, though it did not specifically outlaw perpetual bondage. As blacks sued for freedom, the courts ruled on their behalf, and so by 1790, Massachusetts reported no slaves on the federal census. The Connecticut and Rhode Island legislatures in 1784 followed Pennsylvania's example by passing gradual abolition laws, and Vermont and New Hampshire also banned the institution. New York and New Jersey, where slaveholders were more numerous and powerful, passed gradual abolition acts later, in 1799 and 1804 respectively.

During the 1780s, considerable support for abolition also developed in the Chesapeake region, though enslaved African Americans comprised almost 40 percent of the population. Southern states, like their northern counterparts, continued the First Continental Congress' prohibition of the slave trade. Some people expected cessation of the trade to result in the gradual death of slavery in Virginia and Maryland—a mistake because the African American population there grew naturally by reproduction. Involuntary bondage would persist without positive action for abolition.

Thomas Jefferson exemplified the troubled and confused state of mind of many white Americans about slavery. Though he remained a slaveholder throughout his life and held racist beliefs, Jefferson claimed to support a strategy for gradual abolition in Virginia. The plan, never considered by the assembly, would have freed and educated African American children born after the law went into effect and, when adults, remove them to a separate territory. Jefferson, like most whites who lived in areas with large black populations, wanted desperately to ensure that whites kept political control if African Americans gained freedom. Relocation to a new land was one suggestion for abolishing slavery yet maintaining white power.

Efforts for general abolition failed south of Pennsylvania, yet some progress occurred when Virginia (in 1782), Delaware (in 1787), and Maryland (in 1790) made private emancipation easier. New manumission laws permitted slaveholders who were inspired by antislavery beliefs, whether arising from revolutionary ideals or religion, to free their slaves. A private abolition movement took fire in areas of the Upper South where Quakers and Methodists were numerous and planters were changing from tobacco to wheat as their chief crop, thus requiring fewer field hands. Though declining demand for labor played a role in their decision, still, slaveholders had the choice of whether to emancipate or sell their bondpeople. A market for slaves existed in the Carolinas and Georgia, where abolitionist sentiment had little impact.

The rise in the number of free African Americans in the Upper South was a measure of opposition to slavery. The free black population in Delaware rose to 4,000 in 1790, and over 8,000 by the end of the century; in Maryland to 8,000 in 1790, and 20,000 ten years later; and in Virginia, to nearly 13,000 at the turn of the century. Even with impressive numbers of manumissions, however, in 1800 emancipated blacks were just 8 percent of all African Americans in the region. The majority, by far, remained enslaved.

Defining Religious Liberty

Another question that faced the architects of the new state governments was religious freedom. Revolutionary ideals led many to challenge laws that forced people to attend and financially support an established church. Before the Revolution, the colonies had varied widely in the relationship of church and state. Congregational churches were tax-supported in Massachusetts, New Hampshire, and Connecticut, while the Church of England (Anglican) was established in the Carolinas, Virginia, Maryland, and New York. In contrast, Rhode Island, New Jersey, and Pennsylvania protected a great diversity of religions, giving none of them public funds. All of the colonies, however, placed limits on who could serve in political office. In Pennsylvania, for example, anyone who believed in God could live and worship, but only Protestants could participate in government. The British Crown forbade any province from permitting Roman Catholics to vote and hold office.

The break with Great Britain had the greatest impact on the established Church of England, called the Protestant Episcopal church in the United States after the Revolution. With independence, some of its parishes dissolved, as missionaries departed because the church hierarchy in England stopped paying their salaries. Many Anglican clergymen and laypeople in New England and the Mid-Atlantic region became loyalists, helping to fuel the whig movement for disestablishment. All of the states in which the Anglican church was established promptly ended government support except Virginia, where many leading whigs were Anglicans. Virginia finally acted in 1786, when

PETITION OF PHILADELPHIA JEWS FOR EQUAL RIGHTS, 1783

Though Pennsylvania was renowned for religious liberty, its constitution limited election to the state assembly to Christians. As other states broadened religious liberty during the revolutionary era, Philadelphia Jews called for redress of this inequity. The new Pennsylvania constitution adopted in 1790 removed this religious test.

To the honourable the Council of Censors, assembled agreeable to the Constitution of the State of Pennsylvania. The Memorial of . . . the Synagogue of the Jews at Philadelphia, . . . in behalf of themselves and their brethren Jews, residing in Pennsylvania,

Most respectfully showeth,

That by the tenth section of the Frame of Government of this Commonwealth, it is ordered that each member of the general assembly of representatives of the freemen of Pennsylvania, before he takes his seat, shall make and subscribe a declaration, which ends in these words, "I do acknowledge the Scriptures of the old and new Testament to be given by divine inspiration," to which is added an assurance, that "no further or other religious test shall ever hereafter be required of any civil officer or magistrate in this state."

Your memorialists beg leave to observe, that this clause seems to limit the civil rights of your citizens to one very special article of the creed; whereas by the second paragraph of the declaration of the rights of the inhabitants, it is asserted without any other limitation than the professing the existence of God, in plain words, "that no man who acknowledges the being of a God can be justly deprived or abridged of any civil rights as a citizen on account of his religious sentiments." But certainly this religious test deprives the Jews of the most eminent rights of freemen, solemnly ascertained to all men who are not professed Atheists.

May it please your Honors,

Although the Jews in Pennsylvania are but few in number, yet liberty of the people in one country, and the declaration of the government thereof, that these liberties are the rights of the people, may prove a powerful attractive to men, who live under restraints in another country. Holland and England have made valuable acquisitions of men, who for their religious sentiments, were distressed in their own countries.—And if Jews in Europe or elsewhere, should incline to transport themselves to America, and would, for reason of some certain advantage of the soil, climate, or the trade of Pennsylvania, rather

the assembly passed Thomas Jefferson's statute for religious liberty, which stated,

no man shall be compelled to frequent or support any religious worship, place or ministry whatsoever, nor shall be enforced, restrained, molested, or burthened in his body or

goods, nor shall otherwise suffer on account of his religious opinions or belief.

Nevertheless, the movement to end discrimination stalled, and in the 1780s, religious tests for political office remained common. Americans, who were over-become inhabitants thereof, than of any other State; yet the disability of Jews to take seat among the representatives of the people, as worded by the said religious test, might determine their free choice to go to New York, or to any other of the United States of America, where there is no such like restraint laid upon the nation and religion of the Jews, as in Pennsylvania.—Your memorialists cannot say that the Jews are particularly fond of being representatives of the people in assembly or civil officers and magistrates in the State; but with great submission they apprehend that a clause in the constitution, which disables them to be elected by their fellow citizens to represent them in assembly, is a stigma upon their nation and religion, and it is inconsonant with the second paragraph of the said bill of rights; otherwise Jews are as fond of liberty as their religious societies can be, and it must create in them a displeasure, when they perceive that for their professed dissent to doctrine, which is inconsistent with their religious sentiments, they should be excluded from the most important and honourable part of the rights of a free citizen.

Your memorialists beg further leave to represent, that in the religious books of the Jews, which are or may be in every man's hands, there are no such doctrines or principles established as are inconsistent with the safety and happiness of the people of Pennsylvania, and that the conduct and behaviour of the Jews in this and the neighbouring States, has always tallied with the great design of the Revolution; that the Jews of Charlestown, New York, New-Port and other posts, occupied by the British troops, have distinguishedly suffered for their attachment to the Revolution principles; and their brethren at St. Eustatius, for the same cause, experienced the most severe resentments of the British commanders. The Jews of Pennsylvania in proportion to the number of their members, can count with any religious society whatsoever, the Whigs among either of them; they have served some of them in the Continental army; some went out in the militia to fight the common enemy; all of them have cheerfully contributed to the support of the militia, and of the government of this State; they have no inconsiderable property in lands and tenements, but particularly in the way of trade, some more, some less, for which they pay taxes; they have, upon every plan formed for public utility, been forward to contribute as much as their circumstances would admit of; and as a nation or a religious society, they stand unimpeached of any matter whatsoever, against the safety and happiness of the people.

And your memorialists humbly pray, that if your honours, from any consideration than the subject of this address, should think proper to call a convention for revising the constitution, you would be pleased to recommend this to the notice of that convention.

whelmingly Protestant, thought that only Christian men, preferably Protestants, should govern. The success of the republic, they believed, required "a virtuous people"; Protestant Christianity was the glue that would hold them together. State and local laws required observance of the Sabbath, outlawed gambling and other entertainments, and proclaimed days of thanksgiving and prayer. The states most resistant to disestablishment were the old Puritan strongholds in New England, where Congregational ministers had warmly advocated the whig cause. Massachusetts, New Hampshire, and Connecticut required tax support for Protestant churches well into the nineteenth century.

CHALLENGES TO THE CONFEDERATION

Despite the dominance of the states, the Confederation Congress had important functions that required far more unity and power than it possessed. Of all Congress's difficulties, the inability to tax was most damaging, resulting in the Confederation's quick demise.

Military Demobilization

In the transition to peace in 1783, one of the most remarkable aspects of the American revolutionary experience—in light of revolutions since that time—was the absence of a serious military challenge to civilian control. George Washington was committed to popularly elected government and thus ignored suggestions that he become a military ruler. Even so, Congress faced two problems concerning the armed forces, both arising in part from lack of revenue. During the war, Congress failed to pay or supply the army properly, but had promised generous pensions and bounties to entice men to sign up for the duration of the war. The second question confronting Congress was whether to establish a peacetime army, an issue that had both ideological and financial significance.

For two years after the Battle of Yorktown in 1781, the Continental Army continued to exist, with Washington encamped at Newburgh, New York, where his troops monitored the British army still in New York City. American officers and enlisted men voiced grievances because they needed food, clothing, and wages. Soldiers rioted and insulted their officers, while many simply went home with no compensation except their weapons. Officers at Newburgh drew up a list of complaints for Congress, demanding as much of their back pay as possible and a full reckoning of the entire sum they were owed. The officers suggested that they receive lump sums instead of the promised pensions of half-pay for life. They seemed so disgruntled that Washington remained at Newburgh instead of going home to Mount Vernon as he had planned.

The officers' discontent became more threatening when several politicians, who favored a strong central government, recognized an opportunity to pressure the states into giving Congress the power to tax. In what became known as the Newburgh conspiracy, Robert Morris of Philadelphia and Gouverneur Morris and Alexander Hamilton of New York hatched a plan to use the officers' protests to strengthen the Confederation. Washington would not cooperate, stating that the army was a "most dangerous instrument to play with," even to obtain a national tax. In early 1783, rumors spread that the officers were ready to take "manly" action against the government unless their demands were met. The crisis ended when Washington pledged to negotiate for their back pay and pensions and the officers swore their loyalty to Congress. For its part, Congress agreed to pay troops three months' wages at discharge, while officers would receive pensions of five years' full pay in government bonds. A group of eighty enlisted men stationed at Lancaster, Pennsylvania, found the offer unacceptable, so they mutinied and marched on Philadelphia, barricading the State House where Congress met. Though the soldiers backed down without violence, the frightened congressmen fled to Princeton.

Restitution of military pensions, back wages, and bounties took until the 1790s because Congress lacked the funds to discharge its debts. Soldiers who had been promised land bounties in the west had to wait fifteen years for surveys, in large part because Native Americans refused to give up their territory, which Congress intended to distribute. By the 1790s, most veterans had long since sold their rights to speculators for a fraction of their worth.

The issue of a standing army squared revolutionary ideology against the need for defense. One of the chief causes of the Revolution had been the peacetime quartering in New York and Boston of the British army, which patriots called a "MONSTER of a standing ARMY." But now in the postwar era, the United States faced threats from the Spanish in Florida and Louisiana, the British in Canada, and Native Americans everywhere along the frontier. In April 1783, Congress appointed a committee to consult Washington and other generals on military requirements. The commander-in-chief argued that, despite concerns about armies in peacetime, the United States had to be prepared against its enemies. He suggested retaining 2,600 Continentals in one artillery and four infantry regiments. He also advised Congress to organize a na-

Gouverneur Morris and Robert Morris intended to use the American army's discontent in 1782–1783 to create a strong central government. Portrait by Charles Willson Peale.

tional citizens' militia that would stay in training for ready defense. In 1784, Congress dismissed Washington's plan, stationing a total of eighty men at two forts in New York and Pennsylvania. The following year, it raised another 700 men to supervise the Ohio country, a number that was much too small to support U.S. claims to Indian lands or to force the British from their garrisons. For reasons of principle and finances, the Confederation government virtually disbanded the army during an interval of peace, a pattern the nation would follow well into the twentieth century.

Economic Troubles

The revolution left the United States with a huge debt and an unknown status among trading nations. The Confederation Congress failed to solve the problem of its war debt, which by 1790 amounted to an estimated $10 million owed to other countries and $40 million owed to Americans. During the war, with no power to tax, the government had issued paper currency to pay

for goods and services. It abandoned this policy because of rampant inflation. Congress turned to the states, which refused to contribute sufficient funds, then borrowed from France and from American merchants and farmers for military provisions. It also deferred payment on soldiers' wages. As the principal and interest mounted on these promissory notes and bonds, Congress requested an amendment to the Articles to permit a national duty of 5 percent on all imports. Unanimous agreement of the states was necessary. The legislators tried for five years, but failed on each attempt despite gaining approval from all but one or two states. Through the 1780s the national debt served as the means by which national and state politicians contested power. Nationalists such as Robert Morris and Alexander Hamilton argued for a stronger central government with the power to tax, while state officials used Congress's inability to pay the debt as a reason to ignore the Confederation's authority.

One long-lasting consequence of the war's inflationary crisis was conflict between urban and rural interests over public finance. The spiraling cost of food and fuel in the late 1770s had hurt city residents much more than farmers. In public debate over currency and credit, farmers wanted access to government loans based on the value of their land and its production, similar to the colonial land banks that had allowed them to use real estate as collateral for loans. Though the provincial currency issued by the land banks had been fairly stable, in the 1780s, merchants and urban artisans recalled the more recent inflation of the Revolution. They believed that paper currency based on real estate would send prices sky-high. At the same time, merchants knew that the economy would stagnate if specie (gold and silver) were required for every transaction, so they embraced an alternative method of generating paper currency, the bank.

The first bank in the United States was the Bank of North America, created in 1781 in Philadelphia. Robert Morris proposed the institution, based on the Bank of England, as a way to help solve the wartime fiscal crisis. Morris obtained support from Alexander Hamilton, Thomas Paine, and a committee of Congress for his plan; both the Congress and state of Pennsylvania chartered the institution. Instead of issuing paper currency through a land office, as farmers wanted, the bank issued currency in the form of short-term loans to merchants. These bank notes were backed by gold and silver plate and coins that investors deposited in return for a share of the bank's profits. The attraction for stockholders was that formerly idle gold and silver assets could now earn interest. The Bank of North America earned regular profits during its first two decades, beginning with an 8.74 percent dividend to investors in 1782. If people doubted the security of the bank, they could redeem their bank notes. Bank advocates believed that once a few people tested its soundness and received specie, others would trust the bank and accept the bank notes as currency.

In fact, the Bank of North America followed a conservative course that kept it solvent financially but made it unpopular with many people. The bank's manager, Thomas Willing, lent money only to good credit risks in the mercantile community, thus angering artisans and farmers who viewed the bank as a monopoly created by Congress to benefit the commercial elite. Also, Willing refused to liberalize the bank's loan policy by taking advantage of confidence in the bank's strength. Instead of expanding the money supply as later banks did, the Bank of North America made loans only up to the amount of specie in its vaults.

The Bank of North America helped the mercantile community through a time of uncertainty. Commerce had suffered during the revolution as merchants lost connections with trading partners in Great Britain and the British West Indies. In 1783, Americans expected to reestablish those ties as well as enter new markets in Europe and the French and Spanish colonies. With their newly won independence, they gained release from the restrictions of British mercantilism.

But being part of the mercantilist system had brought advantages as well as constraints. The British did not allow their former colonies to have the best of both worlds. They closed the ports of the British West Indies to American ships, a sharp blow for New England and the Middle Atlantic states, which before the war had found a major market in the islands for exports of fish, grain, flour, lumber, and livestock. To Great Britain and its colonies, the United States was now a foreign country. Americans could sell provisions in the islands and purchase rum, sugar, and molasses, but everything had to be carried on British ships. West Indies planters complained because this resulted in higher prices; American shipowners had to find new routes. On the other hand, Britain was eager to purchase tobacco from the Chesapeake and sell to Americans all the manufactures they would buy. U.S. merchants had access by treaty to ports in France and the French colonies, but were barred from trading in New Spain. Gradually, Americans developed trade with Germany, the Netherlands, Scandinavia, and even China. Some merchants became involved in the Atlantic slave trade, while others found ways to circumvent the British restrictions in the Caribbean. By the end of the 1780s, U.S. exports recovered to approximately their prerevolutionary level.

The road to recovery was rocky, however, because in the immediate postwar years American demand for British manufactures far outstripped exports. During the revolution, American artisans had attempted to supply metal goods and textiles, but had been unable to match British quality and prices. With peace, British manufacturers extended generous credit to American consumers for clocks, watches, furniture, textiles, clothing, mirrors, and other goods. When depression hit in fall 1783 because of the loss of the West Indies market, American farmers, merchants, and shopkeepers found themselves seriously in debt. In New England, for example, the balance of trade with Great Britain was so uneven that exports covered only 13 percent of imports. While the economy improved

EXPLANATION.

I America sitting on that quarter of the globe with the Flag of the United States displayed over her head; holding in one hand the Olive branch, inviting the ships of all nations to partake of her commerce, and in the other hand supporting the Cap of Liberty.

II Fame proclaiming the joyful news to all the world.

III Britannia weeping at the loss of the trade of America, attended with an evil genius.

IV The British flag struck, on her strong Fortresses.

V French, Spanish, Dutch, &c shipping in the harbours of America.

VI A view of New-York, wherein is exhibited the Trator Arnold, taken with remorse for selling his country, and Judas like hanging himself.

America Triumphant and Britannia in Distress, from Weatherwise's *Town and Country Almanack (1782) illustrates the hopes of Americans for prosperity now that they were free from British mercantilism.*

after mid-1785, many farmers had difficulty escaping from debt.

Indeed, estimates of the gross national product suggest that the revolution had an extended negative impact on the American economy, that liberty came at a high price not only in bloodshed but in financial terms as well. Data available for 1774 and 1790 indicate that income declined by over 40 percent, close to the decrease Americans experienced during the Great Depression of the 1930s.

Foreign Affairs

Though the United States had won both the war and the peace, its leaders soon learned that they received little respect among European nations. Ambassadors Thomas Jefferson to France and John Adams to Great Britain had as much difficulty maneuvering among fellow diplomats as have the representatives of new nations in the twentieth century. Despite the boundary provisions of the Treaty of 1783, Spain and Great Britain took advantage of the Confederation's weakness to trespass on territory in the west. The Spanish and English gained allies among Native Americans who were losing their lands to the steady stream of white settlers crossing the Appalachians.

During the 1780s, the Spanish tried to restrict expansion of the United States, which they considered their chief competitor for North America. With a burgeoning population, the former British colonies rivaled the size of New Spain. The Spanish government had refused to accept the treaty boundaries granting the region between the Appalachians and the Mississippi River to the United States. With settlers rapidly filling the area, Spain feared for its control of Louisiana and East and West Florida; it wanted to extend its territory north from West Florida to the Ohio River. The Spanish pursued this objective in a number of ways. They retained forts north of the 31st parallel, which the United States claimed as its southern border on the basis of the peace treaty. Then, in 1784, the

BRITISH CANADA

Lake Superior

Lake Michigan

Ceded by VIRGINIA, 1784

Lake Huron

Ceded by MASSACHUSETTS, 1785
and VIRGINIA, 1784

Lake Ontario

Ceded by
MASS.,
1786

NEW YORK

MAINE
(Mass.)

VT
(1791)

NH

Ceded by CONNECTICUT, 1786
and VIRGINIA, 1784

Lake Erie

Ceded by
CONN.,
1782

MASSACHUSETTS

CONN.   RI

Ceded by
CONNECTICUT,
1800

PENNSYLVANIA

NEW
JERSEY

SPANISH
LOUISIANA

Ceded by VIRGINIA,
1784

Ohio River

MD

DE

VIRGINIA

ATLANTIC
OCEAN

Ceded by VIRGINIA,
1792

Ceded by
SOUTH
CAROLINA,
1787

Ceded by
NORTH CAROLINA,
1790

NORTH
CAROLINA

SOUTH
CAROLINA

Ceded by GEORGIA,
1802

GEORGIA

Mississippi River

Ceded by SPAIN, 1795
Ceded by GEORGIA, 1802

SPANISH
FLORIDA

Gulf of Mexico

Legend:
- States after land cessions
- Ceded territory
- Territory ceded by New York, 1782

MAP 6.1 | WESTERN LAND CESSIONS, 1782–1802

Spanish government closed the port of New Orleans to Americans, apparently hoping to detach from the United States the region that later became Kentucky and Tennessee. Settlers in the trans-Appalachian region protested vigorously because they needed access to the New Orleans market for their goods. Some

threatened to secede from the United States unless Congress convinced Spain to reverse its decision; a few, including James Wilkinson, a former Continental Army officer, actually negotiated with the Spanish. Reporting on a journey in the west, George Washington wrote, "the western settlers (I speak now from my own observation) stand as it were upon a pivot; the touch of a feather would turn them any way."

Congress directed John Jay, the secretary of foreign affairs and a New Yorker, to negotiate with Spain to reopen the port. The Spanish diplomat, Diego de Gardoqui, under instructions from his government, refused to budge, instead offering to open other Spanish ports to U.S. commerce if Americans would relinquish demands for free navigation on the lower Mississippi. With the permission of Congress, Jay agreed to a treaty that provided commercial advantages for eastern merchants but closed New Orleans to westerners for a generation. The west and south erupted in opposition, blocking approval of the Jay-Gardoqui Treaty. The lower Mississippi River remained closed until 1788 when the Spanish permitted Americans to use New Orleans upon payment of duties.

The Spanish government also cooperated with Native Americans to slow the influx of Anglo-American settlers into contested territory. Spanish colonists in the Floridas remained few, so they depended upon good relations with the Creeks, Choctaws, and Chickasaws who controlled the region. Groups of Creeks who had migrated to Florida, and were called Seminoles by the British, could mobilize at least twice as many soldiers as the Spanish. Contrary to Spain's traditional policy of considering Native Americans as subjects to the Crown, its colonial officials in 1784 signed written treaties of alliance with the Indians.

Most threatening of these pacts to the United States was the one with the Creeks, which their leader Alexander McGillivray arranged. The son of a Scottish trader and French-Creek woman, and educated in Charleston, McGillivray could negotiate his way in both European and Indian societies. To protect Creek lands from settlers streaming in from Georgia, he offered the Spanish "a powerful barrier in these parts against the ambitious and encroaching Americans" in return for an alliance and weapons. The Creeks called the invading Georgians "Ecunnaunuxulgee," or "people greedily grasping after the lands of the red people." With Cherokees and Shawnees to the north, the Creeks battled Anglo-Americans through the 1780s, thus slowing settlement on the southwest frontier.

The Confederation government also had difficulty establishing its claims north of the Ohio River, against the British and the Indians of the Ohio Valley. In the treaty of 1783, the British had promised to remove their troops from forts in the Great Lakes region, including Detroit, Oswego, and Niagara. Through the 1780s, however, they refused to withdraw, hoping for return of the territory. They barred American ships from the Great Lakes, placed a customs agent at Oswego, and allied with Native Americans who wanted to halt white settlement. British diplomats justified these actions with the excuse that Americans had failed to pay prewar debts to British creditors and return confiscated loyalist property. While some states were slow in executing these treaty obligations, the British would have kept the garrisons regardless.

Though the British forts bolstered Native American resistance, Great Britain's neglect of their Indian allies in negotiating the peace led the U.S. government to treat them as a conquered people. With great bravado, considering the Confederation's small army, American commissioners said to the Ohio Indians, "You are mistaken in supposing that . . . you are become a free and independent nation, and may make what terms you please. . . . You are a subdued people." Other officials announced, "We claim the country by conquest, and are to give not to receive." Under threat of arms, some Native American leaders acquiesced to U.S. demands. A group of Iroquois yielded rights in the Northwest with the Treaty of Fort Stanwix (1784); Wyandots, Delawares, and others ceded Ohio lands in the Treaty of Fort McIntosh (1785); and Shawnees gave up territory in the Treaty of Fort Finney (1786). Many Native Americans refused to recognize these treaties because the Indian negotiators lacked authority and had been forced to sign. Soon, frontier warfare made U.S. officials realize that they were the ones who were "mistaken" in presuming that the Indians had been "subdued." Theyendanegea (Joseph Brant), the pro-British Mohawk leader who led many Iroquois to Canada after the revolution, rallied Indians against white settlement in the Northwest. In 1786, he urged potential allies, "the Interests of Any One Nation Should be the Interests of us all, the Welfare of the one Should be the Welfare of all the others." Their resistance convinced Secretary of War Henry Knox that the United States must change its tactics or risk a general Indian war that the Confederation could ill afford. He suggested that Congress return to the policy of purchasing lands, instead of demanding them by conquest. The congressmen agreed, incorporating into the Northwest Ordinance of 1787 the futile promise that the Indians' land "shall never be taken from them without their consent."

The Seven Ranges—first area surveyed

GEOGRAPHER'S LINE (BASE LINE)

6 miles

6 miles

FIRST RANGE

SECOND RANGE

THIRD RANGE

FOURTH RANGE

FIFTH RANGE

SIXTH RANGE

SEVENTH RANGE

Tuscarawas R.

Ohio R.

Little Muskingum R.

VIRGINIA
PENNSYLVANIA

Lake Erie

NORTHWEST TERRITORY

OHIO (1803)

PENNSYLVANIA

VIRGINIA

KENTUCKY (1792)

Ohio R.

* Four sections reserved for subsequent sales

Section 16 reserved for school funds

6 miles

1 mile

36	30	24	18	12	6
35	29*	23	17	11*	5
34	28	22	16	10	4
33	27	21	15	9	3
32	26*	20	14	8*	2
31	25	19	13	7	1

A
B C
D E

One Section = 640 acres (1 mile square)
A Half section = 320 acres
B Quarter section =160 acres
C Half-quarter section = 80 acres
D & E Quarter-quarter section = 40 acres

One township (six miles square)

MAP 6.2　│　Land Ordinance of 1785

The Northwest Ordinances

Despite war with the Indians and the presence of British troops, the Confederation Congress moved forward with legislation to create the Northwest Territory. The issue of western lands had divided the thirteen states even during the Revolution. Some states claimed territories from their colonial charters, while others, such as Maryland and New Jersey, had never possessed such claims. Titles stood in conflict with one another, as in the case of the region north of the Ohio River, which Virginia claimed in its entirety and Connecticut and Massachusetts claimed in part. States lacking rights to western lands believed that all should be ceded to the Confederation because together the states had won the trans-Appalachian territory in the Revolution. Virginia, whose charter rights were oldest, resolved the issue in 1781 by agreeing to transfer to the United States the region north and west of the Ohio River, the area that later became the states of

Ohio, Indiana, Illinois, Michigan, and Wisconsin. Virginia offered cession on the condition that the territory eventually be divided into states that would join the Confederation on an equal basis with the original thirteen. The trans-Appalachian lands south of the Ohio River remained temporarily under the control of Virginia, North Carolina, and Georgia.

Congress passed three ordinances to establish guidelines for distributing land and governing the Northwest Territory. Wealthy speculators who had purchased rights from Native Americans had significant influence over the shape these ordinances took. Thomas Jefferson was principal author of the first ordinance, which passed Congress in 1784. This law gave settlers a great deal of autonomy in establishing a territorial government. The Northwest would be divided into seven districts, with the settlers of each to govern themselves by choosing a constitution and laws from any of the existing states. When any district reached the population of the smallest of the original thirteen states, it would be admitted as a state to the Confederation on equal terms. Congress retained responsibility for selling the public lands.

The second ordinance, passed in 1785, set the rules for distributing lands. The influence of speculators was apparent, for the minimum price of a lot was $640, payable in specie or its equivalent, a sum far beyond the means of many potential settlers. All property would be surveyed before sale, laid out in townships six miles square. Each lot would contain 640 acres sold at a minimum of one dollar per acre, with better land offered at a higher price. The government retained lots for public schools and for distribution to Revolutionary War veterans. Because of the relatively high cost, Congress found few individual buyers. In fact, many land-hungry squatters simply set up their farms without government approval, sometimes purchasing rights from neighboring Indians, sometimes not. So Congress accepted a deal offered by a group of New England speculators, the Ohio Company, agreeing to sell them 1.5 million acres for $500,000 in depreciated bonds, or less than ten cents per acre in hard money. Given the Confederation's debt, the sale was welcome.

Congress further cooperated with the Ohio Company in drafting the Northwest Ordinance of 1787. In response to speculators' demands, the law established firmer congressional control over the territory, providing settlers less self-government than under the 1784 ordinance. Initially, a governor, secretary, and three judges appointed by Congress would administer the government. When 5,000 adult males resided in the territory, they could elect an assembly, but the governor held a veto over its actions. Men were eligible to vote if they owned at least fifty acres of land. Three to five states would be created from the Northwest Territory, with each state qualified to enter the union when its population reached 60,000. New states would have equal status with the original thirteen. The ordinance of 1787 also included provisions for individual rights that the Congress and the Ohio Company hoped would attract purchasers. They expected many settlers to come from New England. The ordinance protected private contracts, religious liberty, trial by jury, and habeas corpus (protection against illegal imprisonment). It prohibited slavery from the region forever. Thus, while catering to the interests of speculators, the Northwest Ordinance also extended rights won during the Revolution to new settlers in the west. Further, it limited the spread of slavery, and determined that western territories would achieve the status of states rather than remain colonies.

POLITICAL AND ECONOMIC TURMOIL

Political strife under the Articles of Confederation disappointed Americans who had high hopes for their republic. After all, it was a government of their own making, in which everyone was supposed to be represented adequately. But instead of harmony, economic interests clashed; the states failed to satisfy everybody. Many elites thought the United States was becoming too democratic and anarchic, as farmers revolted, government failed to control the violence, and some legislatures approved the insurgents' demands. Corruption seemed to have contaminated their government, just as in the prerevolutionary period it had ruined the British.

Creditors Versus Debtors

As a result of the postwar depression, farmers throughout the United States faced economic hardship. Many had eagerly purchased British manufactures, expecting to pay for the new clothes and consumer goods by selling their grain and livestock to the West Indies. British merchants offered easy credit to stimulate sales; American merchants and shopkeepers passed the credit on to farm families who would pay with the fall crop.

The house of cards crashed when the British government closed the West Indies to American ships. English mercantile houses called in their debts in specie only, starting a chain of default that extended from London to the frontier. Americans lacked the gold and silver that the British demanded, but merchants refused to accept payment in farm products because they had no market for the goods. So they took farmers to court: In many places, the number of debt cases rose dramatically. For example, in Hampshire County, Massachusetts, from 1784 to 1786, the court heard 3,000 debt cases: Almost one-third of the county's adult males were prosecuted for insolvency.

State governments aggravated the situation by imposing taxes to repay war bonds in full, a policy that worked to the advantage of wealthy speculators who had bought up the bonds from farmers and artisans at a large discount. The Massachusetts government particularly favored mercantile interests, levying on farmers high taxes that also had to be paid in specie. When farmers defaulted, the courts sold their land and cattle, often at only one-third to one-half value. If their assets failed to cover the debts and back taxes, the farmers were imprisoned until they or someone else paid the sum. Often men sat in crowded jails with insufficient ventilation, heat, or food because they owed small debts. Ordinary folk became angry as they feared imprisonment and the loss of their farms.

Farmers Demand Reform

Protesters mobilized as they had in the prerevolutionary period, at first meeting in county conventions to draw up petitions to the state assembly. In Massachusetts, they demanded changes in the state constitution, which many had voted against in 1780, to make the government more responsive to their needs and less costly to run. They wanted abolition of the state senate, which represented the commercial elite; lowering of property qualifications to hold office; and transfer of the capital from Boston to a more central location. Inland towns found it difficult to send representatives to the assembly because expenses were so high. The

farmers also demanded paper money and tender laws, the latter enabling them to settle debts and taxes with goods rather than specie. Both would ease the credit crisis. During the Revolution, the yeomen had benefited from the inflation that resulted from government issued paper money because they received high prices for their produce and were able to pay off prewar debts with cheap dollars. While the farmers stopped short of demanding a return to high inflation, they hoped for a gentle upswing in prices and a larger money supply to help them pay their debts.

When state legislatures emitted paper money or passed tender laws, as in Rhode Island, North Carolina, New York, and Georgia, little unrest ensued. In Rhode Island, political parties channeled conflict, for after the Country party ousted the Mercantile party in spring 1786, the new assembly issued paper money with stiff fines for creditors who refused to accept it. Elites elsewhere referred to "Rogue Island," even suggesting that the state be abolished and divided between Massachusetts and Connecticut.

In other states, mercantile factions maintained control of the government. They detested paper money because debtors would pay in depreciated bills; they opposed tender laws because of the lack of a market for grain and livestock. Merchants argued that paper currency issued as loans on farm property (rather than as notes based on gold and silver deposited in banks) was immoral because it would lose value, allowing debtors to violate contracts by paying back less than they had borrowed. Creditors asserted that their property rights were at risk.

Shays's Rebellion

When state governments failed to help, debtors in New England, New Jersey, Pennsylvania, Maryland, Virginia, and South Carolina protested militantly. Events moved furthest in Massachusetts, where under provocation of the assembly and governor, the farmers rebelled. In fall 1786, armed Massachusetts farmers closed down county courts to prevent further hearings for debt. Perhaps one-fourth of potential soldiers in the state were involved, calling themselves the "Regulators," after the Carolina insurgents of the 1760s. Their opponents first labeled the rebels "Green Bushers" because they wore a sprig of evergreen—the Massachusetts symbol for liberty—then called them Shaysites when Daniel Shays, a forty-year-old veteran

Daniel Shays and Job Shattuck, from the cover of a pamphlet supporting Shays's Rebellion.

of Bunker Hill and Saratoga, emerged as leader. The government, dominated by the eastern elite, frantically requested aid from Congress, which complied by requisitioning $530,000 and 1,340 soldiers from the states. When the states failed to cooperate, the bankruptcy of the Confederation was clear. Congress was powerless, warned those who wanted a stronger central government, even in the face of civil war.

The Massachusetts government acted on its own, taking measures that further alienated angry farmers, inciting greater support for the revolt. The assembly passed the Riot Act, which prohibited armed groups from gathering in public and permitted sheriffs to kill rioters who refused to disband. The legislature also suspended habeas corpus, allowing officials to jail suspected insurgents without showing cause. The farmers refused to back down, as one warned, "I am determined to fight and spill my blood and leave my bones at the courthouse till Resurrection." They protested that the suspension of habeas corpus was "dangerous if not absolutely destructive to a Republican government." Nevertheless, in November 1786, the state government sent 300 soldiers to arrest rebel leaders; when that failed to stop the farmers from closing the courts, Boston merchants raised private funds to outfit 4,400 troops. Residents of Boston and coastal towns who feared the inflationary consequences of paper money filled the ranks. Revolutionary general Benjamin Lincoln commanded the army; in January 1787, they marched to Worcester to protect the county court.

Lincoln's army forced the Shaysites to choose between submission and armed rebellion, for a middle ground of petitions and court closings was no longer

Hand-drawn diagram of the movements of the Shays and Lincoln armies in January–February 1787.

viable. The farmers amassed their own troops, esti-mated at 2,500 men, with Shays, the former Conti-nental Army captain, in charge of one regiment. They unsuccessfully attacked the federal arsenal at Spring-field for weapons to assault Boston, then regrouped to await the merchants' army. Shays was convinced that their cause was just; in a newspaper interview he confi-dently stated that he "knew General Lincoln was com-ing against him, but as he would bring with him no-body but shopkeepers, lawyers, and doctors, he could easily defeat him." Lincoln attacked Shays by surprise in a blizzard, dispersing the rebels within half an hour.

The aftermath of Shays's defeat was more divisive and bloody than the engagements between the armies. The assembly declared a state of "open, unnatural, un-provoked, and wicked rebellion," giving the governor the power to treat the Shaysites as enemies of the state. The legislators passed the Disqualification Act, which barred people implicated in the revolt from voting and holding office for three years, teaching school, or keep-ing inns and taverns. Many of the insurgents escaped to New York and Vermont with their families and pos-sessions. Others, including people who had not been involved, were imprisoned. Militant Shaysites pro-longed the conflict by raiding homes and kidnapping merchants, doctors, shopkeepers, and officials who had sided with the government. As a result of the up-rising and repression, voter turnout skyrocketed in the April 1787 election. A much greater number of west-ern Massachusetts towns sent delegates to the legisla-ture than they had in previous years, making the new assembly somewhat more responsive to rural debtors. While refusing to approve paper money, it enacted a tender law and quickly restored the civil rights of the insurgents.

THE MOVEMENT FOR CONSTITUTIONAL REFORM

The Confederation's helplessness in response to spreading armed rebellion strengthened the hand of nationalists like Robert Morris and Alexander Hamil-ton, who had been arguing for a more powerful cen-tral government. By 1787, Congress had lost much of its authority, and representatives stopped attending,

often preventing action for lack of a quorum. Because it had failed to obtain a national tax and could not force the states to send requisitioned funds, the Con-federation was broke. In 1785, Congress stopped in-terest payments on the French debt and in 1787 ended those on the principal. Nor could it reimburse Ameri-can creditors. In 1787, Congress transferred responsi-bility for the national debt to the states.

The Philadelphia Convention

In September 1786, when Shays's Rebellion was still gathering steam, representatives gathered for a conven-tion in Annapolis, Maryland, to discuss amending the Articles to give Congress power to regulate trade. The convention failed when only five state delegations ar-rived on time. Several of the delegates, including Alexander Hamilton, James Madison, and John Dick-inson, called for another convention to meet in May 1787 at Philadelphia to consider a more thorough re-vision of the Articles. By early 1787, the disorder in Massachusetts and the growing concern about state emission of paper money built support for constitu-tional reform. In February, Congress endorsed a change. Twelve states—all but Rhode Island where farmers controlled the legislature—sent delegates to Philadelphia.

Though the appointed day was May 14, 1787, the convention failed to start until May 25 when enough representatives finally arrived. State legislatures had de-layed choosing their delegations and travel was slow. Among the first were Virginia's representatives, who used the extra time for planning. James Madison, a thirty-six-year-old planter, slaveholder, and intellectual who had served in the Virginia assembly and Con-gress, came to the convention well prepared. A shy man who avoided public speaking, Madison neverthe-less took a dominant role in the proceedings, for which he has been called the father of the Constitu-tion. Propelled by the breakdown of Congress and the problems he witnessed in state government, Madison wanted to reform the Confederation to create a stronger central government. He believed that state constitutions with powerful assemblies were too de-mocratic, giving too much influence to the common people. As a consequence, these legislatures collabo-rated with debtors by circulating paper money, which Madison considered an attack on property. The people

James Madison, *1783, by Charles Willson Peale. Like most of his fellow delegates, Madison was relatively young when he helped frame the Constitution.*

should be represented adequately, Madison thought, but their power must be constrained. The United States needed a new constitution that would place authority in the hands of well-educated, propertied men. Other Virginia delegates included Governor Edmund Randolph and George Washington, whose popularity and prestige made his support for the convention crucial. Washington presided over the proceedings, but participated little in the debates.

A total of fifty-five men served at the Constitutional Convention between opening day and adjournment four months later. Most were wealthy men, members of the political and social elite. Twenty-one were practicing lawyers, another thirteen had been educated in the law, seven were merchants, and eighteen were farmers or planters; nineteen owned African American slaves. Most were relatively young men under the age of fifty, and many had served in the revolution and had held political office. The elder statesman Benjamin Franklin, now eighty-one years old and ailing, was a member of the Pennsylvania delegation.

Several heroes of the revolution were absent, including Thomas Jefferson and John Adams, who were ambassadors abroad; Samuel Adams, who was not chosen as a delegate; and Patrick Henry, who refused to serve because he "smelt a rat." Most of the delegates supported a plan to place more power in the national government.

The Great Compromise

The convention can be divided into two periods. During the first seven weeks, the matter overshadowing all discussion was the power of "large" versus "small" states. After this issue was resolved, delegations formed blocs in new ways, according to concerns about the executive, slavery, and commerce. The basic question that the convention avoided debating at length was whether to amend the Articles of Confederation or write an entirely new constitution. Madison, who thought the Confederation beyond repair, moved the convention along with a document he had drafted in advance, called the Virginia Plan, which scrapped the Articles. Madison was able to set the convention's agenda because at the outset no other delegate had prepared an alternate design.

The Virginia Plan, which Edmund Randolph presented on May 29, proposed a powerful central government, dominated by a National Legislature of two houses (bicameral). The lower house would be elected by qualified voters and would choose the members of the upper house from nominations by state legislatures. The number of delegates from each state depended upon population. This bicameral National Legislature was empowered to appoint the executive and judicial branches of the central government and to veto state laws.

Several states opposed the Virginia Plan because it gave greater representation in the National Legislature to states with large populations. Delaware, Maryland, New Jersey, and Connecticut feared the power of Virginia, Pennsylvania, and Massachusetts, which together comprised almost one-half of the American people. If the Virginia Plan were adopted, just four states could dominate the legislature and ignore the interests of the rest. In dividing on this issue, states considered the possibility of future population expansion as well as present size. Thus states with unsettled territories mostly

This painting of the Constitutional Convention of 1787 by an unknown artist shows George Washington presiding. Because the convention met in secrecy, the artist used his imagination to paint the scene.

sided with the large states, while those without room for growth chose the opposite camp.

The small states preferred a constitution that retained the structure of the Confederation Congress, but expanded its powers. In mid-June, William Paterson introduced the New Jersey Plan, which proposed a one-house, or unicameral, Congress in which the states had equal representation. Congress would appoint an executive council which in turn would choose a supreme court. As in the Virginia Plan, the authority of Congress was much enlarged, with powers to tax, regulate commerce, and compel states to obey its laws. The large states objected to this plan, arguing that Delaware (population 59,000) should not have as much power as Virginia (population 748,000).

The debate over representation in Congress brought the convention to an impasse. It made little progress toward a new constitution until the issue of state representation was resolved. The large states had the votes in the convention but knew they could never get the document ratified if the Virginia Plan prevailed. The Delaware delegation, as instructed by its legislature, threatened to walk out, until Connecticut put forward its proposal, allowing debate to continue. The "great compromise," as Connecticut's plan became known, established a bicameral Congress, with representation in the lower house based upon population. This house, called the House of Representatives, would be elected directly by the voters and have the sole right to initiate revenue bills. Thus, the idea that people with a stake in society should elect the representatives who taxed them was incorporated into the document. In the upper house, called the Senate, states would have equal representation. According to the Constitution, each state legislature chose two senators to serve six-year terms. The House of Representatives would be elected every two years. The bicameral Congress balanced two different sets of interests: It resolved the division between the small and large states and also satisfied those who wanted to limit the influence of ordinary voters. Senators were expected to come from the wealthier, more established segments of society; their long terms and appointment by state legislators would shield them from public opinion. Both houses of Congress had to approve legislation.

The compromise between the large and small states created a government that was both national and federal. It was *national* because the House of Representatives was popularly elected, with not more than one representative per 30,000 people. Upon ratification, the United States would become a single nation rather than a confederacy of states. By expanding legislative powers, the sovereign people vested more authority in the central government. Congress received the powers to tax, coin and borrow money, regulate commerce, establish courts, declare war, and raise armed forces. States were specifically forbidden from keeping troops without the permission of Congress, making treaties, coining money, and issuing paper currency. At the same time, the new Constitution established a *federal* government, one in which the states retained rights, including equal representation in the Senate. Congress was forbidden from giving one state preference over another when levying taxes and regulating trade, nor could it impose export duties, prohibit the slave trade until 1808, or carve a new state from any state's territory without permission. Approval by three-fourths of the states would be necessary to amend the Constitution. But despite these provisions, many Americans believed that the states—the small republics—had lost too much power. The struggle for ratification revolved in large part on this issue.

The Executive, Slavery, and Commerce

Once the question of state representation was solved with the "great compromise," the convention made greater headway, amid conflict and further compromise. Factions within the convention shifted from one debate to the next.

The power of the executive was a concern to people living in a world dominated by kings and princes. Delegates wanted to ensure that their government remained a republic, that it would not become a monarchy or dictatorship. At the same time, they believed that the executive branch should serve as a check on the legislature. The convention debated several questions affecting the executive's power. Should there be a single president or an executive board? While some argued that a plural executive could prevent one person from usurping power, the convention chose a single president, expecting to limit his authority in other ways. Length of term also stimulated discussion, for the longer the term the greater a president's autonomy. The convention reached agreement on a four-year term, without specifying the number of times he could be re-elected.

The question of how the president would be chosen was divisive, between those who preferred direct election by the people and those who wanted Congress or the state legislatures to make the choice. Once again, the issue of states' rights reared its head. A committee appointed by the convention devised an ingenious but complicated formula to satisfy all sides—the electoral college. Though the specifics of its operation were subsequently changed by constitutional amendment, presidential elections still occur through this phantom institution. The electoral college was empowered to elect the president and vice president, with each state allotted as many votes as it had representatives and senators. Thus, even the smallest state received three votes and the large states were represented according to population. The state legislatures could determine how to choose the electors, whether by popular election or by the assembly itself. The electoral college would never meet together as a group. The electors of each state gathered within their states to cast votes, which they sent to Congress for counting. If no candidate received a majority, the House of Representatives made the selection from among the five candidates with the most votes.

Of the Philadelphia convention's decisions on the executive, most crucial to the endurance of the Constitution was the balance of power between the executive and legislative branches. The convention gave the president a veto over laws passed by Congress. The legislators could override the veto if two-thirds of both houses approved. Congress also had authority to remove the president by impeachment and trial for treason, bribery, and "other high Crimes and Misdemeanors." Further balancing came in the areas of foreign affairs and the judiciary. While Congress received power to declare war and raise troops, the president served as commander-in-chief. Only with the "advice and consent" of the Senate could the chief executive negotiate treaties and appoint ambassadors, Supreme Court justices, and other officials.

Slavery was a major factor in the convention's deliberations, though the words "slavery," "slave," and "slave trade" appeared nowhere in the 1787 Constitution. African American bondage affected the debates on representation in Congress, the election of the president, and the regulation of commerce. The southern states wanted to include slaves in a state's population when computing delegates to the House of Representatives and votes in the electoral college. Northerners protested that this gave white southerners an unfair

TABLE 6.1	UNITED STATES POPULATION, 1790	
	Total (all whites and free African Americans)	Slaves
New England	1,009,206	3,763
Middle Atlantic	1,017,087	45,210
Maryland and Virginia	1,067,338	395,663
Lower South	726,626	237,141

advantage (illustrated in Table 6-1) because enslaved people could not vote. As part of the "great compromise," the convention decided that five enslaved Americans would count as three free persons for apportioning representation and direct taxes among the states. Since three-fifths of slaves living in the Chesapeake and Lower South numbered 380,000 people, the power of white voters south of Pennsylvania was significantly magnified. Later called a "covenant with death" by abolitionists, the "three-fifths compromise" perpetuated slavery in the new republic.

Political bargaining resulted in additional provisions that furthered slavery. The convention approved a fugitive slave clause, which prevented free states from emancipating slaves who had escaped from masters in other states. The delegates also adopted a provision that forbade Congress from prohibiting slave importation for twenty years (with no requirement that it ban the slave trade after that time). North and South Carolina and Georgia demanded the option of importing people from Africa because they expected settlement to continue into western Georgia and the present states of Alabama, Mississippi, and Tennessee. Slaves would be needed, they thought, to work the new plantations. Northern delegates, who might have pushed the convention in the direction of their own states— toward the abolition of slavery—did almost nothing to promote that end.

Instead of trying to eliminate slavery under the new government, the northerners made the regulation of commerce their priority. The Lower South obtained the twenty-year protection of the slave trade when New England delegates promised their support in re-

turn for a compromise on international trade. Because the southern states had different economic interests than the north, they feared giving Congress the power to tax exports and regulate commerce. They suspected that the national government, if dominated by northerners in the future, would place heavy taxes on tobacco, rice, and indigo—the south's main exports. Southerners thought that navigation laws could also work to their detriment, because northern merchants owned most American shipping. If Congress passed legislation requiring that all exports be transported in American ships, southerners would lose the choice of using a foreign, perhaps cheaper, carrier. Northerners, on the other hand, wanted Congress to have the authority to negotiate trade agreements on an equal basis with other nations. Congress could then retaliate if a country imposed restrictions such as closing ports. The convention settled these matters, first by forbidding Congress from imposing export duties, then with a deal that empowered Congress to regulate commerce. In return for South Carolina's vote for the latter provision, New England agreed to extend the slave trade for 20 years.

The Philadelphia convention created a Constitution that shifted important powers to a national government, but still vested a great deal of authority in the states. The framers painstakingly created checks and balances among the branches of government to avoid degeneration of their republic into anarchy or despotism. They required direct popular election of only the House of Representatives, giving that body the right to initiate taxes. The convention incorporated flexibility into the document, which had been

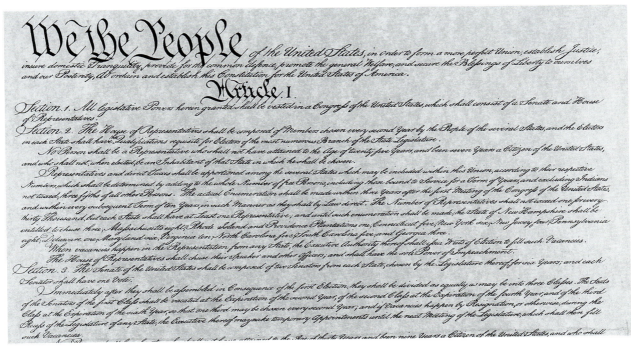

First page of the United States Constitution of 1787.

absent in the Articles of Confederation, by permitting amendment with approval of two-thirds of both houses of Congress and three-fourths of the states. The document shielded some individual rights, though critics argued that many were omitted. The Constitution protected trial by jury in criminal cases and habeas corpus. It banned religious tests for holding office under the United States, ex post facto (retroactive) laws, and bills of attainder, which extinguished a person's civil rights upon sentence of death or as an outlaw. While codifying the principles of self-government and individual liberties, however, the convention—with little dissent—denied them to almost one-fifth of the American population by embedding slavery within the fabric of the new government.

Ratification

After the delegates to the Philadelphia convention signed the Constitution on September 17, 1787, they quickly sent it to the Confederation Congress in New York City. Article 7 of the document required ratification by nine state conventions to establish the new government. States refusing to ratify could remain independent or unite together under another frame of government. The majority of Congress had approved the Constitution as members of the Philadelphia convention, so they forwarded it to the states after little debate. One congressman from Virginia, Richard Henry Lee, tried to bury the document by adding amendments, but was overruled. Advocates of ratification knew that prompt action was necessary to forestall an effective opposition movement.

The group favoring ratification was not particularly well organized but had two advantages over its opponents. One came from the choice of a name, the Federalists, for it undercut the ground on which their adversaries stood. James Madison, Alexander Hamilton, John Jay, and other supporters of the Constitution argued in favor of the federalist provisions that reserved powers to the states as well as the nationalist

AN ANTIFEDERALIST OPPOSES THE CONSTITUTION: RICHARD HENRY LEE TO GEORGE MASON, NEW YORK, OCTOBER 1, 1787

Richard Henry Lee, one of the most ardent opponents of the Constitution drafted in Philadelphia during the summer of 1787, tried to kill the document in the Confederation Congress by adding amendments. Here he explains his opposition on the basis that too much power would reside in the central government, which he expected to be dominated by Northerners. Lee thought, in fact, that if the Constitution were ratified without proper amendment, the result could be "Civil War."

I have waited until now to answer your favor of Septr. 18th from Philadelphia, that I might inform you how the Convention plan of Government was entertained by Congress. Your prediction of what would happen in Congress was exactly verified—It was with us, as with you, this or nothing; & this urged with a most extreme intemperance—The greatness of the powers given & the multitude of Places to be created, produces a coalition of Monarchy men, Military Men, Aristocrats, and Drones whose noise, impudence & zeal exceeds all belief—Whilst the Commercial plunder of the South stimulates the rapacious Trader. In this state of things, the Patriot voice is raised in vain for such changes and securities as Reason and Experience prove to be necessary against the encroachments of power upon the indispensable rights of human nature. Upon due consideration of the Constitution under which we now Act, some of us were clearly of opinion that the 13th article of the Confederation precluded us from giving an opinion concerning a plan subversive of the present system and eventually forming a New Confederacy of Nine instead of 13 States. The contrary doctrine was asserted with great violence in expectation of the strong majority with which they might send it forward under terms of much approbation. Having procured an opinion that Congress was qualified to consider, to amend, to approve or disapprove—the next game was to determine that tho a right to amend existed, it would be highly inexpediant to exercise that right, but merely to transmit it with respectful marks of approbation—In this state of things I availed myself of the Right to amend, & moved the Amendments copy of which I send herewith & called the ayes & nays to fix them on the journal—This greatly alarmed the Majority & vexed them extremely—for the plan is, to push the business on with great dispatch, & with as little opposition as possible; that it may be adopted before it has stood the test of Reflection & due examination—They found it most eligible at last to transmit it merely, without approving or disapproving; provided nothing but the transmission should appear on the Journal— This compromise was settled and they took the opportunity of inserting the word *Unanimously,* which applied only to simple transmission, hoping to have it mistaken for an Unanimous approbation of the thing—It states that Congress having Received the Constitution unanimously transmit it &c.—It is certain that no Approbation was given— This constitution has a great many excellent Regulations in it and if it could be reasonably amended would be a fine System—As it is, I think 'tis past doubt, that if it should be established, either a tyranny will result from it, or it will be prevented by a Civil War.

MAINE
(Mass.)

NEW
HAMPSHIRE
June 21, 1788

NEW YORK
July 26, 1788

MASSACHUSETTS
Feb. 7, 1788

CONN.
Jan. 9,
1788

R.I.
May 29,
1790

PENNSYLVANIA
Dec. 12, 1787

NEW
JERSEY
Dec. 18, 1787

MARYLAND
Apr. 28,
1788

DELAWARE
Dec. 7,
1787

VIRGINIA
June 26, 1788

ATLANTIC
OCEAN

NORTH CAROLINA
Nov. 21, 1789

SOUTH
CAROLINA
May 23, 1788

GEORGIA
Jan. 2, 1788

Lake Michigan   Lake Huron   Lake Ontario   Lake Erie   Ohio R.   Mississippi R.

For
Against
Tie

MAP 6.3 | RATIFICATION OF THE CONSTITUTION

elements of the prospective government. While others denounced the Constitution because it transferred too much power to the national government from the states, the Federalists claimed the document provided balance. The critics were obliged to take the negative name of Antifederalists, which misrepresented their position in favor of states' rights. The Federalists also gained advantage from the fact that many advocates of a strong central government resided in the coastal cities and towns, where public opinion was easier to mobilize than in outlying areas. Most newspapers supported the Constitution. For example, in New York, where the ratification battle became intense, Hamilton, Madison, and Jay published in the newspapers a series of eighty-five essays that provided a detailed argument in favor of the Constitution. The essays also gained wide attention outside New York, and in spring 1788, the authors published them in book form as *The Federalist,* which is considered a major work in American political theory.

Americans chose sides over ratification for both political and ideological reasons. Most Federalists gained their livelihoods as merchants, shopkeepers, professionals, artisans, and commercial farmers. As creditors and consumers, many favored the Constitution because it stopped state emission of paper currency, whose inflationary effects they loathed. Federalists desired a government that would foster the growth of a market economy and facilitate trade with other countries. They believed a national government would provide the stability and strength that were lacking under the Confederation, enabling the United States to gain stature among the nations of Europe. Some frontier settlers, seeking military defense against Native Americans, also supported the Constitution.

The Federalists, who viewed commercial development more favorably than the Antifederalists, thought the purpose of government was to arbitrate among opposing interests. Federalists believed that society benefited when people pursued individual goals. They considered elusive the republican ideal of a community in which everyone could reach consensus because they had similar needs. Madison argued in *Federalist* #10 that people possess different interests because they have unequal abilities and thus varying success in accumulating property. People by nature also have "different opinions concerning religion, concerning government, and many other points." In a free society, they form factions on the basis of both their conflicting ideologies and "the various and unequal distribution of property." He wrote:

> A landed interest, a manufacturing interest, a mercantile interest, a moneyed interest, with many lesser interests, grow up of necessity in civilized nations, and divide them into different classes, actuated by different sentiments and views. The regulation of these various and interfering interests forms the principal task of modern legislation, and involves the spirit of party and faction in the necessary and ordinary operations of the government.

Madison claimed that the Constitution would be beneficial because a large republic contained more safeguards than a small one. In an extended polity, so many factions exist that the ability of a single interest to monopolize power is reduced. With the national government, "you take in a greater variety of parties and interests; you make it less probable that a majority of the whole will have a common motive to invade the rights of other citizens."

Antifederalists disagreed with this analysis, both because they favored small republics and because they feared the actions of men who would likely dominate the central government. Small farmers, many of them

debtors who considered the mercantile elite their enemies, wanted nothing to do with this Constitution. At the core of their opposition was the belief that power should remain in the states. The Antifederalists understood that, despite equal representation in the Senate, the new government was fundamentally different from the Articles. They argued that a republic must be geographically small with a homogeneous population in order to meet the needs of its people. They believed the new central government would be too large and too remote, that the interests of citizens of the thirteen states were too diverse. A congressman could never know the will of 30,000 constituents; with so few persons elected to Congress and such large electoral districts, affluent well-known candidates would have the advantage over ordinary men who ran for office. Thus, even the House of Representatives, the branch of government closest to the people, would become the domain of the rich. To the Antifederalists, the Constitution lacked sufficient barriers against corruption and abuse of power. At the least, term limits on the president and senators were required to prevent these officials from keeping their offices for life. Annual elections (instead of every two years) would make the House of Representatives more responsive to the voters.

Antifederalists also pointed to the omission of a bill of rights as cause for rejecting the Constitution. They advocated freedom of speech, press, assembly, and religion; jury trials for civil cases; judicial safeguards such as the right to a speedy trial and to confront accusers and witnesses; and prohibitions against unwarranted searches and seizures. The Federalists answered that a bill of rights would be superfluous because state constitutions offered these protections (some did, but in no case was protection comprehensive), and because a bill of rights was needed against a powerful king, not when the people themselves were sovereign. This latter argument ignored the vulnerability of the individual to the will of the majority. The Federalists used poor judgment in failing to incorporate a bill of rights into the 1787 Constitution, for the Antifederalists gained momentum as a result. Omitting these rights, for which the patriots had fought, turned many Americans against the proposed frame of government.

Nevertheless, ratification proceeded rapidly at first as state legislatures called elections for the state ratifying conventions. Delaware was the first to ratify when its convention approved the Constitution unanimously on December 7, 1787. In Pennsylvania, where resistance was potentially heavy in the backcountry, Federalists moved quickly, securing approval by a two-to-one margin. New Jersey and Georgia then ratified unanimously. When Connecticut accepted the new government in January 1788 by a three-to-one vote, five states had joined the union. All of these states except Pennsylvania were relatively small and recognized the advantages of joining a union in which they had equal representation in the Senate.

Then the conventions became more acrimonious. North Carolina and Rhode Island rejected the document outright and New Hampshire put off its decision. Maryland and South Carolina ratified easily, but the vote in Massachusetts was close, as animosities from Shays's Rebellion colored the debate. Turnout for the Massachusetts convention was huge, as farmers in the central and western regions of the state believed the Constitution represented the interests of the eastern elite. The convention barely ratified the document by a vote of 187 to 168, recommending a series of amendments to protect individual rights and limit the powers of Congress. In June 1788, New Hampshire finally acted, becoming the ninth state to ratify, the number required to establish the new government. Nevertheless, two states remained crucial, Virginia and New York, whose size and economic importance made their approval necessary if the Constitution was to succeed. Virginia ratified in late June after a fierce debate, recommending to the first Congress a series of amendments, including a bill of rights. New York approved in late July, also with recommended changes, after New York City threatened to secede from the rest of the state if rural districts failed to accept the document.

CONCLUSION

With ratification by eleven states, including the most populous and economically dominant, the United States began a new experiment in republican government. The Articles of Confederation had failed to inspire the thirteen states to work together to solve the Confederation's most pressing problems—the national debt, trade, and protection of U.S. borders against Spain and Great Britain. Even Congress's chief success, the legislation for governing and distributing land in the Northwest Territory, was marred by high land prices, delays in surveying, settlement by squatters, favoritism toward speculators, and conflict with Native Americans. Of course, not all Americans thought the Articles were an utter failure. The Antifederalists preferred a confederacy of sovereign states in which governments stood ready to respond to local needs. But to the Federalists, this had led to paper money and armed rebellion. They demanded a new Constitution, one in which educated, propertied men like themselves would determine national economic policy and foreign affairs. The next challenge for the young United States was to put this new frame of government into effect.

RECOMMENDED READINGS

Beeman, Richard, Botein, Stephen, and Carter, Edward C., eds. *Beyond Confederation: Origins of the Constitution and American National Identity* (1987). These essays provide an excellent introduction to the Confederation period and the making of the Constitution.

Berlin, Ira, and Hoffman, Ronald, eds. *Slavery and Freedom in the Age of the American Revolution* (1983). Important essays on change, or lack thereof, in the status of African Americans during the Revolutionary era.

Doerflinger, Thomas M. *A Vigorous Spirit of Enterprise: Merchants and Economic Development in Revolutionary Philadelphia* (1986). A very good study of Philadelphia merchants and their impact on economic growth in the emergent United States.

Equiano, Olaudah. *The Interesting Narrative of the Life of Olaudah Equiano,* in Henry Louis Gates, Jr., ed., *The Classic Slave Narratives* (1987). Autobiography of a kidnapped African who was enslaved in America, then eventually gained freedom.

Greene, Jack P. *Peripheries and Center: Constitutional Development in the Extended Polities of the British Empire and the United States, 1607–1788* (1986). Links the constitutional structure of Britain and its colonies to the Constitution of 1787.

Hamilton, Alexander, Jay, John, and Madison, James. *The Federalist Papers* (1788). Defense of the Constitution of 1787; seminal treatise of American political thought.

Kenyon, Cecilia M. "Men of Little Faith: The Anti-Federalists on the Nature of Representative Government," *William and Mary Quarterly,* 3rd ser., 12 (1955): 3–43. Insightful essay on the men who opposed ratification of the Constitution of 1787.

Kerber, Linda K. *Women of the Republic: Intellect and Ideology in Revolutionary America* (1980). Evaluates the impact of the revolution on attitudes toward women.

Szatmary, David P. *Shays' Rebellion: The Making of an Agrarian Insurrection* (1980). A detailed study of the western Massachusetts revolt.

Political Ideology, Government, and the Constitution

Appleby, Joyce. *Liberalism and Republicanism in the Historical Imagination* (1992).

Banning, Lance. *The Sacred Fire of Liberty: James Madison and the Founding of the Federal Republic* (1995).

Belz, Herman, Hoffman, Ronald, and Albert, Peter J., eds. *To Form a More Perfect Union: The Critical Ideas of the Constitution* (1992).

Colbourn, Trevor, ed. *Fame and the Founding Fathers: Essays by Douglass Adair* (1974).

"The Constitution of the United States," issue devoted to the Constitution, *William and Mary Quarterly,* 3rd ser., 44 (July 1987).

Greene, Jack P., ed. *The American Revolution: Its Character and Limits* (1987).

Higginbotham, Don. *The War of American Independence: Military Attitudes, Policies, and Practice, 1763–1789* (1971).

Hoffman, Ronald, and Albert, Peter J., eds. *Sovereign States in an Age of Uncertainty* (1981).

Isaac, Rhys. *The Transformation of Virginia, 1740–1790* (1982).

Jensen, Merrill. *The New Nation: A History of the United States During the Confederation, 1781–1789* (1950).

Kurtz, Stephen G., and Hutson, James H., eds. *Essays on the American Revolution* (1973).

Main, Jackson Turner. *The Antifederalists: Critics of the Constitution, 1781–1788* (1961).

Main, Jackson Turner. *Political Parties Before the Constitution* (1973).

Main, Jackson Turner. *The Sovereign States, 1775–1783* (1973).

McDonald, Forrest. *E Pluribus Unum: The Formation of the American Republic, 1776–1790,* 2d ed. (1979).

Miller, William Lee. *The Business of May Next: James Madison and the Founding* (1992).

Morgan, Edmund S. *The Birth of the Republic, 1763–89,* 3rd ed. (1992).

Rakove, Jack N. *The Beginnings of National Politics: An Interpretive History of the Continental Congress* (1979).

Wood, Gordon S. *The Creation of the American Republic, 1776–1787* (1969).

Women and African Americans in Postrevolutionary Society

Berlin, Ira. *Slaves Without Masters: The Free Negro in the Antebellum South* (1974).

Hoffman, Ronald, and Albert, Peter J. eds. *Women in the Age of the American Revolution* (1989).

Gelles, Edith B. *Portia: The World of Abigail Adams* (1992).

Jensen, Joan M. *Loosening the Bonds: Mid-Atlantic Farm Women, 1750–1850* (1986).

Jordan, Winthrop D. *White over Black: American Attitudes Toward the Negro, 1550–1812* (1968).

MacLeod, Duncan J. *Slavery, Race, and the American Revolution* (1974).

McColley, Robert. *Slavery and Jeffersonian Virginia* (1964).

Nash, Gary B., and Soderlund, Jean R. *Freedom by Degrees: Emancipation in Pennsylvania and Its Aftermath* (1991).

Nash, Gary B. *Race and Revolution* (1990).

Ulrich, Laurel Thatcher. *A Midwife's Tale: The Life of Martha Ballard, Based on Her Diary, 1785–1812* (1990).

Zilversmit, Arthur. *The First Emancipation: The Abolition of Slavery in the North* (1967).

Native Americans and the West

Dowd, Gregory Evans. *A Spirited Resistance: The North American Indian Struggle for Unity, 1745–1815* (1992).

McLoughlin, William G. *Cherokee Renascence in the New Republic* (1986).

Onuf, Peter S. *The Origins of the Federal Republic: Jurisdictional Controversies in the United States, 1775–1787* (1983).

Onuf, Peter S. *Statehood and Union: A History of the Northwest Ordinance* (1987).

Wallace, Anthony F. C. *The Death and Rebirth of the Seneca* (1970).

Weber, David J. *The Spanish Frontier in North America* (1992).

White, Richard. *The Middle Ground: Indians, Empires, and Republics in the Great Lakes Region, 1650–1815* (1991).

The Economy and Political Unrest

Ferguson, E. James. *The Power of the Purse: A History of American Public Finance, 1776–1790* (1961).

Foner, Eric. *Tom Paine and Revolutionary America* (1976).

Hall, Van Beck. *Politics Without Parties: Massachusetts 1780–1791* (1972).

Hoffman, Ronald, et al., eds. *The Economy of Early America: The Revolutionary Period, 1763–1790* (1988).

Kulikoff, Allan. *The Agrarian Origins of American Capitalism* (1992).

McCusker, John J., and Menard, Russell R. *The Economy of British America, 1607–1789, With Supplementary Bibliography* (1991).

Merrill, Michael, and Wilentz, Sean, eds. *The Key of Liberty: The Life and Democratic Writings of William Manning, "A Laborer," 1747–1814* (1993).

Pole, J. R. *Political Representation in England and the Origins of the American Republic* (1966).

Rothenberg, Winifred Barr. *From Market-Places to a Market Economy: The Transformation of Rural Massachusetts, 1750–1850* (1992).

Preparation for WAR to defend Commerce.

The Swedish Church Southwark with the building of the FRIGATE PHILADELPHIA.

BUILDING THE *PHILADELPHIA*

Preparation for War to defend Commerce *(1800), illustrating construction of the frigate* Philadelphia. *During the 1790s the United States tried to remain neutral in the European wars while prospering from international trade.*

Chapter 7

THE FEDERALIST REPUBLIC,

1789–1799

AFTER RATIFICATION, THE Federalists took leadership in creating the new government. Everyone expected George Washington to become president, though he was reluctant to assume office. The three authors of *The Federalist,* Alexander Hamilton, James Madison, and John Jay, who had been so important in achieving the Constitution, went on to play a central role in making it work. John Adams and Thomas Jefferson, who were serving as ambassadors in Europe during the convention but supported the document, returned home to become, respectively, vice president and secretary of state.

Though many Federalists disagreed with specific parts of the Constitution, they accepted compromise and knew the weak Confederation had to be replaced. In the flush of victory over the Antifederalists, they set to the task of remedying the nation's ills. Differences soon became clear, however, between Hamilton on the one side, and Madison and Jefferson on the other, as the first administration tackled the national debt and foreign policy. As a result of their conflict over policy, varying interpretations of the Constitution, competition for power, and personal enmity, the nation's first political parties developed.

THE NEW GOVERNMENT

The first national elections went well, from the Federalist point of view, considering the whirlwind of Antifederalist opposition to the Constitution. The great majority of representatives and senators in the first Congress were Federalists. They fulfilled Madison's image of well-to-do men of national reputation and experience in politics. Many had served in the constitutional convention and had signed the document. Most had military or political experience during the Revolution and Confederation period; just a few came from lower-class backgrounds. While the first congressmen were revolutionaries, they were also elites who believed that the country's interests coincided with their own. They wanted a stable government to foster economic growth.

George Washington Becomes President

The choice of George Washington as president was a foregone conclusion, though he would have preferred

CHRONOLOGY

1789	First Congress meets
	Inauguration of George Washington as president
	French Revolution begins
	Judiciary Act of 1789
1790	Site on Potomac River chosen for permanent capital
	Congress approves the funding and assumption plans
	Samuel Slater builds first water-powered textile mill in the United States
	First national census
	Nootka Convention
1791	Bank of the United States is established
	Native Americans of the Ohio Valley destroy Arthur St. Clair's army
	Ratification of Bill of Rights
1793	France declares war on Great Britain and Spain
	Washington begins second term
	Proclamation of Neutrality
	Genêt Affair
	Britain seizes U.S. merchant fleet
	Eli Whitney invents cotton gin
1794	Battle of Fallen Timbers
	Whiskey Rebellion
1795	Senate approves the Jay Treaty
	Treaty of Greenville
	Treaty of San Lorenzo
1797	John Adams becomes second president
1798	XYZ Affair becomes public
	Congress passes Alien and Sedition Acts
	Kentucky and Virginia Resolutions
1798–1800	Quasi-War with France
1799	The Fries Rebellion
	Napoleon takes power in France

to stay at his Mount Vernon estate in northern Virginia. In February 1789, members of the electoral college, selected by popular election in five states, by the governor and council in New Jersey, and by the legislatures of the remaining states, met in their state capitals to cast unanimous votes for the former commander-in-chief. They considered no one else. Washington's leadership during the war, his dignity and character, and his support for republican government made him the obvious choice. He might have tried to grasp power during the shaky Confederation, like a Napoleon or Stalin, but he did not. The first president's commitment to the success of the Constitution ensured the nation's survival during the early years. John Adams, elected vice president, received fewer than half as many votes as Washington.

The president-elect's trip from Mount Vernon to New York City, the temporary federal capital, became an eight-day triumphal march, despite Washington's desire to keep it simple. In large and small towns along his way—Alexandria, Baltimore, Wilmington, Philadelphia—crowds of people, troops of infantry and cavalry, and local officials feted him with ceremonies, cannon fire, and banquets. Philadelphia citizens erected a Roman arch, crowning the Revolutionary hero with a laurel wreath. In New Jersey, throngs saluted his military victories at Trenton and Princeton. On April 23, 1789, Washington crossed into Manhattan on a festooned barge, welcomed by thousands of cheering New Yorkers. He took the oath of office a week later.

The president and Congress, aware that they were setting precedent for the nation, initially placed a great deal of emphasis on titles and the comportment of officials. In this republic, in a world of monarchies, how should they be addressed? Should the president keep his door open and go out to dinner with friends, or should he remain detached? While the questions may

George Washington arrived in New York City for his inauguration as president to the cheers of thousands.

seem trivial, they indicate, at a human level, the novelty of this republican experiment. Sitting as president of the Senate, Vice President Adams, with diplomatic experience in Europe, urged Congress to adopt titles like those of other nations. A Senate committee suggested, for example, that Washington be called "His Highness the President of the United States of America, and Protector of their Liberties." After much debate, Congress dropped the notion of titles, preferring a more republican style. Washington and his successors have been addressed simply as "Mr. President."

For his part, the president wondered how to dignify his office and accomplish his work. He could easily have spent all of his time meeting with visitors, entertaining, and dining out. On the other hand, he did not want complete separation from the people. Washington's personality tended toward aloofness. He decided to hold a one-hour reception once a week, invite a few visitors to dinner, and sometimes attend the theater. In busy New York City, he enforced a distance that nineteenth-century presidents found easier to maintain in more isolated Washington, D.C.

Washington also developed, by trial and error, the way in which the chief executive would deal with Congress. Early in his administration, in advance of negotiating a treaty with the Creek Indians, he attended the Senate to request their "advice and consent," as the Constitution seemed to direct. The senators were unprepared to discuss Washington's proposal, leading to embarrassment on both sides. The president resolved never to consult in formal session again. Instead, he set the precedent of private informal meetings with members of Congress. Heads of executive departments, such as the secretary of the treasury, would attend congressional hearings, not the president. And in the case of treaties, the executive would seek the Senate's consent *after* negotiations were complete, not advice—at least formally—beforehand.

Beyond titles and modes of operating, Congress and the president needed to establish executive departments and courts, and draw up a bill of rights. They filled gaps in the written Constitution. In creating executive departments, which included War, Treasury, State (foreign affairs), and the attorney general, the most crucial constitutional question concerned who would be able to remove the heads of departments from office. The Constitution required that the president appoint officials with the Senate's advice and consent. It said nothing about removal. Some senators hoped to restrict the president's power by requiring Senate approval before officeholders could be fired, thus making them more accountable to the legislature. In rejecting this proposal, Congress clarified one aspect of the Constitution's balance of powers.

THE BILL OF RIGHTS, 1791

During the debates over ratification of the Constitution, many people argued for increased protection of individual rights, including freedom of religion, speech, the press, assembly, and petition, and judicial safeguards such as the right to a speedy trial and prohibition of cruel punishments. The Bill of Rights, or Amendments 1 through 10, added such provisions to the Constitution.

Amendment I
Congress shall make no law respecting an establishment of religion, or prohibiting the free exercise thereof; or abridging the freedom of speech, or of the press; or the right of the people peaceably to assemble, and to petition the government for a redress of grievances.

Amendment II
A well-regulated militia being necessary to the security of a free State, the right of the people to keep and bear arms shall not be infringed.

Amendment III
No soldier shall, in time of peace, be quartered in any house without the consent of the owner, nor in time of war, but in a manner to be prescribed by law.

Amendment IV
The right of the people to be secure in their persons, houses, papers, and effects, against unreasonable searches and seizures, shall not be violated, and no warrants shall issue but upon probable cause, supported by oath or affirmation, and particularly describing the place to be searched, and the persons or things to be seized.

Amendment V
No person shall be held to answer for a capital, or otherwise infamous crime, unless on a presentment or indictment of a grand jury, except in cases arising in the land or naval

With the Judiciary Act of 1789, Congress put some flesh on the skeleton outlined in Article III of the Constitution, which stated that the "judicial power of the United States shall be vested in one Supreme Court, and in such inferior courts as the Congress may from time to time ordain and establish." The Congress might have created a full-blown national court system, unifying state and federal law. Supporters of states' rights, however, opposed such enhancement of national power. Thus, the Judiciary Act, the result of compromise, established a Supreme Court of six justices and a system of federal inferior courts, which were few in number and restricted primarily to consideration of federal crimes. State courts retained original jurisdiction in most civil and criminal cases, with the U.S. Supreme Court taking appeals from the highest state courts. John Jay, one of *The Federalist* authors, became the first chief justice.

forces, or in the militia, when in actual service in time of war or public danger; nor shall any person be subject for the same offense to be twice put in jeopardy of life or limb; nor shall be compelled in any criminal case to be a witness against himself, nor be deprived of life, liberty, or property, without due process of law; nor shall private property be taken for public use without just compensation.

Amendment VI
In all criminal prosecutions, the accused shall enjoy the right to a speedy and public trial, by an impartial jury of the State and district wherein the crime shall have been committed, which district shall have been previously ascertained by law, and to be informed of the nature and cause of the accusation; to be confronted with the witnesses against him; to have compulsory process for obtaining witnesses in his favor, and to have the assistance of counsel for his defense.

Amendment VII
In suits at common law, where the value in controversy shall exceed twenty dollars, the right of trial by jury shall be preserved, and no fact tried by a jury shall be otherwise reexamined in any court of the United States, than according to the rules of the common law.

Amendment VIII
Excessive bail shall not be required, nor excessive fines imposed, nor cruel and unusual punishments inflicted.

Amendment IX
The enumeration in the Constitution, of certain rights, shall not be construed to deny or disparage others retained by the people.

Amendment X
The powers not delegated to the United States by the Constitution, nor prohibited by it to the States, are reserved to the States respectively, or to the people.

Not until the 14th Amendment

The Bill of Rights

During its first months, Congress took up the question of amending the Constitution to satisfy criticisms voiced during ratification, objections that by the summer of 1789, still kept North Carolina and Rhode Island out of the Union. More than the original document, the first ten amendments, called the Bill of Rights, represented the will of the American people, who demanded protection of individual rights.

The ratification campaign had elicited a mountain of proposals for amending the Constitution. Opponents offered two major grounds for altering the document or abandoning it altogether. Antifederalist leaders believed it took too much power from the states, and from themselves as leaders of state and local governments, while popular opinion feared the loss of personal freedoms to a strong national government. State ratifying conventions, even as they voted for the Constitution, suggested amendments to ensure freedom of religion, speech, and the press, and safeguards for fair trials.

James Madison became the chief proponent of the Bill of Rights in Congress, despite his earlier advocacy of the Federalist position that the amendments were unnecessary. In order to get elected to the House of Representatives, he had promised his Virginia constituents to obtain the safeguards. Madison took his vow seriously, pushing his reluctant Federalist colleagues to the task. Antifederalist leaders, who wanted to scrap the Constitution entirely, now denied support to the Bill of Rights because they knew protection of individual freedoms would garner popular support.

After much negotiation between the Senate and the House, on September 25, 1789, Congress sent to the states for ratification a total of twelve amendments. By December 15, 1791, three-quarters of the states approved the ten amendments known as the Bill of Rights, thus putting them into effect. Of the two amendments not approved at the time, one was a rule concerning congressional salaries that was not ratified for two centuries, until 1992, and the other was a complicated formula for computing representation in Congress that was never adopted. Of the Bill of Rights, Articles 1 through 8 enumerated basic individual rights, while the intention of Article 9 was to protect any personal freedoms omitted from this list. Article 10 directed that "powers not delegated to the United States by the Constitution, nor prohibited by it to the States, are reserved to the States respectively, or to the people." It addressed concerns that the national government might assume powers that were not mentioned in the Constitution. Passage of the Bill of Rights by Congress attracted enough support to bring in the two remaining states; North Carolina ratified the Constitution in November 1789 and Rhode Island followed suit in May 1790.

The First Census

Congress also promptly ordered a census of the American population, which the Constitution required within three years of Congress's first meeting and every ten years subsequently. The census, the founders expected, would provide an accurate enumeration for apportioning delegates to the House of Representa-

TABLE 7.1 THE U.S. POPULATION, 1790	Total	Slaves
United States	*3,929,625*	*697,624*
New England	*1,009,206*	*3,763*
Maine (part of Massachusetts)	96,643	0
New Hampshire	141,899	157
Vermont	85,341	0
Massachusetts	378,556	0
Rhode Island	69,112	958
Connecticut	237,655	2,648
Middle States	*1,017,087*	*45,210*
New York	340,241	21,193
New Jersey	184,139	11,423
Pennsylvania	433,611	3,707
Delaware	59,096	8,887
Southern States and Territories	*1,903,332*	*648,651*
Maryland	319,728	103,036
Virginia	747,610	292,627
North Carolina	395,005	100,783
South Carolina	249,073	107,094
Georgia	82,548	29,264
Kentucky	73,677	12,430
Tennessee	35,691	3,417

tives and electoral college. Congress set August 1790 as the date for the first census, appointing marshals to complete their work within nine months, which actually stretched to eighteen. The first census was less complicated than later ones, with just six questions: name of head of household, number of free white males aged sixteen years and over, number of free white males under sixteen, number of free white females, number of other free persons, and number of slaves. The census set categories based on race, sex, and age that would be elaborated in later counts. The separate listing of enslaved persons was required by the clause of the Constitution that counted three-fifths of slaves for representation and taxes. The distinction between free whites and blacks came from cultural values rather than some practical use. The census did not include Native Americans who lived outside areas settled by whites.

This excerpt from the first U.S. Federal Census shows households on several streets in Philadelphia. The census provides much evidence about urban society in 1790, including the names, occupations, sex, and race of heads of household, but less information on other members of their households. Note that many more free blacks than slaves lived in this part of Philadelphia by 1790.

Name of Head of Family.	Free White Males of 16 Years and Upward Including Heads of Families.	Free White Males Under 16 years.	Free White Females Including Heads of Families.	All Other Free Persons.	Slaves.
PHILADELPHIA CITY—continued.					
North Fifth street from Market to Race street, East side.					
Wheelen, Israel (Grocer)	2	3	7		
Leacock, John (Coroner)	3	2	2		
Howell, Samuel (Brush Mak')	1		3		
Bell, Barbary (Widow)	1		2		
Shaw, John (Carpenter)	2	1	1		
Langdell, Margaret (Spinster)			3		
Snowden, George (Carp')	3		4		
Shea, John (Shoe maker)	2	2	4		
Cruds, George (Breeches Mak')	1	3	2		
Paschall, Stephen (Gent^e)	1	3	5	1	
Detrick, Michael (Shoemaker)	3	1	1		
Shearer, Peter (Skinner)	2	3	2		
Church Burial Ground					
Gilmore, Daniel (Negroe)				2	
Davison, William (Gent.)	1	1	2	1	
Elton, Thomas (Joyner; S.)					
Gitz, John (plaisterer)	2	3	2		
Kroll, John (Barber)					
Wyman, Jacob (Taylor)	2	2	4		
Dutch Meeting Burial Ground					
North Fifth street from Market to Race street, West side.					
Cochran, Elizabeth (Widow)			1		
Yeager, Adam (Cedar Cooper)	2	2	4		
Boeush, Adam (Reed Mak')	1	5	5		
Facundus, Peter (Shoe Maker)	2		2		
Wolf, Lewis (Barber)	1	2	3		
Clark, Joseph (School Mast.)	1	1	1		
Enk, Jacob (Taylor)	3	1	5		
Wallace, Burton (Bricklayer & Mason)	1		3	1	
Randell, Thomas (Clerk)	1	1	3		
James, John (Merch')	2	1	2		
Ogle, Cath^e (Widow)	4		2		
Ritter, Henry (Baker)	1	1	7		
Steines, Frederick (Taylor)	1		3		
Field, Eleanor (Tayloress)			3		
Eckfelt, Jacob (Black Smith)	7	6	8		
Wilson, James (Coach Mak'; S.)					
Clark, Samuel (Board Merch')	2	1	4		
Alexander, Margaret (Spinster)			2		
Sadler, Matthew (Carp'; S.)					

Name of Head of Family.	Free White Males of 16 Years and Upward Including Heads of Families.	Free White Males Under 16 years.	Free White Females Including Heads of Families.	All Other Free Persons.	Slaves.
PHILADELPHIA CITY—continued.					
Middle district—Con.					
North Fifth street from Market to Race street, West side—Continued.					
Vandell, George (Negroe)				4	
Whig Quaker Meeting House					
Elwin, Hugh (Shoemaker)	1	1	2		
Weaver, William (Lab')	1	1	2		
Noah, Emanuel (Trader)	1	2	3		
Hartung, William (Scrivener)	1		3		
Robins, Isabella (Widow)	1	1	3		
Dawson, Elias (Merchant)	1	2	4		
Henbury, Thomas (Fish monger)	4		6		
Newman, Frederick (Card maker)	1	1	3		
Kein, Christian (Bl. Smith; S.)	1		3		
Lawrence, Philip (Joyner)	2		2		
Rawlston, George (Custom h° Officer)	1				
Ross, Oliver (Comb Mak')	1	1	3		
Dougherty, Daniel (Shoe Maker)	2	1	3		
Wayne, John & Lab^rs	3	3	5		
Miller, Jacob (Carter)	1		1		
Robinson, Ebenezar (Brush Mak')	1		2		
Dexter, James (Negroe)				7	
Roe, Thomas (Taylor)	3		3		
Howell, Reading (Surveyor)	4	2	4	1	
Evans, Cadwallader (Merch')	1		3		
Taggart, Robert (Gent.)	1		3		
Evans, Robert (Ho. Carp')	4	2	4		
Hudson, Samuel (Gent^n)	2		2		
Seyfried, Jacob (Barber)	1	1	2		
Nail, Henry (Shoemaker)	1		3		
Dennis, John (Shoemaker)	2	1	3		
Meyer, Henry (Inn keeper)	4	3	2		
South Sixth street from Market to Chestnut street, East side.					
Clark, David	7	3	5	1	
Christie, Alexander (painter; S.)	1	2	4		
Gilmore, Samuel (Carp')	1		5		
Hartong, Robert (Lab')	2		1		
South Sixth street from Market to Chestnut street, West side.					
Polk, Adam (Mak')	1		1		
Ellcott, James (Innkeeper)	1	1	4		
Benge, Samuel (Umbrella M.)	2		1	1	

Name of Head of Family.	Free White Males of 16 Years and Upward Including Heads of Families.	Free White Males Under 16 years.	Free White Females Including Heads of Families.	All Other Free Persons.	Slaves.
PHILADELPHIA CITY—continued.					
Middle district—Con.					
South Sixth street from Market to Chestnut street—Con.					
Street, Robert (Shoemaker)	1	1	1		
Welcher, Henry (Lab')	1		2		
Lace, William (Bl. Smith)	1	1	2		
Keen, Reynold. Esqr	4	2	8	2	2
Gray, W^m & Joseph (Brewers)	1				
Matthar, Peter (Inn keeper)	1	1	4	2	1
North Sixth street from Market to Race street, East side.					
Donnalson, Joseph (Gent.)	1		4		
Redman, Joseph (Doct^r P.)					
Simmons, William (Auditors Office)					
Erwin, Robert (Gent^n)	1	1	1		
Elmsley, Alexander (Carp')	1	1	4		
Link, Frederick (Drayman)	3	3	7		
Albright, Michael (Ced^r Cooper)	1	3	2		
Nusshag, Charles Willm (Baker)	1	5	4		
Davis, Sampson (Lab.)	1	3	4		
Hudson, William	4	3	8		
Hawker, Godfrey (Baker)	2	2	4		
Elter, George (Coach Maker; S.)					
Fotter, Matt^e (porter)	2		1		
Branger, William (Lab')	1	1	5		
Brinner, George (Taylor)	1		2		
Greer, Jacob (Butcher)	1	1	2		
Walker, Martha (Widow)			1	1	
Miney, Godfrey (Baker)	1	2	5		
Rust, Leonard (Meal Seller & Innkeeper; S.)	1		3		
Gray, Joseph (Brewer)	1	1	3		
Humphries, Amy (Spinst')	1		3		
Harper, John (Bl. Smith; S.)					
Hallowell, Thomas (Joyner)	1	3	2		
Cunningham, Robert (Weaver)	1	1	4		
McConnell, John (Lab)	1		2		
Venables, Robert (Negroe)				4	
Sandiford, Rowland (Coach Mak')	1		3		
Dietz, Henry (Watchman)	2	1	3		
Guest, James (Taylor)	1	1	2		
Lambert, John (Chair Mak')	1		1		
Haseelback, Philip (Shoemaker)	2	2	2		
Hansell, Jacob (Bl. Smith)	1	3	1		

While sketchy and incomplete, the 1790 census served as a baseline for measuring the growth of a dynamic, expanding people. President Washington reported to Congress a total of 3.9 million people, of whom 60,000 were free African Americans and almost 700,000 were slaves. The census covered the territory included in the thirteen original states, and also Vermont, Kentucky, and Tennessee, which became states respectively in 1791, 1792, and 1796. It did not encompass the area north of the Ohio River where at least 4,000 white settlers had taken up land.

During the 1780s, the white population of the country had swelled by an extraordinary 44 percent, mostly through reproduction; in the 1790s, the increase remained high at 36 percent. After the Treaty of Paris, European immigrants had once again begun crossing the Atlantic Ocean, with the majority coming from Ireland. From 1783 to 1799, 156,000 Europeans entered the United States, of whom 69 percent were Irish, 14 percent were English, Scottish, and Welsh, and 6 percent were German. The African American population also grew quickly during the 1780s and 1790s, at a rate of 32 percent per decade.

Especially striking in the 1790 census are the small numbers of enslaved African Americans in New England and Pennsylvania compared with Maryland, Virginia, and the Carolinas, the result in part of northern abolition. This sectional difference would grow in the nineteenth century as the north focused more on commerce and developed a manufacturing sector, while the south cast its fate with agriculture, adopting cotton as its major crop.

OPPOSING VISIONS OF AMERICA

Almost immediately during Washington's first administration, political divisions arose between sides favoring commerce versus agriculture. Two divergent conceptions of the nation's future emerged among leaders who had formerly cooperated in adopting the Constitution. During the early 1790s, two political parties developed, though their leaders were loathe to call them that because most Americans still considered parties as "evil," as detrimental to unified republican government. As events unfolded in foreign and domestic affairs, the two parties contested one issue after another. Both sides, however, helped to confirm the Constitution by claiming to be its steadfast defenders.

Hamilton Versus Jefferson

Alexander Hamilton, appointed by Washington as secretary of the Treasury, saw the future greatness of the United States in commerce and manufacturing, though in 1790, the country was overwhelmingly agrarian. Born in the West Indies, Hamilton attended King's College in New York City, then served as Washington's aide-de-camp during the Revolution. Highly intelligent, full of energy and enthusiasm, he was a major proponent of the new Constitution. Appointment to the treasury allowed Hamilton to promote his concept of a strong nation, which he modeled on Great Britain for its dominance in international trade, innovations in banking, and burgeoning industry. Hamilton's efforts to foster commerce and manufacturing aroused resistance among former allies, particu-

Alexander Hamilton, *1792, by John Trumbull. The first secretary of the treasury saw Great Britain, with its strong central government and expanding industrial economy, as a model for the new United States.*

larly Madison and Jefferson, leading to bitter partisan disputes.

Hamilton's party, which embraced the name Federalist though it was really nationalist, favored commercial development, a national bank, high tariffs to spur manufacturing, and a strong central government based upon a "loose" interpretation of the Constitution, which allowed expansive powers to Congress and the president. The Federalists favored the British, abhorred the French Revolution after 1792, and were generally suspicious of power wielded by ordinary folk. They were somewhat critical of slavery, however, and gained the allegiance of free blacks. Because their power base lay in New England and the Middle States, the Federalists could generate little enthusiasm for western expansion and sometimes supported the right of Native Americans to retain their lands.

The Republican party, in contrast, favored a "strict" interpretation of the Constitution, opposing a strong central government and federal privileges for manufacturing and commerce. They thought Hamilton's plans for funding the national debt, the bank, and protective tariffs infringed upon states' rights and helped the "few" at the expense of the "many." They disdained the British model and charged Hamilton with advocating a return to monarchy. With their power base in the south, west, and northern cities, the Republicans rejected efforts to abolish slavery and were ardent expansionists on the frontier. They had little sympathy for Indian rights.

Thomas Jefferson became the chief spokesman for the Republican party, though James Madison collaborated in its growth. Jefferson, a wealthy planter and slaveholder, author of the Declaration of Independence, former ambassador to France, and now Washington's secretary of state, argued that Hamilton wanted too much national power. Jefferson rejected the British model of banks and large-scale industry. He believed the root of Britain's effort to destroy American liberty in the 1760s and 1770s had been commercial speculation and greed. Manufacturing in cities created poverty, dependency, and political corruption. Instead, the United States, with limitless land, should foster an agrarian society of small producers. A virtuous republic was one made up of small farmers whose goal was to produce enough to support their families, not make a fortune. Commerce should exist primarily to allow them to sell their surplus in Europe and purchase manufactured goods in return. The farmers should be educated to participate wisely in republican government. Their self-sufficiency and

Thomas Jefferson, *1791, by Charles Willson Peale. The first secretary of state, who favored an agrarian republic, strict construction of the Constitution, and the French, quickly became Hamilton's chief opponent.*

education would make them virtuous, to act for the good of society rather than solely for their own gain.

Paradoxically, a large proportion of the Republicans were not small farmers. Many of the leaders were southern plantation gentry like Jefferson and Madison, or old Antifederalist elites. The party drew together people who had opposed ratification of the Constitution as well as those who favored it but abhorred the government's direction under Washington and Hamilton. The Republicans received solid backing from farmers, especially in the south and west, and from urban craftsmen and small traders who watched wealthy speculators and merchants benefit from Hamiltonian policies.

Funding the National Debt

In becoming secretary of the treasury, Alexander Hamilton's primary challenge, the problem that had helped sink the Confederation, was the Revolutionary war debt. A strong nationalist, he viewed the debt more as an opportunity to enlarge national power than as a financial hurdle. Because the Confederation had gone bankrupt, the United States had poor credit among international and domestic lenders. The United States owed $10 million to foreigners, particularly the French, and $40 million to Americans. The states also owed $25 million in domestic debts. To continue the War for Independence when funds were depleted, Congress and the states had issued certificates to merchants, artisans, and farmers for supplies and to soldiers for wages. After the war, many ordinary folks could not wait for the government to pay—or lost hope that the money was forthcoming—so they sold their certificates to wealthy speculators for a fraction of face value. Often the sellers received only 10 to 15 percent, rates that reflected the risk speculators were taking during the shaky Confederation period.

In his Report on the Public Credit of January 1790, Hamilton formulated a plan by which the U.S. government would honor at face value all Revolutionary war debts, including those of the states. His "funding" proposal involved the exchange of new federal securities for the old debt certificates. He planned to pay off foreign creditors as soon as possible, but retain the domestic debt, paying only interest and a small amount of the principal each year. A customs duty on imports and an excise tax on whiskey would cover the interest; Post Office income would gradually reduce the principal. Hamilton regarded his funding plan as expedient both financially and politically. It would restore the nation's credit internationally as well as in the eyes of its own citizens. Funding would tie wealthy Americans to the new government through their continuing investment. Hamilton's "assumption" plan, by which the federal government assumed state war debts, expanded this strategy by reorienting the loyalty of investors from the states to the nation.

Congress eventually passed Hamilton's proposal to restore public credit, though with great opposition. Many people, including Madison, thought that repaying the domestic debt at face value was unfair, that speculators received a windfall at the expense of the poor. The split between former allies Hamilton and Madison began over this issue. Critics argued that funding allowed the "few" to benefit from the hardships of the "many," who lost money when they sold their war bonds and would pay again through import duties and the excise tax. Opponents feared Hamilton's larger purpose, the expansion of national power, and became convinced that the Treasury secretary was upsetting the balance between the central

government and the states. Assumption raised additional questions because some states had more debt remaining than others. Massachusetts and South Carolina were keen on having the federal government assume their large debts, while Virginians opposed the plan, because they had satisfied most of the state's debt. Despite these divisions, the funding and assumption program passed Congress in July 1790, as part of a bargain struck by Hamilton, Jefferson, and Madison to situate the nation's permanent capital on the Potomac River, in Maryland and Virginia.

Planning Washington, D.C.

The choice of the Potomac for the nation's capital was controversial. Delegates from New England and New York thought the place too far away, while Pennsylvanians argued that their state was ideal. Southerners favored the Potomac. While everyone agreed that a central location was necessary, regional interests surfaced as congressmen recognized the economic and political benefits that the seat of government could bestow. They also debated the question of the temporary capital. Should New York City or Philadelphia host the federal government until the permanent site was ready? The complicated negotiations over funding and assumption resulted in moving the temporary capital from New York to Philadelphia as well as locating the new city on the Potomac.

President Washington and his fellow Virginians who had engineered the bargain, especially Jefferson, supervised the development of the capital. The Residence Act of 1790 gave the president authority to select a ten-mile-square location somewhere along the Potomac; he chose, after consulting with Madison and Jefferson, the land on both sides of the river that included Alexandria, Virginia, and Georgetown, Maryland. The federal city would not be built in either of those towns, but on open land on the east bank of the river. Washington appointed a surveyor, three commissioners to manage the project, and Pierre Charles L'Enfant to design the layout of the capital and its major buildings. L'Enfant's grandiose street plan and Greek and Roman architecture expressed an exalted vision of the republic. The commissioners named the federal city "Washington" and the entire district "Columbia."

The president expected to finance construction by selling lots in the capital, thinking that land prices would skyrocket as citizens valued proximity to the

Pierre Charles L'Enfant's intricate design for Washington, D.C., 1791, far outstripped the country's financial resources and interest in creating a national capital.

seat of government. Instead, land sold poorly and lack of money undermined the project. At one of the failed auctions, even the participation of the president and a parade of two brass bands and an artillery troop could not foster sales. When the commissioners suspended construction temporarily for insufficient funds, L'Enfant protested and was fired. His plan for grand boulevards, public squares, fountains, and imposing buildings was retained, but its execution would wait. For a decade the enterprise limped along, saved by grants from Maryland and Virginia. In 1800, when the government moved to Washington, the president's mansion was still unfinished and only one wing of the Capitol had been built.

The National Bank

The cornerstone of Hamilton's new commercial order was a national bank, to be patterned after the Bank of England. The Bank of the United States and its branches, established in selected cities, would hold the federal government's funds. It would also regulate state banks, which had grown in number since the first

bank, Philadelphia's Bank of North America, was founded in 1781. The chief purpose of the national bank was to expand the money supply, thereby encouraging commercial growth.

First Bank of the United States, Philadelphia. The imposing structure, designed by Samuel Blodget of New Hampshire, was intended to convey confidence in the bank's financial strength.

The Bank of the United States, which Congress chartered in 1791 for a minimum of twenty years, would have assets of $10 million, including $2 million in government deposits. Private investors could purchase the remaining $8 million in stock. At least one-fourth of their investment had to be in hard currency; investors could pay the other three-fourths in federal securities. As the bank prospered, stockholders would receive dividends on their funds. Thus, Hamilton created a way for wealthy Americans, who had just profited from funding the Revolutionary War debt, to benefit further. Because the government was a major stockholder, it also received dividends that could be used to pay off the national debt. The bank made loans to merchants beyond the value of its stock of gold and silver (specie), thus increasing the supply of money, a critically important move for an economy short of specie. The bank notes circulated as currency; the federal government supported their value by accepting them for taxes. To Hamilton and his commercial backers, the Bank of the United States was essential for economic growth. The majority of the House of Representatives agreed, by a vote of thirty-nine to twenty, but the tally indicated important regional differences that fueled party growth. Among northern congressmen, thirty-three voted for the bank and one against, while only six southern delegates supported and nineteen opposed Hamilton's bill.

The plan had many opponents, who variously considered the bank immoral, monopolistic, or unconstitutional. Some believed that all paper money should be based on gold and silver. "Every dollar of a bank bill that is issued beyond the quantity of gold and silver in the vaults," John Adams said, "represents nothing, and is therefore a cheat upon somebody." The wild frenzy to purchase the bank's stock, in which 25,000 shares sold in two hours and then the shares were bid up to 1,300 percent of their face value, reinforced fears that the national bank would undermine republican virtue. Jefferson called the bank's stock "federal filth." Others charged the bank with monopoly, complaining that merchants could secure short-term loans to finance their commercial ventures, but farmers and artisans could not obtain mortgages for purchasing property or making improvements.

In Congress, Madison opposed the national bank on the constitutional grounds that the federal government lacked the power to create corporations. He argued for a strict interpretation of the Constitution, but failed to convince the majority. In particular, Madison said, the Tenth Amendment denied the central government any power not expressly given. Hamilton and his supporters countered with a loose interpretation, that some powers of the federal government are implied. In the case of the bank, for example, the Constitution delegated to Congress and the president the power to lay and collect taxes, pay debts, regulate commerce, and coin and regulate money. It also provided the authority to "make all laws which shall be necessary and proper for carrying into execution the foregoing powers. . . ." Hamilton argued that the bank was a method by which the United States could fulfill its functions, and because some means was necessary, the power to establish the bank was implied. Though President Washington was initially unsure, he accepted Hamilton's reasoning and approved the bill.

Jefferson, like Madison, was convinced the national bank was unconstitutional, advising Washington with this opinion. By 1791, the secretary of state realized the political and economic consequences of the funding act—channeling more power to the federal government and more money to the rich—and thought the bank could only further these trends. He said he had been "duped" by Hamilton and "made a tool for forwarding his schemes" in accepting the assumption of state debts in return for the capital on the Potomac. He now believed that the Treasury secretary's program "flowed from principles adverse to liberty," Jefferson told the president. It was "calculated to undermine and demolish the republic." For his part, Hamilton chafed at this criticism, stating "that Mr. Madison, cooperating with Mr. Jefferson, is at the head of a faction decidedly hostile to me and my administration; and actuated by views, in my judgment, subversive of the principles of good government and dangerous to the Union, peace, and happiness of the country."

As members of Washington's cabinet, both Jefferson and Hamilton found policy making increasingly difficult as positions hardened, especially because foreign policy, in Jefferson's realm, overlapped with domestic fiscal matters. In particular, Jefferson's pro-French leanings conflicted with Hamilton's need to collect tariffs on British imports for funding the debt. If trade with Great Britain ended, Hamilton's financial system fell apart.

Encouragement of Manufacturing

While the Treasury secretary won congressional support for the bank and funding the national debt, he was much less successful in his plan for industry. In

1791, the United States lacked a solid manufacturing base. Hamilton proposed high protective tariffs on certain goods to discourage Americans from buying imports and thus spur U.S. production. He also advocated bounties, or subsidies, on selected products to encourage entrepreneurs. Hamilton believed that a strong nation needed self-sufficiency in manufactures, especially for military defense, but failed to obtain congressional support. Madison contended that granting bounties would expand the power of Congress, while others argued that they were like monopolies and too expensive. A North Carolina congressman advised, "Establish the doctrine of bounties, [and] . . . all manner of persons—people of every trade and occupation—may enter at the breach, until they have eaten up the bread of our children."

In the 1790s, U.S. manufacturing remained on a small scale. Americans appreciated the quality of British imports; what they did not import, they produced themselves or purchased from neighboring artisans. Industry could not be stimulated overnight, for it required technology and the willingness of businessmen to invest time as well as capital for the long term. While some master craftsmen enlarged their shops and hired more workers, mechanized factories with mass production still lay in the future.

During the colonial and Revolutionary periods, urban entrepreneurs had attempted large-scale textile manufacturing to provide employment for poor women and independence from British imports, but these efforts were short-lived and not mechanized. The "factories" had consisted of workhouses, in which large numbers of impoverished widows produced thread and yarn at traditional spinning wheels. Other businessmen used a "putting-out" system, whereby they distributed flax and wool for spinning at home.

In 1788, the Pennsylvania Society for the Encouragement of Manufactures and the Useful Arts introduced spinning jennies to their textile factory in Philadelphia. The jennies, with forty to eighty spindles each and too heavy for women to operate, threatened to displace home spinners by producing cheaper yarn and thread. In 1790, however, the factory and its wooden jennies went up in flames, as did other early textile mills in the Delaware Valley. While the promoters believed that home spinners were sabotaging the factories, the fires may well have been accidental because the mills were highly flammable.

Samuel Slater, a twenty-two-year-old millworker and recent immigrant from Great Britain, in 1790 instituted a new phase in American cloth production by

Until after 1815, households performed one or more steps in textile manufacturing. Here a family works together, with the wife spinning thread, which the husband then wove on his loom. Women also wove cloth, but men rarely—if ever—used a spinning wheel.

building a textile mill in Pawtucket, Rhode Island, using water power to run the spinning machines. From memory he constructed a spinning frame, a machine that produced stronger threads than the jenny. He had left Britain illegally; to keep its advantage in textile making, the government prohibited emigration of craftworkers or export of drawings of the machines. No satisfactory power loom yet existed, so Slater's mill performed only the first two steps of cloth production: carding, or preparing the cotton fibers for spinning, and spinning the thread. Slater then used the putting-out system of distributing the thread to families, who produced the cloth at home. Though Slater established additional mills in Rhode Island and Massachusetts, his workforce stayed fairly small, with about a hundred millworkers in 1800. His manufacturing process also remained dependent on the traditional home production of weavers.

Alexander Hamilton tried an ambitious industrial program in Paterson, New Jersey, with the Society for Establishing Useful Manufactures. The society hoped to create an industrial town on the Passaic River where skilled craftsmen recruited from Britain would produce a variety of cloth and clothing, blankets, carpets, shoes, hats, pottery, metal wire, and paper. After obtaining a state charter from New Jersey, the society sold stock. As in the case of the national bank, the stock sold quickly and appreciated in value. The project lost capital, however, when major stockholders

Samuel Slater's spinning frame. With his water-powered textile mills, Slater removed part of cloth production from the home— carding and spinning—but relied on families to weave the cloth.

sold their shares to make a fast profit. The managers failed to obtain reliable machinery and workers, closing shop in 1796.

While the results of Hamilton's plans were disappointing, with the society's failure and congressional rejection of the protective tariff and bounties, the United States did make progress during the 1790s toward industrialization. In 1790, Congress passed patent legislation, giving inventors exclusive rights to their work for seventeen years, and Slater initiated water-powered textile manufacture. Then, in 1793, while visiting a Georgia plantation, Eli Whitney, a New Englander, invented the cotton engine, or gin. The device, which separated cotton fibers from husks and seeds, greatly increased the productivity of cotton cultivation, swelling the demand for African American slaves and fertile land in the southwest, and spurring cloth production in the north. Because the gin could be duplicated easily, though, Whitney failed to make a fortune from his invention, despite its economic significance. In 1798, he further laid the basis for industrial growth by attempting to manufacture guns with interchangeable parts. After receiving a government contract for 10,000 weapons, he specified that each part be made identical to its counterparts so that it could be exchanged from one rifle to another, allowing less-skilled workers to build and repair the firearms. At this early date, however, such rigid standards were impossible to meet, and as a result, parts needed filing to fit together smoothly.

An inventor who would have benefited from Hamilton's proposed bounties was the Delaware-born artisan Oliver Evans, who apprenticed as a wagon-maker and became fascinated by machines. In 1772, at age seventeen, he heard that the Scottish inventor James Watt had improved the steam engine a few years earlier. Evans began building his own model but, for lack of money and encouragement, thirty years passed before he actually installed a high pressure steam engine in his gypsum fertilizer factory in Philadelphia. This was the first such application of steam power to an industrial setting. In the meantime, in the 1780s, Evans also developed the idea of automating mills, a concept that has grown in significance over two centuries. He devised water-powered machinery for large grist mills that allowed one worker instead of three to supervise all the steps of producing flour. Evans obtained exclusive rights from the states of Pennsylvania and Maryland to his system of automated elevators, conveyors, and hoppers. With insufficient capital, however, he was unable to pursue many of his designs, including steam carriages and trucks, a machine gun, refrigeration, central heating, and gas lighting.

EXPANSION AND CONFLICT IN THE WEST

While Alexander Hamilton's financial policies aided commerce and made wealthy eastern merchants even richer, dynamic growth also occurred in the west. The expansion of settlers from east to west challenged the ability of the new government to keep their loyalty. In particular, Hamilton's excise tax on whiskey weighed heavily on westerners, especially in Pennsylvania, leading to a serious rebellion in 1794. The young nation also contended with the Native Americans, whose lands the settlers were taking; the British military, who kept forts in the northwest; and the Spanish, who contested U.S. territorial claims and rights to navigate the Mississippi.

Kentucky and Tennessee

During the 1780s, the region west of the Appalachians and south of the Ohio River developed quickly, as families, many with African American slaves, left Virginia and North Carolina in search of fertile land and lower taxes. Even before the revolution ended, settlers crossed the mountains in large numbers: Kentucky swelled from 150 settlers in 1775 to 61,000 whites and 12,500 enslaved blacks in 1790; Tennessee reported 32,000 whites and 3,500 slaves in the latter year.

White settlement of Kentucky and Tennessee proceeded quickly as state governments, speculators, and frontiersmen defeated the Cherokees, who claimed ancestral rights to the territory. Understanding that they were renting the land rather than selling it, in 1775 a group of Cherokee leaders, including Attakullaculla and Oconostota, traded 27,000 square miles to Richard Henderson and his associates for a cabin of consumer goods. Called Henderson's Purchase, the sale involved most of Kentucky, comprising the hunting lands of the Shawnees and Iroquois as well as the Cherokees, and was illegal in Indian and English law. With the outbreak of the revolution, most Cherokees and Shawnees joined the British, fighting for return of their lands. Receiving little help from Britain, the Cherokees were defeated in 1777 and forced to sign away even more territory.

Young militants led by Dragging Canoe, Bloody Fellow, and others, assisted by loyalist whites who intermarried and became members of the tribe, rejected these land cessions. In the 1780s and early 1790s, the militant Cherokees, called Chickamaugas, allied with Creeks and Shawnees against settlers along the frontier from Kentucky to Georgia. On both sides, fighting was vicious, with men, women, and children burned, scalped, and shot; and, as in so many cases, the whites

failed to distinguish between enemy Indians and those who wanted peace.

The Washington administration attempted to end the hostilities with the Treaty of Holston in 1791, but gave responsibility for negotiating with the Cherokees to Governor William Blount of the Tennessee Territory, a land speculator the Indians called "dirt king" for his greed after land. Blount ignored Washington's promise to the Cherokees that if they ceded territory on which the whites had settled, the United States would guarantee their remaining lands. Instead, Blount required a cession of over 4,000 square miles in return for an annual payment of $1,000 and no guarantee. When Blount surveyed the border without Cherokee witnesses, the treaty fell apart and war continued. In 1794, after Dragging Canoe died and the Spanish stopped supplying the Indians because of war in Europe, the Chickamaugas met defeat.

By the end of the war, parts of Kentucky and Tennessee had passed the initial stages of settlement. Early on, groups of settlers had gathered in frontier stations consisting of two-story log houses connected by a high wall to create a fort against Indian attack. As the population grew and the threat from Native Americans declined, families moved away from the stations. While, at first, subsistence was primary to frontier settlers, access to markets soon became essential. In the early years, all family members worked to provide food, clothing, shelter, and a few amenities such as soap and rough-hewn furniture. They needed to become familiar with their new environment. One Kentucky pioneer described how "the women the first spring we came out, wo'd follow their cows to see what they ate, that they might know what greens to get. My Wife and I had neither spoon, dish, knife, or any thing to do with when we began life. Only I had a butcher knife." The settlers used skills they had learned at home: They grew corn, tobacco, hemp, cotton, vegetables, and fruits; raised cattle, sheep, horses, and pigs; hunted and fished. Soon the settlers produced a surplus to trade for necessities they could not make themselves, such as nails, rifles, ammunition, needles, tools, and salt, as well as to pay taxes and fees. They sold furs, ginseng, agricultural produce, and livestock. As fertile lands such as Kentucky's Bluegrass region yielded bountiful crops, farmers sought markets by way of the Mississippi River and the port of New Orleans. Because transporting crops overland through the mountains was much more difficult and expensive than sending them downstream, southwestern farmers demanded that the federal government convince Spain to end its restrictions on lower Mississippi shipping.

Even as the number of settlers increased and a market economy developed in the 1790s, the trans-Appalachian region had few schools or church buildings. Most children, if taught at all, learned reading and arithmetic at home. In towns where schools existed, boys might attend for a few months but girls stayed at home. The exception were the children of wealthy families who attended academies with secondary school curricula. One man remembered the experience of most residents of Kentucky in the 1790s: "Our preachers and teachers were, in general, almost as destitute as the people at large, many of whom could neither read nor write, did not send their children to school, and of course, kept no books in the house."

While churches lacked buildings and settled ministers, though, religion was the frontier's chief cultural institution. Throughout the region, Presbyterian, Baptist, and Methodist ministers held services in private homes. Baptist lay ministers farmed beside their neighbors through the week, then led services on Sunday. Methodist circuit riders traveled from one congregation to another, conducting worship services, baptisms, marriages, and prayer meetings. The churches preached a stringent message of salvation and morality. They expected members to avoid sin, including fighting, excessive drinking, adultery, and even celebrating the Fourth of July. If members committed offenses and failed to express sorrow, they were expelled, a serious consequence for people who had few social outlets and whose community revolved around the church. In addition to church, social activities included barn raisings, corn huskings, and log rollings. These events caused trouble when whiskey and frivolity led church members astray, as with one couple a Kentucky Methodist church expelled for "Disorderly Conduct." Another man was "Excluded from this Church for Fighting & Drinking to Excess."

The Ohio Country

White settlement moved more slowly north of the Ohio River than in Kentucky and Tennessee, partly because the U.S. government kept tighter control in the Northwest Territory, but more because Native Americans, with assistance from the British, resisted strongly. Delawares, Shawnees, Iroquois, and many

others refused to cede lands that the federal government wanted to sell to land-hungry easterners. In the 1780s, the United States obtained a series of cessions, but from just some of the people who owned the land. Indians who were not party to the agreements rejected them. Forming a confederacy to withstand U.S. invasion, Ohio Indians attacked whites who risked settling in the region. This northern Indian confederacy allied with the Chickamaugas and Creeks in the south, establishing a pan-Indian defensive that gained help from the Spanish in the south and the British in the north. At one meeting in 1787, the Native Americans agreed to merge their forces "for a general defense against all Invaders of Indian rights."

In the early 1790s, President Washington challenged the northern confederacy by sending two expeditions, both of them unsuccessful. Arthur St. Clair, governor of the Northwest Territory, led the second invasion in 1791, in which 600 of his 1,400 men died. Washington believed that the disaster resulted from

Signatures of Native Americans on the Treaty of Greenville, 1795.

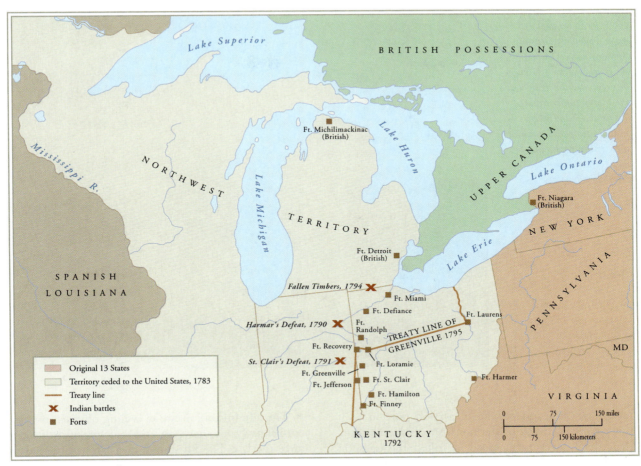

MAP 7.1 | CONFLICT IN THE NORTHWEST TERRITORY, 1790-1796

the use of militia, so instructed General Anthony Wayne to raise 5,000 regulars. Wayne trained the troops for two years, then marched west against the Indian confederacy. On August 20, 1794, the U.S. army defeated the Native Americans decisively at the Battle of Fallen Timbers. Though the British had customarily given aid to the Ohio tribes, this time they closed the gates to Fort Miami, denying refuge to the retreating Indians. A year later, when it became clear to the Native Americans that their alliance with the British had ended, they signed the Treaty of Greenville ceding to the United States most of the land in present-day Ohio. Whether this treaty would last when others had failed, however, depended upon British withdrawal from their garrisons.

The Whiskey Rebellion

In the same year, 1794, the Washington administration also sent troops against western Pennsylvania farmers, who since 1791 had resisted the whiskey tax that Congress passed as part of Hamilton's funding plan. For westerners, the excise was unfair because it took money from their pockets to profit eastern speculators who had bought up debt certificates. Washington and Hamilton decided to take advantage of the unrest to demonstrate the power of the new central government. Farmers throughout the west resented the tax on spirits, for distilling whiskey from grain made their produce less bulky, thus less expensive to transport to eastern markets. They also used the whiskey

Indian Treaty of Greenville, 1795, by an unknown artist. Following General Anthony Wayne's victory at the Battle of Fallen Timbers, he negotiated the treaty with the Miami leader Little Turtle and many other Indians, temporarily ending their military resistance to white settlement in the Northwest Territory.

instead of cash and consumed a good portion of it themselves. In much of the trans-Appalachian region, the federal government failed to collect the excise at all, for under threat of violence from their neighbors, local officials were not inclined to become tax collectors.

The administration found willing officials in western Pennsylvania, however, and there proceeded to enforce the law. The Pittsburgh area farmers resisted in ways reminiscent of the American Revolution. They held protest meetings and refused cooperation with the collectors. They tarred and feathered collaborators,

Pittsburgh in 1790, from a contemporary sketch and later drawing by Seth Eastman. Western Pennsylvania was the center of farmers' protest against Alexander Hamilton's excise tax on whiskey.

burned barns, and destroyed stills of people who paid the tax. The farmers charged that the tax favored large distillers and was collected unevenly. Rebels left notes signed "Tom the Tinker" to warn distillers who registered for the tax that their stills would be "fixed" (that is, ruined) unless they joined the revolt. The insurgents understood their fight as a struggle for "the virtuous principles of republican liberty." But the whiskey tax was only one of the farmers' complaints. Perhaps more important, until August 1794, was the federal government's failure to open up the Ohio country for safe settlement or to convince the Spanish to remove trade restrictions on the Mississippi.

Events came to a climax in July 1794. When officials continued to collect the tax and arrest resisters, 500 men surrounded the excise inspector's home, exchanged gunfire that killed several people, and burned the house. The official and his family escaped. In the days that followed, rebels set more buildings on fire, raised liberty poles, attacked collectors, and rumored secession. In August, 7,000 armed insurgents gathered, some intending to march on the excise headquarters in Pittsburgh, but they stopped before taking further military action. The uprising spread to central Pennsylvania, Virginia, Maryland, and Ohio. Washington sent commissioners to obtain oaths of submission, but the insurrection continued. Hamilton, as acting secretary of war, called up 13,000 eastern troops, who marched west with the president briefly in command. By the time the soldiers reached western Pennsylvania, the revolt was over, as the show of force intimidated the rebels. The administration had demonstrated that armed resistance to federal policies would not be tolerated. Many of the insurgents escaped the grasp of the central government, however, by moving farther west.

The Spanish Frontier

As settlers from the United States migrated across the Appalachians and traders extended their commercial networks, they came into contact with the Spanish. The 1790s marked the high point of Spain's control in North America, its provinces extending from East Florida across the Gulf Coast to Louisiana, Texas, New Mexico, and California. The Spanish government continued to view these borderlands of their empire as a buffer against American and British designs on Mexican silver. Spanish officials recognized the phenomenal population growth of the United States. One warned

that Americans were "advancing and multiplying . . . with a prodigious rapidity," while another took a dim view of the American frontier people, whom he considered "nomadic like Arabs and . . . distinguished from savages only in their color, language, and the superiority of their depraved cunning and untrustworthiness."

Nevertheless, the Spanish decided to open their territory to Americans, hoping to bolster the small settler populations of the borderlands. Spain offered free land in the Floridas and Louisiana, and even changed official policy to allow Protestants to keep their religion as long as they took an oath of allegiance to the Crown and had their children baptized Catholic. Spanish mercantilism also broke down, as plantation owners in the borderlands sold their sugar, cotton, and indigo in the United States. Spain could not provide desired consumer goods or adequate markets, so permitted this trade. These new immigration and economic policies facilitated later acquisition of the Floridas and Louisiana by the United States. In 1791, Jefferson said prophetically that Spain had provided "the means of delivering to us peaceably, what may otherwise cost us a war."

Farther west, in New Mexico, the Spanish finally achieved peace with Native Americans during these years. Abandoning their attempt to integrate Comanches and Apaches as subjects of the Crown, Spain signed a treaty recognizing them as sovereign people. The Indians, through military prowess and endurance, had forced the Spanish to set aside the goal of complete domination and to provide such gifts as guns, ammunition, clothing, mirrors, paint, tobacco, and sugar. Still, the Spanish sent prisoners of war to Cuba as forced laborers and settled other Apaches on reservations called *establecimientos de paz,* or peace establishments. The Spanish had not shed their hope of converting and Hispanicizing the natives. Many Apaches refused to live on the reservations, however, steadfastly maintaining their independence. But the fighting stopped, making Texas, New Mexico, and Arizona safer for travel and economic development. Finally, settlers could journey directly between San Antonio, Santa Fe, and Tucson without fear of attack. The region prospered, providing food and clothing to the silver mines of Mexico.

For several decades, fearing Russian and British incursions along the Pacific coast, Spain had expanded settlement in California. The government sent missionaries and soldiers north from Baja California in 1769 to set up missions and presidios along the coast

This sketch by José Cardero in 1791 shows Native Americans and soldiers working outside the presidio of Monterey, California.

from San Diego as far north as San Francisco. José de Gálvez organized the effort, enlisting Junípero Serra, the zealous Franciscan priest, to establish the missions, which soon dominated Spanish California society. Though fewer than 1,000 Hispanics lived in California by 1790, the missions controlled most of the arable land along the Pacific. With military force and by conversion, they put thousands of California Indians to work on mission lands. Before Spanish colonization, the region's native people possessed neither firearms nor horses; they lived in small villages with neither elaborate political structures nor much experience with war. In the earliest years after Spanish settlement, the natives lacked unity to avenge crimes that Spanish soldiers committed—rape, murder, and theft—or to refuse to serve as agricultural laborers. In 1775, however, one group burned the San Diego mission, followed by rebellions of other coastal Indians.

As elsewhere in North America, the California Indians declined sharply in population after contact with Europeans. People who went to work in the missions lived an average of ten to twelve years; their high death rate probably resulted from close quarters and exposure to disease. According to one missionary, "they live well free but as soon as we reduce them to a Christian and community life . . . they fatten, sicken, and

die." The native population in the mission region along the Pacific coast declined from approximately 60,000 in 1769 to 35,000 at the end of the century.

The Spanish also looked to the Pacific Northwest, which they investigated in 1774, four years earlier than the British explorer Captain James Cook. After Cook publicized the trade for sea otter furs, however, British and American merchants sailed to Nootka Sound, at Vancouver Island, challenging the Spanish claim to the area north of San Francisco. The traders made huge profits by purchasing the silky black otter pelts from the Tlingit, Haida, Nootka, and Chinook peoples, to sell in China for tea, porcelain, and silk. The Indians had formerly hunted the sea otter on a limited basis for fine clothing and food. The Spanish attempted to enforce their rights to the Northwest coast by seizing two British ships. When England threatened war, Spain signed the Nootka Convention (1790), yielding its sole claim to the area and returning the confiscated vessels. Over the next several years, the two countries tried but failed to negotiate a northern boundary of California. Of more concern to Spain, Great Britain, and the United States during the 1790s, was the outbreak of war in Europe and the Atlantic, in the wake of revolution in France.

Dances held by Native Americans for Alejandro Malaspina at Nootka Sound, 1791. Drawing probably by Tomás de Suria.

FOREIGN ENTANGLEMENTS

As Americans built a new government, differed over which direction it should take, and headed west, events in Europe claimed their attention. In 1789, the United States rejoiced when the French abolished noble privileges and formed a constitutional monarchy. Americans believed that France had followed their example, for during the first phase of the French Revolution, its moderate leaders included friends of the United States, notably the Revolutionary War hero, the Marquis de Lafayette. In 1792, however, radicals took control and executed King Louis XVI the next year. The international situation became perilous when the French Republic declared war on Britain and Spain. The king's execution and thousands of deaths by guillotine during the second phase of the revolution cost the French support in the United States, particularly among Federalists, who feared the consequences of ordinary people, "the mob," taking power. Republicans, while not defending the excesses, remained sympathetic toward France because they hated monarchical Britain more.

Neutrality

The European war presented Americans with a tricky situation, for they had no interest in getting involved in the fray, yet had connections with both France and Britain that were potentially dangerous. The U.S.-France commercial and military alliance of 1778 remained in force. While it did not require the United States to enter the war, the French Republic expected favorable trade policies and informal military assistance. Though Secretary of State Jefferson favored France and hated Britain, he agreed that neutrality was essential. American commerce was closely tied with Britain, whose navy could sweep U.S. ships from the sea. Hamilton was particularly concerned that British imports remain high because tariffs paid the lion's share of interest on the national debt. With all of this in mind, President Washington made the only reasonable decision, issuing his Proclamation of Neutrality in April 1793. The message warned citizens to avoid hostile acts against either side, including sale of weapons and privateering. Washington sought the belligerents' recognition of the U.S. right to trade in nonmilitary goods.

Dramatizing the intense party rivalries of the 1790s, this pro-Federalist cartoon shows President Washington leading troops against French radicals, as Thomas Jefferson and Citizen Genêt try to hold him back. The dog graphically shows its disapproval of a Republican newspaper.

American neutrality quickly hit shoals when the activities of the new French ambassador, Edmond Genêt, became known. Citizen Genêt, as he was called in republican France, had arrived in Charleston several weeks before Washington proclaimed neutrality. Following instructions from home, he began enlisting American mercenaries to man privateers and to organize expeditions against the Spanish garrisons at St. Augustine and New Orleans. While the latter plan fell through when the French failed to pay the soldiers, Genêt obtained ships to sail under the French flag against British shipping. The privateers, with largely American crews, seized British vessels, towing them to U.S. ports. There the French consuls sold the ships and their cargoes, paying the mercenaries with part of the proceeds. The French claimed this right under the 1778 alliance. The Washington administration, fearful of British reprisals and outraged by this violation of U.S. sovereignty, closed the ports to Genêt's privateers and requested his recall. The government established specific rules of neutrality and national sovereignty. It prohibited foreign belligerents from arming vessels in U.S. ports and recruiting U.S. citizens in American territory; set the limit of U.S. territorial waters at three miles; and forbade foreign consuls from holding admiralty courts in U.S. cities to auction confiscated ships.

The Washington administration had greater success protecting the nation's sovereignty from French designs than from the British. The American republic's weakness became all too clear when the Royal Navy began impressing—recruiting by force—U.S. citizens from merchant ships. While the navy's official goal was to reclaim British deserters, the commanders often failed to distinguish among deserters, British immigrants who had become U.S. citizens, and native-born Americans.

Then, in November 1793, the British ordered a total blockade of the French West Indies. Any ship intending to trade there would be confiscated. While partly in retaliation for the Genêt affair, the British timed the blockade to coincide with their invasion of St. Domingue, or Haiti, where enslaved blacks had risen up against their French masters in 1791. The British kept the blockade a secret until after U.S. ships headed for the Caribbean. Over the winter, their navy seized more than 250 American vessels, whether they were aimed for French, British, or neutral ports. The British impounded ships, cargoes, and even the sailors' possessions. Because international correspondence was so slow, especially in the winter and during war, Washington received no intelligence of the blockade and confiscations until March 1794.

The United States and Britain seemed headed for war, a course that Americans could ill afford. Exacerbating the crisis was the British refusal to vacate their forts in the Ohio country, as they had agreed to do in the 1783 Treaty of Paris. Americans knew that Britain helped Native Americans resist settlement in the west. In fact, on practically the same day that Washington heard of the confiscations in the Caribbean, he received news that the governor of Canada, Lord Dorchester, had told a group of Indians that they could expect war to break out between the United States and Britain within a year. With British victory, Dorchester promised, the Native Americans could reclaim the lands they had lost north of the Ohio River.

The Jay Treaty

The crisis abated when information soon arrived that the British had ended their total blockade of the French islands, now permitting Americans to trade foodstuffs and consumer goods but not war materiel. Rather than take retaliatory action, the president nominated John Jay, the chief justice of the Supreme Court, to serve as special envoy to the British. Jay's instructions were to convince them to evacuate their forts in the west, pay for African American slaves who had left with the British army after the Revolution, end impressment, open British West Indies trade to American ships, and compensate recent shipping losses in the Caribbean.

Jay completed his negotiations in England in November 1794, obtaining a treaty that was probably as beneficial to U.S. interests as could be expected, given U.S. military weakness. Jay was unable to secure compensation for slaves who departed with the British army over a decade earlier; as a supporter of gradual abolition, he placed low priority on this goal. Nor did he convince the British to stop impressment or to recognize all of the neutral rights that Americans demanded. But Jay actually gained a great deal, including British withdrawal from the western forts by June 1, 1796, payment for confiscated ships in the Caribbean, and the opening of trade in the British West Indies to American vessels of 70 tons or less. He agreed, however, that American shippers would not export from the United States certain tropical products, including cotton, molasses, sugar, coffee, and cocoa, and that Americans would repay British creditors for pre-Revolutionary debts.

Washington received Jay's treaty in March 1795, keeping its contents secret until the Senate debate in June. Twenty Federalist senators voted to ratify while ten Republicans refused. The Federalists struck the provision forbidding U.S. merchants from exporting tropical crops. If they had agreed to this section, American trade would have faced a serious obstacle, particularly with the development of cotton. Thus, the Senate approved the treaty by exactly the two-thirds needed and sent it to the president, who signed the treaty as amended.

When the Jay Treaty became public, Republicans flew into a rage. Their opposition in large part was political: They abhorred *any* treaty with the British and privately bemoaned Jay's success on important issues. Publicly, they complained about his failures on impressment, neutral rights, and compensation for slaves. The Jay Treaty greatly hastened the growth of political parties, as Republicans gained support from former Federalists, particularly in the south. While Hamilton defended the treaty, opponents roared that it surrendered American independence to the former imperial tyrant. John Jay was burned in effigy; mass meetings, petitions, and demonstrations protested the treaty throughout the country.

By spring 1796, however, the tumolt was over, in part because news arrived that Thomas Pinckney had concluded an agreement with Spain the previous October. The Treaty of San Lorenzo opened the Mississippi River to free navigation, allowed Americans to use the port of New Orleans without charge, and fixed the boundary between the United States and West Florida at the 31st parallel as specified in the Treaty of Paris.

Washington Retires

With the threat of war temporarily eased, the west open for settlement and trade, and a flourishing economy, the success of the republic seemed more certain. General Wayne's defeat of the Ohio Indians, the Jay Treaty, and Pinckney's diplomatic success gave westerners—and westward-looking Americans—resolution of their major problems: cession of lands in Ohio, removal of the British from the forts, free access to the Mississippi, and the right of deposit at New Orleans. Eastern merchants and farmers benefited from the lifting of trade restrictions in the British West Indies. Wartime demand for provisions in Europe and the Caribbean drove up farm prices and stimulated production. By the end of the century, American exports and shipping profits were almost five times their 1793 level. As a major neutral maritime nation, the United States assumed a greater place in world trade. With increased transportation profits, merchants invested more heavily in ships. The shipbuilding boom created demand for lumber, rope, and other supplies; wages for craftsmen and laborers rose, though so did the cost of living. Americans took advantage of their newfound prosperity to buy British imports, which in turn paid tariff income toward the national debt. Hamilton's funding plan was a success—the nation's credit was firm—despite resistance to the whiskey tax.

As the election of 1796 approached, George Washington announced his retirement, raising the question of his successor. The president had served two terms, his health had declined, and the battle over the Jay Treaty left him exhausted and angry. In his Farewell Address, Washington surveyed the accomplishments of his administration and gave the nation advice. The United States should avoid as much as possible becoming entwined in international affairs, he counseled. The European war demonstrated how perilous such involvement could be, and how difficult it was to escape. "The great rule of conduct for us in regard to foreign nations is, in extending our commercial relations to have with them as little *political* connection as possible," Washington urged. "So far as we have already formed engagements let them be fulfilled with perfect good faith. Here let us stop." His other major argument concerned factions. The outgoing president warned against parties based on sectional differences—North against South or East against West. And he cautioned against parties more generally, that the "disorders and miseries which result [from factionalism] gradually incline the minds of men to seek security and repose in the absolute power of an individual." In lamenting "the spirit of party," Washington blamed the Republicans for failing to support his administration. They had undercut his authority and the ideal of a consensual republic.

THE ADAMS PRESIDENCY

In fact, the election of 1796 witnessed further development of partisan politics. Though Washington's successors appreciated the wisdom of his "great rule" of foreign policy, they had less enthusiasm for his advice on factions. In 1796, the parties yet lacked full-scale national organization, and candidates did not campaign. But the contest was very much alive, as Federalists supported the policies of Hamilton and Washington, while Republicans opposed them.

John Adams, elected second president of the United States, had been involved in the Revolutionary movement since the 1760s. He was the sole non-Virginian and the only president to serve a single term among the first five chief executives.

Election of 1796

In the third presidential election under the Constitution, both parties had sufficient cohesion to offer national tickets: The Federalist candidates were John Adams for president and Thomas Pinckney for vice president; the Republicans put up Thomas Jefferson for president and Aaron Burr, a senator from New York, for the second spot. The results of the electoral college vote were close: Adams 71, Jefferson 68, Pinckney 59, Burr 30, and a number of other candidates totaling 48. As specified by the Constitution, Adams became president and Jefferson, vice president. Americans quickly realized the problem of this procedure for electing the executive, as the president represented one party and the vice president the other. The framers of the Constitution had not foreseen the development of political parties. In any event, the Federalists kept control of the presidency, though barely, and they increased their votes in Congress by a small margin, to

64 Federalists versus 53 Republicans. Riding on their foreign policy gains and economic prosperity, the Federalists retained control for another four years.

For many Americans, John Adams possessed credentials from service in the revolution and the new republic that made him a worthy heir to Washington. He had contributed to pre-Revolutionary agitation in Boston, served as a delegate to the Continental Congress, promoted the Continental navy, and assisted Jefferson in drafting the Declaration of Independence. He had helped negotiate the 1783 Treaty of Paris, and in 1785, became the first U.S. ambassador to Great Britain. While Adams was a skilled diplomat, an avid student of government, and entirely honest, he lacked the first president's charisma, military bearing, and understanding of executive leadership. As a lawyer, Adams's style was more intellectual and independent; he had no experience as an executive. He preferred to make decisions on his own, without consulting the cabinet or congressional leaders.

Like Washington, Adams denounced parties, adhering to the ideal of a consensual republic. He began his administration with the hope, soon abandoned, that he might bridge the gulf between Federalists and Republicans. Jefferson rebuffed the chief executive's peace overture and directed the Republican opposition from his post as vice president. After the first few days of the Adams administration, the president and vice president never consulted one another.

"Quasi-War" with France

The second president inherited an international situation that had worsened by the time he assumed office in March 1797. The French, now ruled by a dictatorial executive board called the Directory, declared that the Jay Treaty revoked the 1778 alliance. They confiscated American merchant ships and refused to receive the new U.S. ambassador, Charles Cotesworth Pinckney of South Carolina, Thomas Pinckney's brother. In effect, the Directory cut off diplomatic relations. The situation with France was much like the 1794 crisis with Great Britain. Once again, the United States seemed destined for war.

Called by Adams into special session in May 1797, Congress authorized the mobilization of 80,000 militia, completion of three war vessels, and fortification of harbors. Adams also appointed a commission of three men to negotiate with France: John Marshall of Virginia, Elbridge Gerry of Massachusetts, and the Carolinian, Charles Cotesworth Pinckney. Their assignment was to prevent war, stop the confiscation of American ships carrying nonmilitary cargoes, and

"Cinque-têtes," or the Paris Monster, an American cartoon showing the United States negotiators Elbridge Gerry, John Marshall, and Charles Cotesworth Pinckney refusing the demands for money of the French Directory (the five-headed monster).

The Constellation *Capturing the* Insurgente, *February 9, 1799. In the Quasi-War, the U.S. Navy, with British help, quickly outperformed the French.*

obtain compensation for recent losses. In France, the commission corresponded with French Foreign Minister Talleyrand through three intermediaries, who later became known to the American public as X, Y, and Z. The French agents told the commissioners that, like other petitioners to the Directory, they must pay a bribe even to be heard. The amount specified in this case was $250,000. Pinckney exclaimed, "No, no; not a sixpence!" The Directory also required an apology from Adams for criticizing France, a huge loan, and assumption by the U.S. government of any unpaid debts owed by France to American citizens. The commission refused these conditions and returned home. Their experience became known as the XYZ Affair.

In spring 1798, Adams received delayed correspondence that his envoys had been rebuffed. When he called for additional troops and warships, Congress responded by giving him more than he requested. Jefferson denounced the military buildup as "insane"; Republicans demanded to see evidence of France's treachery. When Adams made the commission's dispatches public, war fever engulfed the nation. The cry in the 1798 congressional elections became, "Millions for defense, but not a cent for tribute." Two patriotic songs "Adams for Liberty" and "Hail Columbia" were widely sung, the latter serving as the unofficial national anthem. Congress expanded the regular army and war fleet, established the Department of the Navy, authorized naval vessels to protect American merchant ships, suspended commerce with France, and revoked the French alliance. George Washington assumed command of the army, with

Alexander Hamilton in charge of field operations. To pay for all of this, Congress levied a direct tax of $2 million on dwelling houses, land, and slaves.

Without declaring war, the United States engaged France in hostilities from 1798 to 1800. In what was known as the Quasi-War, the U.S. navy dominated the French, defeating their warships, sinking privateers, and recapturing at least seventy American merchant vessels. The British navy helped by protecting U.S. carriers. While some congressmen feared a French invasion and thereby justified further military preparations, French naval losses to Great Britain and the United States quickly removed that threat.

The Alien and Sedition Acts

The Federalists rode the crest of patriotism in 1798, using their majority in Congress to pass a series of acts that limited the rights of immigrants and critics of the administration. Though Adams later said that he had not recommended the laws, he signed them. Congressional sponsors argued that they were necessary wartime measures. Their practical purpose, however, sought to destroy the Republicans by undermining their support and closing newspapers. The Federalists tried to take advantage of the Quasi-War to link their opponents with the enemy. This strategy worked in the short term, as the pro-French Republicans lost votes in the 1798 congressional election, but proved suicidal for Adams's party after the fear of invasion had passed.

This Federalist design resulted in four restrictive laws. The Naturalization Act of 1798, which aimed to discourage immigration, lengthened the period of residence needed for citizenship from five to fourteen years. The legislation was intended to stop the flow of Irish immigrants who, because they were anti-British and pro-French, swelled the number of Republican voters. The Alien Enemies Act, a compromise measure that had bipartisan support, did not actually go into effect during the Quasi-War. A permanent statute, it established procedures in the event of declared war or invasion for jailing and deporting citizens of the enemy nation who were considered likely to spy or commit sabotage.

Two additional laws gave wide powers to the president during peacetime as well as in war. The Alien Act, which had a term of two years, allowed the president to deport any non–U.S. citizens "he shall judge dangerous to the peace and safety of the United States, or shall have reasonable grounds to suspect are concerned in any treasonable or secret machinations against the government thereof." Like the Naturalization Act, this law potentially threatened Irish immigrants. But because Adams refrained from using it, the Alien Act's importance was more symbolic than real.

The Federalists did enforce the fourth law, the Sedition Act, with serious results. Its term lasted until March 3, 1801, the day before the next president would be inaugurated. Thus the Federalists ensured that if the next chief executive were a Republican, he would not be able to retaliate without obtaining a new statute. In vague language, the Sedition Act made it illegal for "any persons [to] unlawfully combine or conspire together, with intent to oppose any measure or measures of the government of the United States" or to interfere with the execution of a law. Nor could a person "write, print, utter or publish . . . any false, scandalous and malicious writing or writings against the government of the United States, or either house of the Congress . . . or the President." In effect, this law permitted imprisonment and fines for criticizing the government. It applied to U.S. citizens as well as to aliens. Though individuals charged under the Sedition Act could use the truth of their writings as a defense, the law gave a great deal of latitude in making arrests. It was an obvious infringement upon freedom of speech and freedom of the press.

Nevertheless, the administration enforced the law. Adams believed that the Sedition Act was constitutional, that people who censured his policies threatened the future of the republic. The prime targets for prosecution were Republican newspapers. Among the

indicted was Benjamin Bache, the grandson of Benjamin Franklin and editor of the Philadelphia *Aurora,* who was one of Adams's most powerful critics. The official authorized to administer the act was Secretary of State Timothy Pickering, a staunch Federalist, who methodically reviewed the Republican papers for actionable offenses. He even ordered an inquiry into the private correspondence of a Republican congressman who reputedly called Adams a traitor; in this case, however, the investigation was dropped. Under the law, the Federalists indicted and tried at least seventeen people for sedition. They timed cases to reach court in the fall of 1799 or the following spring, with the goal of silencing the Republican press during the 1800 election. Some papers folded and others closed temporarily while their editors were imprisoned. All but one of the cases were prosecuted in New England and the Middle Atlantic states, where the Federalists controlled the courts and could pack juries.

The Republican Opposition Grows

Passage of the Alien and Sedition acts and the jailing of Republican spokesmen shifted the political winds. The war fever from the XYZ Affair subsided with American naval victories and indications that the French were ready to negotiate. In late 1798, the Kentucky and Virginia legislatures approved resolutions that protested the Alien and Sedition acts on the grounds that they were unconstitutional. The Kentucky and Virginia Resolutions, drafted anonymously by Thomas Jefferson and James Madison, respectively, argued that these laws violated the First Amendment and granted powers to the national government not delegated by the Constitution. The Virginia assembly resolved that "in case of a deliberate, palpable, and dangerous exercise of other powers, not granted by the [Constitution], the states . . . have the right, and are in duty bound, to interpose, for arresting the progress of the evil." Virginia and Kentucky sent their resolutions to other legislatures, none of which agreed that states could declare a federal law unconstitutional. Rhode Island, for example, responded that the federal courts held the power to determine constitutionality; "that for any state legislature to assume that authority would be . . . Hazarding an interruption of the peace of the states by civil discord, in case of a diversity of opinions among the state legislatures." Nevertheless, Madison and particularly Jefferson, who drafted yet another set of resolutions for the Kentucky legislature in 1799, contributed toward a theory of "nullification," the idea that a state had the right to veto a federal law it considered unconstitutional. This theory was based upon the strict interpretation of the Constitution that denied, as in the controversy over the national bank, implied powers to the central government.

With the Alien and Sedition acts, the Federalists made a strategic error, one that gave their rivals the political high ground. Where formerly the Republicans could be branded as a faction creating animosity and disunity, one whose program was primarily negative, they now became legitimate defenders of Revolutionary principles. The Republican party justified its opposition by warning that the Federalists were on the road to tyranny. The Sedition Act, Madison argued in the Virginia Resolutions, impeded free investigation of the actions of government officials and "free communication among the people thereon, which has ever been justly deemed the only effectual guardian of every other right." The administration's effort to destroy its adversaries backfired as the Republicans gained respectability among Americans who had formerly supported the Federalists.

The administration fanned the flames of indignation with its heavy-handed reaction to a tax rebellion among Germans of rural eastern Pennsylvania, a group who had previously favored Washington and Adams or had stayed out of politics entirely. The Republicans took advantage of the Pennsylvanians' aversion to the 1798 federal property tax to win their votes in the congressional election. They circulated petitions against the tax, the defense buildup, and the Alien and Sedition laws, petitions that Congress ignored. By early 1799, the people of Northampton and Bucks counties held public meetings and stopped tax assessors from doing their work. In March, after the U.S. marshal jailed eighteen suspected tax resisters in Bethlehem's Sun Tavern, John Fries, a fifty-year-old auctioneer of upper Bucks County, led a band of 140 armed men to release the prisoners.

The Fries Rebellion ended quickly, as the rebels considered the magnitude of their offense. Fries announced that he would pay the tax and would even welcome the assessor to his house for dinner. Nevertheless, the president decided to make an example of the episode. He dispatched troops that failed to march until almost four weeks after the resistance had ceased. The army descended upon Northampton and Bucks counties, entering houses and arresting sixty men. One

army officer wrote "that every hour's experience confirms me more and more that this expedition was not only unnecessary, but violently absurd." Contrary to the Judiciary Act of 1789, the prisoners were taken to Philadelphia for trial. Fries and two others were found guilty of treason by a Federalist court and sentenced to hang, but were subsequently pardoned by the president. The Republicans added the administration's unwarranted use of force to their arsenal of charges against the Federalists. Jefferson could now count Pennsylvania Germans among his strongest supporters.

⚊ CONCLUSION ⚊

George Washington had warned in his Farewell Address that "the spirit of part . . . agitates the community with ill-founded jealousies and false alarms; kindles the animosity of one part against another; foments occasionally riot and insurrection. It opens the door to foreign influence and corruption. . . ." He invoked the ideal of consensual community, challenging his fellow citizens to work together for the good of their country. The flaw of this conception was that Americans could not agree on which policies were best for everyone. The interests of farmers, merchants, and artisans, of residents of the north, south, and west, often diverged. The Federalist and Republican parties grew out of different visions of the nation's future. During the 1790s, the Federalists retained control of the central government, confident that their vision was the correct one. They denounced parties, identifying their government with the republic as a whole. When they tried to eliminate factions by silencing their adversaries with the Sedition Act, ironically they legitimized the party system in the eyes of many Americans.

RECOMMENDED READINGS

Anderson, Margo J. *The American Census: A Social History* (1988). A very good source on the first federal census of 1790.

Charles, Joseph. *The Origins of the American Party System* (1956). Insightful examination of the development of parties in the 1790s.

Cochran, Thomas C. *Frontiers of Change: Early Industrialism in America* (1981). A good introduction to industrialization in the early republic.

Elkins, Stanley, and McKitrick, Eric. *The Age of Federalism* (1993). Detailed narrative of the Washington and Adams administrations.

North, Douglass C. *The Economic Growth of the United States, 1790–1860* (1966). Includes a useful analysis of U.S. trade amid international conflict.

Onuf, Peter S., ed., *Jeffersonian Legacies* (1993). Wide-ranging essays on Thomas Jefferson's character and politics.

Slaughter, Thomas P. *The Whiskey Rebellion: Frontier Epilogue to the American Revolution* (1986). An excellent book on the struggle between Alexander Hamilton and western Pennsylvania farmers over excise taxes.

Smith, James Morton. *Freedom's Fetters: The Alien and Sedition Laws and American Civil Liberties* (1956). Focuses on the Federalists' attempt to curtail civil rights.

White, Richard. *The Middle Ground: Indians, Empires, and Republics in the Great Lakes Region, 1650–1815* (1991). Influential study of Indian-white relations from New France through the War of 1812.

Young, James Sterling. *The Washington Community, 1800–1828* (1966). Interesting work on the development and growth of the new federal capital.

Politics and Diplomacy During the 1790s

Appleby, Joyce. *Capitalism and a New Social Order: The Republican Vision of the 1790s* (1984).

Banning, Lance. *The Jeffersonian Persuasion: The Evolution of a Party Ideology* (1978).

Hoffman, Ronald, and Albert, Peter J., eds. *Women in the Age of the Revolution* (1989).

Beeman, Richard, et al., eds. *Beyond Confederation: Origins of the Constitution and American National Identity* (1987).

Conley, Patrick T., and Kaminski, John P., eds. *The Bill of Rights and the States: The Colonial and Revolutionary Origins of American Liberties* (1992).

Cooke, Jacob E. *Alexander Hamilton* (1982).

Davis, W.W.H. *The Fries Rebellion, 1798–99* (1899).

DeConde, Alexander. *The Quasi-War: The Politics and Diplomacy of the Undeclared War with France, 1797–1801* (1966).

Flexner, James T. *George Washington and the New Nation, 1783–1793* (1970).

Flexner, James T. *George Washington: Anguish and Farewell, 1793–1799* (1972).

Greene, Jack P., ed., *The American Revolution: Its Character and Limits* (1987).

Hoadley, John F. *Origins of American Political Parties, 1789–1803* (1986).

Hofstadter, Richard. *The Idea of a Party System: The Rise of Legitimate Opposition in the United States, 1780–1840* (1969).

Kohn, Richard H. *Eagle and Sword: The Federalists and the Creation of the Military Establishment in America, 1783–1802* (1975).

Kurtz, Stephen G. *The Presidency of John Adams: The Collapse of Federalism, 1795–1800* (1957).

Levy, Leonard. *Legacy of Suppression: Freedom of Speech and Press in Early American History* (1960).

Malone, Dumas. *Jefferson and the Ordeal of Liberty* (1962).

Malone, Dumas. *Jefferson and the Rights of Man* (1951).

Merrill, Michael, and Wilentz, Sean, eds. *The Key of Liberty: The Life and Democratic Writings of William Manning, "A Laborer," 1747–1814* (1993).

Miller, John C. *The Federalist Era, 1789–1801* (1960).

Schwartz, Bernard. *The Great Rights of Mankind: A History of the American Bill of Rights* (1977).

Sharp, James Roger. *American Politics in the Early Republic: The New Nation in Crisis* (1993).

Stourzh, Gerald. *Alexander Hamilton and the Idea of Republican Government* (1970).

Population Growth and the Frontier

Ahlstrom, Sydney E. *A Religious History of the American People* (1972).

Klepp, Susan E., ed. "Symposium on the Demographic History of the Philadelphia Region, 1600–1860," *Proceedings of the American Philosophical Society*, 133:2 (1989).

Rohrbough, Malcolm J. *The Trans-Appalachian Frontier: People, Societies, and Institutions, 1775–1850* (1978).

U.S. Bureau of the Census, *A Century of Population Growth: From the First Census of the United States to the Twelfth, 1790–1900* (1909).

Taylor, Alan. *William Cooper's Town: Power and Persuasion on the Frontier of the Early American Republic* (1995).

Wallace, Anthony F.C. *The Death and Rebirth of the Seneca* (1969).

Weber, David J. *The Spanish Frontier in North America* (1992).

Economic Development and Technology

Browne, Gary Lawson. *Baltimore in the Nation, 1789–1861* (1980).

Doerflinger, Thomas M. *A Vigorous Spirit of Enterprise: Merchants and Economic Development in Revolutionary Philadelphia* (1986).

McGaw, Judith A., ed. *Early American Technology: Making and Doing Things from the Colonial Era to 1850* (1994).

Shelton, Cynthia J. *The Mills of Manayunk: Industrialization and Social Conflict in the Philadelphia Region, 1787–1837* (1986).

Smith, Billy G. *The "Lower Sort": Philadelphia's Laboring People, 1750–1800* (1990).

Tucker, Barbara M. *Samuel Slater and the Origins of the American Textile Industry, 1790–1860* (1984).

SECOND GREAT AWAKENING

Methodist Camp Meeting, *engraving by E. Clay. During the Second Great Awakening, itinerant preachers held outdoor revivals that often lasted for several days.*

Chapter 8

THE NEW REPUBLIC FACES A NEW CENTURY, 1800–1814

AMERICANS CONFRONTED THE nineteenth century with a variety of fears. For the Federalists, the growing Republican opposition warned that the evils of democracy and anarchy stood on the doorstep, ready to take control after the election of 1800. For the Republicans, the Alien and Sedition acts and Federalist repression of the whiskey rebels and John Fries underscored the need for change. Both parties, still members of the Revolutionary generation, thought in terms of the ideals for which they had fought against the British. They also measured events against what was transpiring elsewhere in the world. By 1800, the radical, then reactionary, phases of the French Revolution and Napoleon Bonaparte's rise to power dismayed Americans. The never-ending European war threatened to involve the United States for twenty years, and finally did in 1812. The revolt by slaves in the French West Indies horrified southern slave owners.

Though Thomas Jefferson's presidency proved to be less revolutionary than many Federalists expected, the new century brought indelible changes to American politics and society. The Federalist party shriveled and died, the Louisiana Purchase expanded the nation's territory to the Rocky Mountains and beyond, slavery became more firmly embedded in the southern economy, and the republic fought once more against Great Britain. The Second Great Awakening, the series of religious revivals that had begun in the late 1790s but gained steam after the turn of the century, influenced the ways in which many people interpreted these events.

RELIGION IN AMERICAN SOCIETY

Politics took a back seat in the lives of most Americans during the first decade of the nineteenth century. In many respects, that was the promise of Jefferson's government: low taxes, a small bureaucracy, minimal intrusion by government into the affairs of citizens, peace, religious freedom. In particular, religion absorbed the energies of many different groups: frontier settlers and Native Americans caught up in revivals, organizations to provide welfare relief in towns and cities, new sects like the Shakers, and free African Americans who built separate churches as the cornerstone of their communities. Many people believed that renewed emphasis on religion would transform the nation through individual faith and communal action.

CHRONOLOGY

1800	Washington, D.C., becomes national capital
	Gabriel's Rebellion
	Convention of 1800 with France
	Jefferson's election as president
	Rise of Handsome Lake as a Seneca prophet
1801	Adams's "midnight appointments"
	John Marshall becomes chief justice
	Tripolitan War
	Cane Ridge, Kentucky, camp meeting
1802	Judiciary Act of 1801 repealed
1803	*Marbury* v. *Madison* case
	Great Britain and France resume war
	Louisiana Purchase
1804	Lewis and Clark expedition departs from St. Louis
	Aaron Burr kills Alexander Hamilton
	Twelfth Amendment ratified
	Haiti founded
	Reelection of Jefferson as president
1805	*Essex* decision in Britain
1806	Non-Importation Act
1807	Burr tried for treason
	Leopard-Chesapeake Affair
	Embargo Act
1808	Federal ban on importation of slaves
	Madison elected as president
1809	Giles's Enforcement Act
	Embargo repealed; replaced with Non-Intercourse Act
	Treaty of Fort Wayne
1810	Annexation of West Florida
1811	Charter of national bank expires
	Tecumseh organizes pan-Indian resistance to land cessions
	Battle of Tippecanoe
1812	U.S. declares war on Great Britain
	Hull surrenders Detroit
	Madison elected to second term
1813	Perry defeats British navy on Lake Erie
	Battle of the Thames
1814	Battle of Horseshoe Bend
	British burn public buildings in Washington, D.C.
	Americans repel invasion on Lake Champlain
	Hartford Convention
	Treaty of Ghent

The Second Great Awakening

As the century began, people throughout the country sought spiritual renewal. Among New England Congregationalists, the revivals spread from one town to another between 1797 and 1801. The national Methodist conference of 1800 held in Baltimore witnessed an outpouring of religious fervor. These flames heralded a series of revivals—the Second Great Awakening—which lasted into the 1830s. Women and men of various denominations started voluntary associations to support missionaries, encourage moral behavior, and provide charity. Many followed the lead of young Quaker women in Philadelphia, who in 1795 had established the first female society to provide food, firewood, and clothing to impoverished city folk. Similar groups soon sprang up throughout the middle states, New England, and parts of the South. In accepting the message of revival, large numbers of Americans embraced evangelicalism—the belief that they must take their message of salvation to others. They expected to create a more godly nation through conversion and good works.

In particular, eastern clergy worried that people on the frontier, with few churches, would let sin take control of their lives. As Americans streamed west across the Appalachians, by 1810, Ohio had 230,000 settlers, Kentucky and Tennessee had 668,000, and the Mississippi and Louisiana territories had 117,000. New Englanders moved to western New York State and the Midwest, while southerners carved out new plantations in the southern trans-Appalachian region. Evangelical ministers feared for the nation because so many westerners were unchurched. The clerics expressed their dread in terms of millennialism, the belief that the millennium—Christ's second coming—was at hand, as foretold in Revelation, the last book of the Bible. Pastors urged their congregations to prepare for the millennium by supporting missionary efforts in the west. They believed the kingdom of God could extend to the Pacific Ocean and beyond, but Americans throughout the country must embrace Christianity and convert Native Americans and the people of other lands.

Circuit preachers and missionaries traveled throughout the frontier; the churches they started were often the first social organizations in new communities. The great western revivals of 1800–1815, which built upon this work, began when several Presbyterians summoned the first camp meeting, a religious gathering held outside over the course of several days. People came together, miles from their homes, to hear revivalist preachers. The most famous of the early camp meetings took place in August 1801 at Cane Ridge, Kentucky, where Presbyterian, Methodist, and Baptist clergy preached for about a week to a throng numbering about 20,000. From wagons and crude tents, the crowds listened to the spiritual message that Jesus Christ could save everyone from their sins. The wicked could escape eternal damnation. People reacted emotionally and physically to this message, some jerking their heads or entire bodies, others falling to the ground in a faint.

Reminiscent of the Great Awakening in the South during the 1750s and 1760s (see Chapter 4), the camp meetings spread through Kentucky, Tennessee, and southern Ohio, gathering new congregations. The Methodist and Baptist churches, which placed less importance on the fine points of religious doctrine and a well-educated clergy than the Presbyterians, benefited most from the revivals. The Methodists and Baptists saw extraordinary growth among ordinary people, especially in the South, including African Americans and whites. As one minister wrote, "the illiterate Methodist preachers actually set the world on fire, (the American world at least,) while [pastors of other denominations] were lighting their matches!"

Religion was important to black Americans, whether they remained enslaved or had achieved freedom. In the South, where the expansion of cotton culture ended hopes for the abolition of slavery as tobacco declined, African Americans responded enthusiastically to revivalist preachers. The Methodists and Baptists welcomed free and enslaved blacks into their congregations as equals in spirit though not in governing the church. In hostile northern cities, free black communities depended upon separate churches for leadership and communal fellowship.

Growth of Sects

The period around 1800 witnessed the expansion of several dissenting sects: the Shakers, the Society of the Public Universal Friend, and the Universalists. They are called sects, rather than denominations, because they were new and fairly small in number of adherents. These sectarians held distinctive beliefs that set them apart from mainstream religions, yet had a significant influence on intellectual and social movements of their times.

The Shakers, whose official name was the United Society of Believers in Christ's Second Coming (the Millennial church), came to America in 1774, when Mother Ann Lee arrived from Britain with eight disciples. They left England to escape mob attacks and imprisonment. The group grew slowly at first, but expanded after Lee's death in 1784, as they reaped followers from revivals, especially Baptists. The Shakers even converted the three Presbyterians who had organized the Cane Ridge, Kentucky, camp meeting. The sect offered an avenue for people who had been spiritually reborn in the Awakening and sought a distinctive way to represent that rebirth in their lives.

From visions, Mother Lee believed that she embodied Christ's Second Coming, that the millennium had already arrived. As Christ had appeared as a man, and Lee (called Mother of the New Creation) came as a woman, God had both male and female elements. The

The Shakers of New Lebanon—Religious Exercises in the Dining Room. In religious worship, Shakers abandoned their strict, sex-segregated discipline.

Shakers considered themselves a vanguard to lead everyone to the kingdom of God. They believed in salvation by confession of sin, equality regardless of sex or race, opposition to slavery and war, and assistance to the poor. They abstained from sexual relations. In Shaker communities, which by 1809 existed from Maine to Kentucky, men and women ate, slept, and worked separately. They followed a strict discipline and aspired to economic self-sufficiency. Shakers sat on straight-backed chairs, cut their food into square pieces, and walked along paths laid out in right angles. But in religious worship, they abandoned this right-angle order. In a large open space without pulpit or pews, worshippers danced, shouted, and sang. The Shaker communitarian lifestyle, which yielded plentiful food, a comfortable standard of living, and beautifully designed furnishings, influenced other groups to organize communal, utopian experiments during the years after 1815.

A similar but smaller sect was the Society of the Public Universal Friend, founded by Jemima Wilkinson of Rhode Island. Disowned by Quakers in 1776 for joining the Baptists, Wilkinson became ill, believed that she died, and then returned to life as the Public Universal Friend. Her mission was to convince others to repent their sins and prepare for the millennium. Like Mother Lee, Wilkinson preached celibacy, peace,

and opposition to slavery. She traveled sidesaddle on horseback, attracting a coterie of believers in New England and Pennsylvania. As one convert said, Wilkinson was "the Messenger of Peace . . . Travelling far & wide to spread the glad tidings & news of Salvation to a lost and perishing & dying World who have all gone astray like Lost Sheep." In 1788, upon gathering over 200 Universal Friends, she organized a community called Jerusalem in western New York. They established the first white settlement at Lake Seneca, then later moved to Keuka Lake. The Universal Friends neither organized a communal economy like the Shakers nor continued to seek new members. Nevertheless, the community survived well past Wilkinson's death in 1819.

Another sect, the Universalists, rejected the Calvinist belief that only a minority of people, the elect, could attain salvation. They preached that "it is the purpose of God, through the grace revealed in our Lord Jesus Christ, to save every member of the human race from sin." The American Universalist Church, established in 1779 by an Englishman, John Murray, found a sympathetic audience among ordinary people caught up in the Second Great Awakening in New England and on the frontier. Its message of universal salvation had wide influence, though the Universalist Church itself remained small.

Revivalism Among Native Americans

While the Second Great Awakening and dissenting sects claimed the imagination and souls of white and black Americans, a new wave of revivals drew together Native Americans. Among the Iroquois living on reservations in western New York and the Shawnees, Creeks, Cherokees, and other nations retaining lands in the trans-Appalachian region, prophets warned of imminent doom unless people changed their ways. Native Americans had continued to lose lands to whites throughout the area from the Appalachians to the Mississippi; by 1812, settlers in the region dwarfed the Indian population by seven to one. Decline in the numbers of fur-bearing animals caused economic hardship, while conflict over whether to cooperate with the United States created political factions within tribes.

Like the Delaware prophet Neolin in the 1760s (see Chapter 4), the new nativists blamed loss of land and power on the Indians' failure to maintain traditional rituals and on their adoption of wicked practices from the whites. Among many prophets, Handsome Lake of the Senecas (a nation of the Iroquois) and Tenskwatawa of the Shawnees wielded the greatest influence in the first decade of the nineteenth century.

Handsome Lake, a respected warrior and leader of the Allegany Senecas, fell ill in 1799, seemed to die, then came back to life saying that he had a vision in which messengers told him to become a prophet. In a series of revelations over several years, Handsome Lake received a message of impending catastrophe and a means to salvation. He told his people to stop drinking alcohol and practicing witchcraft. They should perform ancestral rituals such as the white dog ceremony in which a white dog was strangled, then set on fire as a sacrifice to the Creator, then eaten.

Handsome Lake also advocated peace—among his own people as well as toward white settlers and the U.S. government. He embraced the U.S. acculturation policy by which Quakers tried to convince the Iroquois to adopt white farming methods and gender roles, but he opposed further large-scale land cessions, the whiskey trade, social dancing in couples, and gambling with cards. Other Indians opposed acculturation, which required women to leave the fields and take up spinning, and men to farm rather than hunt. They viewed the policy, accurately, as a way to justify further expropriation of hunting lands.

Handsome Lake served as political leader of the Iroquois only briefly, from 1801 to 1803, but his spiritual message remained strong in the years that followed. Most influential was his drive against liquor. A former heavy drinker himself, Handsome Lake advised, in the words of a white observer, that "the Whiskey is the great Engine which the bad Spirit uses to introduce Witchcraft and many other evils amongst Indians." Many Iroquois abstained from hard drink. One Quaker visitor "noted with satisfaction that in the course of our travels among all the Indians on the Allegheny River . . . we have not seen a Single individual the least intoxicated with Liquor—which perhaps would be a Singular Circumstance to Observe in traveling among the same number of white Inhabitants."

Handsome Lake was one of the most influential Indian prophets of the late eighteenth and early nineteenth century. Another was Tenskwatawa, called the Shawnee Prophet, who became prominent among the people of the Great Lakes and Ohio Valley. With his brother, Tecumseh, he inspired a nativist movement to

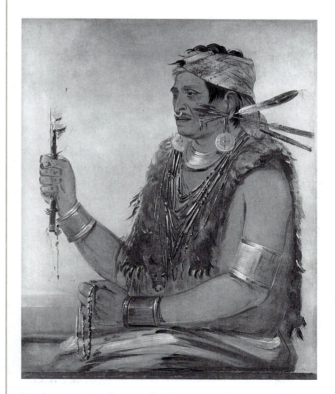

Tenskwatawa, the Shawnee Prophet, *painted by George Catlin, 1830. With his brother Tecumseh, Tenskwatawa organized Native American resistance to white settlement in the Great Lakes region.*

resist the U.S. government's acculturation policy and land grabbing. Tenskwatawa saw visions similar to Handsome Lake's but was less accommodating toward whites. To avoid fiery destruction, he warned, Indians must revitalize their traditional ceremonies, avoid liquor, and reject the new gender roles. One of the prophet's visions promised that the whites would be destroyed if his people obeyed these instructions. Tenskwatawa and Tecumseh summoned nativists to oppose the Indian accommodationist leaders who sold land and adopted white farming. During the War of 1812, as will be discussed below, they organized pan-Indian military resistance in alliance with Great Britain against the United States.

AFRICAN AMERICANS

As slavery ended in the north, blacks faced discriminatory practices that kept the racial caste system in place, including segregation in churches and schools, and restriction from politics and many occupations. Despite this racism, northern blacks created new lives, institutions, and communities that offered a potent draw to African Americans in the south. With the St.

Domingue revolution in mind, southern blacks also considered more violent means to end bondage, as in the case of Gabriel's revolt in Virginia.

Free Blacks in the North

By 1800, Pennsylvania, New York, and all of New England had passed gradual abolition acts or ended slavery outright. New Jersey in 1804 became the last northern state to pass a law for gradual emancipation, which, like those of other states, freed children henceforth born to slave mothers, but retained slaves born before that date in perpetual bondage. The black children who benefited from the law would be required to serve their mother's owner until a certain age—in New Jersey, twenty-five for males and twenty-one for females. In effect, these children became indentured servants as compensation to masters for providing support during their early years.

Despite the gradual nature of these emancipation laws, slavery declined rapidly in the northern states. Responding to their slaves' requests for freedom and to the spirit of the abolition acts, owners freed people whom the laws left in bonds. Masters usually required some additional years of service for the promise of freedom. Frequently, blacks negotiated agreements for

TABLE 8.1	NUMBER OF ENSLAVED AFRICAN AMERICANS, 1800 AND 1810	
	1800	*1810*
New England	1,339	418
New York	20,903	15,017
New Jersey	12,422	10,851
Pennsylvania	1,706	795
Delaware	6,153	4,177
Maryland & District of Columbia	107,707	115,056
Virginia	346,968	394,357
North Carolina	133,296	168,824
South Carolina	146,151	196,365
Georgia	59,406	105,218
Kentucky	40,343	80,561
Tennessee	13,584	44,535
Mississippi Territory	3,489	17,088

TABLE 8.2 FREE BLACK POPULATION IN NORTHERN CITIES			
	1790	*1800*	*1810*
Philadelphia	1,849	6,028	8,942
New York City	1,036	3,333	7,470
Boston	766	1,174	1,484

Reverend Richard Allen, a former slave, was founder of the African Methodist Episcopal Church and a leader of the Philadelphia black community.

themselves or family members. In 1805, a New York slave, Margaret, obtained her owner's pledge of freedom in eight years if she behaved "as she always has done in an orderly manner as a servant ought to do." A New Jersey man promised to pay his owner $50 per year for four years in return for his release. When masters proved recalcitrant, blacks often forced the issue by running away.

The northern cities became magnets for escaped slaves, from the surrounding countryside and the Upper South. In addition, humanitarian concerns touched some southern masters, including George Washington, who freed his slaves in his will. Some owners in Delaware and the Chesapeake region, who held more slaves than they needed, emancipated their slaves, then sold them as indentured servants in the north. Between 1790 and 1810, the free black population of Philadelphia and New York City soared, while that of Boston also grew, though more slowly.

Philadelphia and New York City became centers of free African American culture, with churches fostering autonomous community growth. In Philadelphia, responding to hostility, freed men and women organized separate congregations in the 1780s and 1790s. Reverend Richard Allen, for example, led black worshipers from St. George's Methodist Episcopal Church when whites insisted on segregated seating. Allen described the scene as they were forced to move during prayer:

> We had not been long upon our knees before I heard considerable scuffling and loud talking. I raised my head up and saw one of the trustees, H____ M____, having hold of the Rev. Absalom Jones, pulling him off his knees, and saying, "You must get up, you must not kneel here." . . . we all went out of the church in a body, and they were no more plagued by us in the church.

Allen purchased a blacksmith's shop, converted it into a church, calling it Bethel, which in Hebrew means "house of God." By 1803, the black Methodist church had 457 members, the result of revivals and Allen's fervent preaching. But while the evangelical message of Methodism appealed to African Americans, and "Mother" Bethel grew, the congregation found relations with the hierarchy of the white Methodist church difficult. In the early decades of the nineteenth century, black Methodists in Philadelphia, Baltimore, Wilmington, and New York struggled against white control, finally seceding to form separate denominations. In 1816, Philadelphia's Bethel became the first congregation of the African Methodist Episcopal church.

Urban black churches, which included the Episcopal, Baptist, and Presbyterian as well as the Methodist, provided mutual aid, fellowship, and avenues for leadership. One benefit of belonging to a New York congregation became obvious to an eighty-year-old woman after a fire destroyed her home. When asked where she would find shelter, she answered, "O a sister in the church has promised to take me in." Shunned by white organizations, effectively barred from politics, and lacking equal opportunity for employment, African Americans created alternatives through the church. Talented black men became ministers and elders; from these positions they served as spokesmen for their community.

Like white urban residents, freed men and women formed mutual benefit societies. The names African Americans chose for these organizations demonstrated pride in their African heritage. Philadelphians, for example, formed the Free African Society, Daughters of Ethiopia, Angola Society, Sons of Africa, and many others. The official purpose of these societies was to collect dues to provide relief to poor widows and children, but, just as important, the groups facilitated community involvement.

Though most northern blacks remained impoverished, New York and Philadelphia offered a variety of opportunities that could be found nowhere else. With little money or access to capital, few African Americans, perhaps one in ten, scraped together the funds to purchase a house, shop, or farm. In the first decades of the nineteenth century, many blacks were still completing terms of servitude, while others, though free, lived and worked in white households as domestic servants. Even if they established their own households, women generally washed clothes or performed domestic service for others. Most men were mariners or hired as common laborers—digging foundations, wells, and graves; transporting goods on the docks and through the city streets; and sweeping chimneys. The African American community provided additional opportunity by employing its own. Residents supported black shoemakers, carpenters, food retailers, hucksters, barbers, hairdressers, seamstresses, tailors, cooks, bakers, schoolteachers, and ministers. In Philadelphia, a few African Americans achieved considerable wealth and fame. By 1807, James Forten employed thirty men—blacks and whites—to produce sails for the city's shipbuilders. Robert Bogle developed the idea of catering parties, weddings, and funerals, while Frank Johnson became the city's premier musician. He performed on trumpet and violin, composed dance music and songs, and organized a band that played at balls and public events.

Northern blacks faced daily challenges in earning their bread, while keeping their sights on personal goals of economic success and equal status. But they revered their African roots and remembered fellow

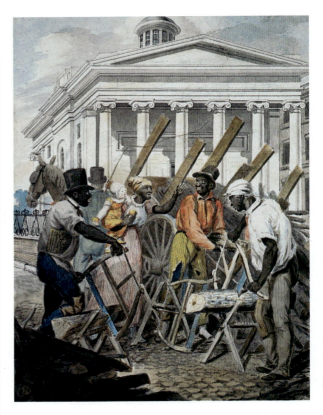

Negroes in Front of the Bank of Pennsylvania, Philadelphia *(1814) shows a group of black workers, the male sawyers laboring in a public space and a female domestic caring for a white child.*

blacks held in slavery. The word African in the name of most mutual aid societies and churches testified to their pride of origins, though many of the founders were two, three, even four generations removed from ancestral lands.

African Americans in northern cities also knew of recent struggles by slaves in St. Domingue and elsewhere; a large number of blacks in Philadelphia and New York City had come from the French island with their masters who fled the black revolt. During the 1790s, blacks on St. Domingue led by Toussaint L'Ouverture, a former slave, defeated local whites and the French, Spanish, and British armies. In 1802, Napoleon tried once again to take control of the island, but failed when disease decimated his forces. In 1804, the victorious rebels of St. Domingue established Haiti as an independent nation. Most white Americans dreaded the importation of black revolt. Thomas Jefferson opposed trade with the island, stating, "We may expect therefore black crews, and super-cargoes and missionaries thence into the southern states. . . . If this combustion can be introduced among us under any veil whatever, we have to fear it."

Slave Rebellion in the South

With more than 850,000 enslaved blacks in the American south in 1800, one-third of the population, whites had reason to be concerned about slave insurgency. After St. Domingue erupted, Georgia and the Carolinas declared black emigrés from the West Indies a threat, prohibiting their entry. South Carolina, in re-opening its international slave trade in 1803, made every effort to avoid admitting rebels. The state excluded blacks from the West Indies and South America, and any who had ever lived in the French West Indies. Every man imported from another state needed a certificate indicating that he had not "been concerned in any insurrection or rebellion."

In August 1800, the worst fears of white southerners were nearly realized when an enslaved blacksmith named Gabriel organized an armed march against the capital of Virginia. With about 600 supporters from Richmond and surrounding counties, Gabriel planned a full-scale insurrection. His strategy included seizing guns from an arsenal, taking Governor James Monroe hostage, and forcing concessions from town officials. Gabriel expected poor whites to join him because they, like slaves, lacked political power. The attack failed when a torrential rainstorm washed out bridges, making travel impossible. Efforts to try again another day collapsed when two informers passed word of the conspiracy to authorities who rounded up suspects. Though Gabriel eluded capture for more than three weeks, he was arrested and hanged, as were twenty-six others implicated in the plot.

White Americans, at the beginning of the nineteenth century, still held the Revolutionary belief that all men and women desired freedom. Masters took seriously the threat of slave revolt. After Gabriel's rebellion, Governor Monroe observed about enslaved African Americans, "Unhappily while this class of people exists among us we can never count with certainty on its tranquil submission." In 1802, Virginians discovered additional conspiracies, with rumors of more violence heightening tensions. In 1805, after four whites had been poisoned in North Carolina, officials burned a slave woman alive, hanged three other slaves,

and whipped and cut off the ears of another. Gabriel's plot, the St. Domingue uprising, and what appeared to be an upsurge of murders and arson by blacks convinced southern lawmakers to enact more stringent slave codes. South Carolina and Georgia tightened requirements for slave patrols and defined as treason any collaboration in slave rebellion. South Carolina and Virginia placed restrictions on meetings after dark, and Virginia increased penalties for arson. Hardening attitudes toward slavery snuffed out southern antislavery societies that were already faltering. The Alexandria, Virginia, association died by 1805; the Virginia Abolition Society expressed little hope for its future work. On a more positive note, as the twenty-year constitutional restriction on prohibiting the slave trade expired (see Chapter 6), Congress officially banned the importation of slaves after January 1, 1808.

JEFFERSON'S REPUBLIC

In 1800, the federal government moved from the nation's cultural capital in Philadelphia to an unfinished village on the Potomac: Washington, D.C. The ruling party also changed, as voters voiced their dissatisfaction with the Federalists by electing Thomas Jefferson and a Republican Congress. Jefferson's promise of reduced government and taxes appealed to a populace concerned about other things besides national politics—their finances, their souls, and local communities. Events prevented the young nation from wrapping itself in isolation, however, for its economic prosperity depended a great deal upon international commerce, a trade severely hampered by the ongoing European war.

Election of 1800

Most recently, the United States had been involved in the Quasi-War with France, in which the French navy ravaged the American merchant fleet. Congress had expanded the army, authorized the U.S. Navy to protect commercial ships, and revoked unilaterally the American-French treaty of 1778, which had pledged a mutual defensive alliance "forever." The Federalists swept the congressional elections of 1798 on the crest of anti-French fervor; they tried to use war fever possible to fulfill: Its mission was to obtain French agreement that the 1778 alliance had ended and indemnities for confiscated American ships. In March 1800, Murray, Ellsworth, and Davie met with Napoleon, who had no intention of paying compensation. The commissioners reached an accord only by ignoring their instructions. The Convention of 1800, signed in France in October and ratified reluctantly by the U.S. Senate in February 1801, echoed provisions of the 1778 commercial treaty in calling for "a firm, inviolable, and universal peace" and recognition of most-favored-nation status between the two nations. The Convention voided the defensive alliance of 1778, however, thus eliminating the French claim to U.S. support against Great Britain. The pact also included a vague confirmation by the French of neutral rights in international trade, but provided no restitution to American shippers, a failing that opponents said made the convention worthless. In fact, it had value in normalizing relations between the two countries and ending the 1778 treaty that had become so dangerous to the United States in the recurring European war.

The chief beneficiary of reduced tensions with France was Thomas Jefferson, named in May 1800 as Republican nominee for president, with Aaron Burr of New York for vice president. John Adams received the Federalist nomination for reelection, with Charles Cotesworth Pinckney of South Carolina as running mate. Many Federalists, including Alexander Hamilton, opposed Adams for making peace with France and for other political reasons. When the electoral votes were tallied, Jefferson and Burr each received 73 votes, Adams had 65, Pinckney 64, and John Jay 1. In lining up votes in the electoral college, the Republicans had failed to take account of the constitutional election procedures that lacked provision for party slates. The drafters of the Constitution had not predicted the development of political parties, so they directed that each elector cast two votes, with the candidate receiving the highest number elected

MAP 8.1   THE ELECTION OF 1800

Legend:
- Adams and other Federalists
- Jefferson and other Democratic-Republicans
- No returns, unsettled, etc.

against the Republicans through the Alien and Sedition acts. Instead, the backlash of concern about civil liberties swelled the opposition, as did suppression of John Fries's rebellion.

As the 1800 election approached, many Federalists expected to take advantage of the unresolved difficulties with France by continuing to paint the Jeffersonian Republicans as pro-French, hence un-American. Nevertheless, to the distress of fellow Federalists, President John Adams moved to end hostilities. He nominated a three-man commission, including William Vans Murray (ambassador to the Netherlands), Chief Justice Oliver Ellsworth, and Governor William R. Davie of North Carolina, to make peace with France. The commission received instructions that proved im-

Aaron Burr, *by Gilbert Stuart. Burr refused initially to follow the script and accept the vice presidency when he tied with Jefferson in the election of 1800.*

president and the runner-up vice president. The electors had no way of designating which candidate they supported for president and which for vice president. The Federalists avoided the difficulty by having one elector vote for John Jay, thus giving Pinckney one less vote than Adams. But the Republicans in the electoral college all cast one vote for Jefferson and one for Burr, resulting in the tie.

If Burr had simply yielded to Jefferson in 1800, the problem would have been resolved without complication. But the New Yorker reached for the presidency, thereby earning the enmity of Jefferson and his party. The tie sent the election to the House of Representatives, which had been elected in 1798 with a Federalist majority. Each state delegation received one vote. Some of the Federalists hatched a plan to support Burr, thinking that they might be able to control him as president. Hamilton, who knew Aaron Burr well, opposed the plot vigorously. To colleagues, Hamilton wrote, "Burr loves nothing but himself; thinks of nothing but his own aggrandizement, and will be content with nothing, short of permanent power in his own hands." The former secretary of the treasury advised his party to make a deal with Jefferson to keep the system of public credit and the navy, retain Federalist appointees in office, and remain neutral in the war between Britain and France. The House of Representatives required thirty-six ballots over six days before the Federalist delegate from Delaware, James A. Bayard, shifted his position to break the tie.

Jefferson's "Revolution"

The third president assumed a conciliatory stance toward the Federalists as he took office. On March 4, 1801, Jefferson delivered his inaugural address to the new Congress, which the Republicans dominated in the House by 69 votes to 36, and in the Senate by an 18–13 majority. He gave the address almost in a whisper, for he was not a good public speaker. The speech reflected his Republican beliefs: emphasis on the power of state governments, freedom of religion and the press, majority rule but protection of minority rights, low government expenditures, and reduction of the federal debt. Jefferson upheld the Convention of 1800 with France implicitly by stating that he desired amity and trade with foreign nations and "entangling alliances with none." His most famous statement, "We are all republicans, we are all federalists," attempted to get beyond the partisan battles that had bedeviled his two predecessors. Jefferson's recapitulation of basic republican principles recalled how recently his generation had fought for these ideals. He later described his election as "the revolution of 1800" that "was as real a revolution in the principles of our government as that of 1776 was in its form; not effected indeed by the sword, as that, but by the rational and peaceable instrument of reform, the suffrage of the people." Despite bitter political enmity, American leaders had created a party system by which power could be contested in elections rather than through bloodshed. With the election of 1800, the Constitution passed a crucial test, with peaceful transfer of power from one party to its opponents.

The new president worked to put his principles into action, to create an agrarian republic in which the federal government kept its role to a minimum. The location in Washington, D.C., seemed the ideal setting for a weak government. In 1800, the town had

THOMAS JEFFERSON'S
FIRST INAUGURAL
ADDRESS,
MARCH 4, 1801

Jefferson wrote this inaugural address, the first given by a president in Washington, D.C., in the two weeks following the confirmation of his election by the House of Representatives. In this speech, the third president sought to heal wounds from the contentious 1800 election and set forth his philosophy of government.

FRIENDS AND FELLOW-CITIZENS   Called upon to undertake the duties of the first executive office of our country, I avail myself of the presence of that portion of my fellow citizens which is here assembled to express my grateful thanks for the favor with which they have been pleased to look toward me, to declare a sincere consciousness that the task is above my talents, and that I approach it with those anxious and awful presentiments which the greatness of the charge and the weakness of my powers so justly inspire. A rising nation, spread over a wide and fruitful land, traversing all the seas with the rich productions of their industry, engaged in commerce with nations who feel power and forget right, advancing rapidly to destinies beyond the reach of mortal eye—when I contemplate these transcendent objects, and see the honor, the happiness, and the hopes of this beloved country committed to the issue and the auspices of this day, I shrink from the contemplation, and humble myself before the magnitude of the undertaking. . . .

During the contest of opinion through which we have past the animation of discussions and of exertions has sometimes worn an aspect which might impose on strangers unused to think freely and to speak and to write what they think. But this being now decided by the voice of the nation, enounced according to the rules of the constitution, all will of course arrange themselves under the will of the law, and unite in common efforts for the common good. All too will bear in mind this sacred principle, that though the will of the majority is in all cases to prevail, that will, to be rightful, must be reasonable; that the minority possess their equal rights, which equal laws must protect, and to violate would be oppression. Let us then, fellow citizens, unite with one heart and one mind, let us restore to social intercourse that harmony and affection without which liberty and even life itself are but dreary things. And let us reflect that, having banished from our land that religious intolerance under which mankind so long bled and suffered, we have yet gained little if we countenance a political intolerance as despotic, as wicked, and capable of as bitter and bloody persecutions. . . . We have called by different names brethren of the same principle. We are all republicans; we are all federalists. If there be any among us who wish to dissolve this Union or to change its republican form, let them stand undisturbed, as monuments of the safety with which error of opinion may be tolerated where reason is left free to combat it. I know, indeed, that some honest

fewer than 400 dwellings, which one government official described as mostly "small miserable huts." The Capitol was incomplete, with wings for the Senate and House but no center. What existed was poorly constructed: The acoustics were dreadful, the roof leaked,

and the heating "noxious." The president's house was not yet finished in 1814 when the British burned it. Construction materials littered the grounds during Jefferson's administration to the extent that, according to one guest, "in a dark night instead of finding your way men fear that a republican government cannot be strong, that this government is not strong enough. But would the honest patriot, in the full tide of successful experiment, abandon a government which has so far kept us free and firm on the theoretic and visionary fear that this government, the world's best hope, may, by possibility, want energy to preserve itself? I trust not. I believe this, on the contrary, the strongest government on earth. I believe it the only one where every man, at the call of the law, would fly to the standard of the law, and would meet invasions of the public order as his own personal concern. Sometimes it is said that man cannot be trusted with the government of himself. Can he, then, be trusted with the government of others? Or have we found angels in the form of kings to govern him? Let history answer this question. . . .

About to enter, fellow citizens, on the exercise of duties which comprehend everything dear and valuable to you, it is proper you should understand what I deem the essential principles of this government, and consequently those which ought to shape its administration. I will compress them in the narrowest compass they will bear, stating the general principle, but not all its limitations. Equal and exact justice to all men, of whatever state or persuasion, religious or political; peace, commerce, and honest friendship with all nations, entangling alliances with none; the support of the state governments in all their rights, as the most competent administrations for our domestic concerns and the surest bulwarks against anti-republican tendencies; the preservation of the general government in its whole constitutional vigor, as the sheet anchor of our peace at home and safety abroad; a jealous care of the right of election by the people, a mild and safe corrective of abuses which are lopped by the sword of revolution where peaceable remedies are unprovided; absolute acquiescence in the decisions of the majority, the vital principle of republics from which is no appeal but to force, the vital principle and immediate parent of despotism; a well disciplined militia, our best reliance in peace and for the first moments of war, till regulars may relieve them; the supremacy of the civil over the military authority; economy in the public expence, that labor may be lightly burthened; the honest payment of our debts and sacred preservation of the public faith; encouragement of agriculture, and of commerce as its handmaid; the diffusion of information and arraignment of all abuses at the bar of the public reason; freedom of religion; freedom of the press, and freedom of person under the protection of the habeas corpus, and trial by juries impartially selected. These principles form the bright constellation which has gone before us and guided our steps through an age of revolution and reformation. The wisdom of our sages and blood of our heroes have been devoted to their attainment. They should be the creed of our political faith, the text of civic instruction, the touchstone by which to try the services of those we trust; and should we wander from them in moments of error or of alarm, let us hasten to retrace our steps and to regain the road which alone leads to peace, liberty, and safety.

to the house, you may, perchance, fall into a pit, or stumble over a heap of rubbish." A foreign visitor thought "this parsimony . . . is a disgrace to the country." Cows grazed on what later became the Mall; hogs ran through the city's streets.

Washington, D.C., remained a village in part because the federal government was small, and Jefferson had no interest in seeing it grow. In 1802, federal personnel throughout the country numbered under 10,000, of whom 6,500 served in military posts. Of

The Capitol in Washington was incomplete at the time of Jefferson's election in 1800. With hogs running through the streets, the town seemed an appropriate seat for his agrarian republic.

the nonuniformed officials, fewer than 300 (including the president and Congress) worked in the capital. The president and Supreme Court each had one clerk, Congress employed thirteen, and the Attorney General none. The central government had relatively little to do, for state and local governments or voluntary associations took primary responsibility for keeping law and order, maintaining roads and bridges, supervising the militia, and providing welfare relief and schools.

Jefferson's lack of attention to building Washington, D.C., revealed his approach to the presidency. In contrast to Federalist efforts to reflect the grandeur of European courts and capitals, he adopted informality and frugality. On one occasion, when a senator visited the executive mansion, he found the tall, thin president in a dirty shirt and worn slippers. Jefferson dealt with members of Congress and foreign diplomats personally, inviting small groups for dinner and conversation. He avoided making speeches, sending written messages to Congress. With only one clerk, he handled many documents himself.

The change of political power from the Federalists to the Republicans raised questions about office-holding and political spoils. At the highest level of executive appointments, the cabinet, Jefferson assumed his right to appoint trusted supporters. He named James Madison of Virginia, his closest ally, as secretary of state, and Albert Gallatin of Pennsylvania as secretary

of the treasury. Both were intelligent and reliable. Gallatin was committed to the president's program to pay off the debt. Other members of the cabinet included Levi Lincoln of Massachusetts as attorney general, Henry Dearborn of Massachusetts as secretary of war, and Robert Smith of Maryland as secretary of the navy.

The question of whether or not to retain bureaucrats was more difficult. Jefferson supported the idea of a civil service in which public officers held their positions on the basis of merit; during the election crisis he suggested that he would allow officeholders to keep their jobs. When he learned that Washington and Adams had appointed only six Republicans to about 600 positions, however, the new president replaced about one-half of the Federalists with Republicans. Most infuriating were the "midnight appointments," as Jefferson called them—the appointments Adams made as a lame duck after he knew that the election was lost. In addition, in February 1801, the Federalist Congress had passed a new Judiciary Act creating additional judgeships and other offices, all of which Federalists received. Jefferson cancelled the appointments, calling upon the new Republican Congress to repeal the law.

Jefferson and Gallatin placed high priority in decreasing government expenditures, taxes, and the national debt. Gallatin opposed all spending by the federal government, including military, because he thought preparedness would incline the nation toward war when a crisis struck. With support of the Republican Congress, the administration cut the defense budget in half and eliminated several ambassadorships in Europe. They repealed all excise taxes, including that on whiskey, relying primarily on import duties for income. Gallatin hoped to pay off the federal debt of $82 million in sixteen years, a goal that was probably impossible even without increased military spending during the War of 1812.

Jefferson's plan to reduce the navy and remain clear of international conflicts hit a snag when Yusuf Karamanli, the leader of Tripoli in North Africa, declared war on the United States. Like the rulers of Algiers, Tunis, and Morocco, Karamanli demanded payments from the United States to "protect" American merchant carriers from pirates. To end this extortion, in 1801 Jefferson sent naval vessels to blockade Tripoli and protect shipping. The United States experienced a major loss when the ship *Philadelphia* ran aground while pursuing pirates, but when a small force of U.S. Marines and Arab mercenaries seized Derna, the Tripolitans agreed to peace. The war had propelled military expenditures upward, however, and convinced Jefferson of the navy's value, thus hindering somewhat the administration's plans for reduced government spending.

The Judiciary

Although the Republicans had captured the presidency and Congress in 1800, the third branch of the federal government, the judiciary, remained firmly in the hands of the Federalists. Adams and the outgoing Congress had tried to solidify their party's power in the courts with the Judiciary Act of 1801, which amended the act of 1789. By appointing additional federal judges, the new law ended the onerous requirement for Supreme Court justices to ride from state to state holding circuit courts twice a year. The act also reduced the number of justices on the Court from six to five, thereby denying Jefferson the opportunity to make an appointment when a seat became vacant. The Republican Congress, in early 1802, repealed this law, reinstating the Judiciary Act of 1789, thus forcing some federal judges out of their jobs and the Supreme Court back to the circuit.

Chief Justice John Marshall, *painted by Ferret de Saint Memin at the time of Marshall's appointment in 1801. During his tenure to 1835, the Chief Justice established federal judicial authority, in particular the court's power to decide the constitutionality of laws.*

Jefferson's bitter relationship with the Supreme Court resulted in part from his antipathy toward Chief Justice John Marshall, his distant cousin, whom Adams had named to the bench in early 1801. Like Jefferson, Marshall was tall, informal in manner, and a native of Virginia. He was educated by tutors, and had joined the patriot forces in 1775, serving until 1781. He attributed his nationalism to that service, saying that he became "confirmed in the habit of considering America as my country, and congress as my government." Marshall began a successful law practice after the war, served as a Virginia assemblyman, supported ratification of the Federal Constitution, then became the leading Federalist in his state. In the legal environment of the new republic, many colleagues appreciated his originality in building cases on logic and natural law rather than depending upon English precedent. On the Supreme Court, too, Marshall followed his own lights, creating the legal basis on which the power of the Court rests. During his long, illustrious career, which lasted until 1835, Marshall solidified the authority of the judicial branch of the federal government.

Marshall's most important decision, *Marbury* v. *Madison* (1803), commenced in a suit by William Marbury, nominated by Adams as a justice of the peace but not commissioned by the Jefferson administration. Marbury sued under the Judiciary Act of 1789, which granted the Supreme Court the power to require Secretary of State Madison to hand over Marbury's commission. Given the partisanship involved, most observers expected Marshall and his Federalist court to direct Madison to comply. Instead, the Chief Justice said that he could not remedy Marbury's situation, though he wished to do so, because the Congress had erred in giving the Court such authority. Marshall declared the provision of the 1789 Judiciary Act unconstitutional, thus establishing the Supreme Court's power of judicial review. Though *Marbury* v. *Madison* was the only case in which Marshall's court struck down an act of Congress, the principle stood.

Jefferson decided that the federal judiciary, still dominated by Federalists and growing in power under his adversary John Marshall, had to be controlled. Because federal judges constitutionally held their seats for life, "during good behavior," the president suggested to congressional Republicans that they start impeachment proceedings against objectionable Federalists. According to the Constitution, officers of the United States should be removed by "Impeachment for, and Conviction of, Treason, Bribery, or other high Crimes and Misdemeanors." The House of Representatives had the duty to impeach, while the Senate's function was to sit in judgment, with a two-thirds vote necessary for conviction. The Republicans impeached John Pickering, an official of the federal district court of New Hampshire, who was an alcoholic and insane, but who had not to anyone's knowledge committed any high crimes. The Senate found him guilty anyway and removed him from his position. Next, in January 1805, the House of Representatives impeached Samuel Chase of Maryland, an associate justice of the Supreme Court and extreme Federalist who castigated Jefferson's administration. But the prosecution failed to convince two-thirds of the Senate that Chase should be expelled from office for misconduct and other charges. Some moderate Republicans refused to adopt Jefferson's strategy to eject troublesome opponents. Thus ended Congress's attempt to remove Federalists from the bench by impeachment. John Marshall probably would have been the next target had the action against Chase succeeded.

Domestic Politics

Jefferson and the Republicans gained in popularity as they steered a course more moderate than the "revolution" of 1800 had promised. The president had reduced taxes and attempted to limit the judiciary, but did not dismantle the Federalist edifice of national power, including the military and the national bank. He mixed republican theory, based upon a nation of small farmers, with practical politics aiding commerce. His policies, combined with booming exports, steadily increased Republican support, as many Federalist voters switched parties. In the election of 1802, the Republicans won 102 seats to the Federalists' 39 in the House of Representatives; the Republican margin in the Senate was 25 to 9.

Looking forward to the next presidential election, Congress acted promptly to avoid the deadlock that had occurred in 1800. The Republicans wanted a formal way (not just an agreement among the electors) to keep the Federalists from conspiring once again to elevate the Republican candidate for vice president to the presidency. The Twelfth Amendment to the Constitution, which required the electors to draw up distinct lists for president and vice president, was ratified by September 1804.

The election of 1804 demonstrated the demise of the Federalists as a national party. They retained power in New England, but Republicans dominated politics elsewhere. Some arch-Federalists, realizing that the nation had moved beyond their control after the Louisiana Purchase (see the next section), briefly plotted to separate the northeastern states from the Union. Jefferson defeated the Federalist presidential candidate, Charles Cotesworth Pinckney, by 162 electoral votes to 14.

Jefferson had replaced Aaron Burr as his running mate with George Clinton, also of New York, thus keeping the ticket balanced geographically. For his part, Burr ran for governor of New York against the Republican candidate, Morgan Lewis. Despite support from Burrite Republicans and some Federalists, the outgoing vice president lost by a landslide. Alexander Hamilton played a decisive role in the defeat by publicly denouncing his longtime enemy. Burr challenged Hamilton to a duel. When the two faced each other at Weehawken, New Jersey, in July 1804, Burr shot Hamilton to death. In doing so, the vice president ended his own political career as well as the life of one of the architects of the American nation-state.

THE LOUISIANA PURCHASE

Jefferson had boosted his popularity prior to the 1804 election with the Louisiana Purchase, which marked the greatest success of his presidency. In pursuing the deal with France, he deviated from one of his beliefs—in limited power of the central government—to obtain land for his agrarian republic. Long interested in the west, he scored a diplomatic coup that doubled the size of the United States and reduced Spain's dominance west of the Mississippi River.

The Bargain with Napoleon

The chain of events leading to the Louisiana Purchase began in 1800, when France signed a secret treaty with Spain for lands in western North America. France would get back the territory it had ceded to Spain in 1763. When Jefferson and Madison heard in 1801 of the impending transfer, they sent the new U.S. ambassador to France, Robert R. Livingston, with instructions to prevent the exchange or at least obtain West Florida. The Americans wanted to prevent France from controlling the Mississippi Valley, for they feared that Napoleon's government would be a greater foe in the west than Spain had been. The dilapidated Spanish empire caused trouble enough. In October 1802, before the French took over the province, the Spanish suspended once again the right of Americans to deposit goods for export at New Orleans. The Americans thought, incorrectly, that Napoleon was behind the ban. Many wanted to take New Orleans by force. Jefferson wrote to Livingston, "The day that France takes possession of N. Orleans . . . we must marry ourselves to the British fleet and nation." Jefferson pushed for negotiations, however, not war.

In response to Livingston's overtures, Napoleon decided to sell the entire Louisiana Territory to the United States. The French leader's zeal to construct an American empire had cooled with the loss of his army in St. Domingue; Louisiana would be too difficult to defend against a hostile United States. And Napoleon needed money, as he was at war with Great Britain once again. In documents dated April 30, 1803, the United States agreed to pay France $15 million, to recognize the rights of the French and Native Americans living in the territory, and to recognize the French residents as American citizens. Spain was furious because

Napoleon had promised not to sell the region to the British or the Americans. Jefferson ignored the Spanish objections, but worried, as a strict constructionist, that the Louisiana Purchase was unconstitutional because the federal government had no specific power to acquire territory. He put aside these concerns, confident that it was right to avoid war and add vast lands for expansion of the American republic. "By enlarging the empire of liberty," the president argued, the nation could maintain its agrarian foundations, thus avoid descent into vice, luxury, and decay. A successful republic was dependent upon broad property holding, for virtuous, independent, middling farmers made ideal citizens. The Louisiana Purchase, Jefferson believed, would extend the life of the republic by providing space for generations of ordinary planters. While some Federalists disagreed, most Americans celebrated the end of friction over the Mississippi River and New Orleans. Western farmers could get their products to market; eastern merchants prospered from the trade.

Disputes with Spain

When U.S. officials gained formal possession of Louisiana in December 1803, the Spanish had only recently transferred control to the French. The ceremonies took place in New Orleans, a city of 8,000 that had been reconstructed in Spanish style since several great fires a decade earlier. With a cathedral, theater, impressive city hall, and mansions, New Orleans served as the cultural and economic center of the lower Mississippi Valley. In population, it was larger than other towns of the Spanish borderlands, including St. Augustine and San Antonio, which each had 1,500 residents; Santa Fe, with 6,000; and Los Angeles, with 850. The entire white population of the Louisiana Territory was approximately 50,000, including French, Spanish, Germans, English, and Americans.

Beyond Spain's objection to the U.S. purchase of Louisiana, the two nations also disputed the territory's boundaries, because the treaties transferring ownership were vague. Thomas Jefferson pushed for the most generous interpretation for the United States. He demanded West Florida, with an eastern boundary at the Perdido River, the present boundary between Alabama and the Florida panhandle. The president also thought his new acquisition extended in the southwest to the Rio Grande, incorporating all of Texas and part of

Plan of New Orleans in 1801, just before the Louisiana Purchase.

New Mexico, and in the northwest to the Rocky Mountains. Spain, on the other hand, said the Louisiana Territory included only a constricted region along the west bank of the Mississippi from northern Missouri to the Gulf of Mexico.

In 1804, Jefferson sent troops to West Florida, hoping to convince Spain by threat of force to give up or sell the province. Americans already outnumbered Spanish residents in the territory, which later comprised parts of Mississippi, Alabama, and Louisiana. Jefferson also wanted East Florida. He decided not to attack, and instead attempted to purchase the Floridas over the next several years, but failed.

The Lewis and Clark Expedition

To strengthen U.S. claims to the west, Jefferson sponsored an exploratory mission to the Pacific Ocean. Several times since 1783, he had tried to organize expeditions for scientific knowledge and to promote American interests in the region. As president, he now had the authority and financial resources to support this major undertaking. By the early nineteenth century, however, others had surveyed parts of the territory. In 1792, an American sea captain Robert Gray explored the Columbia River, and George Vancouver, a British naval officer, sailed the northwest coast. A few years later, fur traders working for the Spanish government ascended the Missouri River to present-

day North Dakota, while British traders from Canada began moving west.

Even before buying Louisiana, the president had decided to send an expedition west; the purchase gave the project greater urgency. He appointed his private secretary, Meriwether Lewis, as captain of the enterprise. Lewis chose his friend William Clark, the brother of George Rogers Clark of Revolutionary fame, to be his partner. Meriwether Lewis and William Clark had served in the army together in the old Northwest, so both were familiar with frontier conditions. Jefferson selected Lewis for his scientific interests as well as his wilderness experience. The president wanted "a person who to courage, prudence, habits & health adapted to the woods, & some familiarity with the Indian character, joins a perfect knoledge of botany, natural history, mineralogy & astronomy."

Jefferson had a long list of goals for his explorers. They were to travel to the source of the Missouri River to find the elusive Northwest Passage, fill in huge blanks in geographic knowledge of the West, and bring back descriptions of unknown species of plants and animals. He also hoped they would make peaceful contact with Native Americans to expand commercial networks for fur traders. Lewis and Clark more than fulfilled their assignment, keeping daily journals of their experiences, including descriptions of Indian societies and culture, systematic weather records, and observations of flora and fauna, as well as

Page 26.

Captains Lewis & Clark holding a Council with the Indians

Meeting of the Lewis and Clark expedition with Native Americans on the Missouri River, 1804. Illustration from the journal of Sergeant Patrick Gass, a member of the expedition.

a detailed map of their journey. Their relations with the people of the Northwest were for the most part amicable.

Lewis and Clark received commissions as army officers to lead the Corps of Discovery of about forty men who departed from St. Louis in May 1804. During that summer and fall they traveled up the Missouri River, using poles and tow ropes against the current. They battled the hot sun, diarrhea, and mosquitoes; several men deserted and one died, the only member of the Corps to perish during the entire trip. The adventurers met with the leaders of Indian nations along the way, telling them that the United States had taken possession of the territory from the Spanish. They arrived in the Mandan and Hidatsa villages of what is now North Dakota, where they spent the winter of 1804–1805.

In April 1805, the Lewis and Clark expedition set out with their guide Sacagawea, a Shoshone woman, and her French husband and infant son. They proceeded up the Missouri River, made an arduous crossing of the Rockies, and reached the mouth of the Columbia River before winter. They had journeyed through lands known to Shoshones and Nez Perces, but not previously to Anglo-Americans. On the way back, the corps divided in two, with Clark leading

a party southeast along the Yellowstone River and Lewis taking a northern route through Montana. They joined forces once again in North Dakota, said farewell to Sacagawea and her family, then returned to St. Louis by September 1806. They had been away so long that many assumed they had been killed by the Spanish or Native Americans.

Spies and Infiltrators

Spanish officials in fact had tried to intercept Lewis and Clark, whom they correctly suspected of making allies for the United States among the western Indians. General James Wilkinson, commander of U.S. troops in the west, governor of the Louisiana Territory, and a double agent known to the Spanish as "Agent 13," had tipped off New Spain about the expedition. The governor of New Mexico sent out search parties but failed to find Lewis and Clark. They did stop the mission of Thomas Freeman and Peter Custis, who in 1806 set out from Louisiana to find the source of the Red River. Another Spanish party nearly intercepted Zebulon Pike, whom Wilkinson had dispatched to explore and spy in the region that is now Kansas, Colorado, and New Mexico. Pike became lost in the southern

THE JOURNALS
OF MERIWETHER LEWIS
AND WILLIAM CLARK
1805

The following entries from the journals of the two explorers demonstrate the challenges the Corps of Discovery faced in mid-winter 1805. In the first paragraph, Lewis describes the birth of a son to Sacagawea, the expedition's Shoshone interpreter and guide. Lewis and Clark used their diaries to record information about the Native Americans they met as well as the plants, animals, weather, and landscape along their route.

[Lewis]   *11th February Monday 1805.*
The party that were ordered last evening set out early this morning. the weather was fair and could wind N. W.   about five oclock this evening one of the wives of Charbono was delivered of a fine boy.   it is worthy of remark that this was the first child which this woman had boarn and as is common in such cases her labour was tedious and the pain violent; Mr. Jessome informed me that he had freequently administered a small portion of the rattle of the rattle-snake, which he assured me had never failed to produce the desired effect, that of hastening the birth of the child; having the rattle of a snake by me I gave it to him and he administered two rings of it to the woman broken in small pieces with the fingers and added to a small quantity of water. Whether this medicine was truly the cause or not I shall not undertake to determine, but I was informed that she had not taken it more than ten minutes before she brought forth   perhaps this remedy may be worthy of future experiments, but I must confess that I want faith as to it's efficacy. —

[Lewis]   12th February Tuesday 1805.
The morning was fair tho' could, thermometer at 14° below naught wind S. E.   ordered the Blacksmith to shoe the horses and some others to prepare some gears in order to send them down with three slays to join the hunting party and transport the meat which they may have pocured to this place—. . . .   I directed some meal brands given [to the horses] moisened with a little water but to my astonishment found that they would not eat it but prefered the bark of the cotton wood which forms the principall article of food usually given them by their Indian masters in the winter season; for this purpose they cause the trees to be felled by their women and the horses feed on the boughs and bark of their tender branches. . . .   The Indians are invariably severe riders, and frequently have occasion for many days together through the whole course of the day to employ their horses in pursuing the Buffaloe or transporting meat to their vilages during which time they are seldom suffered to tast food; at night the Horse returned to his stall where his food is what seems to me a scanty allowance of wood.   under these circumstances it would seem that their horses could not long exist or at least could not retain their flesh and strength, but the contrary is the fact, this valuable anamall under all those disadvantages is seldom seen meager or unfit for service. —   A little after dark

this evening Capt. Clark arrived with the hunting party— since they set out they have killed forty Deer, three buffaloe bulls, & sixteen Elk, most of them were so meager that they were unfit for uce, particularly the Buffaloes and male Elk— the wolves also which are here extreemly numerous heped themselves to a considerable proportion of the hunt— if an anamal is killed and lyes only one night exposed to the wolves it is almost invariably devoured by them.

[Clark]

I returned last night from a hunting party much fatigued, haveing walked 30 miles on the ice and through of wood land Points in which the Snow was nearly Knee Deep

The 1st day [*Feb. 4?*] I left the fort   proceeded on the ice to *new Mandan* Island, 22 miles & Camped   Killed nothing, & nothing to eat,

The 2d day   the morning verry Cold & Windey, I broke thro the ice and got my feet and legs wet, Sent out 4 hunters thro' a point to Kill a Deer & Cook it by the time the party Should get up, those hunters killed a Deer & 2 Buffalow Bulls   the Buffalow too Meagur to eate, we eate the Deer & proceeded on to an old Indian Lodge, Sent out the hunters & they brought in three lean Deer, which we made use of for food,— walking on uneaven *ice* has blistered the bottom of my feat, and walking is painfull to me—

3rd day   Cold morning the after party of the Day worm, Camped on a Sand point near the mouth of a Creek on the S W. Side we Call hunting Creek, I turned out with the hunters, I Killed 2 Deer the hunters killed an Elk, Buffalow Bull & 5 Deer.   all Meager

4th Day   hunted the two bottoms near the Camp   Killed 9 Elk, 18 Deer, brought to camp all the meat fit to eate & had the bones taken out.   every man ingaged either in hunting or Collecting & packing the meat to Camp

5th Day   Dispatched one of the party our Interpeter & 2 french men with the 3 horses loaded with the best of the meat to the fort 44 miles Distant, the remaining meat I had packed on the 2 Slays & drawn down to the next point about 3 miles below, at this place I had all the meat Collected which was killed yesterday & had escaped the wolves, Raven & Magpie, (which are verry noumerous about this Place) and put into a close pen made of logs to secure it from the wolves & birds & proceeded on to a large bottom nearly opposit the Chisscheter (heart) River, in this bottom we found but little game, Great No. of wolves, on the hills Saw Several parsels of Buffalow.— Camped. I killed a Buck

6th Day   The Buffalow Seen last night provd to be Bulls.   lean & unfit for to make uce of as food, the Distance from Camp being nearly 60 miles, and the packing of meat that distance attended with much difficulty deturmined me to return and hunt the points above, we Set out on our return and halted at an old Indian lodge 40 miles below Fort Mandan   Killed 3 Elk & 2 Deer—. . . .

I saw Several old Villages near the Chisscheta River   on enquirey found they were Mandan Villages destroyed by the Sous & Small Pox. . . .

MAP 8.2 | WESTERN EXPLORATION, 1803–1807

Rockies, was rescued by Spanish soldiers, arrested, then released.

Both the United States and Spain knew they were playing for high stakes with these activities. The United States could use exploration of the west and alliances with Native Americans to help confirm their claims to broad boundaries of the Louisiana Territory.

The Spanish had by far superior documentation for Texas, New Mexico, Arizona, California, and western Colorado. But they also denied American rights to what is now western Louisiana. Jefferson sent General Wilkinson with troops to the undefined boundary between Louisiana and Texas; the Spanish dispatched Lt. Col. Simón de Herrera to defend eastern Texas. The two officers avoided fighting by establishing a neutral zone until diplomats could negotiate the border.

Still concerned about protecting their silver mines in Mexico, the Spanish took steps to increase settlement in Texas. They welcomed Indian exiles—Cherokees, Choctaws, and Alabamas—from lands overrun by American settlers east of the Mississippi, but the Hispanic population failed to grow significantly. New Spain officials specifically barred U.S. citizens from Texas, under threat of arrest and imprisonment. The Americans, one Spanish official feared, "are not and will not be anything but crows to pick out our eyes." Anglo-American traders continued to infiltrate Texas, however, to trap animals and bargain for horses with Comanches and other Indians.

The Burr Conspiracy

While Lewis and Clark were reconnoitering the far Northwest, Aaron Burr conceived a plot to create a separate nation in the west. His term as vice president completed, his bid for election as New York governor failed, and indicted for killing Hamilton, Burr contacted the double agent James Wilkinson, various unhappy politicians, and representatives of foreign governments. Burr suggested a variety of plans to those who would listen, including an invasion of New Spain, an attack on Washington, D.C., and secession of the west. Wilkinson cooperated with Burr at first, then turned informer when the conspiracy became public knowledge. Jefferson ordered Burr's arrest for treason, while applauding Wilkinson's "fidelity." Burr tried to escape to Europe, but was captured and taken to Richmond, Virginia, where he was tried in 1807.

The Burr conspiracy case, presided over by Chief Justice Marshall, involved three prosecutors and six defense lawyers, of whom two had served as U.S. attorney general. It might have been called the trial of the century. An unbiased jury could not be found; one juror said before the case was heard that Burr should be hanged. The principal actors in the trial were Marshall, who ignored his responsibility as an impartial judge to favor the defense, and Jefferson, who directed the prosecution from afar. Because Marshall upheld a definition of treason that required actual gathering of troops, not just conspiracy, the case against Burr collapsed. Jefferson blamed Marshall and considered trying to impeach him, but found insufficient congressional support.

MORE FOREIGN ENTANGLEMENTS

While the renewal of war in 1803 between Great Britain and France had impelled Napoleon to sell Louisiana, it also portended trouble for the United States. American merchants flourished, as they took advantage of neutrality and wartime demand for provisions in Europe and the West Indies. But their ships became vulnerable to the British navy and French privateers.

A Perilous Neutrality

Great Britain and France each wanted to prevent the United States from provisioning the other. In particular, the British intended to stop American traders from carrying foreign sugar, coffee, and other tropical products to Europe, even though the merchants conformed technically to British guidelines by taking the goods first to U.S. ports then re-exporting. In the *Essex* case of 1805, British courts stiffened their rules, stating that merely carrying Spanish and French goods to U.S. soil for re-export was insufficient, that only commodities originally meant for sale in the United States, then subsequently redirected to Europe, would be considered exempt from seizure. Few re-exported cargoes met the new guidelines. With the *Essex* rule, the Royal Navy stepped up its confiscations of American ships. Then, in 1806 and 1807, the British and French established blockades of each other's harbors, in combination eliminating neutral trade with Europe and the British Isles. The British Order in Council insisted that neutral ships sail to Britain first for inspection and licensing before trading in Europe. Napoleon's Berlin and Milan decrees banned trade with Britain and threatened neutrals who obeyed the British order with seizure.

After the British destroyed the French and Spanish navies in 1805 at Trafalgar, off the coast of Spain, the British restrictions and impressment of sailors were by far the most troublesome to Americans. Many Federalists and some Republicans cried for war. But Jefferson and the congressional majority looked for ways to avoid hostilities—despite the humiliating British attitude that the United States was still their colony. With a trimmed federal budget and small military, the

The British navy had practiced impressment, or forced recruitment, of American sailors since before the American Revolution. While claiming the men were British deserters, the navy often took native-born Americans, including free blacks.

Republicans were unprepared for war, so looked for alternatives. Congress passed a Non-Importation Act (1806) banning specified British goods, while the president opened negotiations with Great Britain to end impressment and recognize neutral trading rights. No agreement satisfactory to both sides could be reached. Then, in June 1807, the British ship *Leopard* fired upon the American frigate *Chesapeake* for refusing to submit to a search for British deserters. The *Chesapeake,* hit twenty-two times, managed to respond with only one shot. The *Leopard* boarded her, impressing four alleged deserters.

The Embargo of 1807

As Americans briefly clamored for war, Jefferson closed U.S. ports to the British navy and recalled ships from the Mediterranean, where they would have been trapped had war begun. The British refused to stop impressing American sailors, arguing that they only seized British deserters. They challenged Jefferson's port closure by firing on coastal towns in Maine and sailing in Chesapeake Bay. The president resisted a de-claration of war, but placed military posts and gunboats on alert. He chose economic warfare instead. Unfortunately, this policy destroyed the commercial boom that had meant high prices for farmers and employed thousands of sailors.

At the urging of President Jefferson and Secretary of State Madison, Congress passed the Embargo Act in December 1807. The law prohibited exportation to all other countries. The administration hoped in particular to defang the former parent country by withholding provisions to the British Isles and West Indies. A by-product of non-exportation would be a severe drop in imports of British manufactures, of which the United States purchased about one-third of total production. Jefferson and Madison saw the embargo as an act of coercion, one they hoped would be as effective as war. They argued that the boycott would hurt all warring parties, but Britain worst. During 1808, the administration faced difficulty enforcing the embargo because ships, especially from New England, left harbor pretending to sail to American coastal ports but headed for foreign destinations instead. The trade with the British West Indies continued illegally, with encouragement from the British. Federal agents also had little success in preventing smuggling into Canada. In January 1809, the government resorted to an extreme measure, Giles's Enforcement Act, which empowered the president to use the militia against smugglers. The act effectively ended trade.

Despite infractions, the embargo had considerable impact on the U.S. economy. Agricultural prices declined, leading to farm foreclosures. According to official records, exports declined by 80 percent in 1808, though smuggling certainly lessened the effect. The U.S. Treasury suffered a loss in customs revenue, its chief source of income. The embargo stimulated further technological development of the textile industry, particularly in weaving cotton cloth with power looms.

With stern enforcement under Giles's Act, New Englanders became more strident in their demands for termination of the embargo. Jefferson became convinced that civil war was possible, but refused to support repeal at a time when the embargo was starting to work. Republicans in Congress moved anyway, on March 1, 1809, replacing the embargo with a Non-Intercourse Act, which reopened trade with all countries except Great Britain and France. If either of the two belligerents changed its policy to favor neutral rights, the United States would resume commerce with that nation as well. While the new law banned trade with major markets, loopholes offered generous opportunities for smuggling.

Congress made this shift just days before the close of Jefferson's presidency. He was disappointed that the embargo did not have time to succeed; in fact, the British government, under pressure from manufacturers, had come close to easing its restrictions. Thus, Jefferson ended his administration without solving the nation's international troubles, which Americans increasingly defined as an effort by Britain to subjugate its former colonies. As he returned to Monticello, however, the president could reflect favorably upon the goals he had achieved—lower taxes and national debt, smaller government, open doors to immigrants, and peace. He also took pride in an accomplishment he had not foreseen in 1801, the purchase of the Louisiana Territory. Jefferson's administration was remarkable for what it did—and for what it did not do, considering his opposition to Hamiltonian policies in the 1790s. Under Jefferson, the Republicans left intact the national bank, the federal administrative structure, and armed forces. Considering the war-torn world in which the young nation found its way, however, the Republican commitment to minimal government left the United States militarily unprepared.

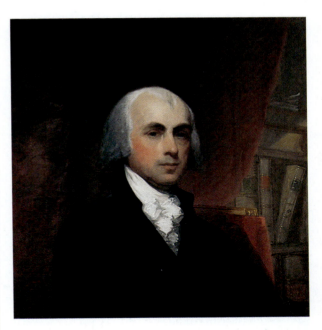

James Madison, *painted by Gilbert Stuart, a few years before he became the fourth U.S. president. Called the "Father of the Constitution," Madison also helped develop the two-party system through opposition to the Federalists in the 1790s.*

MADISON AND THE WAR OF 1812

When Britain continued to impress American sailors and seize ships, Jefferson's successor had two choices: accept humiliation as a third-rate power with near colonial status, or declare war on Great Britain. The British argued that they acted from necessity, as Napoleon conquered Europe. Americans, despite their aversion to the dictator of France, upheld their rights as neutrals to sell provisions to both sides. They considered British impressment of 6,000 seamen as a violation of national sovereignty and human rights. Between 1809 and 1812, these conflicts developed into war.

Election of 1808

Despite the embargo, Jefferson retained enough popularity to win a third term, had he chosen to run. When he withdrew, he designated James Madison, the secretary of state, as his successor. James Monroe, who had served as governor of Virginia and ambassador to Britain, challenged Jefferson's choice; but congressional Republicans, meeting in caucus, endorsed Madison. Dissenting Republicans, called the Quids, gave Monroe some support, but his candidacy died quickly. George Clinton accepted renomination for vice president. The Federalists put up Charles C. Pinckney and Rufus King, hoping that the effects of the embargo might reverse their party's decline.

The Federalists improved upon their performance in 1804 and 1806, gaining twenty-four seats in Congress, but still had much less than a majority. The electoral vote for president was 122 for Madison and 47 for Pinckney. While Americans suffered from the embargo, most were unprepared to desert the Republicans. In electing the new president, citizens ratified Jefferson's political philosophy and policies, which Madison had helped formulate. The third and fourth presidents had jointly founded and nurtured the Republican party; together they had adjusted their ideals to meet the practical needs of the expanding nation. The country could expect a continuation of Jeffersonian

Dolley Payne Madison, by Gilbert Stuart. From a Quaker family, she met and married James Madison in 1794 while he was serving as congressman in Philadelphia. As first lady she brought elegance to the president's mansion.

policies, though the retiring president withdrew entirely from decision making.

In another way, however, the new administration presented a real departure. Madison brought his elegant wife Dolley Payne Madison with him to the executive mansion, which was still unfinished when they arrived. They made a remarkable couple, as one observer noted:

> Mr Madison was a very small man in his person, with a very large head—his manners were peculiarly unassuming; and his conversation lively, often playful. . . . Mrs. Madison was tall, large and rather masculine in personal dimensions; her complexion was so fair and brilliant as to redeem this objection, in its perfectly feminine beauty. . . . There was a frankness and ease in her deportment, that won golden opinions from all, and she possessed an influence so decided with her little Man.

The first lady transformed the president's house into a proper executive mansion. She served as hostess to frequent teas and dinner parties, inviting Federalists and Republicans to socialize together.

Heading for War

After Madison's election, the European struggle continued to embroil the United States. While both Britain and France were hostile to free trade, the British dominated the seas, and as a consequence had substantial impact on U.S. commerce. Over the period to 1812, as Napoleon pushed across Europe, invaded Russia, and met defeat, he became inconsequential as a threat to the Americans. Indeed, his attempt to install his brother Joseph Bonaparte as king of Spain in 1808 undermined Spanish control in the New World. In West Florida, Anglo-Americans who had earlier pledged allegiance to Spain, in 1810 commandeered the Spanish fort at Baton Rouge, declared independence, and petitioned Madison for annexation by the United States. The president promptly claimed West Florida as part of the Louisiana Purchase. American troops occupied Baton Rouge but unsuccessfully attacked Mobile, which remained in Spanish hands. When Louisiana became a state in 1812, it included the western part of West Florida from Baton Rouge to the Pearl River.

In 1811, Madison appointed James Monroe, his former rival for the presidency, as secretary of state. Monroe, who had earlier negotiated a still-born treaty with the British, took office hoping to reach an accord, but soon decided that they wanted nothing less than to put the United States back into its colonial yoke. Great Britain adhered to its Order in Council that American exports go to England before shipment to Europe; the Royal Navy continued to impress American seamen. When Napoleon partially lifted his blockade in 1811, the United States resumed trade with France. Madison tried to convince the British to drop their restrictions as well, but instead they pounced on American ships headed for French ports.

Events in the west also intensified anger toward Britain, because Anglo-Americans believed that the British in Canada were stirring up Native American discontent. In fact, while some Indians traded with the British, many natives distrusted the whites of both Canada and the United States. An alliance between militant Indians and the British took time to evolve, as

Tecumseh in 1811 attempted to unite northern and southern Indians to defend their remaining lands east of the Mississippi River. Portrait from Benjamin Lossing's Pictorial Field Book of the War of 1812 *(1869).*

each group moved independently toward war with the Americans. As a result of the Louisiana Purchase, expanding white settlement, and sales by accommodationist Indian leaders of a large proportion of native lands still remaining east of the Mississippi, the nativist message of Tenskwatawa, the Shawnee Prophet, and his brother Tecumseh found widespread support. Their call to resist white encroachment resonated most clearly in what later became Illinois, Michigan, and Wisconsin, among Chippewas, Potawatomis, and Winnebagos, who could predict that their territory would soon be threatened. Establishment of American forts in the region told the tale.

The cession that spurred nativists into action was the Treaty of Fort Wayne (1809), which turned over 2.5 million acres to the United States. Tecumseh met with William Henry Harrison, governor of the Indiana Territory, to request that the treaty be annulled.

Failing that, the Indian leader went south to seek support from the Creeks, Cherokees, and Choctaws. He found allies among militant factions of Creeks and Seminoles, called the Red Sticks (from their war clubs). The Red Sticks opposed the accommodationists among their own people who sold land to the United States and adopted Anglo-American ways of life. Tecumseh's effort to create a pan-Indian movement throughout the trans-Appalachian west ultimately failed, however, because by 1811, large white populations in Tennessee, Kentucky, and Ohio formed a barrier between north and south. In the fighting of 1811 to 1815, Indian militants battled the United States on two fronts—in the Great Lakes and in the Mississippi Territory and West Florida.

In November 1811, William Henry Harrison decided to cut short Tecumseh's efforts for unity. The governor did not believe the Indian leader's assurance that whites were "unnecessarily alarmed at his measures—that they really meant nothing but peace—the United States had set him the example by forming a strict union amongst all the fires that compose their confederacy." Harrison led a force against Prophetstown (Tippecanoe), the village that Tenskwatawa had founded several years before. Before Harrison struck, the Prophet attacked the encamped soldiers at night, but suffered casualties and withdrew. Harrison also lost men, but burned the town and claimed victory in what became known as the Battle of Tippecanoe. The nativists subsequently rebuilt their settlement; Harrison's action had little effect except to drive them closer to the British.

The War of 1812 Begins

When news of the battle reached Washington, many officials interpreted it as evidence that a British-Indian alliance already existed. The outcome, they mistakenly believed, showed that the British were weak, incapable of sustaining their allies. "War Hawks" in Congress, including the newly elected Speaker of the House Henry Clay of Kentucky and Representative John C. Calhoun of South Carolina, advocated preparations for war. They represented a new generation who had not participated in the revolution and perceived Britain's actions as restoring colonial status. In Calhoun's words, his generation had to prove to "the World, that we have not only inherited that liberty

MAP 8.3 | THE WAR OF 1812

which our Fathers gave us, but also the will and power to maintain it." By April 1812, President Madison agreed. The Federalists, only one-fourth of Congress and primarily from New England, opposed conflict with Great Britain in part to obstruct administration policy, in part for commercial interests. The Republicans were divided. Opponents claimed that Madison intended to wage war for territorial expansion in Canada and Florida.

Congress authorized a 25,000-man regular army and borrowing $11 million. Still, the nation was ill-prepared when Madison issued his war message on June 1. Military funding would prove difficult because the charter of the national bank had been allowed to expire in 1811 due to politics and state banking interests, leaving state banks but no central agency as a source of loans. Lack of federal taxes beyond import duties, which fell sharply when the British blockaded the Atlantic coast, further limited the country's resources. The failure of New England leaders to provide their share of funds—indeed merchants' provisioning of the enemy and the desire of some New Englanders for a separate peace—severely hampered the war effort. The governors of Massachusetts and Connecticut refused to send their militia. Not everyone in New England opposed the war, however, for the majority of representatives from Vermont, New Hampshire, and Maine (still part of Massachusetts) voted in favor of the June 1812 declaration of war. Large numbers of the region's young men enlisted in the army. Former President Adams and his son, John Quincy Adams, also supported what many of their neighbors derisively called "Mr. Madison's War."

Despite military deficiencies and lack of national unity, the Madison administration pushed forward into battle, even after news arrived in August that the British government had lifted, though only for a year, its most odious restrictions on neutral trade. Madison offered an armistice if the British stopped impressment, but they refused. Canada, with only 5,000 regular soldiers, seemed the logical target. The redcoats there had little hope for reinforcements as long as Napoleon marched through Europe.

U.S. military leaders planned three advances, one from Lake Champlain to Montreal, a second at the Niagara River, and the third from Fort Detroit east through Upper Canada. With American victories, they hoped, Canada would fall, forcing Britain to recognize U.S. rights. The Americans moved first in the west, where they expected more support from local militia than from New England. Both the Canadians and the United States needed control of the Great Lakes to retain access to lands farther west. General William Hull received orders to lead about 2,000 troops against Fort Malden, opposite Detroit, under command of British General Isaac Brock and reinforced by Tecumseh and his men. Hull dawdled long enough to allow more British soldiers to arrive. He failed to take Fort Malden and surrendered Detroit. The British and Native Americans then took control of much of the region by capturing Fort Michilimackinac, to the north, and Fort Dearborn, at the present site of Chicago. Another blow came for the United States in October, when the army lost the Battle of Queenston, opposite Fort Niagara, after the New York militia refused to leave American soil to assist the regular troops. William Henry Harrison, commissioned a general, reinforced Fort Wayne against Indian attack. The Americans held Fort Harrison (Terre Haute, Indiana) and other points along a line from Sandusky, Ohio, to St. Louis, and undermined Tecumseh's war effort by destroying Indian towns and cornfields in Ohio, Indiana, and Illinois.

During this frustrating campaign against Canada, James Madison stood for reelection. Some critics claimed that he had started the conflict to win another term. Heading the Federalist ticket was DeWitt Clinton, a New York Republican and nephew of the vice president. Clinton tried to gain support from both political parties by advocating peace to the Federalists while telling the Republicans that Madison had failed to prosecute the war hard enough. The president won by an electoral tally of 128 to 89. Clinton's votes came from New York, New Jersey, part of Maryland, and all of New England except Vermont. Madison received his mandate from Pennsylvania, the south, and west; he obtained substantial Republican majorities in the House and Senate.

In contrast to the army's failures in 1812, the tiny U.S. fleet had surprising success against the mighty

Fort Harrison in 1812, near present-day Terre Haute, Indiana.

Royal Navy. U.S. naval officers, unlike the generals Madison placed in charge of the Canada campaign, proved to be capable leaders. The *Constitution* sank the British *Guerrière* in August; two months later the *United States*, captained by Stephen Decatur, took the *Macedonian*; in December the *Constitution* destroyed the *Java*. While British ships also won some rounds, the American defeats of an enemy considered master of the seas greatly bolstered public opinion.

Victories and Losses, 1813–1814

On land, however, 1813 began with another disaster for the Americans, as the British and Native Americans killed and captured nearly an entire force of 900 troops at Frenchtown, south of Detroit. The United States managed to hold Fort Meigs and Fort Stephenson in northern Ohio. But to destroy British control of Lake Erie and territory to the west, the army needed naval support. The United States began building ships at Presque Isle, Pennsylvania (now Erie), and on September 10, 1813, Oliver Hazard Perry defeated the British squadron at Put-in-Bay, establishing American dominance of the lake. This naval victory cleared the way for General Harrison to attack Fort Malden, from which the British and Indians hastily retreated toward Niagara. The Americans caught up with them at Moraviantown on October 5, winning a decisive victory known as the Battle of the Thames.

Battle of Lake Erie, *painted by an unknown artist, c. 1820, commemorates the victory of Oliver Hazard Perry against the British at Put-in-Bay. The painting shows Perry moving to another vessel when his flagship became disabled.*

Tecumseh died on the battlefield; his brother Tenskwatawa continued to fight alongside the British during the rest of the war, but with little success. To the east, the U.S. Army had burned York (Toronto), the capital of Upper Canada. But the Americans met defeat in an offensive against Montreal and lost Fort Niagara.

In the Mississippi Territory, the nativist Red Sticks waged civil war against Creek leaders who accommodated Anglo-American demands for land. The fratricidal conflict became a war against the United States in July 1813 when 180 American militia struck a much smaller group of Red Sticks. A month later, the nativists killed about 250 settlers who had taken cover in a stockade called Fort Mims. The Red Sticks, with 4,000 warriors but lacking adequate arms, faced overwhelming odds against the combined forces of U.S. troops, accommodationist Creeks, and Cherokee allies. Three armies entered Red Stick territory, destroying homes and dispersing families. The turning point came in March 1814, when General Andrew Jackson, with 3,000 militia and Indian allies, defeated 1,000 Red Sticks in the Battle of Horseshoe Bend, killing 800. The surviving militants escaped to Florida, where they joined nativist Seminoles and continued to fight.

Despite the fact that accommodationist Creeks assisted Jackson's troops in the battle, the United States subsequently forced them to cede one-third of their lands.

In the summer of 1814, the British turned greater attention to the war in America, having defeated Napoleon in April. They sent 10,000 experienced redcoats to Canada, promising trouble for the defense of New York, until the American naval victory on Lake Champlain in September cut short the British invasion. Britain also sent forces to Chesapeake Bay, where in August they attacked the nearly defenseless Washington, D.C. Redcoats burned the Capitol and the president's mansion, shortly after the Madisons fled. The president and Mrs. Madison saved official documents, their own valuable possessions, and the Gilbert Stuart portrait of George Washington. The enemy promptly left the capital, and the U.S. government returned.

The British then assaulted Baltimore, which had time to prepare. Despite heavy bombardment of Fort McHenry by the Royal Navy, the redcoats failed to take the city. James Monroe, who was by then secretary of war as well as secretary of state, took credit for Baltimore's stand. Francis Scott Key memorialized the scene of flaming rockets and exploding bombs in his poem, "The Star Spangled Banner," which was later set to the tune of a popular English song and, in the early twentieth century, became the national anthem. The British sailed south to the Gulf Coast, intending to block off the Mississippi River. In late 1814, Andrew Jackson captured Pensacola, Florida, then organized the defense of New Orleans.

The Hartford Convention

Over the course of the war, sentiment had grown in New England for secession, as the British tightened their blockade of the region and occupied the Maine coast. The Massachusetts governor secretly contacted the British about a separate peace. In late 1814, a group of Federalists organized the Hartford Convention to find a more moderate course to remedy their loss of power within the Union. The convention issued a report supporting the right of states to declare federal laws unconstitutional (similar to the Virginia and Kentucky Resolutions of 1798) and arguing that states should be responsible for their own defense. The Hartford delegates called for significant amendments to the Constitution: removal of the three-fifths clause

"The Fall of Washington or Maddy in full flight," an anonymous English cartoon, 1814. Two British sailors ridicule President Madison and Secretary of State Monroe as they escape the burning capital with state documents.

that counted slaves in apportioning delegates in the House of Representatives and electoral college; a two-thirds majority in Congress to declare war and admit new states; a one-term limit on the president and ban on residents from the same state succeeding one another in the office (obviously targeted at Virginia); and prohibition of naturalized citizens—who were largely Republican—from federal positions. These proposals, calculated to damage Republican power bases in the south and west and among new immigrants in the cities, fell on deaf ears when news of the peace treaty arrived from Europe.

The Treaty of Ghent

Peace came as both the British and the United States recognized that the end of the twenty-year struggle in Europe eliminated the rationale for war in America. The defeat of Napoleon removed Britain's need to regulate neutral trade and impress seamen. Both sides could also see that they had little hope of victory. Britain might continue its blockade and smother U.S. commerce, but to what purpose? Conquest of the former colonies, now expanded into the west, would require huge expenditures of manpower and funds. Victory at New Orleans would plug the Mississippi, but

in late 1814 success was still uncertain. News arrived, as the British considered terms for peace, that the Americans had repelled the offensives at Lake Champlain and Baltimore. While some Britons desired revenge, more wanted to resume trade.

Madison authorized John Quincy Adams, Albert Gallatin, Henry Clay, and two others, to meet the British peace delegation at Ghent, Belgium, in August 1814. After several months of stalemate, the negotiators agreed on Christmas Eve, 1814, to return to the status quo at the outbreak of war. The British dropped their demands for part of Maine and an independent Indian territory north of the Ohio River, while the Americans stopped insisting that the British renounce impressment, which had ceased.

~ CONCLUSION ~

With its simple provision to reinstate the *status quo ante bellum,* the Treaty of Ghent might appear to make the War of 1812 meaningless. The loss of lives and dollars, and disaffection of New England, all seem for nothing. Yet most Americans celebrated the peace, knowing that they had withstood Britain's attempt to treat them as colonials. True, the end of the European war had solved the problems of impressment and neutral trade. Still, a second generation of Americans had proven that they could survive a struggle with what was probably the world's most powerful nation. In addition, the United States had defeated Tecumseh's pan-Indian movement in the west, effectively ending Native American power east of the Mississippi.

Much had changed during the first decade and a half of the nineteenth century. The Federalists transformed themselves from the architects of the national government in the 1790s to advocates of narrow sectional interests in 1814. Thomas Jefferson and James Madison, the Republican authors of the Virginia and Kentucky Resolutions, which had upheld states' rights, moved in the opposite direction during their administrations. Without denying their commitment to limited government, a skeleton military, low taxes, and republican principles, they expanded "the empire of liberty" by purchasing Louisiana and forcing Native Americans from their lands. Jefferson and Madison used every means short of armed conflict to protect commerce, then went to war when all else failed. In purchasing Louisiana, Jefferson relaxed his philosophy of strict interpretation of the Constitution in hope that the additional territory would extend the life of his agrarian republic. Madison facilitated the growth of nationalism—despite New England's lapse—by exacting respect from Great Britain. With the Atlantic world at peace once again, residents from Maine to Louisiana concentrated on making money and building their communities, all with a greater sense that they belonged to an American nation.

RECOMMENDED READINGS

Brant, Irving. *James Madison.* 6 vols. (1941–61). Excellent, detailed biography of the fourth president.

Coles, Harry L. *The War of 1812* (1965). A readable, one-volume study.

Dowd, Gregory Evans. *A Spirited Resistance: The North American Indian Struggle for Unity, 1745–1815* (1992). Demonstrates the significance of religion in Native American resistance.

Horsman, Reginald. *The Causes of the War of 1812* (1961). A good discussion of the circumstances leading to war.

McCoy, Drew R. *The Elusive Republic: Political Economy in Jeffersonian America* (1980). Insightful exploration of Jeffersonian politics and thought.

Malone, Dumas. *Jefferson and His Time.* 6 vols. (1948–81). The benchmark biography of Thomas Jefferson.

Moulton, Gary E., ed. *The Journals of the Lewis and Clark Expedition.* 7 vols. (1983–91). Most comprehensive edition of manuscript maps and journals.

Nash, Gary B. *Forging Freedom: The Formation of Philadelphia's Black Community, 1720–1840* (1988). Insightful study of the challenges of freedom for one community of African Americans in the North.

Smelser, Marshall. *The Democratic Republic, 1801–1815* (1992). A useful, lively overview of the period.

Religion

Ahlstrom, Sydney E. *A Religious History of the American People* (1972).

Bloch, Ruth H. *Visionary Republic: Millennial Themes in American Thought, 1756–1800* (1985).

Butler, Jon. *Awash on a Sea of Faith: Christianizing the American People* (1990).

Hatch, Nathan O. *The Democratization of American Christianity* (1989).

Heyrman, Christine Leigh. *Southern Cross: The Beginnings of the Bible Belt* (1997).

Marini, Stephen A. *Radical Sects of Revolutionary New England* (1982).

Native Americans and the West

Ambrose, Stephen E. *Undaunted Courage: Meriwether Lewis, Thomas Jefferson, and the Opening of the American West* (1996).

Edmunds, R. David. *Tecumseh and the Quest for Indian Leadership* (1984).

McLoughlin, William G. *Cherokee Renascence in the New Republic* (1986).

Rohrbough, Malcolm J. *The Trans-Appalachian Frontier: People, Societies, and Institutions, 1775–1850* (1978).

Wallace, Anthony F. C. *The Death and Rebirth of the Seneca* (1969).

Weber, David J. *The Spanish Frontier in North America* (1992).

White, Richard. *The Middle Ground: Indians, Empires, and Republics in the Great Lakes Region, 1650–1815* (1991).

African Americans

Berlin, Ira, and Hoffman, Ronald, eds. *Slavery and Freedom in the Age of the American Revolution* (1983).

Egerton, Douglas R. *Gabriel's Rebellion: The Virginia Slave Conspiracies of 1800 and 1802* (1993).

Jordan, Winthrop D. *White over Black: American Attitudes Toward the Negro, 1550–1812* (1968).

Nash, Gary B., and Soderlund, Jean R. *Freedom by Degrees: Emancipation in Pennsylvania and Its Aftermath* (1991).

White, Shane. *Somewhat More Independent: The End of Slavery in New York City, 1770–1810* (1991).

Zilversmit, Arthur. *The First Emancipation: The Abolition of Slavery in the North* (1967).

Politics and Foreign Policy

Adams, Henry. *History of the United States During the Administrations of Thomas Jefferson and of James Madison.* Reprint, 2 vols. (1986).

Banner, James M., Jr. *To the Hartford Convention: The Federalists and the Origins of Party Politics in Massachusetts, 1789–1815* (1970).

Banning, Lance. *The Jeffersonian Persuasion: Evolution of a Party Ideology* (1978).

DeConde, Alexander. *This Affair of Louisiana* (1976).

Ellis, Joseph J. *American Sphinx: The Character of Thomas Jefferson* (1997).

Ellis, Richard E. *The Jeffersonian Crisis: Courts and Politics in the Young Republic* (1971).

Fischer, David Hackett. *The Revolution of American Conservatism: The Federalist Party in the Era of Jeffersonian Democracy* (1965).

Hickey, Donald R. *The War of 1812: A Forgotten Conflict* (1989).

Kerber, Linda K. *Federalists in Dissent: Imagery and Ideology in Jeffersonian America* (1970).

Ketcham, Ralph. *James Madison: A Biography* (1990).

Levy, Leonard W. *Jefferson and Civil Liberties: The Darker Side* (1989).

McDonald, Forrest. *The Presidency of Thomas Jefferson* (1976).

Onuf, Peter S., ed. *Jeffersonian Legacies* (1993).

Rutland, Robert Allen. *The Presidency of James Madison* (1990).

Stagg, J.C.A. *Mr. Madison's War: Politics, Diplomacy, and Warfare in the Early American Republic, 1783–1830* (1983).

Young, James Sterling. *The Washington Community, 1800–1828* (1966).

— 1815 TO 1855 —

The United States redefined itself during the forty years after 1815. The boundaries of the nation, the character of its population, the nature of its economy, and the religious beliefs of its people all took new shape. Some of the changes confirmed what the architects of the young nation had expected several decades before; other changes proved to be surprises and the bitterest of disappointments. The speed and scale of transformation astonished everyone.

IN 1815, THE YOUNG United States held only eighteen states, with Louisiana standing exposed at the western boundary, Florida in the hands of the Spanish, and an unsettled line between Canada and the United States. The western half of the continent remained only vaguely known to Anglo-Americans and seemed too far away to be of importance any time soon. Even within the country's sketchy borders, American Indians populated large and rich areas in both the north and the south.

Four decades later, the continental boundaries of the nation had expanded beyond recognition. Florida had come into the Union from Spain. War with Mexico had brought in vast territories from Texas to California. Negotiation with Great Britain had defined the northern boundary from Maine to Oregon. Military and economic pressure on the American Indian nations had driven them across the Mississippi River. A new state entered the Union about every two and a half years; by the end of the 1850s thirty-three

TOTAL POPULATION OF THE U.S.

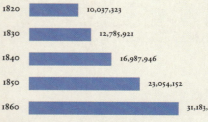

Year	Population
1820	10,037,323
1830	12,785,921
1840	16,987,946
1850	23,054,152
1860	31,183,582

states—including two on the Pacific coast—claimed a place in the nation.

The population exploded. The number of Americans grew from 8.4 million in 1815 to 31.4 million by the end of the 1850s. Nearly 4 million of those people were held in slavery, while 3 million people had crossed the Atlantic from Europe in a mixture of hope and desperation. People spread out across the expanse of the burgeoning country, establishing farms and towns far from the older cities of the east. About half the population of an average town moved every ten years. By the end of the period the United States claimed 5 million more people than England and the new country boasted eight cities of more than 150,000 inhabitants—more than any other country in the world.

Large changes altered the scale of life, tying people together as few could have imagined in 1815. Steamboats transformed water transportation in the 1810s, canals boomed in the 1820s, and railroads arrived in the 1830s. The United States claimed over 35,000 miles of railroad track by the end of the era. In the 1840s,

the first telegraph wires carried information from one city to another in a clatter of keys; by the late 1850s, telegraph wires stretched across the Atlantic Ocean. Novels sold tens of thousands of copies in a few months. Newspapers, confined to just a few major cities in 1815, became staples of American life in the 1830s and 1840s, read and published in hundreds of communities of every size. Daguerreotypes and colorful lithographs decorated homes that had been empty of pictures a generation earlier.

The United States became integrated ever more tightly into the international economy. The capacity of ships arriving in American ports doubled in the 1830s, doubled again in the 1840s, and then again in the 1850s. American vessels plied the Atlantic with cargoes of cotton and wheat for England and Europe. Clipper ships sailed around South America and into the Pacific, carrying prospectors and immigrants along with tea. The United States, anxious about European intervention in Latin America and the Caribbean, claimed the hemisphere as a place under its jurisdiction and protection.

Americans created lodges, clubs, and societies of every sort. Baptists, Methodists, and Presbyterians vied with one another for converts. Reform groups emerged to stamp out alcohol and war, to encourage education and humane treatment of the unfortunate, to improve diet and health, to bring the end of slavery. Women accounted for many members of these organizations, lending their energy and intelligence to activities beyond the home. Political parties mobilized nearly all adult white men, sweeping them up as Democrats, Whigs, Free Soilers, Know Nothings, and Republicans. Men swore allegiance to their party, expressing their passions and beliefs in slogans, songs, and parades. On election days, as many as eight out of ten eligible voters went to the polls, publicly proclaiming their support for their candidates.

The expansion of the United States was the expansion of the largest and most powerful slave society in the modern world. Slavery grew stronger with each passing decade, embracing an ever larger part of the continent to the south and west, holding more people within its bonds, accounting for a larger share of the nation's exports. As the years

TOTAL NUMBER OF SLAVES IN 1820

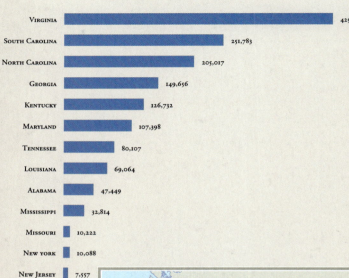

State	Number
VIRGINIA	425,153
SOUTH CAROLINA	251,783
NORTH CAROLINA	205,017
GEORGIA	149,656
KENTUCKY	126,732
MARYLAND	107,398
TENNESSEE	80,107
LOUISIANA	69,064
ALABAMA	47,449
MISSISSIPPI	32,814
MISSOURI	10,222
NEW YORK	10,088
NEW JERSEY	7,557
DELAWARE	4,509
ILLINOIS	917

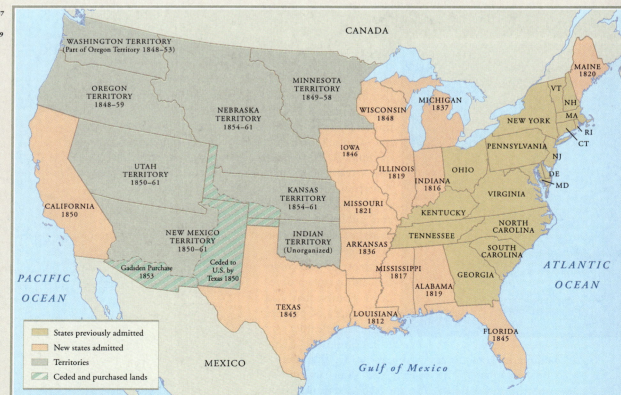

- States previously admitted
- New states admitted
- Territories
- Ceded and purchased lands

1840

1860

AGGR. NUMBER OF SLAVES IN 1860

VIRGINIA	490,865
GEORGIA	462,198
MISSISSIPPI	438,631
ALABAMA	435,060
SOUTH CAROLINA	402,406
LOUISIANA	331,726
NORTH CAROLINA	331,059
TENNESSEE	275,719
KENTUCKY	225,483
TEXAS	182,588
MISSOURI	114,931
ARKANSAS	111,115
MARYLAND	87,189
FLORIDA	61,745
DELAWARE	1,798
NEW JERSEY	18
NEBRASKA	15
KANSAS	2

But the Deacon would keep no overseer on his plantation, who neglected to perform this every morning. I have heard him say that he was no better pleased than when he could hear the overseer's loud complaining voice, long before daylight in the morning, and the sound of the driver's lash among the toiling slaves.

Oh my child my child.

passed, the discussions in the churches, the reform organizations, and the political parties increasingly turned to sectional conflict. Rivalry and distrust between the North and the South infected everything in the public life of the country.

The years between 1815 and 1855, then, did not witness a smooth passage through an "industrial revolution" or "growth of the common man" or "westward expansion." Rather, these years marked a passage filled with rapids and countercurrents and waterfalls. Panics and depressions, internal and external wars, massive migration and immigration, freedom and slavery—all came tumultuously.

	1815	1820	1825	1830	1835

POLITICS & DIPLOMACY

1815: Battle of New Orleans
1816: Monroe elected president; "Era of Good Feelings" begins
Clay calls for "American System"
Indiana admitted to the Union
1817: Mississippi admitted to the Union
1818: Jackson invades Florida
Illinois admitted to the Union
1819: Transcontinental (or Adams-Onís) treaty with Spain
Alabama admitted to the Union
1820: Missouri Compromise
Monroe elected president
Maine admitted to the Union
1821: Missouri admitted to the Union
1822: Denmark Vesey Rebellion, Charleston
1823: Monroe Doctrine announced

1824: Contested election of John Quincy Adams
1828: Tariff of Abominations
Calhoun's *Exposition*
Election of Jackson
1829: David Walker's *Appeal*
Mexico tries to abolish slavery in Texas
1830: Indian Removal Act
Antimasonic party holds first national party convention
1831: Nat Turner's rebellion
Garrison's *The Liberator*
Jackson reorganizes cabinet, Van Buren over Calhoun

1832: Bank War begins
Nullification Crisis
Virginia debates over slavery
Jackson reelected
1833: Force Bill against South Carolina
Compromise Tariff
Slavery abolished in British Empire
1834: Whig party organized
1835: Arkansas admitted to the Union
Revolution breaks out in Texas
Abolitionists' postal campaign
War against Seminoles and runaway slaves in Florida
1836: Congress imposes gag rule
Texas Republic established; Battle of the Alamo

SOCIAL & CULTURAL EVENTS

1816: American Colonization Society founded
American Bible Society founded
1819: Auburn penitentiary established
1824: Lafayette's visit
American Sunday School Union founded

1825: American Tract Society founded
1829: David Walker's *Appeal*
1830: *Book of Mormon*
Finney's revivals begin in Rochester
1831: Garrison's *The Liberator*
Mormons migrate from New York to Ohio
1833: Formation of American Anti-Slavery Society

1837: Grimké sisters lecture to mixed audiences
Horace Mann becomes first secretary of Massachusetts State Board of Education
Ralph Waldo Emerson, "The American Scholar"
1839: Daguerreotypes introduced to the United States

ECONOMICS & TECHNOLOGY

1815: *Enterprise* first steamboat from New Orleans to Pittsburgh
1816: Second Bank of the United States chartered
1817: Mississippi admitted to the Union
1818: Erie Canal begun
National Road completed
1819: *Dartmouth College Case* and *McCulloch* v. *Maryland*
Financial panic and depression

1824: *Gibbons* v. *Ogden*
1825: Completion of Erie Canal
1828: Tariff of Abominations
1831: John Bull begins railroad operation
1832: Bank War begins
1833: Compromise Tariff
1834: National Trades Union formed
Cyrus McCormick patents reaper

1837: Financial panic
Charles River Bridge v. *Warren Bridge* decision
1839: Depression worsens
Daguerreotypes introduced to the United States

1838: John Quincy Adams successfully defeats attempt to annex Texas
1840: Congress passes Independent Treasury Act
Harrison elected president
Frederick Douglass escapes from slavery
American Anti-Slavery Society splits
James G. Birney runs for president as candidate for Liberty party
1841: Harrison dies; John Tyler becomes president
Amistad case heard before the Supreme Court
1844: James K. Polk claims the United States's claim to "all Oregon"

1845: Texas and Florida admitted to the Union
1846: Mexican War begins; Stephen Kearny occupies Santa Fe; Zachary Taylor takes Monterey
Border between Canada and United States established at 49th parallel
Wilmot Proviso ignites sectional conflict
Bear Flag Republic in California proclaimed by John C. Frémont
1847: Taylor defeats Santa Anna at Buena Vista; Winfield Scott captures Vera Cruz and Mexico City
1848: Treaty of Guadalupe Hidalgo
Attempts to buy Cuba from Spain
Free Soil party runs Van Buren for president
Seneca Falls Convention
Zachary Taylor elected president

1849: California seeks admission to Union
1850: Nashville Convention attempts to unify South
Fugitive Slave Law
Taylor dies; Millard Fillmore becomes president
Compromise of 1850
1851: Maine adopts prohibition
Women's rights convention in Akron, Ohio
Indiana state constitution excludes free blacks
1852: Franklin Pierce elected president
1853: Gadsden Purchase
1854: Know-Nothings win unexpected victories
Whig party collapses
Republican party founded
Kansas-Nebraska Act
Ostend Manifesto encourages acquisition of Cuba

1840: Washingtonian temperance movement emerges
1841: Brook Farm founded
P.T. Barnum opens the American Museum
Amistad case heard before the Supreme Court
1842: Edgar Allan Poe, "The Murders in the Rue Morgue"
1844: Methodist Episcopal church divides over slavery
Edgar Allan Poe, "The Raven"

1846: Hiram Powers completes statue "The Greek Slave"
1847: Mormons reach Great Salt Lake Valley
1848: Seneca Falls Convention
Oneida Community established
Mormons settle in Great Basin

1850: Nathaniel Hawthorne, *The Scarlet Letter*
1851: Herman Melville, *Moby-Dick*
Maine adopts prohibition
Women's rights convention in Akron, Ohio
1852: Harriet Beecher Stowe, *Uncle Tom's Cabin*
1854: Henry David Thoreau, *Walden*

1840: Congress passes Independent Treasury Act
1841: California sees arrival of first wagon train
Oregon fever
1843: Oregon sees arrival of first wagon trains
1844: Baltimore-Washington telegraph line
Samuel F. B. Morse patents the telegraph

1848: Gold discovered in California
Regular steamship trips between Liverpool and New York City
1849: "Forty-Niners" race to California
Cotton prices invigorate South

1854: High-point of immigration
Railroad reaches Mississippi River

VALUE OF COTTON EXPORTS AS A PERCENTAGE OF ALL U.S. EXPORTS, 1800–1860
By 1840 cotton accounted for more than half of all U.S. exports.

7.1% — 1800
32.0% — 1820
51.6% — 1840
57.5% — 1860

THE BATTLE OF NEW ORLEANS

The surprising victory of the United States over Britain in 1815 catapulted Andrew Jackson to prominence and bolstered the confidence of the young republic.

Chapter 9

EXPLODED BOUNDARIES:
1815–1826

The military hardships, diplomatic entanglements, political quagmires, and sudden climax of the War of 1812 surprised everyone. Ever since its beginning, even the leaders of the United States had wondered whether a large and lightly governed republic could long endure. Miraculously, the new country did not lose the war. Indeed, upon the war's unexpected end the United States entered upon a period of economic growth and territorial expansion no one could have foreseen. White settlers, newly freed from concern about the British and their American Indian allies, pushed west in remarkable numbers, taking enslaved African Americans with them in the South. Throughout the country, steamboats, canals, and turnpikes tied the countryside to the cities and the cities to one another.

Such rapid growth did not come without a cost. An economic depression suddenly ground the economy to a halt, political crisis emerged out of this time of apparent peace, and slaves staged a revolt. Many Americans worried that their society was changing too fast, that the virtuous time of the Revolution had passed and a time of selfishness had taken its place. Only a resolute determination to redefine the family and to spread the word of God, many believed, would save America.

THE AFTERMATH OF WAR

The United States had little reason to celebrate as 1815 began. For more than two years, bickering grew along with defeats and stalemate. Washington lay in ruins, burned by the enemy. Rumor had it that delegates from the Hartford Convention would soon arrive in the capital threatening to remove New England from the Union unless Congress revised the Constitution. People lost faith in President James Madison and other leaders.

War's End

Throughout the summer and fall of 1814 American and British delegations in the Belgian city of Ghent labored to construct a peace. Britain had just won a long and costly war against France and was eager to bring the hostilities in North America to a close. The United States, for its part, sought to end the fighting and with it the taxation and social division that war bred. After months of deadlock, the two delegations agreed simply to end the war, restoring the previous borders

CHRONOLOGY

1815   Battle of New Orleans

Enterprise first steamboat from New Orleans to Pittsburgh

1816   Monroe elected president; "Era of Good Feelings" begins

Clay calls for "American System"

Second Bank of the United States chartered

Indiana admitted to the Union

American Colonization Society founded

American Bible Society founded

1817   Mississippi admitted to the Union

1818   Jackson invades Florida

Erie Canal begun

Illinois admitted to the Union

National Road completed

1819   Transcontinental (or Adams-Onís) Treaty with Spain

Dartmouth College Case and *McCulloch* v. *Maryland*

Financial panic and depression

Alabama admitted to the Union

Auburn penitentiary established

1820   Missouri Compromise

Monroe elected president

Maine admitted to the Union

1821   Missouri admitted to the Union

1822   Denmark Vesey Rebellion, Charleston

1823   Monroe Doctrine announced

1824   Contested election of John Quincy Adams

Lafayette's visit

Gibbons v. *Ogden*

American Sunday School Union founded

1825   Completion of Erie Canal

American Tract Society founded

---

between U.S. and British territories. Both sides, relieved to be rid of the war, quickly adopted the agreement.

Though the treaty was signed in December, bad weather in the Atlantic delayed until February the ship bringing news of the peace negotiations between the Americans and British. In the meantime, British forces, unaware of the decisions made thousands of miles away, prepared to move against the United States's Gulf Coast. A fleet of sixty ships and 14,000 men planned to attack Mobile, seize control of the coast and the rivers, then move against New Orleans.

Such a plan posed a serious threat to the United States. New Orleans, distant and disconnected from the cities of the east coast, lay vulnerable to invasion. Once the British established a foothold there, American leaders worried, troops could move up the Mississippi River. The United States would be surrounded and harassed by its bitter enemy. Moreover, a British invasion threatened to bring free and enslaved African

Americans, French and Spanish settlers, Native Americans, and even pirates into the conflict throughout the Gulf territories, igniting rebellions against white farmers and traders.

The commander in charge of the American forces, Andrew Jackson, was especially sensitive to the dangers settlers faced on the Gulf Coast. Jackson, a Tennessee lawyer, planter, and militia leader, had capped a tumultuous career by defeating and then enforcing harsh terms on Creek Indians in the early spring of 1814. Jackson pushed the Creeks into ceding 23 million acres of territory to the United States, including most of what was to become Alabama and a fifth of present-day Georgia. Jackson's soldiers shoved the Creeks into the less productive lands of northeastern Alabama, while reserving the fertile black belt for white farmers. Jackson, with the strong support of the governors of the Gulf territories, prepared to continue the war against other groups of Creeks who had fled to Spanish West Florida. After a victory over the British at Mobile, Jackson raced to New Orleans to fight yet more British troops. The American general got there first, in December of 1814. Six hundred free blacks volunteered to help defend the city and Jackson gratefully accepted their offer.

A series of attacks by the British damaged the American forces but did not take New Orleans. The British general in charge, Sir Edward Pakenham, unleashed a frontal assault on January 8, 1815. Two Congreve rockets, launched by the British to signal the beginning of the assault and to frighten their opponents, screamed into the air. Jackson's troops, dug in behind earthworks, fired directly into the charging British troops; wave after wave of the onslaught fell as American troops took turns firing and reloading. In less than an hour it was over: Pakenham and two of his generals lay dead, along with over 2,000 of their troops. The Americans suffered only thirteen dead and a few dozen wounded or missing. Nearly a month later, word of Jackson's remarkable success reached the nation's capital. "ALMOST INCREDIBLE VICTORY!!!," headlines trumpeted. Nine days later word of the Treaty of Ghent, ratified two weeks before the Battle of New Orleans, arrived in Washington.

The Era of Good Feelings

The United States, insecure about its standing in the world of nations, now boasted a new sense of integrity and identity. President Madison announced that the Constitution had proven itself able to "bear the trials of adverse as well as prosperous circumstances." The northern borders of the United States, fluid and in doubt throughout the nation's brief history, took on greater solidity. The Rush-Bagot Treaty of 1817 between the British and the United States calmed conflict on the Great Lakes, while the Convention of 1818 fixed the border with Canada at the 49th parallel.

The War of 1812 suggested to some that the federal government might play a constructive role in American society. Leading members of the Republican party, long known for their opposition to federal power, began to view the central government more favorably. Young Republicans such as Henry Clay of Kentucky and John C. Calhoun of South Carolina urged Congress and the president to encourage the growth of enterprise with the aid of the government, creating

Henry Clay of Kentucky articulated the American System, a plan to encourage national economic growth.

roads, canals, a strong navy, and a national bank. In their eyes, the war with Great Britain had shown the dangers of a sprawling American nation, its resources scattered, its defenses thin. The future of the country, Clay and Calhoun believed, lay in commerce and industry; the government should ally itself with the forces of trade. Although these nationalists called their vision the "American System," representatives from New England objected to projects that seemed so expensive and threatening to local power. Outgoing President James Madison, while unwilling to support all of Clay's and Calhoun's ambitious plans, did decide to support a national bank.

The man who succeeded Madison to the presidency, James Monroe—another in a long line of Virginia Republicans—faced a brief challenge within his party in 1816 but won the national election easily. Monroe was considered an honest man, less intellectually distinguished than Jefferson or Madison, but dependable. He and his wife set a new tone for the presidency, with greater emphasis on etiquette, style, and

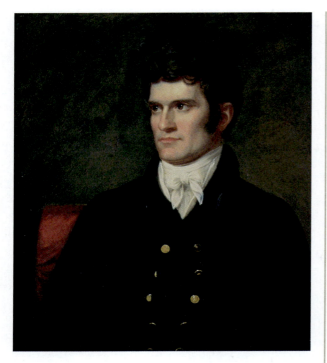

Later famous as a defender of states' rights, John C. Calhoun of South Carolina first became famous as a leading nationalist in Congress.

James Monroe of Virginia, president of the United States between 1817 and 1825, presided over the so-called "Era of Good Feelings" after the War of 1812.

entertaining, on embodying and celebrating the new national stature of the United States. The Monroes had the Executive Mansion painted a brilliant white to cover the smoke stains from its burning during the war with England; it became known as the "White House." After his election, Monroe toured the Northeast, including New England. A journalist there, impressed, talked of a budding "Era of Good Feelings," an era without party rancor—a strong contrast to the bitter conflict of earlier decades.

President Monroe relished the role of peacemaker and conciliator. Adopting John C. Calhoun's ideas for encouraging commerce and industry, Monroe urged Congress to use protective tariffs to protect American manufacturing, to build roads to tie the newly expanded markets and farms together, to connect the abundant rivers and lakes in the United States with a system of canals "the whole coast from its southern tip to its northern extremity in one continued inland navigation." Monroe hoped his plan would be supported by a broad and nonpartisan consensus; he downplayed party divisions and waited for agreement to develop.

The emerging Era of Good Feelings, Monroe assumed, would let the nation move forward without political strife or bitterness.

Native Peoples of the South

Relations with American Indians demanded considerable attention in the years following the peace with England. The war had redefined the relationship of the United States with the native peoples of the southeast. By this time, the American Indians had lived in contact with European culture for more than two centuries. They had long combined their ancient practices with newer ones, especially commercial hunting. Expeditions covered ever-expanding territory to kill enough animals to satisfy the white trading partners upon whose goods the American Indians increasingly depended. Trade networks stretched over thousands of miles. Indians' clothing reflected the combination of cultures, as they combined moccasins with woolen breeches, imported cloth turbans, and jewelry made of melted silver coins. The intermingling worked both ways, for considerable numbers of English and Scots traders lived among the Indians. Many adopted parts of Indian dress and language and married into native families. African Americans, too, often took refuge with the Creeks and Seminoles, so that by 1815 mixed ancestry was common among the people of the southeast.

The removal of the British troops dealt a strong blow to the hopes of the natives of the Gulf Coast. Alliances with the British—both actual and threatened—had been an effective way to hold back the white Americans. Now that that alliance disappeared, the United States quickly sought to exert firm control over the eastern half of the continent. Andrew Jackson

was placed in charge of negotiating with the Creek, Cherokee, Chickasaw, and Choctaw nations of Alabama, Florida, and Mississippi after the peace of 1815. He used heavy-handed treaties to force Indians from their former lands. Many of the natives resisted the removal, objecting that the treaties extracted by Jackson had been signed by men who had no authority to make such concessions. Although the various native peoples, identifying themselves by the location of their villages, their languages, and their traditional enemies, often fought with one another, whites insisted on lumping these diverse people into groups that could be more easily dealt with. Jackson and other officials left the Indians, lacking powerful allies and often in debt to white traders, little choice but to accept bribes and annual grants of money in return for their lands.

As soon as Jackson managed to secure lands from the Creeks, Cherokees, and Chickasaws, white settlers rushed into the territories, hungry for the fertile land

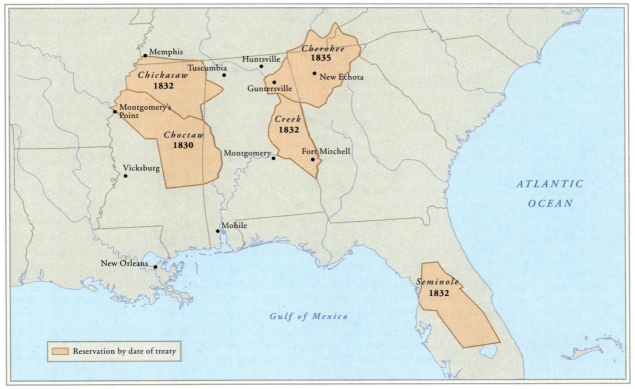

MAP 9.1 | SOUTHERN INDIAN NATIONS AFTER CESSIONS

American Society for Improving Indian Tribes, *The Blessings of Civilization* 1824

In this address to Congress, a prestigious religious group argues that the American Indians have suffered for generations at the hands of the United States. The only way to atone for these "national sins," the commissioners argue, is to educate the Indian people in the ways of white Americans. The document shows the good will that many white Americans held toward the Indians and the limitations of their understanding of the Indians' own desires.

In fulfillment of our commission, we beg leave, respectfully, to state to your honorable body, that a prominent object of the board we represent is, to extend the blessings of civilization and Christianity, in all their variety, to the Indian tribes within the limits of the United States. In carrying on this work of benevolence and charity, we are happy to acknowledge, with much gratitude, the aid received from the government, in making and supporting the several establishments made for accomplishing their purpose. The object of the government and of the Board is one, and, indeed, is common to the whole community. We trust, therefore, that the measure adopted by our board will not be deemed an improper interference with the concerns of the government, a thing at which our feelings would revolt; but, only as a proper act of co-operation of a portion of the citizens, in effecting a great and interesting *national* object.

The history of our intercourse with Indians, from the first settlement of this country, contains many facts honorable to the character of our ancestors, and of our nation— many, also, too many, which are blots on this character; and which, in reflecting on them, cannot fail to fill us with regret, and with concern, lest the Lord of nations, who holds in his hand the scales of equal and everlasting justice, should in his wrath say to us, "As ye have done unto these Indians, so will I requite you." We here allude to the neglect with which these aboriginal tribes have been treated in regard to their civil, moral, and religious improvement—to the manner in which we have, in many, if not most instances, come into possession of their lands, and of their peltry: also, to the provocations we have given, in so many instances, to those cruel, desolating, and exterminating wars, which have been successively waged against them; and to the corrupting vices, and fatal diseases, which have been introduced among them, by wicked and unprincipled white people. These acts can be viewed in no other light, than as national sins, aggravated by our knowledge, and their ignorance; our strength and skill in war, and their weakness— by our treacherous abuse of their unsuspicious simplicity, and, especially, by the light and privileges of Christianity, which we enjoy, and of which they are destitute. In these things we are, as a nation, verily guilty, and exposed to the judgments of that just Being, to whom it belongs to avenge the wrongs of the oppressed; under whose perfect government the guilty, who remain impenitent, can never escape just punishment. The only way, we humbly conceive, to avert these judgments, which now hang, with threatening aspect, over our country—to secure the forgiveness and favor of Him whom we have offended, and to elevate our national character, and render it exemplary in view of the world—is happily, that which has been already successfully commenced, and which the government of our nation, and Christians of nearly all denominations, are pursuing with one consent, and with their combined influence and energies. The American Board of Commissioners for Foreign Missions view these facts as highly encouraging; and it is their earnest desire that the God of nations would speed the course so auspiciously commenced, and give direction, and his blessing, to our joint efforts; add numbers and strength to those already engaged in this good work; convince, and reconcile to the object, those who are now opposed to it; and, ultimately, crown our labors with the desired success.

The work in which we are engaged, we are sensible, is not only noble, and god-like, and worthy to command the best energies of our nature, but it is also a great, arduous, and difficult work, requiring patience, forbearance, perseverance, and unremitted and long continued efforts. Here is scope enough to employ the wisdom, the means, and the power of the nation; and the object is of sufficient magnitude and interest, to command the employment of them all.

We are aware of the great and only objection, deserving notice, that is made to our project, and which has been made by some men of distinction and influence in our country, whose opinion on other subjects is entitled to respect; and this is, that "it is *impracticable;* that Indians, like some species of birds and beasts, their fellow inhabitants of the forest, are *untameable;* and that no means, which we can employ, will prepare them to enjoy with us the blessings of civilization." In answer to this objection, we appeal to facts; facts not distant from us—not of a doubtful nature; but which exist, and are fast multiplying among us, under our own eyes and observation—to facts which cannot be doubted, and in such number and variety, as furnish indubitable evidence of the practicability of educating Indians in such manner, as to prepare them to enjoy all the blessings, and to fulfill all the duties, of civilized life. . . .

It being admitted, then, that the Indians within our jurisdiction *are* capable of receiving an education, which will prepare them to participate with us in all the blessings which we enjoy, these questions will naturally arise: Is it desirable that they should receive such an education? Are they willing to receive it? Have we the means of imparting it to them? These questions, your memorialists conceive, may, with confidence, be answered in the affirmative. It *is* desirable that our Indians should receive such an education as has been mentioned, we conceive, because the civilized is preferable to the savage state; because the Bible, and the religion therein revealed to us, with its ordinances, are blessings of infinite and everlasting value and which the Indians do not now enjoy. It is also desirable as an act of common humanity. The progress of the white population, in the territories which were lately the hunting grounds of the Indians, is rapid, and probably will continue and increase. Their game, on which they principally depend for subsistence, is diminishing, and is already gone from those tribes who remain among us. In the natural course of things, therefore, they will be compelled to obtain their support in the manner we do ours. They are, to a considerable extent, sensible of this already. But they cannot thus live, and obtain their support, till they receive the education for which we plead. There is no place on the earth to which they can migrate, and live in the savage and hunter state. The Indian tribes must, therefore, be *progressively civilized,* or *successively* perish.

SOURCE American Board of Commissioners for Foreign Missions, Memorial to the Senate and the House of Representatives, in American Society for Improving Indian Tribes, *First Annual Report,* 1824, pp. 66–68.

and the fortunes it could build. Such incursions occurred across millions of acres in North Carolina, Kentucky, and Tennessee as well as in Alabama, Mississippi, and Georgia; in each state, the Indians were pushed to the hilly and mountainous lands least desirable for farming. The U.S. government made it easy for white settlers to buy land and sold about a million acres a year throughout the next decade. Not surprisingly, tensions steadily mounted between the ancient residents of the land and those who now claimed it.

While tens of thousands of American Indians continued to live in the southeast, their position grew less tenable each year as white settlers moved onto their hunting lands. The Indians strove to adapt to white ways while maintaining their identity; the Cherokees, in particular, won praise for their "civilized" customs. One Cherokee, Sequoyah, devised an alphabet in his people's language in 1821. The wealthiest Cherokees purchased African American slaves and built substantial cotton plantations. No matter what accommodations they made, the American Indians suffered repeated conflicts with whites who considered themselves the rightful owners of the land.

The Spanish in Florida

Like the American Indians, the Spanish who remained in Florida after 1815 had become vulnerable. Without the assistance of the British, they found it nearly impossible to resist American incursions into their territory. White Americans, for their part, felt they had a right, even an obligation, to drive the Spanish from the mainland, in part because Protestants had long distrusted the Catholic, monarchical Spanish. Many Americans thought it inevitable that Florida and Mexico would become part of the United States. To make relations even more volatile, sixty miles from the southern border of the United States stood the so-called "Negro Fort," occupied by runaway slaves and their Indian allies. In the spring of 1816 Jackson warned the Spanish commandant of Pensacola that the

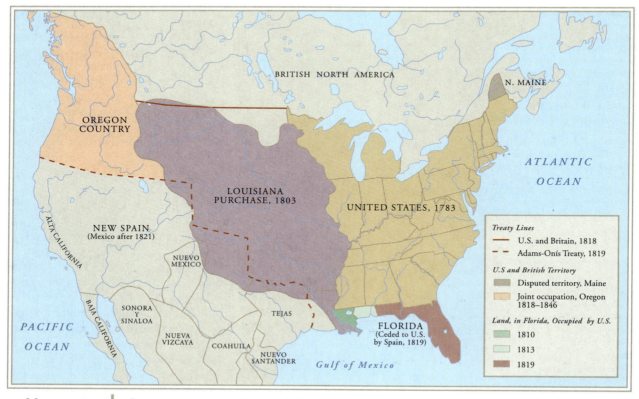

MAP 9.2　　|　　Redrawing the Nation's Boundaries

stronghold was "occupied by upwards of two hundred and fifty negros many of whom have been enticed away from the service of their master—citizens of the United States." The fugitives would "not be tolerated by our government," Jackson warned, "and if not put down by Spanish Authority will compel us in self Defence to destroy them." Spain was eager, in fact, to be rid of the fort as well, but did not have the military power to overthrow it. The Spanish feared, correctly, that Jackson would use the refuge as a pretext to invade Florida. Indeed, the Americans sent an expedition against the fort; a projectile hit a powder magazine, killing 270 of the men, women, and children inside.

In 1818, Jackson's forces also punished groups of Seminoles, who, with their Creek allies, had launched raids of white settlers in south Georgia and then fled into Florida. The American soldiers burned a Seminole town, only to see their foes retaliate by attacking a boat of soldiers, women, and children on the Apalachicola River, killing all but a few on board. Though his authorization from Washington was doubtful, Jackson proceeded to invade Spanish territory, execute a Creek prophet and two British men he accused of abetting the Indian cause, and overrun the weak Spanish presence in the most important outposts. Some in Congress wanted to punish Jackson for what they considered his unauthorized attack. Jackson rushed to Washington to defend himself and his honor. Many white Americans thronged the cities where Jackson appeared along the way, celebrating him as a decisive hero rather than castigating him for being the military despot Henry Clay claimed. The congressional hearings on Jackson's behavior in the war had little effect except to make Jackson suspicious of the men in power in Washington.

Meanwhile, American and Spanish officials negotiated. The U.S. delegation was led by the brilliant and tenacious John Quincy Adams, son of the former president. With Jackson's military victories giving force to his words, Adams held out until the Spanish, in return for 5 million dollars in compensation of private claims, ceded to the United States all territories east of the Mississippi River. In this, the Adams-Onís Treaty of 1819, the Spanish kept the vast territory from Texas to present-day California, while the United States claimed a northern border that ran unbroken to Oregon and the Pacific Ocean. Adams called his handiwork the Transcontinental Treaty, for it stretched the borders of the United States from the Atlantic to the Pacific.

THE TIDES OF TRADE

The end of the Napoleonic Wars in 1815 unleashed the economies of Europe and the countries that dealt with them, including the United States. American prosperity grew as the population boomed, as people moved across the expanse of the continent, and as transportation leaped forward. Slavery expanded along with free labor, farms along with factories, the East along with the South and the West. People made their livings in new ways and participated in an economy of ever-expanding scope.

Banks, Corporations, and Law

No country needed credit more than the United States. Because far too little cash spread across the vast and growing landscape, much business within the country rested on nothing more than trust and promises. Credit relations became tangled and fragile; the fall of one borrower could bring down a chain of lenders. Throughout the years before and during the War of 1812 states chartered banks to help alleviate the problems caused by a shortage of cash. More than 200 such banks had been founded by 1815 and nearly 400 by 1818, issuing notes that served as currency in cash-starved areas. Thomas Jefferson worried that "our citizens are clamoring for more banks, more banks."

Many influential men, including the recently elected President Monroe, supported a new national bank to stabilize the economy and distribute scarce money more uniformly. Advocates of the bank argued that the notes of state banks varied far too much in soundness and value, making the economic system dangerously unstable. The expanding country's economic system needed a central institution to coordinate the flow of money. Accordingly, in 1816 Congress chartered the Second Bank of the United States. Based in Philadelphia, it was authorized to establish branches wherever it wished. The new national bank was an amalgam of public and private enterprise: the federal government deposited its funds in the bank and appointed a fifth of the directors, but the bank ran as a private business. For the privilege of being the only such institution authorized to operate on a national basis, the bank handled, without fees, the funds of the federal treasury. The bank pumped large amounts of paper currency into the system in an

The Second Bank of the United States announced its solidity and strength with its austere classical architecture.

attempt to feed the voracious hunger of the postwar economy, especially in the new states of the West.

The local, state, and federal courts of the United States encouraged the growth of business in the years after the peace of 1815. Courts increasingly favored market forces over custom and stability in property relations, shifting the advantage from farmers and landowners to developers. Those who wanted to dam rivers for factories or build roads enjoyed increasing precedence over those threatened by floods, fires, or disruption caused by development. The courts assumed that the public good from the growth of business outweighed the stability favored by older notions of justice. Because many people bitterly protested this shift in emphasis, state legislatures sometimes sought to curb the power of business interests.

The Supreme Court under Chief Justice John Marshall issued a number of important decisions following

In the absence of a paper currency, notes such as this helped fuel the expansive growth of the American economy in these decades.

the War of 1812 that weakened the power of the states to curb economic development. By establishing a more uniform legal environment that transcended the restrictions of particular states, the court hoped to unleash the beneficial effects of business growth. One decision of 1819 made bankruptcy laws more uniform across the country; another, *Dartmouth College* v. *Woodward,* sheltered corporations from legislative interference; yet another 1819 ruling, *McCulloch* v. *Maryland,* established the constitutionality of the Bank of the United States and protected it from state taxation. A fourth case in this period, *Gibbons* v. *Ogden* (1824), limited the rights of states to interfere in commerce with either special favors and monopolies or restrictive laws. "In all commercial regulations," Marshall pronounced, "we are one and the same people." In this new legal environment, increasingly emulated by state courts and legislators, business flourished in the years immediately following the end of war.

Roads and Canals

Americans threw themselves into a frenzy of road and turnpike building after 1815. New York alone chartered 300 companies that began construction of 5,000 miles of gravel roads. Investors, states, and even the federal government built thousands of miles of private roads — turnpikes — charging tolls to offset the roads'

notoriously high maintenance costs. Some road builders laid logs side-by-side to provide a durable surface, though these so-called "corduroy roads" took a heavy toll on horse, wagon, and rider and wore out quickly besides. In 1818 the U.S. government opened the "National Road," connecting the Potomac River at Cumberland, Maryland, with Wheeling, [West] Virginia, on the Ohio River. The road was the best that technology could provide at the time, with excellent bridges and a relatively smooth stone surface. The road attracted so much business, however, that traffic jams slowed movement to a crawl and the road quickly fell into poor condition. Even on good roads, it often cost more to move bulky items such as corn or wheat than the products could bring at market.

Businesses and state governments began to plan dependable canals with controllable locks and a steady flow of water. Because Baltimore and Philadelphia enjoyed close connections with the West, benefiting from heavily used turnpikes, New York City merchants worried that their dominant position in the East would be lost if they did not establish fast and inexpensive connections as well. Fortunately for New York, a flat passage broke through the Appalachian Mountains within the state's borders. New Yorkers believed that a canal through this area, connecting the Hudson River to Lake Erie, would far surpass any other kind of transportation. Such a canal would be ten times longer than any other canal then in

Corduroy roads, while offering some relief from mud and stones, proved poor competition with newer kinds of transportation such as canals and steamboats.

OHIO BOARD OF CANAL COMMISSIONERS, *ANNUAL REPORT* 1828

The commissioners of Ohio struggle here with a key question of an era when new kinds of transportation were rapidly growing: what role should state and federal government play in economic development? Should the government actively sponsor development, stay out of the way while private businesses competed among themselves, or try to regulate and coordinate private efforts? Here, the Ohio commissioners argue that it is more democratic for the government to take on the responsibility.

An important question may present itself for the consideration of the [Ohio] General Assembly, as connected with the proposed improvements; whether the contemplated canals should be made under the authority, and at the expense of the state, or charters should be granted to private companies for that purpose? The commissioners are of opinion, that the work should be undertaken by the state; chartered companies, possessing exclusive privileges, have always been popular in monarchical governments, because their powers and advantages were so much carved out of the sovereign power for the benefit of subjects—so much in fact gained from the monarchy. The judicial tribunals, influenced doubtless by the popular feeling upon this subject soon found means to secure them to the grantees—gave them a character of *immortality;* changed granted privileges, from the sovereign, into a contract between equals, and placed them beyond the reach of his power, under the protection of that ingenious fiction. Our jurisprudence which borrows its principles and reasonings from England, has very gravely adopted this doctrine of immortality in corporations; naturalized and established it as law in our free governments, and stretched over its dogmas, the aegis of

existence: 364 miles through swamps and solid rock, through places where virtually no white settlers had bothered to migrate.

The mayor of New York City and future governor of the state, De Witt Clinton, became the foremost advocate of the canal, certain it would make his city "the great depot and warehouse of the western world." People scoffed at the money thrown away in "Clinton's Big Ditch." But the largely untrained engineers learned as they went along. Aqueducts had to span rivers and gorges, aqueducts tight and strong enough to withstand the weight of the water and the boats they carried. Locks had to be constructed of heavy timbers and even heavier stone. The canal, 4 feet deep and 40 feet wide at the top, was dug by hands, backs, and shovels. Thousands of laborers, many of them foreign-born, moved with the canal, enlivening and sometimes frightening the more sedentary settlements on the route. Year after year, the canal edged toward Lake Erie, transforming the countryside along the way; by 1819, the canal stretched for seventy-five miles. As soon as workers completed a segment, boats crowded upon its waters, the tolls they paid financing the portions yet unfinished.

Steamboats

Canals, though useful and exciting, reached only a limited part of the vast North American continent.

the Constitution, so that in effect, whatever is granted to a private company by the legislature is holden to be intangible and irrevocable. A grant made under erroneous impressions, and which in its operation is found detrimental to, or even destructive of the public welfare, whether it involves the exercise of sovereign powers or not is, according to established principles of law, altogether irrevocable. The present generation may in this way not only bind themselves, but their posterity forever; and government, instead of being at all times administered for the benefit of the people and in accordance with their will; may be parcelled out into monopolies, swallowing up their interests and counteracting their wishes. How long a free people will sanction such principles, or how consonant they are to the fundamental maxims of our social fabric, it is not our purpose to inquire; the existence of them, we remark, as evincing the risk and danger of granting to private companies any control over matters of public and general interest. Nothing can be more interesting to the whole community, than great navigable highways through the state, from the Lake [Erie] to the Ohio river, on the routes proposed; it does not consist with the dignity, the interest or the convenience of the state, that a private company of citizens or foreigners (as may happen), should have the management and control of them; the evils of such management cannot be fully foreseen, and therefore cannot be provided against; for experience is the only safe guide in legislation and of the operation of such grants we have no experience. Besides, such works should be constructed with a view to the greatest possible accommodation of our citizens; as a public concern, the public convenience is the paramount object; a private company will look only to the best means of increasing their profits, the public convenience will be regarded only as it is subservient to their emolument. We think therefore, that it would be extremely hazardous and unwise, to entrust private companies with making those canals, which can be made by the state.

SOURCE: [Ohio] Board of Canal Commissioners, *Third Annual Report, Civil Engineer* (August 16, 1828), pp. 138–40.

Rivers offered faster and cheaper travel, especially along the Mississippi, Missouri, and Ohio. But their limitations were obvious as well. The rivers could be dangerously fast in some seasons and so slow as to be impassable in others. They often froze for months in the winter. Strong currents ran in only one direction. Those who wanted to transport goods northward had to push their boats against the current, sometimes with poles, sometimes by dragging the boats with ropes as the crews walked along the shore, sometimes merely by grabbing trees and bushes on the banks. It took three or four months to drag a boat upstream. Others simply sold their craft for scrap in New Orleans and walked back to Ohio or Illinois, a long and arduous trip.

Not surprisingly, people dreamed of using steam engines to drive riverboats. Robert Fulton's steamboats had traversed the quieter waters of the Northeast since 1807, but he did not manage to build one for the rigors of the Mississippi until 1811. The War of 1812 slowed development of the steamboats, since engines could not be imported from England, but innovation resumed with the war's end. As soon as Jackson won New Orleans in 1815, the *Enterprise* churned its way upriver from Louisiana all the way to Louisville, Kentucky. Dozens of other craft soon joined, competing with one another. In 1817, the journey from New Orleans to Louisville took twenty-five days; in 1819, fourteen days. "If any one had said this was possible thirty years ago," a journalist marvelled, "we should have been ready to send him to a mad-house." Though the shallow, high-powered, and top-heavy steamboats showed a dangerous propensity to explode, run aground, and slam into submerged obstacles, no one thought of going back to the old way of travel.

The increasing speed and frequency of the steamboats encouraged the growth of villages and towns along the rivers. Huge stacks of wood carted in from the countryside appeared wherever the steamboats regularly stopped for fuel; new stores sold the goods transported on the river; muddy villages dreamed of becoming major cities. Indeed, the populations of Louisville, Pittsburgh, and Cincinnati doubled or more than doubled between 1815 and 1825, developing into centers not only of trade but also of meatpacking and flour milling.

The Growth of the Plantation South

The demand for cotton in England took off after 1815, when cotton became, for the first time, the clothing of choice for large numbers of the world's people. Cotton clothes were cheaper, easier to create, and more comfortable in warm weather than those made from wool or linen. No place in the world was as prepared to supply the burgeoning demand for cotton as the American South. Small farmers as well as planters from the older states of the southern seaboard saw opportunity in the new states of Alabama and Mississippi, especially now that Andrew Jackson had opened Mobile as a port for southern Alabama. Many white farmers also moved to western Tennessee and parts of Louisiana. The steamboat and the cotton gin gave southern planters powerful new tools, while slaves could clear and cultivate land for new plantations far more quickly than would have been otherwise possible. Slaveowners in the older states of the Atlantic seaboard, faced with what they considered a surplus of labor, eagerly sold slaves to planters moving to the "new" lands.

The movement west was not a simple march from the east, but rather followed the geographic and political contours of the areas recently acquired from the American Indians. The first settlements began along the rivers that made it possible to transport cotton to market and in those places where the Creeks and other Indians exercised no claims. The new plantation districts were disconnected from one another, centering on Montgomery in Alabama, Jackson in Mississippi,

The Erie Canal, connecting the Hudson River with Lake Erie, demanded a monumental engineering effort. It soon paid its way, however, as shippers and farmers rushed to use the new waterway.

Steamboats began to ply the Mississippi River and other major waterways in the 1810s and 1820s, accelerating trade and fueling the growth of cities along the way.

and Memphis in Tennessee, all areas taken from the natives of the region since 1814. Small farmers occupied the land farthest from the rivers, supporting themselves with hunting and foraging as well as with growing small amounts of cotton. Young lawyers and editors headed out for the Southwest as well, eager to make their mark in the river towns and county seats growing up across Alabama and Mississippi.

"The *Alabama Feaver* rages here with great violence and has *carried off* vast numbers of our Citizens," wrote one North Carolina planter in 1817. "I am apprehensive, if it continues to spread as it has done, it will almost depopulate the country." The fever proved contagious, "for as soon as one neighbour visits another who has just returned from the Alabama he immediately discovers the same symptoms which are exhibited by the person who has seen the allureing Alabama." Even established men in the older states put their plantations up for sale; others saw the new

states as a place for their grown children to get a fresh start. The combined population of Alabama, Mississippi, and Louisiana more than tripled between 1810 and 1820, growing from 117,000 people to 357,000.

Some ambitious young men from northern states moved to the new cotton lands, the place in the United States, it seemed, where the greatest fortunes could be made in the shortest amount of time. Virgin land could produce a cotton crop in only one year; in two years, a plantation could be in full production. But most of the new residents came from older plantation states. Young southern men were especially eager to move and make their mark. Their wives, mothers, and daughters were often much less enthusiastic about migrating to Mississippi or Alabama, for it meant being removed from the kin who gave those women much of their happiness. The lure of the Southwest overrode concerns husbands may have felt for their wives' opinions, however, for the new states offered a chance at the independence they considered synonymous with manliness. They sought to build a world as much as possible like those of Virginia or Carolina, only more prosperous.

The expansion of the cotton kingdom broadened and deepened the slave trade. Many planters in the East took advantage of the opportunity to sell slaves "down south," especially as the price of slaves — stagnant or declining before 1815 — began to rise. Hundreds of thousands of slaves endured forcible migration to the new states of the Southwest in the 1810s and 1820s; some moved in groups along with their owners to new plantations, but many were sold as individuals to slave traders in the east, who then shipped or marched them to slave markets in New Orleans, Mobile, and other cities to the southwest. The families of many enslaved African Americans were broken apart, as slave traders eagerly bought those in their teens for the hard work of clearing land for plantations from virgin forest.

The new plantations concentrated on cotton at the expense of everything else. Southerners who had just come into the vast and apparently inexhaustible lands of the Creeks and Seminoles worried little about conservation. The finest plantations clung to the rivers, for water offered the only way to get the ever-expanding cotton crop to market. Flatboats carried the bulky product to barges waiting at the docks of Natchez and Vicksburg on the Mississippi or to ships waiting in the bays of Mobile and New Orleans. Food and other provisions for the plantations came down the rivers from

→	Migration patterns
—	Established routes
▨	Settled by 1800
⌐‐	Modern borders

MAP 9.3 | THE PATHS OF SOUTHERN MIGRATION

the new farms and cities to the north. A new national economy knitted together the enormous expanse of the young United States.

Emergence of the Northwest

The area west of the Appalachians, north of the Ohio, and east of the Mississippi—the "Northwest"—was growing at an even faster pace than the Southwest. "Old America seems to be breaking up, and moving westward," one man wrote in 1817 as he watched people move down the Ohio River. The 280,000 white settlers of 1810 in Ohio, Indiana, and Illinois grew to 784,000 ten years later. This immigration in the North bore considerable similarities to its southern counterpart. First of all, many of the settlers to the Northwest came from the states of the upper South; large parts of southern Ohio, Indiana, and Illinois were settled by people from Virginia, Kentucky, Tennessee, and North Carolina. Some southern migrants to the North professed themselves eager to move out of states with slavery, while others merely followed the easiest routes to good land. People from New England and New York filled the towns and farms of the northern parts of the new states of the Northwest.

As in the South, young people dominated migration to the Northwest. Migrants to both regions abandoned areas back east where land had become too expensive, crowded, or depleted. As in the Southwest, settlers to the Northwest did not move in a simple westward wave, but rather flowed up the rivers and

Slave trader, sold to Tennessee,

Arise! Arise! and weep no more dry up your tears, we shall part no more. Come rose we go to Tennessee, that happy shore. To old virginia never — never — return.

the Company going to Tennessee from Staunton. Augusta County, the law of virginia suffered them to go on. I was Astonished at this boldness, the carrier stopped a moment. then Ordered the march, I saw the play it is Commonly in this State, with the negro's in droves sold,

The rapid spread of cotton plantations to the west fueled the domestic slave trade. This coffle of slaves marched from Virginia to Tennessee.

spread from there, sometimes back towards the East. People often emigrated in groups, whether of families or of larger communities. "We are seldom out of sight, as we travel on this grand track towards the Ohio," one traveller noted, "of family groups behind, and before us, some with a view to a particular spot, close to a brother perhaps, or a friend who has gone before, and reported well of the country." Family farms clustered closer together in the Northwest than in the Southwest because the absence of a large slave work-force meant that landholdings remained relatively small.

As in the South, white settlement in the Northwest was made possible by the subjugation of the native peoples. After northern Indians' disastrous losses in the War of 1812, they posed little threat to white settlers. The U.S. government quickly established a series of forts throughout the Northwest to intimidate any American Indians and to make sure that the British and Canadians did not regain a foothold. The growing

MAP 9.4 | THE PATHS OF NORTHERN MIGRATION

numbers of white farmers made it difficult for Native Americans to hunt for a living. President Monroe exulted in the "rapid and gigantic" spread of white settlers into the Northwest, an expansion the "rights of nature demand and nothing can prevent." The president argued that "the earth was given to mankind to support the greatest number of people of which it is capable, and no tribe or people have a right to withhold from the wants of others more than is necessary for their own support and comfort." Whites who moved to the Northwest confronted only scattered remnants of native peoples, trading with white merchants for food, sometimes begging from homesteaders.

Most white settlers proved dissatisfied with the first land they claimed, for about two out of three migrants moved again within a few years. Rumors always circulated about richer land a bit farther west, about a new town certain to be a major city, about opportunity just over the horizon. Many people who had moved once found it easy to move again. Those who remained in a

community became its "leading citizens," consolidating land into larger farms, setting up grist mills and sawmills, running for office, establishing the small towns that served as county seats and trading centers. In many cases, storekeepers were among the first to arrive and among those whose fortunes flourished best. Storekeepers became the bankers and wholesalers of their communities, often buying considerable amounts of land along the way, boosting the towns growing around the stores, churches, and schoolhouses. Courthouses were built early on to formalize land sales and taxation.

Farm and Factory in the Northeast

While the economies of the West and the South were being transformed by settlers and slaves, the economy of the East underwent its own fundamental change. Since the colonial years, people outside the major cities—more than nine out of ten Americans—had made in their own homes much of what they needed. This local production grew stronger when trade dried up during the war with England; in the war's wake, more than two-thirds of the clothes Americans wore were made in their own homes. The year of 1815, in fact, saw the peak of household manufacturing. Local blacksmiths, tailors, cobblers, and other artisans supplied what families could not produce for themselves, while local gristmills and sawmills processed crops and lumber.

Farms averaged a little over a hundred acres, about half improved and the other half occupied by wood lots for fuel and timber. Forests often dominated the farms of younger families while mature families proudly claimed large areas of cultivation, the products of years of labor. Women and men, children and adults, shared and divided the work among themselves. Farm families cleared their fields at spring thaw, manuring, plowing, and planting as soon as danger of frost passed. Livestock and poultry needed constant attention; sheep had to be washed and sheared and geese plucked in the spring. Farm families reaped flax in June, enjoyed a brief respite in August, and then pushed hard for the fall harvest. In winter, men and boys cut wood while women and girls spun thread and wove cloth for clothes. The garden and dairy were the responsibility of women and girls, the cash crops the responsibility of men. Farmers, chronically short of cash, bartered among themselves and with merchants.

After 1815, the farms in many parts of New England, New York, and Pennsylvania would be tied ever more tightly into the economies of the towns and cities. Farm families produced more cash crops and bought more things with money rather than through barter. Women, especially widows and other single females, worked in their homes to produce palm hats, portions of shoes, or articles of clothing that merchants from nearby cities gathered and had assembled in workshops. These women added such work to their farm work, laboring in the evenings and throughout the winters. With so many young men leaving New England for the west, many communities found themselves with considerable numbers of young women who might never marry as well as older women who could not count on the support of sons. Piecework offered these women a chance to contribute to the economies of their households in a way the older farm economy had not, bringing in scarce cash. It was important to everyone in their families that those wage-earning women did not have to leave home to earn those wages.

The expanded cash economy thus overlapped with and conflicted with an older, more self-contained economy. Families sought opportunity in new jobs and new markets even as they feared that the increasingly dense networks of trade would depress the value of their crops, make seasonal farm labor even more difficult to acquire, entice young people from the farm, and undermine local artisans. Rural folk both welcomed and worried over the changes. Although it would be generations before cities and factories dominated the economies of the North, in the meantime, farms, towns, and small factories grew ever more interconnected.

The textile industry of New England stood as the most dramatic example of industrial growth. The cost of cotton clothing fell faster than the cost for any other product as machinery and cheaper cotton lowered the price. Francis Cabot Lowell of Boston

Women provided much of the workforce for the new textile factories that emerged in New England.

MAP 9.5 | LOCATION OF COTTON MILLS, 1820S

designed a power loom in 1813, recreating from memory a machine he had seen on a recent trip to England. The same year, Lowell and a partner, Nathan Appleton, spent over $400,000 to open the first factory in the United States that could integrate all the steps of making cloth under a single roof: the Boston Manufacturing Company, in Waltham, Massachusetts, where a waterfall with a ten-foot drop offered free power. An expanded group of investors in the enterprise—the Boston Associates, they were called—pooled the resources of the city's most prominent merchant families.

Unlike earlier factories, that of the Boston Associates used unskilled labor and machines even for weaving, the most expensive part of the process. Lowell and Appleton, concerned that the introduction of factories

into the United States might create the same alienated and despised working class they saw in England, recruited young New England farm women and girls as operatives. Young females had experience in producing yarn and cloth at home and they would work hard for low wages. Many were eager to earn money for themselves, to move out of crowded homes, and to send money back to their families. As Appleton put it, the young women supplied "a fund of labor, well educated and virtuous" for the factory.

The operatives, considering millwork a three- or four-year commitment before they married and began families of their own, worked fourteen hours a day, six days a week. When they signed a contract with the agents who received a dollar a head for each worker they could recruit, the young women agreed to stay with the mill for at least twelve months or to be put on a blacklist that would prevent them from getting a job elsewhere. The factory was unlike anything the young women had ever confronted: "You cannot think how odd everything seemed," one mill girl recalled; even those who had spun and woven for years could not be prepared for the "frightful" sight of "so many bands, and wheels, and springs in constant motion." Leaving the factory in the evening, an operative could still hear the noise of the mill in her head, "as of crickets, frogs and jewsharps, all mingled together in strange discord."

The social and economic ground for industrialization had been broken in the northeast. Mills, most of them small, grew up along the streams of Connecticut and the Delaware Valley of Pennsylvania and New Jersey, turning out not only textiles but also metal and wood products. These mills, like their bigger and more visible counterparts in Lowell, depended on low wages paid to workers without many other options. Many potential workers, competitors, and outside observers worried about the effects of the factories, even as investors and other supporters saw in the new buildings the hope for a richer and more productive American society.

THE PRICE OF EXPANSION

The prosperity of the immediate postwar years faltered badly in 1819. Apparently boundless growth stopped dead in its tracks. The enlarged scale of the new American economy entangled a far larger number of people than had ever been caught in economic hard times before. Meanwhile, the enlarged boundaries of the American nation brought troubles of their own as the North and the South fought over new territories in the West. Looking out over the world, slaves felt emboldened to revolt and political leaders declared the determination of the United States to control its hemisphere.

The Panic of 1819

A series of events in 1819 abroad and at home conspired to bring a sudden halt to some of the growth in the economy of the United States. Cotton lands in the southeast, the most sought-after property in these

years, saw prices skyrocket as world demand for cotton cloth increased every year. Prices for southern cotton rose to such an extent that in 1818 and 1819 British manufacturers turned to cotton from other sources, especially India. The price of American cotton tumbled, along with the price of the land that produced it. And cotton was not the only crop whose price rapidly declined: the price of tobacco plummeted from 40 cents a pound to 4 cents, wheat fell from $2.41 a bushel to 88 cents. State banks built on inflated, even fraudulent, credit wavered and then crashed. The Panic of 1819 had begun.

The panic proved a sudden and sobering reminder of just how complicated and interdependent the economy of the nation was becoming. The cities were hit the hardest. About half a million workers lost their jobs as business ground to a halt. Americans shuddered to see "children freezing in the winter's storm — and the fathers without coats and shoes." The streets where new goods had been piled now displayed people without homes or food. Charitable groups opened soup kitchens. Wherever they could, families who had moved to towns and cities returned to the countryside to live with relatives. Things were not much safer in the country, however, where the failure of banks meant that apparently prosperous farmers saw household goods, farm animals, and the people they held as slaves sold in humiliating auctions.

Many people, including congressmen, began to call for the revocation of the charter of the Second Bank of the United States. States had chafed throughout the two years of the Bank's life at what they considered its dictatorial power. Several states tried to limit that power by levying extremely high taxes on the branches of the Bank of the United States in their states, but it was at this point that the Supreme Court ruled in *McCulloch* v. *Maryland* that the laws of the federal government "form the supreme law of the land."

Despite the panic, James Monroe was reelected to the presidency in 1820 in one of the quietest and most lopsided elections in the nation's history. The Federalist party, fatally crippled by its opposition to the War of 1812 and its support of the Hartford Convention, offered no effective opposition. Neither did Monroe face an organized contest from others within his own Republican party, which was divided along sectional lines. He received every electoral vote but one. Most Americans seemed to blame someone other than President Monroe for the Panic of 1819 and the lingering hard times that followed it. The Era of Good Feelings somehow managed to survive in the White House—though, it turned out, not in the halls of Congress.

The Missouri Compromise

The recent admission of the new states of the Southwest and Northwest had left a precarious balance in the Senate between slave states and free, though northern states held a strong, and growing, preponderance in the House of Representatives. The Missouri territory posed a special challenge to the balance. Slavery had quickly spread in Missouri, stretching along the richest river lands. If Missouri were admitted with slavery—as its territorial legislature had decreed—then the slave states would hold a majority in the Senate. Slavery in Missouri, an area of the same latitude as much of Illinois, Indiana, and Ohio, seemed to violate the assumption long held by many people in the North that slavery, if it grew at all, would expand only to the south.

The three-fifths clause of the Constitution, northerners complained, gave the slave states twenty more members of Congress and twenty more electors for the presidency than they would have if only white population were counted. The South seemed to be getting extra representation unfairly.

The debates over slavery in Missouri in 1819 and 1820 were not debates between fervent abolitionists in the North and fervent proslavery advocates in the South. Neither of those positions had yet been defined. Instead, white northerners and southerners of all political persuasions agreed that as many blacks as possible should be shipped to Africa. White Americans who could agree on little else about slavery did agree that blacks and whites could not live together in the United States once slavery had ended. That was the message of the American Colonization Society, founded in 1816 and based in Washington, D.C. The society bought land in Africa—naming the new country "Liberia"—and sent about 12,000 African Americans there over the next fifty years. Disease took a terrible toll, however, and many died. Fewer African Americans migrated. In Philadelphia, they even staged protests against the notion of colonization.

In the meantime, slavery caused problems for the political system. A New York congressman, James Tallmadge, Jr., introduced an amendment to the bill that would admit Missouri as a state only if Missouri admitted no more slaves and if those slaves in the territory were freed when they became twenty-five years old. More than eighty of the North's congressmen supported the Tallmadge amendment and only ten opposed it. In the Senate, though, the slave states prevailed by two votes. A deadlocked Congress adjourned in March of 1819 to meet again in December.

During the months in between politicians worked behind the scenes to prepare for the debates and decisions of December. The Union, so celebrated and expansive in the wake of the war with Britain, so peaceful for whites since the Creeks, Seminoles, and Cherokees had been quelled, now seemed in danger of breaking apart from within. Both northern and southern politicians talked openly of ending the Union if need be. Simmering northern resentment, held in check for decades, was suddenly announced, even celebrated. Southerners felt betrayed. In their eyes, slavery was a thing they had inherited, something for which they bore no blame, an institution that would fade away naturally if it were left alone. White southerners thought northerners irresponsible and unrealistic to attack as the Tallmadge amendment did. The denial of Missouri statehood seemed to southerners nothing less than an assault on their character.

In northern states, where abolitionist societies had been relatively sedate, people suddenly announced the depth of their distaste for the institution. Furious meetings erupted in towns and cities across the North, turning out petitions and resolutions in large numbers. Slavery, these petitions thundered, was a blot on the nation, a violation of the spirit of Christianity, an abomination that must not spread into places it had not already ruined. The antislavery advocates of the 1820s expected colonization and abolition to occur simultaneously and gradually. But they also determined to stop the spread of slavery toward the northern part of the continent.

After weeks of debate, a compromise emerged from the Senate: Missouri, with no restriction on slavery, should be admitted to the Union at the same time as Maine, thereby ensuring the balance between slave and free states. Slavery would be prohibited in all the lands acquired in the Louisiana Purchase north of the southern border of Missouri at 36° 30' latitude. Such a provision excluded the Arkansas territory, where slavery was already established, but closed to slavery the vast expanses of the Louisiana Territory—the future states of Iowa, Minnesota, Wisconsin, the Dakotas, Nebraska, and Kansas. Any slaves who escaped to the free states would be returned. Many of the northern

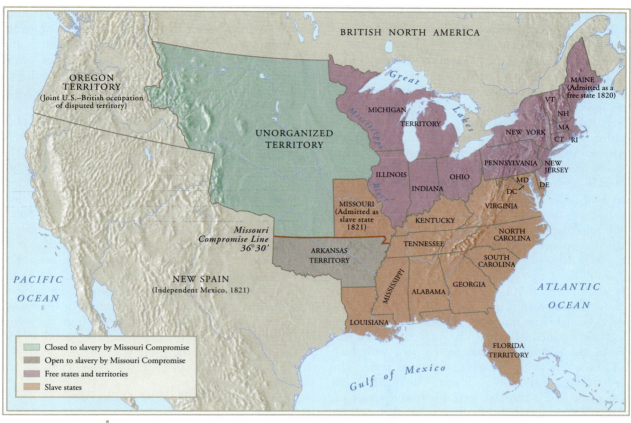

MAP 9.6 | MISSOURI COMPROMISE

men who voted for the measure found themselves burned in effigy back home and defeated when it came time for reelection. The South was no more satisfied than the North, furious to hear itself vilified in the national capital it had long dominated.

The debate broke out again when the Missouri constitutional convention not only authorized slavery but decreed that the state legislature could never emancipate slaves without the consent of their masters; the proposed constitution also pronounced that free blacks would never be permitted to enter the new state. The national House of Representatives refused to admit Missouri under this document and the denunciation by both sides began again where it had paused. Finally, in early 1821, Henry Clay managed to fix a majority in the House in favor of a bill that would admit Missouri as long as the new state promised to pass no law barring the entry of a citizen from any other state. Exhausted, Congress ratified the law.

Northern and southern states had become wary and distrustful of one another as they had never been before. In a real sense, the debates over slavery in Missouri created "the North" and "the South," uniting the new states of the Northwest with the states of New England, New York, and Pennsylvania as they had not been united earlier, forging a tighter alliance between the new states of the Southwest and Virginia, the Carolinas, and Georgia. To the North, the South seemed greedy and corrupt; to the South, the North seemed greedy and hypocritical. The country became polarized as never before.

Vesey's Revolt

An event in 1822 in Charleston, South Carolina, forced white Americans, North and South, to pay greater attention to the people who lived under slavery's dominion. In that city, the heart of South Carolina's richest plantation district, a free black man named Denmark Vesey had closely followed in the papers the debates over the Missouri controversy. What he read there reinforced what he had seen in the Bible and the documents of the American Revolution: Slavery was immoral. Vesey, a middle-aged mulatto of large stature who had bought his freedom twenty years earlier, stood as a commanding presence among the African American people of the low country. He had several wives and many children whose bondage tormented him. A skilled carpenter and preacher, Vesey traveled up and down the coast and into the interior, berating those blacks who accepted racial insult. Many African Americans were attracted to him; most were afraid to oppose him regardless.

Vesey drew not only upon his own strengths, but upon those of a powerful ally, a man known as Gullah Jack. This man, an Angolan, had arrived in South Carolina near the turn of the century, one of the 40,000 slaves brought into the state right before the end of the legal slave trade in 1807. Gullah Jack still looked very much the part of the conjurer he was, with huge whiskers, tiny arms, and unusual gestures setting him apart from American-born blacks. This sorcerer, like Denmark Vesey, hated slavery; his command of the symbols of Africa made his alliance with Vesey all the more powerful. The two men found their most eager audience among the artisans and house slaves of Charleston who had the greatest amount of freedom. Vesey and Gullah Jack found it relatively easy to meet with slaves receptive to their message. Allies in charge of stables and stores gave Vesey access to horses and weapons.

Vesey planned to launch an attack on white Charleston at midnight on a Saturday, when slaves from the countryside came to the city to sell produce. The conspirators hoped to seize the city's poorly protected guardhouse, stores, and roads before the whites could gather themselves in opposition. House slaves would kill their white owners. Once Charleston was secure, the rebels, Vesey planned, would sail to Haiti, where Toussaint L'Ouverture had staged a black rebellion decades earlier and where slavery had been abolished. But the plan met serious difficulties, especially since so many people had to be let in on the secrets. A house servant broke under the pressure and alerted Charleston whites to the danger only two days before the revolt planned for June 16, 1822. The governor

ordered out five military companies and Vesey called off the attack. Over the next two months, white authorities hanged thirty-five alleged conspirators and banished thirty-seven more from the state. Few of the rebels would reveal the names of their allies, going to their deaths with the secrets of the revolt secure. Denmark Vesey was one of those killed.

Though many details remained murky, white South Carolinians believed that they had, by the narrowest of margins, avoided an unimaginable rebellion. The rebels came not from the ranks of the slaves living under the most brutal conditions but from among those most trusted by their owners, those who lived in close association with white women and children. South Carolinians, and white southerners in general, blamed Vesey's Rebellion on the agitation against slavery by northern congressmen in the Missouri debate. "The events of 1822," a leading South Carolinian observed, "will long be remembered, as amongst the choicest fruits of the agitation of that question in Congress." White southerners drew a clear lesson from the events between 1820 and 1822: Northern agitation against slavery invited disaster.

The Monroe Doctrine

The instability of the Spanish regime in Europe, exacerbated by the Napoleonic Wars, sent aftershocks into the colonies in the New World. Throughout the first and second decades of the nineteenth century, one struggle after another disrupted Latin America. Seeing Spain vulnerable in Europe and abroad, leaders in the colonies of the Western Hemisphere—Simón Bolívar in Venezuela, José de San Martín in Argentina, and Miguel Hidalgo in Mexico—pushed ahead with their long-simmering plans for national independence. By 1822, Chile, Mexico, Venezuela, and the Portuguese colony of Brazil had all gained their independence.

Neither the United States nor Great Britain wanted to see France fill the vacuum left by Spain in the New World. A French or Russian empire would pose a potentially dangerous economic and military threat much greater than any posed by the fading Spanish regime. Accordingly, in March of 1822 President Monroe urged Congress to recognize the new republics of Latin America. Throughout the next year, as the French army invaded Spain, the U.S. minister in England proposed that the United States and England

John Quincy Adams was Secretary of State under James Monroe and the author of the so-called "Monroe Doctrine," which announced American opposition to European colonization in the Western Hemisphere.

jointly declare that neither country would annex any part of the tottering empire of Spain, nor permit any other power to do so. Encouraged by former presidents Jefferson and Madison, Monroe wanted to make the joint declaration, but Secretary of State John Quincy Adams persuaded him that it would be more fitting and dignified for the United States to declare its policy independently instead of coming "in as a cockboat in the wake of the British man o'war." Adams's policy was directed more against outside intervention in Latin America than in favor of the new republics, which he considered weak and unlikely to endure an attack by a major power.

Accordingly, in December of 1823 the president used his annual message to Congress to announce what would eventually become known as the Monroe Doctrine: "[T]he American continents, by the free and independent conditions which they have assumed and maintained, are henceforth not to be considered as subjects for future colonisation by any European power." The North American republic had exerted its first claim to recognition by the great powers of the world, making a show of acting independently even though Great Britain was the real power. The Russians and Spanish denounced the American policy as "blustering," "arrogant," "indecent," and "monstrous," meriting only "the most profound contempt." They tolerated the doctrine because the European powers, exhausted by wars among themselves, had little desire to expand their involvement on the other side of the world. The leaders of the Latin American revolts welcomed the warning to the European powers, but were less certain about the United States's own intentions toward Latin America. The Monroe Doctrine, after all, did not say that the United States would not interfere in the Western Hemisphere, only that it would not permit European countries to do so.

THE SWIRL OF PUBLIC LIFE

Two events of 1824 threw into sharp relief the accomplishments and dangers of the emerging nation. The first event was the thirteen-month tour of the United States by one of the heroes of the American Revolution: the Marquis de Lafayette. The second event was the presidential election of 1824. While Lafayette's visit tied the country together with bonds of memory and celebration, the election showed that Americans had become far more divided than had seemed possible only four years earlier.

Lafayette's Return

Lafayette sailed into New York and was met, fittingly enough, with a steamboat, symbol of the strides the United States had made since Lafayette's departure decades earlier. He spent tumultuous and tearful days in New York, where old comrades and young admirers poured out to see the living embodiment of the sacrifices and bravery of the Revolutionary War. Then Lafayette, along with his son, George Washington Lafayette, and his traveling companion, a radical young Scotswoman named Frances Wright, set out to see the rest of the United States. They went first to New England, visiting with John Adams, then down the coast to Philadelphia, Baltimore, Washington, Charleston, and then New Orleans. From there, they went up the Mississippi and on to Nashville, where he met Andrew Jackson. Everywhere Lafayette traveled, the people tried to outdo what had been done before; the hero met with booming guns, torchlight parades, thousands of children dressed in the colors of France, beautiful young women, illuminated pictures, banquet after banquet, speech after speech. Some moments stood out: when the general cried, alone, at the grave of Washington at Mount Vernon, and when he traveled to Monticello to meet with Jefferson. Congress, knowing that the marquis was in serious financial difficulties, presented him with a gift of $200,000 (an enormous sum at the time) and a township of public land. Lafayette met with Cherokees in Georgia. Slaves, hearing of the patriot's opposition to slavery, lined the roads wherever he went to cheer him on.

A toast announced what Americans most admired in Lafayette, "the great apostle of liberty whom the persecutions of tyranny could not defeat, whom the love of riches could not influence, whom popular applause could never seduce." The Frenchman, in other words, was admired for his selflessness at the time of the American Revolution, for putting the cause of liberty before his own self-interest, for putting himself at risk in the pursuit of freedom. Such a posture of noble self-sacrifice was what Americans valued most in their public men and what they expected of those to whom power was given. In Lafayette, they could celebrate the best in themselves.

The Election of 1824

Many people felt, on the other hand, that they saw the worst of the country in the presidential election going on while Lafayette toured the country. Few eligible voters had bothered to cast a ballot four years earlier when James Monroe had won the presidency without opposition, for his election seemed foreordained. But politicians and observers expected a more interesting contest in 1824. Many thought the next president

would be William Crawford, secretary of the treasury, a Georgian and apparent heir to the Virginia dynasty. Others focused on John Quincy Adams, an experienced statesman, New Englander, and the secretary of state—the office from which many presidents had come. Others looked to John C. Calhoun of South Carolina, an impressive secretary of war and advocate of a strong government. Yet others placed their bets on Henry Clay of Kentucky, speaker of the House of Representatives for many years and one of the most visible members of Congress. Finally, Andrew Jackson of Tennessee hoped to parlay the widespread fame he won in the wars against the English and the Indians into the presidency.

Several of these men realized they did not command sufficient national support to win the election outright. They hoped, however, to prevail if the election went into the House of Representatives, where the top three candidates would vie if no candidate won in the electoral college. Cliques spread rumors and alliances of convenience flourished. Openly partisan newspapers sang the praises of their man and published lacerating rumors about his opponents. While the Marquis de Lafayette serenely toured the United States, local and state politicians worked feverishly in taverns, caucuses, and newspaper offices. Many American voters seemed disenchanted with the crass politicking, though, and relatively few voted in 1824. Jackson's popular vote nearly equaled that of Adams and Crawford combined, but the election was thrown into the House of Representatives because no candidate received a plurality in the electoral college. The House could choose among the top three candidates: Jackson, Adams, and Crawford.

Since his fourth-place finish put him out of the running, Clay, the speaker of the House, sought to strike the best deal he could with the other candidates, assuring himself of maximum power, visibility, and opportunities in subsequent elections. Clay, considering Jackson unworthy of the post and a potential military despot, discussed his future with Adams. When the vote came to the House of Representatives in early 1825, Adams won the presidency—taking the three states Clay had won in the electoral college. Two weeks later, Henry Clay received the appointment of secretary of state. "So you see," Andrew Jackson fumed, "the *Judas* of the West has closed the contract and will receive the thirty pieces of silver." Throughout the muddy little city of Washington, people specu-

Martin Van Buren helped invent modern politics in the 1820s, combining publicity and patronage into a powerful machine that would soon be emulated across the country.

lated about the promises the upright John Quincy Adams had made to win the presidency. People often mentioned the cold sweat that broke out on his face when he received word of his election.

Adams wanted a stronger national government, internal improvements, and a tariff to protect American industry. But he could not mobilize support for his positions, either within Washington or among the voters. Adams refused to use patronage to persuade or coerce people to go along with his plans. His administration bogged down into factionalism and paralysis, always with the shadow of his supposed "corrupt bargain" with Clay darkening his reputation. Things seemed far removed, indeed, from the glorious days when Lafayette sacrificed for the American Revolution.

New York politicians sought to harness ambition into useful and organized forms in the 1820s, pioneering the development of the party system. Aaron Burr converted a simple patriotic club in New York City, the Society of Saint Tammany, into the beginnings of a major political machine. De Witt Clinton invented the "spoils system," in which it became the expectation that an incoming officeholder would remove those appointed by his predecessor and put his own supporters in their place. Martin Van Buren, a young lawyer and politician from New York, combined the city machine and the spoils system into a powerful statewide organization. He used newspapers in Albany and New York City to spread the word of the party to the fifty small newspapers he controlled throughout the state, which also published vast numbers of hand bills, posters, and ballots at election time. He built a large network of party men, many of them lawyers who traveled widely in the state and knew many of their counterparts. Van Buren's goal was to combine party unity with personal advancement for party members, creating a powerful and self-reinforcing cycle.

Martin Van Buren opposed John Quincy Adams in the presidential contest of 1824 because Adams's nationally sponsored canals, roads, education, and other services would cut into the power of state government and state politics, elevating what Van Buren saw as dangerous federal power over power closer to home. Partly for this reason, Van Buren cast his lot in 1824 and the years thereafter with Andrew Jackson, who shared Van Buren's preference for localized power. As the next presidential election came closer, Van Buren, now a senator, worked ever more energetically for Jackson, hoping to spread the model of New York politics to the nation as a whole.

CHARACTER DEVELOPMENT

For generations before 1815, Americans had relied on authority and reputation to keep their families and communities stable. Young men and women remained in their parents' households well into their twenties, subordinate to the demands and expectations of their fathers. Workingmen served for years as apprentices and journeymen to master artisans, slowly learning the craft and gradually working toward independence. Men and women carefully cultivated their reputations, projecting a polished image of themselves. Churches aided stability, encouraging deference to the authority of God and institution.

The decade after 1815 saw a new emphasis in American life, a new focus on what people called "character." In a society so mobile, so disconnected from traditional sources of stability and identity, people felt the need for new ways of ensuring appropriate behavior. Americans looked to new kinds of institutions suited for a new age, institutions that could better deal with strangers, new people, those cut off from older forms of social stability. Americans turned first to families, imparting to them primary responsibility for creating virtuous children and husbands.

Women at Home and Beyond

Women had long been recognized as the foundation of a good family. Women directly produced a large portion of the food farm families consumed, while town-dwelling families depended on women for running the household—especially hard work in the days before indoor plumbing and electricity. During the era of the Revolution and early republic, women had been encouraged to raise virtuous children befitting a nation of free people. Churches had long depended on women as the source of spiritual energy and admirable role models.

Women became central in yet another way during the decades following 1815. As Americans looked about them, they became concerned that little seemed to be holding their society together. People moved far beyond the reach of government and beyond the eyes of their parents. Men and women married at younger ages and left home far earlier than their parents had. The opening of land in the West undermined one of the principal forms of control exercised by fathers in earlier generations: the promise of passing on the family farm to sons who stayed at home. Now, sons could acquire land in the West with or without the support of their parents. Daughters might marry earlier and begin families of their own. The American population skyrocketed as so many young families established themselves.

The new economy, too, caused concern for many. Increasingly, men and women seemed pulled in different directions, away from a sole focus on the family farm or family artisan shop. Men found new opportu-

nities in town, in businesses that kept offices or shops in a central area. Young men often worked for wages for a number of employers rather than serving for many years with one master. Middle-class women, too, saw their lives change, especially in towns and cities. Bakeries, butcher shops, clothiers, and candlemakers began to offer, more easily and cheaply, some of the things that women had long labored to produce at home. Schools and academies became more common, providing a place for children to receive education beyond the bounds of the home. Young women from poorer backgrounds came into cities looking for jobs as maids and laundresses, taking away some of the household burden for women well off enough to hire them. Families in towns and cities had fewer children with each passing decade. Women's lives remained hard, as each birth threatened serious illness or death, but those lives began to change in important ways.

As ministers, journalists, and other opinion makers looked upon the changing nature of the households of the Northeast, they began to articulate an ideal of what has been called "domesticity." Families should seize the opportunities provided by the new situations, they said, and help lessen some of the costs created by the new order. Women could put their minds to higher purposes, focusing more on nurturing their children in spirit and mind as well as in body. Women would become the moral center of the household, the guardians of good thoughts, clean living, and a sense of safety for children and husbands. While the world beyond the household seemed increasingly threatening and disorienting, women could make the home a place of refuge and renewal.

Many middle-class women welcomed this message and this mission. It fit well with their own experiences and their own aspirations. In a time when public life made almost no provisions for female participation and when women found virtually no well-paying jobs open to them, the elevation of the home promised an elevation of women's role. Men believed what they said: they thought women naturally better than themselves, more moral and feeling, more intuitive and spiritual. Men worried about the coarseness and callousness of the tumultuous marketplace even as they enjoyed the sense of freedom, excitement, and possibility it offered. Middle-class fathers wanted their children shielded from the hard world as long as possible, if only so they would be better able to handle the world when they emerged after their nurture at home.

Depictions such as this portrait of Catherine Wheeler Hardy and her daughter celebrated the quiet domestic space shared by children and presided over by the mother.

Domesticity asked something of men as well. If the home were to be a haven, the center of society, men would have to make a greater investment in those homes than had their fathers. Men needed to respect the feelings of their wives more, speaking in tones of respect and affection, respecting their wishes about sex and children. Fathers were expected to spend more time with their children, providing a firm male model to accompany the softer nurture of their wives. Drinking and cursing had no place at home.

Such models of domesticity did not emerge overnight, of course. The early 1820s saw only the beginnings of a crusade to make all American homes fit this model. The effort began in towns and cities, making only gradual inroads into the raw and growing countryside. It was stronger in the Northeast than in the South and in the West. Working-class families could not afford this idealized model even if they wanted to follow its example. Women who had to work for others all day had little time to devote to their own families. Women who worked in their own homes mingled the market and the household in a way the creators of the domestic ideal deplored. Men who could not be certain of their next day's wages could not afford to keep children out of the workforce into their late teens. Slave families struggled to stay together in any way they could and could only imagine what it might be like to live in the homes held up as ideal in these years. Nevertheless, that ideal was celebrated and elaborated with each passing year, growing along with the booming towns and cities of the North.

Stirrings of Reform

The same Americans who promoted the Christian, middle-class home as their ideal looked to other institutions and reforms in the early 1820s to help remake

Penal reformers placed great faith in silence, order, and work, helping put the United States in the forefront of the growing penitentiary movement.

American society. They sought to extend the ideals of character, self-control, and education to those who seemed to fall beyond the good effects of family and household. Reformers tapped the domestic impulses of improvement for the society as a whole.

The Panic of 1819 and its aftermath made a deep impression on many town and city dwellers. Wherever they looked in those years, they saw hungry children, desperate fathers, and distraught mothers. They noticed increasing numbers of women selling themselves on the city streets. They decried bulging jails and streets full of people without homes. They worried over the many young men and women who seemed adrift in this rootless new society.

Activist people in the Northeast sought to counter these problems. Some of their efforts grew out of the churches, while others grew out of the ideals of the American Revolution and the marketplace. The churches launched an ambitious drive to put Bibles in every American home, distributing a million Bibles each year. The American Sunday School Union, formed in 1824, wrote and published materials for children to be used in Sunday schools across the country. Those schools, while based in churches, taught reading and writing as well as religion. They

put the churches at the center of community life, giving children beyond the reach of traditional schooling a chance to learn some of the skills and attitudes necessary for spiritual and economic success. The American Tract Society, created in 1825, produced millions of short inspirational pamphlets to reach those who might not set foot in a church or pick up a Bible. The new organizations prided themselves on being national in reach, extending to the Northwest and Southwest, knitting Americans together with a common faith. They preached nothing controversial, claiming only to spread the good news of the Protestant Christian faith. They depended on the hard work of women, who filled the membership rolls and helped raise funds.

Another reform movement of these years took a different kind of strategy. While the idea of the penitentiary had been discussed in Europe and the United States for several decades, support for that institution grew quickly after 1819. In a penitentiary, unlike a common jail, criminals would be locked in individual cells, free from the contamination of others, alone with their conscience and the Bible. There, reflecting on their crimes, they would become "penitent" and would emerge as better people. They would undergo some of the moral nurture they had obviously missed as children and would be ready to take their place in the economy of wages, self-discipline, and delayed gratification growing in the United States.

The most prominent penitentiaries were built in New York and Pennsylvania between 1819 and 1829. Reformers argued over whether prisoners should be isolated at all times, the Philadelphia model, or whether they might be allowed to work together in silence, as they did at Auburn in New York. In either case, Americans were proud of their penitentiaries, among the first in the world, holding them up as examples of what the enlightened new nation could do. Almost every state in the nation, South as well as North, soon built its own penitentiary.

Alongside those institutions appeared other buildings designed to house other kinds of people who could not keep up with rapidly changing American society. Asylums for the deaf and blind, for the insane, for orphans, and for the poor began to appear in the 1820s, replacing more informal kinds of care. Each institution placed its faith in strict order, in moral teaching, and in faith in the inherent good of human nature. The results were not immediately apparent—indeed, many of the inmates of every kind of asylum resisted and protested—but the hope endured.

Reformers launched one other crusade in the 1810s and 1820s, one that many thought might make all the other reforms effective. Many people, religious and otherwise, saw alcohol as the scourge of American life. "You cannot go into hardly any man's house," an English visitor wrote in 1819, "without being asked to drink wine, or spirits, even in the morning." Men drank at work, farmers routinely turned their grain into whiskey, and rum was a major part of New England commerce. Everyone knew the costs of such drinking and groups around the country mobilized locally to slow the drinking, to be more "temperant" in their use of ardent spirits.

The temperance movement slowly stewed until 1825, when Lyman Beecher, a prominent minister delivered and then published six stirring sermons. Beecher argued that temperance was not enough, that only complete abstinence would remove the stain of alcohol from the United States. Drinkers must make a total and immediate break with their addiction. The next year supporters of abstinence formed the American Temperance Society and adopted the strategies of the American Bible Society, spreading the crusade among the Protestant churches of the country. Thou-sands joined, women as well as men, foreshadowing a flood of activity over the next century.

CONCLUSION

The United States saw enormous economic change between 1815 and 1826. As embargo and war ended, as the new nation's armies conquered and contained diverse peoples among the Native Americans, new states in both the Southwest and the Northwest pushed into the national and international economies. Cotton flowed out of Alabama and Mississippi in ever-growing amounts while food flowed from Indiana and Illinois. Banks proliferated with the expanding population and the Second Bank of the United States lent stability to the system. The major ports along the east coast grew as they had never grown before, connecting the expanding United States with the economies of England and Europe. New factory buildings went up along the streams and rivers of Massachusetts, Connecticut, Rhode Island, and Pennsylvania, producing by water power what hands had made only a few years earlier. Turnpikes and roads covered the country in an increasingly dense network. Coming on the heels of the Treaty of Ghent, such change seemed to mark the beginning of a new kind of security and prosperity for the United States.

The completion of the Erie Canal in 1825 demonstrated that Americans could accomplish great things. The constructors of the canal, bragged one speaker, "have built the longest canal, in the least time, with the least experience, for the least money and to the greatest public benefit." Soon after De Witt Clinton ceremoniously poured water from Lake Erie into the Atlantic, thousands of boats were traveling along the canal between Buffalo and New York City, pumping half a million dollars of tolls into the state coffers, sending a surge of prosperity along its route. Other states, busy with their own plans and excavations, looked enviously upon the glorious Erie Canal.

Accompanying this rapid expansion of boundaries of every sort, however, grew considerable anxiety that American society threatened to spin out of control. The government held little power and people worried that many Americans had moved beyond the influence of church, family, school, or employer. The centrifugal forces of the society threatened to pull it apart. No sooner had the postwar boom begun than some Americans began to suggest ways to contain the consequences of change. They offered political compromise, reform societies, and new ideals of the home as ways to counteract what they saw as chaos. But no one expected things to remain settled for long.

RECOMMENDED READINGS

Cashin, Joan E. *A Family Venture: Men and Women on the Southern Frontier* (1991) tells the story of the southwestern migration in a compelling way.

Davis, David Brion. *The Problem of Slavery in the Age of Revolution, 1770–1823* (1975) gives a magisterial overview of the international struggles with slavery.

Horwitz, Morton J. *The Transformation of American Law, 1780–1860* (1977) puts forward a strong and controversial argument about the law and commerce.

Mathews, Jean. *Toward a New Society: American Thought and Culture, 1800–1830* (1990) offers a subtle interpretation of cultural history of this period.

May, Ernest. *The Making of the Monroe Doctrine* (1976) is a solid overview.

Dangerfield, George. *The Awakening of American Nationalism, 1815–1828* (1965) is a classic interpretation of the postwar era.

Freehling, William W. *The Road to Disunion: The Secessionists at Bay, 1776–1854* (1990) portrays the drama of sectional conflict throughout this era.

Sellers, Charles G. *The Market Revolution: Jacksonian America, 1815–1846* (1991) offers a stirring portrayal of the period with economic change at the center.

Sheriff, Carol. *The Artificial River: The Erie Canal and the Paradox of Progress, 1817–1862* (1996) gives a compelling account of the canal's origins, building, and effects.

Rohrbough, Malcolm J. *The Trans-Appalachian Frontier: People, Societies, and Institutions, 1775–1850* (1978) tells this complex story well.

Public Affairs
Fehrenbacher, Don. *The South and Three Sectional Crises* (1980).

Hargreaves, Mary W. M. *The Presidency of John Quincy Adams* (1985).

Moore, Glover. *The Missouri Controversy, 1818–1821* (1953).

Nagel, Paul C. *John Quincy Adams: A Public Life, a Private Life* (1997).

Peterson, Merrill. *The Great Triumvirate: Webster, Clay, and Calhoun* (1989).

Robinson, Donald L. *Slavery in the Structure of American Politics, 1765–1820* (1971).

Young, James Sterling. *The Washington Community, 1800–1828* (1966).

Economic and Legal Change
Bruchey, Stuart. *Enterprise: The Dynamic Economy of a Free People* (1990).

Cochran, Thomas C. *Frontiers of Change: Early Industrialism in America* (1981).

Dublin, Thomas. *Transforming Women's Work: New England Lives in the Industrial Revolution* (1994).

Faulkner, Robert K. *The Jurisprudence of John Marshall* (1968).

Shaw, Ronald E. *Erie Water West: A History of the Erie Canal, 1792–1854* (1966).

Steinberg, Theodore. *Nature Incorporated: Industrialization and the Waters of New England* (1991).

Taylor, George R. *The Transportation Revolution, 1815–1860* (1951).

White, G. Edward. *The Marshall Court and Cultural Change, 1815–1835* (1991).

American Indians
Green, Michael D. *The Politics of Indian Removal: Creek Government and Society in Crisis* (1982).

Finger, John R. *The Eastern Band of Cherokees, 1819–1900* (1984).

McLoughlin, William G. *Cherokee Renascence in the New Republic* (1986).

Perdue, Theda. *Slavery and the Evolution of Cherokee Society, 1540–1866* (1979).

Perdue, Theda. *Cherokee Women: Gender and Culture Change, 1700–1835* (1998).

Washburn, Wilcomb. *The Indian in America* (1975).

Wright, J. Leitch, Jr. *Creeks and Seminoles: The Destruction and Regeneration of the Muscogee People* (1986).

Westward Movement
Atack, Jeremy and Bateman, Fred. *To Their Own Soil: Agriculture in the Antebellum North* (1987).

Bartless, Richard A. *The New Country: A Social History of the American Frontier, 1776–1890* (1974).

Faragher, John Mack. *Sugar Creek: Life on the Illinois Prairie* (1986).

Moore, John Hebron. *The Emergence of the Cotton Kingdom in the Old Southwest: Mississippi, 1790–1860* (1988).

Tadman, Michael. *Speculators and Slaves: Masters, Traders, and Slaves in the Old South* (1989).

Wade, Richard C. *The Urban Frontier: The Rise of Western Cities, 1790–1830* (1964).

Lafayette's Visit
Somkin, Fred. *Unquiet Eagle: Memory and Desire in the Idea of American Freedom, 1815–1860* (1967).

Loveland, Anne. *Emblem of Liberty: The Image of Lafayette in the American Mind* (1971).

Early Reform
Andrew John A., III. *From Revivals to Removal: Jeremiah Evarts, the Cherokee Nation, and the Search for the Soul of America* (1992).

Hirsch, Adam J. *The Rise of the Penetentiary: Prisons and Punishment in Early America* (1992).

Meranze, Michael. *Laboratories of Virtue: Punishment, Revolution, and Authority in Philadelphia, 1760–1835* (1996).

PRESIDENT ANDREW JACKSON

*Andrew Jackson of Tennessee seemed to many people an inspiring leader. Others, however, saw him as a "military chieftain"
dangerous with the power of the presidency.*

Chapter 10

The Years of Andrew Jackson:
1827–1836

Tumultuous change came to the United States in the years Andrew Jackson served as president. Elections became broad public events that involved men of every class. Voters and leaders hotly debated and contested the role of government in American life. Religious revivals swept up entire communities in devotion and prayer. Working people created labor unions and abolitionists launched a bold crusade against slavery.

Growing democracy was not the full story of these years, however. The people of the Creek, Choctaw, Cherokee, Seminole, Sac, and Fox nations were driven from their homes in the South and in the old Northwest. A crisis threatened to ignite a military struggle between South Carolina and the federal government. The revolt of Nat Turner and debates over slavery in Virginia unleashed a proslavery reaction throughout much of the South. The defeat of Mexico in Texas opened a vast new territory to slavery as well as to the settlement of free Americans. Few decades in American history witnessed more important and more sweeping changes.

The Transformation of American Politics

John Quincy Adams had been elected in a fractious election that cast politics in a poor light. The squabbling of leading men over votes in the electoral college seemed clear evidence that the age of the Revolutionary leaders had passed and that a less worthy age had taken its place. As people called for a more democratic kind of politics, states across the Union lowered property requirements for voting and made judges elected rather than appointed officials. Voters seemed restless, hungry for someone to give direction and force to public life. Such a man emerged, along with a new kind of politics.

The Adams Twilight

The second half of John Quincy Adams's administration proved unhappy and unproductive. Neither

CHRONOLOGY

1828 Tariff of Abominations

Calhoun's *Exposition*

Election of Jackson

1829 David Walker's *Appeal*

Mexico tries to abolish slavery in Texas

1830 Indian Removal Act

The Book of Mormon

Finney's revivals begin in Rochester

Anti-Masonic party holds first national party convention

1831 Nat Turner's rebellion

Garrison's *The Liberator*

Jackson reorganizes cabinet, Van Buren over Calhoun

Mormons migrate from New York to Ohio

1832 Bank War begins

Nullification Crisis

Virginia debates over slavery

Jackson reelected

1833 Formation of American Anti-slavery Society

Force Bill against South Carolina

Compromise Tariff

Slavery abolished in British Empire

1834 Whig party organized

National Trades Union formed

1835 Arkansas admitted to the Union

Revolution breaks out in Texas

Abolitionists' postal campaign

War against Seminoles and runaway slaves in Florida

1836 Congress imposes gag rule

Texas Republic established; Battle of the Alamo

Treaty of New Echota

Election of Martin Van Buren

Adams's talents and devotion to the Union had faded, but the public mood seemed little interested in either. The "corrupt bargain," in which Henry Clay allegedly conspired to hand the presidency to Adams, still hung over the White House in 1827. In the eyes of many, Adams had proven himself unfit for office, not only with his reputed bargain, but also, false rumor persisted, by procuring a young American girl for the czar when Adams served as a fourteen-year-old member of the U.S. diplomatic corps in St. Petersburg. The president's elite education and even his purchase of a billiard table and chess set for the White House made him a symbol of "aristocracy." Adams's many and diverse opponents organized against him and his policies almost from the beginning of his administration. It soon became clear that the president would be able to accomplish little of his ambitious agenda of internal improvements, a national university, and western ex-

ploration, ideals that might have won support in earlier years.

Supporters of Andrew Jackson of Tennessee, John C. Calhoun of South Carolina, and William Crawford of Georgia gradually joined forces in anticipation of the election of 1828, when they hoped to unseat Adams and his vision of an active and centralized government. The struggle, Calhoun wrote to Jackson, was between "*power* and *liberty.*" The champion of power had had his turn, Adams's opponents believed; now it was time for the champions of liberty to step forward. After some jockeying, Andrew Jackson emerged as the man to challenge Adams.

Adams supporters warned of the dangers of electing a raw and rough "military chieftain" such as Andrew Jackson to the presidency. Jackson's opponents distributed a handbill marked with eighteen coffins, each one representing a man Jackson had supposedly killed in a

Mrs. Jackson found herself the center of a humiliating scandal as her husband ran for president in 1828. She died soon after the election—the victim, her husband felt certain, of gossip mongers.

duel or ordered executed under his military command. The most incendiary charge, however, was that Jackson had married a woman married to another man, leading her to commit both bigamy and adultery in the process. The facts of the case were unclear—it appears that Rachel Jackson was a religious woman, trapped in a bad marriage, who thought she had received a divorce when she married Jackson—but the anti-Jackson forces made the most of any suspicions to the contrary.

Antimasons

Charges of conspiracy and corruption raged throughout American politics in the 1820s. Some of the suspicions seemed confirmed by events in New York. As the economy of that state prospered along with the Erie Canal, so did fraternal organizations of every sort. The Ancient Order of Masons did especially well, claiming almost 350 lodges in the state. The Masons' exclusive society, surrounded by elaborate ritual and strict secrecy, many non-Masons felt, contradicted American ideals of democracy and openness, taking men away from their families and undermining organized religion. Since Masons were obliged to show business or political preference to a brother over "any other person

in the same circumstances," some of those outside the order feared that Masons might win undue influence in their town, state, or country. As proof, they pointed out that every New York governor but one between 1804 and the late 1820s belonged to the Masons.

Suspicion of the Masons exploded when a brother named William Morgan turned against the order and decided to publish its secret rituals. Local Masonic leaders used their influence with county officials to harass and jail Morgan, who was later kidnapped. He disappeared; many said he had been murdered. The investigation soon stalled, however, as Masonic law enforcement officers and others dragged their feet. Despite twenty trials and three special prosecutors, only a few convictions resulted and those convictions brought only minor jail terms. Fury against the Masons soon spread from New York to the rest of the country, forcing one lodge after another to dissolve.

By 1827, nearly a hundred "Morgan committees" had met and formed in New York and began to spread across the entire northern half of the country. The

Titillating depictions of the supposed Masonic rituals marked a flood of publications from the Antimasons in the late 1820s and early 1830s.

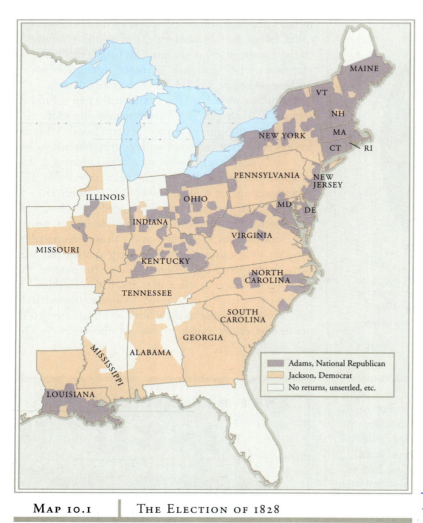

MAP 10.1 | THE ELECTION OF 1828

Legend:
- Adams, National Republican
- Jackson, Democrat
- No returns, unsettled, etc.

cess, in fact, that the movement's leaders dreamed of creating a new party to purify and energize American politics.

Birth of the Democrats

Even while the struggle over the Masons unfolded, Senator Martin Van Buren of New York was building a political coalition behind Andrew Jackson. Van Buren traveled throughout the United States, hammering out a new coalition of ambitious state politicians willing to back Jackson. The members of the coalition called themselves "Democratic Republicans," eventually to be shortened to "Democrats." Their candidates did extremely well in the off-year congressional elections of 1827, exploiting people's disapproval of the ineffectual Adams administration. The Democrats controlled both the House and the Senate.

Throughout 1827 and 1828, Van Buren and the other party leaders organized voters as they had never been organized before. Although Jackson himself was a prominent Mason, Van Buren adopted techniques not unlike those pioneered by the Antimasons in these same years. Using every strategy at their disposal—bonfires, speeches, barbecues, parades, professional writers, and the first campaign song—these Jacksonians claimed that they had found a true man of the people to strip the office from the aristocratic Adams. In towns across the country, "Old Hickory"—Jackson was supposedly as tough as that toughest of trees—was celebrated with hickory poles, brooms, sticks, and trees. The National Republicans, as Adams supporters became known, sniffed at what they considered the unseemly display that diverted attention from real issues, but they could not deny the power of the new methods to win voters' attention.

Voting turnout in 1828 doubled that of the 1824 election. The dramatic confrontation of men and styles contributed to widespread voter interest, while politicians at every level and on both sides made sure

movement gathered around it much of the anger and many of the anxieties of people who resented the growing power of merchants, manufacturers, lawyers, and a new class of professional politicians. Within two years, the "Antimasons" had established more than a hundred newspapers. They held public meetings and launched lobbying campaigns, bypassing local elites and inventing new means of pressuring legislatures directly. Unlike earlier reform organizations, such as those that supported Sunday schools and the distribution of Bibles, the Antimasons thrived on controversy. They devoted themselves to changing public opinion, to mobilizing people against a powerful entrenched force. They succeeded: Masonry lost more than half its members and created virtually no new lodges for the next fifteen years. So great was the Antimasons' sucvoters went to the polls. Jackson won easily over Adams, capturing the critical mid-Atlantic states and all the states of the South except Louisiana and Kentucky. The election proved bittersweet for Jackson, though, for his wife died soon afterward. Jackson blamed the slanderers of the other party for Rachel's death, for she had fallen ill after seeing an editorial denouncing her. The president-elect passed the weeks before his inauguration in sadness and bitterness.

The People's President

Andrew Jackson, still dressed in black in mourning for Rachel, traveled by steamboat from Nashville to Washington in the winter of 1829 to begin his presidency. Ensconced in a hotel suite, Jackson assembled his cabinet, balancing North, South, and West. Van Buren, to no one's surprise, became secretary of state, a position traditionally reserved for the man next in line for the presidency. Vice President Calhoun, ambitious for the

presidency himself, chafed at the appointment but could do little to change it; he and his wing of the party had to satisfy themselves with the appointment of one of their number as secretary of the Treasury. The most controversial appointment, however, proved volatile for reasons that had little to do with political partisanship. Jackson wanted a close friend in the cabinet, someone in whom he could confide, and he chose an old Tennessee associate, John Eaton, as his secretary of war.

Eaton, a widower in middle age, had married Peggy O'Neal Timberlake, an attractive and witty twenty-nine-year-old daughter of a well-known innkeeper in Washington. She was rumored to have driven her last husband to suicide, forcing him to defraud the government to pay debts she had run up. She was also rumored to have had sex with Eaton before their marriage—along with, one contemporary smirked, "eleven doz. others!" Eaton had asked Jackson's opinion of the marriage beforehand, receiving the old general's blessing; the president liked outspoken women

The young wife of Secretary of War John Eaton became the center of a scandal that rocked Washington during Andrew Jackson's first term.

In a scene that soon grew legendary, celebrants at Jackson's inauguration overwhelmed the capacity of the White House to contain their numbers or their rambunctiousness.

and knew from bitter experience the power that unfounded rumors could hold. Jackson, in a gesture of friendship and support as the gossip flew, offered Eaton the cabinet position, apparently hoping he would decline. Unfortunately for Jackson, Eaton accepted. The decision electrified Washington.

Despite his rambunctious youth, Jackson disdained official Washington's fondness for strong drink, endless banquets, and overheated social life. He had witnessed that high life during his time as senator from Tennessee and he held it in contempt when he returned to the capital; he preferred instead to attend the city's churches. Jackson considered himself an outsider despite his power and popularity, an outsider determined to reform Washington, to make the city worthy of the nation it was supposed to serve.

As the inauguration day of March 4 neared, Washington's population doubled as men who considered themselves important in General Jackson's election arrived in the city to claim their fair share of glory, excitement, and jobs. They drank all the whiskey the city had to offer, slept five to a bed, and generally offended the more genteel residents of the capital. At the inauguration, 30,000 people crowded in to see the new president. After Jackson's brief address, members of the excited audience followed him back to the White House—as one observer put it, "country men, farmers, gentlemen mounted and dismounted, boys, women and children, black and white, carriages, waggons and carts all pursuing him." They surged into the White House, spilling barrels of orange punch, standing with muddy boots on expensive chairs to get a better look at the proceedings, smashing thousands of dollars worth of china. Servants attracted the mob outside by moving the liquor. Jackson, literally suffocated by admirers and disgusted by the scene, climbed out a rear window and went for a steak at his boardinghouse.

Jackson Takes Charge

Many people in Washington were as appalled at the events that followed the inauguration as they were with the inauguration itself. As the new administration got under way, Jackson and his advisors cleaned house in the federal government, removing those officials whose competence, honesty, or loyalty to Jackson and the Democrats were suspect. While such a policy had become established practice in several major states, including Van Buren's New York, Jackson was the first president to make such sweeping changes on the federal level. He envisioned himself purging an arrogant bureaucracy of corruption, establishing the democratic practice of "rotation in office." As officeholders quaked and fretted, Jackson's lieutenants decided which custom houses and federal offices would be cleansed. Some of the incumbents clearly deserved to lose their jobs, having served jail terms, embezzled funds, or succumbed to drink, but others were guilty only of being active partisans for the other side in the recent election.

Jackson removed about 900 of 10,000 men from their offices and removed them in an especially brash spirit. One Jackson supporter unwisely announced to the Senate that the Jacksonians saw "nothing wrong in the rule that to the victors belong the spoils of the enemy." This proclamation gave an enduring notoriety to what from then on would be called the "spoils" system, a system that Jackson envisioned as reform, not cynical politics. Jackson further infuriated opponents by appointing partisan newspaper editors to important posts, leading to charges that Jackson was corrupting rather than cleansing American government. One key appointment, the collector of the Port of New York, did indeed prove disastrous, as the man eventually fled the United States with $1.2 million of the people's money. Yet over the course of Jackson's two terms he replaced only about 10 percent of all officeholders, not many more than his predecessors had. As with so much else in the Jackson administration, symbolism seemed to count as much as anything.

The festering conflict within the administration over the so-called "Eaton affair" proved just how important matters of symbolism could be. The wives of the other cabinet members, Vice President Calhoun's wife, and even Emily Donelson—Jackson's daughter-in-law and hostess of the White House—refused to be in the same room with Peggy Eaton. But Jackson would not be swayed in his support for John and Peggy Eaton. The new cabinet found itself bitterly divided between pro-Eaton and anti-Eaton factions. Jackson labored to mend fences, calling an influential pastor to the White House and trying to find evidence to prove Mrs. Eaton's virtue. Nothing proved effective, though, and Jackson decided that the real villain of the story was Vice President Calhoun and his unbending wife Floride. By contrast, Martin Van Buren, a widower, cemented his friendship with the president by treating Mrs. Eaton with ostentatious respect. Jackson, embittered by the refusal of his other advisors to stand by Mrs. Eaton, largely abandoned his official cabinet and relied instead on an informal group of advisors, his so-called "kitchen cabinet," and on Van Buren, the only winner in the Eaton episode.

STRUGGLES OVER SLAVERY

The years around 1830 saw several issues surrounding slavery come to a head. Southern states, worried about the rapidly growing population and power of the North, sought to define the limits of federal power. Feeling themselves neglected and abused by northern interests, South Carolina leaders tried to secure greater autonomy. At the same time, free blacks in both the

Though Andrew Jackson saw his cleansing of federal officeholders as a reform, many critics saw it only as thinly disguised greed.

North and South worked to replace the colonization movement with a campaign to end slavery and create freedom for African Americans in America. Even as these public struggles unfolded, the largest slave revolt in the history of the United States erupted in Virginia. Combined, these events demonstrated that slavery and the issues on which it touched would bedevil the confident and boisterous young country.

Nullification

Before the election, Martin Van Buren and other Democrats had sought to broaden support for Jackson, whose strength lay in the South, by passing a tariff favorable to the economic interests of New Englanders and westerners. After elaborate deal making, the Democrats enacted a major tariff in early 1828. But it came with a high cost: Southerners were furious with what they called this "tariff of abominations," for it raised the price they would have to pay for manufactured items and threatened markets abroad for southern cotton. John C. Calhoun, like other South Carolina planters, feared not only that the tariff would bleed the state dry economically but that it would set a precedent for antislavery forces who might gain control of the federal government at some future date.

Accordingly, in the summer and early fall of 1828, a few months before he would take office as Jackson's vice president, Calhoun sought to find a principled way to reconcile his national ambitions and his local concerns. Rather than argue only against the tariff itself, Calhoun asserted the general rights of individual states within the Union. To do so, he returned to what he called "the primitive principles of our government," the foundations on which everything else rested. Calhoun insisted that interests had become so diverse in the United States that laws appropriate for one state or section might well harm another. Rather than merely letting the majority run roughshod over the minority, Calhoun believed, it made more sense to let a state "nullify" a national law within its own borders. Such nullification was constitutional, he said, because the federal system did not locate sovereignty in any one place, but rather divided it among the states and the nation. Should three-fourths of the states agree that a law must apply to all the country, then that clear majority could overrule the nullification. Calhoun thought he was finding a way to preserve order in an increasingly contentious Union. The document in

which he laid out his ideas, the *South Carolina Exposition,* appeared in December of 1828; the pamphlet was published anonymously because it was too politically dangerous for the vice president of the United States to be publicly on record for nullification.

As Calhoun's position in the Jackson administration deteriorated under the influence of the "Eaton malaria," and as white South Carolinians grew increasingly angry at their helplessness in the face of the tariff, Calhoun remained silent in public on the issue. His dreams of succeeding to the presidency seemed to hang in the balance. Meanwhile, the pressure built. In early 1830 Calhoun's handpicked spokesman, Senator Robert Hayne of South Carolina, engaged in a debate with Massachusetts Senator Daniel Webster over the power of the federal government. The debate was to remain famous for generations, the first clear conflict between the states' rights argument and the defense of what Webster called "liberty and Union, now and forever, one and inseparable." Calhoun, whose position as vice president made him the presiding head of the Senate, could only watch from the podium. Hayne made Calhoun's argument well enough, but most observers agreed that Daniel Webster dominated the debate; the Massachusetts senator's fame sky-rocketed, as people throughout the North gloried in his defense of the Union. Calhoun could not remain in the background much longer; he would have to make his position known.

Calhoun's declaration of principles came at a celebration of Thomas Jefferson's birthday at the Indian Queen Hotel in Washington. Southern and western Democrats hoped that the gathering would reveal the strength of the alliance between the two sections, both of which wanted greater autonomy from the federal government. President Jackson, Vice President Calhoun, and Secretary of State Van Buren were all present. Van Buren urged the president to make clear his own position on nullification and states' rights. No one was really sure what Jackson thought on the issue, since he was identified as a Southerner but had made his reputation fighting for the Union against the British. As the officeholders went around the table, one toast after another proclaiming the rights of the states, Jackson became ever more steely. When it was his turn, the president stood, lifted his glass, and—staring at Calhoun—pronounced words filled with a meaning obvious to those present: "Our Federal Union—it must be preserved." Van Buren climbed on a chair to see how Calhoun would respond to this

As Daniel Webster of Massachusetts speaks, Robert Hayne of South Carolina (front and center, with his hands together) listens. Vice President Calhoun, working with Hayne behind the scenes, presides. The women who fill the galleries show the fascination of the entire country with this constitutional debate. Courtesy Boston Art Commission, 1998.

rebuke. "The Union—next to our liberties the most dear," he retorted, his glass trembling, "may we all remember that it can only be preserved by respecting the rights of the states and distributing equally the benefits and burdens of the Union." There was no going back.

South Carolina planters persuaded themselves that they would have to do something soon. They watched with growing alarm as the newspapers told of the success of British abolitionists in ending slavery in the British West Indies—the place from which many white South Carolina families had come generations earlier. With the memory of Denmark Vesey's plan of 1822 and an 1829 revolt in the low country still fresh in their memory, white Carolinians felt they could display no weakness on the slavery issue. Unlike other southern states, where stark geographic differences between low country and hill country often divided voters and encouraged party differences, South Carolina witnessed broad agreement among its electorate on this crucial issue. Throughout the state, raucous crowds gathered to call for a fight against the federal government on the tariff. Those South Carolinians who favored a more conciliatory stance toward the federal government could not generate nearly as much support for their position.

When the toasts at the Indian Queen Hotel revealed that President Jackson had no sympathy for the nullificationist position, the leaders of the movement in South Carolina were surprised and disappointed. After all, Jackson, like them, was a planter and slaveholder and would suffer economically along with the South Carolinians. While he supported the rights of the states when only their own welfare seemed to be at stake, Jackson considered the tariff to be for the good of the nation as a whole. The tariff provided money for defense and prevented federal debt. The South Carolina challenge would limit the power of the U.S. government to make law for the country in matters that transcended state boundaries. Jackson did not believe the United States could afford to permit such divisiveness to impair its strength in the world of nations. Jackson, the old general, would tolerate no opposition on such matters.

Free Blacks and African-American Abolitionism

Even as the white leaders of South Carolina struggled to define the extent of their powers within the Union, free blacks and slaves struggled to define their freedom. The end had come gradually, fading away in New York only as elderly slaves died. Communities of several thousand free blacks had emerged in every major northern city, establishing their own churches, newspapers, school, and lodges.

Even more numerous were free African Americans in the upper South slave states, especially Maryland and Virginia. Some had been emancipated during the decades after the Revolutionary War, when slavery seemed to be dying and when the ideals of the new nation and Christianity persuaded some masters to free their slaves. Although free blacks in the upper South scattered throughout smaller towns and rural areas, they generally tended to gather in cities as they did in the North. The cities strung along the Atlantic and Gulf coasts—Norfolk, Savannah, Charleston, Mobile, and New Orleans—all contained several thousand free blacks. Outside of Louisiana, few free blacks lived in the deep South.

Free African Americans stayed in the South to be closer to family members held in slavery and because, ironically, southern cities held out greater economic opportunity than the North. Because whites deemed many jobs in the South "nigger work," below the dignity of whites, black Southerners dominated some fields of work. Black men constituted most of the barbers and teamsters, for example, while black women found work as laundresses and domestics. Free blacks in the South had to be careful, making sure that local officials kept records of their freedom, but they could acquire property and educate their children. They stayed in contact with African Americans in the North through newspapers, letters, and word passed by the many black sailors who plied the eastern seaboard.

Free blacks throughout the country debated the merits of leaving the United States altogether, as many whites encouraged them to do. The colonization movement struggled in the 1820s. Few black Americans were willing to be shipped to a place they had never seen; only about 1,400 black Americans went to Liberia in the 1820s. African Americans came to see in colonization an attack on their hard-won accomplishments in the United States, for their leaders insisted that people of color had earned a place in this country. Rather than spending moral energy and money on removing black people, they argued, Americans should work instead on making the United States a fairer place.

David Walker proved to be an important figure in this movement. Walker had lived in Charleston at the time of Denmark Vesey's conspiracy, becoming familiar with the long tradition of revolt and resistance in the Carolina low country. After the suppression of Vesey, Walker moved to Boston. There, he established a used-clothing store, one of the few businesses open to African Americans in the North. Walker did well in the business, bought a home, joined the African Methodist church, and became a black Mason, an organization that fought against slavery and the slave trade. He gave his support to *Freedom's Journal,* an anticolonization paper published by black people in Boston and New York City between 1827 and 1829.

In 1829 Walker released his *Appeal to the Colored Citizens of the World.* Americans, whatever their skin color, had never read such a document. Walker denied that slaves felt or owed any bond to their masters. He called for black spiritual self-renewal, starting with African Americans' recognition of just how angry they were with their lot in the United States. They needed to channel that anger with God's love, Walker urged, making a group effort to end slavery immediately. He did not call for violence but for black Americans to be full Americans in both government and economy.

Within weeks of its publication, Walker's *Appeal* appeared in Savannah, where it was seized, and then in Milledgeville, Georgia (the state capital), then in Virginia, North Carolina, South Carolina, and New Orleans. The *Appeal* created panic and repression wherever it appeared. Southern whites worried at this evidence of invisible networks of communication and resistance among the slaves, free blacks, and, perhaps, sympathetic whites in their midst. Events in Virginia bore out their worst suspicions.

The Crisis of Slavery in Virginia

Nat Turner was a field hand, born in 1800, who felt that God had called him for more than the lot of a slave. Well known even in his youth for his intellectual abilities and his effectiveness as a preacher, on Sundays Turner traveled throughout the countryside around Southampton County, Virginia, coming to know most of the slaves and free black people who lived there. Praying and fasting, Turner saw visions: drops of blood that formed hieroglyphics on leaves, black shadows across the white moon. These things, he became certain, foretold a slave revolt, of the time "fast approaching when the first should be last and the last should be first." Turner, unlike Gabriel in Richmond in 1800 and Vesey in Charleston in 1822, chose to build his revolt around a small group of select lieutenants rather than to risk spreading the word broadly. Their plan was to begin the rebellion on their own and then attract compatriots along the way.

On August 22, 1831, Turner and his band began their revolt. They moved from one isolated farmhouse to the next, killing all the whites they found inside, including children. They gathered horses and weapons. Turner rode at the end of the group, praying for guidance on what plan they should follow. As the night went on, Turner's men had killed about seventy people, starting with the family of Turner's master. By morning, word had rushed to Richmond of the unimaginable events in Southampton. Whites huddled together in Jerusalem, the county seat, and troops arrived to put down the revolt. Blacks, many of whom had no connection with the rebellion, were killed by infuriated and frightened whites hundreds of miles away from Southampton. Turner's troops were all captured or killed, but he managed to escape and to hide in the woods of the county for two months. Once captured, Turner narrated a remarkable "confession" in which he told of his visions and prophecies. He had no regrets and no doubts that God would stand in judgment of the people who held other people in slavery. At his hanging in November, he showed no signs of remorse.

White Southerners saw in Nat Turner their worst nightmares. Here was a literate slave, allowed to travel on his own, allowed to spread his own interpretation of the Bible to dissatisfied slaves eager to listen to Turner's prophecies. The crackdown was not long in coming, as delegates to the state assembly gathered in Richmond a month after Turner's execution. In a series of remarkable debates, these white Virginians, some of them sons and grandsons of Thomas Jefferson, John Marshall, and Patrick Henry, openly admitted the debilitating effect of slavery on Virginia. They worried most about slavery's influence on whites, worried that slavery kept the economy from developing as it did in the North. Delegates from western Virginia, where relatively few slaves lived, expressed their

Nat Turner launched the largest slave revolt in the history of the United States, assembling a devoted band of lieutenants who kept secret the plans of the revolt.

DAVID WALKER,
*APPEAL . . . TO THE
COLORED CITIZENS OF
THE WORLD* (1829)

David Walker, a free black man, argues with Thomas Jefferson's assertion that slavery in the United States was more benign and beneficial than in ancient Greece and Rome, places to which educated Americans
looked for the measure of true civilization. In Walker's eyes, the connection between the ancients and modern whites shows a strain of cruelty
that runs throughout the history of western culture. He attacks the un-
Christian behavior of slavetraders and slaveholders even as he looks to God
for ultimate judgment.

I have been for years troubling the pages of historians to find out what our
fathers have done to the *white Christians of America,* to merit such condign
punishment as they have inflicted on them, and do continue to inflict on us
their children. But I must aver, that my researches have hitherto been to no effect. I have
therefore come to the immovable conclusion, that they (Americans) have, and do continue to punish us for nothing else, but for enriching them and their country. For I cannot conceive of any thing else. Nor will I ever believe otherwise until the Lord shall convince me.

The world knows, that slavery as it existed among the Romans, (which was the primary cause of their destruction) was, comparatively speaking, no more than a *cypher,*
when compared with ours under the Americans. Indeed, I should not have noticed the
Roman slaves, had not the very learned and penetrating Mr. Jefferson said, "When a
master was murdered, all his slaves in the same house or within hearing, were condemned to death."—Here let me ask Mr. Jefferson, (but he is gone to answer at the bar
of God, for the deeds done in his body while living,) I therefore ask the whole American

misgivings most freely, but even large slaveholders
from the East admitted slavery's negative effects. Petitions flowed into Richmond urging the legislators to
take a decisive step to rid Virginia of slavery. Defenders of slavery warned that the debates, published in the
newspapers and discussed on the streets and in the
shops and homes across the state, might result in more
revolts. Enslaved Virginians were not an "ignorant
herd of Africans," one delegate warned, but an "active,
intelligent class, watching and weighing every movement of the Legislature, with perfect knowledge of its
bearing and effect."

Some delegates urged that the state purchase all
slaves born after a certain date—1840 was proposed—and colonize them in Africa or sell them to
plantations farther south. Others argued that the state

could not afford such a step, that the Virginia economy would collapse without slavery, that slaves born
before the date of freedom would revolt, that property
rights guaranteed in the Constitution made it ridiculous to talk about taking slaves from their owners.
Others went much further, arguing that slavery was
not wrong at all but rather God's plan for civilizing
Africans otherwise lost to heathenism and barbarism.
The disparate regions of Virginia found themselves in
deep conflict; some discussed separating themselves
from the rest of the state if one policy or another were
followed. The lawmakers, starkly divided, ultimately
decided that it was "inexpedient" to take any step at all
against slavery at that time, that it would be left for
subsequent legislatures to begin the process that would
free Virginia from slavery. In the meantime, they

people, had I not rather die, or be put to death than to be a slave to any tyrant, who takes not only my own, but my wife and children's lives by the inches? Yea, would I meet death with avidity far! far!! in preference to such *servile submission* to the murderous hands of tyrants. Mr. Jefferson's very severe remarks on us have been so extensively argued upon by men whose attainments in literature, I shall never be able to reach, that I would not have meddled with it, were it not to solicit each of my brethren, who has the spirit of a man, to buy a copy of Mr. Jefferson's "Notes on Virginia," and put it in the hand of his son. For let no one of us suppose that the refutations which have been written by our white friends are enough—they are *whites*—we are *blacks*. We, and the world wish to see the charges of Mr. Jefferson refuted by the blacks *themselves,* according to their chance: for we must remember that what the whites have written respecting this subject, is other men's labors and did not emanate from the blacks. I know well, that there are some talents and learning among the colored people of this country, which we have not a chance to develop, in consequence of oppression; but our oppression ought not to hinder us from acquiring all we can.—For we will have a chance to develop them by and by. God will not suffer us, always to be oppressed. Our sufferings will come to an *end,* in spite of all the Americans this side of *eternity.* Then we will want all the learning and talents among ourselves, and perhaps more, to govern ourselves.—"Every dog must have its day," the American's is coming to an end.

But let us review Mr. Jefferson's remarks respecting us some further. Comparing our miserable fathers, with the learned philosophers of Greece, he says: "Yet notwithstanding these and other discouaging circumstances among the Romans, their slaves were often their rarest artists. They excelled too in science, insomuch as to be usually employed as tutors to their master's children; Epictetus, Terence and Phaedrus, were slaves,—but they were of the race of whites. It is not their *condition* then, but *nature,* which has produced the distinction." See this, my brethren! ! Do you believe that this assertion is

(continued)

passed harsher laws to limit the movement and gathering of free blacks and slaves.

REVIVAL AND REFORM

The power and influence of Protestant churches surged to a new level in the Jacksonian era. Far more than in any previous generation, the Jacksonian years saw the churches take leading roles in every facet of life and in every part of the Union. Revivals pulled in scores of new members, firing them with the desire to remake their lives. Many of those who experienced the spiritual rebirth of the revivals sought ways to demonstrate their faith and their hope for America. A radical new movement against slavery gathered force with stunning speed. At the same time, other Americans sought purer forms of religion itself, listening to prophets who spoke of new churches and new possibilities. Everywhere in the late 1820s and early 1830s, religion seemed on people's lips.

Revivalism

Since the late eighteenth century, revivals led by the major Protestant denominations had periodically inflamed the United States. In those revivals, people who had never declared their faith in Jesus Christ or who had fallen away from the church made public swallowed by millions of the whites? Do you know that Mr. Jefferson was one of as great characters as ever lived among the whites? See his writings for the world, and public labors for the United States of America. Do you believe that the assertions of such a man, will pass away into oblivion unobserved by this people and the world? If you do you are much mistaken — See how the American people treat us — have we souls in our bodies? Are we men who have any spirits at all? I know that there are many *swell-bellied* fellows among us whose greatest object is to fill their stomachs. Such I do not mean — I am after those who know and feel, that we are MEN as well as other people; to them, I say, that unless we try to refute Mr. Jefferson's arguments respecting us, we will only establish them.

But the slaves among the Romans. Every body who has read history, knows, that as soon as a slave among the Romans obtained his freedom, he could rise to the greatest eminence in the State, and there was no law instituted to hinder a slave from buying his freedom. Have not the Americans instituted laws to hinder us from obtaining our freedom? Do any deny this charge? Read the laws of Virginia, North Carolina, etc. Further: have not the Americans instituted laws to prohibit a man of color from obtaining and holding any office whatever, under the government of the United States of America? Now, Mr. Jefferson tells us that our condition is not so hard, as the slaves were under the Romans!!!!

. . .

The whites have always been an unjust, jealous, unmerciful, avaricious and blood thirsty set of beings, always seeking after power and authority. — We view them all over the confederacy of Greece, where they were first known to be any thing, (in consequence of education) we see them there, cutting each other's throats — trying to subject each other to wretchedness and misery, to effect which they used all kinds of deceitful, unfair and unmerciful means. We view them next in Rome, where the spirit of tyranny and de-

expressions of their faith. Thousands of people gathered in the North, South, and West, in town and countryside, to pray and hear ministers tell them of God's love and forgiveness. Hearing of these gifts, and aware of their own sinfulness, men and women sometimes fell to the ground as if stricken. Others cried and screamed. The churches that devoted themselves to spreading the Gospel — known as "evangelical" churches because they sought to bring others to their faith in Scripture — periodically experienced revivals or "awakenings" when numbers of people expressed or renewed their faith. This revivalism burst out again in the mid-1820s.

Many ministers and churches across the country were swept up in the awakening, but one man embodied its new and aggressive spirit: Charles Grandison Finney. Finney, a young attorney from Utica, New York, who had not regularly attended church until encouraged to do so by his fiancée, in 1821 suddenly found himself struck with the power of God's love. "An overwhelming sense" of his wickedness brought Finney to his knees. "I wept aloud like a child [and] the Holy Spirit descended upon me in a manner that seemed to go through me body and soul," he recalled. "I could feel the impression like a wave of electricity, going through and through me." Finney spread the word of the Bible in the plain and straightforward language of everyday life. He told people that they had it within their power to take the first step toward God, that God would listen. Finney told people to seek out salvation, to throw themselves open to the mercy of Jesus.

ceit raged still higher. — We view them in Gaul, Spain and in Britain — in fine, we view them all over Europe, together with what were scattered about in Asia and Africa, as heathens, and we see them acting more like devils than accountable men. But some may ask, did not the blacks of Africa, and the mulattoes of Asia, go on in the same ways as did the whites of Europe? I answer no — they never were half so avaricious, deceitful and unmerciful as the whites, according to their knowledge.

But we will leave the whites or Europeans as heathens and take a view of them as christians, in which capacity we see them as cruel, if not more so than ever. In fact, take them as a body, they are ten times more cruel, avaricious, and unmerciful than ever they were; for while they were heathens they were bad enough it is true, but it is positively a fact that there were not quite so audacious as to go and take vessel loads of men, women and children, and in cold blood and through devilishness, throw them into the sea, and murder them in all kind of ways. While they were heathens, they were too ignorant for such barbarity. But being christians, enlightened and sensible, they are completely prepared for such hellish cruelties. Now suppose God were to give them more sense, what would they do. If it were possible would they not *dethrone* Jehovah and seat themselves upon his throne? I therefore, in the name and fear of the Lord God of heaven and of earth, divested of prejudice either on the side of my color or that of the whites, advance my suspicion of them, whether they are *as good by nature* as we are or not. Their actions, since they were known as a people, have been the reverse, I do indeed suspect them, but this, as I before observed, is shut up with the Lord, we cannot exactly tell, it will be proved in succeeding generations. — The whites have had the essence of the gospel as it was preached by my master and his apostles — the Ethiopians have not, who are to have it in its meridian splendor — the Lord will give it to them to their satisfaction. I hope and pray my God, that they will make good use of it, that it may be well with them.

SOURCE David Walker, *Appeal, in Four Articles; Together with a Preamble to the Colored Citizens of the World. . . .* (Boston: September 28, 1829. 3rd ed. Boston: D. Walker).

By the winter of 1825–1826 Finney found in the young cities of western New York a receptive audience among young men, on their own in a rapidly changing America, and among women of every age. The churches, these people believed, had grown cold in the hands of the established ministry and needed a revival of spirit. They wanted a Christianity of activity, of prayer meetings, of spreading the word any way they could. Finney's influence grew in strength and numbers as women prayed with one another. The district of upstate New York that lay along the path of the Erie Canal became known as "The Burned-Over District," as one revival after another surged through its towns and farms.

The revivals took on a new scale and urgency in 1830 as they ignited Rochester. Like other rapidly growing towns and cities along the Erie Canal, Rochester was ripe for revival. Many people worried that the people of the young city barely knew one another, that husbands and wives, workers and employers, rich and poor, were drifting apart. Politics appeared a morass of selfishness; alcohol seemed to drown hopes of social progress and family happiness; men seemed more concerned with their businesses, lodges, and politics than with their souls. When Finney came to town in 1830, accordingly, he was met by a populace hungry for something to stir them up, hungry for a new message.

Women's prayer groups met daily and traveled from home to home in efforts to bring the word of Jesus. Women pleaded with their husbands to listen to the Reverend Finney. Employers made it clear to the men

This engraving depicts Charles Grandison Finney's moment of conversion as he described the scene in his memoirs.

SAVED IN THE LORD'S OWN TIME AND PLACE

who worked under them that it would be noticed whether or not they attended the revival. These efforts, combined with Finney's masterful sermons and hopeful message, transformed Rochester, bringing hundreds of people into the church who had not come before and reclaiming many who had strayed. All the Protestant denominations worked together, setting aside for a while their differences on baptism and other doctrines.

Such a powerful revival seemed evidence to many people that America could be changed by faith. As they watched saloons shut down, families brought together, and shops and stores closed while the revival was in progress, it appeared that the way was being prepared for God's kingdom on earth. If the United States could be adequately reformed, these people believed, the day of redemption could be hastened. It was up to Americans themselves to purge their country of sin, to make themselves better and then to help others see the way as well. Such faith bred a demand for immediate reforms. When the means of change lay so close at hand, only a prayer away, delay seemed a rejection of God's love.

Abolitionism

Religious ferment stirred some evangelicals to take immediate steps toward improving American society. They believed that they could help prepare the way for God's rule on earth by ridding their society of its nu-

merous evils. While the great majority of white Northerners (and Southerners) thought Christians should seek holiness mainly in their own hearts, others were equally certain that society itself could and should be changed. To many, slavery seemed the place to start.

William Lloyd Garrison was the key person in the emergence of the new antislavery movement. Garrison

William Lloyd Garrison played a key role in persuading many Northern whites that slavery was morally wrong and should be brought to an immediate end.

William Lloyd Garrison's abolitionist newspaper made no compromises, as this celebratory banner proclaims.

had grown up hard, abandoned as an infant by his sea captain father and apprenticed to masters in one craft after another. At twelve, he found himself working in a print shop, where he quickly achieved skill in composing type and writing. At the age of twenty-two, he became the editor of the first newspaper dedicated to the prohibition of alcohol. Believing in the necessity of ending slavery as well as drunkenness, Garrison joined the colonization movement and soon became editor of its paper as well.

In the late 1820s Garrison attended the anticolonizationist meetings held by African Americans in eastern cities, including the group that published the first antislavery newspaper, *Freedom's Journal.* He experienced a mounting desire for a more aggressive antislavery crusade as he saw the limitations of the colonization movement and as he witnessed the passion of people such as David Walker. The balding and bespectacled young Garrison sought out other financial supporters and a partner to launch a paper of his own: *The Liberator.* It called for the immediate start toward emancipation, explicitly rejecting colonization. In 1831, the paper's first year, it had only six subscribers, but it acquired fifty-three by the following year, most of them African American. "I *will* be as harsh as

truth," Garrison announced, "and as uncompromising as justice. On this subject, I do not wish to think, speak, or write, with moderation. . . . I am earnest—I will not equivocate—I will not excuse—I will not retreat a single inch—AND I WILL BE HEARD." He was.

Two hundred antislavery societies emerged in the early thirties. Ground that had been prepared by the evangelical crusades of the preceding few years proved fertile for the antislavery cause. Some northern church members argued that it was the duty of good Christians to cast out slaveholders and to work for immediate emancipation, to use the enormous power of the church as a force for freedom. These "immediatists" called for slaveholders to recognize the truth of what the abolitionists were saying, to free their slaves immediately, hire them as free workers, and help repay the former slaves for their years of unpaid toil. These early abolitionists hoped to convert the slaveholders by persuasion and prayer, by church and newspaper—not by law and force.

The American Anti-slavery Society formed in Philadelphia in 1833. Looking to the example of Great Britain, where the major denominations supported the antislavery movement that was at that moment triumphing over slavery in the British West Indies, the members of the society expected American church leaders to take the lead against American slavery. The North would have to be converted before it could expect the South to follow. To convert the North, antislavery organizations held out the prospect of a free South, where 2 million freed slaves would constitute an "immense market" for the products of Northern "mechanics and manufacturers." These abolitionists expected the former slaves to remain in the South; they spoke little of the competition the freed-people might provide to the workers of the North. Similarly, the antislavery people believed a free South would prosper, with planters and free whites flourishing as they had never flourished before; the South, they claimed, would "exhibit the flush of returning health, and feel a stronger pulse, and draw a freer breath."

The antislavery organizations proved volatile inside as well as out. Far more than any other organizations in the United States at this time, the antislavery cause brought together male and female, black and white, patrician and working class, Quaker and Unitarian, Baptist and Methodist, radical and moderate, political and anti-political people. Each of these groups had its own vision of how the abolitionists should spend their energies and influence. Black abolitionists, in particular, wanted the organizations to do more to help black communities in the North.

The antislavery societies used pamphlets, leaflets, and other literature as their major weapons. Rapid innovations in printing lowered the cost of producing such materials, which flooded post offices and streets. The postal campaign reached its peak in 1834 and 1835, when a million pieces went out through the mail, much of it to the South, where the abolitionists hoped to appeal directly to ministers and others who might be willing to listen to their pleas. That literature, white Southerners furiously protested, virtually invited slaves to follow Nat Turner's example. Georgia slaveholders offered a $12,000 reward for the capture of wealthy merchant Arthur Tappan, who, along with his brother Lewis, funded much of the postal campaign against slavery. Arthur received a slave's severed ear in the mail.

The pamphlets infuriated people in much of the North as well. Mobs, led by some of the wealthiest merchants of northern towns but constituted in large part by white working people, rose up violently against the abolitionists. In 1835 mobs destroyed the home of African Americans, pelted antislavery speakers, and dragged William Lloyd Garrison himself through the streets of Boston at the end of a rope. The leaders of that mob announced that they had assaulted Garrison "to assure our brethren of the South that we cherish rational and correct notions on the subject of slavery." Many white Northerners believed the abolitionists to be hypocrites who cared nothing for America and everything for their own sanctimonious souls. Antislavery speakers risked a mob every time they spoke; one man counted over 150 attacks made on him. Abolitionists' churches were blown up and their school buildings dragged into swamps.

The persecution, ironically, strengthened the abolitionist cause. Denunciation and harassment only made the abolitionists more certain of the need for their efforts, of the moral decay caused by slavery. The 200 antislavery societies of 1835 grew to over 500 in 1836. The reformers flooded Congress with petitions calling for the end of slavery in the District of Columbia, sending over 300 petitions signed by 40,000 people. The acceptance of these petitions by the House, Southerners argued, besmirched slaveholders' honor and threatened to incite slaves to rebellion. The petitions should be rejected out of hand. Congress sought to avoid conflict by merely tabling the petitions, but

the compromise pleased no one. Over the next decade, Northerners of even a mild antislavery bent chafed at this "gag rule," what they saw as a clear violation of American freedom in the interests of slavery.

The Birth of Mormonism

Like so many American families of these years, that of Joseph Smith could not find a secure place. His father dreamed of bringing his family out of poverty, moving them from one community to another. Young Joseph, like hundreds of other people in upstate New York, looked for treasure rumored to have been buried long ago in the mountains; he watched with concern for his soul, too, as revivals came and went without his conversion. Smith reported that he felt the presence of an angel, however, who told him "that God had work for me to do, and that my name should be for good and evil among all nations, kindreds, and tongues. He said there was a book deposited, written upon gold plates, giving an account of the former inhabitants of this continent, and the source from which they sprang. He also said that, the fullness of the everlasting Gospel was contained in it." Smith claimed that the angel directed him to the location of the sacred writings.

In 1827, Smith began to transcribe what he had found; sitting in a tent divided by a partition, he read the plates to an assistant on the other side. *The Book of Mormon* took shape, telling of a struggle between the chosen ones and their persecutors, of a promised land reserved for the righteous. North America, the book said, had been visited by Jesus in the distant past but the people had lost their way and fallen into disputation. Those people had been cursed by God for their sins and marked with dark skins; their descendants were the American Indians, who had forgotten their lost paradise.

Joseph Smith and several followers traveled throughout New York selling copies of what they called the "Gold Bible." They were met with hostility virtually everywhere they went, but they slowly gathered converts to their Church of Jesus Christ of the Latter-Day Saints. Many of the new members were poor, including some free blacks, but others had considerable resources. The most important converts were two brothers, Brigham and Joseph Young. As the movement gathered momentum, hundreds of people joined the church; entire congregations of churches of other faiths joined the Mormons and gladly contributed everything they owned to the church's common fund. The faithful

Joseph Smith was the founder of the Church of Jesus Christ of the Latter-Day Saints, also known as the Mormons.

moved first to Ohio and then to what Smith believed to be the original Eden: Missouri. But other settlers made no secret of their disapproval of the Mormons, firing shots, throwing stones through windows, and burning the crops of the Latter-Day Saints. The Mormons found no peace for the next decade. They were constantly harassed by non-Mormons who feared the growing number of converts and the local economic power that came from the church members' pooled resources and hard work.

POLITICAL TURMOIL

Andrew Jackson made fervent enemies as well as devoted followers throughout his presidency. No one could be neutral about him. Politics quickened in preparation for the election of 1832 as voters and leaders mobilized in opposition or support, latching on to a wide range of issues. Jackson, furious at any resistance, lashed out, determined that his work not be wasted. The nation had not seen such political conflict for decades, as citizens debated issues of the economy, states' rights, and morality.

Taking Sides

In September 1831 the first national political convention in U.S. history met in Baltimore. It was convened by the Anti-Masons. Despite their origins and their name, the Anti-Masons were concerned with the state of American politics in general, not merely with the threat posed by the Masons. They attracted an impressive list of ambitious and accomplished young men to their convention, including many who believed the Jackson White House was too pro-Southern and too callous with the American Indians. The Anti-Masons found little appeal in John Quincy Adams's National Republicans, for that party seemed to be stuck in the past and hapless against the strong Jacksonian Democrats. The Anti-Masons promised to become a powerful third party, a wild card in an already tumultuous American politics.

The Jacksonians held their own convention the following spring. Jackson, fed up with the controversy over Peggy Eaton and alienated from Calhoun, early in 1831 asked all the members of his cabinet to resign. When the president reconstituted the cabinet, he replaced pro-Calhoun men with men more to his own liking. Van Buren, who had suggested the purge as a way of cleaning house before the election of 1832, was nominated by Jackson to be the new ambassador to Great Britain. Calhoun, in a final act of revenge, cast the Senate vote that rejected Van Buren's appointment. Van Buren and Jackson got the last laugh when the convention of 1832 filled the vice presidential slot with Van Buren and removed Calhoun from the ticket. Calhoun, it became clear, would never be Jackon's choice for president; Van Buren had supplanted him as heir apparent.

The radicals in South Carolina, their last connection to the presidency broken, reacted with fury when Jackson signed another high tariff in early 1832. Advocates of nullification won control of the South Carolina legislature and oversaw the election of a state convention. Such a convention, Calhoun and his allies declared, could nullify the U.S. Constitution because state conventions had been elected before the first national constitutional convention and authorized delegates to write a national document in the first place. The South Carolina convention announced that the federal tariffs passed in 1828 and 1832 were null, without force in South Carolina. Any state official who attempted to enforce the tariff, in fact, would be removed from office; South Carolina would secede if the U.S. government turned to arms to enforce the tariff. Calhoun resigned the vice presidency before his final few months in the office expired. He became senator from South Carolina, now free to defend openly the state's resistance to the federal government.

The Bank War

Despite the tariffs intended to serve their interests, most people in the Northeast felt they had received little from Andrew Jackson's first term. They viewed him with distrust and growing anger, perceiving in Old Hickory an enemy to moral and commercial progress, a defender of the backward South and West against the East. The fate of the Second Bank of the United States stood as the key issue in this regard. Many merchants and others deemed it a stabilizing force in the American economy, holding an otherwise decentralized money system in place. It was the job of Nicholas Biddle, the president of the Bank of the United States, to make sure that state banks kept plenty of metal currency—specie—on hand with which to pay the national bank when asked to do so. Such rules kept the state banks from putting out too many notes, from inflating the currency with paper money unsupported by gold or silver. When the economy fell into trouble, on the other hand, Biddle and the Bank of the United States would lessen their demands on the state banks, preventing panics and deflation.

While businessmen appreciated this role of the bank, many other Americans distrusted it. In their eyes, this largely private institution enjoyed far too much power for its own good or the good of the country. Why should privileged stockholders in the bank,

To opponents of the Bank, it seemed a "monster"— unnatural, and hard to kill.

GENERAL JACKSON SLAYING THE MANY HEADED MONSTER.

they asked, profit from the business of the federal government? Why should the national notes be allowed to depress the value of state notes, with their origins closer to home?

For many voters, objections to the Bank of the United States were as much objections to banking and commerce in general as to any specific policies of the national bank. The whole business of banking seemed suspect, with its paper money, its profits seemingly without labor, its government-supported monopolies, its apparent speculation with public money. Andrew Jackson shared these feelings of mistrust. As a young man, he had lost a considerable amount of money to a speculator and nothing he saw as president changed his mind about those who dealt in the mysteries of currency. He disliked monopoly, he disliked paper money, and he disliked the Bank of the United States.

The issue came to a head in 1832 as Henry Clay and other National Republicans, joined by South Carolina nullifiers such as Calhoun, sought to use the bank as a way to defeat Jackson for the presidency. A few months before the election in the fall, the bank's supporters steered its application for rechartering through Congress. Jackson heard of the news while he was ill in bed. "The bank," he told Martin Van Buren, "is trying to kill me, *but I will kill it!*" He vetoed the recharter, proclaiming that the bank was "unauthorized by the constitution, subversive of the rights of the States, and dangerous to the liberties of the people."

Jackson's opponents, in turn, saw the president, not the bank, as the usurper of American rights. How dare he singlehandedly overturn what the people, in the form of Congress, had declared to be their will? Henry Clay and other opponents argued that his action posed a far greater threat to the American people than did the bank. If the president could force his way into the lawmaking process, the division of powers laid out in the Constitution would be violated and the Union would risk falling under the despotic rule of a president who would be king.

Jackson on the Offensive

The election of 1832 turned around these broad issues about the fate of the nation. Jackson portrayed himself as the champion of the common man fighting against a bloated aristocracy of privilege and monopoly. Clay, the candidate of the National Republicans, portrayed

himself as the defender of the Union against an arrogant and power-hungry president, a man who had shown a disregard for morality and justice in his dealing with the American Indians and the spoils system as well as with the Bank. William Wirt, the candidate of the Anti-Masons, declared himself the opponent of conspiracies, corruptions, and subversions larger and more insidious than the bank, all the more dangerous for not being clearly defined.

Despite the challenges on the bank and by the Anti-Masons, Jackson won by a considerable margin, losing South Carolina to a nullifier, Vermont to the Anti-Masons, and the rest of New England and a few other states to Clay. Emboldened by his majority at the polls, the president went on the offensive. Before the bank could deploy its enormous financial resources to gather the two-thirds' majority necessary to override his earlier veto, Jackson quickly moved all federal funds from the Bank of the United States to state banks. The newly appointed secretary of the Treasury followed Jackson's plan and put the government deposits in seven state banks—promptly dubbed "pet banks" by opponents of the new strategy. Congressmen of both parties denounced Jackson's move. Biddle and his bank's supporters fought on for two more years, but without the government's deposits they had little leverage. Jackson's lieutenants efficiently mobilized the votes they needed in Congress to prevent the renewal of the Bank's charter. The Bank of the United States, deprived of government support, began a slow death.

Even as the bank war raised one set of questions about the Constitution and the separation of powers, the nullification crisis brought another constitutional crisis to a climax. Nullification, Jackson announced soon after his reelection, would not be tolerated. He could not have been any clearer: Nullification was "incompatible with the existence of the Union, contradicted expressly by the letter of the Constitution, unauthorized by its spirit, inconsistent with every principle on which it was founded, and destructive of the great object for which it was formed." Disunion was treason, he warned, and would be treated as such; Congress passed a "Force Bill" to permit him to use military power to keep South Carolina in line. Recent opponents of Jackson such as Henry Clay and Daniel Webster were pleased—and surprised—at Jackson's nationalism; they had not expected such convictions from a Tennessee planter. Southerners in general were caught in a difficult position, disapproving of South

Workers from a broad range of jobs found that membership in a union offered them independence and pride as well as economic benefit.

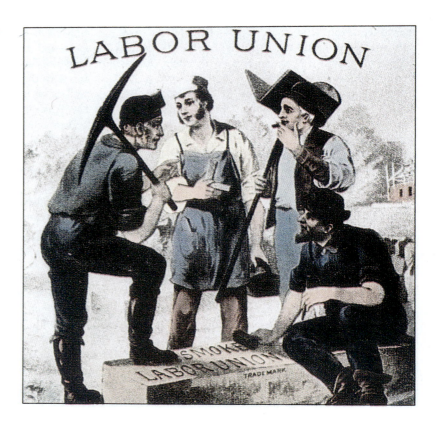

Carolina's radicalism but distrustful of the centralizing precedent of the Force Bill.

Congress twisted and turned on the issue, not wanting South Carolina to get its way but unwilling to see Jackson use arms. After much debate, Congress, under the leadership of Henry Clay, offered compromise in early 1833: The tariff would be slowly but steadily lowered over the next decade, giving northern manufacturers time to adapt. South Carolina, secretly relieved, declared itself the victor and accepted the compromise tariff; in a final display of states' rights defiance, though, the Carolinians nullified the Force Bill. Jackson ignored them, recognizing the emptiness of the gesture.

Those opposed to Jackson began to call themselves "Whigs." Like their British namesakes, the American Whigs saw themselves as the counterbalance to otherwise unchecked monarchical power—in this case "King Andrew I," "the most absolute despot now at the head of any representative government on earth." The men who moved into the Whigs—former National Republicans, former Anti-Masons, and even former Democrats—shared little at first except their opposition to Jackson and his use of power. As the fight against Jackson continued, however, they would find more common ground and become a powerful enemy against Jackson and his party.

Working People

Not everyone prospered during the "flush times" of the 1820s and 1830s. Since prices and rents rose much more quickly than wages, urban working people found themselves falling behind. For generations, artisans and others who worked with their hands prided themselves on their contribution to America. They saw themselves as the bedrock of the republic, the people whose dedication helped win the Revolution, whose sweat helped make the young United States an economic wonder in the world. These working men and women felt their contributions slighted in the new economy, however, their labor no longer bringing the recognition and rewards it deserved. Business owners, eager to bring products to market as quickly and cheaply as possible, increasingly divided the steps of production. Rather than having a journeyman construct an entire shoe for a single customer, for example, merchants employed one set of workers to make only soles and heels, another to stitch uppers to soles, and another to finish the shoes. Such people labored in homes where working and living conditions were abominable, where the lack of light and sanitation destroyed eyes and health.

Workers formed unions to defend their rights. After a failed strike for a ten-hour day by journeymen carpenters in Philadelphia in 1827, artisans pooled their efforts in the Mechanics' Union of Trade Associations, the first citywide federation of workingmen's groups. Members of fifteen different trades joined. In the early 1830s trades' associations appeared in New York, Boston, Baltimore, Washington, and Louisville. They sponsored newspapers, lobbied legislatures, and supported one another during strikes. By the mid-1830s, between 100,000 and 300,000 men and women belonged to unions.

A number of labor and political leaders, recognizing the power of such numbers, sought to mobilize the organized workers into politics. While union members generally liked Andrew Jackson's blows against monopoly, they thought he pulled up short in his attack on privilege. It was not only the Bank of the United States that used power unfairly, they argued, but also large businesses and property holders. They sought to push the political system into doing more to protect working people. Some unions became deeply engaged in politics and put forward their own candidates. Such workingmen's parties seemed full of promise. In 1834, at the movement's high point, workers formed the National Trades Union to "unite and harmonize the efforts of all the productive classes of our country." It appeared that a self-conscious urban working class might become a potent factor in American political life.

THE INDIAN PEOPLES AND THE MEXICAN NATION

The most important "foreign relations" of Andrew Jackson's administration were with the native peoples of North America. The American Indians held immense areas of the South and the West when Jackson took office, land that many whites wanted and demanded. The southwestern border of the United States remained dangerously ambiguous as well. Mexico governed its Texas province loosely and many white Americans coveted that land. Both of these situations would undergo explosive change under Andrew Jackson.

Jackson and the American Indians

Andrew Jackson had announced, and acted upon, his attitudes toward the Indians years before he took office as president. The steady pressing of white population onto the rich lands of the Cherokee, Chickasaw, Creeks, Seminoles, and Choctaws, he thought, left the people of those nations with two choices. They could either become "industrious Citizens" who accepted the sovereignty of the states that claimed the lands on which they lived, or they could "remove to a Country *where* they can retain their ancient customs, so dear to them, that they cannot give up in exchange for regular society." If they could adapt themselves to agriculture and law, they might remain where they were, protected by the laws they pledged to obey; if they could not adapt, they would have to leave. Their only other choice, Jackson thought, was extinction.

White people had mixed feelings about the Indians. Americans of European descent considered the Indians admirable in many ways, dignified and free, able to learn and prosper. Not a few "white" and "black" families were proud to claim some Indian ancestry. Andrew Jackson, for his part, adopted a Creek infant, Lyncoya, educated him, and brought him to live with him and his wife. In fact, the death of Lyncoya from tuberculosis in 1828, at age sixteen, hastened Rachel Jackson's heartbreak and decline. Many other white Americans, including some in Congress, had long contributed time and money to the Indians, helping to build and staff schools, sending seed and agricultural implements to ease the transition to farming.

By the late 1820s the "civilized tribes" had adapted themselves to the dominant society. Many of the tribes were led by chiefs of mixed descent, leaders who lived in cabins, houses, and even mansions. The wealthiest Indians, especially the Cherokee, bought African-American slaves. The children of the Indian leaders and others went to schools established by white missionaries, who persuaded a considerable number of Indians to convert to Christianity. The Cherokees

MEMORIAL AND PROTEST OF THE CHEROKEE NATION (1836)

The Cherokee nation, even while the federal and state governments prepared to force them from their homes in the South, desperately reminded Congress of the treaties struck between the two peoples. The Cherokee pleaded that they had done exactly what white Americans had urged them to do: assimilate, progress, and prosper. The arguments had little effect; the Trail of Tears soon commenced.

The undersigned representatives of the Cherokee nation, east of the river Mississippi, impelled by duty, would respectfully submit, for the consideration of your honorable body, the following statement of facts: It will be seen, from the numerous subsisting treaties between the Cherokee nation and the United States, that from the earliest existence of this government, the United States, in Congress assembled, received the Cherokees and their nation into favor and protection; and that the chiefs and warriors, for themselves and all parts of the Cherokee nation, acknowledged themselves and the said Cherokee nation to be under the protection of the United States of America, and of no other sovereign whatsoever: they also stipulated, that the said Cherokee nation will not hold any treaty with any foreign power, individual State, or with individuals of any State: that for, and in consideration of, valuable concessions made by the Cherokee nation, the United States solemnly guar-

published a newspaper that included articles in both their own language and in English.

Despite these adaptations, the Indians of the Southeast showed no desire to leave the land on which they lived in the late 1820s. In their view, they had already given up more land than they should have—millions of acres over the preceding twenty years—and were determined to hold on to what remained. "We would not receive money for land in which our fathers and friends are buried," they declared. Most whites, especially those who lived nearby and coveted the rich cotton lands under the Indians' control, bristled at the continuing presence of the native inhabitants. Many white people longed to banish the American Indians to land on the other side of the Mississippi River, where, it seemed, whites would not want to live for a very long time, if ever.

In 1827, the Cherokees held a national convention and drew up a written constitution, patterned on that of the United States. They desired both to declare their sovereignty over their lands and to show whites just how devoted they were to American values. But the new constitution, U.S. courts ruled, violated the law of both the nation and the state of Georgia, which petitioned the federal government to remove the Cherokees. An already volatile situation worsened when gold was discovered on the Indian lands and white prospectors rushed in. The Georgia legislature declared the Cherokees' laws null and void, placing Georgia law into effect instead. The Cherokees suddenly found themselves even more vulnerable than before. White settlers invaded northern Georgia, taking Cherokee property.

Jackson told the Indians he was their friend, even their "father," but that he could do nothing to stop their mistreatment except to move them beyond the Mississippi River, where, he promised, they would be safe. The Indians and their supporters, mostly anteed to said nation all their lands not ceded, and pledged the faith of the government, that "all white people who have intruded, or may hereafter intrude, on the lands reserved for the Cherokees, shall be removed by the United States, and proceeded against, according to the provisions of the act, passed 30th March, 1802," entitled "An act to regulate trade and intercourse with the Indian tribes, and to preserve peace on the frontiers." It would be useless to recapitulate the numerous provisions for the security and protection of the rights of the Cherokees, to be found in the various treaties between their nation and the United States. The Cherokees were happy and prosperous under a scrupulous observance of treaty stipulations by the government of the United States, and from the fostering hand extended over them, they made rapid advances in civilization, morals, and in the arts and sciences. Little did they anticipate, that when taught to think and feel as the American citizen, and to have with him a common interest, they were to be *despoiled by their guardian,* to become strangers and wanderers in the land of their fathers, forced to return to the savage life, and to seek a new home in the wilds of the far west, and that without their consent. An instrument purporting to be a treaty with the Cherokee people, has recently been made public by the President of the United States, that will have such an operation, if carried into effect. This instrument, the delegation aver before the civilized world, and in the presence of Almighty God, is fraudulent, false upon its face, made by unauthorized individuals, without the sanction, and against the wishes, of the great body of the Cherokee people. Upwards of fifteen thousand of those people have protested against it, solomnly declaring they will never acquiesce. . . .

SOURCE Memorial and Protest of the Cherokee Nation, June 22, 1836, *Exec. Doc.* No. 286, 24th Cong., 1st sess., pp. 1–2.

religious people in the North, responded bitterly to such claims, arguing that the rights of the Constitution should certainly extend to people who had lived in North America since time immemorial. But the Jacksonians quickly pushed through the Indian Removal Act of 1830. Two Supreme Court decisions in favor of the Cherokees, in 1830 and in 1832, proved to be without effect, since they depended on the federal government to implement them and Jackson had no intention of doing anything of the sort.

In the face of the impending removal, most of the Indian peoples split into pro-assimilation, "progressive" factions and anti-assimilation "conservative" factions. They debated fiercely and sometimes violently among themselves. Missionaries and federal agents dealt primarily with the progressives, but many other Indians resisted, often by moving far into the backwoods. Many thousands of each nation remained behind, either those who had passed into white or black society through marriage or those who lived outside areas of heavy settlement.

Agents, some of mixed blood, swindled the Indians as they prepared for the removal. The Choctaws, the first to move, underwent horrific experiences, suffering greatly and dying in large numbers as they traveled in the worst winter on record with completely inadequate supplies. The Creeks, too, confronted frauds and assaults. The Indians who moved sold whatever they could not take with them, usually at a great loss. Wagons and carts carried the old and the sick, while women and children drove livestock along the trail. Soldiers usually accompanied the Indians, along with an agent to hand out whatever support the government provided. Some of the migrants used steamboats to travel up or down the Mississippi River and then to Oklahoma along the Arkansas or Red River, while others proceeded overland. "To see the remnant of a once mighty people fettered and chained together forced to

MAP 10.2 | THE REMOVAL OF THE AMERICAN INDIANS

depart from the land of their fathers into a country un-known to them," an Alabama newspaper admitted, "is of itself sufficient to move the stoutest heart."

The Cherokee removal was the most prolonged. Af-ter years of negotiating, the government struck a bar-gain with a small and unrepresentative number of the Cherokee in the Treaty of New Echota in 1836. While groups of several hundred at a time left, including some of the wealthiest, 17,000 refused to leave by the deadline. General Winfield Scott then led 7,000 troops against them, driving people from their homes empty-handed, marching them to stockades and ship-ping them out by rail and water. About a quarter of all eastern Cherokees died in what they called "The Trail of Tears." Some Cherokees remained in the mountains of North Carolina and Tennessee, but the power of the eastern Indians had been destroyed.

The Seminoles fought against removal as long as they could. Led by Osceola, the son of an English trader and the husband of an escaped slave, the Semi-noles tried to break the will of the whites by killing soldiers and civilians and by burning their crops and homes. The Second Seminole War launched by the federal government to remove the 5,000 Indians began in 1836 and dragged on for six years. The conflict proved both unpopular and unsuccessful. About 36,000 U.S. soldiers fought and 1,500 died; many more suffered debilitating disease. The federal govern-ment spent $20 million in the fight, even though few white people wanted to settle on the Seminoles' land. The United States captured Osceola only by deception at a supposed peace conference. He died in captivity a few months later, after which some Seminoles finally migrated to Oklahoma. But most of the Seminole

The Cherokee called their forced migration to Oklahoma the Trail of Tears. About 4,000 of the 15,000 Indians forced to move died along the way, as did over 25,000 of the 100,000 southeastern Indians who were driven from their homes in these years.

people, able to use the swampy landscape to hide, were never driven out of Florida.

Fighting also erupted in the Illinois Territory between white settlers and the Sac and Fox Indians. These people, under the leadership of Black Hawk, saw their lands along the Mississippi River taken over by whites while the Indians were on a hunting expedition in 1832. The whites burned the Indians' huts and plowed under their fields. In retaliation, the Sac and Fox destroyed white settlements. A large contingent of volunteers, regular troops, and allied Indians set out after Black Hawk and his people, who also had allies from other Indian nations. Eventually, the whites outnumbered Black Hawk and overran his camp, killing nearly 500 as they tried to cross the Mississippi River. Taken prisoner, Black Hawk refused to repent, telling his captors that he "has done nothing for which an Indian ought to be ashamed. He has fought for his

countrymen, the squaws and papooses, against white men who came, year after year, to cheat them and take away their land." Black Hawk's words and deeds, widely reported in the newspapers of the country, attracted considerable sympathy among whites in the East. Andrew Jackson met with Black Hawk and pardoned him; the chief's autobiography became a best-seller. The United States, using its defeat of the Sac as an example, found it much easier to induce the other Indians of the Old Northwest to cede 190 million acres for $70 million.

Conflict with Mexico

Speculators and settlers from the United States continually moved into Mexican Texas in the 1820s and 1830s. Sometimes the Mexican officials encouraged

A small force of Americans and tejanos *were overwhelmed at the Alamo mission in San Antonio. Although the Mexican army won the battle, their victory unleashed the support of the United States.*

the newcomers; at other times, they sought to slow American settlement. Seeking the end of slavery in Mexico, they wanted settlers but they did not want the slaves white settlers often brought with them. The key leader in the American migration was Stephen F. Austin, a Virginia-born entrepreneur who first arrived in Mexico in 1821 on the heels of Mexican independence. Throughout the 1820s, Austin, negotiating with the changing Mexican governments, oversaw the arrival and settlement of hundreds of Americans. While the Mexican laws on slavery shifted repeatedly, most of the American settlers—the great majority of them Southerners—argued that they had to have slaves if Texas was to develop as they and as Mexican leaders hoped. The Americans, with the tacit approval

of local officials, improvised laws and took advantage of loopholes to keep slavery in fact if not in name.

American settlers and the Mexican government came into increasing conflict, as provincial officials attempted to collect tariffs and slow immigration into the district. Austin and the other Americans petitioned the Mexican government to let them become a separate Mexican state under its own administration, but they were rebuffed when Antonio López de Santa Anna took control of the government. In Santa Anna's eyes, the Texans were clearly inviting an expansionist United States to take this province away from Mexico; he sent in troops to meet the threat. In 1835, a convention of Texans voted to fight against Santa Anna, offering large amounts of land to all who would come help in the struggle.

Volunteers and money flowed into Texas from throughout the United States, where people had been watching the events in that area with great interest. Southern states in particular sent hundreds of men. Nevertheless, they were greatly outnumbered by the Mexicans, who decimated the Americans at several battles. As the Mexican army sought to occupy San Antonio, 188 rebels—including Davy Crockett of Tennessee, famous for his frontier exploits and for his service in Congress—took refuge in the Mission of the Alamo. Most of the people inside were American, but they were joined by *tejanos,* Mexicans of the province who allied themselves with the revolt for independence. The defenders of the Alamo held out against 3,000 Mexican soldiers for nearly two weeks, until the Mexicans finally stormed the mission and killed all inside except three white women, two white children, and an African-American slave. The Mexicans stripped the bodies of the insurrectionaries and burned them. After the Alamo, support for the rebellion grew rapidly in the United States, where it came to be seen as a moral struggle between the forces of freedom and the forces of autocracy. "Remember the Alamo" became the rallying cry.

Santa Anna seemed on the verge of victory until Sam Houston, the general of the American forces, attacked a much larger Mexican force at San Jacinto in April of 1836. Rushing toward the entrenched Mexicans, the Texans overran the artillery and breastworks, winning a decisive battle in only eighteen minutes. Santa Anna himself was captured a day later. As a prisoner, he signed treaties removing Mexican troops from Texas, granting Texas its independence, and recogniz-

The defeat of Santa Anna at San Jacinto brought the fight for Texas independence to a sudden and surprising culmination.

ing the Rio Grande as the boundary. The Mexican Congress, when they heard of this capitulation, announced that they would not be bound by its terms.

Texans and many Americans elsewhere urged the U.S. government to annex the new republic before it could be retaken by the Mexicans. That plea unleashed a heated and protracted debate between advocates of American expansion and those who thought such a step would be immoral and impolitic. Much of the debate raged between Southerners, who saw Texas as a vast new empire, and Northerners, especially abolitionists, who opposed annexation because it would lead to slavery's expansion. The fate of Texas was to be a key political issue for the next decade.

CONCLUSION

The vague and uncertain America of the 1810s and early 1820s became clearer under Andrew Jackson. No longer would politics be a matter of remote personalities in Washington, for now a two-party system mobilized voters and articulated their desires. No longer would slavery be a matter beyond debate, for the nulli-

fication crisis, Walker's *Appeal,* Turner's revolt, and the emergence of an abolitionist movement made slavery a concrete and burning issue. The aggressive young churches of the Second Great Awakening ensured that the Protestant faith became a matter of public action and testimony. After bitter debate and resistance, the power of the American Indians of the eastern United States had been broken and their people removed from homes they had occupied beyond memory. The public culture of the United States had become polarized, sharply conflicted over matters both public and private, full of possibility and full of conflict.

RECOMMENDED READINGS

Feller, Daniel. *The Jacksonian Promise: America, 1815–1840* (1995) offers a recent, upbeat overview.

Freehling, Allison Goodyear. *Drift Toward Dissolution: The Virginia Slavery Debate of 1831–1832* (1982) presents a useful interpretation of the crisis in Virginia.

Freehling, William. *Prelude to Civil War: The Nullification Crisis in South Carolina, 1816–1836* (1966) is the standard account of the subject.

Johnson, Paul. *A Shopkeeper's Millennium: Society and Revivals in Rochester, New York, 1815–1837* (1978) tells the story of revivals in an exciting way.

Laurie, Bruce. *Artisans into Workers: Labor in Nineteenth-Century America* (1989) gives an excellent synthesis of this complicated history.

Roediger, David R. *The Wages of Whiteness: Race and the Making of the American Working Class* (1991) boldly interprets the uses the white working class made of the notion of "race."

Walters, Ronald. *American Reformers, 1815–1860* (1996) offers an updated version of a fine analytical synthesis.

Watson, Harry L. *Liberty and Power: The Politics of Jacksonian America* (1990) provides a helpful and balanced interpretation of a subject that has been much debated by scholars.

Weber, David J. *The Mexican Frontier, 1821–1846: The American Southwest Under Mexico* (1982) tells the complex history of this region before war brought it into the United States.

Wiebe, Robert H. *The Opening of American Society: From the Adoption of the Constitution to the Eve of Disunion* (1984) surveys this entire era.

Andrew Jackson

Schlesinger, Arthur, Jr., *The Age of Jackson* (1945).

Ward, John William. *Andrew Jackson: Symbol for an Age* (1955).

Meyers, Marvin. *The Jacksonian Persuasion* (1957).

Pessen, Edward. *Jacksonian America: Society, Personality, and Politics,* rev. ed. (1979).

Remini, Robert. *The Life of Andrew Jackson* (1988).

Wallace, Anthony F. C. *The Long, Bitter Trail: Andrew Jackson and the Indians* (1993).

The Political System and Political Conflict

Baker, Jean H. *Affairs of Party: The Political Culture of Northern Democrats in the Mid-Nineteenth Century* (1983).

Bartlett, Irving. *John C. Calhoun* (1993).

Bullock, Steven C. *Revolutionary Brotherhood: Freemasonry and the Transformation of the American Social Order, 1730–1840* (1996).

Ellis, Richard. *The Union at Risk: Jacksonian Democracy, States Rights and the Nullification Crisis* (1987).

Formisano, Ronald P. *Transformation of Political Culture: Massachusetts Parties, 1790s–1840s* (1983).

Goodman, Paul. *Towards a Christian Republic: Antimasonry and the Great Tradition in New England, 1826–1836* (1988).

Grimsted, David. *American Mobbing, 1828–1861* (1998).

Howe, Daniel Walker. *The Political Culture of the American Whigs* (1979).

Remini, Robert. *Daniel Webster: The Man and His Time* (1997).

Varon, Elizabeth R. *We Mean to Be Counted: White Women and Politics in Antebellum Virginia* (1998).

Watson, Harry L. *Jacksonian Politics and Community Conflict: The Emergence of the American* (1981).

African-American Resistance

Harding, Vincent. *There Is a River: The Black Struggle for Freedom in America* (1981).

Horton, James Oliver, and Horton, Lois E. *In Hope of Liberty: Culture, Community, and Protest Among Northern Free Blacks, 1700–1860* (1997).

Oates, Stephen B. *The Fires of Jubilee: Nat Turner's Fierce Rebellion* (1975).

Hinks, Peter P. *To Awaken My Afflicted Brethren: David Walker and the Problem of Antebellum Slave Resistance* (1997).

Religion and Reform

Abzug, Robert H. *Cosmos Crumbling: American Reform and the Religious Imagination* (1994).

Cross, Whitney. *The Burned-over District* (1950).

Dillon, Merton L. *Slavery Attacked: Southern Slaves and Their Allies, 1619–1865* (1990).

Hambrick-Stowe, Charles E. *Charles G. Finney and the Spirit of American Evangelicalism* (1996).

Hardman, Keith J. *Charles Grandison Finney, 1792–1875: Revivalist and Reformer* (1987).

Johnson, Curtis D. *Redeeming America: Evangelicals and the Road to Civil War* (1993).

Fogel, Robert. *Without Consent or Contract: The Rise and Fall of American Slavery* (1989).

Friedman, Lawrence J. *Gregarious Saints: Self and Community in American Abolitionism, 1830–1870* (1982).

Harrold, Stanley. *The Abolitionists and the South, 1831–1861* (1995).

Mintz, Steven. *Moralists and Modernizers: America's Pre-Civil War Reformers* (1995).

Richards, Leonard L. *"Gentlemen of Property and Standing": Anti-Abolition Mobs in Jacksonian America* (1970).

Stewart, James Brewer. *Holy Warriors: The Abolitionists and American Slavery,* rev. ed. (1996).

Walters, Ronald G. *The Antislavery Appeal: American Abolitionists After 1830* (1976).

Wyatt-Brown, Bertram. *Lewis Tappan and the Evangelical War Against Slavery* (1969).

The Transformation of the Economy and Work

Bushman, Richard. *The Refinement of America: Persons, Houses, Cities* (1992).

Hammond, Bray. *Banks and Politics in America from the Revolution to the Civil War* (1957).

Hindle, Brooke, and Lubar, Steven. *Engines of Change: The American Industrial Revolution, 1790–1860* (1986).

Wilentz, Sean. *Chants Democratic: New York City and the Rise of the American Working Class, 1788–1850* (1983).

Laurie, Bruce. *Working People of Philadelphia, 1800–1850* (1980).

Dublin, Thomas. *Women at Work: The Transformation of Work and Community in Lowell, Massachusetts, 1826–1860* (1979).

The Mormons

Arrington, Leonard. *The Mormon Experience* (1979).

Bushman, Richard L. *Joseph Smith and the Beginnings of Mormonism* (1984).

Hansen, Klaus J. *Mormonism and the American Experience* (1981).

HARD TIMES, 1837

The irony of a Fourth of July celebration during hard times fills this cartoon, in which symbols of poverty and decay pile on one another.

Chapter 11

Panic and Boom:

1837–1845

IN 1837 THE largest financial panic and depression the nation had ever experienced descended on the United States. Coming after the deep changes of the preceding decade, that depression exerted broad and immediate effects. The hard times shaped reform, literature, politics, slavery, westward migration, and foreign policy, giving a sharp edge to conflict and strong incentives for change. Not surprisingly, these years of economic trouble also saw political turmoil and deep involvement by many aggrieved groups.

These hard years also saw the flowering of the reform spirit that had begun during the heady days of the Second Great Awakening. Men and women energetically championed public education, abstinence from alcohol, antislavery, and a host of other improvements to American life. The popular press also burgeoned, along with art, photography, and literature. A few leading thinkers articulated a bold and distinctive American philosophy, one that bore the marks of its tumultuous time.

DEPRESSION AND INVENTION

The late 1830s and early 1840s produced a surprising mixture of bad and good economic news. The econ-omy fell into prolonged depression, pushing down wages, destroying jobs, eroding labor unions, and undermining confidence in political leaders. At the same time, the creative energies of the American economy persisted. Courts and legislatures fostered an environment favorable to business while inventors and investors plunged ahead despite the hard times. To use a metaphor from the most important innovation of the time, the American economy kept one hand on the brake and the other on the throttle.

Panic and Depression

Andrew Jackson sought to leave a comfortable legacy to his hand-picked successor, Martin Van Buren, but even the inauguration ceremony in March 1837 accentuated the great disparities between the two men. Van Buren had won the election in 1836 against a Whig party that put four different candidates in the field; he hardly enjoyed the sweeping mandate Jackson had claimed four years earlier. While Jackson's gaunt figure symbolized his sacrifices on the frontier and battlefield, Van Buren seemed the plump embodiment of a life spent in political office. While Van Buren's inaugural speech inspired little enthusiasm in the crowd of 20,000, the mere sight of ex-President Jackson roused great cheers. As one observer put it, "the rising sun was

CHRONOLOGY

1837	Financial panic
	Charles River Bridge v. *Warren Bridge* decision
	Grimké sisters lecture to mixed audiences
	Elijah P. Lovejoy murdered in Alton, Illinois
	Horace Mann becomes first secretary of Massachusetts State Board of Education
	Ralph Waldo Emerson, "The American Scholar"
1838	John Quincy Adams successfully defeats attempt to annex Texas
1839	Depression worsens
	Daguerreotypes introduced to the United States
1840	Congress passes Independent Treasury Act
	Harrison elected president
	Frederick Douglass escapes from slavery
	American Anti-Slavery Society splits
	Washingtonian temperance movement emerges
	James G. Birney runs for president as candidate for Liberty party

1841	Harrison dies; John Tyler becomes president
	Brook Farm founded
	California sees arrival of first wagon train
	Oregon fever
	P.T. Barnum opens the American Museum
	Amistad case heard before the Supreme Court
1842	Edgar Allan Poe, "The Murders in the Rue Morgue"
1843	Oregon sees arrival of first wagon trains
1844	Methodist Episcopal church divides over slavery
	James K. Polk claims the United States's claim to "all Oregon"
	Baltimore-Washington telegraph line
	Samuel F. B. Morse patents the telegraph
	Edgar Allan Poe, "The Raven"
1845	Texas and Florida admitted to the Union
	Baptist church divides over slavery

eclipsed by the setting sun." Though Van Buren had been a principal architect of the so-called "spoils" system, he replaced few officeholders on the lower levels of government and made few changes in Jackson's cabinet. The new president seemed content to carry on Jackson's work.

Within weeks of Van Buren's inauguration the American economy hit stormy waters. Complicated changes in international trade played a large role in bringing on the crisis. An unprecedented amount of silver poured into American banks in the mid-1830s, fueling rapid and sometimes dangerous investment. England, concerned that the booming American economy was pulling too much gold and silver out of Britain in the form of investments, demanded repayment in specie just at the time that prices for American cotton—the major element in the Atlantic trade—declined because of record production. As a result, a major New Orleans cotton firm failed when it could not make its payments to British banks. That firm's failure, in turn, led to the closure of a number of banks that had loaned it money. The chain of failures stretched from New Orleans to New York.

Despite the role of international trade in bringing on the crisis, many people blamed the problems on a decision made closer to home: Jackson's policy of accepting only specie, not paper money, for the purchase of public lands. They looked to Van Buren to lead the repeal of this strategy, but Jackson made it clear to Van Buren that he did not want to see his work undone. As usual, Van Buren bowed to Old Hickory's wishes. Delegations of merchants came to the White House to plead with Van Buren, but to no avail. A "run" began on the banks; customers withdrew a million dollars in specie in only two days in early May. The Panic of 1837 had begun. Soon it spread to every city of the

REPRESENTATION OF THE INAUGURATION OF M. VAN BUREN, MARCH 4, 1837.

Martin Van Buren had done more than any other person to create the party system that drove American politics, but he could not meet the expectations for the presidency established by Andrew Jackson nor control the consequences of a debilitating economic depression that hit soon after he took office.

country, to every region. "The immense fortunes which we heard so much about in the days of speculation," one diarist noted, "have melted away like the snows before an April sun."

The panic quickly affected working people as well as the rich. Jobs dried up and many urban families had no idea of where they would get their next meal. The soup kitchens and other charities that had been created in the wake of the last panic, eighteen years earlier, stepped up their operations. In New York City, a poster warned that "Bread, Meat, Rent, Fuel—Their Prices Must Come Down. The Voice of the People Shall be Heard, and Will Prevail." Thousands of people gathered for a public meeting in the freezing weather. Told that a nearby warehouse held 50,000 barrels of flour, the protesters stormed the building and broke in; they took what they could and broke open hundreds of barrels more. The riots continued for days until the police managed to regain order. The working people who made up the crowd blamed "Monopolists and Extortioners" for the widespread misery, hoarding goods to drive up the prices.

The American economy surged up and down over the next five or six years. The panic of 1837 was followed by a better year in 1838, then by another panic in 1839. In the wake of that second panic, the stagnation of the economy spread more deeply and more widely, not ending until 1843. Labor unions weakened as workers grew afraid to risk their jobs. States' plans to finance canals, roads, and other public projects crashed. Several states defaulted on the bonds with which they intended to finance those improvements, leading furious European investors to shun American investments. The flood of capital into the young country dried up, wrecking new projects and causing the failure of those that had already been started. Governors and legislators found themselves under attack from voters angry that the states had permitted themselves to go so far into debt.

Van Buren admitted that allowing state banks to hold federal funds had apparently fueled the speculation, but he would not even consider reinstating a national bank. Instead, he proposed what came to be known as the Sub-Treasury Plan or the Independent

This locomotive in New York State, like its other early counterparts, pulled passenger cars based on old-fashioned carriages. The technology evolved quickly in the 1840s, however, and the United States played an important role in that evolution.

Treasury Plan. In that system, public funds would be disbursed by the secretary of the treasury as the economy seemed to dictate and banks would be kept out of the picture. It would be two more years before the plan passed, but by then it could do neither the country nor Martin Van Buren much good. His foes called him "Martin Van Ruin." The Whigs quickly won state-level offices and looked forward to harvesting more. The Van Buren administration drifted.

The Charles River Bridge Case

Even as the panic unfolded, some of the questions raised by the economic changes of the early 1830s worked their way through the American court system. The Charles River Bridge of Boston, for example, like many others in the late eighteenth and early nineteenth centuries, had been granted a franchise by the state legislature. The owners of the bridge charged a toll for everyone who crossed. As the population of Boston and Charlestown grew rapidly, so did the traffic and the tolls on the bridge. The bridge, which cost about $70,000 to build and improve, was bringing in $30,000 a year by the late 1820s. Another bridge also chartered by the state, the Warren Bridge, went up across the Charles, only 260 feet away. No sooner was the new bridge built than the traffic on the older bridge declined by more than half. The managers of the Charles River Bridge sued in court, claiming that

their original charter implied a monopoly that the state had violated by building a competing bridge. Throughout the 1830s, the case proceeded to the U.S. Supreme Court. It was heard in 1837.

The chief justice of the Supreme Court, Roger B. Taney, recently appointed by Andrew Jackson, shared the Jacksonian animosity against monopolies. His decision regarding the Charles River Bridge case held that a state charter did not imply monopoly, that business must be permitted to flourish in competition. Should old charters be permitted to hinder modern improvements, the country "would be obliged to stand still." The charters had perhaps been necessary in the past, he admitted, when the risks of any commercial undertaking were great in the underdeveloped United States, but by the 1830s such props no longer seemed necessary. Taney's decision in the *Charles River Bridge* reflected a growing consensus among Democrats and Whigs that older forms of economic privilege had to make way for innovation and investment.

Railroads

By the 1830s Americans had devised several means for dealing with the vast spaces of their continent. Thousands of miles of canals cut across the East while steamboats plied the waters of the North and South. Such means of transport, while cheap and dependable, remained relatively slow and limited in their reach. Inland cities longed for fast overland connections with the outside world and they knew of experiments with railroads in England and the United States over the last decade. England, the innovator in railroad technology, enjoyed a head start over America. When New Jersey sponsored a bold rail and canal connection between New York and Philadelphia in 1831 they ordered a custom-built locomotive from the English company—the *John Bull*. The railroad became an immediate success, carrying over 100,000 passengers in 1834.

American companies emulated and improved upon the English designs. By 1841, ten American railroad shops had sprung into existence and they produced 375 of the 500 engines in the United States. Those shops soon began changing the English designs, making the engines more powerful and the rails cheaper, better suited to the rough conditions in the United States. The American shops even exported their engines, including to Britain. Railroad companies quickly grew into some of the largest and most complex American businesses, employing hundreds of people, creating elaborate organizational hierarchies and techniques, pioneering in management as well as engineering. The companies, operating a dangerous business, were among the first to run tight schedules and enforce their rules with fines and firings.

Railroads almost immediately became the key form of transportation in the United States. By 1840, American companies and states had built 3,300 miles of track, matching that of canals; by 1850, the country claimed nearly 9,000 miles of railroad. The trains created whole new industries to serve them, as iron, coal, and steel burgeoned with the railroads' demand. The railroads consumed prodigious amounts of wood for their ties, trestles, and boilers. The trains quickly became integral parts of the American landscape they were doing so much to alter. The railroads gave farmers quick and certain access to markets, permitting them to specialize in certain crops, and towns prospered or died depending on their rail connection. People traveled much farther than they would have imagined before and began to think of themselves as parts of larger networks.

Telegraph poles marched alongside the railroads, speeding the flow of information just as the railroads sped the flow of people and goods. Like the locomotive, the telegraph was the product of inventors in several different countries but received a major impetus from America. Samuel F. B. Morse, the first professor of art in the United States, patented his version of the electronic telegraph in 1840. Morse struggled with the invention—and with poverty—for more than ten years, devising the code of dots and dashes that bears his name as well as ways to make the current travel farther. He finally received support from Congress in 1843, who invested $30,000 to run an experimental line from Washington to Baltimore. Following its success, the telegraph spread across the country with great speed. Americans proudly claimed this invention as their distinctive contribution to the brave new world emerging in the mid-nineteenth century.

CULTURAL FERMENT

A hunger for social— and self—improvement animated many Americans in the 1830s. People were fired by revivals and reform organizations and roused by the hard years of panic and depression. Some took practical routes to progress, focusing their efforts on schools and alcohol, while others explored philosophy and literature. Some used the new printing machinery of the age for entertainment while others turned it to use in the fight against social evils. Each facet of cultural ferment amplified the others, making the late 1830s and early 1840s years of experimentation and excitement.

Public Schools

Many Americans had become dissatisfied with the way young people were schooled in the United States. No state had a statewide school system and local districts ran their own affairs, often wretchedly. The rich attended private schools or employed tutors, while the parents of poorer children had to sign oaths declaring themselves "paupers" before their children could benefit from charity schools. Parents from the middle classes, charged a fee according to the number of children they had, sent their offspring to schools often taught by untrained teachers who enforced rote learning and spasmodic discipline. Many districts, especially in the South, created no schools at all, leaving parents to fend for themselves. Many American children never went to school in the 1820s and 1830s and those who did often attended for only a short time.

Reformers argued that unequal and inadequate education would not suffice in America, a country

Horace Mann successfully championed the idea of tax-supported public schools in Massachusetts, transforming education as a result.

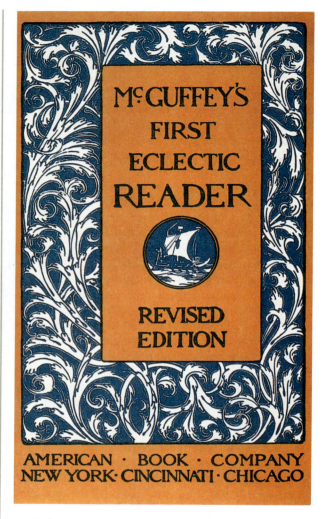

McGuffey's Reader, *the first standardized textbook, offered millions of American schoolchildren moral as well as academic instruction.*

dependent upon informed democracy and economic opportunity. These reformers wanted free schools. Taxes and other state support would make it possible for all children, whatever the wealth of their parents, to go to public schools. The rich would be more likely to send their children to such schools, reformers reasoned, if their tax dollars were supporting them; the poor would be more likely to send their children if they were not stigmatized as paupers. Buildings and teachers could be improved with the increased support.

A Massachusetts lawyer and Whig politician, Horace Mann worked relentlessly to make rich citizens, especially manufacturers, see that a tax in support of schools was a wise investment. Think how much better workers would be, he argued, if they could read and calculate, if they had imbibed regular habits and discipline in schoolrooms. Think to what good use women could be put as teachers, he argued, instilling their virtues of cooperation and peacefulness. Mann gradually persuaded influential people in Massachusetts of the practicability, even the necessity, of com-

mon schools. In 1837 he became the first secretary of the Massachusetts Board of Education.

When Mann took over, about a third of all children in Massachusetts received no schooling at all and many schools were in session for only a couple of months a year. He transformed that system during his tenure as secretary. The minimum school year stretched to six months, buildings and teacher training improved significantly, and teachers' pay increased by more than half. Women teachers became common in the Northeast. Oberlin College in Ohio admitted women in 1837, making it the first coeducational institution in the country. Females attended new "normal schools" that provided teacher training; they read educational journals, underwent professional supervision, and taught with uniform textbooks. These standards spread throughout the North and the West in the 1840s and 1850s, as did McGuffey's Readers. These books, which sold an astonishing 9 million copies in school districts all over the country between 1836 and 1850, blended Christian piety and the virtues of hard work. Though each book aimed at a specific grade, the underlying message was always the same: "God has given you minds which are capable of indefinite improvement."

Transcendentalism

Leading thinkers saw the possibilities of improvement everywhere. Several of those thinkers came out of Unitarianism, a form of liberal Christianity especially strong in New England. Unitarianism encouraged people to emphasize feeling rather than doctrine, to focus on the heart of religion and not on its trappings. Several young people in the 1830s raised within the Unitarian church took these ideas further than their elders intended, rejecting much Christian doctrine. A belief in the literal truth of the Bible, these youthful critics argued, trapped religion in the past, making those who lived in modern times base their faith on miracles that had happened long ago. Better, the rebellious thinkers said, to appeal directly to the heart from the very beginning. These thinkers wanted religion to transcend churches and denominations.

Women played an active role in this effort, with Margaret Fuller becoming especially important. Fuller had grown up in the Unitarian church in Cambridge, Massachusetts, receiving a fine education. But she felt herself adrift, full of "unemployed force," after her male classmates went on to college. She read widely and taught school with two other important figures in the revolt against Unitarianism: Elizabeth Peabody and Bronson Alcott. These three, like Horace Mann, believed that children were innately good and that education should be designed to let that goodness flourish. They argued that school, like church, should not be permitted to get in the way of people's natural connection with nature and with one another. Fuller, Peabody, Alcott, and others were looking for a new and liberating cause.

They soon took their lead from Ralph Waldo Emerson. Emerson had grown up around Concord, Massachusetts. Though descended from a distin-

Ralph Waldo Emerson was America's first popular intellectual, a combination of poet, lecturer, entertainer, and minister.

guished ministerial family, he was raised by a widowed mother and forced to work his way through Harvard College. Uncomfortable as a minister, dissatisfied as a schoolteacher, and widowed while a young man, Emerson set out for Europe. There he met exciting English intellectuals whose works he had read and whose stirring ideas were to influence him so deeply: Samuel Coleridge, Thomas Carlyle, and William Wordsworth. These writers, along with other thinkers such as the mystic Emanuel Swedenborg, provided Emerson with a perspective far removed from the cool Unitarianism on which he had been raised. Emerson perceived humankind as deeply tied to nature, filled with its rhythms and longings. He published such ideas in his first book, *Nature* (1836), a work that gained him considerable attention from the like-minded young people of New England.

But it was Emerson's address before the Phi Beta Kappa initiates at Harvard in 1837 that announced his arrival to a larger audience. That essay was written with a close eye on the events of the year in which it was delivered. In his private life and private journals Emerson worried over the state of the nation after the Panic of 1837, the "calamitous times," the "loud

HORACE MANN,
*ABSOLUTE RIGHT
TO AN EDUCATION,*
1846

Horace Mann abandoned his successful law practice and position in the state legislature to become the first secretary of the Massachusetts Board of Education. Mann argued against those who resisted paying taxes to educate the children of others, insisting that every child had an "absolute right" to an education and that the state had an obligation to provide that education for the public good and at the public's expense.

. . . In the district-school-meeting, in the town-meeting, in legislative halls, everywhere, the advocates for a more generous education could carry their respective audiences with them in behalf of increased privileges for our children, were it not instinctively foreseen that increased privileges must be followed by increased taxation. Against this obstacle, argument falls dead. The rich man who has no children declares that the exaction of a contribution from him to educate the children of his neighbor is an invasion of his rights of property. The man who has reared and educated a family of children denounces it as a double tax when he is called upon to assist in educating the children of others also; or, if he has reared his own children without educating them, he thinks it peculiarly oppressive to be obliged to do for others what he refrained from doing even for himself. Another, having children, but disdaining to educate them with the common mass, withdraws them from the public school, puts them under what he calls "selecter influences," and then thinks it a grievance to be obliged to support a school which he [regards with contempt]. . . .

It seems not irrelevant, therefore . . . to inquire into the nature of a man's right to the property he possesses; and to satisfy ourselves respecting the question, whether any man has such an indefeasible title to his estates, or such an absolute ownership of them, as renders it unjust in the government to assess upon him his share of the expenses of educating the children of the community up to such a point as the nature of the institutions under which he lives, and the well-being of society, require.

cracks in the social edifice." The panic directly touched one of Emerson's friends in Concord, Henry David Thoreau, who graduated from Harvard in the panic year and could find no decent job. Emerson, older than Thoreau, had finally achieved some economic security in the summer of 1837 thanks to an inheritance, but he was well aware of the difficulties facing even the Phi Beta Kappa graduates of Harvard during August of that hard year.

Emerson titled his speech "The American Scholar." He argued that the scholar should be a man of action, a man of nature, a man of risk and endeavor. Books and poetry held tremendous power, Emerson admitted, but it was in activity, in striving, that the American scholar became truly American. It was time to set the teachings of Europe aside long enough to find America's own voice, Emerson told the graduates. "We will walk with our own feet; we will work with our own hands; we will speak our own minds."

Emerson developed these ideas throughout the late 1830s, enjoying growing fame and influence through public lectures. Railroads made it feasible for the first time for speakers to cover a large amount of territory. Public speaking generally paid much better than any

I believe in the existence of a great, immortal, immutable principle of natural law, or natural ethics,—a principle antecedent to all human institutions, and incapable of being abrogated by any ordinance of man,—a principle of divine origin, which proves the *absolute right* to an education of every human being that comes into the world; and which, of course, proves the correlative duty of every government to see that the means of that education are provided for all.

. . .

To any one who looks beyond the mere surface of things, it is obvious that the primary and natural elements or ingredients of all property consist in the riches of the soil, in the treasures of the sea, in the light and warmth of the sun, in the fertilizing clouds and streams and dews, in the winds, and in the chemical and vegetative agencies of Nature. In the majority of cases, all that we call *property*, all that makes up the valuation or inventory of a nation's capital, was prepared at the creation, and was laid up of old in the capacious storehouses of Nature. For every unit that a man earns by his own toil or skill, he receives hundreds and thousands, without cost and without recompense, from the all-bountiful Giver. A proud mortal, standing in the midst of his luxuriant wheat-fields or cotton-plantations, may arrogantly call them his own; yet what barren wastes would they be, did not Heaven send down upon them its dews and its rains, its warmth and its light, and sustain, for their growth and ripening, the grateful vicissitude of the seasons!

. . .

The claim of a child, then, to a portion of pre-existent property, begins with the first breath he draws. The new-born infant must have sustenance and shelter and care. If the natural parents are removed, or parental ability fails; in a word, if parents either cannot or will not supply the infant's wants,—then society at large—the government having assumed to itself the ultimate control of all property—is bound to step in and fill the parent's place. To deny this to any child would be equivalent to a sentence of death, a capital execution of the innocent,—at which every soul shudders. It would be a more cruel form of infanticide than any which is practised in China or in Africa.

SOURCE Horace Mann, *Tenth Annual Report of the Secretary of the Board of Education* (1846), in *The Life and Works of Horace Mann* (Boston: Lee and Shepard, 1891), Vol. IV, pp. 114–17, 128–29, 131–34.

kind of writing, especially in the days before copyright laws. The growth of newspapers and other printing facilitated advertising, getting word of the lectures out beforehand and spreading summaries of the lectures to those unable to attend. People flocked to the lectures. Those who lived in "dreary" towns, one speaker recalled, wanted "to keep pace with the progress of civilization in all its aspects, by informing themselves about the products of literature, the achievements of science, and the aims and appliances of humanitarian movements." In the lecture hall, Emerson exulted, "everything is admissible, philosophy, ethics, divinity, criticism, poetry, humor, fun, mimicry, anecdotes, jokes, ventriloquism. . . ."

Emerson's home in Concord became the gathering place for a group who came to be called the Transcendentalists, who sought to "transcend" the mundane into the mystical knowledge that every human possessed if he or she would listen to it. Margaret Fuller became the editor of the *Dial*, the Transcendentalist magazine, while Elizabeth Peabody opened a bookstore catering to the interests of the group. Bronson Alcott and about eighty others founded Brook Farm, one of the many utopian communities that tried to get off the ground in the 1830s and 1840s. Brook Farm combined manual and intellectual labor, putting people to work in the fields in the morning and on their books in the afternoon. The community produced both crops and an impressive weekly newspaper. Its schools stood as examples of enlightened education. It encouraged idiosyncratic dress and habits, independent thought and action. The experiment failed economically after a few years, but for a while Brook Farm offered the possibility of combining intellectual excitement, physical work, and social responsibility in a way the Transcendentalists craved.

Henry David Thoreau founded, in essence, a one-man utopian community. Since the Transcendentalists believed that people should establish a close connection to nature, Thoreau decided to conduct an "experiment in human ecology." He wanted to see—and show—how a modern man could live in harmony with nature. He built, from some trees he cut on Emerson's land and some boards from an old shanty, an isolated house in the woods near Walden Pond, carefully calculating the cost of nails and other sup-

plies. He strove to be self-sufficient and self-contained (though skeptics charged that he was not *that* far from Concord, where his mother and his fellow Transcendentalists lived and where he frequently visited). The experiment proved important for the beautiful and affecting book Thoreau eventually wrote about his experience, *Walden: Life in the Woods* (1854).

Art and Popular Culture

The Transcendentalists were not alone in their craving for intensity. American painters found an increasing audience for their works in the 1830s as they evolved a style of their own. The United States had never been very receptive to figurative art. Wealthy people bought portraits, but most other Americans had no pictures at all in their homes. Talented young painters born in the United States generally had to travel to Europe for their training and often for their livings as well. This began to change, however, as Americans developed more of a taste for painting and as remarkable young artists came on the scene.

Thomas Cole was the key figure in the emergence of American painting. Though born in England, he came to the Ohio frontier as a small child. Cole, fascinated with the wild scenes of the landscapes around him, taught himself to paint but went to England and Italy to perfect his art. He returned to the village of Catskill in New York to paint the Hudson River Valley in the late 1830s and early 1840s. Soon, other painters, such as Asher Durand and Frederick Church, joined Cole in their fascination with the stirring American landscape, creating what became known as the Hudson River School. They found that landscape full of meaning, speaking of birth and decay, danger and possibility. Their countrymen greeted such works with enthusiasm, celebrating the emergence of an American style as well as American subjects.

Cole also turned to richly symbolic allegorical painting. His journey to Europe had struck him by its contrasts, "both the ruined towers that tell of outrage, and the gorgeous temples that speak of ostentation." He believed America, by contrast, "to be the abode of virtue." He embodied his notions of the cycles of civilization and personal life in two powerful allegorical series, *The Course of Empire* and *The Voyage of Life*. Engravings of these series became popular fixtures in American homes.

Henry David Thoreau, a close friend of Emerson's, embarked on a characteristically American experiment when he went to live alone in the woods at Walden Pond.

This painting by Thomas Cole of Northampton, Massachusetts, after a thunderstorm reflects a common theme in the work of American painters in these years: the power as well as the beauty of nature.

Other important artists followed their own paths through the American landscape. George Catlin spent much of the 1830s living among the American Indians of the Great Plains, making hundreds of drawings and paintings. Even as the Indian removals drew to a close in the East, white Americans remained fascinated with the native peoples farther west. In Catlin's paintings Easterners thought they might catch the last glimpse of a disappearing people. Audiences could also view vanishing wildlife in the remarkable watercolors of John James Audubon. Audubon, born in Haiti and educated in France, settled on the Kentucky frontier as a merchant after he married. He loved the American wilderness too much to stay in his shop, though, and he launched out on daunting journeys to record the environment and appearance of the birds of the young nation. After ten years of work Audubon produced *The Birds of America, from Original Drawings, with 435 Plates Showing 1,065 Figures* in four immense volumes, completing the project in 1838.

The most famous artistic production of antebellum America was a statue: Hiram Powers's *The Greek Slave,* completed in 1846. Powers grew up in the raw country of Ohio but moved to Italy as he prospered. There, Powers sculpted his statue of a nude young woman bound in chains. Many Americans had not deemed such statues suitable for their chaste republic, but Powers found a way to make such a work not only permissible but even morally improving. The young woman represented, Powers said, a Greek girl captured by the Turks in the Greco-Turkish war. As such, she represented Christianity and whiteness, unbowed by the evil and darkness surrounding her. Powers sought, and received, the endorsement of a group of American clergymen, removing any qualms audiences might have. Indeed, the statue became a national fixation and drew enormous crowds when it toured the United States. *The Greek Slave* served as the model for hundreds of miniature copies that appeared in the drawing rooms of the finest homes.

Hiram Power's The Greek Slave *became an American sensation, attracting large crowds and many imitators.*

The same drawing rooms also contained a novelty of the age: daguerreotypes. This form of photography developed in France but arrived in the United States soon after its creation. By the early 1840s all the larger American cities boasted daguerreotype studios. Within a few years, more than eighty young photographers practiced their craft in New York City alone. One of these men on the cutting edge of technology was Matthew Brady, who opened a studio in Washington, D.C., where he and his assistants photographed leading people of the period. This early photography was cumbersome and required long periods of stillness before the camera, but the American people hurried to studios to have their portraits done.

As print became a fixture of everyday life in these years, engravings based on paintings and photographs

soon filled the publications coming off the presses. For the first time, illustrations could be produced cheaply. Anyone with enough money could send messages and images far and wide. Not only did the abolitionists and other reformers use these techniques to great effect, but so did a religious movement, the Millerites, who believed that signs in the Bible foretold the Day of Judgment in 1844. To spread the word, they published 4 million pieces of literature.

Seeing the opportunity afforded by this emergence of a popular audience for print, American writers worked hard to fill the hunger. One especially gifted author, Edgar Allan Poe, skillfully navigated between the market and his art. Poe wrote short stories, the kind of writing most in demand for the burgeoning periodical press and the growing ranks of educated readers, but he brought to the form a kind of self-consciousness few had demonstrated before. Poe tapped into a widespread fascination with the occult, seances, and ghosts, filling his work with ruins, shadows, and legends. Works such as "The Murders in the Rue Morgue" marked the first appearance of the detective story. Poe was not a disturbed man writing out of his

Edgar Allan Poe experimented with new literary forms, crafting remarkable stories and poems of terror and dread.

own fantasies and horrors, but was rather the consummate artist, inventive and controlled. Throughout the hard decade of the 1840s he published stories such as "The Masque of the Red Death," "The Pit and the Pendulum," and "The Tell-Tale Heart" and poetry such as "The Raven." Plagued by the death of loved ones and ill health exacerbated by drink, however, Poe did not survive the decade.

A very different kind of entrepreneur, P. T. Barnum, a Connecticut storekeeper turned newspaper editor turned purveyor of popular entertainment, opened his American Museum in New York in 1841 and people flocked to see what it offered. Barnum played an elaborate game, displaying oddities that strained the limits of belief but that could not be completely disproved. Unlike earlier museums, full of supposedly uplifting displays of minerals and stuffed animals, Barnum's museum frankly offered entertainment, including magicians and midgets such as the famous Tom Thumb. The fact that the "curiosities" were often attacked as fakes by scientists did not seem to deter visitors; controversy was good for business. Barnum's American Museum flourished for the next twenty years, attracting visitors from all over the country and the world.

The Washingtonians

Americans had long waged campaigns against intemperance, but in the depression years of the late 1830s and early 1840s the fight against drink took on a new urgency. With work hard to find, alcohol seemed all the more threatening to laboring people. While earlier temperance movements had mainly enlisted those who were already opposed to alcohol, the new movement of the late 1830s marked an effort by drinkers to reform themselves. Earlier attempts at temperance had often pitted middle- and upper-class reformers against members of the working class, but the new movement grew among people in the lower ranks of American society. Older reform attempts had been largely the efforts of men, but now women became active. The Washingtonian movement, named in honor of George Washington, gave these efforts great force and visibility.

The Washingtonians began in Baltimore in 1840, when six drinkers, regretting their fondness for whiskey, pledged to one another to quit drinking and to persuade other drinkers to do the same. Word of the new movement quickly spread up the eastern seaboard and by 1841 gained over 200,000 members;

This painting captures the atmosphere of fascination and energy that surrounded everything the great American showman P. T. Barnum produced.

two years later, the Washingtonians claimed millions of adherents. Partly as a result of the new organization, Americans' consumption of alcohol plummeted in the 1840s, when the per capita intake of liquor fell to half of what it had been in the 1820s. The success of the Washingtonians outstripped that of any prior temperance organization.

"Martha Washington" societies, for women only, grew rapidly, challenging the men's movement both in size and in fervor. These female temperance advocates were not well-to-do ladies stooping to help the fallen, but rather the wives of artisans and small businessmen. They helped families in distress to get back on their feet. They also provided a new edge to the temperance crusade, reminding men that drunkenness was more often than not a male failing and that it was the wives and children of drunkards who suffered most from their neglect, cruelty, and even violence. The Washingtonian movement provided one of the first forums in which American women could publicly express their grievances and act to remedy them.

Abolitionism

By the late 1830s the American Anti-Slavery Society claimed over a thousand locals and over a quarter of a million members. The same lecture circuits that carried general-interest speakers such as Ralph Waldo Emerson also carried abolitionists, bringing the battle against slavery into places where it had been only a distant rumble a few years earlier. The first female abolitionist speakers—the Grimké sisters, Angelina and Sarah—were prize recruits into the antislavery ranks, for they were the daughters of a prominent South Carolina slave-owning planter. The sisters developed into powerful writers and speakers. By telling New England audiences of their own experiences with slavery, the Grimkés held a credibility that white northern abolitionists could not match. In 1837, the Grimkés decided to exert their power in a new forum by lecturing to mixed audiences of men and women. While some people strenuously objected to such an elevation of women in the public sphere, the Grimkés spoke to over 40,000 people at eighty meetings in sixty-seven towns and cities in nine months in 1837 and 1838.

As it grew stronger, the antislavery cause met with more determined opposition. When abolitionist Elijah P. Lovejoy offended readers of his religious paper in St. Louis—denouncing a local judge who prevented the trial of a mob who had burned a black man alive—citizens of Alton, Illinois, invited Lovejoy to move to their town. Alton prided itself on being a progressive place of 3,000 people, even permitting black children

Temperance advocates called for total abstinence from drink, demonstrating in illustrations such as this that the very first drink could lead to crime and even suicide.

The murder of Elijah Lovejoy, an abolitionist editor in Illinois, revealed the depth of opposition held by many northern whites to anyone who would speak forcefully against slavery.

in its schools. Soon, however, some prominent members of the community, angered at Lovejoy's paper for its dissemination of "the highly odious doctrines of modern Abolitionism," held a public meeting demanding him to quit printing such ideas. Lovejoy only intensified his attacks on slavery. Mobs destroyed two of Lovejoy's presses, but he persisted, bolstered by the support of other members of the community. In November, a mob killed Lovejoy and shattered his press.

Abolitionists debated the proper response to such opposition. William Lloyd Garrison, identified by many as the country's most militant abolitionist, counseled his allies to offer no resistance to violence. He opposed war, capital punishment, and prisons because of their reliance on violence and expanded his crusade to women's rights and the plight of American Indians. Garrison and his supporters renounced all allegiance to the established parties and churches, which had long since shown themselves tolerant of slavery. Other abolitionists, by contrast, focused on slavery alone and used whatever means they could to bring slavery to an end, including political parties.

The differences among the abolitionists came to a head at the annual meeting of the American Anti-Slavery Society in 1839. They differed most visibly in their attitudes toward the role of women. Women constituted perhaps half of all members of the antislavery organizations but some male abolitionists sought to keep females in a subordinate role. Unable to resolve their differences, the abolitionists split. The more conservative group, based in New York, created the Liberty party to run a candidate for president in the upcoming election of 1840. Garrison's organization maintained a more radical stance on the role of women and the strategies through which abolition should be pursued.

Whatever their differences, abolitionists barraged Congress with petitions demanding that slavery be ended in the District of Columbia. Former President John Quincy Adams, now a congressman from Massachusetts, used all his parliamentary skill to fight the gag rule that prevented Congress from recognizing antislavery petitions; he finally succeeded in getting it overthrown in 1845. Adams also successfully defended Africans who had seized a slave ship bound for Cuba, the *Amistad,* and landed in Connecticut. Supported by a large network of abolitionists, Adams took the case before the U.S. Supreme Court and won not only the acquittal of the Africans for murdering the ship's captain but their freedom as well.

Black antislavery speakers greatly strengthened the antislavery cause. Northern blacks had long struggled for the freedom of slaves, but voices from slavery itself proved even more compelling. Speakers such as Henry Box Brown (who had himself mailed from Richmond to Philadelphia in a specially fitted box), Henry Bibb, Solomon Northup, Sojourner Truth, Harriet Tubman, and Ellen Craft electrified audiences with their talks and brought readers to tears with their written testimonies. Slavery, they made clear, was nothing like the benign institution portrayed by the defenders of slavery.

While white abolitionists valued the contributions of their black compatriots, white reformers were not always above racial prejudice. They urged black speakers not to make too much of a fuss when confronted—as they were daily—with the insults and indignities faced by black people in the North. African American abolitionists chafed under the restrictions they faced from fellow reformers and enemies alike; they demanded greater rights for northern as well as southern blacks. Their experiences showed the extent to which race was a national problem.

One of the most remarkable Americans of the nineteenth century burst into visibility in the early 1840s. Frederick Douglass had grown up in Maryland, on the border between slavery and freedom. Like other places in the upper South, Maryland's economy was diversifying in the 1830s and 1840s as towns and cities grew, commerce intensified, and railroads spread. Douglass learned to read from his mistress, though it was against the law for her to teach him, and he began to use that ability to remake himself. In a spirit that would have pleased Horace Mann, the young Douglass carried with him a copy of *Webster's Spelling Book* and *The Columbian Orator*, a book of speeches, including a slave's persuasive argument with his master to set him free. Douglass noticed that his owners spoke bitterly of people called "abolitionists" and he discovered why when he read in a local newspaper of John Quincy Adams's fight against the gag rule.

Sent to Baltimore by his owner, Douglass worked in the shipyards, became skilled as a caulker, continued to read widely, and plotted his freedom. After several attempts at escape, Douglass finally borrowed the papers of a free black sailor and, impersonating his friend, rode a train to freedom. Douglass found himself in New York City, alone and without any notion of what he should do or where he should go. A runaway slave had to be careful, for he or she might be hunted down by a slavecatcher for a reward. Fortunately for Douglass, he met a black man who introduced the young runaway to the New York Anti-Slavery Society. After white abolitionists saw the skill with which he spoke, they sent Douglass to travel throughout the North with William Lloyd Garrison. Throughout the early 1840s, Douglass and other African American abolitionists told their stories of slavery, giving faces and names to the suffering.

One of the most influential and famous Americans of the nineteenth century, Frederick Douglass fought tirelessly against slavery and in favor of a wide range of social reforms.

THE SLAVE SOUTH

The South was an integral part of the United States throughout the antebellum period. Southern cotton drove much of the economy, southern politicians held much of the power, southern concerns guided much foreign policy, and Southerners played important roles in the churches and the armed forces. The South was a prosperous place for white people, whose average per capita incomes compared favorably with those of northern whites. Thanks to the rapid expansion of newspapers and telegraph, white Southerners took part in all the national conversations about race, slavery, and politics.

The South had its trains, newspapers, and reform societies; its white people bought the same books and magazines people read in the North; they had their daguerreotypes taken and sent messages on telegraphs. The growing connections between the regions, in fact, emphasized the differences between the North and the

South. As people in each region read the hard words those across the Mason-Dixon line frequently said about them, their distrust of one another grew. As increasing numbers of people such as Frederick Douglass escaped to the North, Northerners became ever more aware of their region's complicity in perpetuating slavery and even abetting its growth. Even as the two societies developed along similar lines, their single profound difference became ever more potent.

African Americans and the South

By the 1830s, slavery had spread over an enormous area stretching from Frederick Douglass's Maryland to the tumultuous lands of Texas. The decade had seen the domestic slave trade grow at a feverish rate, for the new planters of Mississippi, Alabama, and Louisiana eagerly imported slaves to clear land and plant cotton.

The slaves of the Upper South feared and dreaded being "sold south." By the time of the Panic of 1837, Alabama, Mississippi, and Louisiana grew more than half the nation's cotton, outstripping the older states of the Southeast. American slavery became ever more diverse as it expanded. Enslaved people worked in hemp, wheat, rice, corn, sugar, and tobacco fields as well as cotton. They worked with livestock and racehorses. They practiced carpentry and blacksmithing in the growing towns and small cities of the booming Southwest. They labored on the docks of New Orleans, Mobile, and Memphis and in the shipyards of Baltimore. Some slaves lived where their families had dwelled for generations; others cleared new land of cane brakes and cyprus along the Mississippi frontier. Some knew the white people among whom they lived quite well; others belonged to absolute strangers. Some worked in large groups of black people; others worked alone or beside whites.

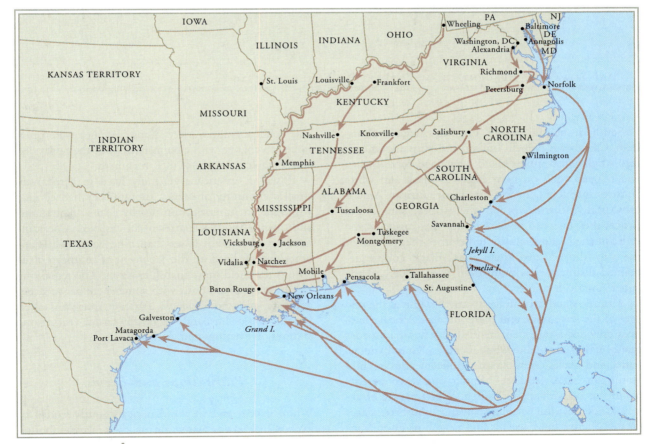

MAP 11.1 | PATHS OF THE SLAVE TRADE

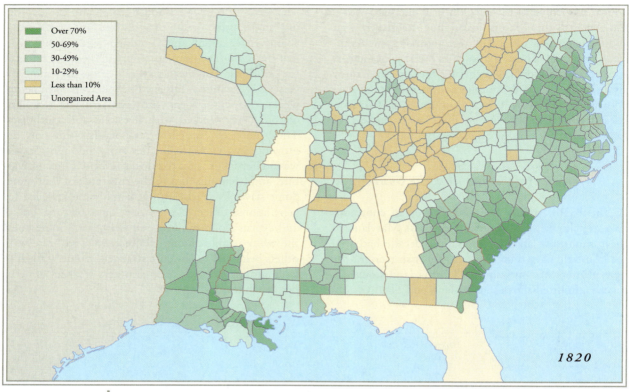

Legend:
- Over 70%
- 50-69%
- 30-49%
- 10-29%
- Less than 10%
- Unorganized Area

1820

MAP 11.2A | PERCENTAGE OF POPULATION ENSLAVED, 1820

Southern culture mixed English, African, Scots-Irish, Caribbean, French, Indian, and Hispanic sources into a rich and complex blend. Language, food, music, and religion took on new shapes as black and white cultures interacted. In the meantime, African Americans prided themselves on the stories, songs, and dances they knew to be particularly their own, on the styles of the baskets, quilts, and clothes they sewed, or the way they carried themselves. Black culture remained distinct and vibrant even as it influenced the larger American culture.

African-American families, partly because of the ravages of the slave trade and partly because African practices provided a precedent, tended to rely on a broader range of kin than did white families. Grandparents, aunts, and uncles often played significant roles in child rearing in black families, helping out when parents could not be with their children. When people of actual blood relation were unavailable, southern slaves created "fictive kin," friends and neighbors given honorary titles of "brother" or "aunt" and treated as such. These arrangements permitted slave families consider-

able resiliency and variety. Those families were often forced to change with circumstance, but they provided considerable strength for their members.

Enslaved Americans generally lived in a relatively small community of others, though they had contact with African Americans on nearby farms, plantations, and towns. About a quarter of all enslaved Americans lived on farms with fewer than nine slaves, while another quarter lived on the 3 percent of southern plantations that held more than fifty slaves. The remaining half lived on plantations with somewhere between ten and forty-nine bondspeople. African Americans often found wives or husbands on nearby farms, visiting one another on evenings and weekends.

Plantations and Farms

White slaveowners in the American South tended to live on the same plantation as their slaves, though some absentee slaveholders held land in the rich low country of South Carolina and in the sugar planta-

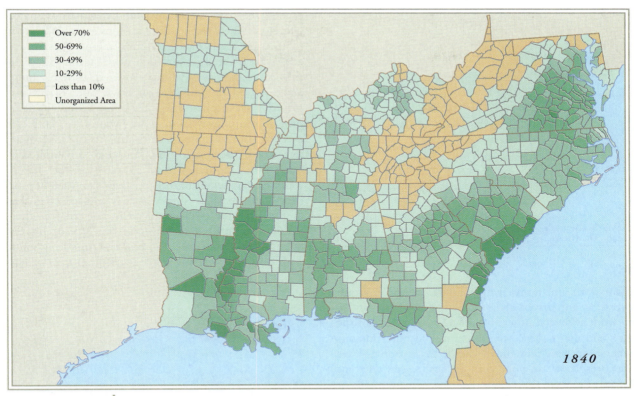

MAP 11.2B | PERCENTAGE OF POPULATION ENSLAVED, 1840

tions of Louisiana. Wealthier whites put day-to-day control of their plantations in the hands of professional overseers. These overseers were seldom so-called "poor white trash," for wealthy planters did not hand over property as valuable as their slaves, land, and crops to people of poor reputation. Rather, overseers were often ambitious young men of middling background who used the overseer position as a stepping stone to their own plantation. If the plantation did not run as smoothly and profitably as the slave owner thought it should, the overseer found himself out of a job. Slaves could and did appeal to the owner if they thought the overseer unfair. Since a master might indeed trust a well-known slave more than a new overseer, the position involved tact as well as brute force.

On larger plantations, where slaves often worked in groups called gangs, trusted male slaves served as "drivers." Such drivers tended to be especially strong and skilled, commanding respect from whites as well as blacks. Especially on plantations with both overseers and drivers, the distribution of power was not a simple matter. Although whites held the ultimate threat of

force, they much preferred to keep the work moving smoothly, with as little trouble as possible. The driver could help both sides, protecting fellow slaves from abuse and assuring that the work got done efficiently. Drivers frequently found themselves caught between the two competing sets of demands, however, and slaves often resented or even hated drivers.

The work that enslaved people did varied by farm, by time of the year, and by gender, but about three out of four worked mainly in the fields. Almost all of them went to the fields during the peak times, for only the richest planters kept able-bodied men employed full-time as house servants or coachmen. Women, who worked in the fields alongside men, also served in the house as cooks and domestics. Slaves were well known for controlling the pace of work, proceeding at a rate that seemed appropriate to them, reporting their tools broken or "lost" when they were forced to work too fast or too long. They traditionally had Sundays to garden for themselves, do their domestic chores, or hunt.

Slaves' lives were by no means simple. Lines of power often became complicated and tangled on

AFRICAN AMERICANS IN THE SLAVE STATES, 1860

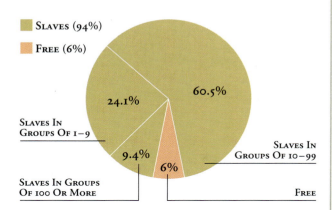

■ SLAVES (94%)
■ FREE (6%)

60.5%
SLAVES IN GROUPS OF 10–99

24.1%
SLAVES IN GROUPS OF 1–9

9.4%
SLAVES IN GROUPS OF 100 OR MORE

6%
FREE

plantations and farms, with masters, mistresses, sons, overseers, and drivers claiming authority. Slaves tended to work at several different jobs over the course of the year and many slaves were hired out to other masters when work was slow on the home place. Some slaves were respected as purveyors of healing or religious knowledge from Africa; some slaves were admired for their musical ability; others won recognition for their ability to read and preach the Gospel. These abilities did not always correspond with the opinions of whites, who frequently underestimated the abilities and character of the people among whom they lived.

Whites told themselves that they knew "their people," that they cared for them and provided them a better life than they would have known in Africa. Indeed, southern masters explained the justice of slavery to themselves and to the North by stressing their Christian stewardship for the slaves and their emotional attachment to them. As one clergyman wrote to his fellow slaveholders in the early 1840s, slaves "were placed under our control . . . not exclusively for our benefit but theirs also." Slaveholders did not want to seem unworthy of the hopeful young nation of which the South was a key part; they did not want to seem antagonistic to spiritual or economic progress.

Throughout the 1830s and 1840s, southern slaveholders and ministers prided themselves on their Christian mission to the slaves, in which thousands of African Americans were inducted into churches along with whites. Most masters would not permit their slaves to learn to read, but they did arrange to have Bible selections read to their slaves. While many slaves

eagerly accepted the Gospel in the white-dominated churches, others resented the obvious and shallow uses the masters made of the sermons, telling the slaves to accept their lot and to refrain from stealing food. In the eyes of the slaves, whites perverted God's teachings and behaved in un-Christian ways. Such slaves displayed their deepest religious feelings only in their own worship, away from prying whites, in the secret meetings in brush arbors and cabins in the slave quarters. There, they prayed to be free and to be united in heaven with those they loved.

Largely oblivious to the lives their slaves led beyond their sight, masters pointed to the physical condition of the slaves as evidence of their concern for "their people." Compared to slaves in other places in the hemisphere, it was true, those of the American South were relatively well-fed and free of disease. They had

Enslaved people of both genders worked in a variety of demanding tasks throughout the year as they brought the South's valuable cotton crop from seed to bale.

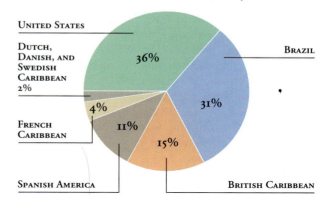

SLAVES IMPORTED, 1500–1870

BRAZIL

DUTCH, DANISH, AND SWEDISH CARIBBEAN

UNITED STATES

SPANISH AMERICA

BRITISH CARIBBEAN

FRENCH CARIBBEAN

38%
17%
6%
6%
17%
17%

PROPORTION OF HEMISPHERE'S SLAVE POPULATION, 1825

UNITED STATES

DUTCH, DANISH, AND SWEDISH CARIBBEAN 2%

FRENCH CARIBBEAN

SPANISH AMERICA

BRAZIL

BRITISH CARIBBEAN

36%
4%
11%
15%
31%

As these two graphs show, the United States accounted for a relatively small proportion of all enslaved people brought from Africa into the Western Hemisphere but, because of the longer lifespans of North American slaves, more than a third of the enslaved population of the New World lived in the United States.

limited and monotonous diets, but generally consumed enough nutrients. Slaves received ineffective or dangerous health care, their houses were small and drafty, and their clothing was limited to a few rough garments per year, but none of these conditions endangered slaves' physical survival. Economic investment as well as community pressure and religious concern helped ensure this minimal support. Slaves in the United States, working in relatively healthy settings and benefiting from a balanced ratio between men and women, generally lived longer than their counterparts elsewhere in the hemisphere.

On the other hand, many slaveowners did not refrain from having their slaves whipped on small provocation, branded, shackled, or locked up in sweltering enclosures. Slave women suffered sexual abuse by overseers, neighboring whites, the owner's sons, or the owner himself. Partly because expectant mothers were often kept in the fields until the last minute, about a third of all black babies died before they reached their first birthday. American slavery, whatever ameliorating features it might have had, was a harsh institution. Its slaves ached for freedom and made the best they could of the hard world into which they were born.

The Politics of the White South

In the South as in the North, the Whigs portrayed themselves as the party of progress and prosperity. The lawyers, editors, and merchants who set up shop in the hamlets and towns of the South proved receptive to such views. The young men who followed such professions eagerly joined organizations such as the Masons, temperance groups, and political parties. They saw themselves as part of the rising generation of Americans and prided themselves on their broad views of national issues. In their eyes, only the Whigs reflected such enlightened perspectives. The large planters on the richest lands were also attracted to the Whigs, for they engaged in trade with northern and English commercial houses, wanted internal improvements, and needed banks and a strong currency. The Whigs drew, too, on the farmers in the mountains of the Upper South, men determined to develop connections to outside markets and to demonstrate their loyalty to the old Union.

The Democrats, on the other hand, found their strongest supporters among the middling farmers and planters of the South. These men tended to be propertied but not wealthy, resentful of the taxes on their lands and slaves. They admired the Democrats' aggressive approach to removing the American Indians and to expanding in the West. Southerners distrustful of Northerners and of commerce found the minimal-government pronouncements of the Democrats appealing and persuasive. Most counties in the South had a substantial number of both Whigs and Democrats; one party tended to breed the other as they built on long-standing rivalries and resentments.

In the South both the Whigs and the Democrats declared themselves the friends of southern slavery, but they differed in their emphases. The Democrats pledged that they would leave the voters alone, protecting slavery by extending the power of the government as little as possible. The Whigs, on the other hand, argued that the best way to protect slavery was for the South to build strong economic and political bridges to the North even as they put a Southerner in the White House. The white South was a touchy democracy. Voter turnout was high and men cared about few things more than they cared about who won in the next election.

THE CHALLENGE OF THE WEST

Americans of every sort kept their eyes to the west. Railroads, telegraphs, canals, and roads strained in that direction; population restlessly flowed there. But thoughtful people recognized that the lack of borders and limits posed threats as well as potential. When everything seemed possible, people placed few checks on their appetites. Every boundary was contested, every obstacle attacked. Politics became a battle between boundless expectation and anxiety.

The Election of 1840

The Whigs should have faced an easy contest in 1840. After all, the Van Buren administration had hardly been a sparkling success. Much of the nation, from the cities of the East to the plantations of the Southwest, remained mired in depression. Van Buren offered little effective leadership during the economic crisis and many people held him to blame for the hard times. But the Whigs were not as strong as they might have been. Their party had been built piece by piece in the 1830s in reaction to Andrew Jackson. As a result, the party was a crazy-quilt of interests and factions. In 1836, the party had even permitted three candidates to run against Van Buren because no one man could command the party's full allegiance. Party leaders vowed that they would not let the same thing happen in 1840. They believed that they would control Amer-

ican politics in the new decade, shaping the country to fit their ideas of what it should be.

The Whigs determined in 1840 to find the one man who stood for the common beliefs that unified Whigs beneath their surface differences. Those beliefs turned around faith in commerce, self-control, Protestantism, learning, and self-improvement. Most important, the Whigs wanted to make an active response to the depression plaguing the nation by putting money in circulation, building internal improvements, and strengthening banks. Such plans appealed to many men appalled at the do-nothing approach of Van Buren and the Democrats. The trick was to find a candidate who embodied their beliefs without appearing to be "aristocratic" or hungry for power, as the Democrats were sure to charge.

The Whigs found such a man in William Henry Harrison. Harrison had made his name as a general—most notably in his defeat of an Indian confederacy in the Battle of Tippecanoe in 1811—and later served in the House of Representatives and in the Senate. Harrison, removed by Andrew Jackson from a position as minister to Colombia, returned to his farm in Ohio, held minor office, and, in his late sixties, expected to live out his days in semiretirement. Harrison had won fame without gathering many political liabilities and was identified with no particular position. The Whigs adopted no platform, not wanting to alienate anyone.

The Whigs sought to balance their ticket with Senator John Tyler of Virginia. This slaveholding Southerner was safe on that issue, but he was also a small-government man. Tyler shared few beliefs with his fellow Whigs, but his embrace of slavery helped mollify Southerners. Moreover, his name made a nice pairing in the phrase that soon became famous: "Tippecanoe and Tyler, Too." One Whig warned that the combination of Harrison and Tyler had "rhyme, but no reason in it." At first, the alliteration seemed reason enough to vote Whig, though, as the party enjoyed a success on the national level that they had never before experienced.

Part of their success grew out of a Democratic blunder. The Democrats were relieved that the Whigs had nominated Harrison. Democrats considered the old general a nonentity; one reporter commented sarcastically that if Harrison were merely given some hard cider and a small pension he would contentedly sit out the rest of his days in a log cabin. The sarcasm backfired, though, for many Americans saw log cabins and home-brewed cider as evidence of American virtue

ALEXIS DE TOCQUEVILLE, *DEMOCRACY IN AMERICA,* 1840

A young French nobleman, Tocqueville came to the United States to observe democracy in action. In the great book from which this selection is drawn, the sympathetic Tocqueville notes a central paradox of American life; all except slaves are free in virtually every facet of their lives and yet that freedom does not seem to bring happiness. Instead, it generates constant anxiety and a ceaseless yearning, as few seem able to grasp all that they can see.

In certain remote corners of the Old World you may still sometimes stumble upon a small district which seems to have been forgotten amid the general tumult, and to have remained stationary while everything around it was in motion. The inhabitants are for the most part extremely ignorant and poor; they take no part in the business of the country, and they are frequently oppressed by the government; yet their countenances are generally placid, and their spirits light.

In America I saw the freest and most enlightened men, placed in the happiest circumstances which the world affords; it seemed to me as if a cloud habitually hung upon their brow, and I thought them serious and almost sad even in their pleasures.

The chief reason of this contrast is that the former do not think of the ills they endure—the latter are for ever brooding over advantages they do not possess. It is strange to see with what feverish ardor the Americans pursue their own welfare; and to watch the vague dread that constantly torments them lest they should not have chosen the shortest path which may lead to it.

A native of the United States clings to this world's goods as if he were certain never to die; and he is so hasty in grasping at all within his reach, that one would suppose he was constantly afraid of not living long enough to enjoy them. He clutches everything, he holds nothing fast, but soon loosens his grasp to pursue fresh gratifications.

In the United States a man builds a house to spend his latter years in it, and he sells it before the roof is on; he plants a garden, and lets it [rents] just as the trees are coming into bearing; he brings a field into tillage, and leaves other men to gather the crops; he embraces a profession, and gives it up; he settles in a place, which he soon afterward leaves, to carry his changeable longings elsewhere. If his private affairs leave him any leisure, he instantly plunges into the vortex of politics; and if at the end of a year of unremitting labor he finds he has a few days' vacation, his eager curiosity whirls him over the vast extent of the United States, and he will travel fifteen hundred miles in a few days, to shake off his happiness. Death at length overtakes him, but it is before he is weary of his bootless chase of that complete felicity which is for ever on the wing.

Among democratic nations men easily attain a certain equality of conditions; they can never attain the equality they desire. It perpetually retires from before them, yet without hiding itself from their sight, and in retiring draws them on. At every moment they think they are about to grasp it; it escapes at every moment from their hold. They are near enough to see its charms, but too far off to enjoy them; and before they have fully tasted its delights, they die. . . .

SOURCE Alexis de Tocqueville, *Democracy in America,* Vol. II (Boston: C. C. Little & J. Brown, 1841), Second Book, Ch. 13

Marching to the slogan of "Tippecanoe and Tyler Too," the Whigs determined to keep their momentum strong. They rolled this ball, for example, all the way across Ohio.

and self-reliance. Even though Harrison drank modern distilled spirits and did not in fact live in a cabin, the image stuck. The Whigs, long frustrated at their reputation as snobs and elitists, seized on hard cider and log cabins as symbols of their party's loyalty to the common American.

All over the country, Whig speakers displayed paintings, signs, flags, and models of log cabins while freely dispensing cider to crowds thirsty from singing the boisterous new campaign songs produced by Whig composers. Harrison himself went out on the campaign trail, the first presidential candidate to do so. A new kind of American political style was being forged before people's eyes and with their eager participation. For the first time, women became prominent at these rallies, encouraging their husbands, fathers, and suitors with smiles and waving kerchiefs. The Whigs embraced causes many women supported, such as temperance and allegiance to the church.

The Democrats had no idea of how to respond to the hard cider and log cabin campaign. To a considerable extent, the Whigs had beaten the Democrats at their own game, playing up their democratic impulses and their reverence for the ways of the past. Martin Van Buren proved an easy target for a Whig campaign that emphasized homespun values. The President's portly figure and penchant for silk vests and doeskin gloves made the Democrats' long-standing claims of representing the common man look hypocritical. Andrew Jackson himself came out to campaign, firing the same charges against the Whigs that had worked so well in the past, charges of elitism, hostility to slavery, and softness on the bank issue. Even these charges failed.

Van Buren received 367,000 more votes than he had four years earlier, but an even higher number of voters cast their ballots for the Whigs. Harrison won nineteen of the twenty-six states, bringing about half a million new voters to the Whigs. Voter turnout surged to a level almost unimaginable just a decade earlier: Eight of every ten eligible voters went to the polls on election day in 1840. Even during the exciting campaigns of the 1820s and 1830s, the turnout had been much lower, between 50 and 60 percent. After 1840, elections would demand the combination of active campaigning, the search for potent symbols, and boisterous public displays that had proven so successful in that year.

Tyler, Webster, and Diplomacy

The Whig celebration did not last long. Harrison, determined to show both his accessibility to the people

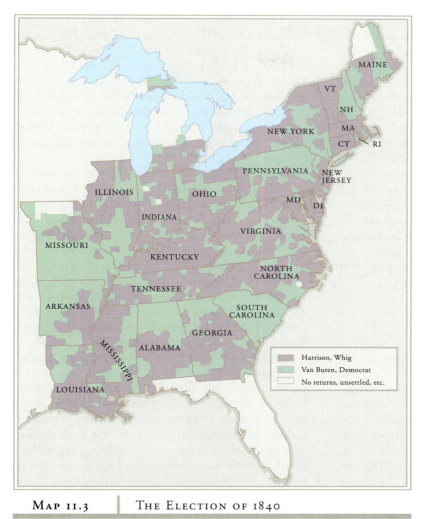

MAP 11.3 | THE ELECTION OF 1840

Harrison, Whig
Van Buren, Democrat
No returns, unsettled, etc.

Many Americans still hated the British. Conflicts between the two countries had broken out over the boundary between the United States and Canada, with areas to the north of Maine and Wisconsin in dispute. In 1837 armed men had fought along the border as Americans aided a rebel movement trying to overthrow British control of Canada; later, a Canadian militia burned an American steamboat carrying supplies for the insurgents, killed one of its crew, and set it adrift, generating intense anger in the northern United States. Armed battle also erupted in the "Aroostock War" over the disputed boundary between Maine and New Brunswick.

Conflict had long been building between the British and the Americans, too, over the African slave trade. Because the United States did not provide any funds for the suppression of the trade, which both nations had prohibited, Great Britain insisted that its vessels be permitted to search American ships off the coast of Africa to prevent the transportation of slaves to British colonies. Americans resented the intrusion in its affairs and refused. The issue threatened to explode in 1841, when American slaves seized the slaving ship the *Creole*, which was taking them from Virginia to New Orleans. The slaves steered the vessel to the Bahamas and claimed their freedom under British law. Much to the anger of southern whites, the British gave sanctuary to the slaves though the ship had been on a domestic, not international, voyage.

Daniel Webster sought to quell this volatile situation. He met with the British representative, Lord Ashburton, to settle these issues before they flamed up into a war that neither nation wanted. After extensive debate and attempts to make sense of poorly drawn maps, the United States and Great Britain decided on a new boundary that gave each about half of what they had claimed in Maine and in the area to the west of Lake Superior. The Webster-Ashburton Treaty also quietened the debate over slavery by establishing joint American-British patrols to intercept ships carrying slaves from Africa.

and his own physical toughness, expounded the longest inaugural speech in American history in March 1841. Unfortunately, the weather was bitterly cold; Harrison contracted pneumonia and died within a month of taking office. John Tyler had become president even though he shared few of the prevailing ideals of the Whigs in Congress. Efforts on the part of Henry Clay and other Whig leaders to expand the power and reach of government with tariffs, banks, and internal improvements proved fruitless in the face of Tyler's opposition. All but one of the members of the cabinet Tyler inherited from Harrison resigned in protest.

The only member to stay on, Daniel Webster, the secretary of state, did so only because he was engaged in important negotiations with England and did not think it proper to step down until they were complete.

Oregon also had troubled relations between the two countries. In the 1820s the United States and Great Britain had signed treaties with Russia, setting the southern boundary of Russia's claims in North America at 54°40′. As a result, the United States and Britain shared the Oregon Territory, a vast region covering present-day Oregon, Washington, Idaho, and British Columbia. Both sides agreed that the 49th parallel, the northern boundary of the United States farther east, would be a reasonable dividing line to the Pacific. Depending on where the boundary line was drawn, either the British or the Americans would possess Puget Sound, a coveted deepwater port. The British, believing that overland migration across the North American continent was virtually impossible, let the issue remain unresolved in the early 1840s so that other, more pressing, issues might be settled. American migration to the Pacific, however, soon proved quite possible.

The Wests

The hard times in the East made moving west seem an increasingly attractive option. Horace Greeley, the most influential newspaper editor of the day, warned people looking for a job in the midst of the depression not to come to the city but rather to "go to the Great West." The "West" included many places. To people in New England, migration to the West in the 1840s often meant migration to the lands of the northern plains and surrounding the Great Lakes. To people from Virginia and Kentucky, migration to the West might mean heading to the free states of Ohio, Indiana, or Illinois or, more often, to Mississippi, Louisiana, and Texas. For people from the cities of the East, the destination might be a booming new city such as Indianapolis, Chicago, or Detroit.

One "West" that captured the imagination of Americans in these years lay far beyond the relatively tame plains and forests of today's Midwest. The new dream of the early 1840s resided in Oregon and California, word of whose beauty and wealth had slowly filtered east throughout the preceding decade. Although many people considered it nothing less than suicide to attempt to cross the Rockies and what was considered "The Great American Desert," a growing stream of families decided to take the chance. Most of those who moved to the Pacific coast gathered in northern Missouri or southern Iowa. They set out in early May across undulating plains, with water and firewood easy to find, their wagons pulled by oxen. They could make up to twenty-five miles a day, though fifteen was more common. The settlers gradually ascended to Fort Laramie, at the edge of the Rockies. By July, they had reached the Continental Divide, the point at which rivers on one side flowed to the east and those on the other flowed to the west. On the trail for more than three months by this point, the settlers had covered two-thirds of the distance of their journey. They still had three months and the hardest traveling yet to come.

From the Divide, the settlers heading to California split off from those going to Oregon. Both faced enormous difficulties in the remainder of their trip: deserts, mountains, fatigue, and dwindling supplies. They raced the weather, for early mountain snowstorms could be deadly. Some of the mountainous areas were so steep that wagons had to be dragged up one side and let down the other with ropes, chains, and pulleys. Finally, by October, 2,000 miles and six months after they had left Missouri or Iowa, the settlers crossed one last ridge and looked down on the sparkling valleys of Sacramento or the Willamette River.

Migration to the Pacific began slowly, with only a few dozen families making the treacherous journey between 1840 and 1842. The numbers mounted between 1843 and 1845, when over 5,000 people passed through Utah on their way to Oregon and California. Throughout the 1840s, the great majority of migrants chose Oregon over California as their destination. In Oregon, settlers found easier places to settle and no Spanish officials to contest their claims. Oregon came to seem a respectable place for literate and upright Protestant families to settle while California seemed a gamble, attractive mainly to single men willing to take their chances in a boom economy that could go bust.

Manifest Destiny

In 1842, the Great United States Exploring Expedition, sent out by the federal government, returned from a journey of 87,780 nautical miles. It had circumnavigated the globe, located Antarctica, and explored the Pacific coast. The captain of the expedition reported that Oregon was a treasure trove of "forests, furs, and fisheries" and that the United States could not afford to give up its claim to any of it. If the United States did not use its military to occupy the territory all the way to the 54°40′ boundary it would

MAP 11.4 | **DISPUTE OVER OREGON BOUNDARY**

The Democrats in Congress and President Tyler supported this expansion, focusing first on Texas. Texas appeared destined to play a key role in the future of the United States, one way or another. If the United States did not quickly annex Texas, Democrats believed, it might fall under the sway of the British. Under British control, they warned, Texas would become not only a barrier to further American migration but also a bastion of antislavery and a haven for runaways. If, by contrast, the United States acted quickly, Texas could become a safety valve for slavery. The vast new territory could attract not only slaveholders and their slaves but also emancipated slaves, pulling them toward their "natural" home in Mexico and Central America, keeping them away from the North and the other attractive lands such as California and Oregon. Midwestern Democrats, for their part, agreed that expansion was essential to the American future. The country simply could not afford to have major ports and potential markets sealed off if it was to avoid another depression such as the one that had recently wracked the country. These Democrats had their eye on Oregon.

James K. Polk, a former governor of Tennessee and an ardent expansionist, got the Democratic nomination for president after an acrimonious convention and nine ballots. The Democrats made their stance: "[O]ur title to the whole of the territory of Oregon is clear and unquestionable." They appealed to both Northerners and Southerners with a program of aggressive expansion, attempting to counter fears of slavery's growth not by rejecting Texas but by embracing Oregon. The first dispatch ever sent by telegraph and then published in a newspaper was a message from this convention about the "Oregon question."

The Election of 1844

In 1844 the Whigs nominated Henry Clay for president on a program explicitly opposed to expansion, expansion that would be "dangerous to the integrity of the

be risking much more than the Oregon territory itself. California might throw off the light Mexican rule under which it rested and join with an independent Oregon to create a nation "that is destined to control the destinies of the Pacific." The Tyler administration sought to downplay this report, not wanting to disrupt negotiations still pending on the boundary of Maine and Wisconsin.

The forces of expansion proved too strong for the administration to contain, however. With increasing numbers of settlers in Oregon, California, and Texas, the issue heated up. In 1845, newspaper editor John Louis O'Sullivan announced that it was the "manifest destiny"—the clear and unavoidable fate—of the United States "to overspread the continent allotted by Providence for the free development of our yearly multiplying millions." In other words, God intended white Americans to fill in every corner of the continent, including all of Canada, Mexico, and Cuba, pushing aside American Indians, Mexicans, English, or anyone else.

Union." The apparently clear-cut choice between Clay and Polk soon became complicated, however. Clay discovered that most white Americans thought westward expansion desirable. He began to waffle on the issue, announcing that he would not oppose Texas annexation if it could be done peacefully and by consensus. Such a strategy backfired, attracting few advocates of expansion but alienating antislavery people in the North.

Meanwhile, the early 1840s witnessed bloody battles over religion that fueled political conflict. A growing stream of immigrants from Ireland, the great majority of them Catholic, flowed into northern cities such as New York, Boston, and Philadelphia. In Protestant eyes, the Roman Catholic Church posed a direct threat to American institutions. That church's hierarchy was undemocratic, critics charged, the concentration of young girls in convents dangerous, the role of nuns and priests suspicious. In 1844 the largest anti-Catholic riot of antebellum America broke out in Philadelphia when Protestants and Irish immigrants erupted into conflict; several Catholic churches burned to the ground while authorities stood by. Because the Democrats proved far more sympathetic to the Irish than did the largely Protestant Whigs, the political differences between the parties now became inflamed with ethnic conflict.

Slavery, too, became an even more explosive issue in the early 1840s. In 1844 the Methodist church divided over slavery and the Baptists split the following year. Though the northern churches had explicitly renounced abolitionism, southern church leaders were angry that many of their northern brethren refused to believe that American slavery was part of God's plan. Five hundred thousand Southerners formed the Methodist Episcopal Church, South, while Baptists from nine southern states created the Southern Baptist Convention. These were the first major splits between Northerners and Southerners.

The conflicts over slavery exerted immediate political consequences. While the abolitionist Liberty party had received only about 7,000 votes in its debut four years earlier, it won 62,000 voters in 1844. In New York, in fact, the Liberty party's strong showing took enough votes from Clay to give the state to Polk. And those electoral votes proved the difference in the national election, as Polk won the presidency by the narrowest of margins thanks to the votes cast in New York.

The Democrats acted on their slim mandate even before Polk took office. The Senate, along party and regional lines, voted to annex Texas, an independent republic since 1836, as soon as Texas consented. Texas gave its approval in the fall of 1845 and won its vote in Washington at the end of that year. The Democrats sought to quiet concerns among Northerners by also annexing Oregon while the fevers of expansion burned. Though some Americans clamored for all of Oregon to its northernmost boundary with Russian territory, chanting "Fifty-four Forty or Fight," neither the United States nor the British proved eager to fight. The boundary was soon set at the 49th parallel, an extension of the northern U.S. boundary from the east.

◆ CONCLUSION ◆

The years between 1837 and 1845 bore the imprint of the largest economic depression in the nation's history up to that time. On the political front, the depression upset what had appeared to be a Democratic stranglehold on the presidency, making Martin Van Buren appear ineffectual and out of touch. Widespread dissatisfaction with the Democrats' handling of the economy laid the foundation for the remarkable Whig victory of 1840, when William Henry Harrison—and Tyler, too—campaigned under the banner of the log cabin and cider, claiming that they stood against economic privilege and corruption. The depression also drove settlers to the West and drove politicians to focus the energies and anxieties of the country on faraway opportunities and dangers.

In a seeming paradox, these same years witnessed American culture at its most ebullient. Painters, philosophers, and poets spoke in a confident new American vernacular. Reformers pushed hard for improvements in education, temperance, antislavery, and much else. Popular culture such as novels, magazines, and Barnum's museum attracted thousands of people. Many Americans focused so much on the future that they often refused to acknowledge the immediate problems surrounding them.

RECOMMENDED READINGS

Genovese, Eugene. *Roll, Jordan, Roll: The World the Slaves Made* (1974) stands as the most powerful portrayal of American slavery.

Kaestle, Carl F. *Pillars of the Republic: Common Schools and American Society, 1780–1860* (1983) is the most thorough and balanced account of education reform.

Kolchin, Peter. *American Slavery, 1619–1877* (1993) offers a nuanced synthesis of much of the recent work.

Rose, Anne C. *Voices of the Marketplace: American Thought and Culture, 1830–1860* (1995) gives a compelling interpretation of cultural history.

Perry, Lewis. *Boats Against the Current: American Culture Between Revolution and Modernity, 1820–1860* (1993) is a stimulating interpretation.

Stevenson, Brenda E. *Life in Black and White: Family and Community in the Slave South* (1996) paints a potent picture of both white and black Southerners.

Thornton, J. Mills, III. *Politics and Power in a Slave Society: Alabama, 1800–1860* (1978) conveys the way democracy and slavery interacted in the South.

Unruh, John I. *The Plains Across: Overland Emigrants and the Trans-Mississippi West, 1840–1860* (1979) tells this story with memorable detail.

Vance, James E. Jr., *The North American Railroad* (1995) shows how the railroad developed in Europe and the United States.

Economic and Political History

Cole, Donald B. *Martin Van Buren and the American Political System* (1984).

Cutler, Stanley. *Privilege and Creative Destruction: The Charles River Bridge Case* (1971).

Holt, Michael. *Political Parties and American Political Development from the Age of Jackson to the Age of Lincoln* (1992).

Howe, Daniel Walker. *The Political Culture of the American Whigs* (1979).

Kohl, Frederick. *The Politics of Individualism: Parties and the American Character in the Jacksonian Era* (1989).

Niven, John. *Martin Van Buren and the Romantic Age* (1983).

Peterson, Norma Lois. *The Presidencies of William Henry Harrison and John Tyler* (1989).

Rezneck, Samuel. "The Social History of an American Depression, 1837–1843," *American Historical Review* (1935).

Temin, Peter. *The Jacksonian Economy* (1969).

Cultural History

Brown, Richard D. *Knowledge Is Power: The Diffusion of Information in Early America, 1700–1865* (1989).

Buranelli, Vincent. *Edgar Allan Poe* (1977).

Cmiel, Kenneth. *Democratic Eloquence: The Fight over Popular Speech in Nineteenth-Century America* (1990).

Emerson, Ken. *Doo-dah! Stephen Foster and the Rise of American Popular Culture* (1997).

Harris, Neil. *Humbug: The Art of P.T. Barnum* (1973).

Laderman, Gary. *American Attitudes Toward Death, 1799–1883* (1996).

Lerner, Gerda. *The Grimké Sisters from South Carolina: Pioneers for Woman's Rights and Abolition* (1967).

Mendelowitz, Daniel M. *A History of American Art* (1970).

Messerli, Jonathan. *Horace Mann* (1972).

Novak, Barbara. *Nature and Culture: American Landscape Painting, 1825–1875* (1980).

Porte, Joel. *Representative Man: Ralph Waldo Emerson in His Time* (1979).

Rose, Anne C. *Transcendentalism as a Social Movement, 1830–1850* (1981).

Tyrrell, Ian R. *Sobering Up: From Temperance to Prohibition in Antebellum America, 1800–1860* (1979).

Zboray, Ronald J. *A Fictive People: Antebellum Economic Development and the American Reading Public* (1993).

The South and Slavery

Blassingame, John., ed., *Slave Testimony: Two Centuries of Letters, Speeches, Interviews, and Autobiographies* (1977).

Boles, John. *Black Southerners, 1619–1869* (1984).

Collins, Bruce. *White Society in the Antebellum South* (1985).

Fox-Genovese, Elizabeth. *Within the Plantation Household: Black and White Women of the Old South* (1988).

Joyner, Charles. *Down by the Riverside: A South Carolina Slave Community* (1984).

Malone, Ann Patton. *Sweet Chariot: Slave Family and Household Structure in Nineteenth-Century Louisiana* (1992).

Martin, Waldo E. *The Mind of Frederick Douglass* (1985).

McFeely, William S. *Frederick Douglass* (1991).

Oakes, James. *The Ruling Race* (1982).

Parish, Peter J. *Slavery: History and Historians* (1989).

Raboteau, Albert J. *Slave Religion: The "Invisible Institution" in the Antebellum South* (1978).

Rose, Willie Lee, ed., *A Documentary History of Slavery in North America* (1976).

White, Deborah Gray. *Ar'n't I a Woman?: Female Slaves in the Plantation South* (1985).

The West and the War with Mexico

Faragher, John Mack. *Women and Men on the Overland Trail* (1979).

Johannsen, Robert W. *To the Halls of the Montezumas: The Mexican War in the American Imagination* (1985).

Merk, Frederick. *History of the Westward Movement* (1978).

Schroeder, John H. *Mr. Polk's War: American Opposition and Dissent, 1846–1848* (1973).

Stephanson, Anders. *Manifest Destiny: American Expansion and the Empire of Right* (1995).

West, Elliott. *The Way to the West: Essays on the Central Plains* (1995).

Winders, Richard Bruce. *Mr. Polk's Army: The American Military Experience in the Mexican War* (1997).

SAN FRANCISCO IN THE DAYS OF THE GOLD RUSH

Ships filled the harbor of the small town of San Francisco as "forty-niners" descended on nearby gold fields.

Chapter 12

EXPANSION AND REACTION: 1846–1854

THE YEARS OF territorial expansion, population growth, and prosperity that accompanied victory in the Mexican War also proved to be years of unprecedented danger and foreboding for the United States. Every hopeful change seemed to bring a reaction. Heightened expectations of a transcontinental empire led to political conflict. Massive immigration from Europe fueled social conflict and sped the disintegration of the party system. Literature took on a more pessimistic tone, expressing doubts about the natural goodness of people and nature. Female activists dicovered that progress for women would come only as a result of prolonged effort. The attempt to open the West to settlement divided Southerners and Northerners against one another. The stopgap compromise on slavery both sides reluctantly signed at the end of all this turmoil satisfied neither side.

WAR WITH MEXICO

Mexico had been a major concern in American foreign policy and politics for generations. Throughout the 1820s American leaders had struggled with the promise and danger posed by the annexation of Texas; throughout the 1830s and 1840s Americans had aided Texans in their fight against the Mexican army. The United States longed for the territories Mexico controlled in western North America, but Mexico pledged to keep those lands. Because the American military remained untested and the battlefields lay far from the centers of population and supplies on the east coast, no one could be sure that the United States could defeat Mexico in a large-scale war. But the United States seemed determined to find out.

The United States at War

No one expected Mexico to accept American annexation of Texas without a struggle. The Mexican government had never recognized the independence of Texas, which Texans claimed as a result of their defeat of Santa Anna in 1836. President James K. Polk made matters worse by insisting that the border between Texas and Mexico lay at the Rio Grande, not at the Nueces River farther north, previously recognized by both nations as the boundary. Even before the formal annexation of Texas took effect in 1845, Polk ordered American troops under the command of General

CHRONOLOGY

1846 Mexican War begins; Stephen Kearny occupies Santa Fe; Zachary Taylor takes Monterey

Border between Canada and United States established at 49th parallel

Wilmot Proviso ignites sectional conflict

Bear Flag Republic in California proclaimed by John C. Frémont

Hiram Powers completes statue "The Greek Slave"

1847 Taylor defeats Santa Anna at Buena Vista; Winfield Scott captures Vera Cruz and Mexico City

Mormons reach Great Salt Lake Valley

1848 Gold discovered in California

Treaty of Guadalupe Hidalgo

Attempts to buy Cuba from Spain

Free Soil party runs Van Buren for president

Zachary Taylor elected president

Seneca Falls Convention

Oneida community established

Regular steamship trips between Liverpool and New York City

Mormons settle in Great Basin

1849 California seeks admission to Union

"Forty-Niners" race to California

Cotton prices invigorate South

Cholera epidemic returns

1850 Nashville Convention attempts to unify South

Fugitive Slave Law

Taylor dies; Millard Fillmore becomes president

Compromise of 1850

Nathaniel Hawthorne, *The Scarlet Letter*

First land-grant railroad: Illinois Central

John C. Calhoun and Henry Clay die

1851 Herman Melville, *Moby-Dick*

Maine adopts prohibition

Woman's rights convention in Akron, Ohio

Indiana state constitution excludes free blacks

1852 Franklin Pierce elected president

Harriet Beecher Stowe, *Uncle Tom's Cabin*

Daniel Webster dies

1853 Gadsden Purchase

Nativism increases

1854 Know-Nothings win unexpected victories

Whig party collapses

Republican party founded

Kansas-Nebraska Act

Ostend Manifesto encourages acquisition of Cuba

Henry David Thoreau, *Walden*

High-point of immigration

Railroad reaches Mississippi River

Zachary Taylor to cross the Nueces; soon, they were proceeding toward the Rio Grande.

Polk had his eyes not only on the border with Texas but on larger prizes still: the sale of California and New Mexico. Polk ordered John C. Frémont, leading an army expedition to map rivers within U.S. borders, to California. Frémont proceeded to support the "Bear Flag Rebellion," an armed struggle by American set-

tlers against the Mexican government. Disrupted, the Mexican provinces might be sacrificed more easily and more cheaply to the United States.

The president prepared for war in Texas, seizing on a skirmish between Mexican and American troops north of the Rio Grande as a convenient excuse. With no apparent sense of irony, Polk declared that "not withstanding all our efforts to avoid it," Mexico had

MAP 12.1 | THE MEXICAN WAR

started a war when it "invaded our territory and shed American blood on the American soil." Even though northern Whigs continually denounced the war and its motives, Whig congressmen believed they had to support appropriations for the soldiers in the field.

American troops under the leadership of Colonel Stephen Kearney took Santa Fe in New Mexico with no casualties late in the summer of 1846. California proved to be a greater struggle, partly because Mexican settlers there put up more of a fight, partly because battle lines there were confused, and partly because Frémont seemed to provoke fights where resistance might not otherwise have appeared. In any case, the American forces won control of California a few months after they had taken New Mexico. The United States Army, under Zachary Taylor and Winfield Scott, achieved a series of victories in Mexico itself in 1846 and 1847, including an impressive amphibious landing at Vera Cruz by Scott's forces that ended in the conquest of Mexico City and "the halls of Montezuma."

Though the Mexicans outnumbered the Americans, the U.S. forces were much better equipped and supplied and enjoyed innovative and impressive leadership from their officer corps. The Mexican War familiarized Americans with names they would come to know all too well a little more than a decade later: Ulysses S. Grant, Jefferson Davis, Robert E. Lee, George McClellan, Joseph Johnston, William T. Sherman, Braxton Bragg, James Longstreet, Thomas Jonathan Jackson, and George Meade. The United States Army proved remarkably effective and won the respect of more established military powers in Europe. But Polk distrusted his two leading generals—Taylor and Scott—suspecting, correctly, that they harbored ambitions of winning the presidency under the Whig banner by capitalizing on their military success.

The Consequences of War

Many Northerners worried about the expansion of slavery and the increased power of the slave states that might accompany victory over Mexico. To put such concerns to rest, David Wilmot, a Pennsylvania Democrat in favor of the war, made a bold move: When a bill to appropriate additional funds for American troops in Mexico came before Congress in 1846, Wilmot offered a "proviso," a condition, that declared that slavery could not be established in any territory the United States might win from Mexico as a result of the war. Wilmot was no abolitionist and no friend of black people—he acted, he said, to protect his party and people of his own skin color—but his proviso became a central topic of debate in the heated battle over slavery. Votes for and against the proviso followed sectional lines to an alarming degree. The Wilmot Proviso went down to defeat and the war proceeded, but from 1846 on the opponents of slavery increasingly distrusted Polk and southern political leaders.

Henry David Thoreau protested the war with Mexico. As he wrote in his essay "On Civil Disobedience," Thoreau considered the Mexican War "the work of comparatively few individuals using the government as their tool." Thoreau decided to signal his disgust with the American government by claiming the higher law of individual conscience and refusing to pay his taxes. He spent only one night in jail before his friends paid his taxes for him, but Thoreau's essay proved influential later in American history when protesters looked for inspiration and justification. Throughout the North, from New England through the old Northwest, many people expressed their disgust with the war.

The war with Mexico limped to an end in late 1847 and the beginning of 1848. American troops controlled Mexico City, the Gulf Coast, and all the northern provinces claimed by the United States, but the Mexican government refused to settle on terms of peace. President James K. Polk, General Winfield Scott, and peace commissioner Nicholas Trist bickered over the treaty. Whigs argued with Democrats even as conflict churned within both parties. Northerners and Southerners viewed one another with undisguised distrust and distaste, as did abolitionists and their many opponents. Some Americans urged Polk to lay claim to all of the conquered country while others insisted that the United States should seize no territory at all from the war. Trist, on his own in Mexico, finally signed a treaty in Guadalupe Hidalgo that brought the negotiations to an end in February 1848.

Mexico, for $15 million and the abandonment of American claims against the Mexican government and its people, agreed to sell California, New Mexico, and all of Texas above the Rio Grande. When the treaty finally appeared before Congress for ratification the following month, many doubted that it would pass, so bitter was the opposition to the war, to Polk, and to expansion. The various cliques, however, found a way to swallow their disagreements long enough to ratify the treaty in March so that the war could end. A prominent newspaper pronounced the treaty "a peace which every one will be glad of, but no one will be proud of." The Mexicans signed the treaty in May and the war finally closed.

War and Politics

James K. Polk, chronically ill and wearied from the presidency, decided not to seek reelection in 1848.

The Democrats, scrambling to find someone to unite the northern and southern branches of the party, decided on Lewis Cass of Michigan. Cass, a rather colorless man except for his red wig, spoke for the majority of northern Democrats who sympathized with white Southerners in their determination to keep black people enslaved and in the South. Antislavery Democrats walked out of the Democratic convention that nominated Cass and called their own convention in New York; there, they nominated Martin Van Buren for the presidency.

Abolitionists who had supported the Liberty party exulted at a candidate who might win a substantial number of votes. Antislavery "Conscience Whigs," watching with disgust as their fellow Whigs fell over one another to decide which general from the Mexican War to nominate, also threw their support behind Van Buren. These various groups forged a working alliance

Zachary Taylor's fame from the war with Mexico translated into votes for the Whig party—even though that party had opposed the war from its outset.

for the election of 1848, declaring their solidarity behind the name of the Free Soil party and its stirring motto: "Free soil, free speech, free labor, and free men." Leading figures such as Charles Francis Adams and Charles Sumner denounced slavery and its defenders.

The mainstream Whigs found themselves in an awkward spot, for they had fervently opposed the Mexican War but now sought to capitalize on the popularity of General Zachary Taylor. Nevertheless, Taylor had several advantages as a candidate. He had no troubling political past; indeed, he had never before cast a ballot in any election. Though he was a slaveholding planter, he had opposed the war with Mexico before he had been sent there to lead American troops. Just what he thought about anything was quite unclear. That lack of clarity suited the Whigs, who counted on repeating their success of 1840 when another vague general, William Henry Harrison, had led them to victory.

Taylor won the election in the electoral college, but the popular vote revealed little consensus. Taylor won eight slave states and seven free ones, while Cass won eight free states and seven slaveholding ones. While Van Buren won over 290,000 votes and came in second in several important states, he did not win enough votes to cement the identity of the new Free Soil party. Free Soilers began drifting back to the Democrats and the Whigs. The election had not clarified the issues that concerned most voters.

AMERICANS ON THE MOVE

Americans, always restless, moved in massive numbers and on a continental scale in the years around 1850. As the economy lifted, transportation developed, boundaries became settled, and gold beckoned, people flooded to the states of the old Northwest and the old Southwest as well as to Texas, Oregon, and California. The suffering of Ireland and political conflict within Germany drove millions across the Atlantic, filling the cities and farms of the East. Nothing seemed settled or permanent.

Rails, Sails, and Steam

The late 1840s and early 1850s saw the emergence of the fastest-growing rail lines and the fastest ships in

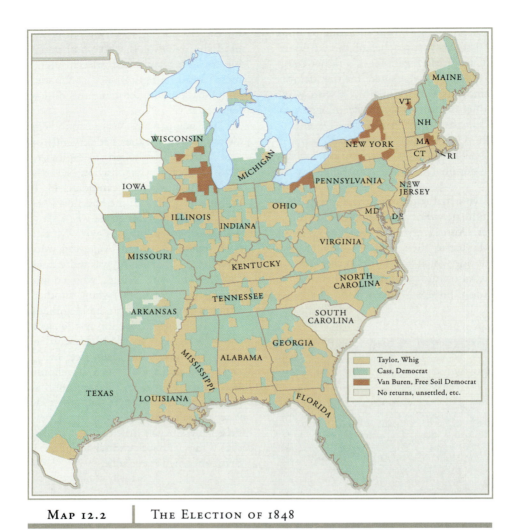

MAP 12.2　|　THE ELECTION OF 1848

the world. The nation's rail network, slowed by the depression of the late 1830s and early 1840s, burgeoned with the return of prosperity. Private investors poured tens of millions of dollars into rail expansion. The federal government aided railroads with free surveys, friendly tariffs, and vast grants of land. The major cities of the eastern seaboard competed against one another to attract as many rail lines as possible. Smaller cities and towns fought to contribute land and cash. Owners of mines and factories subsidized new railroads, as did Wall Street speculators and investors from Great Britain.

Railroads proved more important for some parts of the country than for others. Railroads flourished in New England and New York, where the density of population and manufacturing permitted the new technology to work most efficiently. Midwestern states such as Ohio, Illinois, and Indiana also showed themselves well-suited to the railroads, for their vast flat distances and absence of good river transportation made the extension of the steel rails both necessary and relatively easy. Chicago had no railroads at all in 1850 but by 1860 twelve lines converged in the city, making it the undisputed rail center of the nation—indeed, of the world. Three of those lines stretched from Chicago all the way to New York City; a trip that had taken ten days before the railroad now took only a day and a half.

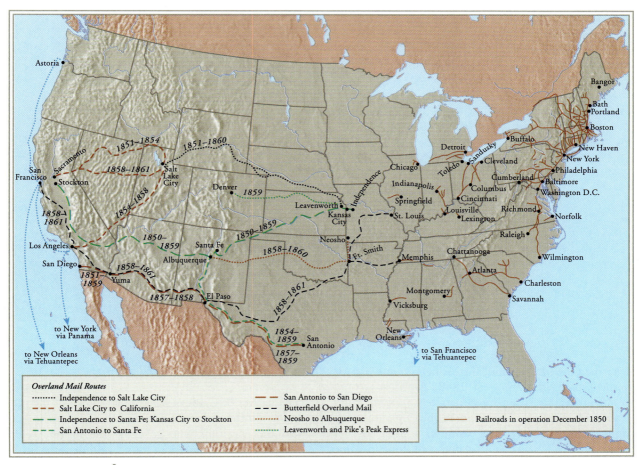

MAP 12.3 | RAILROADS AND OVERLAND MAIL, 1850

Overland Mail Routes

- Independence to Salt Lake City
- Salt Lake City to California
- Independence to Santa Fe; Kansas City to Stockton
- San Antonio to Santa Fe
- San Antonio to San Diego
- Butterfield Overland Mail
- Neosho to Albuquerque
- Leavenworth and Pike's Peak Express
- Railroads in operation December 1850

Rural areas as well as cities immediately felt the effects of the railroad. Farmers now found it profitable to ship their produce to a city a hundred miles away. Farmers specialized, becoming dairymen, vegetable growers, and fruit producers. Steel plows and mechanical reapers drew huge harvests from the rich soil of the upper Mississippi Valley. Corn, wheat, hogs, and cattle flowed out of Ohio, Illinois, Indiana, and Wisconsin. The older farms of New England, New York, and Pennsylvania, facing the competition of the new states of the West, turned to specialty products such as cheese, maple sugar, vegetables, and cranberries. These products, along with thousands of others, rode the railroad tracks to market, tying countryside and city together.

Because the relatively sparse population of the South could not sustain much railroad traffic and because the South's natural system of rivers carried cargo so cheaply throughout the year, railroad building trailed off in the South in the 1840s and did not pick up again until the late 1850s. The South relied instead on the steamboats that plied the Mississippi and other major rivers. The riverboats grew in size, number, and ornateness throughout the period, becoming floating hotels decorated with blazing lights, glittering mirrors, and flying flags. The 1850s marked the glory days of these riverboats, with cotton bales stacked on every square inch of deck.

Elsewhere, packet steamships carried mail, freight, and passengers up and down the eastern seaboard,

Graceful and fast, American clipper ships raced around South America and across the Pacific.

over the Great Lakes, and, increasingly, across the Atlantic Ocean. Beginning in 1848, Americans could count on regular steam travel between New York and Liverpool, England. These innovations in transportation, exciting as they were, came at a steep cost. "I never open a newspaper that does not contain some account of disasters and loss of life on railroads," one diarist observed. "They do a retail business in human slaughter, whilst the wholesale trade is carried on (especially on Western waters) by the steamboats. This world is going on too fast."

Clipper ships enjoyed a brief but stirring heyday in the late forties and early fifties. Clippers used narrow hulls and towering sails to attain speeds that have yet to be reached by any other sailing vessels of their size. The clippers carried expensive tea from China to England, fortune seekers to a gold rush in Australia, and Americans from the east coast to the west. They sailed from New York to San Francisco, all the way around South America, in less than a hundred days. Shipbuilders constructed the vessels as fast as they could and the ships sometimes paid for themselves on their very first voyage. Although they were to be displaced after 1855 by uglier and more efficient steamships, for a few exciting years the clipper ships thrived on the high prices, small cargoes, long voyages, and desperate speed fueled by remarkable discoveries in California.

The Gold Rush

The natives of California had long known of the gold hidden in the rocks and creeks of that vast territory, as had the Mexicans who governed the region. White American settlers, too, had found gold deposits in the early 1840s, when a trickle of men had sought their fortune in California rather than in the more popular destination of Oregon. But it was a discovery in January of 1848 that changed everything.

John Sutter had been one of the first non-Spanish white men to settle in California. In 1839 he had emigrated from Switzerland to the area that became Sacramento, where he established a large fort, trading post, and wheat farm. Sutter hired a carpenter named James Marshall to build a mill on the American River. While working on the project, Marshall happened to notice "something shining in the bottom of the ditch." He realized that the nugget, about half the size of a pea, was gold. Sutter, Marshall, and the other men on the place tried to keep the find a secret, but word leaked to San Francisco. There, sailors abandoned their ships and clerks left their shops to look for gold along the American River. By the end of 1848 such men had gathered nuggets and dust worth about $6 million.

Back east, people remained calm, even skeptical, about the discovery until 230 ounces of almost pure

A diverse population of men rushed to the California gold fields in 1849. Recent immigrants from China worked alongside Indians, whites, and African Americans.

gold went on display in Washington. The Gold Rush began: "The coming of the Messiah, or the dawn of the Millennium could not have excited anything like the interest," one newspaper marvelled. By the end of 1849 over 700 ships carrying over 45,000 Easterners sailed to California. Some of the ships went around South America; others transported their passengers to the Isthmus of Panama, which they crossed by foot and canoe. These trips could be horrific, in part because 1848 and 1849 saw cholera break out across the United States. Once the disease began on board a ship, death swept through the crew and passengers.

About 55,000 settlers rejected the ships and instead followed the overland trails cut across the continent. Some traveled alongside the continuing stream of settlers to Oregon, others followed trails directly to the gold fields from destinations as far south as Mexico. Whether they went by sea or land, the participants in the Gold Rush were quite different from other immigrants to the West. The "Forty-Niners" tended to be either single men or groups of men from the same lo-

cality. In sharp contrast to the Oregon migration, women and children rarely appeared among those rushing to get the gold, accounting for only about 5 percent of all those who came to California in the frantic early days. Most of the men who flooded into California, unlike the Oregon settlers, had little interest in settling there permanently. They intended to find their share of the gold and move on. Once in California, men of all classes, colors, and nations worked feverishly alongside one another in the streams and mountainsides during the day; the miners included Mexicans, Chileans, Frenchmen, Englishmen, Hungarians, and other Europeans. Disease and miserable living conditions hounded all of them, sending thousands to their deaths.

When some Chinese men returned home from California flush with American riches and stories of the "Golden Mountain," the fever spread in Asia as it did in Europe and America. About 70 percent of the Chinese immigrants came from Guangdong Province, where many peasants and artisans had become impoverished and desperate enough to launch the dangerous journey. Young men, in particular, thought California might offer a way to attain the wealth they needed to acquire a farm and a wife back in China; they did not intend to stay long in the alien land. Migrants could buy tickets from brokers on credit, with high interest. Upon their arrival in California, the Chinese immigrants discovered that they had to borrow yet more money from Chinese merchants in San Francisco to be transported to the gold fields. The miners worked continuously in hopes of paying off that debt, fueling resentment and persecution by white miners, but the costs seemed worth the potential reward.

California held out hope for African Americans, too. News of the gold rush spread not only by word of mouth but also through black newspapers and the abolitionist press. Most of the black migrants to California left from the coastal cities of New England. California—unlike Ohio, Illinois, and Indiana—held out the promise of an American West where color really might not matter so much, where a hard-working black man might enjoy the fruits of his own labor. Although abolitionists, black and white, warned that even California might not be safe for black migrants, several thousand African Americans decided to take the chance.

Whatever their race, few miners discovered a fortune. The average miner in 1848 found about an ounce of gold a day, worth around $20. Even though the cost of living was exorbitant in gold-rush California, this $20 was about twenty times what a laborer back east made with a daily wage. As the number of competing miners skyrocketed over the next few years, however, the average take declined until it reached about $6 a day in 1852. Mining became more mechanized and concentrated in fewer hands. Soon, the biggest profits went not to lucky individuals but to companies that assaulted the river beds and ravines with battalions of workers, explosives, and crushing mills.

Although miners of every background went bust, California as a whole flourished. Within four years over $220 million in gold came out of the state. Towns appeared wherever people gathered to look for the gold, and in those towns' stores, physicians, saloons, lawyers, bordellos, and newspapers absorbed the ready cash. Men who tired of mining turned to farming instead, or teaching school, or building houses. San Francisco was the big winner: A dull village before

1848, within a couple of years it had grown into a brash and booming city of 35,000 diverse residents.

The Mormons' Great Migration

A different kind of westward movement was already in full force as the California Gold Rush got underway. These migrants were members of the Church of Jesus Christ of Latter-day Saints, or Mormons. In the face of relentless persecution Joseph Smith, the founder of the church, had led his flock to Illinois. There they established the town of Nauvoo and flourished; by the mid-1840s Nauvoo, with 15,000 residents, had become the largest city in Illinois. But the peace was not to last. Conflict erupted within the church itself when Smith decreed that polygamy was God's will, that men within the church would marry several wives. When Smith ordered the destruction of a Mormon newspaper that opposed the new practice, the paper's owners

Persecuted in Illinois in the 1840s, the Mormons launched a mass migration to the Great Salt Lake in the state they called "Deseret."

signed warrants for his arrest. A mob of non-Mormons broke into the jail where Smith was being held and killed both him and his brother. The Mormons of Nauvoo feared for their lives as vigilantes roamed the area.

The Mormons turned to one of their elders, Brigham Young, to lead them in this time of trial. Young, believing that their church would not be tolerated within settled areas, decided to move to a place beyond the reach of the Mormons' many enemies. Young knew from reading guidebooks for settlers to Oregon and California about the Great Salt Lake, a place of rich land and good water cut off from the east by mountains and from the west and south by deserts. The Mormons carefully planned their migration, sending out scouts and establishing way stations for those who would follow. They abandoned Nauvoo in the spring of 1846. In a well-coordinated migration, 15,000 Mormons moved in stages to the Great Salt Lake. When they first arrived, in 1847, the valley presented a daunting picture of rock and sagebrush but the settlers irrigated the land, turning it into a thriving community.

When frosts, insects, and drought ruined much of the crops in the spring of 1848, Young announced that the Mormons would follow a new strategy: They would pool their labor and their resources even more than before. They designed an ambitious city on the shores of the Great Salt Lake, with wide streets surrounding a temple that would "surpass in grandeur of design and gorgeousness of decoration all edifices the world has yet seen." Young concentrated control of the city and its farms in his own hands and in those of his fellow church leaders. Few Mormons left with the fortune seekers when the gold rush brought thousands of travellers through their new settlement; rather, the Mormons did a profitable business with the forty-niners.

As some non-Mormons settled at the Great Salt Lake, Young decided that a form of government other than the church must be established. He oversaw the creation of a state called "Deseret," a Mormon term meaning "honeybee." The Mormons began a successful campaign to attract new converts from Europe, Asia, and Latin America; thousands of people prepared to move to the new refuge at the Great Salt Lake. In 1849 the residents of Deseret petitioned Congress for admission into the Union as a new state and awaited the decision, knowing that many Americans viewed them with contempt and suspicion.

The High Tide of Immigration

Even as Americans moved west, a vast immigration from Ireland surged into the eastern United States in the late 1840s and early 1850s. Irish immigration itself was not new; about a million people had left Ireland for the United States between 1815 and 1844, though many of those early migrants were Protestant Scots-Irish. The situation in Ireland changed much for the worse beginning in 1845, when the potato harvest failed. A blight suddenly struck healthy fields, turning the leaves black almost overnight and filling the air with "a sickly odor of decay." This, the Great Potato Famine, which would last for nearly a decade, destroyed the basic food for most of the Irish people and created suffering on an immense scale. Over a million people died; another 1.8 million fled to North America as their only hope for survival. In all, about a fourth of the island's population departed, with more people leaving in the eleven years after 1845 than in the preceding 250 years combined. The year of 1854 marked the high point of immigration to the United States before the Civil War.

The Irish emigrants tended to be young, single, poor, unskilled, and Catholic; a large number spoke Irish rather than English; they came over in the dead of winter and with virtually no money or property. While some Irish immigrants spread throughout North America, from Ontario to New Orleans to San Francisco, most congregated in the cities of the North and Midwest. They lived from day to day on whatever money they could earn, moving frequently in hopes of bettering their condition. Most men worked on docks, others in canal and railroad construction, often in competition with free blacks and even slaves, always for the lowest wage. Women worked as domestics and as unskilled laborers in textile mills. Desperately poor, easily identified, widely despised, and often subsisting on the bare edge of starvation, the Irish figured prominently in arrest reports and on penitentiary rolls.

The high tide of Irish immigration occurred simultaneously with the peak of German immigration. Over a million Germans came to America between 1846 and 1854, many of them dislocated by a failed revolution in Germany in 1848. The Germans were much better off financially than the Irish. They tended to be farmers who brought some property with them and established farms in the Midwest. The Germans, more than the Irish, were divided by wealth, generation,

IMMIGRATION TO THE UNITED STATES, 1820–1860

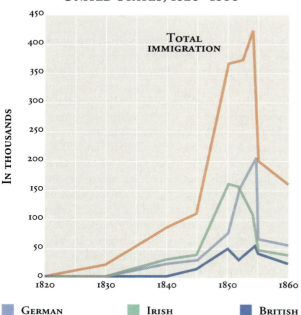

politics, regional background, and religion. Combined, the Irish and German immigrants accounted for almost 15 percent of the entire population of the United States; in some cities, the foreign-born and their children constituted a majority of the population.

In the eyes of many white Protestants, the new arrivals appeared impossible to assimilate, marked, it seemed, by drink, strange languages, and clannishness. The immigrants threatened to drive down wages because they were willing to work for so little. They also threatened to thwart enforced temperance. That movement gained momentum in 1851, when Maine, in reaction to the new immigrants, became the first state to enact statewide prohibition of alcohol. The immigrants often received the vote in state and local elections soon after they landed and they voted heavily against prohibition. Protestants saw in the large numbers of new immigrants an immediate threat to American political institutions.

In the face of such challenges to their values and power, "native Americans" organized against the immigrants. The most powerful manifestation of nativism

Hounded by poverty, Irish people gathered in their villages in search of transportation to America in the late 1840s and early 1850s.

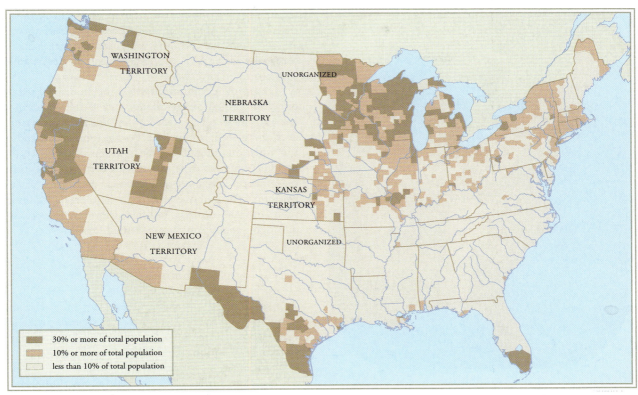

MAP 12.4 | FOREIGN-BORN POPULATION, 1840-1860

Legend:
- 30% or more of total population
- 10% or more of total population
- less than 10% of total population

appeared in New York City in 1849, when Charles Allen founded the Order of the Star Spangled Banner. Its membership was restricted to native-born white Protestants sworn to secrecy. When asked about the order by outsiders, members were instructed to say "I know nothing"—and thus they became popularly known as the "Know-Nothings." The order grew slowly at first, but it drew on deeply held and deepening prejudices. No one knew what the movement might become.

ACTION AND REFLECTION

The late 1840s and early 1850s, though relatively peaceful and prosperous, led a number of people to protest the drift of American life. Some became so disenchanted that they established communities set aside from the rest of society, places where they could experiment with alternative ways of organizing labor, power, and sexuality. Others launched a crusade to make the United States consistent with its highest ideals, defining women as well as men as full citizens. Yet others wrote novels and poetry that reflected, sometimes obliquely and sometimes directly, on the whirl of American life.

Perfect Communities

Most of the hundred or so utopian communities created in the United States between the Revolution and the Civil War were founded in the 1840s. Some communities were secular in origin and some religious, some boldly experimental and others reactionary. They all insisted that people truly dedicated to social improvement had to flee corruption and compromise. Though several prophets and leaders emigrated from Europe to the New World in hopes of establishing

John Humphrey Noyes founded the Oneida community in upstate New York, proclaiming sexual freedom in "complex marriage."

religious utopias, most of the idealistic communities grew directly from American origins.

The most notorious American communal experiment emerged in 1848. It was in that year that John Humphrey Noyes and his 250 followers created the Oneida Association in upstate New York. Noyes, educated as a minister and a lawyer, had become convinced years before that it was possible for humans to be "perfected," made free of sin. Most controversial, he argued that people in a state of perfection should not be bound by conventional monogamous marriages; all belonged to one another sexually in "complex marriage." He gathered a small group of disciples around him who put such beliefs into action, practicing birth control by having males withdraw during intercourse. Without fear of pregnancy, Noyes argued, sexual intercourse could become "a joyful act of fellowship."

Oneida experimented not only with sex but also with economic cooperation. Everyone performed the full range of labor, with few distinctions based on gender. The women of the group cut their hair, wore pantaloons rather than skirts, and played sports with their male compatriots. Unlike other utopian communities,

Oneida focused its energies on manufacturing rather than farming. The community produced an improved and profitable steel animal trap. Later, Oneida transformed itself into a profitable business corporation specializing in silverware.

The utopian communities testified both to the freedom the United States offered and to the yearning it created. In a place with so few visible constraints, everything seemed possible. People took advantage of the isolation offered by the enormous space of the young country to experiment with communities based on religious, sexual, or philosophical principles, or any combination of those principles. The proliferation of such communities also testified, however, to how full of longing many Americans seemed.

Woman's Rights

The seeds for the organized movement for woman's rights in the United States had been planted in 1840, when women attending the World's Anti-Slavery Convention in London, England, found themselves consigned to seats in a separate roped-off area. One of the delegates was Elizabeth Cady Stanton, a well-educated young woman, twenty-five years old, on her honeymoon with her husband, a political abolitionist. Listening to the debates over the place of women in antislavery, Stanton felt "humiliated and chagrined, except as these feelings were outweighed by contempt for the shallow reasoning of the opponents and their comical pose and gestures." Stanton discovered an important ally at the London meeting: Lucretia Mott, twenty-two years Stanton's senior, a devout and activist Quaker and feminist. The two women vowed that they would start a movement back in the States for woman's rights, but they did not soon find the opportunity they sought. Stanton devoted her time to raising her family in Boston, participating only marginally in reform. In 1847, she moved with her family to Seneca Falls, New York, for her husband's health.

While living in Seneca Falls, Stanton revived the idea of holding a convention on woman's rights. She grew frustrated with the narrowness of life in a small town and the limitations placed on women there. Meeting with Lucretia Mott again, Stanton told her friend how miserable she had become. They renewed their determination to start a conversation in the United States over the place of women. The two women joined with three of Mott's Quaker friends to plan a convention in July in Seneca Falls, although

Elizabeth Cady Stanton, one of the founders of the woman's rights movement, about the time of the Seneca Falls Convention of 1848.

people might attend the meeting—held in an obscure town during a busy season for farmers—but over a hundred people came, including a considerable number of men. Of those men the most prominent was Frederick Douglass. Douglass's newspaper, the *North Star,* was one of the few papers to give the convention a positive notice; the rest ridiculed the very notion of equal rights for women.

Despite the skepticism, Stanton and the other organizers of the Seneca Falls Convention succeeded in their major role: getting Americans to talk about woman's rights. Word of the Declaration spread among the many women's groups working in other reform organizations. Stanton, Mott, and their allies determined that they would hold a convention each year to keep the momentum going. Meetings in Rochester, Akron, Worcester, and Syracuse convened over the next decade.

At the Akron meeting in 1851 a black woman spoke, despite the opposition of some who feared that

only Mott had had any experience in organizing a reform meeting. Stanton recalled that they "felt as helpless as if they had been suddenly asked to construct a steam engine." The five women "were neither sour old maids, childless women, nor divorced wives, as the newspapers claimed them to be," Stanton argued; it was not that they themselves had suffered so much, but rather that they had "souls large enough to feel the wrongs of others."

Casting about for a way to express their grievances most effectively, they decided to model their "Declaration of Rights and Sentiments" on the Declaration of Independence. It began with a ringing statement: "The history of mankind is a history of repeated injuries and usurpations on the part of man toward woman, having in direct object the establishment of an absolute tyranny over her." The Declaration drew on the strategies and rhetoric of other reform efforts. It demanded the right to vote and insisted on women's full equality with men in every sphere of life, including property rights, education, employment, divorce, and in court. The organizers worried about how many

Sojourner Truth, a former slave from New York, embodied for many people the pride and strength of black women, for she spoke out for both her gender and her race.

"Declaration of Sentiments" of the Woman Suffrage Movement 1848

Sixty-eight women and thirty-two men signed this declaration, produced at Seneca Falls in 1848. Modeled on the Declaration of Independence, this document provided a touchstone for the woman's movement throughout the rest of the century and beyond.

The history of mankind is a history of repeated injuries and usurpations on the part of man toward woman, having in direct object the establishment of an absolute tyranny over her. To prove this, let facts be submitted to a candid world.

He has never permitted her to exercise her inalienable right to the elective franchise.

He has compelled her to submit to laws, in the formation of which she had no voice.

He has withheld from her rights which are given to the most ignorant and degraded men—both natives and foreigners.

Having deprived her of this first right of a citizen, the elective franchise, thereby leaving her without representation in the halls of legislation, he has oppressed her on all sides.

He has made her, if married, in the eye of the law, civilly dead.

He has taken from her all right in property, even to the wages she earns.

He has made her, morally, an irresponsible being, as she can commit many crimes with impunity, provided they be done in the presence of her husband. In the covenant of marriage, she is compelled to promise obedience to her husband, he becoming, to all intents and purposes, her master—the law giving him power to deprive her of her liberty, and to administer chastisement.

He has so framed the laws of divorce, as to what shall be the proper causes, and in case of separation, to whom the guardianship of the children shall be given, as to be

her appearance would identify the woman's rights movement too closely with abolition. She had escaped slavery in New York in 1827, freed her son in Alabama, and supported her family by working as a domestic. In 1843, she had a vision in which she was commanded to carry the word of God; she renamed herself "Sojourner Truth." In Akron she rebuked the white ministers who had come to argue against the advocates of woman's rights. Those ministers urged women to accept the fact that they were special creatures who should be protected and who should stay in their restricted sphere. "Look at me!" Truth commanded them. "I have ploughed, and planted, and gathered into barns, and no man could head me! And a'n't I a woman? I could work as much and eat as much as a man—when I could get it—and bear de lash as well! And a'n't I a woman?" She had seen most of her thirteen children sold into slavery, and "when I cried out with my mother's grief, none but Jesus heard me! And a'n't I a woman?"

The campaign for woman's rights, as it evolved, developed a complex relationship to abolition and to African Americans. The movement might offer a rare opportunity for women such as Sojourner Truth to be heard, but white woman's rights advocates generally phrased their demands for equal rights in terms of education and refinement that neglected black women and their needs.

Not all activist women, moreover, dedicated themselves to woman's rights. More conservative women, wholly regardless of the happiness of women—the law, in all cases, going upon a false supposition of the supremacy of man, and giving all power into his hands.

After depriving her of all rights as a married woman, if single, and the owner of property, he has taxed her to support a government which recognizes her only when her property can be made profitable to it.

He has monopolized nearly all the profitable employments, and from those she is permitted to follow, she receives but a scanty remuneration. He closes against her all the avenues to wealth and distinction which he considers most honorable to himself. As a teacher of theology, medicine, or law, she is not known.

He has denied her the facilities for obtaining a thorough education, all colleges being closed against her.

He allows her in church, as well as state, but a subordinate position, claiming apostolic authority for her exclusion from the ministry, and, with some exceptions, from any public participation in the affairs of the church.

He has created a false public sentiment by giving to the world a different code of morals for men and women, by which moral delinquencies which exclude women from society, are not only tolerated, but deemed of little account in man.

He has usurped the prerogative of Jehovah himself, claiming it as his right to assign for her a sphere of action, when that belongs to her conscience and to her God.

He has endeavored, in every way that he could, to destroy her confidence in her own powers, to lessen her self-respect, and to make her willing to lead a dependent and abject life.

Now, in view of this entire disfranchisement of one-half the people of this country, their social and religious degradation—in view of the unjust laws above mentioned, and because women do feel themselves aggrieved, oppressed, and fraudulently deprived of their most sacred rights, we insist that they have immediate admission to all the rights and privileges which belong to them as citizens of the United States.

SOURCE Elizabeth Cady Stanton, et al., *History of Woman Suffrage*, Vol. 1 (Rochester, N.Y.: Fowler & Wells, 1889), 58–59.

often socially prominent, had for several decades devoted their energies to acquiring public funds for orphanages, shelters for "fallen" women, and the poor. They continued with these practices throughout the 1840s, using their connections to important men in state legislatures, on city boards, and in prosperous businesses to raise money and garner support. Such women did not hesitate to raise and circulate petitions, gathering the signatures of hundreds of thousands of women. They asked for laws to criminalize seduction and to change property laws, to oppose Indian removal, restrict slavery, and stop the sale of liquor. They often proved successful and effective with these indirect means and saw little need for agitating for the vote for women. American women, in other words, were as politically diverse as the men in their households.

Hawthorne, Melville, and Whitman

Whereas the 1830s and 1840s had been the time of transcendentalism, the 1850s saw American writers grappling with themes very much attuned to their time and place. While Nathaniel Hawthorne's *The Scarlet Letter* and Herman Melville's *Moby Dick* were ironic, dark, and complex allegories, Walt Whitman's *Leaves of Grass* evoked a determinedly hopeful vision. All three captured a key part of the American mood in the 1850s.

A writer deeply engaged with the history of his native New England, Nathaniel Hawthorne wove powerful allegorical stories of sin and regret such as The Scarlet Letter.

Nathaniel Hawthorne's father died at sea and left his family to do the best it could with limited resources and memories of once being a leading family of Massachusetts. Hawthorne went to Bowdoin College despite the family's reduced circumstances and then returned to his mother's home and set up as a writer. Quiet and ambitious, he did not marry until he was thirty-eight years old, devoting his energies to his work. He read almost indiscriminately, gulping down popular crime fiction as well as the latest literary products of Europe. Though he himself was not morose, Hawthorne was fascinated by the lingering consequences of sin, perhaps because one of his ancestors had been a judge in the notorious Salem witch trials. He turned to the history of New England as the setting for his best work, finding there an allegory for the struggles of his own age.

Hawthorne became an active supporter of the Democratic party, largely because of his friendship with an old college friend, Franklin Pierce, a rising figure in the party. Hawthorne wrote for the Democratic papers and won a job in the Salem customs house as measurer

of salt and coal. Hawthorne's political experiences in the late 1840s embittered him, however, for his Whig opponents not only sought to remove Hawthorne from his post but also charged him with corruption. It was at this point that Hawthorne wrote *The Scarlet Letter,* a symbolic story about revenge and its costs. Though set in the colonial era, the novel opened with a biting portrayal of the Salem customs house and its petty (Whig) politicians. The novel propelled Hawthorne into literary fame.

After the arrival of Hawthorne's long-delayed prosperity, he and his family moved to Lenox, Massachusetts, in the Berkshire Mountains in 1850. There he met a younger writer, one who admired Hawthorne for his willingness to write complicated stories of guilt. The young author was Herman Melville. He had left school at the age of fifteen, tried his hand at writing, but, in need of work that paid better and more certainly in the hard times of the late 1830s, went to sea. His experiences on ship, in port, and on the Pacific island where he lived among friendly cannibals gave him the subjects for most of his writing. His first two

Herman Melville became famous as a writer of sea stories but found little public interest in his 1852 masterpiece, Moby-Dick.

books, *Typee* and *Omoo,* adventure stories of the sea, did quite well and made a name for the young author. But Melville was not satisfied to write such books; he envisioned nothing less than an American epic.

Melville's masterpiece, about a ship captain's search for the great white whale "Moby-Dick," created a peculiarly American idiom: part Old Testament, part adventure story, part how-to book, part encyclopedia, part meditation on the enormous and reckless entity that the United States had become by the early 1850s. Good and evil swirled together in *Moby-Dick,* bonded and switched. Unlike *The Scarlet Letter, Moby-Dick,* published in 1852, did not do well on the market. Melville, disenchanted, made his work more cynical and biting. His novel *The Confidence-Man,* published six years after *Moby-Dick,* dwelt on the swindling, corruption, and self-deception that seemed at the heart of the United States in the 1850s, a time when everyone seemed to be on the make. Few people at the time noticed Melville's bold experiments and he gradually fell silent.

Walt Whitman also labored on an epic work, *Leaves of Grass,* throughout the early 1850s. The long poem reflected America at mid-century in all its diversity, roughness, innocence, and exuberance. This poetry of democratic origin and impulse included everything and everyone, speaking in a language stripped of classical allusion and pretension. As Whitman wrote in the preface to this book, anyone who would be a poet in the mid-nineteenth century must "flood himself with the immediate age." Whitman had done just that throughout his entire adult life.

Whitman took the raucous city of New York as his subject. For him, as for so many Americans in these years, cities were frontiers, full of democracy and possibility. Whitman participated fully in the life of the city, writing as a partisan Democratic journalist, running a shop, working as a building contractor, walking the streets, spending days in the public library reading books of science and travel and religion, moving from one editing job to another, attending boisterous political meetings—all the while jotting notes for a new kind of epic poetry taking shape in his head.

As he invented a poetical style to match his kaleidoscopic vision of American life, Walt Whitman also invented an image of himself as the poet who would take in and express everything. Both his life and his poem would be "A Song of Myself." He had his photograph taken, showing him tanned and bearded, shirt open at the collar. Whitman's book was literally self-made; in 1855 he set some of the type and hired

Walt Whitman, exuberant poet of New York and America, gloried in his connection to common people.

friends—printers of legal work—to publish the book for him.

Leaves of Grass came out to no public recognition whatsoever. Whitman sent a few copies to people he admired, however, including Emerson. The reply could not have been more heartening: "I find it the most extraordinary piece of wit and wisdom that America has yet contributed. . . . I greet you at the beginning of a great career. . . ." But most readers of the book, including several leading literary figures who read it on Emerson's recommendation, considered it vulgar, even obscene, shapeless, and crude. The hopeful words of *Leaves of Grass* soon became lost in years when a darker vision of the United States prevailed.

RACE, SLAVERY, AND POLITICS

The decade of the 1850s began with many signs of change and progress. The economy kicked into high gear. People flooded to the recently acquired territories of California and Oregon as well as to the upper and lower Mississippi region. Clipper ships, steamships, and railroads expanded their reach. Abolitionists, perfectionists, and feminists worked for the improvement of American society. Despite the generally positive turn of events, however, a persistent undercurrent of fear and anxiety wore at even the most privileged Americans, a sense that things were becoming undone, going wrong. Even the West, so full of promise, seemed full of threat.

The Crisis of 1850

Some of Americans' anxiety emanated from the new golden land of California. With so many men fighting over access to gold, water, land, and liquor, lawlessness became rampant. The men who had left everything back east or in Europe to come to the goldfields showed little respect for the property rights—and even lives—of the Mexicans, Indians, or white men who were there before. In the eyes of many, anarchy threatened if California could not form a government quickly. A territorial convention created such a government in 1849, helping to restore order, but one of the provisions of the new constitution created great disorder of another kind back in the United States. The new constitution declared that "neither slavery nor involuntary servitude . . . shall ever be tolerated in this state."

This straightforward statement exacerbated conflicts that had been brewing in Washington ever since the Wilmot Proviso three years earlier. The Democrats and Whigs were so divided by region that the House of Representatives could barely elect a speaker. White Southerners of both parties considered the admission of a free California a grave threat to their own status in the Union, giving the Senate a free-labor majority. John C. Calhoun, who had been the most vocal and extreme spokesman for the South ever since the days of the nullification crisis almost twenty years earlier, urged his fellow white Southerners to band together. If they did not cooperate, Calhoun argued, they would be overwhelmed by the numbers and the energy of the free states of the North and the West, abandoned within the Union they had helped create. To lose California was to lose the future. Southern congressmen talked of commercial boycotts, even of secession.

Southern Whigs had put Zachary Taylor forward for the presidency in 1848 assuming that, as a Southerner himself, he would support the expansion of slavery. To their disbelief and disgust, Taylor urged that California be admitted as it wished to be admitted, without slavery. He believed that letting the people of a territory decide their own laws was the surest route to peaceful growth of the country. But Taylor's support of the proposed California constitution unleashed a bitter debate in Congress that many feared would result in disunion or armed conflict. White Southerners argued that to bottle up slavery was to risk war between the races and that to deny the South an equal representation in the Senate was to risk war between North and South. To give in on California, the South's defenders argued, was to lose the sectional balance on which their very safety rested. The most aggressive white Southerners wanted to go on the offensive before Northerners in Congress had time to act; in late 1849 they called a convention of the southern states, to meet in Nashville in June of 1850. Several states agreed to send delegates to the convention.

A fabled session of Congress occurred as a result. In January 1850 the three most famous legislators of the first half of the nineteenth century—John C. Calhoun, Henry Clay, and Daniel Webster—assumed leading roles in the great national drama, drawing the last bits of strength from their aged bodies. Calhoun played the role of the protagonist, delivering fiery warnings and denunciations on behalf of the white South; Clay reprised the role of the Great Compromiser that had made him famous almost exactly three decades earlier in the Missouri controversy; Webster played the role of the conciliator, persuading the angry North to accept, in the name of the Union, the South's demand for respect. Clay and Webster rehearsed their lines in a private meeting before Clay presented his bill to Congress.

Clay's bold plan addressed in one inclusive "omnibus" bill all the issues tearing at the United States on the slavery issue. Balance the territory issue, he suggested, with other concerns that angered people about slavery. Leave slavery in the District of Columbia but abolish the slave trade there. Provide a stronger law to capture fugitive slaves in the North and return them to their owners in the South, but announce that Congress had no power to regulate the slave trade among the states. Admit California as a free state, but leave undetermined the place of slavery in the other territories won from Mexico. Advocates on both sides hoped the compromise would buy time for passions to cool;

In the Great Debate of 1850, Henry Clay, the "Great Compromiser," holds forth while the United States Senate listens. John C. Calhoun sits at a desk on his right, and Daniel Webster to his left, his hand to his ear.

after all, no more new territory remained to fight over that was not covered by either the new compromise or by the Missouri Compromise.

Clay made his plea in January, before a jam-packed Congress, with his characteristic eloquence and power. The eloquence appeared to be to little effect, however, for the same bitter arguments went on for months after Clay's speech. In March, Calhoun gave an address in which he conceded nothing; three days later, Webster claimed to speak "not as a Massachusetts man, nor as a northern man, but as an American. . . . I speak to-day for the preservation of the Union." Webster found himself widely denounced in the North as a traitor, buckling under to the slave mongerers. Moreover, President Zachary Taylor, like Clay and Webster a Whig, refused to support their compromise. William Seward of New York denounced the compromise as "radically wrong and essentially vicious." The "higher law" of God, Seward argued, overruled any human law, including the Constitution.

The Nashville Convention of southern states, meanwhile, turned out to be ineffective, since six states sent no representatives and the representatives who did come disagreed on the proper course of action. While all of them believed in southern rights, most of them did not believe in disunion. The convention took no stand on the pending compromise; they waited to see its provisions.

The omnibus bill appeared doomed. The debates dragged on in committees, the bill torn apart. A series of unanticipated events, however, aided the compromise. Both Calhoun and Taylor died—Calhoun after a long decline, Taylor unexpectedly a few days after a ceremony inaugurating the construction of the Washington Monument. Millard Fillmore was now president. A New Yorker of low visibility before his choice as vice-presidential candidate to balance the Southerner Taylor, Fillmore supported the omnibus bill. Clay and Webster faded from view as younger, less prominent, members of Congress steered the various components of the compromise through committees and votes. The compromisers were led by Stephen A. Douglas, a promising young Democrat of Illinois. The majority of northern and southern senators and

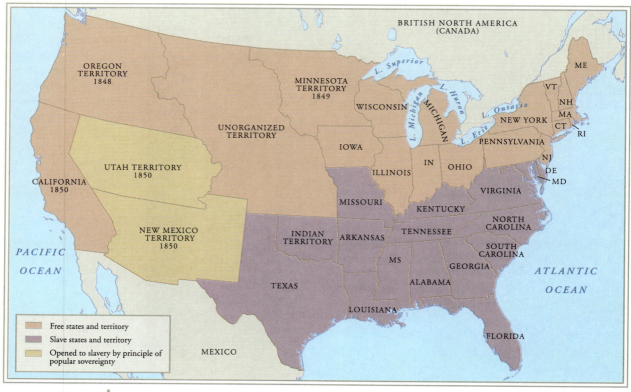

MAP 12.5 | THE COMPROMISE OF 1850

Legend:
- Free states and territory
- Slave states and territory
- Opened to slavery by principle of popular sovereignty

Representatives tenaciously voted against one another, but each part of the compromise passed because a small group of conciliatory congressmen from each side worked together. By September the various components of the compromise of 1850 had become law. "Let us cease agitating," Douglas urged, "stop the debate, and drop the subject." People wanted to forget about the problem of slavery.

The problem of slavery, of course, would not go away merely because of a political compromise. The fugitive slave component of the Compromise of 1850 proved especially troubling. Unlike other parts of the Compromise, provisions regarding fugitive slaves did not concern theoretical issues but rather living and breathing people who risked their lives to escape slavery and flee to the North. The Fugitive Slave Act directly implicated white Northerners and insulted them with blatantly unjust provisions. The commissioners who decided the fate of black Americans accused of being runaway slaves, for example, received ten dollars if an accused fugitive were returned to his or her master but only five dollars if freed. Marshals and sheriffs could force bystanders to aid in the capture of an accused fugitive; if bystanders refused, they faced a substantial fine or even jail term. The alleged runaway could not even testify in his or her own defense or call witnesses. There would be no jury trial. Perhaps most horrifying of all was this provision: No matter how many years before slaves had escaped, no matter how settled or respectable they had become, they could be captured and sent back into bondage. All free blacks stood continually at risk from kidnappers.

Most northern whites offered no opposition and most of the two or three hundred alleged fugitives prosecuted under the law were ruled to be runaways and sent south. But abolitionists raged at the Fugitive

PRACTICAL ILLUSTRATION OF THE FUGITIVE SLAVE LAW.

This cartoon ridicules the law that required Northerners to help capture and return runaway slaves. It glorifies William Lloyd Garrison and assails Daniel Webster, who voted in favor of the law as part of the Compromise of 1850.

Slave Law and they were not alone. Many Northerners, even those unconcerned about slavery in the South, were furious. Armed opposition to the slave catchers immediately arose in cities across the North; it cost $5,000 to capture one fugitive in Boston; mobs broke into jails to free ex-slaves; one slaveowner who came north to claim his property was shot. The Fugitive Slave Law, far from calming the conflict between North and South, made it more bitter.

The White North and African Americans

The years surrounding the crisis of 1850, ironically, were also the years in which black minstrel shows reached their peak of popularity. The traveling troupes of minstrels constituted the most popular form of public entertainment in these years, offering the strange ritual of white men in blackface simultaneously ridiculing and paying homage to the creativity of African-American culture. While white people of all

classes and backgrounds attended the minstrel shows, the quick-paced, humorous, and flashy skits and songs held special appeal for members of the white working class. Over the preceding decades, those workers had seen the value of their skills eroded by mechanization, their wages lowered by depression and competition, their organizations undercut by employers. In their eyes, the minstrel shows offered both a comforting dramatization of their own racial superiority and a way to associate imaginatively with carefree and fun-loving "black" people.

White Northerners revealed their ambivalences about African Americans in other ways as well. Whites who argued that the new territory of the West must be free soil frequently insisted on the exclusion of free blacks as well. Indiana's constitution of 1851, like that of other states in the Midwest and West, specifically barred free blacks from entering the state. Whites in cities associated black people with poverty and crime. A considerable majority of northern whites showed little interest in attending antislavery rallies or reading Frederick Douglass's *North Star.*

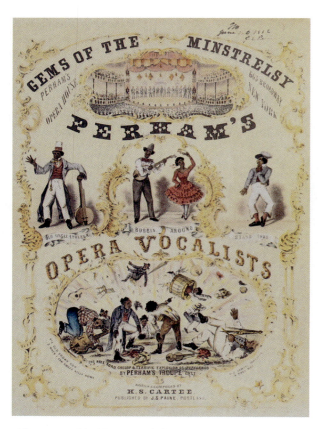

White men in blackface mimicked southern slaves for white audiences in this era, acting out ambivalent feelings of contempt and envy.

Harriet Beecher Stowe, the author of Uncle Tom's Cabin, *wove Christianity and the domestic ideal into a powerful fable of slavery and its consequences.*

Harriet Beecher Stowe's *Uncle Tom's Cabin* helped change white attitudes toward African Americans. Stowe, the daughter of one of the most prominent ministers of the era, had been writing throughout her life, but had not not become prominent. In 1849, when Stowe was thirty-eight years old, her infant son died of cholera in Cincinnati; the next year she moved back to the Beechers' native New England to try to build a new life. There, people talked angrily of the new Fugitive Slave Law and the brutalities it bred. "You don't know how my heart burns within me at the blindness and obtuseness of good people on so very simple a point of morality as this," she wrote to her brother Henry Ward Beecher, a noted minister and an outspoken foe of the new law.

Stowe put her objections to the law and its effects into a story printed serially in a moderate antislavery newspaper over forty issues in 1851. Stowe based her portrayals of black people on the African Americans she had known in Cincinnati, where they worked for her as domestic servants. They told Stowe of their own experiences, of the terrors of being sold south to Louisiana, of their vulnerability to sexual exploitation. Stowe also drew on firsthand narratives of escape, narratives that had long been prominent in the antislavery movement. She switched the usual roles of the freedom narratives, however, making a woman—Eliza—the active heroine and a man—Uncle Tom—the one left behind to endure slavery with Christian suffering and fortitude. The love of a mother for her children drove the story. The image of Eliza crossing the partially frozen Ohio River, baby in her arms, grew into one of the most powerful and familiar scenes of American culture in the nineteenth century and beyond.

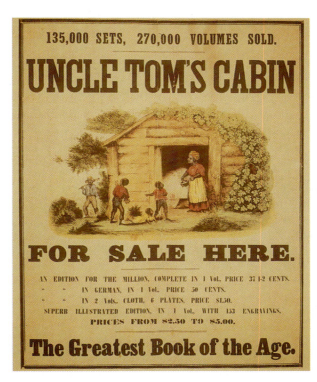

135,000 SETS, 270,000 VOLUMES SOLD.

UNCLE TOM'S CABIN

FOR SALE HERE.

AN EDITION FOR THE MILLION, COMPLETE IN 1 Vol. PRICE 37 1-2 CENTS.
" " IN GERMAN, IN 1 Vol. PRICE 50 CENTS.
" " IN 2 Vols. CLOTH, 6 PLATES, PRICE $1.50.
SUPERB ILLUSTRATED EDITION, IN 1 Vol. WITH 153 ENGRAVINGS,
PRICES FROM $2.50 TO $5.00.

The Greatest Book of the Age.

This book not only helped mobilize the white North's opinions on slavery, but it also proved an immediate and persistent bestseller.

The novel sold 300,000 copies in 1852 alone and became the subject of the most popular play in American history. Readers and theatergoers who had never picked up an antislavery newspaper were shocked at scenes that had long been commonplace in the antislavery press, stories of cruelty, violence, and sexual abuse. Stowe used techniques commonly found in domestic novels—the sanctity of the family, the power of religion, the triumph of endurance—to show that black people had the same feelings as white people, that they experienced the same happiness and despair, that slavery bred misery.

That *Uncle Tom's Cabin* and minstrel shows reached their peak of popularity at the same time gives some idea of the confusion and ambivalence with which white Northerners viewed African Americans in the early 1850s. The most popular cultural icon of the northern United States, Stowe's story, was based on an antislavery message, but thousands of whites laughed at other whites in blackface. Only events could force Northerners to decide what they really thought.

The Know-Nothings

Franklin Pierce, the Democratic candidate for president in 1852, was a Northerner friendly to the white South, a mediocre officer in the Mexican War, and a man known to drink. Fortunately for the Democrats, Pierce's opponent—Winfield Scott—proved to be even less impressive despite his fame as a general in the war with Mexico. The death of Henry Clay in 1850 and Daniel Webster in 1852 left the Whigs, always dependent on strong national leadership, adrift and directionless. Pierce, his campaign biography written by his friend Nathaniel Hawthorne, crushed Scott in every state except four. "General opinion seems to be that the Whig party is dead and will soon be decomposed into its original elements," one diarist commented in the wake of the election. "Shouldn't wonder. Where is its leader or leaders[?]"

Many influential Whigs took the 1852 election as a sign that their party could never win, that the Democrats would always succeed by appealing to the lowest common denominator. The real, substantive issues that had originally shaped the two parties—banks, the tariff, and internal improvements—no longer distinguished them from one another because both the Whigs and the Democrats had moved to the middle on those issues. Neither did slavery and sectional issues sharply define the two parties, for each tried to appease both the North and the South. Even the broader cultural orientation of the two parties had blurred in 1852, as the Whigs appealed to the burgeoning foreign-born vote and the Protestant nativists that had been at the heart of the party grew disgusted with the Whigs.

The Know-Nothings, growing steadily since their emergence in 1849, moved into politics in 1854, but in a way few Democrats or Whigs expected. The Know-Nothings did not announce their candidates beforehand, but rather wrote them in on the ballots, taking incumbents by complete surprise. The Know-Nothings won virtually all the seats in the Massachusetts legislature with this strategy and registered strong showings in New York and Pennsylvania. By 1855, the Know-Nothings dominated New England and displaced the Whigs as the major opponents to the Democrats through the Middle Atlantic states, in much of the South, and in California.

No one in the major parties had anticipated such a turn of events. The Whigs, after all, had long attracted the nativists, fervent Protestants, and temperance

HARRIET
BEECHER STOWE,
UNCLE TOM'S CABIN,
1852

Stowe's remarkable novel captured the moral energy of the antislavery movement. In this episode, the evil New England-born Simon Legree is confronted by the unbending Christian strength of Uncle Tom.

"And now," said Legree, "come here, you Tom. You see I told ye I didn't buy ye jest for the common work; I mean to promote ye and make a driver of ye; and tonight ye may jest as well begin to get yer hand in. Now, ye jest take this yer gal and flog her; ye've seen enough on't to know how."

"I beg Mas'r's pardon," said Tom, "hopes Mas'r won't set me at that. It's what I an't used to—never did—and can't do, no way possible."

"Ye'll larn a pretty smart chance of things ye never did know before I've done with ye!" said Legree, taking up a cowhide and striking Tom a heavy blow across the cheek, and following up the infliction by a shower of blows. "There!" he said, as he stopped to rest, "now will ye tell me ye can't do it?"

"Yes, Mas'r," said Tom, putting up his hand to wipe the blood that trickled down his face. "I'm willin' to work night and day, and work while there's life and breath in me, but this yer thing I can't feel it right to do; and, Mas'r, I *never* shall do it—*never!*"

Tom had a remarkably smooth, soft voice, and a habitually respectful manner that had given Legree an idea that he would be cowardly and easily subdued. When he spoke these last words, a thrill of amazement went through everyone; the poor woman clasped her hands and said, "O Lord!" and everyone involuntarily looked at each other and drew in their breath, as if to prepare for the storm that was about to burst.

Legree looked stupefied and confounded; but at last burst forth—

"What! ye blasted black beast! tell *me* ye don't think it *right* to do what I tell ye! What have any of you cussed cattle to do with thinking what's right? I'll put a stop to it! Why, what do ye think ye are? May be ye think ye're a gentleman, master Tom, to be a telling your master what's right and what an't! So you pretend it's wrong to flog the gal!"

---

advocates to which the Know-Nothings now appealed. But these disgruntled voters proved extremely receptive to the Know-Nothing appeal. The Know-Nothings, unlike the Whigs, left control of the party close to the grassroots; there were no Clays or Websters cutting deals in Washington, no Winfield Scotts appealing to Catholics. The Know-Nothings offered a revitalized political party, one more receptive than the Whigs to the desires of its constituents and one that would attack problems rather than compromise on them. Young men, in particular, seemed drawn to the Know-Nothings, for the new party offered a fresh start, a place for new men. Many rural districts voted heavily for the Know-Nothings as a way

to get back at the cities that had dominated the major parties for so long. For such reasons, the Know-Nothings made strong showings in the South as well as the North.

The appearance of the Know-Nothings reflected a deep-seated change in the American political system, a change that destroyed the delicate balance of power between the two well-established parties. The American party system began disintegrating at the local and state level, with the Whigs fading in some states as early as 1852 and in others not until three years later. Voters defected from the Whigs to both the Know-Nothing and Free Soil parties, depending on which alternative party was strongest in their locality.

"I think so, Mas'r," said Tom, "the poor crittur's sick and feeble; 't would be down-right cruel, and it's what I never will do, not begin to. Mas'r, if you mean to kill me, kill me; but as to my raising my hand agin anyone here, I never shall—I'll die first!"

Tom spoke in a mild voice but with a decision that could not be mistaken. Legree shook with anger; his greenish eyes glared fiercely and his very whiskers seemed to curl with passion; but, like some ferocious beast that plays with its victim before he devours it, he kept back his strong impulse to proceed to immediate violence and broke out into bitter raillery.

"Well, here's a pious dog, at last, let down among us sinners!—a saint, a gentleman, and no less, to talk to us sinners about our sins! Powerful, holy crittur, he must be! Here, you rascal, you make believe to be so pious—didn't you never hear out of yer Bible, 'Servants, obey yer masters'? An't I yer master? Didn't I pay down $1,200 cash for all there is inside yer old cussed black shell? An't yer mine, now, body and soul?" he said, giving Tom a violent kick with his heavy boot. "Tell me!"

In the very depth of physical suffering, bowed by brutal oppression, this question shot a gleam of joy and triumph through Tom's soul. He suddenly stretched himself up, and, looking earnestly to heaven, while the tears and blood that flowed down his face mingled, he exclaimed—

"No! no! no! my soul an't yours, Mas'r! You haven't bought it—ye can't buy it! It's been bought and paid for by one that is able to keep it—no matter, no matter, you can't harm me!"

"I can't!" said Legree, with a sneer, "we'll see—we'll see! Here, Sambo, Quimbo, give this dog such a breakin' in as he won't get over this month!"

The two gigantic Negroes that now laid hold of Tom, with fiendish exultation in their faces, might have formed no unapt personification of the powers of darkness. The poor woman screamed with apprehension and all arose as by a general impulse while they dragged him unresisting from the place. . . .

SOURCE   Harriet Beecher Stowe, *Uncle Tom's Cabin* (Boston: J. P. Jewett, 1852), pp. 419–423.

Dreams of Expansion

The same forces of commerce and transportation that tied together the vastly expanded United States in the late 1840s and early 1850s pulled Americans into world affairs. The steamships and clipper ships that connected New York and San Francisco crisscrossed the oceans of the world. American ships set out not only for Liverpool, but also for South America, Asia, Australia, New Zealand, and Tahiti. The ships carried lumber and hides, tea and silks, missionaries and scientists. American whaling ships restlessly and relentlessly patrolled the South Pacific, stopping for fuel and food at islands scattered over a vast territory. Some entrepreneurs even rushed to mine mountains of bird droppings piled up on remote Pacific islands. The droppings, called guano, offered a nitrogen-rich fertilizer much in demand on the farms and plantations of the eastern United States. American traders eager to break into the Asian market—led by Commodore Matthew C. Perry—appeared in Japanese ports and bargained with the skeptical Japanese.

These exchanges in far-off ports often depended on the Hawaiian Islands as way stations, strategically placed by wind and currents to attract much of the Pacific trade. On a single day in 1852, for example, 131

The Know-Nothings, a party of resentment, secrecy, and violence, attracted criticism as well as voters in the mid-1850s.

whaling ships and eighteen merchant ships tied up in Honolulu. Such trade, while lucrative for some, came at a horrifying cost to the native population because of disease brought by American, Asian, and European ships. Over the seventy-five years since the first contact with outsiders in the late eighteenth century, the Hawaiian population had declined from about 300,000 residents to only about 73,000. Around 2,000 foreigners lived in Hawaii by the early 1850s, a

good many of them Americans, both businessmen and missionaries. Though politicians and editors talked of annexing the islands for the United States, opposition on the islands and in Washington postponed any action. Besides, expansionists' main focus lay elsewhere.

Some well-placed Americans gazed at yet more Mexican territory with covetous eyes, urging the Pierce administration to acquire Baja California and other parts of northern Mexico. Mexico was not inter-

As these three sketches by an American visitor show, European and Polynesian cultures existed side by side in the capital of Hawaii. Protestant and Catholic churches stand beside consulates and native homes.

ested, though, and many Northerners in the United States opposed further acquisitions. Proponents of expansion had to settle for much less than they had wanted: After long wrangling and somewhat inept bargaining, in 1853 the United States paid $15 million for a strip of Mexico to use as a route for a southern transcontinental railroad. This was the Gadsden Purchase, named for the American diplomat who negotiated it. The purchase defined the final borders of the continental United States.

Cuba seemed the most obvious place for further expansion, for it stood as both an opportunity and a threat. It seemed to many Americans that Cuba should be part of the United States, that Havana should stand as the Gibraltar to the entrance of the Gulf of Mexico, a sort of American lake. Cuba was rich and growing, its slave trade flourishing even in the middle of the nineteenth century after the slave trade to the United States had ended. Abolitionists and others talked of freeing Cuba both from slavery and from the Spanish, while white Southerners talked of adding this jewel to the slave empire. Cuban exiles worked in New Orleans and New York to encourage American intervention.

The United States offered to buy Cuba from Spain in 1848, but met a rude rebuff from the weakening European power. Franklin Pierce, pressured by the Southerners in his party and in his cabinet, in the early 1850s renewed the effort to "detach" Cuba from Spain. Southern planters argued that the United States had to act quickly, for they feared that the Spanish would free Cuba's slaves, who would then revolt, take over the island, and threaten the American South. American diplomats in Europe created a furor when they wrote the "Ostend Manifesto," a statement of the policy they wanted the administration to follow: Gain Cuba one way or the other to prevent its "Africanization." The United States would be justified in this action "on the very principle that would justify an individual in tearing down the burning house of his neighbor if there were no other means of preventing the flames from destroying his own home." When the "manifesto" was leaked to the press, the Pierce administration was widely vilified at home and abroad. Pierce publicly renounced any intention of taking over Cuba. The movement to expand the United States into the Caribbean came to a temporary halt.

The Kansas-Nebraska Act

As the Cuban episode revealed, Franklin Pierce proved to be an ineffectual president and party leader, permitting conflicts within the party to overwhelm him. The best hope for the Democrats, Stephen A. Douglas determined, was to deflect attention to the West. Douglas called for two kinds of action: organizing the territories of the West, especially the Kansas and Nebraska area to the west of Iowa and Missouri, and building a railroad across the continent to bind together the expanded United States. The two actions were interrelated, for the railroad could not be built through unorganized territory. Partly to get southern votes for the territorial organization and partly because he believed that slavery would not survive in the northern territories, Douglas agreed to back a bill invalidating the Missouri Compromise line. He proposed that the people of the new territories decide for themselves whether or not their states would permit slaves and slaveholders. Calling this policy "popular sovereignty," Douglas put it forward in the Kansas-Nebraska Bill.

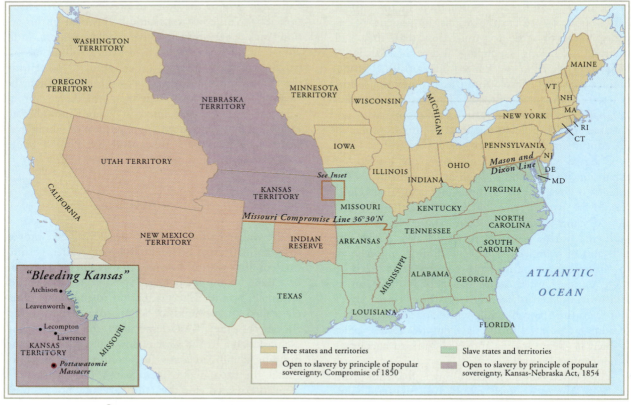

WASHINGTON
TERRITORY

OREGON
TERRITORY

MINNESOTA
TERRITORY

NEBRASKA
TERRITORY

WISCONSIN

MICHIGAN

MAINE

VT

NH

MA

NEW YORK

RI

CT

UTAH TERRITORY

IOWA

See Inset

ILLINOIS

INDIANA

OHIO

PENNSYLVANIA

NJ

*Mason and
Dixon Line*

DE

MD

CALIFORNIA

KANSAS
TERRITORY

MISSOURI

KENTUCKY

VIRGINIA

Missouri Compromise Line 36°30'N

NORTH
CAROLINA

NEW MEXICO
TERRITORY

INDIAN
RESERVE

ARKANSAS

TENNESSEE

SOUTH
CAROLINA

TEXAS

MISSISSIPPI

ALABAMA

GEORGIA

*ATLANTIC
OCEAN*

LOUISIANA

FLORIDA

"Bleeding Kansas"

Atchison •

Leavenworth •

• Lecompton
• Lawrence

KANSAS
TERRITORY

MISSOURI

• Pottawatomie
Massacre

Free states and territories	Slave states and territories
Open to slavery by principle of popular sovereignty, Compromise of 1850	Open to slavery by principle of popular sovereignty, Kansas-Nebraska Act, 1854

MAP 12.6 | KANSAS NEBRASKA AND SLAVERY

Douglas's plan, by reopening the question of slavery in the territories, unleashed political and sectional resentments that had been bottled up by prior compromises. Six prominent Free Soil senators, including Salmon P. Chase, Charles Sumner, and Joshua Giddings, denounced the plan as a plot by a "Slave Power" to make Nebraska a "dreary region of despotism, inhabited by masters and slaves." Northern ministers publicly protested the pending legislation, while newspapers throughout the North scornfully attacked the proposal. Despite the widespread opposition, however, the opponents of the Kansas-Nebraska Bill could not coordinate their efforts sufficiently to stop its passage, supported as it was by virtually all southern congressmen and the Pierce administration.

The fight over Kansas-Nebraska inflamed northern resentment as never before. Many Northerners deter-

mined that they could no longer trust Southerners to keep a bargain and that Northerners were no longer obligated to enforce the Fugitive Slave Act because the Kansas-Nebraska Act had nullified the Compromise of 1850. In the wake of the debate in Congress, attempts to arrest and extradite Anthony Burns, a fugitive slave in Boston, created such a turmoil that the mayor called out 1,500 militia to line the streets along the route between the courthouse and the ship that was to take Burns back to slavery in Virginia.

The Kansas-Nebraska Act sparked a chain reaction. It divided the Democratic party across the North; it upset the fragile balance of power between North and South in Congress; it provided a set of common concerns and language to unite disgruntled Northern Whigs, Free Soilers, and abolitionists. At this juncture, moreover, the Know-Nothings attained their new

This illustrations tells the story of Anthony Burns's sales, escape, arrest, and return to slavery in Virginia. His highly publicized case further inflamed the conflict between the North and the South in the mid-1850s.

prestige and power, pulling voters to their program of nativism and temperance. The Know-Nothings took advantage of the widespread disillusionment with the two major parties to work along lines apparently unrelated to slavery.

Over the next two years the northern political system churned as voters looked for a party that would reflect their concerns and also have a chance of winning power. Each northern state fell into its own kind of confusion and conflict, as politicians and voters jumped from one party to another. The Know-Nothings began to fade almost as quickly as they had emerged. Their descent had several causes. The Know-Nothings came to seem just another political party led by ambitious politicians, violent gangs that terrorized immigrants under the Know-Nothing banner alienated many voters, and Know-Nothing legislators

proved unable to control or punish Catholics as they had promised.

The rise of yet another party also pulled voters away from the Know-Nothings. In 1854 a party was founded in Wisconsin to unite disgruntled voters. The new party appealed to former Whigs, Free Soilers, Know-Nothings, and even Democrats fed up with the pro-Southern party. This new party called itself the "Republican" party. Its platform announced that "no man can own another man" and it would not permit slavery in the territories or in new states. Whether such a bold party could unify the many disaffected voters of the North remained to be seen.

CONCLUSION

The late 1840s and early 1850s saw the United States energized by victory over Mexico and the acquisition of vast new territories, by prosperity in the North and the South, by railroads and clipper ships, by westward migration, and by the arrival of millions of immigrants. As northern family farms spread during the good times, however, so did southern slavery. The gold of the West brought not only wealth but also lawlessness and environmental destruction. The cities of the Atlantic coast seemed full to overflowing with immigrants from Ireland and Germany, while the cities of the Pacific burgeoned with immigrants from China and restless men from back east. Politicians seemed helpless in the face of these changes. Each political compromise only seemed to make things worse. The parties that had held the country together for a quarter of a century began to buckle under the stress.

RECOMMENDED READINGS

Anbinder, Tyler. *Nativism and Slavery: The Northern Know-Nothings and the Politics of the 1850s* (1992) provides a full and balanced account.

Fellman, Michael. *The Unbounded Frame: Freedom and Community in Nineteenth-Century American Utopianism* (1973) offers a helpful overview of perfectionist communities.

Griffith, Elisabeth. *In Her Own Right: The Life of Elizabeth Cady Stanton* (1984) tells the compelling story of this crucial leader of the woman suffrage movement.

Hedrick, Joan D. *Harriet Beecher Stowe: A Life* (1994) paints a detailed portrait of the author of *Uncle Tom's Cabin*.

Hietala, Thomas R. *Manifest Design: Anxious Aggrandizement in Late Jacksonian America* (1985) ties the war with Mexico into the larger patterns of life in the United States.

Lott, Eric. *Love and Theft: Blackface Minstrelsy and the American Working Class* (1993) is an original and challenging analysis.

Miller, Kerby A. *Emigrants and Exiles: Ireland and the Irish Exodus to North America* (1985) gives a full account of the origins and impact of this migration.

Potter, David M. *The Impending Crisis: 1848–1861* (1976) is a superb overview of American politics from the wake of the Mexican War to the outbreak of the Civil War.

Reynolds, David S. *Beneath the American Renaissance: The Subversive Imagination in the Age of Emerson and Melville* (1988) is a brilliant exploration of the "classic" era of American literature.

Rohrbough, Malcolm J. *Days of Gold: The California Gold Rush and the American Nation* (1997) offers a fresh and exciting account of its subject.

Politics and Sectional Relations

Ashworth, John. *Slavery, Capitalism, and Politics in the Antebellum Republic. Volume 1: Commerce and Compromise, 1820–1850* (1995).

Campbell, Stanley. *The Slave Catchers* (1968).

Carwardine, Richard J. *Evangelicals and Politics in Antebellum America* (1993).

Gara, Larry. *The Presidency of Franklin Pierce* (1991).

Gienapp, William E. *The Origins of the Republican Party, 1852–1856* (1987).

Johannsen, Robert W. *Stephen A. Douglas* (1973).

Johannsen, Robert W. *The Frontier, the Union, and Stephen A. Douglas* (1989).

Peterson, Merrill D. *The Great Triumvirate: Webster, Clay, and Calhoun* (1987).

Rayback, Joseph G. *Free Soil: The Election of 1848* (1970).

Transportation and Its Effects

Alvarez, Eugene. *Travel on Southern Antebellum Railroads, 1828–1860* (1974).

Faragher, John Mack. *Sugar Creek: Life on the Illinois Prairie* (1986).

Fishlow, Albert. *American Railroads and the Transformation of the Antebellum Economy* (1965).

Hahn, Steven and Prude, Jonathan eds., *The Countryside in the Age of Capitalist Transformation: Essays in the Social History of Rural America* (1985).

Stover, John. *American Railroads* (1961).

Taylor, George Rogers. *The Transportation Revolution, 1815–1860* (1951).

The Gold Rush

Billington, Ray Allen. *The Far Western Frontier, 1830–1860* (1956).

Lapp, Rudolph M. *Blacks in Gold Rush California* (1977).

Saxton, Alexander. *The Indispensable Enemy: Labor and the Anti-Chinese Movement in California* (1971).

White, Richard. *It's Your Misfortune and None of My Own: A New History of the American West* (1991).

Utopian Communities

Bestor, Arthur E. *Backwoods Utopias: The Sectarian and Owenite Phases of Communitarian Utopianism in America, 1663–1829* (1950).

Lockwood, Carden, *Oneida: Utopian Community to Modern Corporation* (1969).

Klaw, Spencer. *Without Sin: The Life and Death of the Oneida Community* (1993).

Kolmerten, Carol. *Women in Utopia* (1990).

Women and Women's Rights

DuBois, Ellen C. *Feminism and Suffrage: The Emergence of an Independent Women's Movement in America, 1848–1869* (1978).

Hoffert, Sylvia D. *When Hens Crow: The Woman's Rights Movement in Antebellum America* (1995).

Ginzburg, Lori D. *Women and the Work of Benevolence: Morality, Politics, and Class in the Nineteenth-Century United States* (1990).

Hewitt, Nancy. *Women's Activism and Social Change: Rochester, New York, 1822–1872* (1984).

Lebsock, Suzanne. *The Free Women of Petersburg: Status and Culture in a Southern Town, 1784–1860* (1984).

Painter, Nell Irvin. *Sojourner Truth: A Life, a Symbol* (1996).

Ryan, Mary P. *Women in Public: Between Banners and Ballots, 1825–1880* (1990).

Sklar, Kathryn Kish. *Catherine Beecher: A Study in American Domesticity* (1973).

Stansell, Christine. *City of Women: Sex and Class in New York, 1789–1860* (1986).

Yellin, Jean Fagan. *Women and Sisters: The Antislavery Feminists in American Culture* (1989).

The American Renaissance

Callow, Philip. *From Noon to Starry Night: A Life of Walt Whitman* (1992).

Halttunen, Karen. *Confidence Men and Painted Women: A Study in Middle-Class Culture in America, 1830–1870* (1982).

Kirby, David. *Herman Melville* (1993).

Mellow, James R. *Nathaniel Hawthorne in His Times* (1980).

Rogin, Michael Paul. *Subversive Genealogy: The Politics and Art of Herman Melville* (1983).

Zweig, Paul. *Walt Whitman: The Making of the Poet* (1984).

Immigration

Knobel, Dale T. *Paddy and the Republic: Ethnicity and Nationality in Antebellum America* (1986).

Ripley, LaVern J. *The German-Americans* (1976).

AMERICANS OF THE 1850s had no idea that the Civil War awaited them. They could not imagine that a vast war, larger than any Europe had known, could overwhelm the new republic. New farms and plantations, after all, spread rapidly in expectation of more boom years like the 1850s. Villages and workshops spread throughout the North while cities, fed by millions of immigrants from Europe, grew rapidly at harbors and along railroads and rivers. In the South, cotton and slavery created a per capita income for white Southerners higher than that of any country in Europe except England. Slavery, it was clear, would not collapse of its own contradictions any time soon; the institution had never been more profitable. Telegraphs, newspapers, steamboats, and railroads tied the North and South together more tightly every year.

The two sections viewed each other as aggressive and expansionist, intent on making the nation all one thing or another. The North claimed that the slaveholder South would destroy the best government on earth rather than accept the results of a fair election. The white South claimed that the arrogant and greedy North would destroy the nation rather

CHARLESTON
MERCURY
EXTRA:

Passed unanimously at 1.15 o'clock, P. M., December 20th, 1860.

AN ORDINANCE

To dissolve the Union between the State of South Carolina and other States united with her under the compact entitled "The Constitution of the United States of America."

THE
UNION
IS
DISSOLVED!

PASSAGES

Rates of Travel from New York City, 1857

Within a day	Within 4 days	Within 1 week	Within 4 weeks	Over 6 weeks
Within 2 days	Within 5 days	Within 2 weeks	Within 5 weeks	
Within 3 days	Within 6 days	Within 3 weeks	Within 6 weeks	

New York

than acknowledge what the Constitution had established. Both sides were filled with righteous rage, accepting violence to gain the upper hand, whether that involved capturing fugitive slaves or applauding John Brown's failed insurrection. Americans could not stop the momentum they had themselves created. Despite desperate efforts at compromise and delay, the war came.

Once the war could no longer be avoided,

most people threw themselves into the conflict alongside their neighbors, whatever doubts they had held before. Confident that the war would be brief, young men on both sides enlisted to teach their enemies a lesson. Both the North and the South proved excellent at war. They innovated freely and successfully, fought relentlessly, discovered effective generals, and mobilized women as well as men. Indeed, the North's strengths and the South's strengths balanced so that the war went on for four years, killing 630,000 people, a proportion of the population equivalent to 5 million people in the United States today and a number larger than the country was ever to sacrifice in another war.

Throughout the conflict, from Lincoln's election to his death, the role of slavery remained both powerful and unclear. Lincoln announced that the war was for Union, not abolition. The Confederacy announced that the war was for independence, not merely slavery. Enslaved Americans in the South, however, forced slavery as an issue on both the Union and the Confederacy, risking their lives to flee to Union camps, undermining plantations and farms. Lincoln and much of the North came to see that ending slavery would end the Confederacy and help redeem the death and suffering. Two hundred thousand black men enlisted as soldiers and played a key role in bringing Union victory.

The North and the South struggled with themselves even as they fought one another. The North broke apart along lines of class, ethnicity, party, and locale. By 1864 a considerable portion of the northern population wanted the war to end, with compromise if necessary. The opponents of Lincoln expected to overwhelm him in the election that fall and even Lincoln shared that expectation. The white South broke apart along lines of class, locale, and gender. Poor soldiers deserted; upcountry communities shielded deserters and resisted the Confederate government; impoverished white women rioted and resisted. Slaves rushed to the Union army at the first opportunity, every escape weakening the southern economy and Confederate morale.

Events on the battlefield, through 10,000 conflicts large and small, exerted their own logic and momentum. The Union army grew stronger as the Confederate army thinned and weakened. The victories of Grant and Sherman in 1864 destroyed the South's best hope of a negotiated peace. The relentless spread of the Union army throughout the South divided the Confederacy into smaller and smaller pieces, each helpless to aid the other. When Lee's army fell into defeat the Confederate nation dissolved almost immediately.

Whatever Lincoln's plans for reuniting the nation, those plans ended at Ford's Theater in April of 1865. His successor, Andrew Johnson, took the most cautious route possible, limiting the scope of black freedom in every way he could. The white South's resolve, indeed, seemed greater than any power the Union wielded in the South. African Americans struggled to make their freedom real: they mobilized politically, founded churches and schools, and reconstituted families. They demanded rights as Americans and did all they could to secure those rights. Black Southerners found many white northern allies but many more white southern enemies who quickly turned to violence, as well as white Northerners who supported or tolerated the violence. The years of 1866 and 1867 were full of a promise and a terror no one could have imagined ten years before. In many ways, the Civil War had not yet ended; its consequences had hardly begun.

CIVIL WAR LOSSES

Civil War deaths compared with U.S. deaths in other wars (estimated)

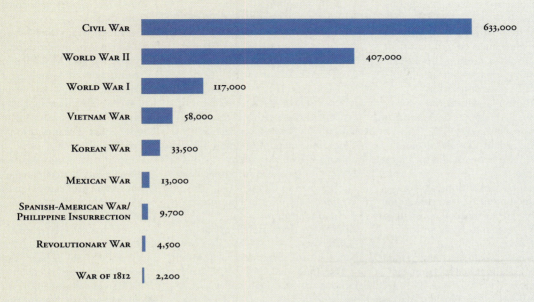

CIVIL WAR	633,000
WORLD WAR II	407,000
WORLD WAR I	117,000
VIETNAM WAR	58,000
KOREAN WAR	33,500
MEXICAN WAR	13,000
SPANISH-AMERICAN WAR/ PHILIPPINE INSURRECTION	9,700
REVOLUTIONARY WAR	4,500
WAR OF 1812	2,200

For the next decade, Reconstruction in the South gradually receded. The process left blacks with greater political rights in law because of the Fourteenth and Fifteenth Amendments, but a more limited role in the day-to-day process of governing. The presidency of Ulysses S. Grant was a disappointment because the hero of the war proved unable to provide effective leadership, sectional reconciliation, or honest government. An economic collapse in 1873 helped the Democrats restore the national political balance and hasten the end of Reconstruction. The disputed election between Rutherford B. Hayes and Samual J. Tilden in 1876 saw the abandonment of black southerners to the rule of those who believed in white supremacy. The Civil War had preserved the Union and abolished slavery, but the unsettled problem of race cast a long shadow into the future.

POLITICS & DIPLOMACY

1855: Proslavery and free-soil forces clash in Kansas

Massachusetts desegregates public schools

1856: John Brown's raid in Kansas

James Buchanan elected president

Congressman Preston Brooks canes Senator Charles Sumner

1857: *Dred Scott* decision

Lecompton Constitution

Hinton R. Helper, *The Impending Crisis of the South*

1858: Lincoln-Douglas debates

1859: John Brown's raid on Harpers Ferry

Vicksburg convention calls for reopening of African slave trade

Kansas ratifies free-soil constitution

1860: Democratic convention divides

Abraham Lincoln elected president

South Carolina secedes from the Union

1861: Mississippi, Florida, Alabama, Georgia, Louisiana, and Texas secede

Montgomery Convention creates Confederate States of America

Lincoln inaugurated

Firing on and surrender of Fort Sumter

Arkansas, Tennessee, Virginia, and North Carolina secede

Confederate victory at Bull Run (Manassas)

Jefferson Davis elected president of Confederacy with six-year term

Union navy seizes Confederate commisioners Mason and Slidell from British ship *Trent*

1862: Confederates surrender Fort Donelson to Grant

Virginia v. *Monitor* in Hampton Roads, Virginia

Grant wins dramatic victory at Shiloh

New Orleans surrenders to Admiral Farragut

Jackson's Shenandoah Valley Campaign

Lee takes command of Army of Northern Virginia

Lee drives McClellan from Richmond in Seven Days' Battles

Confederate victory at Second Bull Run (Manassas)

Battle of Antietam (Sharpsburg)

First Emancipation Proclamation

Burnside replaces McClellan as commander of Army of the Potomac

Lee overwhelms Burnside at Fredericksburg

1863: Second Emancipation Proclamation

Culmination of Lee's victory over Hooker at Chancellorsville

Grant's successful campaign in Mississippi

Death of Stonewall Jackson

Union victory at Gettysburg

Vicksburg surrenders to Grant

Black troops fight at Fort Wagner, South Carolina

Lincoln's Gettysburg Address

Union victory at Chattanooga

SOCIAL & CULTURAL EVENTS

1857: Mass revivals

1858: Frederick Law Olmsted begins design for Central Park in New York City

1863: Lincoln's Gettysburg Address

ECONOMICS & TECHNOLOGY

1857: Financial panic and depression

Baltimore–St. Louis rail service completed

1861: Suspension of specie payments

Mathew Brady begins photography of Civil War

1862: Legal Tender Act in North authorizes "greenbacks"

Homestead Act passed by Union Congress

Virginia v. *Monitor* in Hampton Roads, Virginia

1863: Confederate Congress passes Impressment Act

Union Congress passes National Bank Act

Bread riot in Richmond

1864: Grant assumes command of all Union forces

Battle of the Wilderness in Virginia

Union victory at Cold Harbor

Sherman captures Atlanta

Lincoln re-elected president

Beginning of Sherman's march from Atlanta to the Atlantic

1865: Congress passes Thirteenth Amendment, abolishing slavery

Congress creates Bureau of Refugees, Freedmen, and Abandoned Lands (Freedmen's Bureau)

Lincoln's second inauguration

Fall of Richmond to Union

Lee surrenders to Grant at Appomattox Court House

Lincoln assassinated; Andrew Johnson becomes president

Former Confederate states hold constitutional conventions through December; pass "black codes"

Thirteenth Amendment to Constitution ratified, abolishing slavery

1866: Congress passes Civil Rights Act and Freedmen's Bureau renewal over Johnson's veto

Riots in New Orleans and Memphis

Congress approves Fourteenth Amendment

Ku Klux Klan formed

1867: Congress passes Reconstruction Act and Tenure of Office Act

Johnson dismisses Secretary of War Stanton, triggering impeachment proceedings

First elections in South under Reconstruction Act

Passage of Reconstruction Act

Alaska Purchase negotiations

1868: Andrew Johnson impeached and acquitted

U.S. Grant elected President

1869: Fifteenth Amendment passes Congress

Woman suffrage starts in Wyoming Territory

1870: Ku Klux Klan conducts terror raids in South

1871: Tweed Ring exposed in New York City

1872: Grant reelected

1873: Salary Grab and Credit Mobilier Scandals

1874: Democrats gain in congressional elections

1875: Civil Rights Act passes Congress

1876: Hayes and Tilden in disputed election

1877: Hayes declared president after compromises settle election dispute

---

1865: First woman professor of astronomy appointed at Vassar College

1866: American Equal Rights Association founded to seek black and woman suffrage

1867: Horatio Alger begins publishing series of books for young boys

1868: Louisa May Alcott publishes *Little Women*

1869: Licensing of women lawyers begins

First intercollegiate football game played between Princeton and Rutgers

1870: First Greek letter sorority, Kappa Alpha Theta, founded

1871: Cable car invented

1872: American Public Health Association starts

1873: Mark Twain and Charles Dudley Warner publish *The Gilded Age*

1874: Women's Christian Temperance Union founded

1875: Smith and Wellesley College open to provide higher education for women

1876: Centennial Exposition in Philadelphia

1864: Confederate Congress assumes new powers of taxation, impressment of slaves

George Pullman invents sleeping car

1866: National Labor Union organized

1867: Patrons of Husbandry (Grange) founded

1868: First 8-hour day for federal workers

1869: Gold Corner scheme of Jay Gould and Jim Fisk

Transcontinental Railroad completed

1870: Standard Oil Company of Ohio organized

1871: Chicago fire burns center of city

1872: Adding machine invented

1873: Panic of 1873 starts depression

1874: Sale of typewriters begins

Tomkins Square riot of unemployed in New York City

1875: First dynamo for outdoor lighting constructed

1876: Heinz tomato ketchup marketed

1877: National railroad strike

"BORDER RUFFIANS"

The northern press depicted what they took to be the seedy character of the proslavery men who came over the border from Missouri into Kansas to support slavery.

Chapter 13

Broken Bonds:

1855–1861

The United States had never seemed stronger than at the beginning of 1855. The economy was booming, settlers pushed into the West, steamers and clippers plied the oceans of the world, railroads spread at a relentless rate, and immigrants streamed into American farms and factories. Churches, schools, asylums, and reform organizations grew faster than ever. Many people believed that the nation was entering upon its brightest day.

But the signs of danger were not hard to see. The conflict between the North and the South grew more bitter with each passing political crisis. Those crises came in a stunning succession in the late 1850s and early 1860s, every year bringing a clash more divisive than the one before. The battle between North and South broke out in the Kansas territory, in state politics, in the village of Harpers Ferry, and finally in the contest for president. The party system, weakened by nativism and loss of faith by voters, seemed powerless to stop the disintegration.

SECTIONAL CONFLICT

Conflict between the North and the South had been a staple of American politics for decades before 1855. Ter-

ritories proved a persistent problem, but Northerners and Southerners also argued over the tariff, nominees for high office, and religion. They sometimes confronted the issue of slavery head-on, but more often they talked around it. The arguments grew hot, but eventually calmed down until the next outbreak. Events of the late 1850s, however, broke the pattern. New crises came before the old ones could dissipate. The crises embroiled every political, economic, moral, and practical difference between the North and the South.

Bleeding Kansas

The Kansas-Nebraska Act, steered through Congress in 1854 by Senator Stephen A. Douglas of Illinois, declared that settlers would decide for themselves, in their "popular sovereignty," what kind of society they would create. But partisans from both the North and the South determined to fill the territory with settlers of their own political persuasion. "Come on, then, Gentlemen of the slave States," New York's Senator William H. Seward proclaimed soon after the Kansas-Nebraska Act passed. "Since there is no escaping your challenge, I accept it in behalf of the cause of freedom. We will engage in competition for the virgin soil of Kansas, and God give the victory to the side which is stronger in numbers as it is in right."

CHRONOLOGY

1855 Proslavery and free-soil forces clash in Kansas

Massachusetts desegregates public schools

1856 John Brown's raid in Kansas

James Buchanan elected president

Congressman Preston Brooks canes Senator Charles Sumner

1857 Financial panic and depression

Dred Scott decision

Lecompton Constitution

Baltimore–St. Louis rail service completed

Hinton R. Helper, *The Impending Crisis of the South*

Mass revivals

1858 Lincoln-Douglas debates

Frederick Law Olmsted begins design for Central Park in New York City

1859 John Brown's raid on Harpers Ferry

Vicksburg convention calls for reopening of African slave trade

Kansas ratifies free-soil constitution

1860 Democratic convention divides

Abraham Lincoln elected president

South Carolina secedes from the Union

1861 Mississippi, Florida, Alabama, Georgia, Louisiana, and Texas secede

Montgomery Convention creates Confederate States of America

Lincoln inaugurated

Firing on and surrender of Fort Sumter

The Massachusetts Emigrant Aid Company announced that it planned to dispatch $5 million and 20,000 settlers to Kansas to ensure that the embattled territory became a free state. Though the Emigrant Aid Society only managed to send about 1,200 settlers to Kansas under its sponsorship, and about a third of those soon left, advocates of slavery in Kansas believed that the forces of abolition would overwhelm the territory before slaveholders could move there. The abolitionist press, building on over thirty years of experience, encouraged the impression that the antislavery settlers constituted a formidable foe.

Proslavery advocates across the Kansas border in Missouri fought what they saw as Yankee invaders. On election day, these Missourians flooded across the border to vote in support of the proslavery candidates for the territorial legislature. This illegal and inflammatory action by the "border ruffians," as the northern press quickly labeled them, was not necessary, for Southerners already accounted for six of every ten men settled in Kansas by 1855. In any case, the proslavery forces

triumphed and took control of the territorial legislature in Lecompton. There, they passed a series of aggressive laws against free-soil advocates. Forbidding antislavery men to serve on juries or hold office, the legislature also decreed the death penalty for any person who assisted a fugitive slave. Ironically, only about 200 slaves lived in Kansas.

Faced with the blatant acts of the proslavery legislature and encouraged by their allies back east, antislavery Kansans decided that their only recourse was to establish a rival government. They worked through the summer and fall of 1855 in Topeka to write a constitution of their own. Over the winter, the free-soil advocates "ratified" the constitution—though they had no legal authority to do so—and elected their own legislature and governor. The free-soil delegates felt justified by the obvious injustice of their proslavery opponents. Both sides were certain that the future of the country lay in their hands.

Antislavery forces in New England and New York, including church congregations, sent rifles to Kansas

These settlers in Topeka, Kansas, armed themselves against their proslavery adversaries.

to arm what they saw as the side of righteousness. Southerners, in turn, organized an expedition to reinforce their comrades. Not surprisingly, this volatile situation soon exploded into violence. On May 21, 1856, a group of slave-state supporters, angered by free-state newspapers and rumors of military drills by their opponents, marched into the free-soil stronghold of Lawrence, threw printing presses into the river, and fired cannon at the Free State Hotel, which, they believed, had been established as a free-soil fortress. The cannon shot proving inadequate, the slave-state men burned the hotel to the ground. Free-soilers labeled the episode the "sack of Lawrence."

The very next day, in Washington, D.C., Representative Preston Brooks of South Carolina searched out Senator Charles Sumner of Massachusetts. Sumner had delivered a series of bitter speeches against slavery, the last one focusing on the "crime against Kansas." Sumner attacked Brooks's relative and fellow South Carolinian, the elderly Senator Andrew P. Butler, for taking "the harlot, slavery" as his "mistress" and ridiculed the old man for spitting when he talked. Brooks, defending the honor of his family and his

state, demonstrated his contempt for Sumner by striking him repeatedly about the head with a heavy rubber cane. Sumner, seated at a Senate desk screwed to the floor, ripped the chair from its moorings as he tried to rise. He did not return to his seat for two and a half years, the victim of shock. The empty seat became a symbol in the North of southern brutality, even insanity, on the slavery issue; the incident became a symbol in the South of the only sort of response the arrogant North would respect. Supporters from across the South sent Representative Brooks dozens of new canes to replace the one he had broken on their behalf.

The next day, an event back in Kansas intensified the already volatile conflict. The episode swirled around one John Brown, a free-soil emigrant to Kansas. Brown was fifty-six years old, a man who had failed in twenty different businesses in six states. He had been a supporter of abolitionism since 1834 and followed five of his sons to Kansas in 1855. There, he became furious at the proslavery forces and entered into the fight against them. Brown accompanied a group of free-staters to defend Lawrence, but they heard of the hotel's destruction before they arrived.

Preston Brooks's attack on Charles Sumner in the United States Senate electrified the nation in the spring of 1856.

SOUTHERN CHIVALRY ─ ARGUMENT versus CLUB'S.

Brown persuaded four of his sons and a son-in-law, along with two other men, to exact revenge for the defeat. Sharpening their broadswords to razor-like edges, the band set out for Pottawatomie Creek. There, acting in the name of the "Army of the North," they took five men from three houses and, after questioning them, split open their skulls. The men who were killed had been associated in some way with the territorial district court, but no one was, or is, sure of Brown's precise motives. He was never punished for the killings, though his responsibility was widely reported.

In the wake of the "sack of Lawrence," the caning of Sumner, and the "Pottawatomie Massacre"—exploding in just a three-day period in May of 1856—the territory became known as "Bleeding Kansas." A new governor finally helped quieten the conflict in September and Kansans seemed eager to settle the conflict and get to work building farms and towns. But the legitimacy of the territorial government remained an issue of heated contention both in Kansas and in Washington. The South, as it had in recent years with the Fugitive Slave Act and the Kansas-Nebraska Act, won a hollow victory when it seized the first election for the territorial government in Kansas. That government would soon pass, but the symbolic value of Bleeding Kansas would long endure.

The Election of 1856

The events in Kansas proved a disaster for the Democrats. In one state after another, Democratic senators lost office in the off-year elections of 1855. To many Southerners, the Democrats seemed a mere tool of Stephen Douglas and his northern allies; to many Northerners, it seemed that Douglas's call for popular sovereignty was a cover for greedy slaveholders. President Franklin Pierce seemed incapable of leadership, many in his party decided, and they set about looking for a new candidate for the fall election. The Democrats, needing someone who had not been tarnished by the events of the preceding two years, turned to James Buchanan to run in 1856. As minister to England, Buchanan had conveniently been out of the country during the entire Kansas mess.

The Know-Nothings alienated voters on both sides of the slavery issue by refusing to address the territorial problem directly. Southerners who had voted with the Know-Nothings had nowhere to turn but to the Democrats, but Northerners could devote their attention to the new Republican party. While many Republicans viewed the extreme nativism of the Know-Nothings with distaste, the Republican party did not denounce the anti-immigrant movement. They bypassed their most outspoken antislavery men for the 1856 nomination and turned to John C. Frémont, famed as an explorer of the West and expander of liberty's empire in California. He had taken almost no public positions and had accumulated almost no political experience. The Republicans thought they had found just the sort of vague candidate who would give few potential voters a reason to vote against him.

The new Republican party was antislavery but not pro-black; Republicans avoided talking about race at all if they could help it. What they did talk about was the goodness of the North: its free labor, its free speech, its free soil. The North, they argued, was everything the South was not, a place where hardworking white men could build a life for their families free from the threat of arrogant, powerful, and greedy slaveholders.

The Republicans talked of the "Slave Power," a political conspiracy of the most powerful slaveholders. Republicans saw everything from the three-fifths clause to the Missouri Compromise to the gag rules to the war with Mexico to the bloodshed in Kansas as the fruit of the Slave Power. How else to explain the long list of southern victories at a time when the North grew more populous and wealthy? Kansas and the caning of Sumner showed that the Slave Power, a Cincinnati paper raged, "cannot tolerate free speech anywhere, and would stifle it in Washington with the bludgeon and the bowie-knife, as they are now trying to stifle it in Kansas by massacre, rapine and murder." By speaking of the Slave Power, the Republicans could denounce the South without calling for the end of slavery and could rail at the richest slaveholders without denouncing the majority of southern whites.

Republicans attacked Catholics as well, repeating the charges that nativists had made for decades. Ironically, rumors that Frémont was a Catholic quickly surfaced and refused to subside, undercutting his support. Moreover, Frémont refused to give direction to the national campaign. To make matters worse, Millard Fillmore, the former president, ran under the banner of the American party, as the Know-Nothings called themselves, appealing to those nativists for whom the Republicans seemed too weak. Fillmore and his die-hard supporters hoped that the three-way election would split the electorate so that the final decision would rest with the House; there, Fillmore thought, he would appear as a compromise candidate.

On election day in 1856, 83 percent of the eligible voting men went to the polls, one of the highest turnouts of the era. Although Buchanan won all of the South except Maryland, he received only 45 percent of the popular vote in the country as a whole. A difference of a few thousand votes in a few states would have denied Buchanan the election. The Democrats had won, but were filled with anxiety; the Republicans had lost, but were filled with confidence. It was clear to everyone that the American political system was in flux and transition. No sooner was the 1856 election over than political leaders and editors began planning for the next one.

Observers of all political persuasions believed that James Buchanan had it within his power to strengthen the Democrats in both the North and the South. His party, after all, still controlled both houses of Congress and the Supreme Court as well as the presidency. The Republicans, moreover, had drawn much of their power from the chaos in Kansas. Should that situation

The Republicans, putting forward John C. Frémont for president, depicted themselves as the party of free-soil prosperity.

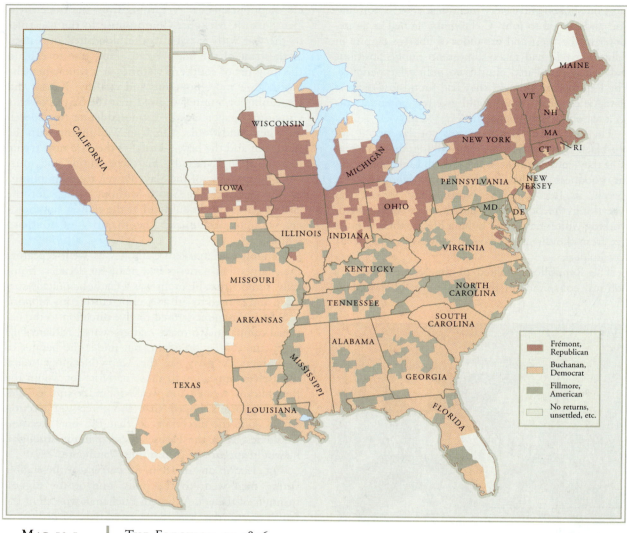

MAP 13.1 | THE ELECTION OF 1856

stabilize, the Republicans would lose their most effective weapon. Once Kansas had peacefully entered the
Union as a free state under the banner of popular sovereignty, Democrats happily observed, no other territory awaited in which similar conflicts might be expected. Slavery, everyone seemed to agree, had no
chance in Oregon, Nebraska, Minnesota, Washington,
Utah, or New Mexico. The territorial issue that had
torn at the country since 1820 might finally die down.
When it did, moderates on both sides hoped, reason
would return to American politics.

Dred Scott

In his inaugural address, James Buchanan mentioned a
case pending before the Supreme Court, the case of
Dred Scott, a slave. That case had moved its way
through various levels of courts for more than a
decade. Scott, born in Virginia around 1800, had in
the 1830s been taken by his master, an army surgeon
named John Emerson, to territories far in the upper
Midwest. Scott had married Harriet Robinson, the
slave of a federal Indian agent. Dr. Emerson bought

Harriet and thus owned the two daughters she bore with Scott. When Emerson died in 1843, Scott and his family became the property of Emerson's widow, who moved to St. Louis. Scott pleaded with her to let him hire out his own time—to work for wages and pay her from his earnings, as many urban slaves did—but Mrs. Emerson refused. In 1846 the Scotts petitioned for their freedom, claiming that their residence in the free territory entitled them to free status.

Suits such as the Scotts' had been brought successfully before Missouri courts in years past and at first there seemed nothing remarkable about their case. A long series of postponements and delays dragged the case on into the early 1850s, however, when the legal environment had become much more divided by political controversy over slavery. Democratic judges and lawyers worked to deny the Scotts their freedom on the grounds that such a precedent would undermine the right of Southerners to take slaves, constitutionally protected property, into the territories. A Republican lawyer agreed to carry the Scotts' case before the Supreme Court to counter the Democrats' aggressive claims. Unfortunately for the Republicans and the Scotts, five southern Democrats sat on the court, along with two northern Democrats, one northern Whig, and one northern Republican. Presiding was Chief Justice Roger B. Taney (pronounced "tawney"), an eighty-year-old Marylander first appointed to the court by Andrew Jackson in 1835, well known for his determination to defend slavery at every opportunity.

The *Dred Scott* case came before the Supreme Court during the superheated months of 1856, when Kansas, the Brooks/Sumner affair, and the presidential election commanded the country's attention. Although the case could have been decided on relatively narrow grounds, the Democratic members of the court wanted to issue a sweeping pronouncement that would settle once and for all the question of slavery in the territories. President-elect Buchanan pressured a fellow Pennsylvanian on the court to side with the Southerners. Two days after Buchanan took office in March of 1857, the court announced its decision in the *Dred Scott* case. It took Chief Justice Taney two hours to read the opinion. What he read shook the nation.

Taney spent half his time denying that Scott had the right to bring a case in the first place. Black people, Taney decreed, could not become citizens of the United States nor exercise the rights of citizenship because "they were not included, and were not intended

The Dred Scott *case attracted the attention of the entire country in 1856. This northern newspaper depicted Scott and his family sympathetically, emphasizing family ties and the women of the family.*

to be included, under the word 'citizens' in the Constitution." In chilling language and with distorted history, Taney declared that at the time the Constitution was written, throughout the "civilized and enlightened portions of the world," members of the "negro African race" were held to be "altogether unfit to associate with the white race . . . and so far inferior, that they had no rights which the white man was bound to respect; and . . . might justly and lawfully be reduced to slavery for his benefit." Therefore, Dred Scott had never been a citizen of Missouri and had no right to sue his mistress. Taney also decreed that Congress had never held a constitutional right to restrict slavery in the territories and that therefore the Missouri Compromise of 1820 was invalid. Two justices dissented from the majority's opinion, but the decision stood as the law of the land. In the meantime, a descendant of

Dred Scott's original owner bought the slave and set him free; Scott died the next year.

White Southerners exulted that they had been vindicated by the *Dred Scott* decision, that the Supreme Court was on their side, that the Republicans' demand for territories free of slavery was simply unconstitutional. The Republicans, however, sneered at the decision, which they saw as one more corrupt act by the Slave Power Conspiracy. A New York newspaper held that the court's decision was "entitled to just so much moral weight as would be the judgment of a majority of those congregated in any Washington barroom." The Republicans reprinted the dissenting opinions in the *Dred Scott* case and denounced the decision in the state legislatures they controlled throughout the North. They argued that the Founding Fathers had never intended slavery to be a permanent part of the United States, that the founders had carefully avoided using the word "slavery" in the Constitution and merely tolerated bondage because they expected it to die of its own weight. If the *Dred Scott* decision were followed to its logical conclusion, these northern Republicans warned, the United States would reopen the slave trade with Africa and even extend slavery into northern states where it had been banned.

The Republicans thought the court's audacious statement "the best thing that could have happened" to the Republican party. As an abolitionist newspaper put it, the "fiercer the insult, the bitter the blow, the better." The Republicans expected the *Dred Scott* decision, like the events in Kansas and the caning of Sumner, to "galvanize" their party, to make it stronger. The Republicans needed to sweep the government in 1860, they argued, to clean out corruption and conspiracy from top to bottom.

Arguments over Slavery

Slavery had never been stronger in the United States than it was in 1857. The three and a half million slaves of the South extended over a vast territory stretching from Delaware to Texas. Four hundred thousand slaveowners possessed slaves worth $3 billion. Theorists devised ever more elaborate and aggressive defenses of slavery, no longer depicting it merely as a necessary evil or an unfortunate inheritance from the English or a burden that had to be shouldered with Christian forbearance. Rather, they claimed, slavery was an instrument of God's will, a progressive force in the world, a means of civilizing and Christian-izing Africans otherwise lost to barbarism and heathenism. Southern physicians went to great lengths to prove that Africans and their descendants were physically and intellectually inferior to whites, dependent upon white guidance for their very survival.

Some defenders of slavery argued that slavery was *better* than free labor, more humane and Christian. If

THE NEGRO IN HIS OWN COUNTRY.

THE NEGRO IN AMERICA.

This proslavery cartoonist imagined an Africa of cannibalism and an America of refinement to claim that slavery was a force for good in the world.

the hypocritical and self-righteous men of the North would admit it, white Southerners argued, free labor exacted a great cost. Men, women, and children went hungry when unemployment, ill health, or old age struck because no one in the North felt any responsibility for anyone else. In the South, by contrast, theorists such as George Fitzhugh of Virginia insisted in *Cannibals All!* of 1857, slaveholders cared for their slaves even when those slaves had grown too old or feeble to work. The South's relative lack of schools, orphanages, asylums, and prisons, the defenders of the region insisted, testified not to backwardness but to a personalized society where individual responsibility replaced impersonal institutions. Compare the status of free blacks in the North and the South, white Southerners challenged, and you will find that white Northerners showed much less concern for the black people who lived in their own communities than they did for slaves they never saw.

Some white Southerners in the late 1850s argued for the expansion of American territory in Cuba or Central America, places where slavery could flourish. William Walker, a young Tennesseean, dreamed of personal glory, an isthmian canal, and a new territory for slavery. After several attempts at "filibustering," small-scale military efforts, in Mexico, Walker took advantage of a civil war to gain power in Nicaragua in

1855 and 1856, attracting great attention and 2,000 American settlers. But Central American leaders united against him, cholera wiped out his army, and the United States rejected his claims to legitimacy. White Southerners enthusiastically supported several attempts by Walker in the late 1850s to take Nicaragua, but he failed repeatedly. Finally, a firing squad in Honduras put an end to Walker's crusade by executing him.

Despite the highly publicized adventures of the filibusters and the agitation of a few editors and politicians for the reopening of the African slave trade, most white Southerners wanted above all to keep and protect what they had, not jeopardize slavery by brashly expanding it. Not only would a renewed slave trade with Africa ignite the opinion of the world against the South, they recognized, but it would also drive down slave prices and create new problems of discipline and revolt. The white South prided itself on having created a stable and prosperous society during its two and a half centuries of slavery and did not want to endanger that society.

Moreover, the slave economy boomed in the late 1850s. Planters took advantage of improved cotton gins, river boats, railroads, and new kinds of seed to double, in the 1850s alone, their production of cotton. The claim of southern politicians that "Cotton is

SCENE ON A COTTON PLANTATION. GATHERING COTTON.

The southern cotton economy boomed in the late 1850s even as the sectional crisis grew more threatening.

Hinton Helper, *The Impending Crisis of the South,* 1857

This book, a lacerating critique of slavery by a racist white Southerner, proved even more incendiary in the South than had Harriet Beecher Stowe's *Uncle Tom's Cabin.* The Republican party seized on the book as a revelation from inside the slave power's empire, arguing that it revealed the secret resentments of the white majority. To the Republicans' surprise and dismay, however, the book bred anger against the North instead of Republican recruits in the South.

It is a fact well known to every intelligent Southerner, that we are compelled to go to the North for almost every article of utility and adornment, from matches, shoepegs and paintings, up to cotton-mills, steamships and statuary; that we have no foreign trade, no princely merchants, nor respectable artists; that, in comparison with the Free States, we contribute nothing to the literature, polite arts and inventions of the age; that, for want of profitable employment at home, large numbers of our native population find themselves necessitated to emigrate to the West, while the Free States retain not only the larger proportion of those born within their own limits, but induce, annually, hundreds of thousands of foreigners to settle and remain amongst them; that almost everything produced at the North meets with ready sale, while, at the same time, there is no demand, even among our own citizens, for the productions of Southern industry; that, owing to the absence of a proper system of business among us, the North becomes, in one way or another, the proprietor and dispenser of all our floating wealth, and that we are dependent on Northern capitalists for the means necessary to build our railroads, canals and other public improvements; that if we want to visit a foreign country, even though it may lie directly south of us, we find no convenient way of getting there except by taking passage through a Northern port; and that nearly all the profits arising from the exchange of commodities, from insurance and shipping offices, and from the thousand and one industrial pursuits of the country, accrue to the North, and are there invested in the erection of those magnificent cities and stupendous works of art which dazzle the eyes of the South, and attest the superiority of free institutions!

. . .

And now that we have come to the very heart and soul of our subject, we feel no disposition to mince matters, but mean to speak plainly and to the point, without any equivocation, mental reservation, or secret evasion whatever. The son of a venerated parent, who, while he lived, was a considerate and merciful slaveholder, a native of the South, born and bred in North Carolina, of a family whose home has been in the valley of the Yadkin for nearly a century and a half, a Southerner by instinct and by all the influences of thought, habits and kindred, and with the desire and fixed purpose to reside permanently within the limits of the South, and with the expectation of dying there also—we feel that we have the right to express our opinion, however humble or unimportant it may be, on any and every question that affects the public good. . . .

And now to the point. In our opinion, an opinion which has been formed from data obtained by assiduous researchers and comparisons, from laborious investigation, logical reasoning, and earnest reflection, the causes which have impeded the progress and prosperity of the South, which have dwindled our commerce and other similar pursuits, into the most contemptible insignificance; sunk a large majority of our people in galling poverty and ignorance, rendered a small minority conceited and tyrannical, and driven the rest away from their homes; entailed upon us a humiliating dependence on the Free States; disgraced us in the recesses of our own souls, and brought us under reproach in the eyes of all civilized and enlightened nations—may all be traced to one common source, and there find solution in the most hateful and horrible word, that was ever incorporated into the vocabulary of human economy—*Slavery.*

. . .

In making up these [statistical] tables we have two objects in view; the first is to open the eyes of the non-slaveholders of the South to the system of deception that has been so long practiced upon them, and the second is to show slaveholders themselves—we have reference only to those who are not too perverse, or ignorant, to perceive naked truths—that free labor is far more respectable, profitable, and productive, than slave labor. In the South, unfortunately, no kind of labor is either free or respectable. Every white man who is under the necessity of earning his bread, by the sweat of his brow, or by manual labor, in any capacity, no matter how unassuming in deportment, or exemplary in morals, is treated as if he were a loathsome beast, and shunned with disdain. His soul may be the very seat of honor and integrity, yet without slaves—himself a slave—he is accounted as nobody, and would be deemed intolerably presumptuous, if he dared to open his lips, even so wide as to give faint utterance to a three-lettered monosyllable, like yea or nay, in the presence of an august knight of the whip and the lash.

. . .

The lords of the lash are not only absolute masters of the blacks, who are bought and sold, and driven about like so many cattle, but they are also the oracles and arbiters of all the non-slaveholding whites, whose freedom is merely nominal, and whose unparalleled illiteracy and degradation is purposely and fiendishly perpetuated. How little the "poor white trash," the great majority of the Southern people, know of the real condition of the country, is, indeed, sadly astonishing. The truth is, they know nothing of public measures, and little of private affairs, except what their imperious masters, the slave-drivers, condescend to tell, and that is but precious little, and even that little, always garbled and one-sided, is never told except in public harangues; for the haughty cavaliers of shackles and handcuffs will not degrade themselves by holding private converse with those who have neither dimes nor hereditary rights in human flesh.

Whenever it pleases, and to the extent it pleases, a slaveholder to become communicative, poor whites may hear with fear and trembling, but not speak. They must be as mum as dumb brutes, and stand in awe of their august superiors, or be crushed with stern rebukes, cruel oppressions, or downright violence. If they dare to think for themselves, their thoughts must be forever concealed. The expression of any sentiment at all conflicting with the gospel of slavery, dooms them at once in the community in which they live, and then, whether willing or unwilling, they are obliged to become heroes, martyrs, or exiles. . . .

Non-slaveholders are not only kept in ignorance of what is transpiring at the North, but they are continually misinformed of what is going on even in the South. Never were the poorer classes of a people, and those classes so largely in the majority, and all inhabiting the same country, so basely duped, so adroitly swindled, or so unpardonably outraged.

SOURCE   Hinton R. Helper, *The Impending Crisis of the South* (New York: A. B. Burdick, 1859), pp. 25–26, 28–29, 40, 42–43.

King" proved no empty boast. Even though northern factories and farms grew rapidly in the 1850s, cotton still accounted for fully half of all U.S. exports. Without cotton, many thousands of northern and British workers would have had no jobs, along with a large number of merchants, lawyers, bankers, insurance agents, dock workers, and clerks.

The prosperity created by the cotton boom resonated throughout the southern economy. Small towns emerged in the 1850s and southern cities grew quickly, attracting immigrants and businesses. Although the South could not keep up with the North—one of the most rapidly developing economies in the world—the South actually did quite well by international standards. Considered as a separate economy, the South stood second in the world in the number of miles of railroad, sixth in cotton textile factories, and eighth in iron production. The South was roughly the equal of France, Germany, or Austria-Hungary in its level of industrial output. Slaves proved to be adaptable both to factories and cities. The number of slaves in cities declined in the 1850s mainly because the demand for slaves in the countryside was so strong.

The southern economy, then, was not weak or weakening in the 1850s. Slavery and cotton had never been more profitable. On the other hand, the South was not urbanizing or industrializing nearly as quickly as the North. The South did not create a large class of entrepreneurs or skilled workers, nor did the region invest much money in machinery to make its farms and plantations more efficient; the purchase of a slave was a more certain investment. The southern plantation economy, in effect, was too profitable for its own good. The short-term gains of the 1850s dissuaded wealthy Southerners from investing in businesses that held greater potential for long-term development, businesses that were not as dependent on other regions and countries for their continued prosperity.

Northerners considered the southern economy the mirror image of the North: sick rather than healthy, backward rather than dynamic, inegalitarian rather than democratic. Critics of the South argued that slavery victimized not only slaves but also "poor whites." In the antislavery portrayal, the Slave Power's domination began at home, where haughty self-proclaimed aristocrats lorded over ignorant whites, bullying them into supporting parties and policies that worked against their own interests. Antislavery people charged that slaves degraded white labor in the South, made manual labor shameful, and substituted a cheap sense of racial superiority for actual accomplishment.

The most effective criticism of the South in this vein came from a Southerner: Hinton Rowan Helper, the son of a small slaveholding farmer in western North Carolina. In 1857, a northern press published

GRAPH 13-1 EXTENT OF SLAVEHOLDING IN THE SOUTH
POPULATION OF 7,981,000

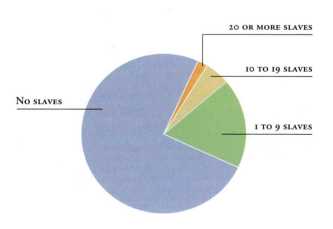

GRAPH 13.2 PATTERNS OF SLAVEHOLDING IN THE SOUTH, 1850
347,525 FAMILIES

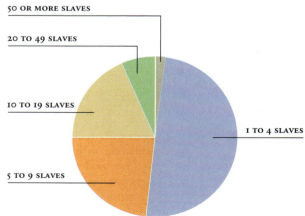

More than half of all slaveholders owned four or fewer slaves in 1850.

Helper's book, *The Impending Crisis of the South*, which argued that the South's growth, prosperity, and cultural development were being held back by slavery. He charged that "the lords of the lash are not only absolute masters of the blacks . . . but they are also the oracles and arbiters of all non-slaveholding whites." Helper deployed statistics from the census to prove his case, showing that land values, literacy levels, and manufacturing rates in the South were substantially lower than those in the North. Helper, no friend to black Southerners, proposed that slaveholders be taxed to colonize all free blacks in Africa or Latin America.

Though many Northerners believed that Helper spoke for a large number of yeomen farmers in the South, there is little indication that many southern whites agreed with Helper's assessment of their status. Most whites saw slavery as an avenue for their own advancement, not a hindrance. Many men and women bought a slave before they bought land, even if only to rent the slave to other whites. Slaveowners included women, shopkeepers, industrialists, lawyers, ministers, and even a few free blacks. No investment seemed to offer a more certain return than a slave, especially in the 1850s when slave prices rose rapidly. While that rise in prices meant that a growing proportion of white people would be unable to afford a slave—so that the percentage of whites who owned slaves declined from about a third in 1840 to about a quarter in 1860—most nonslaveholding whites apparently reconciled themselves to their situation or determined that they, too, would eventually join the slaveowning ranks.

Southern Solidarity and Differences

Politics reinforced the sense among southern white men that they lived in a fair and democratic society. While many nonslaveholders in mountainous districts across the South voted against the large slaveholding districts, most southern white men voted in concert with the richest men in their immediate neighborhoods. And in every county in the South, including the mountains, those richest men were slaveholders. In the eyes of the poorer men, their wealthy neighbors could act as spokesmen and brokers for the community in the state capital. Common people identified themselves as members of communities, congregations, and parties.

Southern whites identified themselves most of all as white people, tied to other whites by blood and her-

itage, transcending obvious differences of wealth and background. Whites held black people in contempt despite their knowledge that many African Americans were more intelligent, hard-working, and Christian than many whites. To be white was to be the inheritor of all the accomplishments of the ancients, of Christendom, and the modern world. It was to be inherently, undeniably, free. Such attitudes were reinforced at every level, from the daily rituals of life to the writings of leading thinkers from Europe. White Southerners railed against the Republicans because that party threatened this bond of race between the white North and the white South. When southern whites called the Republicans "Black Republicans," they seized on the most charged and degrading language they could imagine.

Despite the solidarities of racial thinking, important political differences divided Southerners. At one extreme were the so-called "fire-eaters," virulent defenders of the South and slavery. These men were diverse in age, wealth, occupation, slaveholding, and

Edmund Ruffin of Virginia was a "fire-eater"—a proponent of southern independence—as well as a proponent of agricultural reform. He hoped that both would make the South stronger.

James D. B. DeBow, "The Interest in Slavery of the Southern Non-Slaveholder" 1860

DeBow used his statistical expertise as a former Superintendent of the United States Census to refute arguments such as Hinton Helper's in the preceding document. DeBow argued that the South was actually more democratic in property holding than the North and that slavery actually helped the non-slaveholding white Southerner in many ways.

. . . When in charge of the national census office, several years since, I found that it had been stated by an abolition Senator from his seat, that the number of slaveholders at the South did not exceed 150,000. Convinced that it was a gross misrepresentation of the facts, I caused a careful examination of the returns to be made, which fixed the actual number at 347,255, and communicated the information, by note, to Senator Cass, who read it in the Senate. I first called attention to the fact that the number embraced slaveholding families, and that to arrive at the actual number of slaveholders, it would be necessary to multiply by the proportion of persons, which the census showed to a family. When this was done, the number was swelled to about 2,000,000.

Since these results were made public, I have had reason to think, that the separation of the schedules of the slave and the free, was calculated to lead to omissions of the single properties, and that on this account it would be safe to put the number of families at 375,000, and the number of actual slaveholders at about two million and a quarter.

Assuming the published returns, however, to be correct, it will appear that one-half of the population of South Carolina, Mississippi, and Louisiana, excluding the cities, are slaveholders, and that one-third of the population of the entire South are similarly circumstanced. The average number of slaves is nine to each slaveholding family, and one-half of the whole number of such holders are in possession of less than five slaves.

It will thus appear that the slaveholders of the South, so far from constituting numerically an insignificant portion of its people, as has been malignantly alleged, make up an aggregate, greater in relative proportion than the holders of any other species of property whatever, in any part of the world; and that of no other property can it be said, with equal truthfulness, that it is an interest of the whole community. Whilst every other family in the States I have specially referred to, are slaveholders, but one family in every three and a half families in Maine, New Hampshire, Massachusetts and Connecticut, are holders of agricultural land; and, in European States, the proportion is almost indefinitely less. The proportion which the slaveholders of the South, bear to the entire population is greater than that of the owners of land or houses, agricultural stock, State, bank, or other corporation securities anywhere else. No political economist will deny this. Nor is that all. Even in the States which are among the largest slaveholding, South Carolina,

party affiliation. Some lived in cities, others on plantations. Some, such as J.D.B. DeBow, wanted to make the South more industrial and modern, while others rejected such development as a Yankee blight on the rural South. Whatever their differences, these men saw themselves as the voice of honesty. They did not consider themselves hotheads. Men such as Robert Barnwell Rhett and Edmund Ruffin argued that the abolitionists and their Republican supporters intended to destroy the South. The only sane response, they be-

Georgia and Tennessee, the land proprietors outnumber nearly two to one, in relative proportion, the owners of the same property in Maine, Massachusetts and Connecticut, and if the average number of slaves held by each family throughout the South be but nine, and if one-half of the whole number of slaveholders own under five slaves, it will be seen how preposterous is the allegation of our enemies, that the slaveholding class is an organized wealthy aristocracy. *The poor men of the South are the holders of one to five slaves, and it would be equally consistent with truth and justice, to say that they represent, in reality, its slaveholding interest.*

[How does slavery benefit the non-slaveholding white man?]

1. The non-slaveholder of the South is assured that the remuneration afforded by his labor, over and above the expense of living, is larger than that which is afforded by the same labor in the free States.

2. The non-slaveholders, as a class, are not reduced by the necessity of our condition, as is the case in the free States, to find employment in crowded cities and come into competition in close and sickly workshops and factories, with remorseless and untiring machinery.

3. The non-slaveholder is not subjected to that competition with foreign pauper labor, which has degraded the free labor of the North and demoralized it to an extent which perhaps can never be estimated.

4. The non-slaveholder of the South preserves the status of the white man, and is not regarded as an inferior or a dependent.

5. The non-slaveholder knows that as soon as his savings will admit, he can become a slaveholder, and thus relieve his wife from the necessities of the kitchen and the laundry, and his children from the labors of the field.

6. The large slaveholders and proprietors of the South begin life in great part as non-slaveholders.

7. But should such fortune not be in reserve for the non-slaveholder, he will understand that by honesty and industry it may be realized to his children.

8. The sons of the non-slaveholder are and have always been among the leading and ruling spirits of the South; in industry as well as in politics.

9. Without the institution of slavery, the great staple products of the South would cease to be grown, and the immense annual results, which are distributed among every class of the community, and which give life to every branch of industry, would cease.

10. If emancipation be brought about as will undoubtedly be the case, unless the encroachments of the fanatical majorities of the North are resisted now the slaveholders, in the main, will escape the degrading equality which must result, by emigration, for which they would have the means, by disposing of their personal chattels: whilst the non-slaveholders, without these resources, would be compelled to remain and endure the degradation.

SOURCE "The Non-Slaveholders of the South," in DeBow and others, *The Interest in Slavery of the Southern Non-Slaveholder. The Right of Peaceful Secession. Slavery in the Bible.* (Charleston: Evans & Cogswell, 1860), pp. 3–5, 7–12.

lieved, was to face the issue squarely and aggressively, to agitate the slavery issue constantly, to refuse to yield an inch in the territories or anywhere else. The fire-eaters were calling for secession as early as 1857. They sought to keep secessionism in people's minds so they could act quickly when events drove the two regions apart once again.

At the other end of the political spectrum in the South were the former Whigs and Know-Nothings. They considered the Democrats, especially the fire-eaters, great threats to the future of the South and slavery. The Democrats' relentless calls for southern rights and the expansion of slavery, they argued, did as much as the abolitionists to inflame northern sentiment against the South. Former leaders of the Whigs and the nativist American party did their best to pull their allies into a new party opposed to the Democrats and attractive to a "thoughtful, sedate, constitution-abiding, conservative class of men." The many Unionists in the upper South, in cities, and even in some of the richest plantation districts felt drawn to this position. The editors of the former Whig and American papers chided the Democrats for continually agitating the slavery question. They warned voters that the Democrats would sell out the South in Kansas, that the Democrats talked a tough game but always ended up caving in to the North.

In the North, too, the major parties had to contend with activists on the fringes of respectable opinion. By 1857, the abolitionists had become both entrenched and somewhat discouraged. They had succeeded in making slavery detested throughout the North and had created much of the anti-southern energy that flowed into the Republican party. But abolitionists distrusted that party. The Republicans seemed interested only in the welfare of the white North, in keeping the territories open to northern men. Republicans denied any intention of ending slavery in the South, the very reason the immediate abolitionists had come into being over a quarter of a century before. The Republicans even resurrected talk of colonization, the movement the abolitionists had abandoned twenty-five years earlier. The Republicans, while better than the pro-southern Democrats, still dissatisfied the abolitionists.

A SOCIETY IN CRISIS

The American economy boomed in the mid-1850s. Not only did cotton do well, but so did the farms, factories, railroads, and cities of the North and West. People cheered the laying of a telegraphic cable all the way across the Atlantic Ocean, an incredible feat. New York City began the construction of its glorious Central Park. Currier and Ives prints became the rage, brightening homes across the country with charming scenes of American life. The sale of newspapers, books,

and magazines surged, including an impressive new publication, *Atlantic Monthly.* Working people's organizations staged a comeback. Churches and schools spread with remarkable speed. The mileage of railroads tripled, to more than 30,000 miles. The United States had become a marvel of the modern world.

But underlying this prosperity ran a deep current of unease. Some people were uncomfortable with the prosperity itself, worried that Americans were growing soft and self-indulgent. Others felt guilt that as the economy boomed slavery became stronger. Others despaired at the state of American politics, which seemed in disarray under the control of selfish men who cared for nothing other than their own advancement. The conflict between the North and the South embodied all these anxieties, focusing them, giving them concrete shape.

Financial Panic and Spiritual Revival

Late in the summer of 1857, people warned that there had been too much speculation recently, that companies and individuals had borrowed too much money. The end of the Crimean War in Europe seemed ominous for the United States, for now the countries of the Old World could turn their energies toward growing their own food, undermining the heavy demand for American farm products that had buoyed the economy for several years. When a major insurance company went under in 1857, a panic spread among New York banks and railroad stocks plummeted along with western land values. Soon, banks and companies across the country began to fail.

Working people of all ranks lost their jobs. Not only unskilled laborers, domestics, and millworkers found themselves without work, but so did educated bookkeepers and clerks. Not only were recent Irish immigrants homeless, but so were white Protestant native-born workers. Across the North, hundreds of thousands of people had no income and many were forced to rely on charity to feed and clothe themselves. Workers tried to organize, but employers shut down the mills and factories. As winter approached, many people wondered whether their families would survive through the cold months. Others worried that the poor would rebel against the rich.

The white South used the panic for rhetorical advantage. Southerners blamed northern financiers for bringing on the Panic of 1857, for dragging the pros-

THE PANIC IN WALL STREET. 1857

The sudden financial panic of 1857 seemed to many Americans a sign of moral corruption and social decay.

perous South into depression. Though the white and free black working people of southern cities suffered along with their counterparts to the north, white Southerners bragged that their region quickly recovered from the panic, showing the greater stability of their agrarian social order. They also bragged that their slaves, unlike white workers, never starved or went without a roof over their heads. Slaveholders, unlike employers, could not—would not, they said—abandon their workers when hard times arrived.

Throughout the country, the panic and depression of 1857 caused people to pause and take stock of their situation. How could it be, they asked, that the country could go so quickly from prosperity to poverty? Some said that the political system had betrayed the country, that selfish politicians had allowed banking to become too loose or the tariff too strict—or vice versa, since no one could be certain. Others warned that Americans had grown too rich and lazy for their

own good, borrowing and spending too freely, becoming too wrapped up in their material welfare at the expense of everything and everyone else.

A wave of religious revivals emerged in response to the panic and the moral failures it reflected. Almost as soon as the crisis began in the fall of 1857, revivals commenced. They lasted for over a year, sweeping back and forth across the country. Unlike earlier revivals, the religious spirit emerged not in rural districts or in raw new canal towns but in the largest cities of the Northeast. Unlike earlier revivals, too, those of 1857 attracted a conspicuously large number of men as well as women. Both businessmen and workingmen attended sermons and prayer meetings on their lunch hour. The revivals also witnessed the first active participation of denominations such as the Episcopalians and Unitarians. It seemed to many people, in fact, that the revivals were the most heartening and significant in American history, showing that the people in the forefront of modern America were trying to change their ways. And as people read their newspapers they saw plenty that needed to be changed—especially in Kansas, where events in the fall of 1857 reclaimed the front page from both the hard times and the revivals.

Kansas—Again

Most of the settlers who had arrived in Kansas in 1856 and 1857 were nonslaveholding migrants from the upper South. They did not appear eager to establish slavery in Kansas. An open election, therefore, would likely install a constitutional convention in favor of free soil at the time Kansas became a state. The proslavery legislature elected in the earliest days of the territory, however, still controlled Kansas in 1857 and a prosouthern Democrat still sat in the White House. Free state advocates fought back, touring the North, preaching their cause, and raising money for the struggle against the Slave Power. Leading abolitionists, as well as leading thinkers such as Henry David Thoreau and Ralph Waldo Emerson, warmly supported John Brown for what they saw as his bravery in Kansas.

As the curtain opened in Kansas in November of 1857, the small band of unregenerate proslavery delegates who still controlled the legislature proposed a new constitution. Kansas had to produce a constitution that the U.S. Congress would accept. The legislature, after a drawn-out and drunken convention, provided that voters would choose between the constitution with slavery or without slavery. In either case, slaveowners already in Kansas would be permitted to keep their slaves. The Republicans portrayed the constitution as one more audacious act of the Slave Power, but in fact the "Lecompton Constitution" posed a serious problem for the Democrats. Northern members of the party could not support it without appearing too sympathetic to the South and losing already queasy constituents to the Republicans; they could not oppose it without alienating the southern Democrats that made up the bulk of the party's strength.

Stephen Douglas refused to endorse the Lecompton Constitution as a violation of popular sovereignty but President Buchanan, the other leading Democrat, urged its adoption. He persuaded himself that the constitution was in fact a moderate compromise, letting Kansas enter the Union as a free state in the long run while protecting the slaveholders who were already

James Buchanan, a Pennsylvania Democrat, became the object of contempt among many Northerners for his sympathy for the South in the political struggles of the late 1850s.

there. Once Kansas was a state, he reasoned, its legislature could decide what to do with those slaves without dragging all of Congress into the conflict. Most northern voters saw the matter differently: though it was obvious that the great majority of Kansans wanted to enter the Union as a free state, those antislavery Kansans would be forced to accept slavery in their midst.

Republicans could hardly believe that Buchanan had handed them such an easy way to portray him as a tool of the South. And neither could Stephen Douglas, who recognized that Buchanan's actions would create enormous problems for the Democrats, for popular sovereignty, and for Stephen Douglas. The Democrats fought bitterly among themselves for months, Douglas denouncing the president and seeking to use the Senate to block the Lecompton Constitution,

Buchanan using the powers of the presidency to mobilize senators against Douglas. Southern senators sneered at Douglas and called him a traitor to the party, even as they delivered blustering proslavery arguments from the Senate floor.

Moderate southern and northern Democrats warned that the South, drunk with its power on the Supreme Court, in Congress, and in the White House, was destroying its only hope for continued success: a strong Democratic party in the North. When Kansas voters overwhelmingly rejected the Lecompton Constitution in the spring of 1858, they rejected Buchanan and the South as well. The Democrats suffered widespread defeat in the state elections that spring and lost control of the House. The prospects were not much better for the fall. Douglas himself faced a tough election battle and Buchanan did everything he could to destroy this rival in his own party. Running against a promising Republican candidate, Abraham Lincoln, Douglas needed all the help he could get.

The Lincoln-Douglas Debates

Abraham Lincoln, though possessing considerable political assets, was still very much the underdog in the Illinois senatorial race of 1858. As a Whig in a heavily Democratic state, Lincoln had not found it easy to win or hold office in the 1840s and 1850s. He had lost repeatedly, occupying national office for all of two years: elected to the House of Representatives in 1845, Lincoln lasted only one term. He opposed the war with Mexico, an unpopular stance in Illinois, and was sent back to his law office in Springfield. There, Lincoln made a good living for himself and his family, drawing on his own abilities and the connections that came with his marriage to Mary Todd, a member of a prominent family in the booming town. Lincoln's modest beginnings on the Kentucky and Illinois frontier, where he had received only one year of formal education, lay comfortably in the past. Still, he longed for a major public office.

Though the short, portly, experienced, pragmatic, and famous Stephen Douglas seemed the opposite of the tall, thin, inexperienced, principled, and obscure Abraham Lincoln, the two men in fact shared a great deal. Douglas, too, had grown up poor and Douglas too had made himself into what he had become by the late 1850s. Douglas, although the most prominent Democrat in the country, was actually four years younger than Lincoln, who had watched Douglas with some envy over the preceding two decades. Both Lincoln and Douglas identified quite easily with the voters of Illinois, sharing their constituents' moderate positions on most national issues.

Illinois held within its borders a considerable share of American diversity, its population composed of many New England migrants in the northern half of the state, upcountry southern migrants in the bottom half, and German and Irish immigrants in Chicago. Both the factories and the farms of Illinois prospered in the 1850s, as did abolitionists, Know-Nothings, Whigs, and southern-leaning Democrats. The Illinois senatorial election of 1858 promised to throw all these groups into contention. "The battle of the Union is to be fought in Illinois," a Washington newspaper announced. At stake was this question: Could the Democrats survive as a national party, with Douglas as their leader, or were they doomed to become a party of the South?

Douglas traveled by private railroad car from Chicago to Springfield, the state capital and Lincoln's base. All along the way, Douglas gave speeches to thousands of people, telling them that he was the voice of experience, principled compromise, and popular sovereignty. He also told them that Lincoln, while "a kind-hearted, amiable, good-natured gentleman," held "monstrous revolutionary doctrines" of abolitionism. To Douglas's great annoyance, Lincoln followed the senator to rebut his arguments and charges, sometimes appearing in the crowd, sometimes arriving the next day. Douglas, though reluctant to give the relatively unknown Lincoln a share of attention, finally agreed to hold seven joint debates in the late summer and early fall. The candidates took turns opening and closing the debates, every word transcribed by reporters from across the country.

Lincoln was far from an abolitionist, refusing to join the antislavery Liberty and Free Soil parties and staying with the Whigs far longer than most of the men who became Republicans. Unlike the abolitionists, Lincoln venerated the Constitution and the spirit of compromise it embodied. He repeatedly brought up the Dred Scott decision from the previous year, however, arguing that it was a corruption of the Constitution. The Supreme Court decision, Lincoln warned, would permit slavery to spread into lands where Illinois men or their sons would otherwise migrate. Douglas offered what he saw as practical, commonsense responses to such charges, arguing that slavery would not spread anywhere the majority of the

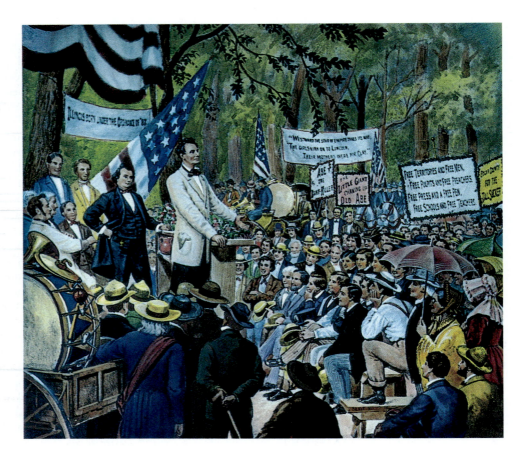

Abraham Lincoln and Stephen Douglas vied for a U.S. Senate seat from Illinois in 1858, debating the most troubling issues that faced the entire nation.

white population did not want it to. A far greater and more immediate threat, Douglas argued, was that the Republicans would force the South into desperate acts by dragging moral issues into political contexts where they could not be resolved. Let the sovereign white people of each state decide for themselves, in the fullness of time, whether they would have slavery or not, Douglas counseled. Douglas did not defend slavery—which he hoped and expected would eventually fade away through natural causes—but he declared that "I care more for the great principle of self-government, the right of the people to rule, than I do for all the negroes in Christendom."

Lincoln charged that Douglas's strategy merely postponed an inevitable reckoning between the slave states and the free states. He argued that "a house divided against itself cannot stand. . . . Either the opponents of slavery will arrest the further spread of it, and place it where the public mind shall rest in the belief that it is in the course of ultimate extinction, or its

advocates will push it forward till it shall become alike lawful in all the States, old as well as new, North as well as South." Notwithstanding Douglas's efforts to dismiss the morality of slavery as beside the point in a northern senatorial campaign, that morality repeatedly surfaced in the debates. Lincoln argued that he, not Douglas, was the one defending true self-government. Douglas's policy permitted the forces of slavery to grow stronger and more aggressive, while Lincoln's would place slavery on the path toward "ultimate extinction." It would likely be several generations before that extinction occurred, Lincoln believed, and it would probably need to be accompanied by the colonization of the former slaves out of the United States, but the process could begin in 1858.

Lincoln made a distinction between different kinds of rights. African Americans, he thought, had economic rights: "In the right to eat the bread, without leave of anybody else, which his own hand earns, he is my equal and the equal of Judge Douglas, and the equal of every living man." But Lincoln did not believe in social equality between blacks and whites. He would not grant black men the right to intermarry with whites, serve on juries, or vote, but he did believe that black people had the right not to be slaves. Lincoln, though not offering a coherent or consistent vision of African-American freedom, took the offensive, making Douglas appear more of a defender of slavery than at heart he was.

The election was close, the Douglas Democrats defeating the Republicans by about 4000 votes out of 250,000 cast. The state legislature, which elected U.S. senators in these decades, went to the Democrats and they returned Douglas to Washington. But Abraham Lincoln had won as well. He had become nationally famous, identified as the spokesman for a principled yet restrained antislavery. All across the North, in fact, the Republicans made impressive gains in 1858. In every state, many people—perhaps the majority of whites—wanted the conflict to quieten, wanted the nation to find some compromise. But the political environment did not have a chance to calm in 1859, for it was then that John Brown returned to the national scene.

John Brown and Harpers Ferry

John Brown had become famous in the three years since he had burst into prominence in Bleeding Kansas in 1855. Antislavery people back east, assured by journalists that Brown had not personally killed anyone at Pottawatomie, admired the hard man for his firsthand opposition to slaveholders. He acted on what other antislavery people only talked about. Thus, as he toured New England in search of funds to carry on the cause, he found willing listeners and open hands. Antislavery advocates were eager to contribute to the fight against slavery in Kansas, not realizing they were contributing to a fight against slavery much closer to home.

Throughout 1857 and 1858 Brown planned for an attack on the federal arsenal at Harpers Ferry, Virginia. He had a thousand iron pikes forged to arm the slaves he believed would rise in rebellion once he and his men triggered the revolt. He revealed his plans to black ministers and to the so-called "Secret Six," leading white abolitionists who helped fund his attack on slavery where it lived. He tried to win the support of Frederick Douglass, who while sympathetic thought

The campaign launched by John Brown and twenty-one black and white allies in 1859 failed in its immediate aims of unleashing a rebellion of the enslaved but succeeded in heightening the moral and political debate over slavery.

the plan doomed logistically. But Brown pressed on. One of his lieutenants moved to Harpers Ferry and even established a family there, preparing the way for the attack. In the meantime, Brown continued the fight against slavery in the West, freeing eleven slaves in Missouri, killing their master and leading them into Canada. Such exploits, though illegal, only heightened Brown's visibility and appeal in New England, where he was welcomed by leading industrialists and politicians.

The assault on Harpers Ferry started in earnest in the summer of 1859, when Brown rented a farm seven miles away and assembled his men and munitions. To his disappointment, he could recruit only twenty-one men, five of them African Americans. Brown's sons accounted for three of the number, while runaway slaves, free blacks, abolitionist editors, and college students made up the rest. Most of them were quite young, in their twenties.

The raid began easily enough on Sunday, October 16, as Brown's men quickly seized the arsenal and a rifle-manufacturing plant. Rather than merely taking the weapons and freeing local slaves, however, Brown and his men occupied the small armory building and waited for word to spread among the slaves of Virginia that their day of liberation had come. The word spread instead among local whites, who quickly surrounded the armory and Brown's men, killing or capturing eight of them. Militia from Virginia and Maryland arrived the next day, followed soon after by federal troops under the command of Robert E. Lee and J. E. B. Stuart. The troops rushed the armory, easily overwhelming Brown's men. Ten of the abolitionist forces were killed, five (including Brown) wounded, and seven escaped to Canada or the North. Brown was tried within two weeks and found guilty. He was sentenced to be hanged exactly a month later, on December 2.

The entire episode, from the raid to Brown's execution, took only about six weeks in late 1859 to unfold. Yet those six weeks saw opinion in both the North and the South change rapidly. Contradictory reports and rumors eventually settled into an accepted narrative of events. Public opinion in the North and South, mixed at first, crystallized into sharply opposing viewpoints. Even those Northerners who were appalled at the violence were also appalled at the speed with which Brown was tried and condemned. Even those Southerners who read with reassurance early denunciations of Brown in the North were appalled when they realized that many Northerners refused to condemn the raid and even applauded it.

The rhetoric surrounding John Brown showed none of the careful phrasing and hedging that had marked the Lincoln-Douglas debates, none of the calculation about votes that might be won or lost. Rather, the rhetoric seemed almost cathartic, as both Northerners and Southerners said the worst they could imagine about the other. The many people of moderate sympathies on both sides watched, appalled, as common ground eroded beneath their feet, as whatever goodwill that had survived Bleeding Kansas, the Fugitive Slave Law, and *Uncle Tom's Cabin* disappeared.

Brown had not set out to become a martyr. He fully expected to unleash a massive slave rebellion, bringing the end of American slavery. While his precise plans remain obscure, maps in his possession marked places where slaves outnumbered their masters and might overwhelm them with force. Brown wanted to play the role of Moses, leading the oppressed and chosen out of captivity. Once captured, however, Brown seemed to fit another role, that of Christ, selflessly dying for the salvation of others. No longer the Old Testament figure of blood and vengeance, Brown now appeared to many in the North as a New Testament figure of suffering and dignified sacrifice. The metaphorical struggle did not end with that resolution. Many Northerners came to believe that John Brown's body could be redeemed only with a return to the stern violence he had championed. Even pacifist abolitionists began to think that the time for a more direct attack on slavery had come.

THE FIRST SECESSION

Everyone knew the election of 1860 held enormous meaning for the United States, but no one could be sure what that meaning might be. Would this be the election that brought everyone to their senses so that the conflict between North and South could be resolved? Would the border states be able to control the election, putting men of moderation in the White House? Would northern voters suddenly realize the South meant what it said and pull back? The actual events proved far more threatening than most Americans had believed possible.

The Election of 1860

White Southerners automatically linked John Brown with the Republican party, though leading Republicans explicitly denied any connection and even denounced Brown. The Republicans, hoping to win support from the nonslaveholders in the South, arranged for the distribution of Hinton Helper's *Impending Crisis of the South*. The book had little effect in the South, however, and the Republicans realized that they would be a purely northern party. Not only had any southern base of support disappeared, but Harpers Ferry had made the Republicans far more attractive in the North than before.

The Democrats, more determined than the Republicans to remain a national party, also felt the effects of Brown's raid. Meeting in Charleston in April 1860 to

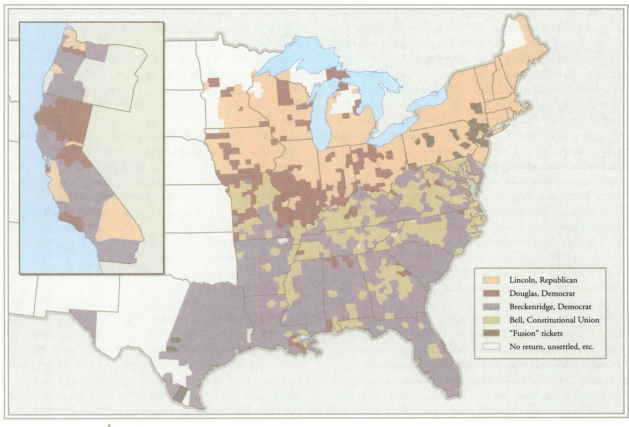

MAP 13.2 | THE ELECTION OF 1860

decide on their presidential nominee for the fall election, the northern Democrats attempted to carry out the strategy everyone expected: nominating Stephen Douglas and popular sovereignty. The northern Democrats saw this as a compromise with the South. But southern Democrats, outraged at the northern response to Dred Scott, Kansas, and John Brown, demanded that the party explicitly support the rights of slaveholders to take their slaves into the territories. Northern Democrats, already besieged by the Republicans in the North, could not afford to make that concession and still have a chance to win back home. The Southerners proved heedless of this plea, however, and walked out of the convention. Several weeks later, the Northerners met in Baltimore and nominated Douglas. The Southerners, meeting in Charleston, nominated John C. Breckinridge of Kentucky.

Before the two Democratic conventions met again in June, Unionists in both the North and the South tried to avert catastrophe by nominating a compromise candidate, a candidate who would strictly follow the Constitution as it was interpreted by the Supreme Court. Calling themselves the Constitutional Union party, they settled on John Bell of Tennessee. Many of these Unionists were former Whigs who no longer had a political home. They counted on the other candidates to create a deadlock that would have to be settled in the House of Representatives. There, the Unionists hoped, cooler heads would prevail and legislators would gratefully turn to their compromise candidate.

As the Democrats tore themselves apart, the Republicans met in Chicago. There, in efforts to put southern concerns at rest, the Republicans denounced the John Brown attack on Harpers Ferry and announced their belief in the right of each state to decide for itself whether it would have slavery. The Republicans cemented their appeal to voters unconcerned with the slavery issue by calling for protective tariffs, internal improvements, and free homesteads for anyone—even those who were not yet citizens—who would settle the West. The Republicans were much stronger than they had been only four years earlier in their first presidential campaign. Party strategists calculated that they need only win Pennsylvania and one other state they had lost to the Democrats in 1856 to wrap up the election. The states they needed to take were Illinois, Indiana, or New Jersey—all of them on the border with the South and all of them far more moderate on the slavery question than states farther north. Thus, the Republicans, after tumultuous struggle among various factions, turned to a moderate who had recently come to the nation's attention and who was a favorite son of one of the crucial states: Abraham Lincoln of Illinois.

A certain air of unreality surrounded the election of 1860. People did not know that the way that they voted would bring on a civil war, or even secession. While Stephen Douglas constantly warned of such a danger, both Breckinridge and Lincoln downplayed any such dire consequence, insisting, and believing, that the other side was bluffing. Ironically, all the years of conflict, all the series of crises and near-crises, had persuaded both the North and the South that the other talked tougher than it would act. The parties, especially the Republicans, staged loud and raucous political events that proved long on emotion and short on clearly defined positions. Lincoln said nothing and stayed close to home while his party leaders displayed split fence rails and touted his honesty.

Northerners and Southerners were willing to believe the worst of each other because the election of 1860 was actually two separate elections, one in the North and one in the South. Lincoln made no attempt to explain himself to the South; Breckinridge made little attempt in the North. They never met face to face, either in cooperation or in debate. Bell spoke mainly to the already converted. Douglas, speaking from New England to Alabama and everywhere in between, tried to warn people what could happen if they voted along sectional lines, but few were willing to believe their opponents would have the nerve to act on their threats.

On election day, November 6, Lincoln won in every northern state except New Jersey, which divided between Douglas and Lincoln. Douglas won outright only in Missouri, and that barely. Breckinridge won all the South except the border states of Virginia, Ten-

nessee, and Kentucky, which went with Bell. Even at this late stage of sectional division voters did not fit into easy categories. It was hardly a contest between a rural South and an industrial urban North, for northern cities tended to vote for compromise candidates, not for Lincoln. Similarly, over half of Southerners voted for Bell or Douglas, supporting the Union over the South.

Once the election returns were in, though, these complications and reservations seemed to evaporate. Even though Lincoln won only in the North, the election was not even close in the electoral college, where electors representing each state cast ballots for only two candidates and thus concentrated their votes, and where the North's greater population gave him an advantage. Lincoln won 180 electoral votes to Breckinridge's 72, Bell's 39, and Douglas's 12. In southern eyes, the North had arrogantly placed its own interests above those of the Union, insisting on electing a man who made no effort to win a single vote in the South. In northern eyes, the South was to blame, walking out of nominating conventions and talking of disunion. The election of 1860 completed what John Brown's raid had started: the estrangement of North and South. Of all the candidates, only one received electoral votes from both a northern and southern state. And Stephen Douglas, the recipient of those few votes, soon died.

The Quest for Southern Independence

Some white men in the South had talked for years about what they would do if an avowed enemy of slavery became president. These fire-eaters declared Abraham Lincoln's 1860 victory a sign that the North valued neither the Union nor the Constitution on which it was based. The South, they said, had every right, every incentive, to leave the Union. Although the Republicans claimed to work within the political system, Southerners charged, Lincoln's supporters had violated an honored tradition of compromise necessary for the country's survival.

Even though the Democrats still controlled Congress and the Supreme Court, Southerners believed that Lincoln would use the patronage of the federal government to install Republican judges, customs collectors, federal marshals, and postmasters throughout the South. Such officials could undermine slavery from within, Southerners worried, eroding the author-

As "Dred Scott" fiddles, the
four candidates of 1860
dance to the tune of slavery.
While Lincoln is
accompanied by a black
woman, Breckenridge, in the
upper left, dances with the
devil in the form of
secessionist William L.
Yancey, Stephen Douglas
cavorts with an Irishman in
the lower left corner, and
John Bell solemnly steps with
an American Indian—all
references to supposed
liabilities each candidate
carried with him.

ity of slaveowners and permitting abolitionist literature to circulate. For years, Lincoln had talked of "a
house" that had to be unified, of a nation that had to
be all one thing or all another, all slave or all free.
Would he not act to undermine slavery now that he
was in power?

The nation's eyes turned to South Carolina. Influential men there, after all, had talked of secession since
the nullification crisis nearly thirty years earlier. The
same states that had created the Union, they believed
in 1861 as they had believed before, could also dissolve that Union when it no longer served their purposes. South Carolinians remembered that they had
lost the nullification struggle, however, and did not
want to act alone again. Therefore, the South Carolina
legislature met on the day after Lincoln's election but
did not secede immediately. Its members called for an
election two months later to select delegates who
would then decide the course the state should follow.
In the meantime, they hoped, support for secession
would grow and other southern states would join
South Carolina in leaving the Union. One South Carolina lawmaker, scoffing at the idea that the North
would offer military resistance, laughingly offered to
drink all the blood shed over secession.

States of the Deep South quickly lined up behind
South Carolina, as secession rallies erupted across the
region. Carolina leaders, heartened by the response, seceded earlier than they had planned, on December 20.
By February 1, Mississippi, Florida, Alabama, Georgia,
Louisiana, and Texas had joined the secession movement. On February 9, delegates from these states met
in Montgomery, Alabama, and created a provisional
constitution, similar to that of the United States except in its explicit guarantee of slavery and states'
rights. On February 18, the convention inaugurated a
provisional president, Jefferson Davis of Mississippi,
and vice president, Alexander H. Stephens of Georgia.
Davis, long a national figure, was a moderate, a strong
states' rights advocate but not a fervent secessionist.
The states of the new Confederacy portrayed themselves as a calm and conservative people, not wild-eyed
revolutionaries.

Though the South appeared united against the
North, it was not. The advocates of secession knew
they had to strike while Lincoln remained more image
than substance. Two bad things could happen if they
waited to see what the new president did once in office. He might either attack the South by force or he
might prove to be as moderate as he claimed to be. In

On December 20, 1860, South Carolina declared its connection to the Union dissolved. Within six weeks, six other southern states joined in the dissolution.

Jefferson Davis, of Mississippi, a former U.S. Senator and Secretary of War, became the first—and only—president of the Confederate States of America in 1861.

the latter case, secessionists feared, white Southerners would let the moment pass, giving the North time to build its strength and the Republicans time to tighten their hold on the nation.

Divisions over Secession

Many thousands of white Southerners, some of them quite powerful and influential, resisted secession.

Some argued that secession was treason. Others warned that the South was committing suicide. Others argued that slavery would be far safer within the Union than in a fragile new country bordered by an antagonistic United States. Other opponents of immediate secession argued that the southern states should wait until they could cooperate with one another more formally and fully. By presenting a united front to the North, these "cooperationists" insisted, the South would not need to secede at all. The North, recognizing that the South really was not bluffing, would grant concessions protecting slavery forever.

The arguments against immediate secession appealed to a large portion of Southerners. Even in the southern states that rushed to secede in January of 1861, almost half of all votes went to delegates who had not supported immediate secession. The opposition to secession proved stronger still in the upper

South, in Virginia, North Carolina, Tennessee, Kentucky, and Maryland. Under the name of Douglas Democrats, Constitutional Unionists, or simply the Opposition, men of moderate impulse in the upper South mobilized to resist immediate secession. These upper-South moderates warned that their states would bear the brunt of any conflict between the lower South and the North, whatever form that conflict might take. And voters listened: more than a month after the first seven states seceded, secession lost in Virginia by a two-to-one margin. The secessionists were stymied, too, in Tennessee, North Carolina, and Arkansas. The leaders of these border states believed they could bargain between the Gulf Confederacy and the North, winning the concessions the South wanted while maintaining the Union.

Northerners, too, remained quite divided at the beginning of 1861. Many recent immigrants from Ireland and Germany viewed the conflict between the North and the South as none of their business. Northern Democrats loathed Lincoln and feared his policies. They called for conciliation with the South, for a quieting of the rhetoric. Many black Northerners urged caution, warning that a war for Union alone did not deserve black support. A war to end bondage would be worth fighting, such African-American spokesmen argued, but in 1861 only the most aggressive white abolitionists, few in number, spoke of such a cause.

People had plenty of opportunity to air their opinions, for events did not move quickly after Lincoln's election. After the first flush of secessionist victory at the beginning of 1861, people throughout the nation watched and waited to see what would happen when the new president officially assumed office on March 4. In the meantime, no one appeared to be in charge. James Buchanan, as lame-duck president, could not do much, and neither could the lame-duck Congress. Lincoln, for his part, remained at home in Illinois, saying little.

Most Republicans, including Lincoln, viewed the rhetoric and even the votes for southern secession as negotiating strategies rather than actual steps toward dissolving the Union. The Republicans showed no inclination to bargain with the South over what remained the key question: federal support for slavery in the territories. The tensions that had built up in the 1850s, Lincoln thought, could no longer be avoided. There had to be some sort of conflict and resolution before the nation could move forward. "The tug has to come," he argued, "and better now, than any time hereafter." If the North postponed action, Lincoln and other Republicans thought, the South would step up its efforts to gain new slave territories in the Caribbean and Central America, dragging the United States into war and perpetuating human bondage far into the future. Like the secessionists, Lincoln did not think the "tug" between North and South would require bloodshed.

The Situation in Charleston

While Americans fixed their attention on political leaders in the winter of 1861, the center of the conflict gradually shifted to two obscure forts in the harbor of Charleston, South Carolina. A Kentucky-born U.S. army officer, Major Robert Anderson, worried that secessionists would attack his small federal force at Fort Moultrie in Charleston and force him either to surrender or to fire on American citizens. Determined to avoid a war, on December 26 Anderson moved his small garrison from Fort Moultrie to Fort Sumter, a facility still under construction but occupying a safer position in the center of the Charleston harbor. Anderson hoped that his strategic retreat would prevent an attack on the federal fort. When South Carolina guns drove away a ship President Buchanan had sent with supplies for Anderson and his men, Buchanan chose not to force the issue; like the rest of the nation, he would wait for Lincoln's inaugural. Meanwhile, South Carolina troops strengthened their position around the Charleston harbor. Anderson's food reserves began to run dangerously low.

Men from both the North and the South worked frantically, but fruitlessly, to find a compromise during these weeks. Some urged the passage of a new constitutional amendment that would permit slavery forever; some urged the purchase of Cuba to permit slavery to expand; some urged that war be declared against another country to pull the United States together again. All the compromises were designed to placate the South, to draw it back into the Union with guarantees of its safety. Abolitionists viewed such maneuvering with disgust and told their countrymen to let the South go, purifying the country and hastening the end of slavery in the process. "If the Union can only be maintained by new concessions to the slaveholders," Frederick Douglass argued, "if it can only be stuck together and held together by a new drain on the negro's blood, then . . . let the Union perish."

Such views were not popular. Mobs blamed the abolitionists for the South's secession and attacked antislavery advocates throughout the North.

On February 11, Abraham Lincoln began a long and circuitous railway trip from Illinois to Washington, pausing frequently along the way to speak to well-wishers. At first, he played down the threat of secession—"Let it alone," he counseled, "and it will go down of itself." But as the train rolled on and the Confederate convention in Montgomery completed its provisional government, Lincoln became more wary. Warned of attempts on his life, Lincoln slipped into Washington under cover of darkness.

Lincoln Assumes Office

Lincoln assembled his government under the growing shadow of war. He sought to balance his cabinet with men of various temperaments, backgrounds, and strategies. The two most formidable cabinet members were Secretary of State William H. Seward, a moderate Republican who still dreamed of compromise, and Secretary of the Treasury Salmon P. Chase, a radical Republican inclined to take a harder line with the South. Fort Sumter stood as the most pressing issue facing the new administration. Any show of force to reclaim the fort from South Carolina, southern Unionists warned, and the secessionists would sweep border states such as Virginia into the Confederacy.

Lincoln, with Seward's advice, toned down the speech he delivered at his inauguration in March. As sharpshooters stood on nearby rooftops to watch for assassins, Lincoln told the South that he had no intention of disturbing slavery where it was already established, that he would not invade the region, that there would be no shedding of blood, that he would not attempt to fill offices with men repugnant to local sensibilities. But he also warned that secession was illegal, "the essence of anarchy." It was his duty to maintain the integrity of the federal government, and to do so he had to "hold, occupy, and possess" federal property in the states of the Confederacy, including Fort Sumter. Lincoln pleaded with his countrymen to move slowly, to take their time, to let passions cool. "We must not be enemies. Though passion may have strained it, it must not break our bonds of affection."

People heard in Lincoln's inaugural what they chose to hear. Republicans and Unionists in the South thought it a potent mixture of firmness and generosity.

Lincoln took over the presidency at a time when the sectional conflict had reached a crisis; he had little time or room in which to maneuver as the federal soldiers in Fort Sumter ran out of food and had to be abandoned or supplied.

Skeptics in the North, South, and Europe, on the other hand, focused on the threat of coercion at Fort Sumter. If Lincoln attempted to use force of any kind, they warned, war would be the inevitable result. Lincoln did not plan on war; he was trying to buy time, hoping that southern Unionists could gather their strength and that compromisers in Washington would come up with a workable strategy.

The Crisis at Fort Sumter

But there was less time than Lincoln realized. On the very day after Lincoln's speech, Major Anderson reported to Washington that he would be out of food within four to six weeks and that it would take at least 20,000 troops to resupply the fort. After weeks of lis-

South Carolina troops fire cannon at the federal forces under the command of Captain Robert Anderson. Although no one was killed in the assault, the shots opened the Civil War.

tening to various counsellors, Lincoln finally decided that he had to act: he would send provisions but not military supplies to Fort Sumter. By doing so, Lincoln would maintain the balance he promised in his inaugural speech, keeping the fort but not using coercion unless attacked first.

The president recognized that this distinction would not matter to the Confederacy. Jefferson Davis and his government, goaded by impatient editors and would-be soldiers, had decided a week earlier that any attempt to reprovision the fort would be in and of itself an act of war, a violation of the territorial integrity of the Confederacy. Davis recognized that no foreign power would respect a country, especially one as new and tenuous as the Confederate States of America, if it allowed one of its major ports to be occupied by an-

other country. The Union's resupply of the fort would mean they still controlled it.

The Confederate government decided that their commander in Charleston, P.G.T. Beauregard, should attack Fort Sumter before the relief expedition had a chance to arrive. On April 12, at 4:30 in the morning, Beauregard (a former student of Major Anderson's at West Point) opened fire on the Union garrison. The shelling continued for thirty-three hours. Anderson held out for as long as he could, but when fire tore through the barracks and his ammunition ran low he decided the time for surrender had come. Although no one on either side died in the battle, Northerners, even those who had little faith in their new president or his policies, agreed that the events in South Carolina could not go unanswered. Southerners, even those who resented South Carolina for precipitating the war, agreed that they would have no choice but to come to that state's aid if the North raised a hand against their fellow Southerners.

⁓ C O N C L U S I O N ⁓

It was no accident that the slave states and free states experienced mounting animosity and distrust in the late 1850s. The rapid expansion of both the North and the South led people to focus their eyes on the West; the struggles in Kansas, Washington, Illinois, and state capitals would determine the character of the American nation. The struggles carried great symbolic weight, testifying to the worth of the northern and southern people, to their justice and courage.

Watching the events of those years unfold, however, it is clear that the conflict could most certainly have taken other forms. Had Kansas been handled more adroitly by Buchanan and the Democrats, had Preston Brooks not caned Charles Sumner, had Chief Justice Taney not issued the *Dred Scott* decision, and had John Brown not given violence a martyr's sanction, the election of 1860 would not have become the watershed it did. This cascade of events washed the United States toward dissolution. Another cascade of events would soon push it into war.

RECOMMENDED READINGS

Crofts, Daniel W. *Old Southampton: Politics and Society in a Virginia County, 1834–1869* (1992) provides a wonderfully detailed account of the way politics worked in communities.

Fehrenbacher, Don E. *The Dred Scott Case: Its Significance in American Law and Politics* (1978) is the classic account of this complicated episode.

Finkelman, Paul, ed., *His Soul Goes Marching On: Responses to John Brown and the Harpers Ferry Raid* (1995) contains fascinating articles about this much-interpreted event.

Foner, Eric. *Free Soil, Free Labor, Free Men: The Ideology of the Republican Party Before the Civil War* (1970) masterfully demonstrates the power of free labor ideology.

Holt, Michael F. *The Political Crisis of the 1850s* (1978) stresses the dynamics of the two-party system in bringing on the Civil War.

Morrison, Michael A. *Slavery and the American West: The Eclipse of Manifest Destiny and the Coming of the Civil War* (1997) is a subtle and up-to-date survey of this critical topic.

Stampp, Kenneth. *America in 1857: A Nation on the Brink* (1990) shows the advantages of examining the simultaneous processes and events of this period.

Wyatt-Brown, Bertram. *Southern Honor: Ethics and Behavior in the Old South* (1982) is a bold and powerful interpretation of white southern culture.

Zarefsky, David. *Lincoln, Douglas, and Slavery: In the Crucible of Public Debate* (1990) recasts our understanding of these famous political debates.

Political Crisis

Cooper, William J. Jr., *The South and the Politics of Slavery, 1828–1856* (1978).

Dykstra, Robert R. *Bright Radical Star: Black Freedom and White Supremacy on the Hawkeye Frontier* (1993).

Fehrenbacher, Don E. *Prelude to Greatness: Lincoln in the 1850s* (1962).

Finkleman, Paul, *An Imperfect Union: Slavery, Federalism, and Comity* (1981).

Forgie, George B. *Patricide in the House Divided: A Psychological Interpretation of Lincoln and His Age* (1979).

Kelly, Robert. *The Cultural Pattern in American Politics: The First Century* (1979).

Knupfer, Peter. *The Union As It Is: Constitutional Unionism and Sectional Compromise* (1991).

Levine, Bruce. *Half Slave and Half Free: The Roots of Civil War* (1992).

Oates, Stephen B. *To Purge This Land with Blood: A Biography of John Brown* (1970).

Rawley, James A. *Race and Politics: Bleeding Kansas and the Coming of the Civil War* (1969).

Gupta, Gunja Sen. *For God and Mammon: Evangelicals and Entrepreneurs, Masters and Slaves in Territorial Kansas, 1854–1860* (1996).

Sewell, Richard. *A House Divided: Sectionalism and the Civil War, 1848–1865* (1988).

Smith, Elbert B. *The Presidency of James Buchanan* (1975).

Stampp, Kenneth. *The Imperiled Union* (1980).

Summers, Mark W. *The Plundering Generation: Corruption and the Crisis of the Union, 1849–1861* (1987).

Von Frank, Andrew. *The Trials of Anthony Burns: Freedom and Slavery in Emerson's Boston* (1998).

Walther, Eric H. *The Fire-Eaters* (1992).

The White South

Ayers, Edward L. *Vengeance and Justice: Crime and Punishment in the Nineteenth-Century American South* (1984).

Burton, Orville Vernon. *In My Father's House Are Many Mansions: Family and Community in Edgefield, South Carolina* (1985).

Ford, Lacy K. Jr., *Origins of Southern Radicalism: The South Carolina Upcountry, 1800–1860* (1988).

Harris, J. William. *Plain Folk and Gentry in a Slave Society: White Liberty and Black Slavery in Augusta's Hinterlands* (1985).

Huston, James L. *The Panic of 1857 and the Coming of the Civil War* (1987).

Inscoe, John C. *Mountain Masters: Slavery and the Sectional Crisis in Western North Carolina* (1989).

Jaffa, Harry. *Crisis of the House Divided: An Interpretation of the Issues in the Lincoln-Douglas Debates* (1959).

McCardell, John. *The Idea of a Southern Nation: Southern Nationalists and Southern Nationalism, 1830–1860* (1979).

Owsley, Frank L. *Plain Folk of the Old South* (1949).

Takaki, Ronald T. *A Pro-Slavery Crusade: The Agitation to Reopen the African Slave Trade* (1971).

Wright, Gavin. *The Political Economy of the Cotton South: Households, Markets, and Wealth* (1978).

ROBERT E. LEE

Lee rejected Lincoln's offer of command of the Union armies before he resigned his U.S. commission
and swore allegiance to the Confederacy, dramatizing the divided loyalties of many Americans at the beginning of the war.

Chapter 14

DESCENT INTO WAR,
1861–1862

At the beginning of 1861, Americans could not imagine anything like the war that soon consumed their nation. Events piled on one another in ways that few would have wished and that no one could have predicted. The men who voted for Lincoln did not think the South would secede, the architects of secession did not think the North would resist, and neither side thought the other would or could fight for long. Events proved no more predictable once the war began. Last-minute reinforcements and retreats changed the outcome of battles; news from the battlefield shaped every political and diplomatic decision. Circumstance and timing shaped everything.

WAR BEGINS: APRIL 1861 TO JULY 1861

Neither the Union nor the Confederacy was ready for conflict in the spring of 1861. A number of states had yet to declare their loyalties and other states, communities, and families found themselves divided against themselves. In a matter of months, both the North and the South had to prepare for war and throw themselves into the first battle.

Lincoln Calls for Troops

Two days after the Confederate flag went up over Fort Sumter on April 15, President Lincoln declared South Carolina in rebellion against the United States and called for 75,000 militiamen from states north and south to help put the rebellion down. Lincoln could have called up far more troops, for men clamored to serve throughout the North. But the president sought to appear restrained in his response. He still hoped that Unionists in southern states besides South Carolina would rally to the nation's defense if he showed that he was no extremist. Lincoln also acted cautiously because he had not received the approval of Congress, which would not convene until July.

Lincoln's attempt to blend firmness and conciliation failed. Southern states saw the call to the militia as an act of aggression against South Carolina and state sovereignty. The upper South states replied with defiance to Lincoln's requests for their militia. "Tennessee will furnish not a single man for the purpose of coercion," its governor responded, "but fifty thousand if necessary for the defense of our rights and those of our Southern brothers." Virginia seceded two days later. Although many people in Virginia, especially in the mountainous western counties, still clung to hopes of avoiding war, two delegates to every one voted for

CHRONOLOGY

1861

April	15	Lincoln calls for 75,000 militia
	17–20	Arkansas, Tennessee, Virginia, and North Carolina secede
May	29	Richmond becomes capital of Confederacy
July	21	Confederate victory at Bull Run (Manassas)
	25	Frémont takes command in the West
	27	McClellan takes command of Union forces near Washington
August	30	Frémont declares martial law, and frees slaves, in Missouri
September	6	Kentucky remains in the Union
November	1	McClellan assumes command of all Union armies
	6	Jefferson Davis elected president of Confederacy with six-year term
	7	Union capture of Port Royal, South Carolina
	8	Union navy seizes Confederate commisioners Mason and Slidell from British ship *Trent*
	19	Halleck replaces Frémont as Union commander in West
December	26	Union government releases Mason and Slidell
	30	suspension of specie payments

1862

February	6	Union captures Fort Henry on Tennessee River
	16	Confederates surrender Fort Donelson to Grant
	22	Inauguration of Jefferson Davis
	25	Legal Tender Act in North authorizes "greenbacks"
		Confederates evacuate Nashville
	27	Confederate Congress authorizes martial law and suspends habeas corpus
March	8–9	*Virginia* v. *Monitor* in Hampton Roads, Virginia

secession on April 17. These Virginians, like white Southerners of all inclinations and temperaments, refused to permit northern troops to march through their states to defeat South Carolina. Southerners considered this an invasion by an arrogant central government, the very sort of coercion that had triggered the American Revolution. Recognizing the importance of Virginia's addition to their ranks, the Confederacy immediately voted to move their capital to Richmond in May of 1861.

The States Divide

Arkansas, Tennessee, and North Carolina, despite the continuing vitality of the Unionist cause in all three states, quickly followed Virginia's example. The Okla-homa Territory, too, aligned itself with the Confederacy. There, leaders of the Five Civilized Tribes, slaveholders themselves, used the opportunity to fight against the U.S. government that had dispossessed them from their homes three decades earlier. The leaders of other Indian nations sided with the Union, however, and began to fight for control of the Indian Territory. The Pamunkey of Virginia and the Lumbee of North Carolina aided the Union behind Confederate lines, while the Eastern Cherokee and Catawba fought hard for the Confederates among whom they lived.

State leaders elsewhere frantically struggled with one another. In Maryland, rioters attacked Massachusetts troops as they marched through Baltimore two days after the secession of neighboring Virginia—spilling the first blood of the war when twelve civil-

CHRONOLOGY

	17	McClellan begins move to James River Peninsula
April	5	McClellan begins siege of Yorktown
	6–7	Grant wins dramatic victory at Shiloh
	16	Confederacy passes Conscription Act
	25	New Orleans surrenders to Admiral Farragut
May	8–9	Jackson's Shenandoah Valley Campaign
	20	Homestead Act passed by Union Congress
	31	Lee takes command of Army of Northern Virginia
June	6	Confederates evacuate Memphis
	26	Lee drives McClellan from Richmond in Seven Days' Battles
July	11	Halleck appointed general-in-chief of Union armies
	12	Border states reject Lincoln plan for gradual emancipation
	17	Second Confiscation Act
	22	Cabinet hears Lincoln's draft of emancipation proclamation
August	3	Union decides to evacuate McClellan's troops from peninsula
	29–30	Confederate victory at Second Bull Run (Manassas)
September	4–6	Lee invades Maryland
	17	Battle of Antietam (Sharpsburg)
	22	First Emancipation Proclamation
October	3–4	Union victory at Corinth
November	7	Burnside replaces McClellan as commander of Army of the Potomac
		Republicans lose widely in mid-term elections in North
December	13	Lee overwhelms Burnside at Fredericksburg
	16–20	Crisis in Lincoln's cabinet
	27–29	Sherman defeated near Vicksburg

ians and four Union soldiers died in the gunfire. Maryland bitterly divided along lines of geography and sentiment, the southern portion of the state sympathizing with the Confederacy, Baltimore and the western portion generally supporting the Union. Should the United States lose Maryland, the District of Columbia would be completely surrounded by Confederate territory. Accordingly, Lincoln acted quickly to keep Maryland in line, jailing secession advocates before they could persuade others and suspending the writ of habeas corpus so those leaders could not be released.

Kentucky, after months of determined attempts to remain neutral, narrowly decided for the Union in September. Missouri, after chaotic bloodshed reminiscent of the events in Kansas seven years earlier, officially remained in the Union but was ravaged from within for the next four years. Dissension took different form in the mountains of western Virginia. In June, delegates from fifty counties met in Wheeling to renounce the Virginia secession convention, begin the gradual abolition of slavery, and declare their loyalty to the Union. After a complicated series of conventions and elections, the state of West Virginia came into being in 1862 and joined the Union the following year. As in Maryland and Kentucky, the presence of Union troops in western Virginia provided protection against Confederate forces and sympathizers.

As it turned out, the Union and the Confederacy divided about as evenly as possible. Virginia, Tennessee, North Carolina, and Arkansas, all of which went into the Confederacy, might well have decided to remain with the Union; had they done so, the Confederacy would have had little hope of sustaining a

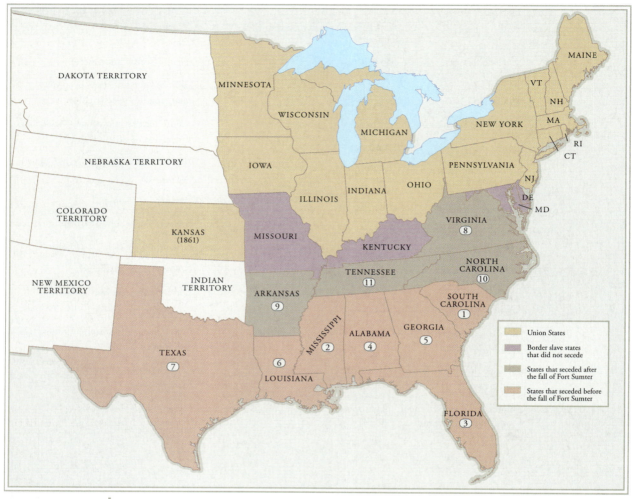

MAP 14.1 | THE COURSE OF SECESSION

successful war against the North. Those states, the three most populous in the South among them, accounted for half of all manufacturing and half of all food production in the Confederacy. Maryland, Kentucky, and Missouri, on the other hand, might well have joined the Confederacy; had they done so, the Union cause would have been weakened, perhaps fatally. Kentucky and Missouri, possessing white populations and economic resources larger than those of any Confederate state except Virginia, occupied crucial positions along the major rivers that led into the South. Even the dissidents balanced out. About 100,000 men

from these border states that went with the Union ended up fighting for the Confederacy. About 90,000 men—half of them white, the other half black—of the border states that went with the Confederacy ended up fighting for the Union.

Although Abraham Lincoln was criticized from every angle in these months—for acting too arrogantly and for acting indecisively, for taking too much power into his hands and for not taking enough—he managed to bring into the Union fold the states he had to win. Had he lost these struggles, he might well have failed in all the other struggles that awaited him.

The Numbers

Looking back, knowing that the war dragged on for four years, the cards seem heavily stacked in the North's favor. The Union, after all, had vastly greater industrial capacity, railroads, canals, food, draft animals, ships, and entrepreneurial talent, all the things a mid-nineteenth-century war required. The Union could also claim four times as many white residents as the South—22 million versus 5.5 million. And while the 3.5 million enslaved people who lived in the Confederacy were extraordinarily valuable to the South, everyone recognized that the slaves could become equally valuable allies for the North under the exigencies of war.

Since the South acknowledged the North's advantages, many people then and since assumed that the Confederates must have been driven either by irrational rage or heedless bravery. Neither the Confederates nor the North, however, expected the secession crisis to turn into a full-fledged war, much less a four-year war of attrition and endurance. When Lincoln called for the 75,000 militia he called them for only ninety days' service. When southern boys and men rushed to enlist for the Confederacy in the spring of 1861, they assumed they would be back home in time to harvest their crops in the autumn.

Southerners considered themselves natural soldiers, comfortable on horseback and with a rifle, caricaturing their new enemies as clerks and factory workers. Though the Union did have more city men and immigrants than the South, most Northerners, like Southerners, were young men raised on farms. Since both sides believed that the other was bluffing and that their opponents were weak and divided, Northerners and Southerners thought the conflict would likely come to a swift, and peaceful, resolution. In such a struggle, sheer numbers did not seem nearly as important as they eventually became.

The Strategies

The military strategies of both sides sought to minimize actual fighting. The South saw itself as purely on the defensive; it would wait for northern armies to invade and then defeat them with the determination of people defending their own homes and farms. The North, for its part, counted on what became known as the "Anaconda Plan," named after the snake of that name that slowly squeezes its prey to death. That plan depended on sending an overpowering force down the Mississippi River, both by water and by land, dividing the South in two. At the same time, the Union navy would seal off the South from outside supplies. The goal, general-in-chief Winfield Scott said, was to "envelop the insurgent states and bring them to terms with less bloodshed than any other plan." Ground troops and land battles would be kept to a minimum.

The Confederacy, from the perspective both of its own strategy and that of the North, possessed considerable military advantages. It occupied an enormous area, larger than today's United Kingdom, France, Italy, and Spain combined. It possessed dozens of harbors and ports, connected by an excellent system of rivers and an adequate network of railroads. The Confederacy's long border with Mexico made it difficult to seal off outside supplies. The Confederacy could wage a defensive war, drawing on its own resources, fighting on its own land, moving its troops internally from one point to another while the Union had to move around the perimeter. The many country roads of the South, known only to locals, would provide routes for Confederate surprise attacks or strategic retreats. Every white Southerner could be a spy or an ally when a fellow Confederate needed food or medical aid.

For a model of how such a defensive plan might work, Southerners looked to the American Revolution, when the thirteen colonies absorbed everything the powerful British army and navy could throw at them. Like the American colonies eighty years earlier, the Confederates did not have to win every battle nor conquer northern territory. Southerners thought they had only to keep fighting long enough for the North to lose heart, for the North's political, economic, regional, and ethnic divisions to overwhelm its temporary unity. Indeed, the Confederacy enjoyed advantages the American colonies had not enjoyed. The new southern nation covered twice as much territory as the colonies and the North possessed nowhere near the military power of the British at the time of the Revolutionary War.

Leadership

There was also the matter of leadership. In 1861, many observers would have given the advantage to the Confederates in this regard. Abraham Lincoln, after all, had held public office for only two years before he assumed

Lincoln's Cabinet: seated from the left, Secretary of State William H. Seward; Secretary of the Treasury Salmon P. Chase; Secretary of War Edwin M. Stanton; Postmaster General Montgomery Blair; Secretary of the Navy Gideon Welles. Lincoln is seated at the head of the table.

the presidency, and his only military service had been a brief battle against Indians. Jefferson Davis, by contrast, had graduated from West Point and distinguished himself in the war with Mexico. He had been secretary of war under Franklin Pierce and had served in the United States Senate. Davis, unlike Lincoln, directed his forces' military strategy with the confidence born of firsthand knowledge and experience.

At the beginning of the war, too, it appeared that the South had the better generals. The southern generals certainly had more experience: the average age of the Union generals in 1861 was thirty-eight; of Confederate generals, forty-seven. At the outbreak of hostilities, Lincoln actually offered Robert E. Lee of Virginia command of the Union army. Lee had graduated second in his class at West Point in 1829 and had served as an engineer, an officer in the Mexican War in the 1840s, and superintendent of West Point in the late 1850s. He had opposed secession. But Lee was descended from a long line of distinguished Virginians and had married into another prominent Virginia family. He declined the Union generalship and then resigned his U.S. military commission altogether;

within a week he had accepted command of Virginia's forces. Lee made the same tortured decision so many Southerners made when secession finally came: "With all my devotion to the Union and the feeling and loyalty of an American citizen, I have not been able to make up my mind to raise my hand against my relatives, my children, my home."

After Lee rejected overall command of the Union troops, Lincoln decided to forego a single commander for the time being. The Confederacy, with Jefferson Davis in the presidency, also felt no need for a commanding general. Many lesser generals still had to be named quickly, however: 126 by the Union and 89 by the Confederacy. Military experience and ability did not always prove to be the major considerations in these appointments, as both Lincoln and Davis used generalships to cement the loyalty and support of politically important men. About a third of Union generals and half their Confederate counterparts had not been professional soldiers, though most had undergone some military training; overall, the North and the South placed roughly similar proportions of professional soldiers in command. Lincoln, forced to unify a people far more divided than the white population of the Confederacy, chose generals from the ranks of various constituencies he needed to appease: abolitionists, Democrats, Irish, and Germans. The northern generals, not surprisingly, tended to have more business experience than their southern counterparts, expertise that proved useful in the modern warfare then emerging.

Neither the Union nor the Confederacy enjoyed a clear advantage in civilian leadership. Both Lincoln and Davis assembled cabinets that balanced geography, political faction, personality, and expertise; both leaders continually rearranged their cabinets as dissension broke out, incompetence became obvious, or politics demanded. The Confederates had to create a government from scratch, including the design of flags, stamps, and money. Davis ran through several secretaries of war and secretaries of state before finding the two men on whom he felt he could rely, James A. Seddon and Judah P. Benjamin, respectively.

The Union enjoyed a head start in such matters—it at least had a flag and office furniture—but the Republicans had never been in federal power before and had many problems to iron out. Several of Lincoln's cabinet members—Seward and Chase, in particular—let it be known that they considered themselves better qualified for the presidency than Lincoln. Office-seekers besieged Washington at the very time Lincoln was trying to keep the South in the Union; he felt like an innkeeper, he said, faced with customers demanding rooms in one wing while he tried to put out a fire in another wing. Lincoln's cabinet ended up containing men whom he barely knew and upon whom he was not always sure he could rely.

The First Conflicts

Battles began before anyone was ready, even before the alignment of states was complete. On the day following Lincoln's call for troops in April, federal officers in charge of the arsenal at Harpers Ferry and the naval yard in Norfolk, Virginia, sought to destroy the weapons under their command before secessionists could seize them. Despite their efforts, Virginia troops managed to recover valuable gun-making machinery, artillery, and ships for the Confederate cause. At almost exactly the same time, southern sympathizers in Missouri raided the arsenal at St. Louis. A few weeks later, battles broke out along the B&O Railroad in

what would become West Virginia, with Robert E. Lee, the new general for Virginia, leading an unsuccessful and embarrassing chase of troops under the command of George McClellan. Meanwhile, nearly four thousand Confederates, most of them from Texas, pushed into New Mexico. They hoped to win the mineral riches of Colorado and perhaps even California for the southern cause.

All these struggles showed both sides to be far from ready to fight a war in 1861. Not only were guns and uniforms scarce, but so were combat experience and even battlefield training. Even those men who had attended West Point had learned more about engineering than they had about tactical maneuvers; many of the men who were to become leading generals over the next few years had left the army for civilian pursuits in the years before the war. The United States Army contained only about 16,000 men, and most of them were scattered across the vast territory west of the Mississippi River. Neither side had accurate maps of the terrain on which they would be fighting. The militiamen who first responded to the calls of the Union and Confederacy had scarcely been trained at all. Militia companies had long been famous for drinking and socializing, not teaching men how to fight.

Mobilization

Both sides took immediate steps to create new armies, organized within local communities and led by local men. The Confederate Congress authorized 400,000 volunteers in May of 1861, only weeks after the secession of the upper South states. In its special session beginning in July of 1861, the Union Congress authorized 500,000 troops, each signing on for three years; 700,000 eventually enlisted under this law. Much mobilization took place on the local level. Prominent citizens often supplied uniforms, guns, and even food for the troops from their localities. Men signed on in communities and for communities, their official names identifying their states, their nicknames identifying their town or county. Units elected their own officers. States competed to enlist the largest numbers of men. Governors chose military leaders who could strengthen political bonds, satisfy calls for patronage, and assuage enemies. Local newspapers sought to make sure that state-level leaders dealt fairly with local troops and officers.

Some Northerners wondered whether their society had grown too rich and soft to fight the South, whether the many divisions among classes, occupations, religions, and ethnic groups would hinder the Union war effort. Such doubters took heart at the response to the crisis of 1861. Both workingmen and wealthy men eagerly signed up, even in places recently divided by labor conflict. Members of ethnic groups took pride in forming their own units; the Irish and Germans, recent immigrants to the United States, supplied over 150,000 men each. Northerners congratulated themselves that patriotism and self-sacrifice had not been killed, as many feared, by the spirit of commerce so strong in the land.

Southerners, too, found reason to be proud in 1861. The leaders of the South had secretly worried that some of what the abolitionists had said was true, that when push came to shove the nonslaveholders would not fight for a cause that many identified with the defense of slavery. But southern boys and men were activated by the same impulses that drove their northern counterparts: idealized images of the American Revolution, dreams of glory, youthful self-confidence, and a burning desire to impress family, friends, and young women with their bravery. At this point in the war, white southerners talked less about slavery than they had before or than they would later. In their eyes, they fought to defend their farms and homes from "foreign" invaders. That helped account for the fact that four-fifths of military-age white men in the South fought in the army or navy, compared to about half of those in the North.

Editors, politicians, and citizens of both the North and the South, impressed with the outpouring of volunteers, impatiently demanded that the conflict be wrapped up immediately. Confident of victory, such people on both sides itched for the fight that would settle things once and for all.

The First Battle

Northerners soon grew impatient with the passive Anaconda Plan of cutting the South off from the outside. "Forward to Richmond," one influential New York paper trumpeted day after day in June and July of 1861. With so many men eagerly signing on to fight, Northerners thought they should get the war over with early, before the South had time to consolidate its forces—maybe even before the Confederate

Congress met on July 20. The Union already had 35,000 men poised in northern Virginia, about twenty-five miles away from a Confederate force of 20,000 under the command of P. G. T. Beauregard. Beauregard's troops protected an important rail junction at Manassas, along Bull Run (a "run" is a stream). Confederate and Union troops also watched one another warily in the Shenandoah Valley, about fifty miles to the west.

These troop deployments reflected a primary goal of each side in the early stages of the war: capturing the capital of their enemies. Both Washington and Richmond seemed tantalizingly vulnerable to their enemies. Union leaders thought that if they could win Richmond, the industrial, commercial, and administrative center of the South, the rest of the Confederacy would soon follow. Confederate leaders thought that if they could conquer the capital of the United States, forcing Lincoln and his cabinet to flee, European powers would recognize the Confederacy's sovereignty and legitimacy. Each side's men and resources arrayed around the two capitals.

The officers of both the Union and the Confederacy had learned their strategy at West Point, a strategy based on the experience of European armies in the Napoleonic Wars of several decades earlier. These officers usually attempted to concentrate their force in hopes of overwhelming the enemy at the point of attack. The Union tried to take advantage of its greater numbers of men and resources; the Confederacy sought to use its interior lines, its knowledge of the Virginia landscape, and aggressive maneuvers to gain an advantage. Both sides knew what the other hoped and planned to do, making it difficult for either to strike the decisive blow.

In the first major battle of the war, the South's advantages outweighed the North's. Both sides attempted to coordinate their troop movements near Washington and in the Shenandoah Valley. The valley, shielded from the east by the Blue Ridge Mountains, had long served as a major corridor between the North and the South. If that corridor was left unprotected by the Union, Confederate forces could rush up the valley and capture Washington. But if too many troops protected the valley, the North would tie up men and resources that could be used more effectively elsewhere. The Confederacy employed cavalry, under the command of the flamboyant young colonel James E.B. (Jeb) Stuart, to move quickly up and down the valley, keeping the North off balance.

Despite his flamboyant appearance and cavalry tactics, J. E. B. Stuart, like a number of other Confederate generals, adhered to a strict religious discipline that prohibited drinking and swearing.

Early in the war, Thomas J. "Stonewall" Jackson was the most beloved Confederate leader, admired for his military daring and his devout religious belief.

The Union, under the command of General Irvin McDowell, tried to concentrate most of their forces at Manassas by moving them from the valley. On July 21 the northern troops were finally ready to attack. Congressmen and other spectators drove their carriages out from Washington to "see the Rebels get whipped." At first, it appeared that the ladies and gentlemen would see what they came for. Union troops flooded over the battlefield, fording the creeks, flanking the strongest points in the Confederate lines. The southern forces fell back to more defensible positions. When it looked as if the Confederates were to be routed, a southern general found inspiration in the actions of a unit under the command of Thomas J. Jackson. "Look!," the general pointed out to his men, "There is Jackson standing like a stone wall! Rally behind the Virginians!" The man who made the plea was soon killed, but "Stonewall Jackson," until recently an undistinguished mathematics professor at the Virginia Military Institute, had been christened.

Confederate reinforcements that poured off the train at Manassas gave Beauregard a renewed spirit. The Union forces, spent from days of marching and long hours of fighting, suffered confusion when the lack of a common uniform led some Northerners to mistake Confederates for their own troops. They began to pull back and then to run, throwing away their equipment along the way. Some civilian carriages got caught in the panicked flood of troops rushing back to Washington; the Confederates gleefully captured a congressman.

The South had claimed its first victory. Each side had engaged about 18,000 soldiers, making Bull Run by a considerable margin the largest battle ever waged in the United States up to that time. Both the North and the South lost about 600 men. Although each side had about an equal number of soldiers and although defending ground was much easier than taking it offensively, the humiliating rout confirmed the Confederate belief that one Rebel could whip ten Yankees.

Key parts of Confederate lore emerged from Bull Run as well: the rebel yell and the Confederate battle flag. The yell was not merely a scream or a roar, but a high wail, unnerving and strange. No one knew where

The first major battle of the war, at Manassas, Virginia, on July 21, 1861, suddenly turned into a rout of Union forces when confusion and Confederate reinforcements abruptly turned the tide.

it came from—fox-hunting, perhaps—but it served as the rallying cry for southern troops for the rest of the war. Union soldiers admitted that it affected them, for "there is nothing like it this side of the infernal region." The first flag of the Confederacy, the "Stars and Bars," looked a great deal like that of the United States, leading to confusion in the heat of battle. After Bull Run, Beauregard designed a new flag—a square banner, red with a blue cross and white stars—to ensure that southern troops did not fire on one another. It was that battle flag, never the official flag of the Confederacy, that later generations came to consider synonymous with the South.

For the next two years, the Battle of Bull Run emboldened southern forces who fought in Virginia. The Confederacy, feeling itself invulnerable, fought aggressively, even recklessly, in the east. The Union fought cautiously, even tentatively, in Virginia. Neither side forgot this conflict even though they called it by different names. Northern forces generally named battles after physical features such as rivers and mountains; thus, they deemed this the Battle of Bull Run. Southerners usually named battles after nearby towns or villages; they called this one Manassas. Later, after tens of thousands more had died, both the Union and the Confederacy would have to change their name for this

The Confederate battle flag, on the right, was adopted after Bull Run because the official flag—the so-called "Stars and Bars" (at left)—looked too much like the U.S. flag and led to deadly confusion in battle.

battle, adding a "first" to distinguish it from blood later poured on the same battlefield.

Women and War

Women North and South had avidly studied the debates over the elections and secession being waged in the newspapers. They had expressed their opinions in private conversation, in their letters, and in their diaries. Many had listened to the speeches on all sides, applauding the speakers they liked and avoiding those they did not. They had counseled their sons and husbands, sometimes resisting the drift of opinion and sometimes urging their men on to join others of their community. They had worn cockades displaying their loyalties and had sung the latest songs. The testimonials and tributes that officials and soldiers offered to women were not hollow gestures, but heartfelt. Men believed they were fighting for their families.

Once the speeches, songs, and toasts had come to an end and the fighting begun, women became even more active. Since neither the Union nor the Confederacy had prepared for a fight, the women had much to do. Within two weeks of the war's beginning, women on the two sides had formed 20,000 aid societies. These societies devoted themselves to supplying the armies' needs, especially clothing and medical supplies. One such organization in Alabama provided, in just one month, "422 shirts, 551 pairs of drawers, 80 pairs of socks, 3 pairs of gloves, 6 boxes and one bale of hospital supplies, 128 pounds of tapioca, and a donation of $18 for hospital use." Such women's groups in the South worked independently of one another, but in the North the United States Sanitary Commission coordinated their efforts, producing supplies worth over $15 million.

With the first battles, women claimed positions as nurses even though men had served before as military nurses. Despite some initial grumbling by men and gossiping by cautious women, women converted themselves immediately into competent and devoted nurses. Wounded men poured into Washington and Richmond after First Manassas, with only women in private homes and institutions to take care of them. Dorothy Dix, long known as the champion of the mentally ill and neglected people in the antebellum era, took matters in hand for the North. She became superintendent of nurses for the Union army, organizing 3,000 women who volunteered to serve. Concerned both about the effectiveness and propriety of

Women in both the North and South quickly stepped forward, sometimes against opposition, to save lives and relieve suffering.

LOUISA MAY ALCOTT,
"JOURNAL"
APRIL 1861

Thirty years old in 1862, Alcott, who had lived in her father's home her entire life, applied to become a nurse. She had no formal training, though she had cared for her dying sister. Her journal tells of her feelings at the beginning of her service, "full of hope and sorrow, courage and plans." She threw herself into the work, but grew ill with typhoid fever and endured mercury poisoning from the medication she received. She had to come home for the duration of the war. Alcott became a best-selling author with her enduring novel, *Little Women,* published in 1868.

April. [1861]—War declared with the South, and our Concord company went to Washington. A busy time getting them ready, and a sad day seeing them off, for in a little town like this we all seem like one family in times like these. At the station the scene was very dramatic, as the brave boys went away perhaps never to come back again.

I've often longed to see a war, and now I have my wish. I long to be a man, but as I can't fight, I will content myself with working for those who can. . . .

September, October. [1862]— . . . War news bad. Anxious faces, beating hearts, and busy minds.

I like the stir in the air, and long for battle like a warhorse when he smells powder. The blood of the Mays is up! . . .

November.—Thirty years old. Decided to go to Washington as a nurse if I could find a place. Help needed, and I love nursing, and *must* let out my pentup energy in some new way. Winter is always a hard and a dull time, and if I am away there is one less to feed and warm and worry over.

I want new experiences, and am sure to get 'em if I go. So I've sent in my name, and bide my time writing tales, to leave all snug behind me, and mending up my old clothes,—for nurses don't need nice things, thank Heaven!

December.—On the 11th I received a note from Miss H. M. Stevenson telling me to start for Georgetown next day to fill a place in the Union Hotel Hospital. Mrs. Ropes of

women ministering to young male strangers, Dix decreed that she wanted only "plain" women, women over thirty, and women who would dress in brown and black. Such women did come forward in large numbers, but so did women of other descriptions as well. Patriotism and mercy activated them, but the forty-cents-a-day wage was certainly welcome too during these harsh days.

Women's efforts soon became legendary, North and South. Women labored until they could no longer stand, until their long dresses trailed blood from amputations and wounds, until they had watched one young man after another die. Kate Cumming and Phoebe Pember played leading roles in the Confederacy, and Clara Barton, formerly a clerk at the Patent Office in Washington, took her aid to the front lines of the Union and later founded the American Red Cross. Most women stayed closer to home, working in factories or doing piecework in their households under ever harsher circumstances.

Boston was matron, and Miss Kendall of Plymouth was a nurse there, and though a hard place, help was needed. I was ready, and when my commander said "March!" I marched. Packed my trunk, and reported in B.[oston] that same evening.

We had all been full of courage till the last moment came, then we all broke down. I realized that I had taken my life in my hand, and might never see them all again. I said, "Shall I stay, Mother?" as I hugged her close. "No, go! and the Lord be with you!" answered the Spartan woman, and till I turned the corner she bravely smiled and waved her wet handkerchief on the doorstep. Shall I ever see that dear old face again?

So I set forth in the December twilight, with May and Julian Hawthorne as escort, feeling as if I was the son of the house going to war.

Friday, the 12th, was a very memorable day, spent in running all over Boston to get my pass, etc., calling for parcels, getting a tooth filled, and buying a veil,—my only purchase. A. C. gave me some old clothes, the dear Sewalls money for myself and boys, lots of love and help, and at 5 P.M., saying "goodby" to a group of tearful faces at the station, I started on my long journey, full of hope and sorrow, courage and plans.

A most interesting journey into a new world full of stirring sights and sounds, new adventures, and an evergrowing sense of the great task I had undertaken.

I said my prayers as I went rushing through the country white with tents, all alive with patriotism, and already red with blood.

A solemn time, but I'm glad to live in it, and am sure it will do me good whether I come out alive or dead.

All went well, and I got to Georgetown one evening very tired. Was kindly welcomed, slept in my narrow bed with two other room-mates, and on the morrow began my new life by seeing a poor man die at dawn, and sitting all day between a boy with pneumonia and a man shot through the lungs. A strange day, but I did my best, and when I put mother's little black shawl round the boy while he sat up panting for breath, he smiled and said, "You are real motherly, ma'am." I felt as if I was getting on. The man only lay and stared with his big black eyes, and made me very nervous. But all were well behaved, and I sat looking at the twenty strong faces as they looked back at me,—hoping that I looked "motherly" to them, for my thirty years made me feel old, and the suffering round me made me long to comfort every one. . . .

SOURCE Alcott's journals are located at Houghton Library, Harvard University, and have been published in Joel Myerson and Daniel Shealy, editors, *The Journals of Louisa May Alcott* (Boston, 1989).

WAR TAKES COMMAND: AUGUST 1861 TO MARCH 1862

The war spread across the continent in the fall, winter, and spring of 1861–1862. Armies consolidated command and launched campaigns thousands of miles from headquarters. Governments transformed their economies, invented or reinvented navies, conducted diplomacy, and cemented the loyalties of those at home. Families steeled themselves for a war longer than they had been willing to imagine.

McClellan Assumes Control

The North, while embarrassed by Bull Run, took from that defeat a determination to fight more effectively.

Early in the war, Lincoln and the rest of the North placed great faith in the "Young Napoleon," General George B. McClellan. Events would later lessen their admiration.

Volunteers flooded into recruitment offices. Lincoln removed the leaders responsible for that battle and replaced them with George B. McClellan. McClellan was the logical choice. Although short of stature and only thirty-four years old, he exuded great authority. He was known as the "young Napoleon." McClellan had distinguished himself in the Mexican War, studied military tactics in Europe, and served as a railroad president. Moreover, he had already frustrated Confederate forces with Robert E. Lee in western Virginia. Drawing on all these experiences, McClellan threw himself into reorganizing and reenergizing the Union troops under his command.

McClellan's men loved him and the press lavished praise on the young general. Already inclined toward grandiose visions of his abilities, McClellan developed an exalted sense of himself. The cocky commander considered Lincoln an "idiot" and his cabinet incompetent "geese." McClellan ignored, avoided, and in-

sulted those men at every opportunity. A Democrat deeply suspicious of abolitionists and Republicans, McClellan wanted only to restore the Union, not to dislodge slavery in the South or to damage his prospects as a presidential candidate in 1864. As a result, McClellan wanted to make his army perfectly prepared before he risked it, and his reputation, in battle against Confederates whose numbers his spies consistently exaggerated. Meanwhile, months dragged by. Lincoln and newspaper editors became furiously impatient but McClellan would not be moved. Everyone in the east waited for McClellan to attack the Confederates in Virginia.

The War in the West Begins

There was to be no waiting in the West, where troops fought on a smaller but more vicious scale. Four days after the battle at Bull Run, the Union installed a new commander in charge of the forces in Missouri: John C. Frémont, the "pathfinder of the West" and unsuccessful Republican candidate for president in 1856. While the situation in Virginia unfolded slowly, the situation in Missouri burst into chaos in July and August of 1861. Guerilla forces ranged throughout the state, sharply divided between northern and southern partisans. Confederate armies built up on the southern border, ready to attack in both the eastern and western parts of the state. Frémont decided that he had to protect the Mississippi River in the East and therefore left a weak force in the West. That force, outnumbered by the Confederates, staged a desperate attack, with terrible losses, at Wilson's Creek. As at Bull Run, the lack of a standard uniform color created deadly confusion; Union troops withheld fire against men in blue only to realize, too late, that they were Confederates. The northern units fell into ragged retreat, exposing Missouri to Rebel incursions.

Not only had Frémont lost much of Missouri, but he faced problems McClellan, back in the East, never confronted. With the army desperate for war materiel and supplies so far from Washington, contractors took advantage of the situation, selling substandard goods to the Union army at inflated prices. With the populace of Missouri so divided in its loyalties, Frémont did not know whom to trust; spies and guerillas seemed everywhere. Frantic, he declared the entire state under martial law, decreed the death penalty for captured guerillas, and seized the slaves and other property of all Confederate sympathizers. While anti-slavery advocates in the North applauded Frémont for doing what they thought Abraham Lincoln should be doing for the entire South, slaveholders in the border states of Kentucky and Maryland threatened to throw their allegiances to the South if Lincoln did not over-rule Frémont. The president, desperate to keep the border states within the Union, publicly reprimanded his general. When Frémont resisted, Lincoln felt that he had no choice but to remove Frémont from his post. Missouri, like Bull Run, embarrassed the Union in the summer of 1861.

Events on the battlefield in the earliest stages of the war proved to be a poor guide to the long term. Although the North had been shaken by Bull Run and Missouri, it had lost neither Washington nor the border states. Although the South had apparently won at Bull Run, the Confederate forces, exhausted and bogged down in mud, had not taken advantage of the situation to attack the Union capital. Although the Confederacy had driven Union troops from much of Missouri, that state was eventually to supply 100,000 men to the North and only 30,000 to the South. Although slaveholders in the border states fumed at the Union government and military leaders, they remained in the Union. As a result, the South was deprived of a key strategic advantage: access to the Ohio River and a defensible border with the North. With the Union army able to move up and down the Ohio at will, the Confederates had to defend a vast, vague, and shifting border in Kentucky and Tennessee.

To virtually everyone's surprise, the war was not to be won by a decisive battle within a few months of the war's start. Instead, slower and less dramatic processes proved decisive. Armies and navies had to be built from scratch; economies had to be converted to wartime demands; politics had to be reoriented; diplomacy had to adjust to the complexities of the battlefield and the international order; households and families had to absorb growing sacrifices. These transformations began in earnest in the summer of 1861.

Paying for War

The Civil War, involving so many men over such an enormous territory, immediately became breathtakingly expensive. It was by no means clear how either side was going to pay. Although the Union and the Confederacy were, by any international standard, rich

societies, neither had ever supported a large army or an active government. Taxes on imported goods and the sale of apparently endless public lands paid for what government there was. Ever since the Bank War of the 1830s the federal and state governments did little to manipulate the currency. As a result, when the war came, the men responsible for paying for it had only a few options—loans, new taxes, or the creation of paper money—all of them long suspect in America.

Loans met the least resistance in both the North and the South, but this borrowing could provide only a third of the cost of the war. Taxes proved even less effective, never supplying more than a small portion of the funds despite considerable effort to raise them. The Confederacy, enjoying far fewer resources than the North, quickly decided that it had no choice but to turn to paper money. As soon as they could find adequate engravers and printing presses, the South began producing millions of dollars in the new currency in an ever-growing stream. Catastrophic inflation began to grow as early as the winter of 1861–1862.

The situation was not quite as bad in the North, where taxes and bonds carried much more of the burden of financing the war, but the Union, too, was forced to issue paper money by the first winter of the war. As the secretary of the treasury warned, *"immediate action is of great importance. The treasury is nearly empty."* People hoarded gold in anticipation of the deprivations a widened war would cause. New York banks felt they had no choice but to suspend specie payments in December of 1861. The Union Congress, faced with strong warnings from constituents and colleagues, reluctantly decided in February of 1862 that it had no choice but to create paper money as well. The Legal Tender Act of that month permitted the treasury to release up to $10 million of the new currency, quickly dubbed "greenbacks." The paper money provided critical fuel for the northern economy and for the burgeoning military.

The Confederate Homefront

Southerners, black and white, watched helplessly as armies stripped their farms of food and livestock. They cowered as rifle and cannon shot ripped through their homes. They ministered to the bleeding young men dragged into their parlors and bedrooms. The residents of places where both Unionists and

Much of the Civil War turned around conflicts such as the one depicted in this painting, in which small groups of soldiers confronted one another and civilians far from the scenes of major battles.

Confederates remained strong—such as Missouri and eastern Tennessee—became caught in internal civil wars that pitted roving gangs of thugs against one another and against those who happened to be in their path. Governors received letters from women, their husbands and sons gone, who worried that they faced starvation if they did not get help soon.

Inflation ate away at the Confederacy like a cancer. The rapid rise in prices made currency worth less every day, food and cotton worth more. Speculators could make money simply by buying up supplies and holding them while prices escalated. Farmers faced the temptation to grow cotton despite the needs of the armies in the fields. Cotton stored well and everyone knew that cotton would fetch a high price after the war, no matter who won. As a result, land and labor that could have grown food bent under the weight of cotton.

White Southerners began to worry that the slaves would rise in rebellion if permitted to grow ever more "insolent." Confederate leaders worried that the plantations could not produce the food the armies so desperately needed if white men did not force the slaves

to work. African Americans wanted to hunt, fish, or work for themselves and their own families rather than to labor for the white people. Plantation mistresses often discovered, to their fury and fear, that slaves would not work when the master—and the overseer, whips, and guns he wielded—no longer hung over the slaves. Accordingly, the Confederate Congress passed what became known as the "twenty negro law," exempting from the draft one white man on every plantation that had at least twenty slaves. That a government in such need of every available soldier felt compelled to write such laws revealed how central slavery and its control remained even in the midst of war.

The twenty slave law came at additional cost as well: to many poorer Southerners, the law was another in a growing list of grievances against the rich and the Confederate government. Resentment against wealthy men and women, mediated during peacetime by family ties, common church membership, careful manners, and democratic politics, quickly came to the surface in the context of war. Common people were quick to notice when plantation slaves labored over cotton rather than corn, when mistresses appeared in public in their finery, when the well-to-do hoarded gold or dodged taxes. Wealthy young men sometimes entered the Confederate army as privates—Robert E. Lee's son did so—but others considered an officer's commission, preferably in the cavalry, their just due as gentlemen. Scions of plantation fortunes often did little to disguise their disgust or amusement at the speech or clothing of the poorer men alongside whom they fought. The poorer soldiers noticed, as did their wives.

Navies

The navies of the North and South had to adapt most quickly. In the mid-nineteenth century, water vied with railroads as the most vital means of transportation. Just as many battles, starting with Bull Run,

broke out at rail junctions, so did the leaders on both sides recognize the centrality of ports and rivers. The North's Anaconda Plan depended on control of the waterways, stopping the shipment of the South's immensely valuable cotton crop, cutting the region off from importations of weapons and other manufactured goods, and dividing the Confederacy along the Mississippi River. While ground troops back east dug in for the winter of 1861–1862, the navies of both sides struggled for control of the seas and rivers.

The Union enjoyed a great initial advantage in its number of ships, but at the time of the war many of those ships were scattered around the globe. It took months to track them down and bring them home. Moreover, most of the Union's vessels were deep-sea ships, not very useful for the sort of river and port fighting the war was likely to bring. With remarkable speed, however, the Union naval department built new

The Confederacy depended on English shipyards, such as this one in Liverpool, to construct vessels to run the Union blockade, attack Union ships on the seas, and defend their ports.

craft and deployed them against the South. The skilled workers of the shipbuilding towns of the east coast produced hundreds of ships and boats.

Although a number of naval officers resigned their Union commissions to join the Confederacy, the South had virtually no ships at the beginning of the war. The Confederacy immediately contracted with large shipbuilding companies in England to produce craft the South did not have the time or facilities to make for itself. Jefferson Davis also authorized sailors to attack northern ships on the high seas and turn them in for a share of the booty. For a few months these "privateers" preyed on any unguarded ship they could find, but the Union navy quickly shut them down. The Confederates then used their naval officers to man ships that would attempt to sink rather than claim enemy ships. One intrepid officer, Raphael Semmes, escaped through the blockade in 1861 and seized eighteen Union ships before he was trapped at Gibraltar on the other side of the Atlantic and forced to sell his ship and escape to England.

In the meantime, the North pushed its advantage. Larger ships began to blockade 189 harbors and ports from Virginia to Texas, patrolling 3,500 miles of coastline. Such enormous territory obviously proved difficult to control, especially because northern ships periodically had to travel to ports hundreds of miles away for supplies and fuel. When Union craft left for such journeys, southern blockade runners rushed into the unprotected ports. The Union navy decided to seize several southern ports for use as supply stations. The federal ships moved first in August, at Cape Hatteras in North Carolina, shelling the forts there and cutting off the supplies that dozens of blockade runners had brought into the Confederacy. The northern navy also took a station near Biloxi, Mississippi, from which they could patrol the Gulf of Mexico. The most valuable seizure, however, was Port Royal, South Carolina. Not only did that place offer an excellent harbor, but it stood midway between the major southern ports of Charleston and Savannah. In November of 1861, the Union navy overwhelmed Confederate forts on the Sea Islands that stretched along the coast. The federal army and navy now had invaluable bases of operations.

Diplomacy and the Trent *Affair*

On the day after the capture of Port Royal, another event on the seas drew attention on both sides of the Atlantic. A Union ship stopped a British mail packet, the *Trent,* as it traveled from Cuba to St. Thomas. The *Trent* carried James Mason and John Slidell, Confederate commissioners sailing to London and Paris to negotiate for the support of the British and French governments. The captain of the Union ship, Charles Wilkes, after firing two shots across the bow of the British vessel, boarded it and seized the Confederate emissaries. When Wilkes arrived in Boston to deposit Mason and Slidell in prison, he met with a hero's welcome. A northern public that had been frustrated by the inability of its leaders to achieve success on the battlefield roared its approval of Wilkes's bold and decisive action. Congress ordered a medal struck in his honor.

The excitement began to wane, however, when people realized the possible repercussions of Wilkes's actions. Despite the growth of the Union navy, Great Britain still ruled the oceans—and Great Britain was furious at the boarding of their ship by the Americans. British newspapers and politicians called for war against the arrogant Americans. The *Trent* affair reflected the uneasy state of international relations created by the war. The Confederacy hoped that England or France, even both, would come to its aid. The importance of cotton in the international marketplace was such, Southerners argued, that the industrial powers of Europe could not long afford to allow the northern navy to enforce its blockade. Moreover, many Southerners—and Northerners, for that matter—expected the European powers to take advantage of the American war for their own purposes. The United States had been growing with daunting speed in population, territory, and trade; surely it would benefit France and England to support the Confederacy and weaken the Union.

The situation in the winter of 1861–1862 proved more complicated than people had expected, however. International law did not offer a clear ruling on whether Captain Wilkes had acted legally. And neither did self-interest offer a clear guide to whether England should declare war on the United States or aid the Confederacy. The factories of Britain had stockpiled cotton in expectation of the war and did not clamor for intervention as Southerners had hoped. France and England watched one another warily, neither country eager to upset the fragile balance of power between themselves by taking the first step in America. Besides, the United States seemed to be doing a good job of destroying itself without the intervention of Europe.

Public opinion within England and France divided, for it was by no means clear to most Europeans in this first year of the war which side had the better claim to their sympathies. Lincoln repeatedly declared that the war was not a war against slavery. That declaration, Lincoln believed, was necessary to cement the support of the border states and dubious Democrats, but it undercut the support of English and European abolitionists for the Union cause. The Confederates claimed to be fighting for self-determination, a cause with considerable appeal in Europe, but potential supporters often viewed southern slaveholding with disgust and distrust. Both the English and the French waited for events on the battlefields of North America to clarify issues.

The *Trent* affair, however, had to be settled at once. Its settlement came through diplomatic evasion and maneuvering. The U.S. officials decided that, despite the enthusiasm with which Wilkes's actions were greeted by Congress, he had acted on his own, unauthorized by the government of the Union. Mason and Slidell were freed from prison and permitted to continue their journey to London and Paris. The English, eager for a solution, put the incident behind them. Although the Confederacy was jubilant at having "won," the underlying situation had not changed. Mason and Slidell, along with the Confederate emissaries to other countries, found that though many powerful people elsewhere were sympathetic to the rebellious Southerners and hopeful of their success, they were unwilling to go to war against the United States.

The international situation remained tense and unsettled throughout the war. Leaders of both the North and the South could imagine situations in which England or France would intervene with weapons and supplies, tipping the balance of the war. Foreign intervention remained a fervent hope for the Confederacy and a great fear of the North. Abraham Lincoln and Jefferson Davis would always pay close attention to Europe.

The Rivers of the West

The Union felt starved for victories at the beginning of the hard winter of 1862. Northern troops remained bogged down in the eastern theater, where George McClellan lay immobile with typhoid fever, but Union generals in the West moved aggressively. Deprived of control of the Ohio River when Kentucky

Ulysses S. Grant distinguished himself in key battles in Tennessee and Mississippi in 1862. Many months and battles would pass, however, before Grant would assume command in the East.

sided with the Union, the Confederates under Albert Sidney Johnston desperately needed to stop the Union in the West. Troops under the command of Ulysses S. Grant, a relatively obscure general from Illinois, confronted a Confederate line of defense across southern Kentucky, based at the most important railroad junctions. Grant decided to use the rivers rather than the railroads for his assault, however. Employing the Union's new river gunboats to great effect, Grant pushed down both the Tennessee and the Cumberland rivers across the Kentucky border into Tennessee.

Important Confederate forts stood on both these rivers, but Grant hoped to overwhelm them by combined attacks on water and land. He assaulted Fort Henry on the Tennessee River in early February, easily overcoming the fort's defenses with the big guns on his river craft. The Union now commanded a river that flowed all the way through Tennessee into northern Alabama. Grant, buoyed by this remarkable victory, sent his boats steaming back up the Tennessee River to

MAP 14.2 | THE CIVIL WAR IN THE WEST, 1861-1862

the Cumberland while he marched his men overland to Fort Donelson. There, the Confederates enjoyed a more strategic position for their fort and fought desperately, destroying several of the gunboats that had seemed so indestructible only a few days earlier. Despite the Confederacy's efforts, however, Grant pressed his advantage and overwhelmed southern troops that attempted to break out of the fort and retreat to nearby Nashville.

When the Confederate general in charge of the 13,000 troops who remained in the fort attempted to negotiate with Grant (an old friend) for their surren-

der, Grant brusquely responded: "No terms except an unconditional and immediate surrender can be accepted. I propose to move immediately upon your works." Grant's phrase soon echoed through northern newspapers, jokes, and even mildly risqué love letters. Grant's first two initials, northern newspapers crowed, actually stood for Unconditional Surrender. Within days, Union troops pushed into nearby Nashville, the capital of Tennessee, making it the first great conquest of the war. Europe noticed: One of the Confederate emissaries released after the *Trent* affair morosely reported from London that "the late reverses at Fort

The Union's use of river boats provided a decided advantage when they quickly overran this fort on the Tennessee River in February 1862.

Henry and Fort Donelson have had an unfortunate effect on the minds of our friends here."

The Monitor *and the* Virginia

Even as Grant's troops seized their victories on the rivers of Tennessee, the Union navy continued its relentless attack on the eastern seaboard of the Confederacy. A well-planned amphibious attack allowed the northern navy to consolidate its control of the North Carolina coast, sealing off every city except Wilmington. The blockade steadily tightened.

Despite the Union's success, the southern navy had reason for hope in early 1862. Confederate Secretary of the Navy Stephen Mallory—a former U.S. senator quite experienced in naval affairs—had created an effective and innovative department. Mallory sought to take advantage of recent developments in shipbuilding and naval warfare such as steam power, the screw propeller, and armor. The Confederacy eagerly experimented, too, with mines in their harbors.

Most important, the South examined the possibilities of iron-plated ships. In the years immediately preceding the Civil War, the French and British had been experimenting with such vessels but the United States remained far behind. The Confederacy began building an ironclad almost from the very beginning of the war, converting a Union ship captured in Norfolk in April of 1861. They added walls of two-feet-thick solid oak, covered with four-inch-thick iron plate, and installed an iron ram on the front to rip through the wooden hulls of enemy ships. It carried ten heavy guns. The Confederacy changed the ship's name from the U.S.S. *Merrimack* to the C.S.S. *Virginia*.

The Union, for its part, hired a Swiss inventor to design a different kind of ironclad; his innovative plan called for a ship most of which would be submerged except for a rotating turret on top. The result resembled "a tin can on a shingle," one observer commented, and it was by no means clear how such a craft might work in battle. No one was even sure it would stay afloat, much less fight effectively with its two guns. It was called the *Monitor*.

On March 8, 1862, with the Union navy consolidating its control of the eastern seaboard, the Confederates decided the time had come to unleash their new weapon. The *Virginia* attacked several Union ships occupying the harbor at Hampton Roads, Virginia. The ironclad overwhelmed two wooden ships and drove

In one of the most memorable episodes of the war, the U.S.S. Monitor *and the C.S.S.* Virginia *bruised one another in the harbor of Hampton Roads, Virginia, in March 1862. Though neither ship won, the Union's* Monitor *proved the superior vessel.*

THE FIRST BATTLE BETWEEN IRON SHIPS OF WAR.
The "Monitor" 2 Guns and Merrimac 10 Guns.
The Merrimac was crippled and the whole Rebel Fleet driven off.

three others aground; their guns proved useless against the heavy iron sheathing. The Confederates looked forward to the next day, when they planned to finish off the grounded ships.

In one of the more dramatic episodes of the young war, however, the Union happened to be sending its own ironclad to a Virginia port thirty miles away on the morning after the *Virginia* launched its attack. Hearing the sound of the guns in Hampton Roads, the *Monitor* steamed down and arrived just in time. The two vessels pounded one another for hours, the cannonballs bouncing off both ships. The imposing southern ironclad had been neutralized and the blockade would continue. Although neither iron ship actually won the battle of March 9, the advantages of the northern *Monitor* quickly became evident. Not only did that craft provide a much smaller target and a more maneuverable set of guns, but the *Monitor* required only half as much water in which to operate. The *Virginia* proved too big to retreat into rivers and too unwieldy for open seas; it would pose no threat to Washington or New York. The Union began a crash campaign to build as many ironclads as possible, using the *Monitor* as their model.

THE UNION ON THE OFFENSIVE: MARCH TO SEPTEMBER 1862

The Union strategy had long pivoted around the effort to take Richmond. With their most illustrious general in command and enjoying apparently unlimited resources, Northerners expected to make quick work of Virginia. Although the Confederacy had put up a surprisingly effective campaign, the Union expected to win the war in the spring and summer of 1862. As with all things in this war, however, events followed directions no one could foresee.

The Peninsular Campaign Begins

On the very day that the C.S.S. *Virginia* emerged at Hampton Roads, Abraham Lincoln gave his approval of General George McClellan's long-delayed plan to win the war in the East. Rather than fighting in northern Virginia, McClellan would attack on the peninsula

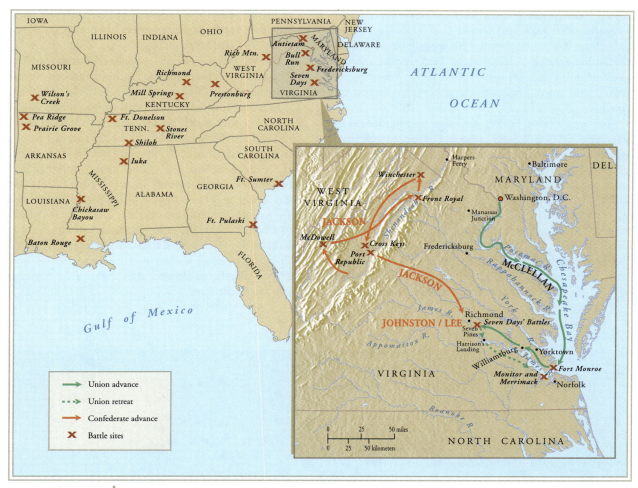

MAP 14.3 | THE CIVIL WAR IN THE EAST, SPRING 1862

between the James and York rivers farther south, using the Chesapeake Bay as a supply route. By moving the war away from Washington, McClellan argued, he would lessen the threat to the nation's capital and find better roads from which to attack Richmond. His army, after months of marching and polishing (and criticism from the northern public, press, and president), was finally ready to do its job.

Four hundred watercraft of every description began transferring Union soldiers to the tip of the peninsula at Fortress Monroe, about seventy miles from Richmond. The march that McClellan envisioned would, ironically, push through two of the most famous places in American history: Jamestown and Yorktown. The

transfer of 100,000 men took weeks to unfold. McClellan required several more weeks to arrange them just so in preparation for what he expected to be his triumphant march into Richmond.

Shiloh

In the meantime, U. S. Grant and his fellow general William T. Sherman pushed their troops ever deeper into Tennessee. The Confederates, under the leadership of Albert Sidney Johnston, had retreated to Corinth, Mississippi, where they regrouped and joined with other units. They planned to attack Grant to regain momentum if not the enormous territory and strategic rivers they had lost at Fort Henry and Fort Donelson. Grant established his own base of operations only twenty miles away, at Pittsburgh Landing, Tennessee. To the surprise of the Union, Johnston attacked the larger Union force at Shiloh Church on April 6.

The area around Shiloh was no classic battlefield of sweeping vistas and high ground. Rather, its scattered woods and rough terrain turned the battle into a series of brutal fights among desperate groups of scattered men with little coordinated leadership. Johnston, killed leading an attack, was replaced by Beauregard, who succeeded in pushing the Union men back two miles. The Confederates' dominance proved short-lived, however, for 25,000 northern reinforcements arrived overnight. The Southerners received no new men. The next day saw Grant and his men regain the ground they had lost, driving the Confederates back to Corinth. Though the southern forces had been badly hurt, the northern forces were themselves too exhausted and shaken to pursue.

The carnage at Shiloh exceeded anything anyone had ever seen. The bloodiest battle in the hemisphere up to that point, Shiloh exacted a horrible toll: about 1,700 killed and 8,000 wounded on each side. About 2,000 of the wounded men in both the Union and the Confederacy forces would soon die. Sherman wrote of the "piles of dead soldiers' mangled bodies . . . without heads and legs. . . . The scenes on this field would have cured anybody of war." Newspapers and generals debated the outcome of the battle for months, trying to decide the hero and the loser, but it eventually became clear that the southern attempt to halt northern momentum in the Mississippi Valley had failed. It also became clear that commanders on both sides would fight desperately, and with enormous costs, when cornered.

In one of the bloodiest days of fighting in the war, the troops of Grant and William T. Sherman clashed with those of Albert Sidney Johnston and P. G. T. Beauregard. Johnston was killed and the Union forces seized a desperate, last-minute, and costly victory.

The fleet of David Farragut accomplished what the Confederates considered impossible, pushing past the elaborate defenses of New Orleans. Using the cover of darkness, much of the fleet managed to survive a thundering artillery assault.

New Orleans

The Federals' success in Tennessee, along the Carolina coast, and in Hampton Roads in the spring of 1862 heartened Union supporters who had begun to doubt the success of their cause. Yet another drama played itself out in New Orleans. There, a Union naval force under David Farragut—a sixty-year-old Tennesseean married to a Virginian—determined to do what Confederates considered impossible: overwhelm their largest city and largest port from the Gulf. Confederates recalled that the mighty British of 1815 had been unable to take New Orleans and fully expected the same fate to befall the Yankees. The city lay under the protection of two forts claiming 115 guns as well as a river blocked with logs and thick cables. So safe did they consider New Orleans that Confederate troops abandoned the city to fight at Shiloh, leaving the port protected only by militiamen.

Farragut had his own weapons, however: 20 mortar boats, 17 ships with 210 guns, and 15,000 soldiers.

The Union navy pounded the forts for days with the mortars, unsuccessfully. Frustrated, on April 24 Farragut audaciously led his ships, single-file, past the forts and past Confederate ships that tried to ram the Union craft or set them on fire with flaming rafts. Once they had run this gauntlet, the Union ships had clear sailing right up to the docks of New Orleans. There, they confronted no resistance, only thick smoke from the bales of cotton the Southerners had set on fire to keep out of Yankee hands. Troops under the command of Benjamin Butler occupied New Orleans while Farragut continued to drive up the Mississippi River. He took Baton Rouge and Natchez, but Vicksburg held Farragut off, thanks to its position on bluffs high above the river. River boats coming from the north soon took Memphis as well, giving the Union control of all the Mississippi River except the area near Vicksburg. Northern forces used the river as a major supply route. Rather than a highway uniting the upper and lower South, the Mississippi became a chasm separating one half of the Confederacy from the other.

Sarah Morgan, "Diary" March 1864

Sarah Morgan was a high-spirited teenager when the Civil War broke out, the daughter of a respected judge. Though she and her father supported the Union during the secession crisis, both invested their loyalty in the Confederacy once the Civil War began. This part of her diary, begun in 1862, records the grief that struck the hundreds of thousands of American families who lost sons, brothers, and fathers in the war. Despite her sense of helplessness, Morgan went on to write for a leading newspaper in South Carolina after the war.

March

Dead! dead! Both dead! O my brothers! what have we lived for except you? We who would so gladly have laid down our lives for yours, are left desolate to mourn over all we loved and hoped for, weak and helpless; while you, so strong, noble, and brave, have gone before us without a murmur. God knows best. But it is hard—O so hard! to give them up without a murmur!

We cannot remember the day when our brothers were not all in all to us. What the boys would think; what the boys would say; what we would do when the boys came home, that has been our sole thought through life. A life time's hope wrecked in a moment—God help us! In our eyes, there is no one in the world quite so noble, quite so brave, quite so true as our brothers. And yet they are taken—and others useless to themselves and a curse to their families live on in safety, without fear of death. This is blasphemy. God knows best; I will not complain. But when I think of drunken, foolish, coarse Will Carter with horses and dogs his sole ambition, and drinking and gambling his idea of happiness, my heart swells within me. He lives, a torment to himself and a curse to others—he will live to a green old age as idle, as ignorant, as dissipated as he is now.

And Gibbes, Harry, and George, God's blessings he bestowed on us awhile—are dead. My brothers! my dear brothers! I would rather mourn over you in your graves, remembering what you were, than have you change places with that man. Death is nothing in comparison to dishonor.

If we had had any warning or preparation, this would not have been so unspeakably awful. But to shut ones eyes to all dangers and risks, and drown every rising fear with "God will send them back; I will not doubt his mercy," and then suddenly to learn that your faith has been presumption—and God wills that you shall undergo bitter affliction—it is a fearful awakening! What glory have we ever rendered to God that we should expect him to be so merciful to us? Are not all things His, and is He not infinitely more tender and compassionate than we deserve?

We have deceived ourselves willfully about both. After the first dismay on hearing of Gibbes' capture, we readily listened to the assertions of our friends that Johnson's Island was the healthiest place in the world, that he would be better off, comfortably clothed and under shelter, than exposed to shot and shell, half fed, and lying on the bare ground during Ewell's winter campaign. We were thankful for his safety, knowing Brother would leave nothing undone that could add to his comfort. And besides that, there was the sure hope of his having him paroled. On that hope we lived all winter—now confident that in a little while he would be with us, then again doubting for awhile, only to have the hope grow surer afterwards. And so we waited and prayed, never doubting he would come at last. He himself believed it, though striving not to be too hopeful lest he should disappoint us, as well as himself. Yet he wrote cheerfully and bravely to the last. Towards the middle of January, Brother was sure of succeeding, as all the prisoners had been placed under Butler's control. Ah me! How could we be so blind? We were sure he would be with us in a few weeks! I wrote to him that I had prepared his room.

On the 30th of January came his last letter, addressed to me, though meant for Sis. It was dated the 12th—the day George died. All his letters pleaded that I would write more frequently—he loved to hear from me; so I had been writing to him every ten days. On the third of February I sent my last. Friday the fifth, as I was running through Miriam's room, I saw Brother pass the door, and heard him ask Miriam for mother. The voice, the bowed head, the look of utter despair on his face, struck through me like a knife. "Gibbes! Gibbes!" was my sole thought; but Miriam and I stood motionless looking at each other without a word. "Gibbes is dead" said mother as he stood before her. He did not speak; and then we went in.

We did not ask how, or when. That he was dead was enough for us. But after a while he told us uncle James had written that he had died at two o'clock on Thursday the twenty first. Still we did not know how he had died. Several letters that had been brought remained unopened on the floor. One, Brother opened, hoping to learn something more. It was from Col. Steedman to Miriam and me, written a few hours after his death, and contained the sad story [of] our dear brother's last hours. He had been in Col. Steedman's ward of the hospital for more than a week, with headache and sore throat; but it was thought nothing; he seemed to improve, and expected to be discharged in a few days. On the twenty first he complained that his throat pained him again. After prescribing for him, and talking cheerfully with him for some time, Col. Steedman left him surrounded by his friends, to attend to his other patients. He had hardly reached his room when someone ran to him saying Capt. Morgan was dying. He hurried to his bedside, and found him dead. Capt. Steedman, sick in the next bed, and those around him said he had been talking pleasantly with them, when he sat up to reach his cup of water on the table. As soon as he drank it he seemed to suffocate; and after tossing his arms wildly in the air, and making several fearful efforts to breathe, he died.

O Gibbes! Gibbes! When you took me in your arms and cried so bitterly over that sad parting, it was indeed your last farewell! My brothers! my brothers! Dear Lord how can we live without our boys?

Sewed to the paper that contained the last words we should hear of our dear brother, was a lock of hair grown long during his imprisonment. I think it was a noble, tender heart that remembered that one little deed of kindness, and a gentle, pitying hand that cut it from his head as he lay cold and stark in death. Good heart that loved our brave brother, kind hand that soothed his pain, you will not be forgotten by us!

SOURCE   *The Civil War Diary of Sarah Morgan,* Charles East, ed. (Athens: University of Georgia Press, 1991), pp. 597-600.

The Confederate Draft

The end of April, then, seemed to promise the early end to the war that people had expected at its outbreak. Although many of the battles had been close that spring, they all seemed to turn out in favor of the North. The first year-long enlistments in the Confederate army were running out in April, just when the southern army met its worst defeats. Many soldiers, deciding they had done their part, left for home. Jefferson Davis and the Confederate Congress, fearful that their armies would be short of men as the Union stepped up its attacks in the late spring and summer, decided that they had no choice but to initiate a compulsory draft, the first centrally administered draft in American history. All white men between the ages of eighteen and thirty-five were required to fight for three years. Those soldiers who had been fighting for the last year would have to fight for three more. If men enlisted or reenlisted within the thirty days following passage of the law, they could choose the unit with which they fought and bear the proud title of volunteer. If they waited, they would have no such options.

Although the Confederacy eventually abolished substitution, in which men with enough money could pay a substitute to fight in their place, it still permitted men from many occupations to claim an exemption from military service. Governors, resentful of the power of the Confederacy, appointed many men to positions in their state governments and militia so that they would be exempted from the draft. Within a few months, the Confederacy, concerned about the productivity and safety of the South's plantations, also exempted one white man for every twenty slaves he supervised in the twenty negro law. Conscription ran against everything the South saw itself fighting for: freedom, a weak state, manly bravery, a common cause that would unite all white southern men. The draft, necessary though it was—providing a fifth to a third of all Confederate soldiers—divided Southerners more profoundly than anything else in the Civil War.

The Seven Days

"Every blow tells fearfully against the rebellion," a New York newspaper declared at the end of May. "The rebels themselves are panic-stricken or despondent. It now requires no very far reaching prophet to predict the end of this struggle." From the viewpoint of the

battlefields in Tennessee and Mississippi, and from the viewpoint of the ports of Norfolk and New Orleans, the war did indeed seem to be nearing its end. And in Virginia George McClellan's troops, the pride of the Union and 100,000 strong, had pushed their way up the peninsula toward Richmond. By the end of May only five miles separated them from their destination.

Not that it would be easy for the Union troops to take Richmond. The river assaults that had worked so well two months earlier in Tennessee failed in Virginia. The Confederates were able to attack the river gunboats from the heights of Drewry's Bluff, raining artillery and rifle shot down on the craft below. Even the *Monitor,* fresh from its impressive showing in Hampton Roads, proved ineffectual when faced with an enemy one hundred feet above. Moreover, the Confederates, knowing that the Union would try to take their capital, had established imposing defenses around Richmond and concentrated many of their troops in the vicinity.

Defensive positioning proved more important in the American Civil War than in any prior conflict, including the war with Mexico, in which so many of the generals on both sides of the Civil War had gained their experience of battle. Defenders gained their advantage from a new kind of weapon: the rifle. A rifle, unlike a musket, used a spiral groove in the barrel to put spin on a bullet, like a football pass, giving the bullet much greater stability and accuracy. A musket had been accurate at only about eighty yards but a rifle could hit a target at four times that distance. While the benefits of rifling had long been recognized, it was not until the 1850s that a French inventor, Charles Minie, devised a way to make it possible for a rifled gun to fire without requiring the grooves to be cleaned. While the rifles still had to be loaded from the end of the barrel, preventing even the most skillful soldiers from firing more than three times a minute, rifles nevertheless made it much more difficult for attacking troops to overwhelm a defense. Far more northern troops than southern troops had rifles in 1862, but the Confederates around Richmond still benefited from the trenches and walls of their defenses.

Lincoln and McClellan believed that Washington faced a direct threat from Confederate troops in the Shenandoah Valley under the command of the increasingly impressive Stonewall Jackson. Jackson had already developed a reputation as a general who fought cleverly, quickly, and unpredictably. For three months in the spring of 1862, Jackson maneuvered his men back and forth, up and down the valley, creating the impression that his forces were larger than they were and that they could attack anywhere, any time. As a result, the Union divided its forces, depriving McClellan's invasion of tens of thousands of soldiers that would have otherwise been available for the assault on Richmond.

The Union and the Rebel forces tested one another around Richmond in May and June, inflicting heavy casualties in battles that settled nothing. Robert E. Lee replaced Joseph Johnston, wounded in battle, as general of the Confederate forces in Virginia. Lee had no towering reputation at that point; the South did not exult nor did the North tremble. But Lee quickly proved himself aggressive and daring, much like Jackson. He almost immediately planned an attack against the larger force under McClellan's command. Lee sent out J. E. B. Stuart, his cavalry leader, who rode all the way around McClellan's troops, reconnoitering their position, stealing their supplies, and humiliating them with his skill and bravery. Stuart reported that part of McClellan's troops were vulnerable to attack. Lee brought Jackson and his men to join in an assault. The resulting prolonged conflict around Richmond, which became known as the Seven Days' Battles, did not distinguish either side. The Confederates' offensive did not work as planned and Jackson failed to carry out his part of the assault. For the North's part, McClellan, though possessing far more troops than his opponents, believed himself outnumbered and sacrificed his advantage. Thirty thousand men had been killed and wounded.

Slavery Under Attack

By the summer of 1862 the war seemed to have reached a stalemate, strength against strength. Both the Union and the Confederacy claimed important victories and both believed a decisive battle could still win the war. The North took heart because Union ships controlled the coasts and rivers on the perimeter of the South even as Union troops pushed deep into Tennessee and Mississippi. The Confederacy took comfort because vast expanses of rich southern farmland and millions of productive slaves remained beyond the reach of Union control.

President Lincoln, while detesting slavery personally, feared that a campaign against bondage would di-

vide the North and undermine his administration. As the war dragged into its second year, however, even Northerners who did not oppose slavery on moral grounds could see that slavery offered the South a major advantage. Slaves in the fields meant more white Southerners on the battlefields; slaves in the cooking tents and at the reins of wagons meant more Confederate soldiers shouldering guns. Most important, black Southerners themselves pressed slavery as a problem on the Union armies. Wherever those armies went, slaves of every description fled to the Federals as refugees. The Union called the black people who made their way to the Union ranks "contrabands," a word usually used to describe smuggled goods. The term revealed the confusion among white Northerners about the status of the black people in their midst. Were they fugitive slave property or people who had made themselves free by escaping bondage? While some Union officers returned the slaves to their owners, other officers seized the opportunity to strike against slavery.

Northern leaders confronted such issues most directly near Port Royal, South Carolina. When the Union forces overran the Sea Islands along the coast in 1862, the relatively few whites who lived there fled, leaving behind 10,000 slaves. Almost immediately, various groups of Northerners began to vie for the opportunity to reshape southern society as they thought it should be shaped. The Sea Islands claimed some of the largest and richest plantations in the South, growing rare and expensive long-staple cotton. Union leaders felt it crucial that freed slaves prove they would work willingly and effectively. Female abolitionist schoolteachers journeyed down from New England, while men mixing motives of profit and reform came from New York City and the Northwest to demonstrate that plantations run on the principles of free labor could be both productive and humane.

The black South Carolinians who lived on the islands both welcomed and struggled with these white Northerners. While the former slaves valued the opportunity to learn to read and write and wanted land of their own, they did not always appreciate lessons from the newcomer whites about religion and agriculture. Black people knew how to farm and knew their God. Not only in South Carolina, but wherever the Union army penetrated, officers and civilians sought to control black labor and rich land. Sometimes, federal officials decreed that the freed people could sign contracts with whomever they chose—but they had to sign contracts with someone. In other times and

The Sea Islands of South Carolina quickly became a testing ground for northern ideals. Missionaries and teachers of both genders came to the islands to instruct the newly liberated residents in matters both secular and religious.

places, Union leaders followed bolder experiments, permitting black people to take responsibility for some of the land they had worked as slaves. Some white Northerners, including military leaders, proposed seizing land from former slaveholders to give to the former slaves.

General David Hunter, a man of abolitionist sympathies, took advantage of his position in Port Royal in the late spring of 1862 to organize a number of black military units and to declare slavery abolished in South Carolina, Georgia, and Florida. Lincoln revoked Hunter's proclamation, however, determined that he, not generals in the field, would control the volatile issue of slavery. Lincoln did not envision the immediate emancipation decreed by Hunter, with no compensation to slaveholders and with former slaves living alongside their former masters. Lincoln thought that sectional reunion demanded that slavery end in the United States as it had elsewhere in the Western Hemisphere: gradually, with payments to the slaveholders for their loss of property. Ideally, Lincoln argued, the former slaves would be colonized beyond the borders of the United States, perhaps in Haiti or Liberia.

Lincoln also resisted those members of his party and his cabinet who thought that black men should be enlisted into the Union army. Such Republicans, often called "Radicals" for their support of black rights, did all they could to turn the Union cause into an antislavery cause. The Radicals passed laws that forbade northern commanders to return refugee slaves to their former masters and they ended (albeit gradually and with compensation) slavery in the District of Columbia. Many northern Democrats bitterly opposed such expansion of the war's purposes and means, warning that abolition would only embitter and embolden the Confederates, making peace that much more difficult to attain. Democrats sympathetic to the South, called "Copperheads" by their opponents, marched under the motto "The Constitution as it is and the Union as it was." They wanted slavery to remain in place so that the South would come back into the nation and the bloodshed would stop.

Lincoln sought to steer a course between the Radicals and the Copperheads, between the immediate abolitionists on the one hand and those who would leave slavery entrenched in a reunified United States on the other. But in the summer of 1862 he moved closer to an assault on slavery. The Union army had strengthened its position in Kentucky and Missouri and it no longer appeared that the border states could effectively align themselves with the Confederates, no matter how disgruntled they might be with the Union. Similarly, Lincoln came to see that the southern

Unionists, upon whom he had pinned so many hopes in 1860 and 1861, could not or would not organize effective opposition to the Confederacy from within. Lincoln decided that to win the war he would have to hit slavery. "It may as well be understood, once for all," Lincoln announced, "that I shall not surrender this game leaving any available card unplayed."

On July 22, 1862, Lincoln and his cabinet authorized Federal military leaders to take whatever secessionist property they needed and to destroy any property that aided the Confederacy. That meant that Union officers could protect the black men and women who fled to northern camps, using them to work behind the lines. Lincoln decided to wait for a victory on the battlefield before announcing the most dramatic part of his plan: that as of January 1, 1863, he would declare all slaves in areas controlled by the Confederates free. While this proclamation would free no slaves under Union control in the border states, it ruled out compromise that would end the war and bring the South back into the Union with slavery. Knowing that this announcement would unleash harsh criticism in the North, Lincoln wanted to wait until the North was flush with confidence before he announced this Preliminary Emancipation Proclamation. When and where that victory might occur, however, was by no means clear in July of 1862.

Second Manassas and Antietam

Confidence actually ran higher in the Confederacy than in the Union during the second summer of the war. The Union, after all, could draw little solace from McClellan's sluggish performance in the ferocious Seven Days' Battles outside of Richmond in June. His insistence in the battles' aftermath that no Virginia property, including slaves, should be confiscated showed that he was out of step with the Republican leadership. Lincoln placed Henry Halleck, who advocated a more aggressive stance toward southern civilians and their slaves, in charge of all Union troops. The president put John Pope, who had been fighting in the West, in charge of the new Army of Virginia. Pope prided himself on his harshness toward Confederate property, spies, and guerillas. McClellan still commanded troops, but his role had been restricted.

The new Union leaders decided to remove McClellan's troops from the peninsula of Virginia and consolidate them, under the joint command of Pope, with

troops from the Shenandoah Valley. The forces began to move from the peninsula in August, transported by water to an area closer to Washington. Lee watched this process with a mixture of excitement and concern. Even though a massive unified army in northern Virginia posed a long-term threat of considerable consequence, the withdrawal created a temporary opportunity for the Confederacy. Lee decided to attack Pope's troops while McClellan's were withdrawing. Lee hoped to occupy as much territory as possible, resting and re-supplying his troops while complicating Union efforts to unify their forces.

Lee's plan worked better than he could have expected. Stonewall Jackson attacked Pope's men and pillaged a large federal supply depot at Manassas—on virtually the same ground where the first battle of that name had been fought a long year before. Pope then fell under attack by James Longstreet's troops, who drove the new Yankee commander back into Washington. With McClellan no longer threatening Richmond and Pope posing no danger to northern Virginia, Lee decided to seize the advantage and push into Maryland. He believed that large numbers of Marylanders would rush to the Confederate cause, showing the North that the Confederacy could not be defeated. Lee had another audience in mind as well: England and France. In the wake of Union indecision and defeat in the summer of 1862, leaders in both countries were leaning toward recognition of the Confederacy. A major victory in northern territory, Lee felt certain, would prove that the South deserved the support of the major powers.

Lee acted so confidently because he knew he would face George McClellan again. On September 17, the two old adversaries fell into battle once more, this time at Antietam Creek, near Sharpsburg, Maryland. The Confederates had 35,000 men to McClellan's 72,000, but the Southerners held the defensive ground. The terrible battle ended as so many had ended in the eastern battlefields over the preceding months, in confusion and stalemate. More men were killed, wounded, or declared missing on this day than on any other day in the Civil War: 13,000 for the Confederacy and 12,000 for the Union. Lee had lost nearly a third of his army; McClellan, despite his numerical advantage, had been unable to destroy the enemy.

Neither side could be satisfied with the battle's outcome, but the North made the best of the situation. Lincoln decided that Antietam represented enough of

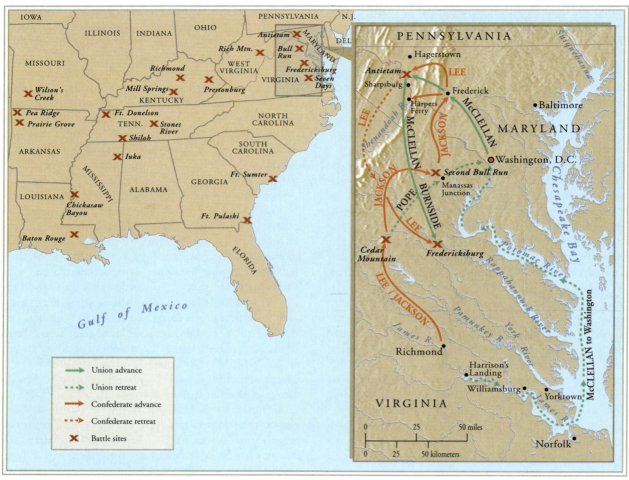

MAP 14.4 | THE CIVIL WAR IN THE EAST, SUMMER AND FALL 1862

a victory to justify his announcement of the Preliminary Emancipation Proclamation. The European powers decided that they would withhold their support for the Confederacy for the time being. The Confederacy decided that they would pull back into Virginia to fight another day. Things could have turned out very differently at this juncture. Had McClellan destroyed Lee's army—and it appears in retrospect that he might have done so—the Confederacy might have given up its claims for independence before slavery had been ended. Had Lee merely held his ground in Virginia after driving McClellan away from Richmond and Pope back into Washington, on the other hand, England and France might have offered mediation—

and the North might well have accepted, again without the end of slavery. As it was, however, both the North and the South would fight again and again.

Stalemate

While Northerners and Southerners slaughtered one another in Maryland with little clear advantage gained by either side, troops also ranged over Kentucky and Tennessee. Southern forces under the command of Braxton Bragg pushed far into Kentucky in the fall of 1862, determined to regain ground lost early in the war. Confederates believed that Kentuckians, like

The sunken road where Confederates battled Union soldiers on this Maryland battlefield became known as "Bloody Lane." Bodies piled up six deep on the bloodiest single day of the Civil War.

Marylanders, would rush to the southern flag if given a chance. Both in Kentucky and in Maryland, sympathy for the Confederacy did not lead people to enlist or even to share their food or horses. People had little confidence that the Confederates could prevail in Kentucky and did not want to risk all they had in support of a losing cause. Although the Confederates never suffered sharp defeat in Kentucky, they had too few men to occupy the state. Rather than risk losing his army, Bragg pulled his men into a more defensible position in Tennessee. As in Maryland at about the same time, bold Confederate offensives had ended without any tangible gain.

By the summer and fall of 1862, many men had died to little apparent purpose. Lincoln decided that generals in both the East and the West must be removed; George McClellan and Don Carlos Buell seemed too slow to react, too cautious—and perhaps too inclined to side with the Democrats. Lincoln replaced Buell with William S. Rosecrans and replaced McClellan with Ambrose E. Burnside, an appealing man uncertain that he was qualified for the job entrusted to him. His doubts proved to be well founded.

In November, Burnside decided to establish a new base for yet another assault on Richmond. He moved his troops to Fredericksburg, Virginia, and launched an attack on a virtually impregnable Confederate position at Marye's Heights. With Southerners able to fire down on them at will from protected positions, over 12,000 Union soldiers died as they tried repeatedly to ford the Rappahannock River and storm the heights. At battle's end, both armies remained where they had been at the battle's beginning.

The North fell into mourning, humiliation, and anger at this sacrifice. Officers as well as enlisted men made no secret of their loss of faith in Burnside, complaining bitterly through official and unofficial channels. In Tennessee, Rosecrans felt that he had to move against Bragg to demonstrate Union resolve and power. The two armies clashed on the last day of 1862 at Stones River near Murfreesboro, ending the year with a battle like so many others in this year. The two sides, losing about a third of their men each, the worst proportion in the entire war, fought to a virtual draw.

The winter of 1862–1863 saw the North and the South precariously balanced, both against one another

After the slaughter at Marye's Heights in December 1862, Confederates stripped the bodies of Union soldiers of their boots and uniforms. Here, northern burial parties inter their dead.

and within their own societies. On the battlefield, the South had made impressive showings at Fredericksburg and at Second Manassas, but the northern army had held Kentucky and Maryland. The Confederacy still possessed Vicksburg, high on a bluff on the Mississippi River, but Grant and Sherman were planning ways to take the city. Slaves ran to Union armies at every chance and plantations decayed. The Preliminary Emancipation Proclamation had given the Union effort a new purpose and new credibility with liberals in Europe, especially in England, but Lincoln faced mounting criticism within his own party and a growing threat from disgruntled Democrats. The North needed victories. Everything depended on the men in the field.

CONCLUSION

The bloody sacrifice without decisive victory of the Seven Days and Antietam fed disillusionment on both sides. The governments in both the North and the South found themselves the objects of bitter criticism from political opponents, newspapers, the public, and even former supporters. Military officers squabbled among themselves and with civilian leaders. The only thing people could agree on was that the war would

not end soon, that the death and suffering would continue.

The preceding year and a half had seen events and changes no one could have predicted, warfare on a scale no one could have imagined. Eighteen months after Lincoln had begun his journey to Washington to become president, war had become a way of life. The boundaries between the Union and the Confederacy had been firmly drawn. The governments of both sides had begun to function effectively. The first volunteer units of both armies had been mobilized and had seen action. Both the South and the North had claimed military victories. The Confederacy recalled the battle at Manassas with pride, while the Union took comfort in the steady success of its navy. The first international crisis, the *Trent* affair, had passed without dragging a major European power into the conflict. But in late 1862 both the North and the South felt that their cause must be clarified and given greater purpose if the war were to be anything more than sheer carnage.

RECOMMENDED READINGS

Boritt, Gabor. *Why the Civil War Came* (1996) gives a useful overview of recent thinking on this much-debated historical topic.

Crofts, Daniel W. *Reluctant Confederates: Upper South Unionists in the Secession Crisis* (1989) analyzes the crucial border states with keen insight.

Jones, Howard. *The Union in Peril: The Crisis over British Intervention in the Civil War* (1992) provides a fresh interpretation of a critical episode.

McPherson, James M. *Battle Cry of Freedom: The Civil War Era* (1988) is the fullest one-volume account of the Civil War.

Paludan, Phillip Shaw. *A People's Contest: The Union and the Civil War, 1861–1865* (1988) paints a full portrait of the North during war.

Parish, Peter J. *The American Civil War* (1975) offers an elegant synthesis.

Royster, Charles. *The Destructive War: William Tecumseh Sherman, Stonewall Jackson, and the Americans* (1991) is an original and disturbing meditation on war.

Simpson, Brooks D. *America's Civil War* (1996) is a fine brief interpretation with a useful bibliography.

Thomas, Emory M. *The Confederate Nation, 1861–1865* (1979) is the standard account.

Overviews

Catton, Bruce. *The Centennial History of the Civil War*, vol. 1: *The Coming Fury* (1961); vol. 2: *Terrible Swift Sword* (1963); and vol. 3, *Never Call Retreat* (1965).

Freehling, William W. *The Reintegration of American History: Slavery and the Civil War* (1994).

McPherson, James M. *What They Fought For, 1861–1865* (1994).

Nevins, Allan. *The War for the Union*, 4 vols. (1959–1971)

Foote, Shelby. *The Civil War: A Narrative* (1958–1974).

Secession and the South

Barney, William L. *The Secessionist Impulse: Alabama and Mississippi in 1860* (1974).

Channing, Steven A. *A Crisis of Fear: Secession in South Carolina* (1970).

Davis, William C. *"A Government of Our Own": The Making of the Confederacy* (1994).

Faust, Drew Gilpin. *The Creation of Confederate Nationalism: Ideology and Identity in the Civil War South* (1988).

Johnson, Michael P. *Toward a Patriarchal Republic: The Secession of Georgia* (1977).

Klein, Maury. *Days of Defiance: Sumter, Secession, and the Coming of the Civil War* (1997).

Rable, George C. *The Confederate Republic: A Revolution Against Politics* (1994).

Snay, Mitchell. *The Gospel of Disunion* (1993).

Biographies

Davis, William C. *Jefferson Davis: The Man and His Hour* (1991).

Fellman, Michael. *Citizen Sherman: A Life of William Tecumseh Sherman* (1995).

McFeely, William S. *Grant: A Biography* (1981).

Oates, Stephen B. *A Woman of Valor: Clara Barton and the Civil War* (1994).

Paludan, Phillip Shaw. *The Presidency of Abraham Lincoln* (1994).

Robertson, James I. Jr., *Stonewall Jackson: The Man, the Soldier, and the Legend* (1997).

Sears, Stephen W. *George B. McClellan: The Young Napoleon* (1988).

Simpson, Brooks D. *Let Us Have Peace: Ulysses S. Grant and the Politics of War and Reconstruction, 1861–1868* (1991).

Thomas, Emory M. *Robert E. Lee: A Biography* (1995).

The Border States

Curry, Richard O. *A House Divided: A Study of Statehood Politics and the Copperhead Movement in West Virginia* (1964).

Fellman, Michael. *Inside War: The Guerilla Conflict in the Civil War* (1989).

Harrison, Lowell. *The Civil War and Kentucky* (1975)

Naval History

Fowler, William M. Jr., *Under Two Flags: The American Navy in the Civil War* (1990).

Merrill, James M. *Battle Flags South: The Story of the Civil War Navies on Western Waters* (1970).

Wise, Stephen R. *Lifeline of the Confederacy: Blockade Running During the Civil War* (1988).

Foreign Policy

Crook, David P. *The North, the South, and the Powers, 1861–1865* (1974).

Owsley, Frank L. *King Cotton Diplomacy* (1959).

Warren, Gordon H. *Fountains of Discontent: The "Trent" Affair and the Freedom of the Seas* (1981).

Paying for War

Ball, Douglas B. *Financial Failure and Confederate Defeat* (1990).

Hammond, Bray. *Sovereignty and the Empty Purse: Banks and Politics in the Civil War* (1970).

The War in the West

Hauptman, Laurence M. *Between Two Fires: American Indians in the Civil War* (1995).

Josephy, Alvin M. Jr., *The Civil War in the American West* (1991).

THE WOUNDED

Many of the men waiting to be taken to the hospital tent would not emerge alive.

Chapter 15

BLOOD AND FREEDOM:

1863–1867

It was not clear in 1863 or even 1864 that the North was going to win the Civil War. Over the course of those years, people on both sides believed that Lincoln might not be reelected, that European powers might intervene, that the North might lose its will to fight, that one key battle could swing the outcome in the favor of the South. The Civil War enveloped the entire nation, home front and battlefield alike. The outcome of a battle could win an election or trigger a riot, while events at home affected the leaders' decisions of when and where to fight. In the North, the strong political opposition to Abraham Lincoln and his policies exerted a constant pressure on his policies and his conduct of the war. In the South, slaves abandoned plantations and white families' hardship led soldiers to rethink their loyalties. Those struggles continued after the guns had fallen silent.

PEOPLE AT WAR: SPRING 1863

Both Northerners and Southerners expected the spring of 1863 to bring the climax of the Civil War. Much

had been decided, organized, and mobilized over the preceding two years. The generals and the battlefields determined the outcome of battles, but perhaps the wives, slaves, workers, bureaucrats, draft dodgers, and politicians behind the lines would determine the outcome of the war.

Life in the Field

Soldiers eventually got used to the miseries of sleeping on the ground, poorly cooked food, driving rain, and endless mud. They might even become adjusted to the lice and dirt that flourished in the camps of both the Union and the Confederacy. They learned to adapt to gambling, drinking, cursing, and prostitution, either by succumbing to the temptations or by steeling their resolve against them. They could toughen themselves to the intermittent mails and the arrival of bad news from home. Confederates managed to march with shoes falling off their feet. Over time, veterans could even learn to absorb the deaths of men with whom they had shared so much.

But even the most stalwart of soldiers could not adapt to the constant threat of diseases such as diarrhea, dysentery, typhoid, malaria, measles, diphtheria,

CHRONOLOGY

1863

January	1	Second Emancipation Proclamation
	25	Hooker replaces Burnside as commander of Army of the Potomac
February	25	Union Congress passes National Bank Act
		Grant unsuccessfully looks for "back door" to Vicksburg
		Trans-Mississippi area comes under command of Confederate General Kirby Smith
March	3	Union Congress passes Conscription Act
	26	Confederate Congress passes Impressment Act
April	2	Bread riot in Richmond
May	1	Confederate Congress gives more power to War Department
	5	Clement Vallandigham, "copperhead leader," arrested
	6	Culmination of Lee's victory over Hooker at Chancellorsville
	1–18	Grant's successful campaign in Mississippi
	10	Death of Stonewall Jackson
June	3	Lee begins advance to North
	15	Lee's army crosses Potomac
	28	Meade replaces Hooker as commander of Army of Potomac
July	1–3	Union victory at Gettysburg
	4	Vicksburg surrenders to Grant
	8	Port Hudson surrenders to Union
	13–14	Lee retreats across Potomac into Virginia
	13–16	New York City draft riots

	18	Black troops fight at Fort Wagner, South Carolina
September	8	Union captures Fort Wagner
	19–20	Rosecrans defeated by Bragg at Chickamauga
		Confederate congressional elections go against Jefferson Davis
October	17	Grant assumes control of Union forces in West
		Elections show Republicans growing stronger
November	19	Lincoln's Gettysburg Address
	25	Union victory at Chattanooga
December	8	Lincoln proclamation of amnesty and proposals for reconstruction

1864

January		Widening rift between Lincoln and Congress on reconstruction
February		Confederate Congress assumes new powers of taxation, impressment of slaves
March	9	Grant assumes command of all Union forces
	16	Alexander Stephens attacks "despotism" of Davis administration
April	12	Confederate general Nathan Bedford Forrest captures Fort Pillow, Tennessee; allegedly massacres African-American troops
May	4	Union begins offensive in Virginia and Georgia
	5–6	Battle of the Wilderness in Virginia
June	3	Union victory at Cold Harbor
	7	Lincoln renominated by Republicans; Andrew Johnson as vice president

CHRONOLOGY

	15–18	Union fails in attack on Petersburg; begins nine-month siege
	27	Sherman defeated at Kennesaw Mountain, Georgia
July	4	Lincoln pocket vetoes Wade-Davis Reconstruction bill
	17	Hood replaces Johnston as Confederate commander in Atlanta
	30	Union failure at Battle of the Crater near Petersburg
August	5	Union victory at Mobile Bay
		Republicans discuss removal of Lincoln as candidate
	29	Northern Democrats nominate McClellan for president
September	2	Sherman captures Atlanta
	19–22	Sheridan's victories in Shenandoah Valley
October	19	Union victory at Cedar Creek, ending Confederate threat in Shenandoah
	23	Union victory in Missouri ends fighting west of the Mississippi
November	8	Lincoln reelected president
	15–16	Beginning of Sherman's march from Atlanta to the Atlantic
	30	Union victory at Franklin, Tennessee
December	15–16	Union victory at Nashville
	21	Savannah falls to Sherman
1865		
January	31	Congress passes Thirteenth Amendment, lending federal sanction of slavery
February	1	Sherman begins march through Carolinas

	6	Lee becomes commander of all Confederate forces
	17	Columbia, South Carolina, burned; Confederates evacuate Charleston
March	3	Congress creates Bureau of Refugees, Freedmen, and Abandoned Lands (Freedmen's Bureau)
	4	Lincoln's second inauguration
		Sherman completes march through Carolinas
	13	Confederate army authorizes recruitment of slaves into army
	30	Grant begins final assault in Virginia
April	2	Fall of Petersburg to Union
	3	Fall of Richmond to Union
	4	Jefferson Davis's last appeal to people of the South
	9	Lee surrenders to Grant at Appomattox Court House
	14–15	Lincoln assassinated
	26	Joseph E. Johnston surrenders in North Carolina
May	10	Jefferson Davis captured
	26	Edmund Kirby Smith surrenders trans-Mississipp region, bringing the war to formal end
		Former Confederate states hold constitutional conventions through December; pass "black codes"
		African Americans hold conventions in South
December	18	Thirteenth Amendment to Constitution ratified, abolishing slavery

CHRONOLOGY

1866	
February	Johnson vetoes Freedmen's Bureau Bill
April	Congress passes Civil Rights Act and Freedmen's Bureau renewal over Johnson's veto
May	Riots in New Orleans and Memphis
June	Congress approves Fourteenth Amendment
	Ku Klux Klan formed
	Most ex-Confederate states reject Fourteenth Amendment

1867		
March	2	Congress passes Reconstruction Act and Tenure of Office Act
		Constitutional conventions in southern states
August	12	Johnson dismisses Secretary of War Stanton, triggering impeachment proceedings
		First elections in South under Reconstruction Act

and scarlet fever. As bloody as the battles were, disease killed twice as many men as died from the guns of the enemy. Many doctors of the Civil War era used the same instruments of surgery on soldier after soldier, unwittingly spreading disease to patients already suffering from amputation or bullet wounds. After every battle, screams filled the night as surgeons sawed off legs and arms, feet and hands, in often vain hopes of stopping gangrene.

Purposes

The North fought for ideals of union and democracy; the South fought for ideals of self-determination. But soldiers fought for more personal purposes as well. Men acted courageously not only because they believed in the official political purposes for which they were fighting, but also because they wanted to be admired by the people at home, because they wanted to be manly, because they wanted to do their part for their comrades, because they wanted to bring the war to a quicker end, and because they grew to hate the enemy.

Soldiers enlisted in their communities, as members of communities. Many men fought alongside their brothers, uncles, cousins. A steady stream of letters flowed back and forth between the units and the families and neighbors back home. Gossip, praise, and condemnation flourished, as acts of bravery or cowardice became magnified through distance and repetition. Any soldier who planned to return home knew that his deeds in the war would live with him the rest of his life. As a result, even fearful or halfhearted soldiers might throw themselves into battle to demonstrate their courage.

While about three-fifths of Civil War soldiers were over twenty-one at the age of enlistment—considerably older than the armies of the twentieth century—the largest single group of soldiers was eighteen. They came of age during the war, defined themselves during the war. For those who passed the birthdays of their late teens or early twenties on the battlefields, the transition to manhood became inseparable from the war. To be manly meant more than the simple ability to inflict violence on the enemy. It meant pride, responsibility, loyalty, and obedience. Every battle became a test of manhood, which could not be won once and forever but had to be proven every time it was challenged under fire. Some of the bravery and sacrifice of the war grew out of boys' desperate desire to be thought men.

Courage developed, too, out of hatred. While neither the Union nor the Confederacy developed effective twentieth-century style propaganda machinery, people on both sides spread the worst stories and rumors about one another. Newspapers printed exaggerated or fabricated atrocity reports about the enemy.

The longer the war went on the more people felt they had to hate one another to justify so much bloodshed. Violence, on the battlefield and against property and civilians, was often sheer vengeance.

The sermons men heard in the camps told them they were fighting on the side of the right. The Old Testament afforded rich imagery and compelling stories of violence inflicted for good causes. Many Americans believed that God enacted His will directly in human affairs. As the war ground on, the leaders, the soldiers, and the civilians of both sides came to feel that events were more than the product of human decision or even courage. Surely, they told themselves, so much suffering and sacrifice had to be for a larger purpose.

The Problems of the Confederate Government

Convinced that greedy merchants were holding supplies of flour until prices rose even higher, in the spring of 1863 poor women in Richmond rushed into the streets of the Confederate capital. They broke open the stores of merchants accused of hoarding the precious staple, taking what they needed and what they considered fairly to be theirs. Jefferson Davis went to plead with the angry women. The threat of being arrested and the promise of free supplies broke up the riot, but similar events occurred in several other southern cities. No one could tell when even larger riots might erupt again.

The rioters were not the only ones who took what they needed. Confederate officers in the field took—"impressed"—what their troops required. The officers forced reluctant farmers to accept whatever prices the army offered, in an increasingly worthless currency. In the spring of 1863, the Confederate government attempted to curb the worst abuses of this practice in the Impressment Act. If a farmer did not think the prices he or she received were fair (and they were almost never as high as they could get through private sale), the case could be appealed before local authorities. In practice, however, this cumbersome system failed. Farmers hid their produce from officers and resented it when they were forced to sell. Impressment, like the draft and the "twenty negro law," eroded civilian support for the Confederate government.

The southern government could not afford to lose this or any other kind of support, for its power, weak at the beginning of the conflict, became even weaker over time. While the absence of political parties originally appeared to be a sign of the South's consensus, that absence eventually undermined what original consensus the Confederacy had enjoyed. Jefferson Davis, without a party mechanism to discipline those who spoke out against him, could not remove enemies from office or threaten them with loss of party patronage. Davis's own vice president, Alexander Stephens, turned against the president soon after the war began. Stephens became a persistent and outspoken critic of the Confederate president throughout the rest of his term, actively undermining support for Davis and even allying with avowed enemies of Davis and his policies.

The Confederate government faced a fundamental dilemma. The whole point of secession had been to move political power closer to localities, protecting slavery in particular and self-determination in general. States' rights had been the rallying cry. The government of the Confederacy, however, had to centralize power in order to protect the states. If the armies were to be fed and clothed, if diplomats were to make a plausible case for the Confederacy's nationhood, if soldiers were to be mobilized, then the Confederate government had to exercise greater power than its creators had expected or intended. Jefferson Davis continually struggled with this tension. For every Southerner who considered Davis too weak, another considered the president dangerously powerful.

The Northern Homefront

In the North, the war heightened the strong differences between the Democrats and the Republicans. The Democrats won significant victories in congressional elections throughout much of the North in the fall and winter of 1862, testifying to the depth and breadth of the opposition to Lincoln and his conduct of the war. Wealthy businessmen in the cities of the northeast were eager to reestablish trade with their former southern partners, while Irish immigrants wanted to end the risk of the draft and competition from freed slaves. Some Democrats in the northwest talked of seceding from both the South and the East, which they saw as the base of the rich and the Republicans. Many citizens of Ohio, Indiana, and Illinois, whose families had come from the South, wanted to renew the southern connections that had been broken by the war.

Black men had called for their inclusion in the U.S. Army from the beginning of the war. In the spring of 1863 the U.S. Colored Troops were formed and over 180,000 African-American men fought for the Union over the next two years.

The Union passed its Conscription Act in March of 1863 because disease, wounds, and desertion had depleted the ranks faster than they could be replaced. When drafted, a man could appear for duty, hire a substitute to fight in his place, or simply pay a fee of $300 directly to the government. State and federal governments often paid bounties—signing bonuses—to those who volunteered. More than a few men, struck by the possibilities of such ready cash, took the bounties and then promptly deserted and moved to another locality to claim another bounty.

The opposition to the Lincoln government raised crucial issues. How much dissent could a wartime government tolerate? With the North claiming to fight for liberty, what limitations on freedom of speech and protest could it enforce? A Democratic congressman from Ohio, Clement Vallandigham, tested those limits in the spring of 1863. Hating both secessionists and abolitionists, Vallandigham refused to obey a general's orders to stop criticizing the Lincoln administration. He was arrested, tried before a military court, and sentenced to imprisonment for the rest of the war. Lincoln was dismayed by these events. They fueled the charge common throughout the North that he was a tyrant, trampling on the rights of Americans. The president commuted Vallandigham's sentence, sending him to the Confederates in Tennessee, hoping to make Vallandigham appear a southern sympathizer rather than a martyr to the cause of free speech. Vallandigham quickly escaped to Canada, however, where he continued his criticisms. Ohio Democrats defiantly nominated Vallandigham for governor in the elections to be held in the fall of 1863. If things continued to go badly for the Union, who knew what kind of success a critic of Lincoln might find?

African-American Soldiers

Though northern civilian and military leaders remained deeply divided and ambivalent about black freedom, it became clear to everyone that freed slaves could be of great value to the Union. In May 1863, the War Department created the Bureau of Colored Troops. White men of abolitionist leanings sought to become officers for these units, eager to show what they and their men could do. Generals in the field accepted into service many southern black men who had traveled to northern camps.

At first, black recruits found themselves restricted to noncombat roles and a lower rate of pay: ten dollars a month versus the thirteen dollars a month and three-fifty clothing allowance given white soldiers. Black men, though eager to serve, protested that they could not support their families on such amounts and that their lives were worth just as much as their white compatriots. African Americans knew, and coveted, the rights and privileges of other Americans. They wrote petitions and appealed to higher authorities, often in the language of the Declaration of Independence and the Constitution.

Confederate officials who expected black soldiers to make reluctant or cowed fighters soon discovered otherwise. In May of 1863 two black regiments stormed, seven times, a heavily fortified Confederate installation at Port Hudson, Louisiana. Soon thereafter, black soldiers found themselves on the other side of the barricades. At Milliken's Bend, Louisiana, they fought Confederates hand-to-hand, desperately wielding swords and bayonets against white men. Northern newspapers echoed the words of praise from generals in the field: "No troops could be more determined or more daring."

African-American men in the North rushed to the recruiting tables. Frederick Douglass, the leading spokesman for black Americans, celebrated the enlistments: "Once let the black man get upon his person the brass letters, *U.S.*; let him get an eagle on his button, and a musket on his shoulder, and bullets in his pocket, and there is no power on earth which can deny that he has earned the right to citizenship in the United States." From Rhode Island to Ohio, black troops prepared to head south. Even more African-American units formed in the states of the occupied South, as formerly enslaved men became soldiers of the United States Army.

THE BATTLEFIELDS OF SUMMER: 1863

Everything seemed in place for a climactic culmination of the war in the summer of 1863. The Union had almost severed the western half of the Confederacy from the eastern; the Union army received a relentless flow of men and arms; the Union had penetrated deep into Tennessee and stood on the threshold of Georgia. On the other hand, the Confederate army had toughened itself to its disadvantages and learned to make the most of the advantages it enjoyed. It appeared to be strength against strength as the mud dried and the fighting season began.

Vicksburg and Chancellorsville

Union leaders needed all the help they could get in early 1863, for pivotal battles clearly loomed in the summer to come. Grant and Sherman remained frustrated in their goal of seizing Vicksburg; Rosecrans faced Bragg in Tennessee; Lee's army had yet to be decisively defeated despite the men, resources, and determination thrown into battle against him. Lee would face General Joseph Hooker. Lincoln, in one more attempt to find an effective leader, had chosen Hooker to replace Ambrose Burnside. Throughout the spring, "Fighting Joe" Hooker energized his men and repaired some of the damage to morale and readiness inflicted at Fredericksburg. But no one knew if he would be able to handle Lee.

The Northern public was especially impatient with Grant and Sherman, who, it seemed, would be stranded forever outside Vicksburg. Grant knew the delays threatened his command. Vicksburg, heavily fortified by both geography and the Confederates, seemed most vulnerable to attack from the southeast, but to get there Grant would have to find a way to move his men across the Mississippi River without landing them in swamps that could swallow an army. Throughout the long wet winter, Grant had tried one experiment after another, including digging canals. Nothing worked.

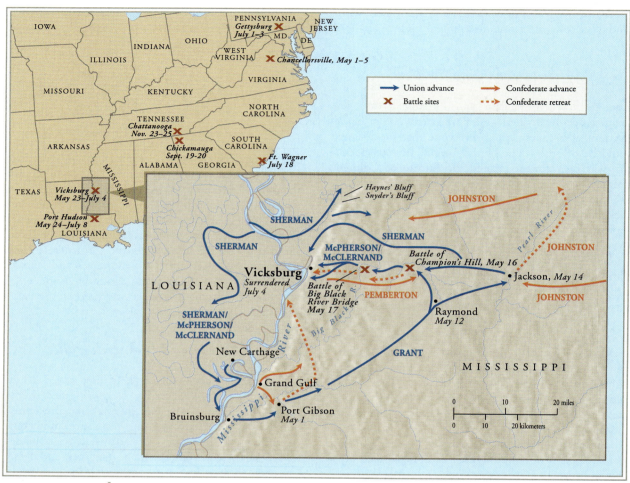

| MAP 15.1 | THE CIVIL WAR, SUMMER 1863: VICKSBURG |

Grant finally set aside his complicated engineering plans and decided on a bold move: he would run a flotilla of gunboats and barges past Vicksburg under the cover of night to ferry his men across the Mississippi south of the city, where the land was better. The guns of Vicksburg stood two hundred feet above the river, ready to fire down on any passing craft, but the Union men covered their boilers with sacks of grain and bales of cotton to protect them from the shelling. Most of the boats made it through. Grant, now equipped with means of transport and supply, took the advice of a local slave about the best place to land his men on the other side of the river. He had Sherman create a diversion far away from Grant's landing place, confusing the Confederates, and then ferried his

entire army across the Mississippi. Grant's army remained vulnerable, cut off from his allies and his major supply base, but by late April he was finally where he wanted to be.

In the same week Grant made his landing near Vicksburg, Hooker began his attack on Lee, still based in Fredericksburg. Hooker commanded 130,000 men, the largest army in the war thus far. Unlike Burnside, however, Hooker intended to outsmart Lee rather than try to overwhelm him with numbers and bravery. A large Union force would sweep around Lee and attack him from behind even as another force attacked from the front. To keep from being bottled up in Fredericksburg, Lee would have to emerge from his well-entrenched defensive

MAP 15.2 | THE CIVIL WAR, SUMMER 1863: VIRGINIA AND PENNSYLVANIA

position, either fighting in the open or retreating to Richmond. Lee met this bold move with an even bolder one. He would divide his forces, already much smaller than Hooker's, and send Stonewall Jackson to attack Hooker's men from the rear, outflanking Hooker's own flanking maneuver.

On May 2, Jackson assaulted Hooker's troops near Chancellorsville. The outnumbered Confederates defeated the surprised and indecisive Hooker, achieving a major victory. Southern jubilation, though, ended the very night of their triumph, for nervous Confederate soldiers accidentally shot Stonewall Jackson while he surveyed the scene near the front lines. The surgeons removed his arm that evening and hoped that he might live.

While Jackson lay in his tent, fading in and out of consciousness, Lee managed to contain another assault on Fredericksburg and to push the Union troops away from their positions. The losses had once again been staggering, for the South even more than for the North, but Lee had overcome a larger opponent. After the last battles quieted, however, Jackson died. His death took with it Lee's most trusted general and a kindred spirit, a quiet man who loved the attack.

Gettysburg

Despite his victory at Chancellorsville, Lee recognized that the Confederacy was in trouble. Rosecrans still

A battle in an obscure town in southern Pennsylvania, Gettysburg, provided some of the most memorable struggles of the entire war, especially the Confederate charge up an unprotected slope to Cemetery Ridge, where massed Union troops awaited.

threatened to break through Tennessee into Georgia, Grant clawed his way closer to Vicksburg, and the Union blockade drew an ever tighter net around the coast. While the North seemed to have an inexhaustible supply of men, the South did not. The Confederacy could not fight everywhere at once. Some of his generals urged Lee to rush with his troops to Tennessee to defend the center of the Confederacy and pull Grant away from Vicksburg. But Lee decided that his most effective move would be to invade the North again, taking the pressure off Virginia and replenishing his troops, heartening the South and disheartening the Union. A successful strike into the North might even yet persuade Britain and France to recognize the Confederacy.

In early June, Lee began to move up through the Shenandoah Valley into southern Pennsylvania. Hooker seemed confused, certain that Lee had the Union outnumbered even though he did not. When, after a minor dispute, Hooker offered his resignation to Lincoln, the president quickly accepted and put General George Meade in charge. Meade, while experienced, knew little of Hooker's plans and even less of Lee's. He quickly had to decide how best to stop the

greatest threat the Confederate army had yet posed to the North. Washington and Baltimore lay in danger, along with the cities, towns, and farms of Pennsylvania. There, the Confederate troops enjoyed taking food and livestock from the rich land.

Although Lee and his men moved unchecked across the Potomac and deep into Pennsylvania, they found themselves in a dangerous situation. Lee had permitted Jeb Stuart's cavalry, his "eyes," to range widely from the main army; as a result, the Confederates had little idea where the Union army was or what moves they were making. For their part, Meade and his fellow officers decided to pursue Lee, but not too aggressively, looking for a likely time and place to confront the enemy. Neither side had a clear plan or desire to fight immediately; both waited to see what the other would do.

On June 30, units from the Confederacy and the Union stumbled over one another at a small town neither side knew or cared much about: Gettysburg. Ironically, the Confederates flowed down from the northwest while the Union soldiers came in from the southeast. On July 1 they began to struggle for the best defensive position near the town, fighting over the highest and most protected land. It appeared at first that the Southerners had the better of the first day's battle, but as the smoke cleared both sides could see that late in the day the Union army, larger in any case, had consolidated itself on the most advantageous ground. Meade's men, after fierce fighting at the ends of their line, occupied a fishhook-shaped series of ridges and hills that permitted them to protect their flanks and to repel the Confederates spread around them. The second day saw the Confederates slowly mobilize their forces for assaults on those positions and launch attacks late in the afternoon. The resulting battles in the peach orchard, the wheat field, Little Round Top, and the boulder-strewn area known as the Devil's Den proved horrific—with 35,000 men dead or wounded—but left the Union in control of the high ground.

Despite the Union's superior position and some misgivings by his generals, Lee decided on a frontal attack the next day. The Confederates hoped their artillery would soften the middle of the Union lines. The Confederates did not realize how little damage their guns had done until well-entrenched Union troops decimated waves of an attack led by George E. Pickett. Only a few southern men made it to the stone wall that protected the Northerners, and even those Confederates quickly fell. It proved a disastrous charge and a disastrous three days for Lee and the Confederacy. They lost 23,000 men through death or wounds, about a third of their entire force. While the Union lost similar numbers of men, they had more to lose. The Northerners and their new general had fought a conservative, defensive battle; the southern side, short on supplies and men, had gambled, somewhat desperately, on an aggressive assault. The strategic and political consequences of the battle remained to be seen on the evening of July 3, when men lay dead or dying all across the somber fields of Gettysburg.

The next morning, a thousand miles away, Vicksburg surrendered to Ulysses S. Grant. Unlike Gettysburg, where the battle had been fought in a place no one would have foretold and which no one considered strategically important, Vicksburg held enormous tactical and psychological importance. It had been the symbol of Confederate doggedness and Union frustration. After six weeks of siege, after six weeks of near starvation behind the Confederate defenses, Vicksburg fell. The Mississippi River now divided the Confederacy while it tied the Union to the Gulf of Mexico.

Some Southerners, including Jefferson Davis, did not perceive Gettysburg as a defeat. In their eyes, Lee and his men had pushed deep into the Union, inflicted heavy losses, and damaged northern morale without being trapped there. Northerners at the time often agreed, pronouncing themselves more frustrated than satisfied with Meade, who had not destroyed Lee's army despite his greater numbers and the friendly terrain. During the Confederate retreat to Virginia the Southerners found themselves caught between a swollen Potomac River and pursuing Federal troops. Meade, his army exhausted and weakened from losing tens of thousands of men, chose not to fight against the defenses Lee's men hurriedly put up against their pursuers. Meade could not know that the condition of the southern troops was even worse than his own, full of demoralization and desertion. Fortunately for the Confederates, the river soon calmed enough that they were able to escape back into Virginia. Meade could have ended the war at the Potomac, Lincoln felt certain, but "as it is, the war will be prolonged indefinitely."

The New York City Draft Riots

On the very day that Lee struggled across the Potomac to safety, riots broke out in New York City. Northern working people held complicated feelings about the war. Many of those who labored in the North's factories, mines, farms, and railroads had come to the United States in the last few years. These people, mostly Irish and Germans, valued the opportunity the American economy offered as well as the nation's avowed commitment to freedom. They volunteered in large numbers, often in units comprised solely of immigrants from their country, to fight for the Union cause. Immigration to the North continued to flow heavily even during the war, as men and women eagerly filled the jobs vacated by those who fought.

On the other hand, many of the immigrants viewed black Americans with dread and contempt, seeing them as competitors for jobs and housing. Urban labor organizations divided over Lincoln's election and over the response to secession. Many Irishmen, almost all of them Democrats, proclaimed that they had no quarrel with white Southerners and that they resented the federal government's draft. The conspicuous success of northern businessmen and the obvious effect of inflation on the wages of workers created strong resentments as well. Working people sneered at those men who had enough money to hire substitutes to fight in their place. Three hundred dollars, after all, constituted half a year's wage for a workingman.

Irish immigrants despaired at the losses among Irish-American units in the field. When their regiments were decimated at Fredericksburg, Gettysburg, and elsewhere, Irish people began to wonder if commanders valued their lives as highly as those of the native-born. When word came, just as the draft lottery was to take place in New York City on July 11, 1863, of the 23,000 men lost at Gettysburg, the fury of working people rose. On July 13, it exploded. Mobs began by assaulting draft officials, then turned their anger on any man who looked rich enough to have hired a substitute, then on pro-Lincoln newspapers and abolitionists' homes. Most viciously, they turned on black citizens. The rioters burned a black orphanage and assaulted any African Americans they encountered on the streets.

The police struggled for three days to control the riot, the largest the United States had ever seen. Eventually, troops (including all-Irish units) rushed from the battlefields of Pennsylvania to aid the police. The troops fired into the rioters; over a hundred people, most of them protesters, died and another 300 were injured. The working people got some of what they wanted: more welfare relief, exemptions from the draft for those whose families would have no other means of support, and an exodus of black people who feared for their lives. Resistance to the draft and to blacks erupted, too, in the mining districts of Pennsylvania, in the immigrant sections of Chicago, and in the quarries of Vermont. As in the South, women rioted alongside men. The war threatened to pull the North apart in 1863 even as it attempted to save the Union.

Ironically, a few days after the New York draft riots scores of black troops died during a bold nighttime assault on Fort Wagner near Charleston, South Carolina. Despite the bravery of the African Americans, the assault failed. The Confederates made a point of burying the African-American soldiers in a mass grave along with their white officer, Robert Gould Shaw, intending to insult him and his memory. Instead, they elevated him as a northern martyr.

Chickamauga

After Gettysburg, Vicksburg, and the New York riots in July, events slowed until September, when Union General William Rosecrans left Chattanooga, near the Georgia border, and began moving toward Atlanta. His opponent, Braxton Bragg, was reinforced by Longstreet from Virginia and hoped to entice Rosecrans into dividing his forces so that they could be cut off. They confronted one another at Chickamauga Creek—a Cherokee name meaning "river of death." The Confederates took advantage of Union mistakes on the heavily wooded battlefield, inflicting harrowing damage and driving Rosecrans back into Chattanooga. The Union troops were trapped there, the Confederates looming over them on Lookout Mountain and Missionary Ridge, with few routes of escape and limited supplies. The Northerners had gone from a position of apparent advantage to one of desperation.

Lincoln, judging Rosecrans "confused and stunned" by the battle at Chickamauga, used this opportunity to put Grant in charge of all Union armies between the Appalachian Mountains and the Mississippi River. In the fall of 1863, Grant traveled to Chattanooga, where Sherman joined him from Mississippi and Hooker came from Virginia. Lincoln had growing faith in Grant, the man who had taken the Tennessee and Mississippi rivers for the Union. Now the president trusted Grant to save Chattanooga, a crucial outpost on the Union's drive into Georgia.

The Gettysburg Address

The North's victories in the summer of 1863 aided Lincoln's popularity. The draft riots in New York City damaged the reputations of Democrats while the bravery of black soldiers on the battlefields of Louisiana and South Carolina led white Northerners to rethink some of their prejudices. In the fall of 1863, the Republicans won major victories in Pennsylvania and Ohio, the latter especially sweet because the Democrats had nominated Clement Vallandigham, the Copperhead whom Lincoln had exiled from the state only a few months earlier. Lincoln determined to make the most of these heartening events, for the good fortune might not last.

When Lincoln received an invitation to speak at the dedication of the cemetery at Gettysburg on November 19, he saw it as a chance to mend political fences, offer words of comfort to grief-stricken parents and wives, and persuade reluctant governors to give

ABRAHAM LINCOLN "THE GETTYSBURG ADDRESS," 1863

Perhaps the most influential and memorable brief passage in American history, Lincoln's "remarks" at the opening of the Gettysburg battle-field in November of that year articulated the highest ideals with which the war could be associated: a government "of the people, by the people, for the people." The "new birth of freedom" Lincoln invoked proved, however, to take generations to come to pass.

Four score and seven years ago our fathers brought forth on this continent, a new nation, conceived in Liberty, and dedicated to the proposition that all men are created equal.

Now we are engaged in a great civil war, testing whether that nation, or any nation so conceived and so dedicated, can long endure. We are met on a great battle-field of that war. We have come to dedicate a portion of that field, as a final resting place for those who here gave lives that that nation might live. It is altogether fitting and proper that we should do this.

But, in a larger sense, we can not dedicate—we can not consecrate—we can not hallow—this ground. The brave men, living and dead, who struggled here, have consecrated it, far above our poor power to add or detract. The world will little note, nor long remember what we say here, but it can never forget what they did here. It is for us the living, rather, to be dedicated here to the unfinished work which they who fought here have thus far so nobly advanced. It is rather for us to be here dedicated to the great task remaining before us—that from these honored dead we take increased devotion to that cause for which they gave the last full measure of devotion—that we here highly resolve that these dead shall not have died in vain—that this nation, under God, shall have a new birth of freedom—and that government of the people, by the people, for the people, shall not perish from the earth.

even more to the Union cause. The event had not been planned with him in mind and the president was not even the featured speaker. Edward Everett, a scholar and famed lecturer, had been asked weeks before to give the main address. But Lincoln, seeing a chance to impart a sense of direction and purpose to the Union cause, recognized that a battlefield offered the most effective backdrop for the things he wanted to say.

Burial crews had been laboring for weeks to inter and reinter swollen and stinking remains on the Gettysburg battlefield. Thousands of horse carcasses had been burned; thousands of human bodies had been hastily covered with a thin layer of soil. Speculators hurriedly bought up land in expectation of government-sponsored cemeteries. Pennsylvania purchased seventeen acres and hired a specialist in rural cemetery design to lay out the burial plots so that no state would be offended by the location or amount of space devoted to its fallen men. Only about a third of the reburials had taken place when Lincoln arrived; caskets remained stacked at the station.

Lincoln, contrary to legend, did not dash off his speech on the back of an envelope. He had reworked and polished it for several days. The "remarks," as the program put it, lasted three minutes. Lincoln used those minutes to maximum effect. He looked beyond the muddy fields, the decaying bodies, the shattered hopes for a decisive northern victory. He said virtually nothing about the details of the scene surrounding the 20,000 people at the ceremony. Neither did he mention slavery directly. Instead, he spoke of equality as the fundamental purpose of the war. He called for a "new birth of freedom."

Lincoln was attempting to shift the purpose of the war from Union for Union's sake to Union for freedom's sake. He spoke as if all the white Union men who died at Gettysburg had willingly given their lives for black freedom and even equality, though he knew that many had not. Lincoln sought to salvage something from the deaths of the 50,000 men at Gettysburg. Democratic newspapers rebuked Lincoln for his claim, arguing that white soldiers had "too much self-respect to declare that negroes were their equals." But other Northerners accepted Lincoln's exhortation as the definition of their purpose. They might not believe that blacks deserved to be included as full participants in a government of, by, and for "the people," but they did believe that the Union fought for liberty broadly conceived. As battles and years went by, the words of the Gettysburg Address would gain force and resonance as Americans looked back to see the war's purposes portrayed in their most flattering light.

Just four days after Lincoln's speech, Grant gave the North new reason to believe their ideals might triumph. On November 23, Grant's men overwhelmed the Confederates on Lookout Mountain outside Chattanooga; two days later, Union soldiers accomplished the improbable task of fighting their way up Missionary Ridge because Confederate artillery could not reach opponents coming up directly from below. The Union, now in control of Kentucky and Tennessee, had a wide and direct route into Georgia. Lincoln had finally found in Grant a general who seemed to value action over preparation.

England and France finally determined in late 1863 that they would not try to intervene in the American war. England even decided against delivering two powerful ships being built there for the Confederacy. The northern public, encouraged by events on the battlefield, supported Republican candidates in the congressional elections of 1863 more vigorously than had seemed possible just a few months before, when the New York draft riots and Chickamauga had thrown shadows over the Union purpose.

THE WINTER OF DISCONTENT: 1863–1864

The battles of the summer had been horrific; more men had died than anyone had thought possible. Both sides held their victories close to their hearts and brooded over their losses. The resolve and fury of summertime faded into the bitterness and bickering of winter. As the cycle rolled around again, people grew profoundly weary of the sacrifice but steeled themselves for a final push.

Politics North and South

Lincoln hoped to end the war as soon as possible, using persuasion as well as fighting to entice white Southerners back into the national fold. In early December 1863, Lincoln issued his proclamation of amnesty and reconstruction. To those who would take an oath of loyalty to the Union, Lincoln promised a full pardon and the return of all property other than slaves. Though he excluded Confederate leaders and high officers from this offer, Lincoln tried to include as many white southern men as possible. As soon as 10 percent of the number of voters in 1860 had sworn their loyalty to the Union, he decreed, the Southerners could begin forming new state governments. Slavery would come to a gradual end. Education and apprenticeship programs would aid former slaves in the transition to full freedom. He did not provide for African-American participation in the new governments of the South. Though he did comment that some "very intelligent" black men, including veterans, might be permitted to vote, Lincoln would not risk alienating an already skittish white northern electorate with radical plans for the postwar world.

Abolitionists and their allies attacked Lincoln's reconstruction plan as far too lenient to the rebel masters and not helpful enough for the former slaves. "To free the slave, and then to abandon him . . . betwixt bondage and manhood, is not this as cruel as slavery?" asked one critic. In the Wade-Davis bill of February 1864, Republican congressmen attempted to institute more stringent demands on former Confederates and offer more help to former slaves. They wanted to use the power of the national government to enforce a standard set of laws across the South. Just as Lincoln feared that too strong a plan of reconstruction would galvanize white Southerners against peace, Republicans in Congress and in his cabinet feared that too weak a plan would permit former slaveowners and Confederates to negate much of what the war might win. Congressmen and Secretary of the Treasury Salmon P. Chase worked behind the scenes in opposition to Lincoln's plan.

While Jefferson Davis did not have to worry about his own re-election in late 1863—the Confederacy had established the presidential term at six years—he did have to worry about congressional elections. They did not go well: forty-one of the new 106 representatives expressly opposed Davis and his policies, while he held only a slight majority in the Senate. Just as northern Democrats called for compromise and peace, so did some Southerners. When Davis took a hands-off policy, he was criticized for doing too little. When he tried to assert more control, he found himself called "despotic" by his own vice president. When he tried to use slaves to the South's advantage, he was criticized for meddling with the very institution the war was supposed to protect. When he tried to use the power of the Confederate government to coordinate the war effort, he was criticized for undermining the rights of the states in whose name the war was being fought.

The Confederacy stumbled through the winter and into the spring of 1864, arguing with itself, desperately watching for signs that the North might be losing heart.

Prisons

Early in the Civil War, both sides had exchanged prisoners of war rather than spend men and resources maintaining prisons. Such arrangements worked well enough into 1863, but then things began to break down. Not only did the battles of that year fill the ramshackle prisons of both sides to capacity and beyond, but the Confederates decreed that any former slave captured would be executed or reenslaved, not taken prisoner. The Union, as a matter of principle, refused to participate in any exchanges so long as this policy remained in effect. Prisoners began piling up on both sides and stories of mistreatment became more frequent and more horrifying. Men spent months in abandoned warehouses or exposed to the elements in the roughest of camps.

Northerners who heard of the Confederate camp at Andersonville, Georgia, became livid. The camp was built early in 1864 when the Confederates decided to

The Confederate prisoner of war camp in Andersonville, Georgia, witnessed great brutality and appalling death rates from disease and hunger.

move prisoners from Richmond. Not only would they be less likely to be rescued by northern troops farther south, but they could more easily be supplied by railroad away from the heavy fighting in Virginia. The camp, built for 10,000 men, soon became overcrowded; it held 33,000 by August. The prisoners, without shade, had to drink polluted water. Gangs of northern soldiers controlled daily life within the prison, routinely beating and robbing new arrivals. Of the 45,000 men eventually held at Andersonville, 13,000 died. Even higher proportions died at smaller camps in North Carolina. While Confederates held in northern prisons were better supplied, even their death rates reached as high as 24 percent. Overall, about 16 percent of northern soldiers died in prison, 12 percent of Southerners. Many in the North criticized Lincoln for refusing to reinstitute exchanges, but Lincoln would not sacrifice the former slaves. Moreover, he knew that exchanges helped the soldier-starved Confederacy more than they did the North. Lincoln wanted to push the war to the earliest possible conclusion, even if that meant, much to his regret, that suffering would have to increase before it could end.

Union Resolve

In March 1864 Lincoln gave new direction and purpose to the Union effort by putting Ulysses S. Grant in charge of all northern forces. By then, with victories stretching from Fort Donelson to Vicksburg to Chattanooga, Grant had gained confidence both in himself and from others. He and Lincoln agreed that the Union had to use its superiority in materiel, manpower, and navy to attack the Confederacy on every front at once, forcing the South to decide what terri-

African-American men worked at a wide range of tasks for the Union army, both behind the lines and at the front.

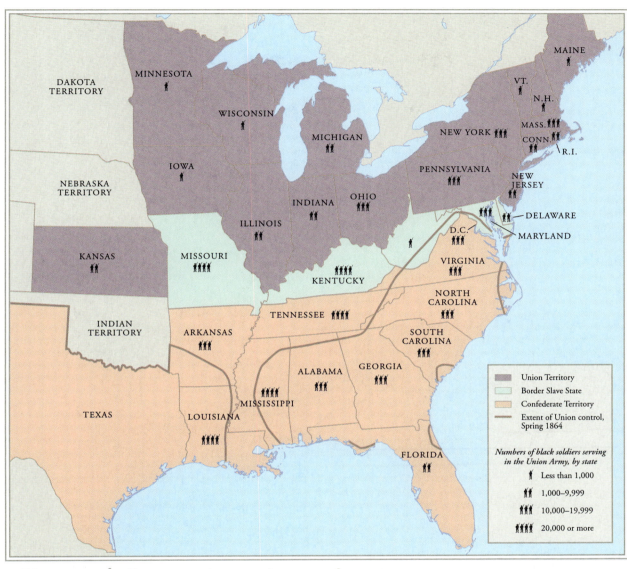

MAP 15.3 | ORIGINS OF AFRICAN-AMERICAN SOLDIERS

tory it would sacrifice. While Grant would fight in Virginia, he left William T. Sherman in charge in Chattanooga. Sherman would attack the young railroad center of Atlanta, cutting the Gulf South off from the Upper South. With the trans-Mississippi South lost to the Confederacy since 1863 and much of Louisiana, Tennessee, Mississippi, western Virginia, and Alabama under Union control, the loss of Atlanta

would chop the Confederacy into pieces too small to resist the northern army.

In retrospect, knowing how the war turned out, the events of 1864 may appear anticlimactic. Lee and the Confederates seemed to face overwhelming odds. Yet Southerners recognized that everything turned around holding the Northerners off until the presidential election in the North. Many Northerners

MAP 15.4 | THE CIVIL WAR, 1864-1865

called for peace and compromise. If the Southerners could inflict enough damage on the Union army, Northerners might elect someone willing to bring the war to an end through compromise and recognition of Southern independence. The Confederates knew, too, that the three-year terms of the most experienced veterans in the Union army expired in 1864. More than half of those veterans, willing to let someone else fight the Rebels, chose to leave the army even though the war was not over. They would be replaced with soldiers younger, less seasoned, and perhaps less committed to the Union cause. The Confederates also realized that Grant, new to his command, would be confronting Robert E. Lee, who was fighting with an experienced army on battlefields where he had already

seized victory. All things considered, it was by no means clear in 1864 that the Union would win Virginia or the war.

African Americans played an increasingly large role in Union plans, for over 180,000 black soldiers enlisted just when the North needed them most, upon the departure of so many men who had enlisted for three years. By the spring of 1864, the means of recruitment, training, and pay for these soldiers had become well established. The Confederates, however, refused to recognize the same rules of warfare for black soldiers that they acknowledged for whites. In April of 1864, at Fort Pillow in western Tennessee, Confederate cavalry under the command of Nathan Bedford Forrest shot down black Union soldiers who at-

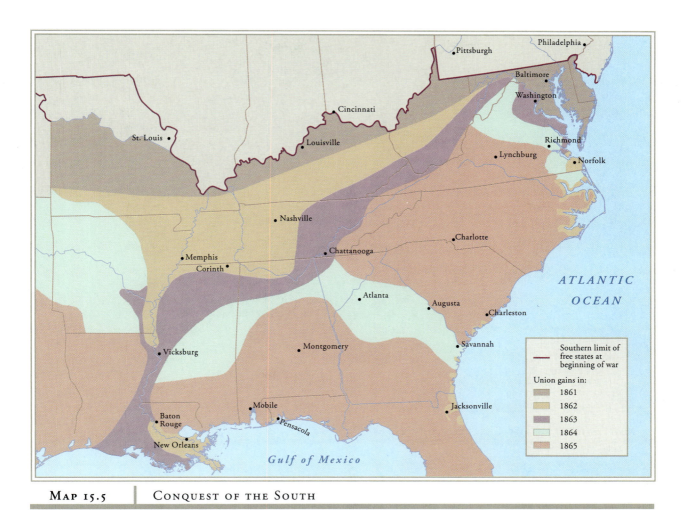

MAP 15.5 | CONQUEST OF THE SOUTH

Legend:
— Southern limit of free states at beginning of war

Union gains in:
- 1861
- 1862
- 1863
- 1864
- 1865

tempted to surrender. More than once thereafter, the Confederates would hear black soldiers yell "Remember Fort Pillow!" as they attacked.

With the election clock running, Grant set out in May 1864 to destroy Lee's army. The Battle of the Wilderness near Chancellorsville, close to the site where Stonewall Jackson had died a long year before, saw brutal fighting and horrible losses. Fire in the tangled woods trapped wounded men, burning them alive. Grant lost more men than Hooker had in the battle of the previous year, but whereas Hooker treated such losses as a decisive defeat, Grant pushed on, relentlessly pressuring Lee's men.

The two armies fought again and again over the next two months in the fields of Virginia, the casualties mounting in a sickening spiral. The Confederates turned the Union army back to the east of Richmond and rushed up the Shenandoah Valley to threaten Washington itself. The North repulsed the invasion and dispatched Philip Sheridan to the valley to make sure the Confederates did not regroup. With the Confederates pinned down in Petersburg, near Richmond, Pennsylvania coal miners volunteered to tunnel under the fortifications and plant explosives. Throughout July, they dug; finally, at the end of the month, they detonated a charge and blew an enormous crater in the Confederate lines. The attack that followed the explosion, however, failed. Union soldiers piled into the crater, where the rallying Confederates trapped them. Petersburg did not fall. Once again, Virginia had seen desperate fighting but few decisive results.

Fortunately for Lincoln, things were going better farther south. Throughout June and July, Sherman pushed relentlessly through north Georgia toward

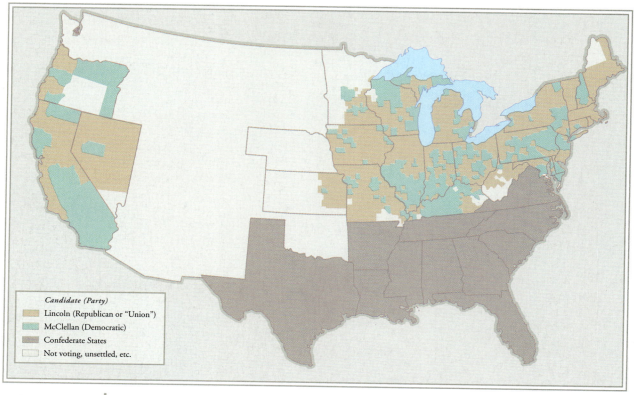

MAP 15.6 | THE ELECTION OF 1864

Atlanta. By the end of July, the southern army had fallen back into Atlanta, preparing to defend it from siege. It seemed only a matter of time before the Union triumphed. But how much time? The offensives by Grant and Sherman had come at the cost of high casualty rates. How many more tens of thousands would the North sacrifice? How many more months under the leadership of Abraham Lincoln?

The Northern Election of 1864

The president had to fight off challenges even within his own party, for some Republicans called for Chase, Frémont, or even Grant to carry the banner in 1864. Some party leaders considered Lincoln too radical; others considered him too cautious. Through adroit use of patronage, however, Lincoln managed to win renomination in June. The Republican party tried to broaden its appeal to Democrats by nominating An-

drew Johnson, military governor of Tennessee and a former Democrat, to the vice presidency.

In the meantime, the Democrats confidently moved forward. They knew that many Northerners distrusted, even hated, Lincoln. In the eyes of his critics, Lincoln had caused the war, trampled on constitutional rights, consolidated too much power, and refused to end the war when he had a chance. The Democrats intended to take full advantage of such criticisms, especially by nominating George McClellan as their candidate. McClellan retained great renown as a general and demonstrated that a person could oppose Lincoln's political purposes of the war without being a coward or traitor. McClellan and the Democrats portrayed themselves, not the Republicans, as the truly national party, for they were determined to restore the United States to its prewar unity and grandeur. McClellan said he would end the war if the South would reenter the Union— bringing slavery with it. It was a bargain that appealed to many in the North.

Just when it appeared that the Democrats would unseat Lincoln, however, news from the battlefield changed everything. Sherman swung around Atlanta and began destroying the railroads that made the small city an important junction. The Confederates, afraid they would be encircled and trapped within the city, set much of Atlanta on fire and abandoned it. Sherman and his army marched into the city on September 2. Two weeks later, Sheridan attacked the Confederates in the Shenandoah Valley, pushing them far beyond any threat to Washington and systematically destroying the valley's ability to support them again.

Even with these victories, and even with the heavy support of Lincoln by men in the army, Lincoln won only 55 percent of the popular vote. He did much better in the electoral college, sweeping every state except three. The Republicans also elected heavy majorities to both houses of Congress. For the time being, the Republicans closed ranks.

The March to the Sea

A week after Lincoln's election Sherman judged that he could not remain in Atlanta, where he could be cut off from his supply line. He decided to set out across Georgia, provisioning his army along the way, taking the war to the southern people themselves. Such a march would be as much a demonstration of northern power as a military maneuver, proving to the Confederate populace that they could no longer resist. The triumphant army of 60,000 made its way across the state throughout the fall of 1864, living off the land. Large numbers of deserters from both sides, fugitive slaves, and outlaws took advantage of the situation to inflict widespread destruction and panic. Sherman arrived at Savannah on December 21. "I beg to present to you, as a Christmas gift, the city of Savannah," Sherman buoyantly telegraphed Lincoln.

FROM WAR TO RECONSTRUCTION: 1865–1867

Americans had lived with war for four years; they had learned how to hate. As the war ground to a halt in

This picture, taken four days before his assassination, shows the toll four years of war had taken on the 56-year-old president.

early 1865, Americans had to wonder if they remembered how to share a country with their former enemies. They had to wonder, too, how different the country would be with African Americans no longer as slaves. Of all the changes the United States had ever seen, emancipation stood as the most profound.

War's Climax

Events moved quickly at the beginning of 1865. In January, Sherman issued Special Field Order 15, which reserved land in coastal South Carolina, Georgia, and Florida for former slaves. Those who settled on the land would receive forty-acre plots. Four days later, the Republicans in Congress passed the Thirteenth Amendment, abolishing slavery forever—a bill

The mountains of Tennessee, North Carolina, and Georgia saw brutal fighting far from the front lines. Here, guerillas attack Confederate cavalry pursuing deserters and Union sympathizers.

that had failed only seven months before. The lawmakers may have been influenced by petitions from the Women's National Loyal League with 400,000 signatures in favor of the amendment. At the beginning of February, Sherman's troops began to march north into the Carolinas. Columbia, South Carolina, burned to the ground, with both Confederate and Union troops contributing to the conflagration. Growing numbers of Confederate soldiers deserted from their armies to return to their homes. Lincoln met with Confederate officials to try to bring the war to an end, offering slaveowners compensation for their freed slaves if the Southerners would immediately cease the war. Jefferson Davis refused and Lincoln's cabinet persuaded him never to speak of compensation again.

At the beginning of March, Lincoln was inaugurated for his second term. Rather than gloating at the impending victory on the battlefield, Lincoln called for his fellow citizens to "bind up the nation's wounds." That same month, Congress created the Bu-

reau of Refugees, Freedmen, and Abandoned Lands to ease the transition from slavery to freedom, helping destitute whites as well as blacks. Nine days later, the Confederate government, after hotly debating whether to recruit slaves to fight as soldiers if their owners agreed, finally decided to do so after Lee, desperate for men, supported the measure.

Appomattox and Assassination

The Confederates' slave recruitment law did not have time to convert slaves to soldiers, however, for Grant soon began his final assault on Confederate troops in Virginia, systematically cutting off the rail lines that offered reinforcements and supplies. Petersburg fell on April 2, Richmond the next day. Jefferson Davis vainly appealed for southern resolve. Lee hoped to lead his army to the train station at Appomattox Court House to resupply them, but on April 9 Grant intercepted Lee's men just short of their destination. Lee, with

While John Wilkes Booth had been killed by Union troops twelve days after Lincoln's assassination in April of 1865, it was not until July that four of the eight convicted co-conspirators—including a woman—were hanged.

nowhere else to go and no ally to come to his aid, surrendered.

A number of Confederate armies, scattered from North Carolina to Texas, had yet to surrender, and Jefferson Davis had yet to be captured, but it was clear that the war had ended. Lee refused the pleas of some of his men to fight the Yankees as guerrillas. Grant permitted the Confederates to keep their animals for farming. The Southerners began to straggle home. Two days later, Lincoln addressed a Washington audience about what would come next for the freedmen. He admitted that Northerners differed "as to the mode, manner, and means of Reconstruction" and that the white South was "disorganized and discordant."

Lincoln did not live to take part in the planning, for he was assassinated on April 14 by John Wilkes Booth, a failed actor and southern sympathizer. Booth attacked Lincoln while the president sat with Mrs. Lincoln at Ford's Theater in Washington, shooting him in the back of the head and then leaping to the stage. Lincoln lingered for the night but never recovered consciousness; he died early the next morning. After a long and frantic search, Booth was captured and killed in a burning barn. Several conspirators, including a female accomplice, were executed several months later.

The Costs and Consequences of the War

The North lost almost 365,000 men to death and disease in the Civil War, the South 260,000—a fifth of its adult white male population. Another 277,000 Northerners were wounded, along with 195,000 Southerners. Many of these wounded men carried the legacy of the war through the rest of their lives; empty sleeves, blank stares, disfigured faces, and incessant pain continued long after the armies had gone home. Black Americans lost 37,000 men in the Union Army and another 10,000 men, women, and children in the contraband camps. Widows and orphans, black and white, northern and southern, faced decades of struggling without a male breadwinner. Many people found their emotional lives shattered by the war, unable to forget what they had seen and done. Alcohol, drug abuse, crime, and violence became widespread problems in postwar America.

The southern economy fell to its knees. Major southern cities had been reduced to ash. Railroads had been ripped from the ground, engines and cars burned. Fields had grown up in weeds and brush, drainage ditches choked. Farm values fell by half. Livestock, tools, barns, and fences stolen or destroyed by

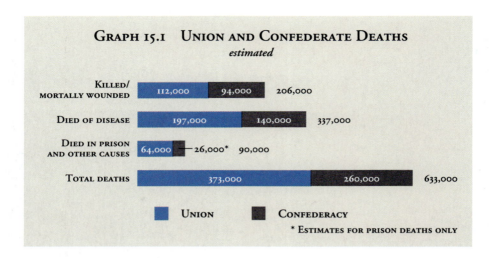

GRAPH 15.1　UNION AND CONFEDERATE DEATHS
estimated

	Union	Confederacy	Total
KILLED/ MORTALLY WOUNDED	112,000	94,000	206,000
DIED OF DISEASE	197,000	140,000	337,000
DIED IN PRISON AND OTHER CAUSES	64,000	26,000*	90,000
TOTAL DEATHS	373,000	260,000	633,000

■ UNION　　■ CONFEDERACY

* ESTIMATES FOR PRISON DEATHS ONLY

the armies of both sides would take years to replace. Just as damaging in the long run, lines of credit had been severed. Before emancipation, planters had used slaves as collateral for loans. Now, without that basis, few people outside the South were willing to loan money to planters or other investors. Moreover, during the war Congress had passed banking acts that favored the North at the expense of the South, directing capital away from the credit-starved South. Southerners who had supported the Confederacy by purchasing its bonds and currency found that they had lost the inheritance of generations.

The Civil War did not mark a sudden turn in the northern economy, but it did accelerate processes already well underway. The nationalization of markets, the accumulation of wealth, and the dominance of larger manufacturing firms all became more marked after 1865. Greenbacks, bonds, and a national banking system regularized the flow of capital and spurred the growth of business. The Republicans used the opportunity of the war years to enact their vision of progress, passing the Department of Agriculture Act, the Morrill College Land Grant Act, the Homestead Act, and the Union Pacific Railroad Act, all using the power of the federal government to encourage settlement of the West, strengthen public education, and spur economic development. Northern farmers saw prices for their products remain high, as the demands of the war coincided with poor harvests in Europe. Despite the prosperity in the North, the hundreds of thousands of veterans faced many dislocations and

readjustments as they returned to the farms, factories, and shops they had left months or years before.

Emancipation and the South

As the battles ground to a halt, slaves became former slaves. For some, the process proved dramatic and sudden, while for others freedom emerged only gradually. Some, especially the young, greeted freedom confidently, while others, especially the elderly, could not help but be wary of anything so strange, no matter how long and how much they had prayed for it. Some seized their freedom at the first opportunity, taking their families to Union camps or joining the army. Others celebrated when the Yankees came to their plantations, only to find that their owners and white neighbors retaliated when the soldiers left. Others bided their time, waiting to make sure the war had really ceased and their bondage had come to an end. Some refused to believe the stories of freedom at all until their master or mistress called them together to announce that they were indeed no longer slaves.

Upon hearing the news, the freed people gathered to discuss their options. For many, the highest priority was to reunite their families. Such people set off on journeys short or long, south or north, in desperate efforts to find a husband, wife, child, or parent sold away in earlier years. For others, sheer survival was the highest priority. Freedom came in the late spring,

GRAPH 15.2   THE BLOODIEST BATTLES
Total Casualties

1863 GETTYSBURG — Union 23,053 / Confederacy 28,063
1864 SEVEN DAYS' BATTLES — Union 15,849 / Confederacy 20,614
1864 CHICKAMAUGA — Union 16,170 / Confederacy 18,454
1863 CHANCELLORSVILLE/SECOND FREDERICKSBURG — Union 16,845 / Confederacy 12,764
1862 ANTIETAM — Union 12,410 / Confederacy 10,316
1862 SECOND MANASSAS/CHANTILLY — Union 16,054 / Confederacy 9,286
1862 SHILOH — Union 13,047 / Confederacy 10,694
1863 FREDRICKSBURG — Union 12,653 / Confederacy 5,309

■ UNION   ■ CONFEDERACY

After four years of war, little remained in the besieged cities of the Confederacy.

barely in time to get crops in the ground. Some former slaves argued that their best bet was to stay where they were for the time being. They had heard rumors that the government would award them land in the South just as it had given lands in the West to northern settlers. Between July and September of 1865, however, those dreams died. Union officers promised land to former slaves in Virginia, Louisiana, Mississippi, and South Carolina, but then Washington revoked the promises. The land would be returned to its former owners. Black people would have no choice but to strike bargains with white Southerners.

Former slaveowners also responded in many different ways. Some, unable to conceive of living in a South without slavery, fled to Latin America. Others tried to keep as much of slavery as they could by whipping and chaining workers to keep them from leaving. Other former masters and mistresses attempted to keep as much of slavery as possible by of-

fering to let former slaves stay in their cabins and work for wages. Some callously evicted older and less productive slaves even as others assured the elderly that they had a home on the plantation for the rest of their lives.

Plantation owners came to realize that all the land in the world was worthless without someone to work it. African Americans had no choice but to compromise with white landowners. At first, in the spring of 1865, planters insisted that the former slaves work as they had worked before emancipation, in "gangs." In return for their work, they would receive a portion of the crop, shared among all the workers. Many black people chafed at this arrangement, preferring to work as individuals or families. In such places, landowners found that they had little choice but to permit black families to take primary responsibility for a portion of land. The former slaves provided the labor and received part of the crop as a result. Planters, though

Black Southerners took advantage of the presence of Union troops to leave the farms and plantations on which they had been held. Many set out to find family members.

reluctant to give up any control over the day-to-day work on their land, realized they had few choices. They possessed little cash to pay wage workers and no alternative labor. The black families who worked the land often found themselves in debt despite their hard work, as declining cotton prices and high credit rates undermined their efforts.

The Bureau of Refugees, Freedmen, and Abandoned Lands—the Freedmen's Bureau—oversaw the transition from a slave economy to a wage economy.

The Freedmen's Bureau, created in the spring of 1865, adjudicated conflicts between white landowners and black workers.

Black Southerners established schools for themselves across the region, often at considerable sacrifice.

Much of the work of its agents, military officers, involved keeping people alive in the ravaged South. They dispensed medicine, food, and clothing from the vast stores of the federal government to white and black alike. The Bureau created courts to adjudicate conflicts and to draw up labor contracts between landholders and laborers. It established schools and coordinated female volunteers who came from the North to teach in them. While many white Southerners resented and resisted the Freedmen's Bureau, it helped smooth the transition from slavery to freedom, from war to peace, in 1865.

Black Mobilization

Black Southerners mourned and feared the loss of Abraham Lincoln. He had helped bring their freedom, a freedom that remained new and tenuous. Without his leadership, former slaves rightly worried, the forces of reaction might overwhelm their freedom. Southerners of both races watched to see what Andrew Johnson might do.

African Americans in the South quickly mobilized. Throughout the South, former slaves and former free blacks gathered in conventions to announce their vision of the new order. They paraded and petitioned, making the case for their full citizenship. They wanted, above all else, equality before the law and the opportunity to vote. The delegates, while insistent, spoke to southern whites in conciliatory terms. By and large, they did not demand confiscation of land nor did they speak extensively of economic concerns in general. Let us have our basic rights before the courts and at the ballot box, they said, and we will take care of ourselves. Such concerns and confidence reflected the perspective of the conventions' leadership: former free blacks, skilled artisans, ministers, and teachers. The great mass of southern blacks—former slaves desperate for a chance at some economic independence in the countryside—found their concerns neglected.

Black Southerners agreed on the centrality of two institutions, however: the church and the school. At the very moment of freedom, they began to form their own churches. For generations, African Americans had been forced to worship alongside whites, sitting in

"*Letter to the Union Convention, 1865*"

Black Citizens of Tennessee

In this petition by black Tennesseans to their white Unionist couterparts in the waning days of the Civil War, the themes of the Gettysburg Address receive eloquent endorsement. The fifty-nine men who signed the petition articulated the highest ideals of the American nation. There is no record of a response.

[Nashville, Tenn., January 9, 1865]

To the Union Convention of Tennessee Assembled in the Capitol at Nashville, January 9th, 1865:

We the undersigned petitioners, American citizens of African descent, natives and residents of Tennessee, and devoted friends of the great National cause, do most respectfully ask a patient hearing of your honorable body in regard to matters deeply affecting the future condition of our unfortunate and long suffering race.

First of all, however, we would say that words are too weak to tell how profoundly grateful we are to the Federal Government for the good work of freedom which it is gradually carrying forward; and for the Emancipation Proclamation which has set free all the slaves in some of the rebellious States,as well as many of the slaves in Tennessee.

After two hundred years of bondage and suffering a returning sense of justice has awakened the great body of the American people to make amends for the unprovoked wrongs committed against us for over two hundred years.

Your petitioners would ask you to complete the work begun by the nation at large, and abolish the last vestige of slavery by the express words of your organic law.

Many masters in Tennessee whose slaves have left them, will certainly make every effort to bring them back to bondage after the reorganization of the State government, unless slavery be expressly abolished by the Constitution.

We hold that freedom is the natural right of all men, which they themselves have no more right to give or barter away, than they have to sell their honor, their wives, or their children.

We claim to be men belonging to the great human family, descended from one great God, who is the common Father of all, and who bestowed on all races and tribes the priceless right of freedom. Of this right, for no offence of ours, we have long been cruelly deprived, and the common voice of the wise and good of all countries, has remonstrated against our enslavement, as one of the greatest crimes in all history.

We claim freedom, as our natural right, and ask that in harmony and cooperation with the nation at large, you should cut up by the roots the system of slavery, which is not only a wrong to us, but the source of all the evil which at present afflicts the State. For slavery, corrupt itself, corrupted nearly all, also, around it, so that it has influenced nearly all the slave States to rebel against the Federal Government, in order to set up a government of pirates under which slavery might be perpetrated.

In the contest between the nation and slavery, our unfortunate people have sided, by instinct, with the former. We have little fortune to devote to the national cause, for a hard fate has hitherto forced us to live in poverty, but we do devote to its success, our hopes, our toils, our whole heart, our sacred honor, and our lives. We will work, pray, live, and, if need be, die for the Union, as cheerfully as ever a white patriot died for his country. The color of our skin does not lessen in the least degree, our love either for God or for the land of our birth.

We are proud to point your honorable body to the fact, that so far as our knowledge extends, not a negro traitor has made his appearance since the beginning of this wicked rebellion.

Whether freeman or slaves the colored race in this country have always looked upon the United States as the Promised Land of Universal freedom, and no earthly temptation has been strong enough to induce us to rebel against it. We love the Union by an instinct which is stronger than any argument or appeal which can be used against it. It is the attachment of a child to its parent.

Devoted as we are to the principles of justice, of love to all men, and of equal rights on which our Government is based, and which make it the hope of the world. We know the burdens of citizenship, and are ready to bear them. We know the duties of the good citizen, and are ready to perform them cheerfully, and would ask to be put in a position in which we can discharge them more effectually. We do not ask for the privilege of citizenship, wishing to shun the obligations imposed by it.

Near 200,000 of our brethren are to-day performing military duty in the ranks of the Union army. Thousands of them have already died in battle, or perished by a cruel martyrdom for the sake of the Union, and we are ready and willing to sacrifice more. But what higher order of citizen is there than the soldier? or who has a greater trust confided to his hands? If we are called on to do military duty against the rebel armies in the field, why should we be denied the privilege of voting against rebel citizens at the ballot-box? The latter is as necessary to save the Government as the former.

The colored man will vote by instinct with the Union party, just as uniformly as he fights with the Union army. . . .

If colored men have been faithful and true to the Government of the United States in spite of the Fugitive Slave Law, and the cruel policy often pursued toward them, will they not be more devoted to it now than ever since it has granted them that liberty which they desired above all things? Surely, if colored men voted without harm to the State, while their brethren were in bondage, they will be much more devoted and watchful over her interests when elevated to the rank of freemen and voters. If they are good law-abiding citizens, praying for its prosperity, rejoicing in its progress, paying its taxes, fighting its battles, making its farms, mines, work-shops and commerce more productive, why deny them the right to have a voice in the election of its rulers?

This is a democracy—a government of the people. It should aim to make every man, without regard to the color of his skin, the amount of his wealth, or the character of his religious faith, feel personally interested in its welfare. Every man who lives under the Government should feel that it is his property, his treasure, the bulwark and defense of himself and his family, his pearl of great price, which he must preserve, protect, and defend faithfully at all times, on all occasions, in every possible manner.

This is not a Democratic Government if a numerous, law-abiding, industrious, and useful class of citizens, born and bred on the soil, are to be treated as aliens and enemies, as an

continued next page

inferior degraded class, who must have no voice in the Government which they support, protect and defend, with all their heart, soul, mind, and body, both in peace and war.

This Government is based on the teachings of the Bible, which prescribes the same rules of action for all members of the human family, whether their complexion be white, yellow, red or black. God no where in his revealed word, makes an invidious and degrading distinction against his children, because of their color. And happy is that nation which makes the Bible its rule of action, and obeys principle, not prejudice.

Let no man oppose this doctrine because it is opposed to his old prejudices. The nation is fighting for its life, and cannot afford to be controlled by prejudice. Had prejudice prevailed instead of principle, not a single colored soldier would have been in the Union army to-day. But principle and justice triumphed, and now near 200,000 colored patriots stand under the folds of the national flag, and brave their breasts to the bullets of the rebels. As we are in the battlefield, so we swear before heaven, by all that is dear to men, to be at the ballot-box faithful and true to the Union.

The possibility that the negro suffrage proposition may shock popular prejudice at first sight, is not a conclusive argument against its wisdom and policy. No proposition ever met with more furious or general opposition than the one to enlist colored soldiers in the United States army. The opponents of the measure exclaimed on all hands that the negro was a coward; that he would not fight; that one white man, with a whip in his hand could put to flight a regiment of them; that the experiment would end in the utter rout and ruin of the Federal army. Yet the colored man has fought so well, on almost every occasion, that the rebel government is prevented, only by its fears and distrust of being able to force him to fight for slavery as well as he fights against it, from putting half a million of negroes into its ranks.

The Government has asked the colored man to fight for its preservation and gladly has he done it. It can afford to trust him with a vote as safely as it trusted him with a bayonet. . . . .

balconies and listening to sermons exhorting slaves not to steal. For many ex-slaves, one of their first acts of freedom was to form their own churches with their own ministers. People who owned virtually nothing somehow built churches across the South. Those churches often served as schools as well. Hundreds of northern white women aided black Southerners in their quest for an education in 1865 and 1866, but the former slaves did not wait for outside help before creating their own schoolhouses and choosing teachers from among themselves.

Andrew Johnson

In the meantime, events in Washington undermined the efforts of black Southerners to build a new world for themselves. Andrew Johnson wanted to attract moderates from both the North and the South to a party that would change as little as possible; he was willing to sacrifice black Southerners to create that alliance. Johnson had been selected to run for the vice presidency because he was a Southerner who had remained true to the Union. As a result, both Northerners and Southerners

One other matter we would urge on your honorable body. At present we can have only partial protection from the courts. The testimony of twenty of the most intelligent, honorable, colored loyalists cannot convict a white traitor of a treasonable action. A white rebel might sell powder and lead to a rebel soldier in the presence of twenty colored soldiers, and yet their evidence would be worthless so far as the courts are concerned, and the rebel would escape. A colored man may have served for years faithfully in the army, and yet his testimony in court would be rejected, while that of a white man who had served in the rebel army would be received. . . .

There have been white traitors in multitudes in Tennessee, but where we ask, is the black traitor? Can you forget how the colored man has fought at Fort Morgan, at Milliken's Bend, at Fort Pillow, before Petersburg, and your own city of Nashville?

When has the colored citizen, in this rebellion been tried and found wanting? . . .

In this great and fearful struggle of the nation with a wicked rebellion, we are anxious to perform the full measure of our duty both as citizens and soldiers to the Union cause we consecrate ourselves, and our families with all that we have on earth. Our souls burn with love for the great government of freedom and equal rights. Our white brethren have no cause for distrust as regards our fidelity, for neither death nor life, nor angels, nor principalities, nor powers, nor things present, nor things to come, nor height, nor depth, nor any other creature, shall be able to separate us from the love of the Union.

Praying that the great God, who is the common Father of us all, by whose help the land must be delivered from present evil, and before whom we must all stand at last to be judged by the rule of eternal justice, and not by passion and prejudice, may enlighten your minds and enable you to act with wisdom, justice, and magnanimity, we remain your faithful friends in all the perils and dangers which threaten our beloved country.

SOURCE *Free at Last: A Documentary History of Slavery, Freedom, and the Civil War.* Ira Berlin, et al., eds. (New York: New Press, 1992) pp. 497–505.

[*59 signatures*]
And many other colored citizens of Nashville

distrusted Johnson. A longtime Democrat before the crisis of the Union, Johnson maintained a limited, Jacksonian view of government in opposition to the rapid expansion in the power of government in the war years. The new president's well-known disdain for the wealthy planters of the South appealed to equally disdainful Republicans in Washington. Unlike them, however, Johnson held little sympathy for black people and little interest in promoting their interests. Johnson saw himself following Lincoln's plan and pursuing Lincoln's highest goal: reuniting the Union. Johnson believed that reunification should start by winning the support of white Southerners.

Johnson could hardly have been placed in a more difficult position and could hardly have made worse of it. Congress was not in session at the time of Lincoln's death and would not be for seven months, so Johnson used the opportunity to implement his vision of reunion. In what became known as "Presidential Reconstruction," Johnson offered amnesty to former Confederates who would take an oath of loyalty to the Union, restoring their political and civil

Andrew Johnson attempted to forge a new alliance between white Northerners and white Southerners, callously abandoning black Southerners in the process.

flaunted their opinions of the North. Some refused to fly the American flag, some refused to ratify the Thirteenth Amendment, some even refused to admit that secession had been illegal. Former Confederates filled important posts in state governments throughout the South. Georgia elected Alexander H. Stephens, the ex-vice president of the aborted nation, to Congress. Johnson personally pardoned such men, reasoning that reunion could best be served by acknowledging the decisions of the white South.

The North erupted in outrage when the new state governments enacted the so-called "black codes," laws for the control of the former slaves. The southern white legislatures granted only the barest minimum of rights to black people: the right to marry, to hold property, to sue and be sued. Most of the laws decreed what African Americans could not do: move from one job to another, own or rent land, practice certain occupations. When the members of Congress convened in December of 1865, they reacted as many of their constituents did—with fury. To Northerners, even those inclined to deal leniently with the South, the former Confederates seemed to deny all the war had decided. And many Northerners blamed the man who had overseen this travesty, Andrew Johnson.

Johnson and the Radicals

It was not that most Northerners, even most Republicans, wanted the kind of policies promoted by Radicals such as Thaddeus Stevens, who called for land to be seized from wealthy planters and given to the former slaves, or of Charles Sumner, who wanted immediate and universal suffrage for blacks. But neither did they want the sort of capitulation that Johnson had tolerated. Moderates tried to devise plans that would be acceptable to both sides, that would protect black freedom while still permitting white Southerners to reclaim a place in the nation.

The moderates sought to continue the Freedmen's Bureau, which was not only saving people, white and black, from starvation in the South but was also providing for schools and at least some measure of justice for the former slaves. The Bureau was understaffed and underfunded—only about 900 agents covered the entire South—but it offered some measure of

rights and immunizing them against the seizure of their property or prosecution for treason. While Johnson withheld such amnesty from political leaders of the rebellion, the Confederate military, and the largest planters, he soon began to grant pardons to such men when they applied to him personally. Johnson's plans for political reunion made no provisions at all for black voting. Indeed, his plan threatened to return the South to even greater national power than it had held before because the entire African-American population would now be considered when the number of representatives was calculated, not merely as three-fifths of a people as before the war.

White Southerners could hardly believe their good fortune, for they had told themselves to expect harsher peace terms. The state conventions elected in 1865

Thaddeus Stevens, a congressman from Pennsylvania, was among the leaders of the Radical Republicans.

hope for former slaves. The Bureau, under the leadership of the deeply religious General O. O. Howard, saw itself as a mediator between blacks and whites. It insisted on the innovation of formal contracts between laborer and landlord, specifying the duties and responsibilities of all involved. Although these contracts infuriated southern white men, who resented the implied challenge to their honor and who resisted treating former slaves with such dignity, the Freedmen's Bureau ended up supporting landowners as often as black laborers. The moderates also attempted to institute a Civil Rights bill to define American citizenship for all those born in the United States, thereby including blacks. Citizenship would bring with it equal protection under the laws, though the bill said nothing about black voting and gave African Americans only the most rudimentary guarantees of freedom.

Republicans of widely varying perspectives supported the Freedmen's Bureau and Civil Rights bills as the starting place for rebuilding the nation. But Johnson vetoed both bills, claiming that they violated the rights of the states and of white Southerners who had been excluded from the decision making. Republicans, furious and determined, closed ranks to override Johnson's veto. Recognizing their ability to overrule any presidential vetoes, in fact, the Republicans proceeded to neutralize Johnson altogether.

To prevent any future erosion of black rights, the Republicans proposed the Fourteenth Amendment, which, as eventually ratified, guaranteed citizenship to all American-born people and equal protection under the law for those citizens, making it illegal to deprive any person of life, liberty, or property without due process of law. The amendment decreed that any state that abridged the voting rights of any male inhabitants who were twenty-one and citizens would suffer a proportionate reduction in its congressional representation. (It did not simply guarantee universal male suffrage because all but five northern states still refused black men the right to vote.) Johnson urged the southern states to refuse to ratify the amendment, advice they promptly followed.

Throughout the second half of 1866 the North watched, appalled, as much that the Civil War had been fought for seemed to be brushed aside in the South. Not only did the southern men who met in the state conventions refuse to accept the relatively mild Fourteenth Amendment, but they made clear their determination to fight back in every way they could against further attempts to remake the South. The spring of that year saw riots in Memphis and New Orleans in which policemen and other whites brutally assaulted and killed black people with little or no provocation.

It was in 1866, too, that the Ku Klux Klan appeared. This group was the strongest and most visible of many paramilitary organizations created by whites after the war. Founded in Tennessee, the Ku Klux Klan dedicated itself to maintaining white supremacy and everything it associated with that supremacy: law and order, Christian morals, and home rule. The Klan dressed in costumes designed to overawe the former slaves, hiding behind their anonymity to avoid retaliation from the black community and from government authorities. The Klan became in effect a military wing of the Democratic party, devoting much of its energy to warning and killing white and black men who dared associate with the Republicans.

Johnson toured the country in the fall of 1866 to denounce the Republicans and their policies. The

In the Memphis riot of July 1866, southern whites killed thirty-seven blacks and three white supporters after a Republican meeting.

tour was a disaster. The voters rejected both Johnson and the Democrats, as the governorship and legislature of every northern state came under the control of the Republicans. The Republicans who returned to Congress in December of 1866 felt they held a mandate to push harder than they had before. They had only a few months, however, until their term ended in March, to decide what to do and how to do it. They bitterly disagreed with one another over the vote, land distribution, the courts, and education. Some wanted to put the South under military control for the indefinite future while others sought to return things to civilian control as soon as possible. Finally, on March 2, 1867, as time was running out on the session, they passed the Reconstruction Act.

The Reconstruction Act

The Reconstruction Act, coming two tumultuous years after the end of the war, placed the South under military rule. All the southern states except Tennessee, which had been readmitted to the Union after it ratified the Fourteenth Amendment, were put

in five military districts. The military commander of each district held broad power to punish those who imperiled the rights or property of others. Once order had been instituted, then the states would proceed to elect conventions to draw up new constitutions. The elections for those conventions would include black voters, but not former Confederates who had been disfranchised. The constitutions written by those conventions had to accept the Fourteenth Amendment and provide for universal manhood suffrage. Once a majority of the state's citizens and both houses of the national Congress had approved the new constitution, the state could be readmitted to the Union. White Southerners resisted the plan as tyrannical, but submitted to it when it became clear they had no choice.

To ensure that Andrew Johnson did not undermine this plan—which soon became known as "Radical Reconstruction"—Congress sought to curb the president's power. With no threat of his veto after the 1866 elections, the Republicans could do much as they wanted. Congress decreed that it could call itself into special session. There, they limited the president's authority as commander-in-chief of the army and, in the Tenure of Office Act, prevented him from removing officials who had been confirmed by the Senate. Some Republicans were queasy about such steps, but they had no intention of letting Johnson undermine Reconstruction.

Johnson, characteristically, did not quietly accept such restrictions of his power. He saw the Republicans as power-hungry tyrants, writing unconstitutional laws, and he determined to challenge them. When he intentionally violated the Tenure of Office Act by removing Secretary of War Edwin Stanton in the summer of 1867, many in Congress decided that Johnson warranted impeachment. Matters stewed throughout the fall, while the first elections under the Reconstruction Act took place in the South.

Reconstruction Begins

Secession and the war had dissolved the old party system in the South, forcing former Whigs and former Democrats into awkward and testy alliances. Whites argued openly with one another about the best route to restoring their former power. Some called for cooperation with the North while others called for resistance. Some called for cooperation with blacks, while other whites declared themselves dedicated to a party of unalloyed white supremacy.

After word of the Reconstruction Act circulated in the spring and summer, both black men and white claimed leadership roles within the Republican party. Black Northerners came to the South to use their educations in the service of Reconstruction, looking for appointive and elective office. Ambitious black Southerners, many of whom had been free and relatively prosperous before the Civil War, put themselves forward as the natural leaders of the race. Such men became the backbone of the Republican party in black-belt districts, giving speeches, visiting with voters, often risking their lives to mobilize former slaves into citizens.

White Southerners sneered at white Northerners who supported the Republican cause. They called them "carpetbaggers." These men, according to the insulting name, were supposedly so devoid of

The Ku Klux Klan emerged in 1866, devoting itself to the maintenance of white supremacy in all its forms.

African-American men could vote in the South during Reconstruction, but often risked their livelihoods or their lives to do so.

connections and property in their northern homes that they could throw everything they had into a carpetbag—a cheap suitcase—and head south as soon as they read of the opportunities created by Radical Reconstruction. The majority of white Northerners who became Republican leaders in the South, however, had in fact moved to the region long before Reconstruction began. Many were former Union soldiers who had decided to try their lot in the South at war's end, becoming planters or merchants. Many had been well educated in the North before the war and many held property in the South. Like white Southerners, however, the northern-born Republicans found the postwar South a difficult place in which to prosper. Black people were no more inclined to work for low wages for white Northerners than for anyone else and southern whites often went out of their way to avoid doing business with the Yankees. As a result, when Reconstruction began, a considerable number of Northerners took up the Republican cause as a way to remake

the South and find a place for themselves in the new order.

White southern Republicans, labeled "scalawags" by their enemies, risked being called traitors to their race and region. Few white Republicans emerged in the plantation districts, because they endured ostracism, resistance, and violence for violating white unity in the face of Radical Reconstruction. In the upcountry districts, however, former Whigs and Unionists asserted themselves against the planters and Confederates. The Republican party became strong in the mountains of east Tennessee, western North Carolina, eastern Kentucky, north Alabama, and northern Georgia. Many whites in these districts, though unwilling to join with low country African Americans or their white leaders in true party feeling or common purpose, struck alliances of convenience with them. Black voters and white voters generally wanted and needed different things. Blacks, largely propertyless, called for an activist government to provide schools, orphanages, and hospitals. Most whites, on the other hand, owned land and called mainly for lower taxes.

Throughout the South, most whites watched, livid, as the Republicans mobilized black voters in enormous numbers in the fall of 1867. While many white Democrats boycotted the elections, the Republicans swept into the constitutional delegate positions. Most white Republicans came from the up-country, but about a sixth of the delegates were of white northern background. Although many black men voted, African-American delegates made up only a relatively small part of the convention's delegates. They held the majority in South Carolina and Louisiana, but much smaller proportions elsewhere. About half of the 265 African Americans elected as delegates to the state conventions had been free before the war, about forty had served in the Union army, and most were ministers, artisans, farmers, and teachers. Over the next two years, these delegates would meet to write new, much more democratic, constitutions for their states.

At the very moment of the success of the southern Republicans, however, ominous signs came from the North. Republicans were dismayed at the election returns in the North in 1867, for the Democrats' power surged from coast to coast, reducing by three-quarters the gains the Republicans had made just the preceding year. Many white voters thought that the Radicals had gone too far in their concern with black rights and wanted officeholders to devote their energies to problems closer to home. The Republicans in Washington heard the message. They began scaling back their support for any further advances in Reconstruction. No sooner had the experiment in the South begun, in other words, than the North began to undermine it.

CONCLUSION

The Civil War changed the United States more deeply than any other event in the nineteenth century. The conflict brought the deaths of over 625,000 soldiers and the shattering of families North and South. It saw bitter rioting in the streets and the first assassination of a president. It saw fortunes made and lost. It brought a major shift in the balance of power among the regions and an expansion of the federal government. Most important, the war brought what few Americans, regardless of their region or their color, could have imagined at the end of 1860: the immediate emancipation of 4 million enslaved people.

Freedom emerged from the war through a circuitous route. The war began as a war for Union. As the deaths mounted and African Americans seized freedom at every opportunity, abolitionists and Republicans increasingly insisted that the war become a war to end slavery. Many white Northerners supported emancipation because it seemed the best way to end the war, crippling the Confederate ability and will to fight. Abraham Lincoln worked desperately to keep the support of both the advocates and foes of emancipation, knowing that moving too quickly would shatter the fragile support that kept him in office. The New York City draft riots and the close elections of 1863 demonstrated that many Northerners resisted the continuation of the war and its embrace of black freedom. Only Union success on the battlefield in late 1864 permitted Lincoln's re-election. His assassination made an already confused situation far more so, ending slavery and restoring the Union without a blueprint and without leadership. The end of the war resolved the question of secession and the continuance of slavery, but it left much undecided.

The end of the fighting saw the conflict shift in the South, as people struggled to determine what freedom would mean. For black Southerners, the goal was autonomy and respect, a chance to work for themselves and enjoy the fundamental rights of American citizens. For white Northerners, the goal was to reconstruct the South in an idealized image of the North, with orderly free labor and the rule of law at its heart. For white Southerners, the goal was the reassertion of the power they had held before the war, especially power over the black people in their midst. Such goals could not be reconciled. The era of Reconstruction would be devoted to the struggle among them.

RECOMMENDED READINGS

Berlin, Ira, Barbara J. Fields, Steven F. Miller, Joseph P. Reidy, and Leslie S. Rowland, eds., *Freedom,* (1985–) is a fascinating multivolume documentary collection.

Donald, David. *Lincoln* (1995) stands as the most elegant biography.

Faust, Drew Gilpin. *Mothers of Invention: Women of the Slaveholding South in the American Civil War* (1995) offers a challenging and interesting interpretation.

Fellman, Michael. *Inside War: The Guerilla Conflict in Missouri During the American Civil War* (1989) makes palpable the internal struggles in the border areas.

Foner, Eric. *Reconstruction: America's Unfinished Revolution, 1863–1877* (1988) is a magisterial interpretation of the struggle over black freedom.

Gallagher, Gary W. *The Confederate War: How Popular Will, Nationalism, and Military Strategy Could Not Stave Off Defeat* (1997) explores why the Confederacy could fight as long as it did.

Harris, William C. *With Charity for All: Lincoln and the Restoration of the Union* (1997) offers a fresh assessment of Lincoln's attitudes toward the white South.

Hattaway, Herman, and Jones, Archer. *How the North Won: A Military History of the Civil War* (1983) authoritatively describes strategy and tactics.

Litwack, Leon. *Been in the Storm So Long: The Aftermath of Slavery* (1979) beautifully evokes the conflicting emotions and motives surrounding freedom.

Roark, James L. *Masters Without Slaves: Southern Planters in the Civil War and Reconstruction* (1978) describes the war from the perspective of those who lost the most in southern defeat.

Rose, Willie Lee. *Rehearsal for Reconstruction: The Port Royal Experiment* (1964) is a classic account of the first efforts to create northern policy toward the freed people.

Interpretations

Aaron, Daniel. *The Unwritten War: American Writers and the Civil War* (1973).

Beringer, Richard E. Herman Hattaway, Archer Jones, and William N. Still, Jr., *Why the South Lost the Civil War* (1986).

Frederickson, George. *The Inner Civil War: Northern Intellectuals and the Crisis of Disunion* (1965).

Vinovskis, Maris A. *Toward a Social History of the American Civil War: Exploratory Essays* (1990).

Warren, Robert Penn. *The Legacy of the Civil War* (1961).

Wills, Garry. *Lincoln at Gettysburg* (1992).

Wilson, Edmund. *Patriotic Gore: Studies in the Literature of the American Civil War* (1962).

Battles

Castel, Albert. *Decision in the West: The Atlanta Campaign of 1864* (1992).

Cozzens, Peter. *The Shipwreck of Their Hopes: The Battles for Chattanooga* (1994).

Glatthaar, Joseph T. *The March to the Sea and Beyond: Sherman's Troops in the Savannah and Carolina Campaigns* (1985).

Hennessy, John H. *Return to Bull Run: The Campaign and Battle of Second Manassas* (1993).

Kennett, Lee. *Marching Through Georgia: The Story of Soldiers and Civilians During Sherman's Campaign* (1994).

Rhea, Gordon H. *The Battle of the Wilderness, May 5–6, 1864* (1994).

Sears, Stephen W. *Landscape Turned Red: The Battle of Antietam* (1983).

Sears, Stephen W. *Chancellorsville* (1996).

Sword, Wiley. *Shiloh: Bloody April* (1974).

Tucker, Glenn. *Chickamauga: Bloody Battle in the West* (1961).

Northern Politics and Leadership

Klement, Frank L. *Clement L. Vallandigham and the Civil War* (1970).

Neely, Mark. *The Fate of Liberty: Abraham Lincoln and Civil Liberties* (1991).

Richardson, Heather Cox. *The Greatest Nation on the Earth: Republican Economic Policies During the Civil War* (1997).

Silbey, Joel H. *A Respectable Minority: The Democratic Party in the Civil War Era, 1860–1868* (1977).

Waugh, John C. *Reelecting Lincoln: The Battle for the 1864 Presidency* (1997).

The Homefronts

Ash, Stephen V. *Middle Tennessee Society Transformed, 1869–1870* (1988).

Ash, Stephen V. *When the Yankees Came: Conflict and Chaos in the Occupied South, 1861–1865* (1995).

Bernstein, Iver. *The New York City Draft Riots: Their Significance for American Society and Politics in the Age of the Civil War* (1990).

Cook, Adrian. *The Armies of the Streets: The New York City Draft Riots of 1863* (1974).

Durrill, Wayne K. *War of Another Kind: A Southern Community in the Great Rebellion* (1990).

Grimsley, Mark. *The Hard Hand of War: Union Military Policy Toward Southern Civilians, 1861–1865* (1995).

O'Connor, Thomas H. *Civil War Boston: Home Front and Battlefield* (1997).

Sutherland, Daniel E. *Seasons of War: The Ordeal of a Confederate Community, 1861–1865* (1995).

Soldiers' Experiences

Cornish, Dudley Taylor. *The Sable Arm: Negro Troops in the Union Army, 1861–1865* (1956).

Glatthaar, Joseph T. *Forged in Battle: The Civil War Alliance of Black Soldiers and White Officers* (1990).

Hess, Earl J. *The Union Soldier in Battle: Enduring the Ordeal of Combat* (1997).

Linderman, Gerald F. *Embattled Courage: The Experience of Combat in the Civil War* (1987).

Marvel, William. *Andersonville: The Last Depot* (1994).

McPherson, James M. *For Cause and Comrades: Why Men Fought in the Civil War* (1997).

Mitchell, Reid. *Civil War Soldiers* (1988).

Mitchell, Reid. *The Vacant Chair: The Northern Soldier Leaves Home* (1993).

Trudeau, Noah Andre. *Like Men of War: Black Troops in the Civil War, 1862–1865* (1998).

Wiley, Bell I. *The Life of Johnny Reb* (1943).

Wiley, Bell I. *The Life of Billy Yank* (1952).

Women's Experiences

Clinton Catherine, and Nina Silber, eds., *Divided Houses: Gender and the Civil War* (1992).

Massey, Mary E. *Bonnet Brigades* (1966).

Rable, George C. *Civil Wars: Women and the Crisis of Southern Nationalism* (1991).

Rose, Anne E. *Victorian America and the Civil War* (1992).

Venet, Wendy Hamand. *Neither Ballots nor Bullets: Women Abolitionists and the Civil War* (1991).

Emancipation and Aftermath

Carter, Dan T. *When the War Was Over: Self-Reconstruction in the South, 1865–1867* (1985).

Cimbala, Paul A. *Under the Guardianship of the Nation: The Freedmen's Bureau and the Reconstruction of Georgia, 1865–1870* (1997).

Fields, Barbara Jeanne. *Slavery and Freedom on the Middle Ground: Maryland During the Nineteenth Century* (1985).

Holt, Thomas. *Black over White: Negro Political Leadership in South Carolina During Reconstruction* (1977).

McFeely, William S. *Yankee Stepfather: General O. O. Howard and the Freedmen* (1966).

Mohr, Clarence L. *On the Threshold of Freedom: Masters and Slaves in Civil War Georgia* (1986).

Perman, Michael. *Reunion Without Compromise: The South and Reconstruction, 1865–1868* (1973).

Ransom, Roger L., and Sutch, Richard. *One Kind of Freedom: The Economic Consequences of Emancipation* (1977).

THE FIFTEENTH AMENDMENT ADOPTED

When the Fifteenth Amendment was approved in 1870, a lithograph artist depicted the moment when race, color, and having been a slave were no longer barriers to male voters. The prominent individuals shown include the most famous African American of the day, Frederick Douglass, in the group at the top of the illustration.

Chapter 16

RECONSTRUCTION ABANDONED,

1867–1877

AFTER 1867 THE nation continued to struggle over the gains that black Americans had earned during the Civil War. The battle raged in the minds of Northerners and in the halls of Congress, but it was fought with the greatest intensity in the South. There, whites sought to recapture as many of the features of slavery as they could. Violence, brutality, election fraud, and economic intimidation ended the experiment in multiracial politics known as Reconstruction.

Racial prejudice was at the heart of the problem, but other circumstances hastened the abandonment of Reconstruction. Settlement of the West claimed the energies of many people. In the mid-1870s an economic depression made civil rights seem less relevant. White Americans worried that the national government was becoming too powerful, and they reverted to traditional beliefs in localism and state rights. For many in the North, the issue of race seemed a dreary and hopeless legacy of the war, a commitment easier to forget than to fulfill. The hum of industry, the spread of railroads, the rise of cities, all seemed more in tune with an era of progress than preserving the rights of former slaves. Slowly, painfully, the nation retreated from the principles for which the Civil War had been fought. In 1877 an informal sectional compromise sealed the return to white rule in the South.

Outside the political arena, industrialization transformed the economy. The completion of the two transcontinental railroads in 1869 symbolized the rapid pace of technological change. Four years later, however, the Panic of 1873 demonstrated that progress did not always move forward along an unbroken path. The 1870s produced social unrest and deprivation for many.

A PERIOD OF UNREST

The waning of Reconstruction left African Americans and Indians further removed from the mainstream of society. As the drive to expand freedom for black Americans stalled, white dominance in the South hardened. Military defeat of the Indians confined them to reservations. Women of all colors and ancestries found that their future remained subject to the wishes of a male-dominated nation. After the upheaval of the Civil War, the 1870s were a time to pause and react, a time of political mediocrity and governmental caution.

CHRONOLOGY

1867	Alaska purchase treaty signed
1868	Andrew Johnson impeached and then acquitted
	Purchase of Alaska completed
	Ulysses S. Grant wins presidency
1869	Ulysses S. Grant inaugurated as president
	Transcontinental railroads link up
	Licensing of women lawyers begins
	Fifteenth Amendment passes Congress
	"Gold Corner" scheme of Jay Gould and Jim Fisk
	Woman suffrage enacted in Wyoming Territory
1870	Santo Domingo annexation treaty defeated
	Ku Klux Klan terror raids in the South
	First Greek letter sorority (Kappa Alpha Theta) founded
1871	Ku Klux Klan Act passes Congress
	Tweed Ring exposed in New York City
	Chicago fire burns three and a half miles of the city
1872	Liberal Republican movement challenges Grant
	Grant wins reelection over Horace Greeley
1873	Panic of 1873 starts economic depression
	Salary Grab and Crédit Mobilier scandals
	Mark Twain and Charles Dudley Warner publish *The Gilded Age*
1874	Women's Christian Temperance Union founded
	Democrats make substantial gains in the congressional elections
	Sale of typewriters begins
	Chautauqua movement for summer education starts
1875	Civil Rights Act passes Congress
	Smith College and Wellesley College open to provide higher education for women
1876	Custer defeated at Little Big Horn
	Heinz tomato ketchup is marketed
	Centennial Exposition opens in Philadelphia
	Tilden and Hayes are candidates in presidential election which remains contested as year ends
1877	Hayes declared winner of the presidency after series of compromises settles disputes
	Reconstruction comes to an end

The Impeachment of Andrew Johnson

As President Andrew Johnson sought to block the Radical Reconstruction program, sentiment to impeach him grew among Republicans in Congress. The president's effort to oust Secretary of War Edwin M. Stanton in August 1867 also resulted in demands for his impeachment. The Republicans could do little until December when Congress reassembled. By that time, impeachment efforts had faltered, and it appeared that the political momentum had turned toward Johnson. After the Senate refused to accept his dismissal of Stanton in January 1868, Johnson replaced him anyway—an act of defiance that Republicans claimed was a clear breach of the Tenure of Office Act (see Chapter 15).

Emboldened by Johnson's action, the solidly Republican House voted for his impeachment and brought eleven charges against him. None of the charges involved violations of criminal law; they dealt instead with Johnson's Reconstruction policies. The trial got underway in March. Two months later the Senate failed to produce a two-thirds' vote to convict the president.

The impeachment attempt failed for several reasons. Moderate Republicans feared that if a president were impeached and convicted on political grounds a bad precedent would be set. Johnson temporarily eased obstructive tactics and the situation in the South became more favorable to the Republicans. The approach of the 1868 election also made ousting Johnson seem less urgent.

Although he was acquitted, Johnson did not become more conciliatory; he opposed Reconstruction until the end of his term. His intransigence encouraged southern whites and contributed to the resistance against African-American equality that marked the 1870s. Few presidents have done less to capitalize on their historic opportunities than Andrew Johnson.

The Purchase of Alaska

During the months that Andrew Johnson's impeachment case dominated the headlines, the Congress also moved to complete a major territorial acquisition. In March 1867 the Russian minister to the United States hinted to Secretary of State William H. Seward that the tsarist government in St. Petersburg would respond favorably to an American offer to purchase Alaska. The Russians knew that they could not defend their northern possession against the British in Canada, and they worried about a potential American occupation. The Russian diplomat and Seward worked out a treaty that was signed on March 30, 1867. The United States paid $7,200,000 for Alaska. On April 9, the Senate gave its approval by a vote of thirty-seven to two.

Paying for the Alaska purchase required an appropriation from the House. The members did not take up the subject until July 1868, after the House had impeached the president. Faced with a *fait accompli* in that the occupation of the territory had occurred a year earlier, the House approved the money solidly on July 14, and the measure became law two weeks later. The purchase of Alaska represented a major strategic and geographic victory for the country, but it would be another twenty-five years before overseas expansion once again took place.

The Election of 1868

The leading candidate for the Republican nomination was Ulysses S. Grant. His association with the Union victory gave him a popularity that transcended

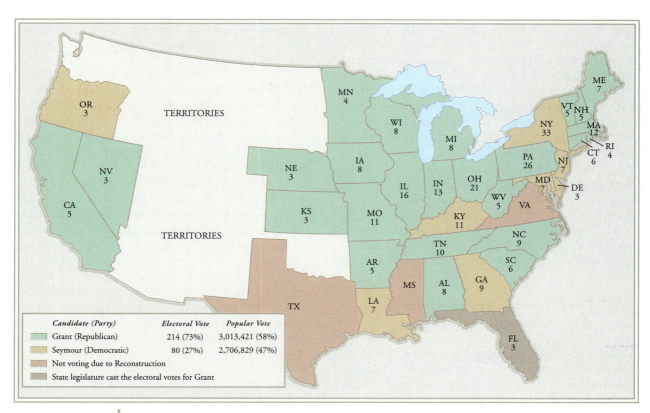

Candidate (Party)	Electoral Vote	Popular Vote
Grant (Republican)	214 (73%)	3,013,421 (58%)
Seymour (Democratic)	80 (27%)	2,706,829 (47%)
Not voting due to Reconstruction		
State legislature cast the electoral votes for Grant		

MAP 16.1 | THE ELECTION OF 1868

THE FIFTEENTH AMENDMENT 1870

The last of the three Reconstruction amendments, the Fifteenth Amendment said that race or color could not be a reason for denying a citizen the right to vote.

Sect. 1. The right of citizens of the United States to vote shall not be denied or abridged by the United States or by any State on account of race, color, or previous condition of servitude.

Sect. 2. The Congress shall have the power to enforce this article by appropriate legislation.

partisanship and would draw key Democratic votes in what shaped up to be a close election contest. In his letter of acceptance, Grant concluded with the phrase "let us have peace" and that phrase became the theme of his campaign. To run against Grant, the Democrats turned to the former governor of New York, Horatio Seymour. Along with his running mate, Frank Blair, Seymour made a campaign based on the philosophy of white supremacy. As the New York *Herald,* a Democratic newspaper, reported, "Universal Nigger Suffrage is the Great Issue of the Campaign." Seymour made several speaking tours; Grant stayed home. When the votes were counted, Grant had 53 percent and Seymour had 47 percent. In the electoral college, however, Grant had a more secure margin of 214 electoral votes to 80. The relatively close result indicated that white voters were cooling toward Reconstruction and that the high point of post–Civil War racial reform was past.

The Fifteenth Amendment and Woman Suffrage

After the 1868 election Republicans pushed for adoption of the Fifteenth Amendment to the Constitution, which stated that the federal and state governments could not abridge the right of a citizen to vote "on account of race, color, or previous condition of servitude." Legislative approval came in February 1869.

Because the amendment reduced the legal ability of the southern states to exclude African Americans from voting, Democrats attacked it as "a step toward centralization and consolidation." Republicans responded that "we are one nation."

The new amendment had striking limitations. It did not assure African Americans the right to hold office, nor did it address the restrictions that northern states imposed on the right of other males to vote. These limits included literacy tests, and property qualifications. In California, immigrant Chinese were barred from voting. State legislatures outside the South endorsed the amendment promptly and it was ratified in 1870.

The Fifteenth Amendment ignored women, despite the major contribution they had made to the abolition movement through antislavery societies, pamphlets, and petition drives. Some advocates of woman suffrage, such as Susan B. Anthony, opposed the amendment because it excluded women. She favored voting barriers for black and Asian men if women did not have the vote. Despite his earlier support for woman suffrage, Frederick Douglass now said that "this hour belongs to the negro," meaning black males. At a meeting of the Equal Rights Association in May 1869, differing views about the right strategy for achieving woman suffrage caused an open rift.

The split led to the formation of two distinct groups. The National Woman Suffrage Association

Susan B. Anthony was a leading advocate of a woman's right to vote in the post-Civil War era. Her connection with that reform continued throughout the late nineteenth century.

(NWSA) reflected the position of Susan B. Anthony and Elizabeth Cady Stanton who believed that the Fifteenth Amendment should not be supported until it included women. The American Woman Suffrage Association (AWSA), led by Lucy Stone and Alice Stone Blackwell, endorsed the amendment and focused their suffrage efforts on the states. The new territory of Wyoming granted women the right of suffrage in 1869. The goal of the Wyoming legislature was to advertise its underpopulated territory, not to expand women's rights, but a small step forward had nonetheless been taken. The discord between the two suffrage organizations lasted for two decades, however, and slowed the progress toward reform.

GRANT'S FIRST TERM

The new president entered the White House with little political experience. He intended to administer the government rather than promote new programs. "I shall on all subjects have a policy to recommend," he said in his inaugural address, "but none to enforce against the will of the people."

Grant's limited view of the presidency meant that Congress played a dominant role during his adminis-

tration. Republicans did not look to the White House for leadership in developing programs or shaping policy. As a result, the office of the presidency lost some of the authority it had acquired during the Civil War. A generation passed before the balance shifted back toward the executive branch.

The new administration faced hard choices. Southern Republicans wanted help from Washington against resurgent Democrats. A growing number of northern party members questioned whether continuation of Reconstruction was wise or practical. Some had backed off from the commitment to African Americans that Reconstruction implied. Within the Republican ranks, party reformers wanted to limit the power of the leaders to dole out patronage. They wanted to adopt a merit system for appointing officials; this was referred to as "civil service reform." Party regulars hoped that Grant would side with them against the reformers and recognize the power of congressional leaders.

At first Grant tried to avoid partisan battles. For example, he had no clear policy on appointments. In selecting his cabinet he did not follow the advice of influential Republicans but relied instead on men who shared his cautious governing style. Cabinet officers

When he took office, President Grant was seen as a constructive change from the turmoil of Andrew Johnson's administration. In office, he found that politics was more of a challenge to him than military success in the Civil War.

were given free rein in using merit rather than political connections to staff their departments. Some worked with Congress; other did not.

In the South, the Democrats endeavored to split the Republicans. They collaborated with party members who had become alienated from the Republican leadership. Playing down their dislike of black voters, they centered their arguments on whether former Confederates should be allowed to cast ballots. The elections in 1869 produced mixed results. Republicans did well in Mississippi and won narrowly in Texas while Democrats prevailed in Virginia and Tennessee. The latter outcomes foreshadowed an erosion of Republican electoral strength as the Democrats reestablished their power in the South. Grant's passive style meant that Republicans and their black allies in the South found themselves at a disadvantage.

The Railroads Meet

While politics dominated Washington, an event in Utah captured the attention of the rest of the nation. Throughout the 1860s two transcontinental railroads had been laying track across the country. The Union Pacific had built westward and the Central Pacific eastward. The competing lines faced significant obstacles of money and geography. The Central Pacific had

In the work of building the transcontinental railroad, the grueling labor of Chinese workers was indispensable. They worked for low pay in difficult conditions in a society that scorned them and often subjected them to harsh discrimination.

crossed the heights of the Sierra Nevada mountains through rocky gorges and treacherous rivers. Several thousand Chinese laborers did the most dangerous work. They tunneled into snowdrifts to reach their work sites and then toiled on sheer cliffs with picks and dynamite. On the Union Pacific side, more than 10,000 construction men, many of them Irish immigrants, laid track across Nebraska and Wyoming.

On May 10, 1869, the two rail lines met at Promontory, Utah. The occasion was marked by a dramatic ceremony. Engine 119 of the Union Pacific stood with its cowcatcher touching the cowcatcher of the Central Pacific's Engine No. 60. A gold spike was driven into the ground with a silver sledgehammer, though railroad executives failed to hit the spike on their first few tries. The transcontinental lines had been built so quickly in part because of loans and subsidies from the federal government to the rail companies. The process by which the financing had occurred would soon become one of the more notorious scandals of the Grant presidency.

The completion of the first transcontinental railroad in 1869 ushered in a period of railroad construction in which the nation developed one of the best and most comprehensive transportation systems in the world. It meant that the opening of the entire

The completion of the transcontinental railroad at Promontory, Utah, in 1869 symbolized the joining together of the nation's two coasts. As the presence of photographers indicates, it also became an important media event.

MAP 16.2 | INDIAN RESERVATIONS IN THE WEST

Indian reservations, 1880

ARIZONA TERRITORY
1. Colorado River
2. Gila River
3. Moqui Pueblo
4. Papago
5. White Mountain
6. Suppai

CALIFORNIA
7. Hoopa Valley
8. Mission
9. Round Valley
10. Tule River
11. Klamath River

COLORADO
12. Ute

DAKOTA TERRITORY
13. Crow Creek
14. Devils Lake
15. Flandreau
16. Ft. Berthold
17. Lake Traverse
18. Old Winnebago
19. Ponca
20. Sioux
21. Yankton

IDAHO TERRITORY
22. Coeur d'Alene
23. Ft. Hall
24. Lapwai
25. Lemhi

IOWA
26. Sac and Fox

KANSAS
27. Black Bob
28. Chippewa and Munsee
29. Kickapoo
30. Miami
31. Potawatomi

MINNESOTA
32. Bois Forte
33. Fond du Lac
34. Grand Portage
35. Leech Lake
36. Mille Lac
37. Red Lake
38. White Earth
39. Winnebagoshish

MONTANA TERRITORY
40. Blackfeet
41. Crow
42. Jocko

NEBRASKA
43. Iowa
44. Niobrara
45. Omaha
46. Oto
47. Sac and Fox
48. Winnebago

NEVADA
49. Duck Valley
50. Moapa Valley
51. Pyramid Lake
52. Walker River

NEW MEXICO TERRITORY
53. Jicarilla Apache
54. Mescalero Apache
55. Navajo
Pueblos
56. Jémez
57. Acoma
58. San Juan
59. Picurís
60. San Felipe
61. Pecos
62. Cochiti
63. Santo Domingo
64. Taos
65. Santa Clara
66. Tesuque
67. San Ildefonso
68. Pojoaque
69. Zia
70. Sandia
71. Isleta
72. Nambé
73. Laguna
74. Santa Ana
75. Zuñi

OREGON
76. Grande Ronde
77. Klamath
78. Malheur
79. Siletz
80. Umatilla
81. Warm Springs

UTAH TERRITORY
82. Uinta Valley

WASHINGTON TERRITORY
83. Chehalis
84. Colville
85. Makah
86. Nisqually
87. Puyallup
88. Shoalwater
89. Squaxin Island
90. Lummi
91. Muckleshoot
92. Port Madison
93. Snohomish or Tulalip
94. Swinomish
95. Quinaielt
96. Skokomish
97. Yakima
98. Columbia

WYOMING TERRITORY
99. Wind River

INDIAN TERRITORY (OKLAHOMA)
100. Quapaw
101. Peoria
102. Ottawa
103. Pawnee
104. Wyandot
105. Modoc
106. Seneca
107. Seminole
108. Choctaw
109. Chickasaw
110. Potawatomie-Shawnee
111. Apache
112. Comanche
113. Kiowa
114. Wichita
115. Arapaho
116. Cheyenne
117. Creek
118. Sauk-Fox
119. Kickapoo
120. Iowa
121. Oto Missouri
122. Tonkawa
123. Ponca
124. Chilocco
125. Kansa
126. Osage
127. Cherokee

West was now possible. Settlement of the region resumed in the post–Civil War years. Farmers pushed out on to the fertile plains of what had once been erroneously labeled "The Great American Desert." No area of the country seemed isolated any longer. This rapid expansion raised anew the question of what should happen to the Native Americans who had been pushed westward before the Civil War and to the nomadic tribes of Plains Indians, who now saw their hunting grounds and traditional domains imperiled.

Grant's "Peace Policy"

In its relations with Native Americans, the Grant administration pursued what became known as the "peace policy." While many settlers in the West would have welcomed the extermination of the Indian tribes, most Americans favored the peace policy strategy.

This approach had first taken shape in the years just before Grant took office. Those who sought better treatment of Indians argued that negotiations with hostile tribes would lead to resettlement in the western parts of Dakota Territory and in the western portion of what was then dubbed Indian Territory (now Oklahoma). Instead of treating the entire West as a huge Indian reservation as had been the case before the Civil War, the government would allocate areas to the tribes. These "reservations" would become places where Native Americans could be instructed about the cultural values and habits of white society, taught to grow crops, and paid a subsistence income until they were able to support themselves. Implementation of this program lagged, however, during 1868, and no reservations for peaceful tribes had yet been established when Grant became president.

The Peace Policy in Action

To supervise Indian policy, Grant named Jacob D. Cox as secretary of the interior. Cox, in turn, selected Ely Parker, a Seneca Indian, as commissioner of Indian affairs. The administration persuaded Congress to appropriate $2 million for Indian affairs and to set up a Board of Indian Commissioners to distribute the money. Instead of leaving the selection

Chief Red Cloud of the Sioux sits for a photographer in his regalia. Fear and fascination were mingled in popular attitudes toward Native Americans after the Civil War.

of Indian agents to political patronage, the administration relied on nominations from the Christian churches.

The peace policy mixed kindness with coercion. If the Indians accepted the supervision of the church officials on the reservations, the government would leave them alone. Resistance to the peace policy, on the other hand, served as a reason for the U.S. Army to drive the Indians onto reservations and open new lands for white settlement. In its early months, the peace policy appeared to be a humane improvement over earlier practices. For the Indians, however, the new approach represented another assault on their traditional way of life. Moreover, it remained to be seen how the peace policy would fare in the face of economic and political pressures that continued white settlement generated.

AN ERA OF SCANDALS

Scandals plagued the Grant administration from the outset. In the summer of 1869, two speculators, Jay Gould and Jim Fisk, sought to manipulate the market in gold so as to achieve huge profits. Their efforts caused a rise in the price of gold that produced financial turmoil on September 24, 1869, when investors who had contracted to sell gold at lower prices faced ruin. The government ordered the sale of its own gold supplies, and the crisis eased when the price returned to its normal level. The details of the controversy soon faded away but the administration was embarrassed by revelations that some members of Grant's family, along with an official in the Treasury Department, had aided Gould and Fisk in carrying out their plan. Some critics suggested that First Lady Julia Grant had participated. Even though Grant and his wife were not implicated, the episode raised serious doubts about the ethical standards of his presidency.

To this impression of corruption the Grant administration also added a sense of confusion and incompetence. In foreign policy, there was talk of confronting Spain in an attempt to acquire Cuba. Secretary of State Hamilton Fish forestalled that potential crisis.

The railroad operator Jay Gould was a favorite subject of cartoonists who derided his financial schemes and treated him as a menace to the welfare of society. Gould's sharp dealings gave his enemies ample ammunition for their attacks.

Grant also wanted to annex the Dominican Republic (Santo Domingo). A presidential agent negotiated an annexation treaty with Santo Domingo's rulers, and the pact was sent to the Senate. Grant pushed hard for approval of the treaty, but the Senate, fearful of the influence of speculators and lobbyists, was suspicious of the president's goals and balked at endorsing what Grant had done with the treaty.

One diplomatic area in which Grant had some success was in the resolution of American claims for maritime losses against Great Britain over the *Alabama,* one of several Confederate merchant raiding ships that had been constructed in Great Britain during the Civil War. The *Alabama* had sunk numerous Union vessels. Charles Sumner, chair of the Senate Foreign Relations Committee, wanted to use the claims as leverage in an effort to acquire Canada. In 1871, Secretary of State Fish negotiated a treaty that led to an amicable settlement of the issue but left Canada undisturbed.

Grant and the Congress

Other issues troubled Grant's relations with Congress. Congressional Republicans split on a number of economic issues such as the protective tariff and the currency question. The mainstream of the party now believed that a tariff policy to "protect" American industries against foreign competition would be in the best interests of the business community, workers, and the Republican party. A minority of party members viewed the protective policy as unwise economically and a potential source of corrupt influence from protected industries. On the currency question, eastern Republicans favored the gold standard and what was known as "hard money"; western colleagues advocated an expansion of the money supply, government use of paper money or "greenbacks," and even some reliance on silver dollars as an alternative to gold.

Equally divisive was the issue of civil service. Calls for reform in the way government employees were selected intensified as the movement for a nonpartisan civil service gathered momentum. Republicans who wanted to reduce the tariff, implement the civil service, and treat the South more leniently defected from the administration and formed what they called Liberal Republican alliances with Democrats in such states as West Virginia and Missouri. In the 1870s, "liberal" meant a person who favored a smaller government, lower tariffs, and an end to Reconstruction.

Grant and His Party

Faced with a series of challenges to his presidency during 1870, Grant displayed greater reliance on the Republican party and its leaders in Congress. These Republican regulars had little taste for civil service reform, lower tariffs, or an end to Reconstruction. The president's turn to traditional politicians made sense, but it alienated Liberal Republicans. The possibility of a split in the party increased.

The president's resolve to depend more on regular Republicans strengthened after the Senate defeated his treaty with Santo Domingo during the summer of 1870. Following this episode, Grant knew that he could not work with Republican opponents of his presidency or satisfy the clamor for milder Reconstruction policies, civil service reform, and a less active national government. The Democrats could always outbid him on those issues, and courting them would only weaken the Republicans further. Failure to maintain good relations with his own party would mean political disaster. Grant was not an astute politician, but he could read that lesson clearly.

Toward the 1870 Elections

As a result, in 1870 Grant turned to groups within the party that could ensure his renomination and reelection two years later. He made conciliatory gestures toward the party mainstream. When Secretary of the Interior Jacob D. Cox complained about the practice of compelling government employees to make campaign contributions, Grant dismissed him. The president nominated his attorney general, Ebenezer R. Hoar, for the Supreme Court. When the Senate rejected him, Grant decided that Hoar too should leave the cabinet. To succeed him, he chose Amos T. Akerman, a southern Republican.

In the 1870 elections the Grant administration aligned itself with Republicans who defended Congress and the White House. Officeholders who supported Liberal Republican candidates or Democrats were removed. Despite these actions, the fall elections produced a setback for the president and his party. Liberal Republicans won in West Virginia and Missouri. Nationwide, the Democrats gained forty-one seats in the House of Representatives as the members from all the southern states rejoined the Congress. The Republicans retained control, however. The Demo-

crats also gained six seats in the Senate, although the Republicans still held a decisive edge in that chamber as well. Given Grant's relatively narrow victory in 1868, the enemies of the president looked forward to the 1872 election with some optimism.

The Ku Klux Klan in the South

By the summer of 1870 reports reached Washington of growing violence against blacks as well as white Republicans in the South. Roving bands of whites calling themselves the Ku Klux Klan (see Chapter 15) were responsible for the attacks. Throughout the South the Klan repressed any challenge to white dominance. One Republican in Louisiana said that "murder and intimidation are the order of the day in this state."

The Klan and its offshoots, such as the Knights of the White Camellia and the White Brotherhood, acted as paramilitary agents of the Democratic party to stamp out Republicanism through any means available. In Tennessee a black Republican was beaten after he won an election for justice of the peace. His

A cartoon attacks the Ku Klux Klan and the "white leagues" of the South for their terrorist tactics toward the African-American population. The result for the freed slaves is a condition that is "worse than slavery."

assailants told him "that they didn't dispute I was a very good fellow . . . but they did not intend any nigger to hold office in the United States."

The Klan would stop at nothing to eliminate its opponents. Leaders of the Republican party were hunted and killed. Campaign rallies sparked terror raids. In an incident in Alabama, in October 1870, four blacks died in a Klan attack on an election meeting. A "negro chase" in South Carolina left thirteen blacks dead.

The Klansmen rode in white robes and hoods; their aim, they said, was to frighten their racial foes. The disguises also hid their identity as white leaders employing extralegal violence to subvert the democratic process. Throughout 1870 a wave of shootings and brutality swept across the South, undermining the Republican party's chances of surviving below the Mason-Dixon line.

The Government and the Klan

During the 1870 election, the Klan violence had a devastating impact on Republicans in the South. In North Carolina, Georgia, Florida, and Alabama, the Klan's terror tactics intimidated voters and demoralized the party's leadership. In county after county the night riders attacked and murdered local black leaders. After the elections the Klan, emboldened by its success, became more active than ever.

By 1871 the Republicans had less stomach for military intervention in the political affairs of the South. As an Illinois newspaper put it, "the negro is now a voter and a citizen. Let him hereafter take his chances in the battle of life." Republican leaders asked themselves whether the cost of helping to maintain party organizations in the South justified the effort and time that had to be expended in the face of resolute Democratic opposition.

The Klan's violence, however, presented a challenge that could not be ignored. If violence could not be stopped, the Republican party in the South might simply vanish and the achievements of Reconstruction would be nullified. As a result, Congress adopted legislation to curb election fraud, bribery, and coercion in elections. When these measures proved inadequate, the lawmakers passed the Ku Klux Klan Act of 1871. This legislation outlawed conspiracies to deprive voters of their civil rights and prohibited efforts to bar any citizen from holding public office. If the Klan in-

In the aftermath of the Civil War, the old labor system of slavery and the plantation gave way to other forms of agricultural labor that kept African Americans tied to the land. Sharecropping meant that farmers had to provide a substantial portion of their crops to the white owner of the land.

terfered with equal protection of the laws, it could be prosecuted. The government received expanded powers to deal with such actions through the use of federal district attorneys to override state laws and, as a last resort, through military force.

The Democrats labeled these laws an unconstitutional interference with the rights of the states. Their passage was the "crowning act of centralization and consolidation," said one critic. A Republican countered by saying: "Tell me nothing of a constitution which fails to shelter beneath its rightful power the people of a country."

Breaking the Klan's Power

Events in the South renewed the Republicans' resolve to end the law-breaking and violence that the Klan represented. Attorney General Akerman argued that the threat the Klan posed to democratic government amounted to war. Akerman and his solicitor general,

Benjamin H. Bristow, were now part of the Department of Justice, which had been established in 1870, and they mobilized federal district attorneys and U.S. marshals to enforce prosecutions against the Klan.

During 1871 the legal offensive against the Klan went forward. In state after state indictments came down against Klan leaders. In North Carolina, hundreds of men faced trial; many went to prison. Similar prosecutions began in Mississippi and South Carolina. Federal troops assisted the Justice Department's work in South Carolina. The Klan was discredited as a public agent in southern politics and its violence became more covert and less visible. Although the Klan prosecutions showed that effective federal action could force the southern states to comply with the rule of law, in the North sentiment for such stern measures was ebbing. Soon the popular mood would move toward virtual abandonment of Reconstruction.

Scandals and Corruption: New York's Tweed Ring

The willingness to use national power that had marked the Reconstruction era receded in part because Americans increasingly believed that politics everywhere had become hopelessly corrupt. The most celebrated example of corruption in this period was the Tweed Ring, which dominated New York City during the late 1860s.

The leader of the ring was William Magear Tweed, Jr., who had risen through various city offices such as alderman and supervisor of elections and by the early 1870s had won a seat in the state senate. He was closely identified with the Democratic party organization which met at a political clubhouse called Tammany Hall to plan electoral strategy. The expanding cities of the post–Civil War years offered politicians countless chances to profit from the allocation of lucrative contracts and official services. Tweed and his allies turned these new opportunities to their personal advantage. They padded the city's accounts, and extracted kickbacks from contractors doing business with the city.

"Boss" Tweed's power rested on the votes of the city's heavily Democratic population. Long loyal to the Democrats who shared their suspicion of Republican efforts to regulate moral behavior, Irish Catholic immigrants supported the party that spoke to their needs and was receptive to their lifestyle and religious

Few individuals were more notorious in the 1870s than William M. "Boss" Tweed of New York City. The Tweed Ring and the lavish expenditures of money that it made in New York City came to symbolize the corruption and boss rule that many Americans associated with the rise of the city.

values. Their votes were crucial if the party expected to carry the state in a presidential contest. Tammany Hall also made sure that city services and jobs were available to those who supported them at the polls. By the end of the 1860s, Tweed seemed to hold New York City's political destiny in his hands.

In fact, Tweed's moment at the top of New York politics was very brief. He came under assault from the *New York Times,* which devoted endless columns to exposing the misdeeds of the Democratic party and its leaders. More significant from a national perspective, a cartoonist named Thomas Nast used artistic skill to make Tweed an object of derision. Nast's drawings depicted Tweed as the leader of a band of criminal freebooters, a money-grabbing scoundrel, a ludicrous caricature of an official in a democratic society. Tweed was aware of the damage the cartoons did to his reputation and political standing. As he told one editor, "I don't care a straw for your newspaper articles. My constituents don't know how to read, but they can't help seeing them damned pictures."

In mid-1871, a resentful member of the Tweed Ring, angered at being left out of the spoils, gave city account books to a reporter. The revelation of how much had been spent on city projects stunned the population. A courthouse that had been projected to cost $250,000 came to $13 million. Other reports of corruption abounded as Tweed's pursuers closed in. Within a year, Tweed had been indicted, ousted from his position at Tammany Hall, and placed on trial. He escaped conviction in his first trial but was later retried and found guilty on 204 counts. He fled the country and took refuge in Spain. Arrested there when an official recognized him from a Nast cartoon, he returned to New York a broken man and died in 1878.

For many fearful Americans Tweed's story symbolized the decline in ethical standards that they believed had followed the Civil War. They had short memories. American politics in the 1850s had not been famous for the honesty and moral standards of those who led the nation. Nonetheless, citizens began to think that the expanded power of the state and the extension of the franchise to all white males and many freed slaves threatened the nation's political future. "We are in danger of going the way of all Republics," said one critic of the existing system. "First freedom, then glory; when that is past, Wealth, vice, corruption." A North Carolina newspaper echoed this sentiment: "As things go, the thieves will soon be in the majority."

The Liberal Republican Challenge to Grant

Restoring "higher" ethical standards was the stated purpose of the Liberal Republicans, who sought a presidential candidate to run against President Grant in the 1872 election. Their political creed included ending Reconstruction, returning good men like themselves to national power, and curbing the influence of political patronage through expanded use of the merit system. The leaders of the campaign were Senator Carl Schurz, a Missouri Republican, Edwin L. Godkin, editor of The Nation, and Charles Francis Adams, the son of former President John Quincy Adams.

Liberal Republicans believed in smaller government. "The Government," wrote E.L. Godkin, "must get out of the 'protective' business and the 'subsidy' business and the 'improvement' business and 'development' business. . . . It cannot touch them without breeding corruption." Such Republican programs as the protective tariff appalled them. Most of all, they saw Reconstruction as a failed experiment in racial democracy that should be abandoned. As Grant's one-time secretary of the Interior, Jacob D. Cox, contended: "the South can only be governed through the part of the community that embodies the intelligence and the capital." In effect, black Americans in the South would have to look to whites in that region for protection of their rights and privileges.

The Liberal Republicans lacked a national candidate with the stature to challenge a popular president whose reputation had not been diminished by the problems of his first term. Although many party leaders were unhappy with the policies of the Grant administration, few were commanding political figures. Senator Carl Schurz had been born in Germany and therefore was ineligible under the Constitution. Other presidential hopefuls included Charles Francis Adams, Senator Lyman Trumbull of Illinois, and Horace Greeley, the editor of the New York Tribune.

In May 1872, the Liberal Republicans gathered in Cincinnati. According to the Tribune, "there had never been a better class of men gathered on such an occasion." The balloting revealed that the contest lay between the colorless Adams and the well-known and eccentric Greeley. Greeley won the nomination on the sixth ballot.

The sixty-one-year-old editor was an odd choice. He favored the protective tariff, which most reformers disliked, and was indifferent to civil service reform. Once a harsh critic of the South, he had mellowed and now favored ending Reconstruction. A lifetime of passions for such offbeat remedies as vegetarianism and the use of human manure in farming made him seem a political oddball in the eyes of many Americans. "That Grant is an Ass no man can deny," said one Liberal Republican, "but better an Ass than a mischievous idiot."

The 1872 Election

The Republican convention renominated Grant and chose Henry Wilson of Massachusetts to be his running mate. In its platform the party stressed the

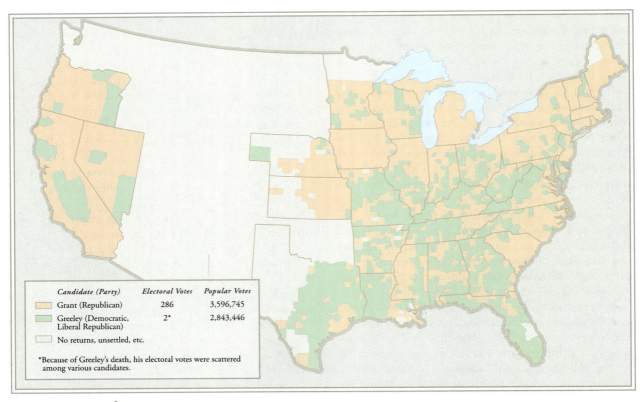

Candidate (Party)	Electoral Votes	Popular Votes
Grant (Republican)	286	3,596,745
Greeley (Democratic, Liberal Republican)	2*	2,843,446
No returns, unsettled, etc.		

*Because of Greeley's death, his electoral votes were scattered among various candidates.

MAP 16.3 | THE ELECTION OF 1872

continuing problem of Reconstruction. The black leader Frederick Douglass said of the impending contest: "If the Republican party goes down, freedom goes down with it." The Republican appeal urged voters to preserve what had been achieved during the Civil War. One Republican orator told the crowd that they could either "Go vote to burn school houses, desecrate churches and violate women or vote for Horace Greeley, which means the same thing."

When the Democrats held their national convention in early July, they faced a dilemma. If they failed to nominate Greeley, they had no chance of winning. Nominating him, however, would alienate southern voters. In the end the delegates accepted Greeley as their only alternative. The Liberal Republican-Democratic nominee made a vigorous campaign while Grant observed the tradition in which an incumbent president did not campaign actively. Grant did, however, influence the campaign from behind the scenes.

The outcome was a decisive victory for Grant and his party. The president swamped Greeley in the popular vote and in the electoral tally. There were still enough Republicans in the South to enable Grant to carry all but five of the southern states. Worn out by the rigors of the campaign, Greeley died in late November 1872. Because of Greeley's ineptitude and divisions within the party, the election marked a low point for the Democrats. Grant would continue as president, but his second term would prove to be even more difficult and scandal-ridden than his first administration.

Recurrent Scandals

As the excitement of the 1872 election died down, political attention turned to sensational allegations of corruption in Congress. The first scandal concerned the efforts of the Crédit Mobilier Company (named after a French company) to purchase influence with lawmakers during the late 1860s. The directors of the Union Pacific Railroad had established Crédit Mobilier to raise money to build the transcontinental line. By paying themselves to construct the railroad, the participants in the venture made large profits and the company's shareholders did as well. The only problem was that much of the money in effect came from the federal government through loans and guarantees.

To forestall a congressional probe into the company, Crédit Mobilier's managers gave leading Republicans in Congress a chance to buy shares in the company at prices well below their actual market value. When the lawmakers sold their shares, they pocketed the difference—the equivalent of a bribe. One beneficiary was a future president, James A. Garfield, of Ohio, but he sold his stock soon after he received it and made a profit of only $329. When a newspaper broke the story in late 1872, an investigation followed. The inquiry produced a few scapegoats but cleared most of the lawmakers involved. Nevertheless, the episode damaged the credibility of public officials.

Another embarrassing episode occurred in February 1873. At the end of a congressional session, a last-minute maneuver gave senators and representatives a retroactive pay increase. The public denounced the action, calling it the "Salary Grab." The Chicago *Tribune* said it was "nothing more nor less than an act of robbery." When Congress reconvened in December 1873, repeal of the salary increase sailed through both houses in a burst of political contrition. These two incidents generated widespread calls for reducing government expenditures and rooting out corruption. As Mark Twain said, "It could probably be shown by facts and figures that there is no distinctly native American criminal class except Congress."

Twain himself captured the spirit of the times in his novel, *The Gilded Age.* The main character, Colonel Beriah Sellers, was an engaging confidence man who embodied the boosterism and economic looseness of the postwar years, along with the healthy amount of fraud and chicanery that accompanied the rapid growth of business. In time, the title of Twain's book came to be used as a label for the entire era between the end of Reconstruction and the start of the twentieth century. "The Gilded Age" was, however, a richer and more complex time than the stereotype of corrupt politicians and fraudulent entrepreneurs that Twain portrayed.

THE PANIC OF 1873 AND ITS CONSEQUENCES

The sense of national crisis deepened in September 1873 when the banking house of Jay Cooke and Company failed. The disaster was triggered by the bank's inability to market the bonds of the Northern Pacific Railroad, in which it had invested heavily. An economic downturn ensued that rivaled similar panics that had occurred in 1819, 1837, and 1857; however, the Panic of 1873 was worse than any of them.

The immediate effects of the downturn lasted until 1879. In fact, an extended period of economic hard times had begun that would extend through the 1890s. A hallmark of the "Great Depression," as it was then called, was declining prices for agricultural products and manufactured goods. Americans grappled with the consequences of an economy in which falling prices placed the heaviest burdens on people who were in debt or who earned their living by selling labor. An abundance of cheap unskilled labor proved a boon for capitalists who wanted to keep costs down. For the

Cartoonists reacted when the Panic of 1873 began with the failure of the Northern Pacific Railroad and Jay Cooke's banking interests. Here the "Northern Pole R.R." and the "Bank of Inflation" are consumed in the general collapse.

Table 16.1 Railroad Mileage, 1869–1876	
1869:	46,844
1870:	52,922
1871:	60,301
1872:	66,171
1873:	70,268
1874:	72,385
1875:	74,096
1876:	76,808

poor, however, it meant that they had little job security and could easily be replaced if they protested against working conditions. Industrialization went forward at a substantial human cost.

The panic occurred because of a speculative post–Civil War boom in railroad building that produced an overexpansion of transportation facilities. In 1869, railroad mileage stood at about 47,000 miles; four years later it had risen to 70,268 miles. The new railroad lines employed tens of thousands of workers and extended across a far larger geographical area than any earlier manufacturing enterprises. Bigness in railroad operations portended the future expansion of the industrial sector. When large railroads such as the Northern Pacific failed because of their overexpansion and inability to pay their debts, the resulting impact rippled through society. Economic activities such as car making, steel rail production, and passenger services, which were dependent on the rail lines, declined as well. Layoffs of employees and bankruptcies of businesses followed. More than 10,000 companies failed in 1878, the worst year of the depression.

The Plight of the Unemployed

Americans who were thrown out of work during the 1870s had no system of unemployment insurance to fall back on. In some cities up to a quarter of the labor force looked for work without success. Tramps roamed the countryside. The conventional wisdom held that natural forces had to operate to restore prosperity; any form of political intervention would be futile and dangerous. When President Grant proposed that the national government generate jobs through public works, the secretary of the Treasury informed him: "It is not part of the business of government to find employment for people."

Those who were out of a job during the mid-1870s could not afford such a philosophical attitude. Laborers in the Northeast mounted a campaign calling for

The hard times that arose from the Panic of 1873 produced labor unrest in many cities. Here an artist recreates the riot in Tompkins Square in New York in 1874.

"Work or Bread" that included large public demonstrations in major cities. The marchers asked city and state governments to sponsor projects to create parks and construct streets, thereby providing work. In January 1874 a demonstration at Tompkins Square in New York City pitted a crowd of 7,000 unemployed laborers against police. Many marchers were arrested; others were injured in the confrontation.

Labor unrest marked the first half of the decade. Numerous and prolonged strikes occurred in 1874 and 1875. In Pennsylvania the railroads used their control of police and strikebreakers to put down the "Long Strike" of coal miners and their supporters. Twenty alleged members of a secret society called the Molly Maguires were hanged. Conservative Americans feared that the nation was on the verge of revolution.

Distress and Protest Among the Farmers

In agricultural regions, the drop in farm prices also produced discontent. The price of wheat stood at $1.16 per bushel in 1873; it fell to ninety-five cents a bushel a year later. The price of corn reached a high of sixty-four cents a bushel in 1874 but had slipped to forty-two cents a bushel in 1875. The resulting decline in income meant that debts on land and equipment were a greater burden on the hard-pressed farmers. Faced with the economic power of the railroads and grain merchants, the farmer was "a mere bushwhacker, confronting organized and well-equipped armies."

Farmers' protests were led by the Patrons of Husbandry, also known as the Grange. Created in 1867, the nonpartisan Grange focused on complaints about the high mortgages farmers owed, the prices they had to pay to middlemen such as the operators of grain elevators, and the discrimination that they suffered at the hands of railroads that charged high rates for shipping agricultural commodities.

Regulating the Railroads

The answer to the railroads' power, the angry farmers argued, lay in using the power of state governments to force the railroads to end their discriminatory practices. That meant the creation of state railroad commissions with the power to establish equitable rates and prevent unfair treatment of those who shipped agricultural products. Shippers of manufactured goods in many states added their political clout to the campaign for state commissions. In 1870 Illinois adopted a new state constitution that mandated that the legislature "pass laws establishing maximum rates of charges for the transportation of passengers and freight." The legislature responded a year later, giving the Illinois Railroad Commission wide powers. Neighboring states such as Iowa, Minnesota, and Wisconsin followed suit in the next several years. Railroad companies challenged some of these laws in the courts, and a case involving the constitutionality of the Illinois law began working its way toward the Supreme Court under the title *Munn* v. *Illinois*.

The pressure for regulatory legislation affected Congress in 1873–1874. An Iowa Republican introduced legislation in the House to establish a national railroad commission. As an anonymous spokesman for the West told a journalist, "Sir, you will never make me doubt that a government which could put down that mighty Rebellion can regulate the details of a few tariffs of some railroad corporation." The bill passed in the House, but the Senate never acted upon it. Federal legislation would not be enacted until 1887.

The decline in consumer prices and the burden of debt on farmers and businessmen in the South and West stimulated pressure for laws to put more money in circulation. That would make debts easier to pay. The Treasury Department's decision to end the coinage of silver in 1873 aroused particular ire among southern and western advocates of inflation; they called it the "Crime of 1873." Proponents contended that an overabundance of silver in the marketplace required the move to a gold standard. By coining silver into money at a price above its market levels, the government was in effect subsidizing American silver production and cheapening the currency. Opponents of the change, however, were suspicious of the dominance of eastern bankers over financial policy.

An effort to inject a modest amount of inflation into the economy came in 1875. A currency bill cleared both houses of Congress, providing some $64 million in additional money for the financial system. President Grant considered signing the bill, but he encountered economic conservatism among eastern Republicans. Their advice led him to veto the bill in April 1875, and Congress failed to override his action. The federal government would not intervene in the deepening economic crisis.

WOMEN IN THE 1870S

Amid the male-dominated political scenes that marked this period, occasional episodes reminded the nation that women were not allowed to play a direct part in public life. Susan B. Anthony sought the opportunity to address the Liberal Republican and Republican national conventions in 1872, but without success. On election day she and fifteen other women registered and voted at their polling place in Rochester, New York. Anthony and the voting officials were arrested. Her trial in federal court led to a $100 fine, which she refused to pay. Rather than giving Anthony a reason for appealing the case to a higher court, authorities did not collect the fine against her.

Another champion of woman's rights was Victoria Claflin Woodhull. A faith healer and spiritualist from Ohio, she and her sister Tennessee Claflin came to New York, where in 1870 Victoria announced her candidacy for president of the United States. She published a weekly newspaper that endorsed the right of women to practice free love outside of marriage. In 1872 she denounced one of the nation's leading ministers, Henry Ward Beecher, for having had an affair with a member of his congregation. The exposé led to one of the most sensational public trials of the nineteenth century. The proceedings ended in a hung jury, and Victoria Woodhull and her sister fled to England to escape from public outrage. Woodhull's experience and social disgrace demonstrated the perils that faced women who defied the strict social conventions of the post–Civil War era.

Overcoming Barriers to Equality

For women from the middle and upper classes the 1870s brought expanding educational opportunities. The number of women graduating from high school stood at nearly 9,000 in 1870, as compared with 7,000 men. Aware of these trends, state universities and private colleges opened their doors to women students in growing numbers. The University of Minnesota, the University of Kansas, and Indiana University did so in 1869; universities in Missouri, California, and Michigan followed suit a year later. By 1872 nearly one hundred institutions of higher learning admitted women. This process went forward despite the fears of male academics. Edward Clarke, a retired Harvard medical professor, warned in 1873 that when women expended their "limited energy" on

The spread of industrialism brought new products into the home that were advertised as labor-saving devices for women. The reality was that the amount of work women did expanded as a result of the new machinery for domestic use.

higher education, they put their "female apparatus" at risk. Nevertheless, Cornell University began accepting women applicants in 1875.

One of the first female students at Cornell was M. Carey Thomas, who received her B.A. at Cornell in 1877. Five years later she received her Ph.D. at a German university. By the 1890s she had become the president of Bryn Mawr, a woman's college outside Philadelphia. Like other women in male-dominated institutions, she endured rudeness and indifference from her male colleagues. She later recalled that "it is a fiery ordeal to educate a lady by coeducation."

Obtaining an education did not ensure access to male-dominated professions, however. Myra Bradwell tried to become a lawyer in Illinois, but the state bar association rejected her application. She sued in federal court, and in 1873 the U.S. Supreme Court ruled that the law did not grant her the right to be admitted to the bar. One Justice said that "the paramount destiny and mission of woman are to fulfill the noble and benign offices of wife and mother." That decision gave the Illinois legislature the authority to deny women the chance to practice law. In fact, in 1870 there were only five female lawyers in the entire country.

The Supreme Court also rebuffed efforts to secure woman suffrage through the courts. Virginia Minor, president of the Woman Suffrage Association in Missouri, tried to vote in the 1872 election, but the registrar of voters turned her away. She sued on the grounds that the action denied her her rights as a citizen. In the case of *Minor* v. *Happersett* (1875) the Supreme Court ruled unanimously that suffrage was not one of the rights of citizenship because "sex has never been made one of the elements of citizenship in the United States." To achieve the right to vote, women would have to amend the Constitution or obtain the right of suffrage from the states, a process that took another four decades to complete.

The Rise of Voluntary Associations

Blocked off from politics, women created a public space of their own through voluntary associations. Notable in this process were the efforts of black churchwomen, who established missionary societies to work both in the United States and abroad on projects to assemble funds and create institutions such as Spelman College in Atlanta, founded in 1881. Clubs and literary societies sprang up among white women as well.

In New York City women created Sorosis, a club for women only, after the New York Press Club barred women from its membership. In 1873 delegates from local Sorosis clubs formed the Association for the Advancement of Women. The New England Woman's Club, located in Boston, represented "the social force of the women of New England." Its members succeeded in the early 1870s in changing local laws to allow women to serve on the School Committee. Later the club founded the Women's Education Association to expand educational opportunities for their sex. During the two decades that followed, the women's club movement established strong roots in all parts of the nation.

Despite their inability to vote, women made their presence felt in public affairs in an unexpected way in 1873. Protests against the sale and use of alcohol erupted among women in New York, Ohio, and Michigan. Their anger was a response to the growing number of liquor dealers in these states and the spread of saloons and bars. Women marched in the streets and demanded that saloons and liquor dealers close their establishments. They also exhorted drunkards to reform. Middle-class women went down on their knees in front of bars and smashed barrels of liquor in public. "The women are in desperate earnest," said a Missourian who witnessed one of these crusades. The temperance movement was not limited to women, but the upsurge of activity among women gave the crusade a new militance.

The Woman's Christian Temperance Union

As their successes grew, women sought to make their campaign more than a transitory episode. In August 1874 a group of temperance leaders assembled at Lake Chautauqua, New York, where they called for a national meeting that developed into the Woman's Christian Temperance Union. During the next five years temperance leagues and local organizations of the WCTU crusaded against intoxicating beverages. By the end of the 1870s a thousand unions had emerged, with an estimated 26,000 members. In 1879, Frances Willard became president of the Union. Under her leadership, the WCTU went beyond its original goal of temperance and ventured into broader areas of social reform such as woman suffrage and the treatment of children.

MINOR V. HAPPERSETT
21 WALLACE, 162
1875

This case involved the question of whether women were entitled to vote as citizens under the Fourteenth Amendment.

WAITE, C. J. The question is presented in this case, whether, since the adoption of the Fourteenth Amendment, a woman, who is a citizen of the United States and of the State of Missouri, is a voter in that State, notwithstanding the provision of the constitution and laws of the State, which confine the right of suffrage to men alone. . . .

It is contended that the provisions of the Constitution and laws of the State of Missouri, which confine the right of suffrage and registration therefore to men, are in violation of the Constitution of the United States, and therefore void. The argument is, that as a woman, born or naturalized in the United States and subject to the jurisdiction thereof, is a citizen of the United States and of the State in which she resides, she has the right of suffrage as one of the privileges and immunities of her citizenship, which the State cannot by its laws or constitution abridge.

There is no doubt that women may be citizens. They are persons, and by the Fourteenth Amendment "all persons born or naturalized in the United States and subject to the jurisdiction thereof" are expressly declared to be "citizens of the United States and of the State wherein they reside." But, in our opinion, it did not need this amendment to give them that position. Before its adoption the Constitution of the United States did not in terms prescribe who should be citizens of the United States or of the several States, yet there were necessarily such citizens without such provision. . . .

For convenience it has been found necessary to give a name to this membership. The object is to designate by a title the person and the relation he bears to the nation. For this purpose the words "subject," "inhabitant," and "citizen" have been used, and the choice between them is sometimes made to depend upon the form of the government. Citizen is now more commonly employed, however, and as it has been considered better suited to the description of one living under republican government, it was adopted by nearly all of the States upon their separation from Great Britain, and was afterwards adopted in the Articles of Confederation and the Constitution of the United States. When used in this sense it is understood as conveying the idea of membership of a nation, and nothing more. . . .

Women at Work

The 1870s also brought greater economic opportunities for women in sales and clerical work. The typewriter was developed in the early 1870s and young, college-educated women were an abundant source of skilled labor to operate the new machines. E. Remington and Sons, which produced the typewriter, said in 1875 that "no invention has opened for women so broad and easy an avenue to profitable and suitable employment as the 'Type-Writer.'" At the end of the decade women accounted for 40 percent of the total number of stenographers and typists in the country. The developments of the 1870s laid the foundation for the growth in

. . . Sex has never been made one of the elements of citizenship in the United States. In this respect men have never had an advantage over women. The same laws precisely apply to both. The Fourteenth Amendment did not affect the citizenship of women any more than it did of men. In this particular, therefore, the rights of Mrs. Minor do not depend upon the amendment. She has always been a citizen from her birth, and entitled to all the privileges and immunities of citizenship. . . .

If the right of suffrage is one of the necessary privileges of a citizen of the United States, then the constitution and laws of Missouri confining it to men are in violation of the Constitution of the United States, as amended, and consequently void. The direct question is, therefore, presented whether all citizens are necessarily voters.

The Constitution does not define the privileges and immunities of citizens. For that definition we must look elsewhere. In this case we need not determine what they are, but only whether suffrage is necessarily one of them.

It certainly is nowhere made so in express terms. The United States has no voters in the States of its own creation. The elective officers of the United States are all elected directly or indirectly by state voters. . . .

The [Fourteenth] Amendment did not add to the privileges and immunities of a citizen. It simply furnished an additional guaranty for the protection of such as he already had. No new voters were necessarily made by it. Indirectly it may have had that effect, because it may have increased the number of citizens entitled to suffrage under the constitution and laws of the States, but it operates for this purpose, if at all, through the States and the state laws, and not directly upon the citizen.

It is clear therefore, we think, that the Constitution has not added the right of suffrage to the privileges and immunities of citizenship as they existed at the time it was adopted. This makes it proper to inquire whether suffrage was co-extensive with the citizenship of the States at the time of its adoption. If it was then it may with force be argued that suffrage was one of the rights which belonged to citizenship, and in the enjoyment of which every citizen must be protected. But if it was not, the contrary may with propriety be assumed.

When the Federal Constitution was adopted, all the States, with the exception of Rhode Island and Connecticut, had constitutions of their own. . . . Upon an examination of these constitutions we find that in no State were all citizens permitted to vote. . . .

(continued)

numbers of female office workers during the rest of the nineteenth century. For most women, however, these opportunities remain edelusive.

The most typical experience of American women was toil. Black women in the South labored in the fields alongside their husbands who were tenant farmers or sharecroppers. They did "double duty, a man's share in the field, and a woman's part at home." In the growing cities, immigrant and native-born women worked in textile factories or became domestic servants. Women accounted for more than a quarter of the workforce in Philadelphia at the end of the 1870s. Many urban women took in boarders; their routine equalled that of a small hotel.

In this condition of the law in respect to suffrage in the several States it cannot for a moment be doubted that if it had been intended to make all citizens of the United States voters, the framers of the Constitution would not have left it to implication. . . .

It is true that the United States guarantees to every State a republican form of government. . . . The guaranty is of a republican form of government. No particular government is designated as republican, neither is the exact form to be guaranteed, in any manner especially designated. Here, as in other parts of the instrument, we are compelled to resort elsewhere to ascertain what was intended.

The guaranty necessarily implies a duty on the part of the States themselves to provide such a government. All the States had governments when the Constitution was adopted. In all the people participated to some extent, through their representatives elected in the manner specially provided. These governments the Constitution did not change. They were accepted precisely as they were, and it is, therefore, to be presumed that they were such as it was the duty of the States to provide. Thus we have unmistakable evidence of what was republican in form, within the meaning of that term as employed in the Constitution.

As we have seen, all the citizens of the States were not invested with the right of suffrage. In all, save perhaps New Jersey, this right was only bestowed upon men and not upon all of them. Under these circumstances it is certainly now too late to contend that a government is not republican, within the meaning of this guaranty in the Constitution, because women are not made voters. . . .

Certainly if the courts can consider any question settled, this is one. For nearly ninety years the people have acted upon the idea that the Constitution, when it conferred citizenship, did not necessarily confer the right of suffrage. . . .

Being unanimously of the opinion that the Constitution of the United States does not confer the right of suffrage upon any one, and that the constitutions and laws of the several States which commit that important trust to men alone are not necessarily void, we affirm the judgment.

Middle-class women with domestic servants had some assistance, but they still did an incredible amount of work. Sewing machines had become more common, but preparing food, doing laundry, keeping the house warm, and disposing of waste all required hand labor. Mary Mathews, a widowed teacher in the 1870s, "got up early every Monday morning and got my clothes all washed and boiled and in the rinsing water; then commenced my school at nine." Other days of the week passed in the same fashion for her and other women.

To assist women in performing these tasks in the separate sphere of the home and family, manuals about housework became popular in the 1870s, along with private cooking schools and college courses in home economics. Catherine Beecher, who had written about the ways in which women could exercise influence in the domestic aspects of life since the early 1840s, collaborated with her famous sister, Harriet Beecher Stowe, in writing *The American Woman's Home* (1869). In this work, she argued "that family labor and care tend not only to good health, but to the *Highest culture of the mind.*" Women were, she contended, "ministers of the family state." In the new coeducational colleges and universities, home economics programs offered instruction in operating kitchens and dining

As women became more involved in public life after the Civil War, they found outlets for their social concerns beyond the ballot box. One of the most important organizations was the Woman's Christian Temperance Union (WCTU). The artist evokes the imagery of the medieval Crusades to show women attacking the liquor industry and its political connections.

As industrialism took hold, women moved into the workplace. New inventions such as the typewriter gave women a larger place in offices and stores as secretaries and clerks.

rooms in an efficient manner. Cooking schools appeared in large cities with a separate class for "plain cooks" and a "Ladies Class" for affluent women who sought to link "the elegancies of artistic cookery with those economical interests which it is the duty of every woman to study."

The ease with which divorces could be obtained in many states produced a movement to tighten the conditions under which marriages could be dissolved. Laws to limit the sale of birth control devices and restrict abortions reflected the same trend. The New York Society for the Suppression of Vice was formed in 1872 under the leadership of Anthony Comstock. It lobbied successfully for a national law barring obscene materials, including information about birth control and abortion, from the mails. Comstock and

his allies pushed for a similar law in New York and obtained the power to make arrests for violations of the statute. Thus, while women had made some gains after the Civil War, they remained second-class citizens within the masculine political order of the Gilded Age.

POLITICS IN THE GILDED AGE

After the presidential election of 1872, the North's already weakened commitment to the continuation of Reconstruction ebbed more rapidly. The Panic of 1873 distracted attention from the rights of black Americans. The Grant administration was less willing to intervene in southern politics and the Justice Department prosecuted fewer individuals for violations of the Enforcement Acts against the Klan and pardoned some of those who had earlier been convicted of terrorist activity.

Northern support for Reconstruction had fallen away because the experiment in multiracial government appeared to have failed. Liberal Republicans and northern Democrats used racist propaganda against the political aspirations of southern blacks. The editor of *The Nation,* E. L. Godkin, said that black residents of South Carolina had an "average of intelligence but slightly above the level of animals." White northerners found it easier to believe that the South would be better off when whites were once again dominant. Black Americans should be left "to the kind feeling of the white race of the South."

A damaging setback to African Americans' economic aspirations occurred with the failure of the Freedmen's Savings and Trust Company in Washington, D.C. Since its founding in 1865 the bank had managed the deposits of thousands of former slaves. It was supposed to provide lessons in thrift for its depositors. However, its managers sought larger returns by investing in speculative railroad projects. The Panic of 1873 caused huge losses, and the bank failed in the following year. Some depositors received 60 percent of what they had put in, but many lost their entire accounts.

The Stigma of Corruption

Corruption among southern Republican governments became a favorite theme of critics of Reconstruction. There were some genuine instances of corruption: Black and white Republicans accepted bribes from lobbyists or benefited from government contracts. But these actions were far from widespread or typical. Moreover, the white governments that took over after Reconstruction also displayed lax political ethics and committed more serious misdeeds than their predecessors had. Nevertheless, the corruption issue gave the opponents of black political participation a perfect weapon which they exploited fully during the 1870s. Of course, it would not have mattered if Reconstruction governments lacked any moral flaws. Any government that represented a biracial community was intolerable to white southerners.

While participation of African Americans in southern politics increased dramatically during Reconstruction, their role in the region's public life remained limited compared to whites. Sixteen blacks served in Congress during the period, most only briefly, and several were unseated by white opponents. Many more held offices in the state legislatures, but even their numbers were comparatively modest. In 1868, for example, the Georgia legislature had 216 members, of whom only thirty-two were black. In only one state,

South Carolina, did blacks ever hold a majority in the legislature, and they did so in only one house. One black man, P.B.S. Pinchback, served as governor in Louisiana for a little more than a month. Six African Americans held the office of lieutenant governor in the states of Louisiana, Mississippi, and South Carolina.

Two blacks served in the U.S. Senate. Hiram Revels of Mississippi became the first African American to enter the Senate. His term began in 1870 but lasted only one year. From 1875 to 1881 Blanche K. Bruce represented Mississippi for a full term. Thus, whites retained statewide and national offices throughout the Reconstruction era. By the 1870s blacks had begun to make their presence felt in southern legislatures, but the decline of Reconstruction made that trend a short-lived one.

The Resurgence of the Democrats

The changing political situation across the nation further diminished support for Reconstruction outside the South. Hard economic times arising from the Panic of 1873 worked against the Republicans. Discontented farmers wanted the government to inflate the currency and raise prices on their crops. Factory workers wanted to see more jobs become available. The fate of African Americans in the South became a secondary concern. Accordingly, angry voters turned to the Democrats in the 1874 congressional races. The party used the issue of Republican corruption to regain control of the House of Representatives for the first time in sixteen years, adding seventy-seven seats to their total. Democrats elected 169 members, compared to 109 for their opposition. The Democrats also picked up ten Senate seats. It was a "Tidal Wave" said one happy Democrat.

In the South, the resurgent Democrats "redeemed," as they called it, several states from Republican dominance. They began with Texas in 1873, then took back Arkansas and elected most of the region's members in the U.S. House of Representatives. Louisiana experienced the emergence of the White League, which was determined that "the niggers shall not rule over us." In September open fighting erupted in New Orleans between armed Republicans and more than 3,000 White League partisans. President Grant sent in federal troops to restore calm. In Alabama the Democrats also relied on violence and murder to oust the Republicans. Some blacks who attempted to vote in the Barbour County election were shot; seven were killed and

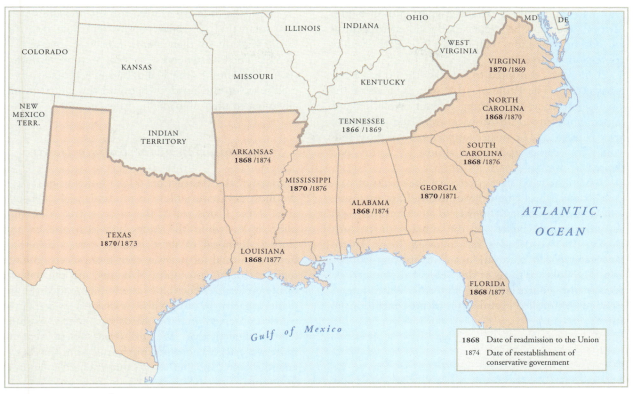

MAP 16.4 | RECONSTRUCTION IN THE SOUTH

nearly seventy wounded. Given the wide support for the Democratic party among southern whites, honest elections might have produced similar victories for their party at the polls; but intimidation and violence were key elements in the victories that the Democrats secured in the South in 1874.

The Democrats intended to use their control of the House of Representatives afterward to roll back Reconstruction and also prevent any further expansion of black rights. During the lame-duck congressional session of 1874–1875 Republicans enacted a path-breaking civil rights law that gave black citizens the right to sue in federal courts when they confronted discrimination in public accommodations. The law involved an additional expansion of national power; it remained to be seen how the federal courts North and South would rule when black plaintiffs sued to enforce their rights under the new civil rights statute.

Early in 1875 the Grant administration used troops to prevent occupation of the Louisiana state capitol and illegal seizure of the state government by the Democrats in the midst of an election dispute. The action drew widespread protests from many northern Democrats and a growing number of Republicans who argued in favor of allowing the white South to handle its own affairs. Meanwhile, the Democrats used more violence to overturn Republican rule in Mississippi. The state governor, Adelbert Ames, stated that he was "fighting for the Negro, and to the whole country a white man is better than a 'Nigger.'" Without a national consensus behind civil rights and Reconstruction, the fate of black Americans lay in the hands of white southerners who were determined to keep African Americans in economic, political, and cultural subjection.

Why Reconstruction Failed

Reconstruction failed to change American race relations because it challenged long-standing racist arrangements in both the North and South. The Civil

War had called these arrangements into question. African Americans had acted to expand their political role and become more than passive recipients of white oppression or largesse.

Then events conspired to frustrate the hopes of Reconstruction. The Panic of 1873, the scandals of the Grant presidency, and waning interest in black rights caused white Americans to back away from expansion of racial justice. The missed opportunity of the 1870s would not come again until almost a century had elapsed.

To help the freed slaves overcome the effects of slavery and racial bias would have involved an expansion of national governmental power to an extent that went beyond political beliefs of the nineteenth century. During the two decades that followed, black Americans experienced segregation and deepening oppression. The political gains of the Reconstruction era, especially the Fourteenth and Fifteenth Amendments remained unfulfilled promises for future generations to pursue.

THE END OF NATIVE AMERICAN RESISTANCE

While the United States was in the process of abridging its Civil War commitments to African Americans, the long struggle of Native Americans to resist white encroachment also ended. Pressures for white expansion onto Indian lands intensified during the Reconstruction period. Indians' efforts to push back the wave of white encroachment failed, and after 1876 Native Americans lacked the power to determine their own destiny.

During the 1870s Easterners and new immigrants surged westward to the prairies. The census reported over 2,660,000 farms in 1870 and just over 4 million ten years later. The newcomers competed with the Indians for space and resources. The amount of land devoted to wheat cultivation, for example, rose from nearly 21 million acres at the beginning of the decade to 62,545,000 in 1880. An African-American man who moved to Kansas at this time explained what drove him westward: "That's what white men go to new countries for, isn't it? You do not tell them to stay back because they are poor."

The cattle industry exerted further pressure on the Indians in the late 1860s. Texans returning from the Civil War drove their herds north to markets in Kansas. These cattle and others in western territories such as Wyoming, the Dakotas, and Colorado occupied space on the prairies where Indians had traditionally pursued their nomadic hunting culture.

Annihilation of the Buffalo Herds

The systematic destruction of the buffalo herds dealt the most devastating blow to the Indians. In the societies of the Plains tribes, the meat of the bison supplied food, while the hides provided shelter and clothes. Removal of these resources was calamitous, but the cultural impact was even more severe. Buffalo represented the continuity of nature and the renewal of life cycles. Destruction of the buffalo ended the Indians' capacity to resist white incursions. As one Crow warrior observed after the herds had gone, "Nothing happened after that. We just lived. There were no more war parties, no capturing horses from the Piegan and the Sioux, no buffalo to hunt. There is nothing more to tell."

The decline of the buffalo herds began during the 1860s, when drought, disease, and erosion shrank the animals' habitat. Then an expanding eastern market for buffalo robes and such products as pemmican (dried buffalo meat, berries, and fat) spurred intensive hunting of buffalo. As railroads penetrated the region, hunters could transport their products to customers with relative ease. The result was virtual extermination of the buffalo. More than *5 million* buffalo were slaughtered during the early 1870s. Along the Arkansas River, a British traveler reported, "there was a continual line of putrescent carcasses, so that the air was rendered pestilential and offensive to the last degree." Within a decade the once huge buffalo herds had vanished. By the end of the nineteenth century only a few buffalo remained alive.

A Last Stand for Custer and the Indians

During the mid-1870s, as the buffalo vanished and white incursions into Indian territories increased, Native American tribes mounted a last, futile effort to stem the tide that was overwhelming their way of life. The renewed strife on the Plains occurred in spite of

The opening of the West to white settlement in the 1870s produced the extermination of the huge buffalo herds that had roamed the prairies and sustained the Native American tribes. This picture shows some forty thousand hides piled up in a "hide yard" in Dodge City, Kansas.

President Grant's peace policy. The president's original appointees either resigned or left because of political attacks and the churches' influence over the operation of Indian policy receded as corruption and politics again shaped the treatment of Native Americans. Fewer Indians trusted the promises that they would receive fair treatment on the reservations, and the tribes that retained their nomadic way of life confronted ever-increasing numbers of settlers and a hostile military.

Fighting erupted on the southern plains in 1874 when Comanches and Kiowas attacked wagon trains. The Indians were arrested when they returned to their reservations, but raiding continued. A confrontation ensued between U.S. soldiers and Cheyennes, Kiowas, and Comanches that became known as the Red River War. The army did not win on the battlefield. Instead, the Indians' resistance collapsed because of lack of food and supplies.

In the North, the discovery of gold in the Black Hills of Dakota produced a wave of treasure seekers and increased pressure on the Sioux to relinquish the area for white development. The Indians refused, and the U.S. government sent soldiers to protect the miners. The Indian leaders, Crazy Horse and Sitting Bull, rallied their followers to stop the army. Near what the Indians called the Greasy Grass (known to whites as the Little Big Horn), Colonel George Armstrong

Custer led a force of 600 men. With a third of his detachment, he attacked more than 2,000 Sioux warriors. The result was the annihilation of Custer and his force on June 25, 1876. The Indian victory shocked the country, but it was only a momentary success. The army pursued the Indians during the months that followed, and in the process the ability of the Sioux to resist white soldiers declined. By the end of the Grant administration, the only Indians who were able to fight actively against the army were the Apaches in the Southwest. The bad treatment that the Apaches received from the government produced sporadic clashes during the 1880s and the army triumphed by the end of the decade.

One more tragic encounter, the Battle of Wounded Knee in 1890, lay ahead for the Plains Indians. For the most part the Grant presidency brought an end to the centuries of white–Indian warfare that had marked the history of the West in the United States.

THE ELECTION OF 1876

Several themes of late-nineteenth-century American life came together as the 1876 presidential election approached. The centennial of the Declaration of

Independence offered citizens an opportunity to reflect on the nation's progress and the social issues that remained unresolved. The race question confronted leaders and citizens even as the passions and commitments of Reconstruction faded. The contest for the White House seemed unusually important as it would shape the direction of the country during the rest of the century. As a result, the year achieved more than usual significance.

The Continuing Shadow of Scandal

Toward the end of Grant's second term, political corruption continued to cast a shadow over the White House. Attention focused on the "Whiskey Ring" in the Treasury Department. The officials involved took kickbacks from liquor interests in return for not collecting federal excise taxes on whiskey. Grant had appointed a new secretary of the Treasury, Benjamin H. Bristow, a Kentucky Republican who began a campaign to expose the ring. At first Grant said to Bristow: "Let no guilty man escape if it can be avoided." Later he changed his mind. When Bristow's probe discovered that the president's own secretary, Orville E. Babcock, had ties to a leader of the conspiracy, Grant allowed Babcock to avoid prosecution and sought Bristow's resignation. The episode further damaged Grant's credibility.

The final incident involved the secretary of War, W.W. Belknap. For some time Belknap's wife had been receiving regular cash gifts from a man who sold supplies to the army. When these financial ties were revealed, Belknap faced impeachment by a congressional committee. He resigned abruptly, and Grant accepted his hasty departure. The trail of scandal had now touched the White House, or so the president's critics argued. In the end, the most that could be laid at Grant's door was a too-trusting nature and bad judgment in some of his appointments. Grant presided over what became known as one of the most corrupt administrations in the nation's history, but his personal honesty remained unquestioned and his popularity high.

Marking the Centennial

As the nation's one hundredth birthday neared, attention focused on the Centennial International Exhibi-

tion to be held in Philadelphia in May of 1876. It was the second such fair to be held in the United States; New York had held an exposition in 1851. On 285 acres of fairgrounds stood several hundred buildings and pavilions crammed with exhibits, specimens, and artifacts from thirty-seven nations. The fair opened on May 10 with 200,000 spectators, the entire Congress in attendance, and a welcoming address by President Grant. Handel's "Hallelujah Chorus" and a salute from one hundred guns ended the ceremonies. The crowd poured into the buildings to see what had been assembled as evidence of the advance of civilization in the United States.

For spectators the huge Corliss steam engine was a stellar attraction. Standing forty feet tall, it weighed

At the Centennial Exposition in Philadelphia in 1876, one of the great attractions was the Corliss steam engine. To those who flocked into the grounds, the massive machine became a symbol of the promise and the dangers of industrial growth.

700 tons. The engine was shut down at noon each day for one hour; throngs assembled to see it start up again. Seventy-five miles of shafts and belts made the gigantic machine move. This massive example of technology symbolized the nation's faith in its industrial future.

Equally fascinating was the "harmonic telegraph" of Alexander Graham Bell, as the telephone was then called. To help publicize Bell's invention, Emperor Dom Pedro II of Brazil listened to the receiver and heard Bell deliver a soliloquy from "Hamlet" from across the hall. Dom Pedro exclaimed: "I hear, I hear! To be or not to be."

For all its technological marvels, the exhibition did not do justice to the complexity of American life in the 1870s. African Americans had almost no recognition at the fair. Native American cultures were depicted as "curiosities" consisting of totem poles, tepees, and trinkets. The Woman's Pavilion stressed homemaking. The exhibit evoked a protest from Elizabeth Cady Stanton and Susan B. Anthony. On July 4, 1876, they read a "Women's Declaration of Independence" that contrasted their aspirations with the traditional attitudes toward women expressed at the fair.

Nearly 10 million Americans came to the fair during its run, which ended on November 10. There they learned to eat bananas, and hot popcorn became a fad among city dwellers who soon made it a staple at other entertainment and sporting events. Although the fair lost money, its organizers pronounced it a great success. "We had a nation to show," said one U.S. senator. The Centennial exhibition contributed to a sense of national pride and confidence as the nation completed its first one hundred years. The presidential election that marked the year proved to be a more troubling symbol of the problems that the country faced.

The Race for the White House

A key test of the nation's institutions occurred during the election of 1876. The closest result in history produced a dispute that threatened to renew hostilities between North and South. As the election year began, the Democrats were optimistic about their ability to regain power for the first time since 1860. The repudiation of the Republicans in the 1874 elections seemed to foreshadow a Democratic triumph in the race for the presidency. The South would return to its usual Democratic allegiance; the Democrats could also capitalize on unhappiness with the difficult economic times in the North and Midwest.

To run as the Democratic candidate, the party selected the governor of New York, Samuel J. Tilden. Tilden was known as "Whispering Sammy" for his soft-spoken demeanor and as the "Great Foreclocer" for his business dealings. He had been an opponent of the Tweed Ring and was regarded as a political reformer. A corporate lawyer, he believed in the gold standard and governmental economy. His platform spoke of a "revival of Jeffersonian democracy" and called for "high standards of official morality." Since Tilden was not in good health, the fact that presidential candidates did not campaign during that era worked to his advantage.

Among the Republicans there was some talk of a third term for President Grant, who remained very popular. The scandals of his presidency, however, made him a political burden rather than an asset. The front-runner for the nomination was the charismatic and exciting James G. Blaine of Maine, a former speaker of the House of Representatives. With the nomination seemingly in his grasp, Blaine encountered questions about his dealings with an Arkansas railroad while he was in the House. He answered the charges vigorously, but the episode raised problems about his ethics at a time when the party wanted to run a "clean" candidate against Tilden.

At the national convention Blaine took an early lead, but as the balloting continued, his candidacy lost momentum. Instead, the Republicans chose Governor Rutherford B. Hayes of Ohio as the nominee. Hayes had a good military record in the Civil War; there were no questions about his honesty; and he been able to carry the key state of Ohio on three occasions. He had all the assets of a man such as Blaine without any of the liabilities. The Republicans chose William A. Wheeler of New York as their candidate for vice president.

In the campaign the Democrats stressed Republican corruption and Tilden's honesty. A campaign song contained this message:

The night of gloom is gliding out,
Forth breaks the rosy day.
And Tilden is the sun of hope,
That lights the nation's way.

In response, the Republicans used the Reconstruction issue, as they had in the 1868 and 1872 contests.

Americans brought the military experience of the Civil War to their political campaigning in the 1870s. The massive parade of the "Boys in Blue" in 1876 indicates how strong were the memories of the recent war. Many feared that the disputed election in which Hayes finally defeated Tilden might spark a renewal of the fighting.

The rhetoric invoking the Civil War became known as "waving the bloody shirt," in memory of a Republican orator who had held up a bloodstained Union tunic and urged voters to remember the sacrifices of the Men in Blue. As one Republican put it, "Soldiers, every scar you have on your heroic bodies was given to you by a Democrat." Hayes saw the wisdom of this strategy. "It leads people away from hard times, which is our deadliest foe."

When the election results came in, it seemed at first that Tilden and the Democrats had won. With most of the South in his column, the Democratic candidate had also carried New York, Connecticut, and New Jersey. Preliminary counts indicated that Tilden had won 184 electoral votes, one short of the 185 needed for victory. Hayes, on the other hand, had 165 electoral votes, and seemed to have been defeated. Yet three southern states—Louisiana, Florida, and South Carolina—and a disputed elector in Oregon were still in doubt because both Democrats and Republicans claimed victory. They might give Hayes the White House. On election night that seemed an unlikely scenario, but the Republicans acted quickly to build a case for Hayes.

Republican operatives moved to contest the outcome in the three undecided states. Telegrams to party members called for evidence of intimidation of African-American voters. Honest returns from these states, the Republicans argued, would show that Hayes had carried each one; they disputed the results provided by Democratic election officials. The Republicans believed that they held a trump card. In the three states that they were contesting, the Republicans could rely on federal troops to safeguard state governments that were loyal to their cause. Otherwise, Democrats could simply occupy the state capitals and count the election returns their way. Both parties began maneuvering to control how the electoral votes of these three states were recorded.

The Constitution did not specify how a contested presidential election was to be decided. With each of the states in question sending in two sets of election returns, the House of Representatives had the responsibility for electing a president if no one won a majority in the electoral college. At the same time, the Senate had the constitutional duty to tabulate the electoral vote. With Republicans in control of the Senate and Democrats in control of the House, neither

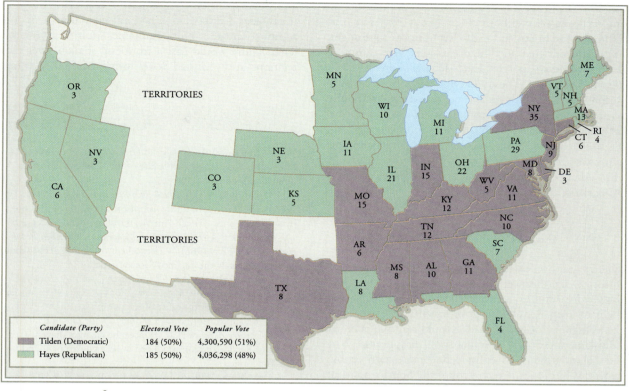

Candidate (Party)	Electoral Vote	Popular Vote
Tilden (Democratic)	184 (50%)	4,300,590 (51%)
Hayes (Republican)	185 (50%)	4,036,298 (48%)

MAP 16.5 | THE ELECTION OF 1876

side could proceed without the support of the other. A stalemate ensued.

To resolve the crisis, Congress created an electoral commission of fifteen members, ten from the House and Senate and five from the Supreme Court. As originally conceived, the panel was to have seven Republicans, seven Democrats, and a politically independent Supreme Court justice named David Davis. Then Davis was elected to the U.S. Senate by the Illinois legislature with Democratic votes in a move to defeat a Republican incumbent. Their ploy won a Senate seat, but wounded Tilden's chances. Davis resigned from the commission and a Republican justice took his place. In a series of 8–7 votes along straight party lines, the electoral commission accepted the Republican returns from Louisiana, Florida, and South Carolina, allocated the single disputed Oregon electoral vote to Hayes as well, and declared that Hayes had received 185 electoral votes and Tilden 184.

The question of who had really been elected president depended on the political perspective from which the contest was viewed. Tilden had a margin of 250,000 popular votes over Hayes and had carried sixteen states. Hayes had won eighteen states in addition to the three contested southern states. In Louisiana, Florida, and South Carolina, Tilden had received a majority of the white vote, but black Republican voters had been intimidated and terrorized to such an extent that an honest count was in doubt. Resolving the issue of which man deserved to be president became a matter for political compromise between the two major parties.

Despite the electoral commission's decision, the Democratic House still had to declare Hayes the winner. With the March 4, 1877, inauguration date approaching, the Democrats postponed tallying the electoral vote in an effort either to make Tilden president after March 4 or to extract concessions from the

Republicans. To prevent a crisis, negotiations began among leaders from both sides to put Hayes in the White House in return for the Republicans' agreement to end Reconstruction. The discussions were complex; they involved a variety of issues such as railroad subsidies for the South. The underlying issue, however, was Reconstruction. If Hayes became president, the South wanted assurances that Republican rule would not be maintained through federal military intervention. After much maneuvering, an unwritten understanding along these lines led Congress to decide on March 2, 1877, that Rutherford B. Hayes had been elected the president of the United States.

CONCLUSION

The events that led to Hayes's inauguration had great historical significance. Although Hayes did not withdraw federal troops from the South, neither did he use them to keep Republican governments in power, and the remnants of an official Republican presence in Louisiana and South Carolina soon disappeared. Nor did Hayes attempt to enforce Reconstruction in the courts. Whites regained control of the South's political institutions, while black southerners remained second-class citizens with limited political and economic rights. Reconstruction had ended in name as it had been ending in fact during Grant's second term.

Several powerful historical forces produced that sad result. Pervasive racism in both the North and the South labeled African Americans as unfit for self-government and accepted a return to white rule in the South. Pursuing Reconstruction into the 1880s would have involved giving to the national government more power over the lives of individual Americans than would have been tolerated in that era. Weary of Reconstruction and its moral claims, the generation of white Americans who had fought the Civil War turned their attention to other national problems. In so doing, they condemned black citizens to continued segregation and oppression.

The Civil War and Reconstruction period did have a positive legacy despite the tragic abandonment of African Americans. Slavery was abolished and the Union preserved. Black Americans had demonstrated that they could fight and die for their country, help make its laws, and function as full citizens when given an honest chance to do so. The Fourteenth and Fifteenth Amendments at least contained the promise of a further expansion of the rights of black Americans in the future. But the nation had missed a historic opportunity to create a more equitable, multiracial society. That failure would cast a troubling shadow over race relations in the United States for generations to come.

RECOMMENDED READINGS

Bordin, Ruth. *Frances Willard: A Biography* (1986) is a biography of the important leader of the Women's Christian Temperance Union.

Du Bois, W.E.B. *Black Reconstruction in America* (1935), the first important revisionist study of Reconstruction by a distinguished African-American historian and leader.

Foner, Eric. *Reconstruction: America's Unfinished Revolution, 1863–1877* (1988), is an excellent treatment of the whole period, especially the decline of Reconstruction.

Hoogenboom, Ari. *Outlawing the Spoils: A History of the Civil Service Reform Movement, 1865–1883* (1961) considers an important reform cause of the period.

Keller, Morton. *Affairs of State: Public Life in Late Nineteenth-Century America* (1977) traces the changes that the Civil War and Reconstruction produced in how government and politics functioned.

McFeely, William S. *Grant: A Biography* (1981), a prize-winning biography that examines Grant's life from the perspective of the 1970s.

Sproat, John G. *"The Best Men": Liberal Reformers in the Gilded Age* (1968) is a critical examination of the reformers who disliked the political system of the 1870s.

Summers, Mark Wahlgren. *The Era of Good Stealings* (1993) uses the corruption issue of the 1870s to write the closest thing to a political history of the decade.

Woodward, C. Vann. *Reunion and Reaction: The Compromise of 1877 and the End of Reconstruction* (1951) offers a provocative treatment of the disputed election of 1876.

Politics and Public Policy

Hoogenboom, Ari. *Rutherford B. Hayes: Warrior & President* (1995).

Polakoff, Keith I. *The Politics of Inertia: The Election of 1876 and the End of Reconstruction* (1973).

Summers, Mark. *The Press Gang: Newspapers and Politics, 1865–1878* (1994).

Thompson, Margaret Susan. *The "Spider Web": Congress and Lobbying in the Age of Grant* (1984).

Unger, Irwin. *The Greenback Era: A Social and Political History of American Finance, 1865–1879* (1964).

Women

Beeton, Betty. *Women Vote in the West: The Woman Suffrage Movement, 1869–1896* (1986).

Davis, Margery W. *Women's Place Is at the Typewriter: Office Work and Office Workers, 1870–1930* (1982).

Jeffrey, Julie Roy. *Frontier Women: The Trans-Mississippi West* (1979).

Jones, Jacqueline. *Soldiers of Light and Love: Northern Teachers and Georgia Blacks, 1865–1873* (1980).

Kugler, Israel. *From Ladies to Women: The Organized Struggle for Women's Rights in the Reconstruction Era* (1987).

The West

Ambrose, Stephen. *Crazy Horse and Custer: The Parallel Lives of Two American Warriors* (1976).

Gould, Lewis L. *Wyoming: From Territory to Statehood* (1989).

Lamar, Howard R. *Dakota Territory, 1861–1889: A Study of Frontier Politics* (1956).

Utley, Robert. *The Indian Frontier of the American West, 1846–1890* (1984).

Wooster, Robert. *The Military and United States Indian Policy, 1865–1890* (1988).

The South

Abbott, Richard H. *The Republican Party and the South, 1855–1877: The First Southern Strategy* (1986).

DeSantis, Vincent. *Republicans Face the Southern Question* (1959).

Gillette, William. *Retreat from Reconstruction, 1869–1879* (1979).

Perman, Michael. *The Road to Redemption: Southern Politics, 1869–1879* (1984).

Seip, Terry. *The South Returns to Congress: Men, Economic Measures, and Intersectional Relationships, 1869–1879* (1983).

Appendix

The Declaration of Independence

THE UNANIMOUS DECLARATION OF
THE THIRTEEN UNITED STATES OF AMERICA

When in the Course of human events it becomes necessary for one people to dissolve the political bands which have connected them with another, and to assume among the Powers of the earth, the separate and equal station to which the Laws of Nature and of Nature's God entitle them, a decent respect to the opinions of mankind requires that they should declare the causes which impel them to the separation.

We hold these truths to be self-evident, that all men are created equal, that they are endowed by their Creator with certain unalienable Rights, that among these are Life, Liberty and the pursuit of Happiness. That to secure these rights, Governments are instituted among Men, deriving their just Powers from the consent of the governed. That whenever any Form of Government becomes destructive of these ends, it is the Right of the People to alter or to abolish it, and to institute new Government, laying its foundation on such principles and organizing its Powers in such form, as to them shall seem most likely to effect their Safety and Happiness. Prudence, indeed, will dictate that Governments long established should not be changed for light and transient causes; and accordingly all experience hath shewn, that mankind are more disposed to suffer, while evils are sufferable, than to right themselves by abolishing the forms to which they are accustomed. But when a long train of abuses and usurpations, pursuing invariably the same Object evinces a design to reduce them under absolute Despotism, it is their right, it is their duty, to throw off such Government, and to provide new Guards for their future security. Such has been the patient sufferance of these Colonies; and such is now the necessity which constrains them to alter their former Systems of Government. The history of the present King of Great Britain is a history of repeated injuries and usurpations, all having in direct object the establishment of an ab-

solute Tyranny over these States. To prove this, let Facts be submitted to a candid world.

He has refused his Assent to Laws, the most wholesome and necessary for the public good.

He has forbidden his Governors to pass Laws of immediate and pressing importance, unless suspended in their operation till his Assent should be obtained; and when so suspended, he has utterly neglected to attend to them.

He has refused to pass other Laws for the accommodation of large districts of people, unless those people would relinquish the right of Representation in the Legislature, a right inestimable to them and formidable to tyrants only.

He has called together legislative bodies at places unusual, uncomfortable, and distant from the depository of their Public Records, for the sole Purpose of fatiguing them into compliance with his measures.

He has dissolved Representative Houses repeatedly, for opposing with manly firmness his invasions on the rights of the People.

He has refused for a long time, after such dissolutions, to cause others to be elected; whereby the Legislative Powers, incapable of Annihilation, have returned to the People at large for their exercise; the State remaining in the mean time exposed to all the dangers of invasion from without, and convulsions within.

He has endeavoured to prevent the Population of these States; for that purpose obstructing the Laws for Naturalization of Foreigners; refusing to pass others to encourage their migrations hither, and raising the conditions of new Appropriations of Lands.

He has obstructed the Administration of Justice, by refusing his Assent to Laws for establishing Judiciary Powers.

He has made Judges dependent on his Will alone, for the tenure of their offices, and the amount and payment of their salaries.

He has erected a multitude of New Offices, and sent hither swarms of Officers to harass our People, and eat out their substance.

Text is reprinted from the facsimile of the engrossed copy in the National Archives. The original spelling, capitalization, and punctuation have been retained. Paragraphing has been added.

He has kept among us, in times of peace, Standing Armies without the Consent of our legislatures.

He has affected to render the Military independent of and superior to the Civil Power.

He has combined with others to subject us to a jurisdiction foreign to our constitution, and unacknowledged by our laws; giving his Assent to their Acts of pretended Legislation:

For Quartering large bodies of armed troops among us:

For protecting them, by a mock Trial, from Punishment for any Murders which they should commit on the Inhabitants of these States:

For cutting off our Trade with all parts of the world:

For imposing Taxes on us without our Consent:

For depriving us in many cases, of the benefits of Trial by Jury:

For transporting us beyond Seas to be tried for pretended offences:

For abolishing the free System of English Laws in a neighbouring Province, establishing therein an Arbitrary government, and enlarging its Boundaries so as to render it at once an example and fit instrument for introducing the same absolute rule into these Colonies:

For taking away our Charters, abolishing our most valuable Laws, and altering fundamentally the Forms of our Governments:

For suspending our own Legislatures, and declaring themselves invested with Power to legislate for us in all cases whatsoever.

He has abdicated Government here, by declaring us out of his Protection, and waging War against us.

He has plundered our seas, ravaged our Coasts, burnt our towns, and destroyed the lives of our people.

He is at this time transporting large Armies of foreign Mercenaries to compleat the works of death, desolation and tyranny, already begun with circumstances of Cruelty and perfidy scarcely paralleled in the most barbarous ages, and totally unworthy the Head of a civilized nation.

He has constrained our fellow Citizens taken Captive on the high Seas to bear Arms against their Country, to become the executioners of their friends and Brethren, or to fall themselves by their Hands.

He has excited domestic insurrections amongst us, and has endeavoured to bring on the inhabitants of our frontiers, the merciless Indian Savages, whose known rule of warfare, is an undistinguished destruction of all ages, sexes and conditions.

In every stage of these Oppressions We have Petitioned for Redress in the most humble terms: Our repeated Petitions have been answered only by repeated injury. A Prince, whose character is thus marked by every act which may define a Tyrant, is unfit to be the ruler of a free People.

Nor have We been wanting in attentions to our British brethren. We have warned them from time to time of attempts by their legislature to extend an unwarrantable jurisdiction over us. We have reminded them of the circumstances of our emigration and settlement here. We have appealed to their native justice and magnanimity, and we have conjured them by the ties of our common kindred to disavow thee usurpations, which, would inevitably interrupt our connections and correspondence. They too have been deaf to the voice of justice and of consanguinity. We must, therefore, acquiesce in the necessity, which denounces our Separation, and hold them, as we hold the rest of mankind, Enemies in War, in Peace Friends.

WE, THEREFORE, the Representatives of the UNITED STATES OF AMERICA, in General Congress, Assembled, appealing to the Supreme Judge of the world for the rectitude of our intentions, do, in the Name, and by Authority of the good People of these Colonies, solemnly publish and declare, That these United Colonies are, and of Right ought to be FREE AND INDEPENDENT STATES; that they are Absolved from all Allegiance to the British Crown, and that all political connection between them and the State of Great Britain, is and ought to be totally dissolved; and that, as Free and Independent States, they have full Power to levy War, conclude Peace, contract Alliances, establish Commerce, and to do all other Acts and Things which Independent States may of right do. And for the support of this Declaration, with a firm reliance on the protection of divine Providence, we mutually pledge to each other our Lives, our Fortunes and our sacred Honor.

The Constitution of the United States of America

We the People of the United States, in Order to form a more perfect Union, establish Justice, insure domestic Tranquility, provide for the common defence, promote the general Welfare, and secure the Blessings of Liberty to ourselves and our Posterity, do ordain and establish this Constitution for the United States of America.

ARTICLE I.

SECTION 1. All legislative Powers herein granted shall be vested in a Congress of the United States, which shall consist of a Senate and House of Representatives.

SECTION 2. The House of Representatives shall be composed of Members chosen every second Year by the People of the several States, and the Electors in each State shall have the Qualifications requisite for Electors of the most numerous Branch of the State Legislature.

No Person shall be a Representative who shall not have attained to the Age of twenty five Years, and been seven Years a Citizen of the United States, and who shall not, when elected, be an Inhabitant of that State in which he shall be chosen.

Representatives and direct Taxes[1] shall be apportioned among the several States which may be included within this Union, according to their respective Numbers, which shall be determined by adding to the whole Number of free Persons, including those bound to Service for a Term of Years, and excluding Indians not taxed, three fifths of all other Persons.[2] The actual Enumeration shall be made within three Years after the first Meeting of the Congress of the United States, and within every subsequent Term of ten Years, in such Manner as they shall by Law direct. The Number of Representatives shall not exceed one for every thirty Thousand, but each State shall have at Least one Representative; and until such enumeration shall be made, the State of New Hampshire shall be entitled to chuse three; Massachusetts eight; Rhode Island and Providence Plantations one; Connecticut five; New York six; New Jersey four; Pennsylvania eight; Delaware one; Maryland six; Virginia ten; North Carolina five; South Carolina five; and Georgia three.

When vacancies happen in the Representation from any State, the Executive Authority thereof shall issue Writs of Election to fill such Vacancies.

The House of Representatives shall chuse their Speaker and other Officers; and shall have the sole Power of Impeachment.

SECTION 3. The Senate of the United States shall be composed of two Senators from each State, chosen by the Legislature thereof, for six Years; and each Senator shall have one Vote.[3]

Immediately after they shall be assembled in Consequence of the first Election, they shall be divided as equally as may be into three Classes. The Seats of the Senators of the first Class shall be vacated at the Expiration of the second Year, of the second Class at the Expiration of the fourth Year, and of the third Class at the Expiration of the sixth Year, so that one third may be chosen every second Year; and if Vacancies happen by Resignation, or otherwise, during the Recess of the Legislature of any State, the Executive thereof may make temporary Appointments until the next Meeting of the Legislature, which shall then fill such Vacancies.[4]

No Person shall be a Senator who shall not have attained to the Age of thirty Years, and been nine Years a Citizen of the United States, and who shall not, when elected, be an Inhabitant of that State for which he shall be chosen.

The Vice President of the United States shall be President of the Senate, but shall have no Vote, unless they be equally divided.

The Senate shall chuse their other Officers, and also a President pro tempore, in the Absence of the Vice President, or when he shall exercise the Office of President of the United States.

Text is from the engrossed copy in the National Archives. Original spelling, capitalization, and punctuation have been retained.

[1]Modified by the Sixteenth Amendment.

[2]Replaced by the Fourteenth Amendment.

[3]Superseded by the Seventeenth Amendment.

[4]Modified by the Seventeenth Amendment.

The Senate shall have the sole Power to try all Impeachments. When sitting for that Purpose, they shall be on Oath or Affirmation. When the President of the United States is tried, the Chief Justice shall preside: And no Person shall be convicted without the Concurrence of two thirds of the Members present.

Judgment in Cases of Impeachment shall not extend further than to removal from Office, and disqualification to hold and enjoy any Office of honor, Trust or Profit under the United States: but the Party convicted shall nevertheless be liable and subject to Indictment, Trial, Judgment and Punishment, according to Law.

SECTION 4. The Times, Places and Manner of holding Elections for Senators and Representatives, shall be prescribed in each State by the Legislature thereof, but the Congress may at any time by Law make or alter such Regulation, except as to the Places of chusing Senators.

The Congress shall assemble at least once in every Year, and such Meeting shall be on the first Monday in December, unless they shall by Law appoint a different Day.[5]

SECTION 5. Each House shall be the Judge of the Elections, Returns and Qualifications of its own Members, and a Majority of each shall constitute a Quorum to do Business; but a smaller Number may adjourn from day to day, and may be authorized to compel the Attendance of absent Members, in such Manner, and under such Penalties as each House may provide.

Each House may determine the Rules of its Proceedings, punish its Members for disorderly Behaviour, and, with the Concurrence of two thirds, expel a Member.

Each House shall keep a Journal of its Proceedings, and from time to time publish the same, excepting such Parts as may in their Judgment require Secrecy; and the Yeas and Nays of the Members of either House on any question shall, at the Desire of one fifth of those Present, be entered on the Journal.

Neither House, during the Session of Congress, shall, without the Consent of the other, adjourn for more than three days, nor to any other Place than that in which the two Houses shall be sitting.

SECTION 6. The Senators and Representatives shall receive a Compensation for their Services, to be ascertained by Law, and paid out of the Treasury of the United States. They shall in all Cases, except Treason, Felony and Breach of the Peace, be privileged from Arrest during their Attendance at the Session of their respective Houses, and in going to and returning from the same; and for any Speech or Debate in either House, they shall not be questioned in any other Place.

No Senator or Representative shall, during the Time for which he was elected, be appointed to any civil Office under the Authority of the United States, which shall have been created, or the Emoluments whereof shall have been encreased during such time; and no Person holding any Office under the United States, shall be a Member of either House during his Continuance in Office.

SECTION 7. All Bills for raising Revenue shall originate in the House of Representatives; but the Senate may propose or concur with Amendments as on other Bills.

Every Bill which shall have passed the House of Representatives and the Senate shall, before it become a Law, be presented to the President of the United States; If he approve he shall sign it, but if not he shall return it, with his Objections to that House in which it shall have originated, who shall enter the Objections at large on their Journal, and proceed to reconsider it. If after such Reconsideration two thirds of that House shall agree to pass the Bill, it shall be sent, together with the Objections, to the other House, by which it shall likewise be reconsidered, and if approved by two thirds of that House, it shall become a Law. But in all such Cases the Votes of both Houses shall be determined by yeas and Nays, and the Names of the Persons voting for and against the Bill shall be entered on the Journal of each House respectively. If any Bill shall not be returned by the President within ten Days (Sundays excepted) after it shall have been presented to him, the Same shall be a Law, in like Manner as if he had signed it, unless the Congress by their Adjournment prevent its Return, in which Case it shall not be a Law.

Every Order, Resolution, or Vote to which the Concurrence of the Senate and House of Representatives may be necessary (except on a question of Adjournment) shall be presented to the President of the United States; and before the Same shall take Effect, shall be approved by him, or being disapproved by him shall be repassed by two thirds of the Senate and House of Representatives, according to the Rules and Limitations prescribed in the Case of a Bill.

SECTION 8. The Congress shall have power To lay and collect Taxes, Duties, Imposts and Excises, to pay the Debts and provide for the common Defence and general Welfare of the United States; but all Duties, Imposts and Excises shall be uniform throughout the United States;

---

[5]Superseded by the Twentieth Amendment.

To borrow Money on the credit of the United States;

To regulate Commerce with foreign Nations, and among the several States, and with the Indian Tribes;

To establish an uniform Rule of Naturalization, and uniform Laws on the subject of Bankruptcies throughout the United States;

To coin Money, regulate the Value thereof, and of foreign Coin, and fix the Standard of Weights and Measures;

To provide for the Punishment of counterfeiting the Securities and current Coin of the United States;

To establish Post Offices and post Roads;

To promote the Progress of Science and useful Arts, by securing for limited Times to Authors and Inventors the exclusive Right to their respective Writings and Discoveries;

To constitute Tribunals inferior to the supreme Court;

To define and punish Piracies and Felonies committed on the high Seas, and Offences against the Law of Nations;

To declare War, grant Letters of Marque and Reprisal, and make Rules concerning Captures on Land and Water;

To raise and support Armies, but no Appropriation of Money to that Use shall be for a longer Term than two Years;

To provide and maintain a Navy;

To make Rules for the Government and Regulation of the land and naval Forces;

To provide for calling forth the Militia to execute the Laws of the Union, suppress Insurrections and repel Invasions;

To provide for organizing, arming, and disciplining, the Militia, and for governing such Part of them as may be employed in the Service of the United States, reserving to the States respectively, the Appointment of the Officers, and the Authority of training the Militia according to the discipline prescribed by Congress;

To exercise exclusive Legislation in all Cases whatsoever, over such District (not exceeding ten Miles square) as may, by Cession of particular States, and the Acceptance of Congress, become the Seat of the Government of the United States, and to exercise like Authority over all Places purchased by the Consent of the Legislature of the State in which the Same shall be, for the Erection of Forts, Magazines, Arsenals, dock-Yards, and other needful Buildings;—And

To make all Laws which shall be necessary and proper for carrying into Execution the foregoing Powers, and all other Powers vested by this Constitution in the Government of the United States, or in any Department or Officer thereof.

SECTION 9. The Migration or Importation of such Persons as any of the States now existing shall think proper to admit, shall not be prohibited by the Congress prior to the Year one thousand eight hundred and eight, but a Tax or duty may be imposed on such Importation, not exceeding ten dollars for each Person.

The Privilege of the Writ of Habeas Corpus shall not be suspended, unless when in Cases of Rebellion or Invasion the public Safety may require it.

No Bill of Attainder or ex post facto Law shall be passed.

No Capitation, or other direct, Tax shall be laid, unless in Proportion to the Census or Enumeration herein before directed to be taken.

No Tax or Duty shall be laid on Articles exported from any State.

No Preference shall be given by any Regulation of Commerce or Revenue to the Ports of one State over those of another: nor shall Vessels bound to, or from, one State, be obliged to enter, clear, or pay Duties in another.

No Money shall be drawn from the Treasury, but in Consequence of Appropriations made by Law, and a regular Statement and Account of the Receipts and Expenditures of all public Money shall be published from time to time.

No Title of Nobility shall be granted by the United States: And no Person holding any Office of Profit or Trust under them, shall, without the Consent of the Congress, accept of any present, Emolument, Office, or Title, of any kind whatever, from any King, Prince, or foreign State.

SECTION 10. No State shall enter into any Treaty, Alliance, or Confederation; grant Letters of Marque and Reprisal; coin Money; emit Bills of Credit; make any Thing but gold and silver Coin a Tender in Payment of Debts; pass any Bill of Attainder, ex post facto Law, or Law impairing the Obligation of Contracts, or grant any Title of Nobility.

No State shall, without the Consent of the Congress, lay any Imposts or Duties on Imports or Exports, except what may be absolutely necessary for executing its inspection Laws: and the net Produce of all Duties and Imposts, laid by any State on Imports or Exports, shall be for the Use of the Treasury of the United States; and all such Laws shall be subject to the Revision and Controul of the Congress.

No State shall, without the Consent of Congress, lay any Duty of Tonnage, keep Troops, or Ships of War in time of Peace, enter into any Agreement or Compact with another State, or with a foreign Power, or engage in War, unless actually invaded, or in such imminent Danger as will not admit of delay.

ARTICLE II.

SECTION 1. The executive Power shall be vested in a President of the United States of America. He shall hold his Office during the Term of four Years, and, together with the Vice President, chosen for the same Term, be elected, as follows:

Each State shall appoint, in such Manner as the Legislature thereof may direct, a Number of Electors, equal to the whole Number of Senators and Representatives to which the State may be entitled in the Congress: but no Senator or Representative, or Person holding an Office of Trust or Profit under the United States, shall be appointed an Elector.

The Electors shall meet in their respective States, and vote by Ballot for two Persons, of whom one at least shall not be an Inhabitant of the same State with themselves. And they shall make a List of all the Persons voted for, and of the Number of Votes for each; which List they shall sign and certify, and transmit sealed to the Seat of the Government of the United States, directed to the President of the Senate. The President of the Senate shall, in the Presence of the Senate and House of Representatives, open all the Certificates, and the Votes shall then be counted. The Person having the greatest Number of Votes shall be the President, if such Number be a Majority of the whole Number of Electors appointed; and if there be more than one who have such Majority, and have an equal Number of Votes, then the House of Representatives shall immediately chuse by Ballot one of them for President; and if no Person have a Majority, then from the five highest on the List the said House shall in like Manner chuse the President. But in chusing the President, the Votes shall be taken by States, the Representation from each State having one Vote; A quorum for this Purpose shall consist of a Member or Members from two thirds of the States, and a Majority of all the States shall be necessary to a Choice. In every Case, after the Choice of the President, the Person having the greatest Number of Votes of the Electors shall be the Vice President. But if there should remain two or more who have equal Votes, the Senate shall chuse from them by Ballot the Vice President.[6]

The Congress may determine the Time of chusing the Electors, and the Day on which they shall give their Votes; which Day shall be the same throughout the United States.

No Person except a natural born Citizen, or a Citizen of the United States, at the time of the Adoption of this Constitution, shall be eligible to the Office of President, neither shall any Person be eligible to that Office who shall not have attained to the Age of thirty five Years, and been fourteen Years a Resident within the United States.

In Case of the Removal of the President from Office, or of his Death, Resignation, or Inability to discharge the Powers and Duties of the said Office, the Same shall devolve on the Vice President, and the Congress may by Law provide for the Case of Removal, Death, Resignation or Inability, both of the President and Vice President, declaring what Officer shall then act as President, and such Officer shall act accordingly, until the Disability be removed, or a President shall be elected.[7]

The President shall, at stated Times, receive for his Services, a Compensation, which shall neither be encreased nor diminished during the Period for which he shall have been elected, and he shall not receive within that Period any other Emolument from the United States, or any of them.

Before he enter on the Execution of his Office, he shall take the following Oath or Affirmation:—"I do solemnly swear (or affirm) that I will faithfully execute the Office of President of the United States, and will to the best of my Ability, preserve, protect and defend the Constitution of the United States."

SECTION 2. The President shall be Commander in Chief of the Army and Navy of the United States, and of the Militia of the several States, when called into the actual Service of the United States; he may require the Opinion, in writing, of the principal Officer in each of the executive Departments, upon any Subject relating to the Duties of their respective Offices, and he shall have Power to grant Reprieves and Pardons for Offences against the United States, except in Cases of Impeachment.

He shall have Power, by and with the Advice and Consent of the Senate, to make Treaties, provided two thirds of the Senators present concur; and he shall nominate, and by and with the Advice and Consent of the Senate,

---

[6]Superseded by the Twelfth Amendment.

[7]Modified by the Twenty-fifth Amendment.

shall appoint Ambassadors, other public Ministers and Consuls, Judges of the supreme Court, and all other Officers of the United States, whose Appointments are not herein otherwise provided for, and which shall be established by Law; but the Congress may by Law vest the Appointment of such inferior Officers, as they think proper, in the President alone, in the Courts of Law, or in the Heads of Departments.

The President shall have Power to fill up all Vacancies that may happen during the Recess of the Senate, by granting Commissions which shall expire at the End of their next Session.

SECTION 3. He shall from time to time give the Congress Information of the State of the Union, and recommend to their Consideration such Measures as he shall judge necessary and expedient; he may, on extraordinary Occasions, convene both Houses, or either of them, and in Case of Disagreement between them, with Respect to the Time of Adjournment, he may adjourn them to such Time as he shall think proper; he shall receive Ambassadors and other public Ministers; he shall take Care that the Laws be faithfully executed, and shall Commission all the Officers of the United States.

SECTION 4. The President, Vice President and all civil Officers of the United States, shall be removed from Office on Impeachment for, and Conviction of, Treason, Bribery, or other high Crimes and Misdemeanors.

ARTICLE III.

SECTION 1. The judicial Power of the United States, shall be vested in one supreme Court, and in such inferior Courts as the Congress may from time to time ordain and establish. The Judges, both of the supreme and inferior Courts, shall hold their Offices during good Behaviour, and shall, at stated Times, receive for their Services, a Compensation, which shall not be diminished during their Continuance in Office.

SECTION 2. The judicial Power shall extend to all Cases, in Law and Equity, arising under this Constitution, the Laws of the United States, and Treaties made, or which shall be made, under their Authority;—to all Cases affecting Ambassadors, other public Ministers and Consuls;—to all Cases of admiralty and maritime Jurisdiction;—to Controversies to which the United States shall be a Party;—to Controversies between two or more States;—between a State and Citizens of another State;[8]—between Citizens of different States,—between Citizens of the same State claiming Lands under Grants of different States, and between a

State, or the Citizens thereof, and foreign States, Citizens or Subjects.

In all Cases affecting Ambassadors, other public Ministers and Consuls, and those in which a State shall be Party, the supreme Court shall have original Jurisdiction. In all the other Cases before mentioned, the supreme Court shall have appellate Jurisdiction, both as to Law and Fact, with such Exceptions, and under such Regulations as the Congress shall make.

The Trial of all Crimes, except in Cases of Impeachment, shall be by Jury; and such Trial shall be held in the State where the said Crimes shall have been committed; but when not committed within any State, the Trial shall be at such Place or Places as the Congress may by Law have directed.

SECTION 3. Treason against the United States, shall consist only in levying War against them, or in adhering to their Enemies, giving them Aid and Comfort. No Person shall be convicted of Treason unless on the Testimony of two Witnesses to the same overt Act, or on Confession in open Court.

The Congress shall have Power to declare the Punishment of Treason, but no Attainder of Treason shall work Corruption of Blood, or Forfeiture except during the Life of the Person attainted.

ARTICLE IV.

SECTION 1. Full Faith and Credit shall be given in each State to the public Acts, Records, and judicial Proceedings of every other State. And the Congress may by general Laws prescribe the Manner in which such Acts, Records and Proceedings shall be proved, and the Effect thereof.

SECTION 2. The Citizens of each State shall be entitled to all Privileges and Immunities of Citizens in the several States.

A Person charged in any State with Treason, Felony, or other Crime, who shall flee from Justice, and be found in another State, shall on Demand of the executive Authority of the State from which he fled, be delivered up, to be removed to the State having Jurisdiction of the Crime.

No Person held to Service or Labour in one State, under the Laws thereof, escaping into another, shall, in Consequence of any Law or Regulation therein, be discharged from such Service or Labour, but shall be

[8]Modified by the Eleventh Amendment.

delivered up on Claim of the Party to whom such Service or Labour may be due.

SECTION 3. New States may be admitted by the Congress into this Union; but no new State shall be formed or erected within the Jurisdiction of any other State, nor any State be formed by the Junction of two or more States, or Parts of States, without the Consent of the Legislatures of the States concerned as well as of the Congress.

The Congress shall have Power to dispose of and make all needful Rules and Regulations respecting the Territory or other Property belonging to the United States; and nothing in this Constitution shall be so construed as to Prejudice any Claims of the United States, or of any particular State.

SECTION 4. The United States shall guarantee to every State in this Union a Republican Form of Government, and shall protect each of them against Invasion; and on Application of the Legislature, or of the Executive (when the Legislature cannot be convened) against domestic Violence.

ARTICLE V.

The Congress, whenever two thirds of both Houses shall deem it necessary, shall propose Amendments to this Constitution, or, on the Application of the Legislatures of two thirds of the several States, shall call a Convention for proposing Amendments, which, in either Case, shall be valid to all Intents and Purposes, as Part of this Constitution, when ratified by the Legislatures of three fourths of the several States, or by Conventions in three fourths thereof, as the one or the other Mode of Ratification may be proposed by the Congress; Provided that no Amendment which may be made prior to the Year One thousand eight hundred and eight shall in any Manner affect the first and fourth Clauses in the Ninth Section of the first Article; and that no State, without its Consent, shall be deprived of its equal Suffrage in the Senate.

ARTICLE VI.

All Debts contracted and Engagements entered into, before the Adoption of this Constitution, shall be as valid against the United States under this Constitution, as under the Confederation.

This Constitution, and the Laws of the United States which shall be made in Pursuance thereof; and all Treaties made, or which shall be made, under the Authority of the United States, shall be the supreme Law of the Land; and the Judges in every State shall be bound thereby, any Thing in the Constitution or Laws of any State to the Contrary notwithstanding.

The Senators and Representatives before mentioned, and the Members of the several State Legislatures, and all executive and judicial Officers, both of the United States and of the several States, shall be bound by Oath or Affirmation, to support this Constitution; but no religious Test shall ever be required as a Qualification to any Office or public Trust under the United States.

ARTICLE VII.

The Ratification of the Conventions of nine States, shall be sufficient for the Establishment of this Constitution between the States so ratifying the Same.

Done in Convention by the Unanimous Consent of the States present the Seventeenth Day of September in the Year of our Lord one thousand seven hundred and Eighty seven and of the Independence of the United States of America the Twelfth. In witness whereof We have hereunto subscribed our Names,

Articles in Addition to, and Amendment of, the Constitution of the United States of America, Proposed by Congress, and Ratified by the Legislatures of the Several States, Pursuant to the Fifth Article of the Original Constitution.

AMENDMENT I[9]

Congress shall make no law respecting an establishment of religion, or prohibiting the free exercise thereof; or abridging the freedom of speech, or of the press; or the right of the people peaceably to assemble, and to petition the Government for a redress of grievances.

AMENDMENT II

A well regulated Militia, being necessary to the security of a free State, the right of the people to keep and bear Arms shall not be infringed.

[9]The first ten amendments were passed by Congress September 25, 1789. They were ratified by three-fourths of the states December 15, 1791.

AMENDMENT III

No Soldier shall, in time of peace, be quartered in any house, without the consent of the Owner, nor in time of war, but in a manner to be prescribed by law.

AMENDMENT IV

The right of the people to be secure in their persons, houses, papers, and effects, against unreasonable searches and seizures, shall not be violated, and no Warrants shall issue, but upon probable cause, supported by Oath or affirmation, and particularly describing the place to be searched, and the persons or things to be seized.

AMENDMENT V

No person shall be held to answer for a capital or otherwise infamous crime, unless on a presentment or indictment of a Grand Jury, except in cases arising in the land or naval forces, or in the Militia, when in actual service in time of War or public danger; nor shall any person be subject for the same offence to be twice put in jeopardy of life or limb; nor shall be compelled in any criminal case to be a witness against himself, nor be deprived of life, liberty, or property, without due process of law; nor shall private property be taken for public use, without just compensation.

AMENDMENT VI

In all criminal prosecutions, the accused shall enjoy the right to a speedy and public trial, by an impartial jury of the State and district wherein the crime shall have been committed, which district shall have been previously ascertained by law, and to be informed of the nature and cause of the accusation; to be confronted with the witnesses against him; to have compulsory process for obtaining witnesses in his favor, and to have the Assistance of Counsel for his defence.

AMENDMENT VII

In suits at common law, where the value in controversy shall exceed twenty dollars, the right of trial by jury shall be preserved, and no fact tried by a jury, shall be otherwise reexamined in any Court of the United States, than according to the rules of the common law.

AMENDMENT VIII

Excessive bail shall not be required, nor excessive fines imposed, nor cruel and unusual punishments inflicted.

AMENDMENT IX

The enumeration in the Constitution, of certain rights, shall not be construed to deny or disparage others retained by the people.

AMENDMENT X

The powers not delegated to the United States by the Constitution; nor prohibited by it to the States, are reserved to the States respectively, or to the people.

AMENDMENT XI[10]

The Judicial power of the United States shall not be construed to extend to any suit in law or equity, commenced or prosecuted against one of the United States by Citizens of another State, or by Citizens or Subjects of any Foreign State.

AMENDMENT XII[11]

The Electors shall meet in their respective States and vote by ballot for President and Vice-President, one of whom, at least, shall not be an inhabitant of the same State with themselves; they shall name in their ballots the person voted for as President, and in distinct ballots the person voted for as Vice-President, and they shall make distinct lists of all persons voted for as President, and of all persons voted for as Vice-President, and of the number of votes for each, which lists they shall sign and certify, and transmit sealed to the seat of the government of the United States, directed to the President of the Senate;—The President of the Senate shall, in the presence of the Senate and House of Representatives, open all the certificates and the votes shall then be counted;—The person having the greatest number of votes for President, shall be the President, if such number be a majority of the whole number of Electors appointed; and if no person have such majority, then from the persons having the highest numbers not exceeding three on the list of those voted for as President, the House of Representatives shall choose immediately, by ballot, the President. But in choosing the President, the votes shall be taken by states, the representation from each state having one vote; a quorum for this purpose shall consist of a member or members from two-thirds of the states, and a majority of

---

[10] Passed March 4, 1794. Ratified January 23, 1795.
[11] Passed December 9, 1803. Ratified June 15, 1804.

all the states shall be necessary to a choice. And if the House of Representatives shall not choose a President whenever the right of choice shall devolve upon them, before the fourth day of March next following, then the Vice-President shall act as President, as in the case of the death or other constitutional disability of the President.— The person having the greatest number of votes as Vice-President, shall be the Vice-President, if such number be a majority of the whole number of Electors appointed, and if no person have a majority, then from the two highest numbers on the list, the Senate shall choose the Vice-President; a quorum for the purpose shall consist of two-thirds of the whole number of Senators, and a majority of the whole number shall be necessary to a choice. But no person constitutionally ineligible to the office of President shall be eligible to that of Vice-President of the United States.

AMENDMENT XIII[12]

SECTION 1. Neither slavery nor involuntary servitude, except as a punishment for crime whereof the party shall have been duly convicted, shall exist within the United States, or any place subject to their jurisdiction.

SECTION 2. Congress shall have power to enforce this article by appropriate legislation.

AMENDMENT XIV[13]

SECTION 1. All persons born or naturalized in the United States, and subject to the jurisdiction thereof, are citizens of the United States and of the State wherein they reside. No State shall make or enforce any law which shall abridge the privileges or immunities of citizens of the United States; nor shall any State deprive any person of life, liberty, or property, without due process of law; nor deny to any person within its jurisdiction the equal protection of the laws.

SECTION 2. Representatives shall be apportioned among the several States according to their respective numbers, counting the whole number of persons in each State, excluding Indians not taxed. But when the right to vote at any election for the choice of electors for President and Vice-President of the United States, Representatives in Congress, the Executive and Judicial officers of a State, or the members of the Legislature thereof, is de-

nied to any of the male inhabitants of such State, being twenty-one years of age, and citizens of the United States, or in any way abridged, except for participation in rebellion, or other crime, the basis of representation therein shall be reduced in the proportion which the number of such male citizens shall bear to the whole number of male citizens twenty-one years of age in such State.

SECTION 3. No person shall be a Senator or Representative in Congress, or elector of President and Vice-President, or hold any office, civil or military, under the United States, or under any State, who, having previously taken an oath, as a member of Congress, or as an officer of the United States, or as a member of any State legislature, or as an executive or judicial officer of any State, to support the Constitution of the United States, shall have engaged in insurrection or rebellion against the same, or given aid or comfort to the enemies thereof. But Congress may by a vote of two-thirds of each House, remove such disability.

SECTION 4. The validity of the public debt of the United States, authorized by law, including debts incurred for payment of pensions and bounties for services in suppressing insurrection or rebellion, shall not be questioned. But neither the United States nor any State shall assume or pay any debt or obligation incurred in aid of insurrection or rebellion against the United States, or any claim for the loss or emancipation of any slave; but all such debts, obligations, and claims shall be held illegal and void.

SECTION 5. The Congress shall have the power to enforce, by appropriate legislation, the provisions of this article.

AMENDMENT XV[14]

SECTION 1. The right of citizens of the United States to vote shall not be denied or abridged by the United States or by any State on account of race, color, or previous conditions of servitude—

SECTION 2. The Congress shall have power to enforce this article by appropriate legislation.

AMENDMENT XVI

The Congress shall have power to lay and collect taxes on incomes, from whatever source derived, without

---

[12]Passed January 31, 1865. Ratified December 6, 1865.

[13]Passed June 13, 1866. Ratified July 9, 1868.

[14]Passed February 26, 1869. Ratified February 2, 1870.

apportionment among the several States, and without regard to any census or enumeration.

AMENDMENT XVII[15]

The Senate of the United States shall be composed of two Senators from each State, elected by the people thereof, for six years; and each Senator shall have one vote. The electors in each State shall have the qualifications requisite for electors of the most numerous branch of the State legislatures.

When vacancies happen in the representation of any State in the Senate, the executive authority of such State shall issue writs of election to fill such vacancies: *Provided,* That the legislature of any State may empower the executive thereof to make temporary appointments until the people fill the vacancies by election as the legislature may direct.

This amendment shall not be so construed as to affect the election or term of any Senator chosen before it becomes valid as part of the Constitution.

AMENDMENT XVIII[16]

SECTION 1. After one year from the ratification of this article the manufacture, sale, or transportation of intoxicating liquors within, the importation thereof into, or the exportation thereof from the United States and all territory subject to the jurisdiction thereof for beverage purposes is hereby prohibited.

SECTION 2. The Congress and the several States shall have concurrent power to enforce this article by appropriate legislation.

SECTION 3. This article shall be inoperative unless it shall have been ratified as an amendment to the Constitution by the legislatures of the several States, as provided in the Constitution, within seven years from the date of the submission hereof to the States by the Congress.

AMENDMENT XIX[17]

The right of citizens of the United States to vote shall not be denied or abridged by the United States or by any State on account of sex.

Congress shall have power to enforce this article by appropriate legislation.

AMENDMENT XX[18]

SECTION 1. The terms of the President and Vice-President shall end at noon on the 20th day of January, and the terms of Senators and Representatives at noon on the 3d day of January, of the years in which such terms would have ended if this article had not been ratified; and the terms of their successors shall then begin.

SECTION 2. The Congress shall assemble at least once in every year, and such meeting shall begin at noon on the 3d day of January, unless they shall by law appoint a different day.

SECTION 3. If, at the time fixed for the beginning of the term of the President, the President elect shall have died, the Vice-President elect shall become President. If a President shall not have been chosen before the time fixed for the beginning of his term, or if the President elect shall have failed to qualify, then the Vice-President elect shall act as President until a President shall have qualified; and the Congress may by law provide for the case wherein neither a President elect nor a Vice-President elect shall have qualified, declaring who shall then act as President, or the manner in which one who is to act shall be selected, and such person shall act accordingly until a President or Vice-President shall have qualified.

SECTION 4. The Congress may by law provide for the case of the death of any of the persons from whom the House of Representatives may choose a President whenever the right of choice shall have devolved upon them, and for the case of the death of any of the persons from whom the Senate may choose a Vice-President whenever the right of choice shall have devolved upon them.

SECTION 5. Sections 1 and 2 shall take effect on the 15th day of October following the ratification of this article.

SECTION 6. This article shall be inoperative unless it shall have been ratified as an amendment to the Constitution by the legislatures of three-fourths of the several States within seven years from the date of its submission.

AMENDMENT XXI[19]

SECTION 1. The eighteenth article of amendment to the Constitution of the United States is hereby repealed.

---

[15]Passed May 13, 1912. Ratified April 8, 1913.

[16]Passed December 18, 1917. Ratified January 16, 1919.

[17]Passed June 4, 1919. Ratified August 18, 1920.

[18]Passed March 2, 1932. Ratified January 23, 1933.

[19]Passed February 20, 1933. Ratified December 5, 1933.

SECTION 2. The transportation or importation into any State, Territory, or possession of the United States for delivery or use therein of intoxicating liquors, in violation of the laws thereof, is hereby prohibited.

SECTION 3. This article shall be inoperative unless it shall have been ratified as an amendment to the Constitution by conventions in the several States, as provided in the Constitution, within seven years from the date of the submission hereof to the States by the Congress.

AMENDMENT XXII[20]

No person shall be elected to the office of the President more than twice, and no person who has held the office of President, or acted as President, for more than two years of a term to which some other person was elected President shall be elected to the office of the President more than once.

But this Article shall not apply to any person holding the office of President when this Article was proposed by the Congress, and shall not prevent any person who may be holding the office of President, or acting as President, during the term within which this Article becomes operative from holding the office of President or acting as President during the remainder of such term.

AMENDMENT XXIII[21]

SECTION 1. The District constituting the seat of Government of the United States shall appoint in such manner as the Congress may direct:

A number of electors of President and Vice President equal to the whole number of Senators and Representatives in Congress to which the District would be entitled if it were a State, but in no event more than the least populous State; they shall be in addition to those appointed by the States, but they shall be considered, for the purposes of the election of President and Vice President, to be electors appointed by the State; and they shall meet in the District and perform such duties as provided by the twelfth article of amendment.

SECTION 2. The Congress shall have power to enforce this article by appropriate legislation.

AMENDMENT XXIV[22]

SECTION 1. The right of citizens of the United States to vote in any primary or other election for President or Vice President, or for Senator or Representative in Congress, shall not be denied or abridged by the United States or any State by reason of failure to pay any poll tax or other tax.

SECTION 2. The Congress shall have power to enforce this article by appropriate legislation.

AMENDMENT XXV[23]

SECTION 1. In case of the removal of the President from office or of his death or resignation, the Vice President shall become President.

SECTION 2. Whenever there is a vacancy in the office of the Vice President, the President shall nominate a Vice President who shall take office upon confirmation by a majority vote of both Houses of Congress.

SECTION 3. Whenever the President transmits to the President pro tempore of the Senate and the Speaker of the House of Representatives his written declaration that he is unable to discharge the powers and duties of his office, and until he transmits them a written declaration to the contrary, such powers and duties shall be discharged by the Vice President as Acting President.

SECTION 4. Whenever the Vice President and a majority of either the principal officers of the executive department or of such other body as Congress may by law provide, transmit to the President pro tempore of the Senate and the Speaker of the House of Representatives their written declaration that the President is unable to discharge the powers and duties of his office, the Vice President shall immediately assume the powers and duties of the office of Acting President

Thereafter, when the President transmits to the President pro tempore of the Senate and the Speaker of the House of Representatives his written declaration that no inability exists, he shall resume the powers and duties of his office unless the Vice President and a majority of either the principal officers of the executive department or of such other body as Congress may by law provide, transmit within four days to the President pro tempore of the Senate and the Speaker of the House of Representatives their written declaration that the President is unable to

[20]Passed March 12, 1947. Ratified March 1, 1951.

[21]Passed June 16, 1960. Ratified April 3, 1961.

[22]Passed August 27, 1962. Ratified January 23, 1964.

[23]Passed July 6, 1965. Ratified February 11, 1967.

discharge the powers and duties of his office. Thereupon Congress shall decide the issue, assembling within forty-eight hours for that purpose if not in session. If the Congress, within twenty-one days after receipt of the latter written declaration, or, if Congress is not in session, within twenty-one days after Congress is required to assemble, determines by two-thirds vote of both Houses that the President is unable to discharge the powers and duties of his office, the Vice President shall continue to discharge the same as Acting President; otherwise, the President shall resume the powers and duties of his office.

AMENDMENT XXVI[24]

SECTION 1. The right of citizens of the United States, who are eighteen years of age or older, to vote shall not be denied or abridged by the United States or by any State on account of age.

SECTION 2. The Congress shall have power to enforce this article by appropriate legislation.

AMENDMENT XXVII[25]

No law, varying the compensation for the service of the Senators and Representatives, shall take effect, until an election of Representatives shall have intervened.

[24]Passed March 23, 1971. Ratified July 5, 1971.

[25]Passed September 25, 1789. Ratified May 7, 1992

ADMISSION OF STATES

Order of admission	State	Date of admission	Order of admission	State	Date of admission
1	Delaware	December 7, 1787	26	Michigan	January 26, 1837
2	Pennsylvania	December 12, 1787	27	Florida	March 3, 1845
3	New Jersey	December 18, 1787	28	Texas	December 29, 1845
4	Georgia	January 2, 1788	29	Iowa	December 28, 1846
5	Connecticut	January 9, 1788	30	Wisconsin	May 29, 1848
6	Massachusetts	February 6, 1788	31	California	September 9, 1850
7	Maryland	April 28, 1788	32	Minnesota	May 11, 1858
8	South Carolina	May 23, 1788	33	Oregon	February 14, 1859
9	New Hampshire	June 21, 1788	34	Kansas	January 29, 1861
10	Virginia	June 25, 1788	35	West Virginia	June 20, 1863
11	New York	July 26, 1788	36	Nevada	October 31, 1864
12	North Carolina	November 21, 1789	37	Nebraska	March 1, 1867
13	Rhode Island	May 29, 1790	38	Colorado	August 1, 1876
14	Vermont	March 4, 1791	39	North Dakota	November 2, 1889
15	Kentucky	June 1, 1792	40	South Dakota	November 2, 1889
16	Tennessee	June 1, 1796	41	Montana	November 8, 1889
17	Ohio	March 1, 1803	42	Washington	November 11, 1889
18	Louisiana	April 30, 1812	43	Idaho	July 3, 1890
19	Indiana	December 11, 1816	44	Wyoming	July 10, 1890
20	Mississippi	December 10, 1817	45	Utah	January 4, 1896
21	Illinois	December 3, 1818	46	Oklahoma	November 16, 1907
22	Alabama	December 14, 1819	47	New Mexico	January 6, 1912
23	Maine	March 15, 1820	48	Arizona	February 14, 1912
24	Missouri	August 10, 1821	49	Alaska	January 3, 1959
25	Arkansas	June 15, 1836	50	Hawaii	August 21, 1959

POPULATION OF THE UNITED STATES

Year	Total population	Number per square mile	Year	Total population	Number per square mile	Year	Total population	Number per square mile
1790	3,929	4.5	1808	6,838		1826	11,580	
1791	4,056		1809	7,031		1827	11,909	
1792	4,194		1810	7,224	4.3	1828	12,237	
1793	4,332		1811	7,460		1829	12,565	
1794	4,469		1812	7,700		1830	12,901	7.4
1795	4,607		1813	7,939		1831	13,321	
1796	4,745		1814	8,179		1832	13,742	
1797	4,883		1815	8,419		1833	14,162	
1798	5,021		1816	8,659		1834	14,582	
1799	5,159		1817	8,899		1835	15,003	
1800	5,297	6.1	1818	9,139		1836	15,423	
1801	5,486		1819	9,379		1837	15,843	
1802	5,679		1820	9,618	5.6	1838	16,264	
1803	5,872		1821	9,939		1839	16,684	
1804	5,065		1822	10,268		1840	17,120	9.8
1805	6,258		1823	10,596		1841	17,733	
1806	6,451		1824	10,924		1842	18,345	
1807	6,644		1825	11,252		1843	18,957	

Figures are from *Historical Statistics of the United States, Colonial Times to 1957* (1961), pp. 7, 8; *Statistical Abstract of the United States: 1974,* p. 5, Census Bureau for 1974 and 1975; and *Statistical Abstract of the United States: 1988,* p. 7.

Note: Population figures are in thousands. Density figures are for land area of continental United States.

(continued)

POPULATION OF THE UNITED STATES, CONTINUED

Year	Total population	Number per square mile	Year	Total population[1]	Number per square mile	Year	Total population[1]	Number per square mile
1844	19,569		1896	70,885		1948	147,208	
1845	20,182		1897	72,189		1949	149,767	
1846	20,794		1898	73,494		1950	150,697	50.7
1847	21,406		1899	74,799		1951	154,878	
1848	22,018		1900	76,094	25.6	1952	157,553	
1849	22,631		1901	77,585		1953	160,184	
1850	23,261	7.9	1902	79,160		1954	163,026	
1851	24,086		1903	80,632		1955	165,931	
1852	24,911		1904	82,165		1956	168,903	
1853	25,736		1905	83,820		1957	171,984	
1854	26,561		1906	85,437		1958	174,882	
1855	27,386		1907	87,000		1959	177,830	
1856	28,212		1908	88,709		1960	178,464	60.1
1857	29,037		1909	90,492		1961	183,672	
1858	29,862		1910	92,407	31.0	1962	186,504	
1859	30,687		1911	93,868		1963	189,197	
1860	31,513	10.6	1912	95,331		1964	191,833	
1861	32,351		1913	97,227		1965	194,237	
1862	33,188		1914	99,118		1966	196,485	
1863	34,026		1915	100,549		1967	198,629	
1864	34,863		1916	101,966		1968	200,619	
1865	35,701		1917	103,414		1969	202,599	
1866	36,538		1918	104,550		1970	203,875	57.5[2]
1867	37,376		1919	105,063		1971	207,045	
1868	38,213		1920	106,466	35.6	1972	208,842	
1869	39,051		1921	108,541		1973	210,396	
1870	39,905	13.4	1922	110,055		1974	211,894	
1871	40,938		1923	111,950		1975	213,631	
1872	41,972		1924	114,113		1976	215,152	
1873	43,006		1925	115,832		1977	216,880	
1874	44,040		1926	117,399		1978	218,717	
1875	45,073		1927	119,038		1979	220,584	
1876	46,107		1928	120,501		1980	226,546	64.0
1877	47,141		1929	121,700		1981	230,138	
1878	48,174		1930	122,775	41.2	1982	232,520	
1879	49,208		1931	124,040		1983	234,799	
1880	50,262	16.9	1932	124,840		1984	237,001	
1881	51,542		1933	125,579		1985	239,283	
1882	52,821		1934	126,374		1986	241,596	
1883	54,100		1935	127,250		1987	234,773	
1884	55,379		1936	128,053		1988	245,051	
1885	56,658		1937	128,825		1989	247,350	
1886	57,938		1938	129,825		1990	250,122	
1887	59,217		1939	130,880		1991	254,521	
1888	60,496		1940	131,669	44.2	1992	245,908	
1889	61,775		1941	133,894		1993	257,908	
1890	63,056	21.2	1942	135,361		1994	261,875	
1891	64,361		1943	137,250		1995	263,434	
1892	65,666		1944	138,916		1996	266,096	
1893	66,970		1945	140,468		1997	267,901	
1894	68,275		1946	141,936		1998	269,501	
1895	69,580		1947	144,698				

[1]Figures after 1940 represent total population including armed forces abroad, except in official census years.
[2]Figure includes Alaska and Hawaii.

PRESIDENTIAL ELECTIONS

Year	Number of states	Candidates[1]	Parties	Popular vote	Electoral vote	Percentage of popular vote[2]
1789	11	**George Washington**	No party designations		69	
		John Adams			34	
		Minor Candidates			35	
1792	15	**George Washington**	No party designations		132	
		John Adams			77	
		George Clinton			50	
		Minor Candidates			5	
1796	16	**John Adams**	Federalist		71	
		Thomas Jefferson	Democratic-Republican		68	
		Thomas Pinckney	Federalist		59	
		Aaron Burr	Democratic-Republican		30	
		Minor Candidates			48	
1800	16	**Thomas Jefferson**	Democratic-Republican		73	
		Aaron Burr	Democratic-Republican		73	
		John Adams	Federalist		65	
		Charles C. Pinckney	Federalist		64	
		John Jay	Federalist		1	
1804	17	**Thomas Jefferson**	Democratic-Republican		162	
		Charles C. Pinckney	Federalist		14	
1808	17	**James Madison**	Democratic-Republican		122	
		Charles C. Pinckney	Federalist		47	
		George Clinton	Democratic-Republican		6	
1812	18	**James Madison**	Democratic-Republican		128	
		DeWitt Clinton	Federalist		89	
1816	19	**James Monroe**	Democratic-Republican		183	
		Rufus King	Federalist		34	
1820	24	**James Monroe**	Democratic-Republican		231	
		John Quincy Adams	Independent Republican		1	
1824	24	**John Quincy Adams**	Democratic-Republican	108,740	84	30.5
		Andrew Jackson	Democratic-Republican	153,544	99	43.1
		William H. Crawford	Democratic-Republican	46,618	41	13.1
		Henry Clay	Democratic-Republican	47,136	37	13.2
1828	24	**Andrew Jackson**	Democratic	647,286	178	56.0
		John Quincy Adams	National Republican	508,064	83	44.0
1832	24	**Andrew Jackson**	Democratic	687,502	219	55.0
		Henry Clay	National Republican	530,189	49	42.4
		William Wirt	Anti-Masonic	33,108	7	
		John Floyd	National Republican		11	2.6

[1]Before the passage of the Twelfth Amendment in 1804, the Electoral College voted for two presidential candidates; the runner-up became vice president. Figures are from *Historical Statistics of the United States, Colonial Times to 1957* (1961), pp. 682–83; and the U.S. Department of Justice.

[2]Candidates receiving less than 1 percent of the popular vote have been omitted. For that reason the percentage of popular vote given for any election year may not total 100 percent.

Year	Number of states	Candidates	Parties	Popular vote	Electoral vote	Percentage of popular vote[1]
1836	26	**Martin Van Buren**	Democratic	765,483	170	50.9
		William H. Harrison	Whig		73	
		Hugh L. White	Whig		26	
		Daniel Webster	Whig	739,795	14	
		W. P. Mangum	Whig		11	
1840	26	**William H. Harrison**	Whig	1,274,624	234	53.1
		Martin Van Buren	Democratic	1,127,781	60	46.9
1844	26	**James K. Polk**	Democratic	1,338,464	170	49.6
		Henry Clay	Whig	1,300,097	105	48.1
		James G. Birney	Liberty	62,300		2.3
1848	30	**Zachary Taylor**	Whig	1,360,967	163	47.4
		Lewis Cass	Democratic	1,222,342	127	42.5
		Martin Van Buren	Free Soil	291,263		10.1
1852	31	**Franklin Pierce**	Democratic	1,601,117	254	50.9
		Winfield Scott	Whig	1,385,453	42	44.1
		John P. Hale	Free Soil	155,825		5.0
1856	31	**James Buchanan**	Democratic	1,832,955	174	45.3
		John C. Frémont	Republican	1,339,932	114	33.1
		Millard Fillmore	American	871,731	8	21.6
1860	33	**Abraham Lincoln**	Republican	1,865,593	180	39.8
		Stephen A. Douglas	Democratic	1,382,713	12	29.5
		John C. Breckinridge	Democratic	848,356	72	18.1
		John Bell	Constitutional Union	592,906	39	12.6
1864	36	**Abraham Lincoln**	Republican	2,206,938	212	55.0
		George B. McClellan	Democratic	1,803,787	21	45.0
1868	37	**Ulysses S. Grant**	Republican	3,013,421	214	52.7
		Horatio Seymour	Democratic	2,706,829	80	47.3
1872	37	**Ulysses S. Grant**	Republican	3,596,745	286	55.6
		Horace Greeley	Democratic	2,843,446	[2]	43.9
1876	38	**Rutherford B. Hayes**	Republican	4,036,572	185	48.0
		Samuel J. Tilden	Democratic	4,284,020	184	51.0
1880	38	**James A. Garfield**	Republican	4,453,295	214	48.5
		Winfield S. Hancock	Democratic	4,414,082	155	48.1
		James B. Weaver	Greenback-Labor	308,578		3.4
1884	38	**Grover Cleveland**	Democratic	4,879,507	219	48.5
		James G. Blaine	Republican	4,850,293	182	48.2
		Benjamin F. Butler	Greenback-Labor	175,370		1.8
		John P. St. John	Prohibition	150,369		1.5
1888	38	**Benjamin Harrison**	Republican	5,477,129	233	47.9
		Grover Cleveland	Democratic	5,537,857	168	48.6
		Clinton B. Fisk	Prohibition	249,506		2.2
		Anson J. Streeter	Union Labor	146,935		1.3

[1]Candidates receiving less than 1 percent of the popular vote have been omitted. For that reason the percentage of popular vote given for any election year may not total 100 percent.

[2]Greeley died shortly after the election; the electors supporting him then divided their votes among minor candidates.

Year	Number of states	Candidates	Parties	Popular vote	Electoral vote	Percentage of popular vote[1]
1892	44	**Grover Cleveland**	Democratic	5,555,426	277	46.1
		Benjamin Harrison	Republican	5,182,690	145	43.0
		James B. Weaver	People's	1,029,846	22	8.5
		John Bidwell	Prohibition	264,133		2.2
1896	45	**William McKinley**	Republican	7,102,246	271	51.1
		William J. Bryan	Democratic	6,492,559	176	47.7
1900	45	**William McKinley**	Republican	7,218,491	292	51.7
		William J. Bryan	Democratic; Populist	6,356,734	155	45.5
		John C. Wooley	Prohibition	208,914		1.5
1904	45	**Theodore Roosevelt**	Republican	7,628,461	336	57.4
		Alton B. Parker	Democratic	5,084,223	140	37.6
		Eugene V. Debs	Socialist	402,283		3.0
		Silas C. Swallow	Prohibition	258,536		1.9
1908	46	**William H. Taft**	Republican	7,675,320	321	51.6
		William J. Bryan	Democratic	6,412,294	162	43.1
		Eugene V. Debs	Socialist	420,793		2.8
		Eugene W. Chafin	Prohibition	253,840		1.7
1912	48	**Woodrow Wilson**	Democratic	6,296,547	435	41.9
		Theodore Roosevelt	Progressive	4,118,571	88	27.4
		William H. Taft	Republican	3,486,720	8	23.2
		Eugene V. Debs	Socialist	900,672		6.0
		Eugene W. Chafin	Prohibition	206,275		1.4
1916	48	**Woodrow Wilson**	Democratic	9,127,695	277	49.4
		Charles E. Hughes	Republican	8,533,507	254	46.2
		A. L. Benson	Socialist	585,113		3.2
		J. Frank Hanly	Prohibition	220,506		1.2
1920	48	**Warren G. Harding**	Republican	16,143,407	404	60.4
		James N. Cox	Democratic	9,130,328	127	34.2
		Eugene V. Debs	Socialist	919,799		3.4
		P. P. Christensen	Farmer-Labor	265,411		1.0
1924	48	**Calvin Coolidge**	Republican	15,718,211	382	54.0
		John W. Davis	Democratic	8,385,283	136	28.8
		Robert M. La Follette	Progressive	4,831,289	13	16.6
1928	48	**Herbert C. Hoover**	Republican	21,391,993	444	58.2
		Alfred E. Smith	Democratic	15,016,169	87	40.9
1932	48	**Franklin D. Roosevelt**	Democratic	22,809,638	472	57.4
		Herbert C. Hoover	Republican	15,758,901	59	39.7
		Norman Thomas	Socialist	881,951		2.2

[1]Candidates receiving less than 1 percent of the popular vote have been omitted. For that reason the percentage of popular vote given for any election year may not total 100 percent.

Year	Number of states	Candidates	Parties	Popular vote	Electoral vote	Percentage of popular vote[1]
1936	48	**Franklin D. Roosevelt**	Democratic	27,752,869	523	60.8
		Alfred M. Landon	Republican	16,674,665	8	36.5
		William Lemke	Union	882,479		1.9
1940	48	**Franklin D. Roosevelt**	Democratic	27,307,819	449	54.8
		Wendell L. Willkie	Republican	22,321,018	82	44.8
1944	48	**Franklin D. Roosevelt**	Democratic	25,606,585	432	53.5
		Thomas E. Dewey	Republican	22,014,745	99	46.0
1948	48	**Harry S. Truman**	Democratic	24,105,812	303	49.5
		Thomas E. Dewey	Republican	21,970,065	189	45.1
		J. Strom Thurmond	States' Rights	1,169,063	39	2.4
		Henry A. Wallace	Progressive	1,157,172		2.4
1952	48	**Dwight D. Eisenhower**	Republican	33,936,234	442	55.1
		Adlai E. Stevenson	Democratic	27,314,992	89	44.4
1956	48	**Dwight D. Eisenhower**	Republican	35,590,472	457	57.6
		Adlai E. Stevenson	Democratic	26,022,752	73	42.1
1960	50	**John F. Kennedy**	Democratic	34,227,096	303	49.9
		Richard M. Nixon	Republican	34,108,546	219	49.6
1964	50	**Lyndon B. Johnson**	Democratic	43,126,506	486	61.1
		Barry M. Goldwater	Republican	27,176,799	52	38.5
1968	50	**Richard M. Nixon**	Republican	31,785,480	301	43.4
		Hubert H. Humphrey	Democratic	31,275,165	191	42.7
		George C. Wallace	American Independent	9,906,473	46	13.5
1972	50	**Richard M. Nixon**	Republican	47,169,911	520	60.7
		George S. McGovern	Democratic	29,170,383	17	37.5
1976	50	**Jimmy Carter**	Democratic	40,827,394	297	50.0
		Gerald R. Ford	Republican	39,145,977	240	47.9
1980	50	**Ronald W. Reagan**	Republican	43,899,248	489	50.8
		Jimmy Carter	Democratic	35,481,435	49	41.0
		John B. Anderson	Independent	5,719,437		6.6
		Ed Clark	Libertarian	920,859		1.0
1984	50	**Ronald W. Reagan**	Republican	54,281,858	525	59.2
		Walter F. Mondale	Democratic	37,457,215	13	40.8
1988	50	**George H. Bush**	Republican	47,917,341	426	54
		Michael Dukakis	Democratic	41,013,030	112	46
1992	50	**William Clinton**	Democratic	44,908,254	370	43.0
		George H. Bush	Republican	39,102,343	168	37.4
		Ross Perot	Independent	19,741,065		18.9
1996	50	**William Clinton**	Democratic	45,628,667	379	49.2
		Robert Dole	Republican	37,869,435	159	40.8
		Ross Perot	Reform	7,874,283	0	8.5

[1]Candidates receiving less than 1 percent of the popular vote have been omitted. For that reason the percentage of popular vote given for any election year may not total 100 percent.

PRESIDENTIAL ADMINISTRATIONS

President	Vice President	Secretary of State	Secretary of Treasury	Secretary of War	Secretary of Navy	Postmaster General	Attorney General
George Washington 1789–1797	John Adams 1789–1797	Thomas Jefferson 1789–1794 Edmund Randolph 1794–1795 Timothy Pickering 1795–1797	Alexander Hamilton 1789–1795 Oliver Wolcott 1795–1797	Henry Knox 1789–1795 Timothy Pickering 1795–1796 James McHenry 1796–1797		Samuel Osgood 1789–1791 Timothy Pickering 1791–1795 Joseph Habersham 1795–1797	Edmund Randolph 1789–1794 William Bradford 1794–1795 Charles Lee 1795–1797
John Adams 1797–1801	Thomas Jefferson 1797–1801	Timothy Pickering 1797–1800 John Marshall 1800–1801	Oliver Wolcott 1797–1801 Samuel Dexter 1801	James McHenry 1797–1800 Samuel Dexter 1800–1801	Benjamin Stoddert 1798–1801	Joseph Habersham 1797–1801	Charles Lee 1797–1801
Thomas Jefferson 1801–1809	Aaron Burr 1801–1805 George Clinton 1805–1809	James Madison 1801–1809	Samuel Dexter 1801 Albert Gallatin 1801–1809	Henry Dearborn 1801–1809	Benjamin Stoddert 1801 Robert Smith 1801–1809	Joseph Habersham 1801 Gideon Granger 1801–1809	Levi Lincoln 1801–1805 John Breckinridge 1805–1807 Caesar Rodney 1807–1809
James Madison 1809–1817	George Clinton 1809–1813 Elbridge Gerry 1813–1817	Robert Smith 1809–1811 James Monroe 1811–1817	Albert Gallatin 1809–1814 George Campbell 1814 Alexander Dallas 1814–1816 William Crawford 1816–1817	William Eustis 1809–1813 John Armstrong 1813–1814 James Monroe 1814–1815 William Crawford 1815–1817	Paul Hamilton 1809–1813 William Jones 1813–1814 Benjamin Crowninshield 1814–1817	Gideon Granger 1809–1814 Return Meigs 1814–1817	Caesar Rodney 1809–1811 William Pinkney 1811–1814 Richard Rush 1814–1817
James Monroe 1817–1825	Daniel D. Tompkins 1817–1825	John Quincy Adams 1817–1825	William Crawford 1817–1825	George Graham 1817 John C. Calhoun 1817–1825	Benjamin Crowninshield 1817–1818 Smith Thompson 1818–1823 Samuel Southard 1823–1825	Return Meigs 1817–1823 John McLean 1823–1825	Richard Rush 1817 William Wirt 1817–1825
John Quincy Adams 1825–1829	John C. Calhoun 1825–1829	Henry Clay 1825–1829	Richard Rush 1825–1829	James Barbour 1825–1828 Peter B. Porter 1828–1829	Samuel Southard 1825–1829	John McLean 1825–1829	William Wirt 1825–1829
Andrew Jackson 1829–1837	John C. Calhoun 1829–1833 Martin Van Buren 1833–1837	Martin Van Buren 1829–1831 Edward Livingston 1831–1833 Louis McLane 1833–1834 John Forsyth 1834–1837	Samuel Ingham 1829–1831 Louis McLane 1831–1833 William Duane 1833 Roger B. Taney 1833–1834 Levi Woodbury 1834–1837	John H. Eaton 1829–1831 Lewis Cass 1831–1837 Benjamin Butler 1837	John Branch 1829–1831 Levi Woodbury 1831–1834 Mahlon Dickerson 1834–1837	William Barry 1829–1835 Amos Kendall 1835–1837	John M. Berrien 1829–1831 Roger B. Taney 1831–1833 Benjamin Butler 1833–1837
Martin Van Buren 1837–1841	Richard M. Johnson 1837–1841	John Forsyth 1837–1841	Levi Woodbury 1837–1841	Joel R. Poinsett 1837–1841	Mahlon Dickerson 1837–1838 James K. Paulding 1838–1841	Amos Kendall 1837–1840 John M. Niles 1840–1841	Benjamin Butler 1837–1838 Felix Grundy 1838–1840 Henry D. Gilpin 1840–1841

(continued)

President	Vice President	Secretary of State	Secretary of Treasury	Secretary of War
William H. Harrison 1841	John Tyler 1841	Daniel Webster 1841	Thomas Ewing 1841	John Bell 1841
John Tyler 1841–1845		Daniel Webster 1841–1843 Hugh S. Legaré 1843 Abel P. Upshur 1843–1844 John C. Calhoun 1844–1845	Thomas Ewing 1841 Walter Forward 1841–1843 John C. Spencer 1843–1844 George M. Bibb 1844–1845	John Bell 1841 John C. Spencer 1841–1843 James M. Porter 1843–1844 William Wilkins 1844–1845
James K. Polk 1845–1849	George M. Dallas 1845–1849	James Buchanan 1845–1849	Robert J. Walker 1845–1849	William L. Marcy 1845–1849
Zachary Taylor 1849–1850	Millard Fillmore 1849–1850	John M. Clayton 1849–1850	William M. Meredith 1849–1850	George W. Crawford 1849–1850
Millard Fillmore 1850–1853		Daniel Webster 1850–1852 Edward Everett 1852–1853	Thomas Corwin 1850–1853	Charles M. Conrad 1850–1853
Franklin Pierce 1853–1857	William R. King 1853–1857	William L. Marcy 1853–1857	James Guthrie 1853–1857	Jefferson Davis 1853–1857
James Buchanan 1857–1861	John C. Breckinridge 1857–1861	Lewis Cass 1857–1860 Jeremiah S. Black 1860–1861	Howell Cobb 1857–1860 Philip F. Thomas 1860–1861 John A. Dix 1861	John B. Floyd 1857–1861 Joseph Holt 1861
Abraham Lincoln 1861–1865	Hannibal Hamlin 1861–1865 Andrew Johnson 1865	William H. Seward 1861–1865	Salmon P. Chase 1861–1864 William P. Fessenden 1864–1865 Hugh McCulloch 1865	Simon Cameron 1861–1862 Edwin M. Stanton 1862–1865
Andrew Johnson 1865–1869		William H. Seward 1865–1869	Hugh McCulloch 1865–1869	Edwin M. Stanton 1865–1867 Ulysses S. Grant 1867–1868 John M. Schofield 1868–1869
Ulysses S. Grant 1869–1877	Schuyler Colfax 1869–1873 Henry Wilson 1873–1877	Elihu B. Washburne 1869 Hamilton Fish 1869–1877	George S. Boutwell 1869–1873 William A. Richardson 1873–1874 Benjamin H. Bristow 1874–1876 Lot M. Morrill 1876–1877	John A. Rawlins 1869 William T. Sherman 1869 William W. Belknap 1869–1876 Alphonso Taft 1876 James D. Cameron 1876–1877

Secretary of Navy	Postmaster General	Attorney General	Secretary of Interior
George E. Badger 1841	Francis Granger 1841	John J. Crittenden 1841	
George E. Badger 1841 Abel P. Upshur 1841–1843 David Henshaw 1843–1844 Thomas Gilmer 1844 John Y. Mason 1844–1845	Francis Granger 1841 Charles A. Wickliffe 1841–1845	John J. Crittenden 1841 Hugh S. Legaré 1841–1843 John Nelson 1843–1845	
George Bancroft 1845–1846 John Y. Mason 1846–1849	Cave Johnson 1845–1849	John Y. Mason 1845–1846 Nathan Clifford 1846–1848 Isaac Toucey 1848–1849	
William B. Preston 1849–1850	Jacob Collamer 1849–1850	Reverdy Johnson 1849–1850	Thomas Ewing 1849–1850
William A. Graham 1850–1852 John P. Kennedy 1852–1853	Nathan K. Hall 1850–1852 Sam D. Hubbard 1852–1853	John J. Crittenden 1850–1853	Thomas McKennan 1850 A. H. H. Stuart 1850–1853
James C. Dobbin 1853–1857	James Campbell 1853–1857	Caleb Cushing 1853–1857	Robert McClelland 1853–1857
Isaac Toucey 1857–1861	Aaron V. Brown 1857–1859 Joseph Holt 1859–1861 Horatio King 1861	Jeremiah S. Black 1857–1860 Edwin M. Stanton 1860–1861	Jacob Thompson 1857–1861
Gideon Welles 1861–1865	Horatio King 1861 Montgomery Blair 1861–1864 William Dennison 1864–1865	Edward Bates 1861–1864 James Speed 1864–1865	Caleb B. Smith 1861–1863 John P. Usher 1863–1865
Gideon Welles 1865–1869	William Dennison 1865–1866 Alexander Randall 1866–1869 William M. Evarts 1868–1869	James Speed 1865–1866 Henry Stanbery 1866–1868 O. H. Browning 1866–1869	John P. Usher 1865 James Harlan 1865–1866
Adolph E. Borie 1869 George M. Robeson 1869–1877	John A. J. Creswell 1869–1874 James W. Marshall 1874 Marshall Jewell 1874–1876 James N. Tyner 1876–1877	Ebenezer R. Hoar 1869–1870 Amos T. Akerman 1870–1871 G. H. Williams 1871–1875 Edwards Pierrepont 1875–1876 Alphonso Taft 1876–1877	Jacob D. Cox 1869–1870 Columbus Delano 1870–1875 Zachariah Chandler 1875–1877

President	Vice President	Secretary of State	Secretary of Treasury	Secretary of War	Secretary of Navy
Rutherford B. Hayes 1877–1881	William A. Wheeler 1877–1881	William M. Evarts 1877–1881	John Sherman 1877–1881	George W. McCrary 1877–1879 Alexander Ramsey 1879–1881	R. W. Thompson 1877–1881 Nathan Goff, Jr. 1881
James A. Garfield 1881	Chester A. Arthur 1881	James G. Blaine 1881	William Windom 1881	Robert T. Lincoln 1881	William H. Hunt 1881
Chester A. Arthur 1881–1885		F. T. Frelinghuysen 1881–1885	Charles J. Folger 1881–1884 Walter Q. Gresham 1884 Hugh McCulloch 1884–1885	Robert T. Lincoln 1881–1885	William E. Chandler 1881–1885
Grover Cleveland 1885–1889	T. A. Hendricks 1885	Thomas F. Bayard 1885–1889	Daniel Manning 1885–1887 Charles S. Fairchild 1887–1889	William C. Endicott 1885–1889	William C. Whitney 1885–1889
Benjamin Harrison 1889–1893	Levi P. Morton 1889–1893	James G. Blaine 1889–1892 John W. Foster 1892–1893	William Windom 1889–1891 Charles Foster 1892–1893	Redfield Procter 1889–1891 Stephen B. Elkins 1891–1893	Benjamin F. Tracy 1889–1893
Grover Cleveland 1893–1897	Adlai E. Stevenson 1893–1897	Walter Q. Gresham 1893–1895 Richard Olney 1895–1897	John G. Carlisle 1893–1897	Daniel S. Lamont 1893–1897	Hilary A. Herbert 1893–1897
William McKinley 1897–1901	Garret A. Hobart 1897–1899 Theodore Roosevelt 1901	John Sherman 1897–1898 William R. Day 1898 John Hay 1898–1901	Lyman J. Gage 1897–1901	Russell A. Alger 1897–1899 Elihu Root 1899–1901	John D. Long 1897–1901
Theodore Roosevelt 1901–1909	Charles Fairbanks 1905–1909	John Hay 1901–1905 Elihu Root 1905–1909 Robert Bacon 1909	Lyman J. Gage 1901–1902 Leslie M. Shaw 1902–1907 George B. Cortelyou 1907–1909	Elihu Root 1901–1904 William H. Taft 1904–1908 Luke E. Wright 1908–1909	John D. Long 1901–1902 William H. Moody 1902–1904 Paul Morton 1904–1905 Charles J. Bonaparte 1905–1906 Victor H. Metcalf 1906–1908 T. H. Newberry 1908–1909
William H. Taft 1909–1913	James S. Sherman 1909–1913	Philander C. Knox 1909–1913	Franklin MacVeagh 1909–1913	Jacob M. Dickinson 1909–1911 Henry L. Stimson 1911–1913	George von L. Meyer 1909–1913
Woodrow Wilson 1913–1921	Thomas R. Marshall 1913–1921	William J. Bryan 1913–1915 Robert Lansing 1915–1920 Bainbridge Colby 1920–1921	William G. McAdoo 1913–1918 Carter Glass 1918–1920 David F. Houston 1920–1921	Lindley M. Garrison 1913–1916 Newton D. Baker 1916–1921	Josephus Daniels 1913–1921

Postmaster General	Attorney General	Secretary of Interior	Secretary of Agriculture	Secretary of Commerce and Labor
David M. Key 1877–1880 Horace Maynard 1880–1881	Charles Devens 1877–1881	Carl Schurz 1877–1881		
Thomas L. James 1881	Wayne MacVeagh 1881	S. J. Kirkwood 1881		
Thomas L. James 1881 Timothy O. Howe 1881–1883 Walter Q. Gresham 1883–1884 Frank Hatton 1884–1885	B. H. Brewster 1881–1885	Henry M. Teller 1881–1885		
William F. Vilas 1885–1888 Don M. Dickinson 1888–1889	A. H. Garland 1885–1889	L. Q. C. Lamar 1885–1888 William F. Vilas 1888–1889	Norman J. Colman 1889	
John Wanamaker 1889–1893	W. H. H. Miller 1889–1893	John W. Noble 1889–1893	Jeremiah M. Rusk 1889–1893	
Wilson S. Bissel 1893–1895 William L. Wilson 1895–1897	Richard Olney 1893–1895 Judson Harmon 1895–1897	Hoke Smith 1893–1896 David R. Francis 1896–1897	J. Sterling Morton 1893–1897	
James A. Gary 1897–1898 Charles E. Smith 1898–1901	Joseph McKenna 1897–1898 John W. Griggs 1898–1901 Philander C. Knox 1901	Cornelius N. Bliss 1897–1898 E. A. Hitchcock 1898–1901	James Wilson 1897–1901	
Charles E. Smith 1901–1902 Henry C. Payne 1902–1904 Robert J. Wynne 1904–1905 George B. Cortelyou 1905—1907 George von L. Meyer 1907–1909	Philander C. Knox 1901–1904 William H. Moody 1904–1906 Charles J. Bonaparte 1906–1909	E. A. Hitchcock 1901–1907 James R. Garfield 1907–1909	James Wilson 1901–1909	George B. Cortelyou 1903–1904 Victor H. Metcalf 1904–1906 Oscar S. Straus 1906–1909
Frank H. Hitchcock 1909–1913	G. W. Wickersham 1909–1913	R. A. Ballinger 1909–1911 Walter L. Fisher 1911–1913	James Wilson 1909–1913	Charles Nagel 1909–1913

				Secretary of Commerce	Secretary of Labor
Albert S. Burleson 1913–1921	J. C. McReynolds 1913–1914 T. W. Gregory 1914–1919 A. Mitchell Palmer 1919–1921	Franklin K. Lane 1913–1920 John B. Payne 1920–1921	David F. Houston 1913–1920 E. T. Meredith 1920–1921	W. C. Redfield 1913–1919 J. W. Alexander 1919–1921	William B. Wilson 1913–1921

President	Vice President	Secretary of State	Secretary of Treasury	Secretary of War	Secretary of Navy	Postmaster General	Attorney General
Warren G. Harding 1921–1923	Calvin Coolidge 1921–1923	Charles E. Hughes 1921–1923	Andrew W. Mellon 1921–1923	John W. Weeks 1921–1923	Edwin Denby 1921–1923	Will H. Hays 1921–1922 Hubert Work 1922–1923 Harry S. New 1923	H. M. Daugherty 1921–1923
Calvin Coolidge 1923–1929	Charles G. Dawes 1925–1929	Charles E. Hughes 1923–1925 Frank B. Kellogg 1925–1929	Andrew W. Mellon 1923–1929	John W. Weeks 1923–1925 Dwight F. Davis 1925–1929	Edwin Denby 1923–1924 Curtis D. Wilbur 1924–1929	Harry S. New 1923–1929	H. M. Daugherty 1923–1924 Harlan F. Stone 1924–1925 John G. Sargent 1925–1929
Herbert C. Hoover 1929–1933	Charles Curtis 1929–1933	Henry L. Stimson 1929–1933	Andrew W. Mellon 1929–1932 Ogden L. Mills 1932–1933	James W. Good 1929 Patrick J. Hurley 1929–1933	Charles F. Adams 1929–1933	Walter F. Brown 1929–1933	J. D. Mitchell 1929–1933
Franklin Delano Roosevelt 1933–1945	John Nance Garner 1933–1941 Henry A. Wallace 1941–1945 Harry S. Truman 1945	Cordell Hull 1933–1944 E. R. Stettinius, Jr. 1944–1945	William H. Woodin 1933–1934 Henry Morgenthau, Jr. 1934–1945	George H. Dern 1933–1936 Harry H. Woodring 1936–1940 Henry L. Stimson 1940–1945	Claude A. Swanson 1933–1940 Charles Edison 1940 Frank Knox 1940–1944 James V. Forrestal 1944–1945	James A. Farley 1933–1940 Frank C. Walker 1940–1945	H. S. Cummings 1933–1939 Frank Murphy 1939–1940 Robert Jackson 1940–1941 Francis Biddel 1941–1945
Harry S. Truman 1945–1953	Alben W. Barkley 1949–1953	James F. Byrnes 1945–1947 George C. Marshall 1947–1949 Dean G. Acheson 1949–1953	Fred M. Vinson 1945–1946 John W. Snyder 1946–1953	Robert P. Patterson 1945–1947 Kenneth C. Royall 1947 *Secretary of Defense* James V. Forrestal 1947–1949 Louis A. Johnson 1949–1950 George C. Marshall 1950–1951 Robert A. Lovett 1951–1953	James V. Forrestal 1945–1947	R. E. Hannegan 1945–1947 Jesse M. Donaldson 1947–1953	Tom C. Clark 1945–1949 J. H. McGrath 1949–1952 James P. McGranery 1952–1953
Dwight D. Eisenhower 1953–1961	Richard M. Nixon 1953–1961	John Foster Dulles 1953–1959 Christian A. Herter 1957–1961	George M. Humphrey 1953–1957 Robert B. Anderson 1957–1961	Charles E. Wilson 1953–1957 Neil H. McElroy 1957–1961 Thomas S. Gates 1959–1961		A. E. Summerfield 1953–1961	H. Brownell, Jr. 1953–1957 William P. Rogers 1957–1961
John F. Kennedy 1961–1963	Lyndon B. Johnson 1961–1963	Dean Rusk 1961–1963	C. Douglas Dillon 1961–1963	Robert S. McNamara 1961–1963		J. Edward Day 1961–1963 John A. Gronouski 1961–1963	Robert F. Kennedy 1961–1963
Lyndon B. Johnson 1963–1969	Hubert H. Humphrey 1965–1969	Dean Rusk 1963–1969	C. Douglas Dillon 1963–1965 Henry H. Fowler 1965–1968 Joseph W. Barr 1968–1969	Robert S. McNamara 1963–1968 Clark M. Clifford 1968–1969		John A. Gronouski 1963–1965 Lawrence F. O'Brien 1965–1968 W. Marvin Watson 1968–1969	Robert F. Kennedy 1963–1965 N. deB. Katzenbach 1965–1967 Ramsey Clark 1967–1969

Secretary of Interior	Secretary of Agriculture	Secretary of Commerce	Secretary of Labor	Secretary of Health, Education and Welfare	Secretary of Housing and Urban Development	Secretary of Transportation
Albert B. Fall 1921–1923 Hubert Work 1923	Henry C. Wallace 1921–1923	Herbert C. Hoover 1921–1923	James J. Davis 1921–1923			
Hubert Work 1923–1928 Roy O. West 1928–1929	Henry C. Wallace 1923–1924 Howard M. Gore 1924–1925 W. J. Jardine 1925–1929	Herbert C. Hoover 1923–1928 William F. Whiting 1928–1929	James J. Davis 1923–1929			
Ray L. Wilbur 1929–1933	Arthur M. Hyde 1929–1933	Robert P. Lamont 1929–1932 William N. Doak 1930–1933	James J. Davis 1929–1930			
		Roy D. Chapin 1932–1933				
Harold L. Ickes 1933–1945	Henry A. Wallace 1933–1940 Claude R. Wickard 1940–1945	Daniel C. Roper 1933–1939 Harry L. Hopkins 1939–1940 Jesse Jones 1940–1945 Henry A. Wallace 1945	Frances Perkins 1933–1945			
Harold L. Ickes 1945–1946 Julius A. Krug 1946–1949 Oscar L. Chapman 1949–1953	C. P. Anderson 1945–1948 C. F. Brannan 1948–1953	W. A. Harriman 1946–1948 Charles Sawyer 1948–1953	L. B. Schwellenbach 1945–1948 Maurice J. Tobin 1948–1953			
Douglas McKay 1953–1956 Fred Seaton 1956–1961	Ezra T. Benson 1953–1961	Sinclair Weeks 1953–1958 Lewis L. Strauss 1958–1961	Martin P. Durkin 1953 James P. Mitchell 1953–1961	Oveta Culp Hobby 1953–1955 Marion B. Folsom 1955–1958 Arthur S. Flemming 1958–1961		
Stewart L. Udall 1961–1963	Orville L. Freeman 1961–1963	Luther H. Hodges 1961–1963	Arthur J. Goldberg 1961–1963 W. Willard Wirtz 1962–1963	A. H. Ribicoff 1961–1963 Anthony J. Celebrezze 1962–1963		
Stewart L. Udall 1963–1969	Orville L. Freeman 1963–1969	Luther H. Hodges 1963–1965 John T. Connor 1965–1967 Alexander B. Trowbridge 1967–1968 C. R. Smith 1968–1969	W. Willard Wirtz 1963–1969	Anthony J. Celebrezze 1963–1965 John W. Gardner 1965–1968 Wilbur J. Cohen 1968–1969	Robert C. Weaver 1966–1968 Robert C. Wood 1968–1969	Alan S. Boyd 1966–1969

President	Vice President	Secretary of State	Secretary of Treasury	Secretary of Defense	Postmaster General[1]	Attorney General	Secretary of Interior	Secretary of Agriculture
Richard M. Nixon 1969–1974	Spiro T. Agnew 1969–1973 Gerald R. Ford 1973–1974	William P. Rogers 1969–1973 Henry A. Kissinger 1973–1974	David M. Kennedy 1969–1970 John B. Connally 1970–1972 George P. Schultz 1972–1974 William E. Simon 1974	Melvin R. Laird 1969–1973 Elliot L. Richardson 1973 James R. Schlesinger 1973–1974	Winton M. Blount 1969–1971	John M. Mitchell 1969–1972 Richard G. Kleindienst 1972–1973 Elliot L. Richardson 1973 William B. Saxbe 1974	Walter J. Hickel 1969–1971 Rogers C. B. Morton 1971–1974	Clifford M. Hardin 1969–1971 Earl L. Butz 1971–1974
Gerald R. Ford 1974–1977	Nelson A. Rockefeller 1974–1977	Henry A. Kissinger 1974–1977	William E. Simon 1974–1977	James R. Schlesinger 1974–1975 Donald H. Rumsfeld 1975–1977		William B. Saxbe 1974–1975 Edward H. Levi 1975–1977	Rogers C. B. Morton 1974–1975 Stanley K. Hathaway 1975 Thomas D. Kleppe 1975–1977	Earl L. Butz 1974–1976
Jimmy Carter 1977–1981	Walter F. Mondale 1977–1981	Cyrus R. Vance 1977–1980 Edmund S. Muskie 1980–1981	W. Michael Blumenthal 1977–1979 G. William Miller 1979–1981	Harold Brown 1977–1981		Griffin Bell 1977–1979 Benjamin R. Civiletti 1979–1981	Cecil D. Andrus 1977–1981	Robert Bergland 1977–1981
Ronald W. Reagan 1981–1989	George H. Bush 1981–1989	Alexander M. Haig, Jr. 1981–1982 George P. Shultz 1982–1989	Donald T. Regan 1981–1985 James A. Baker 1985–1988 Nicholas F. Brady 1988–1989	Caspar W. Weinberger 1981–1987 Frank C. Carlucci 1987–1989		William French Smith 1981–1985 Edwin Meese 1985–1988 Richard Thornburgh 1988–1989	James G. Watt 1981–1983 William P. Clark 1983–1985 Donald P. Hodel 1985–1989	John R. Block 1981–1986 Richard E. Lyng 1986–1989
George H. Bush 1989–1992	J. Danforth Quayle 1989–1992	James A. Baker 1989–1992 Lawrence S. Eagleburger 1992	Nicholas F. Brady 1989–1992	Richard Cheney 1989–1992		Richard Thornburgh 1989–1990 William Barr 1990–1992	Manuel Lujan 1989–1992	Clayton Yeutter 1989–1990 Edward Madigan 1990–1992
William Clinton 1993–	Albert Gore 1993–	Warren M. Christopher 1993–1996 Madeleine K. Albright 1997–	Lloyd Bentsen 1993–1994 Robert E. Rubin 1994–	Les Aspin 1993–1994 William J. Perry 1994–1996 William S. Cohen 1997–		Janet Reno 1993–	Bruce Babbitt 1993–	Mike Espy 1993–1994 Dan Glickman 1995–

[1]On July 1, 1971, the Post Office became an independent agency. After that date, the Postmaster General was no longer a member of the Cabinet.
[2]Acting Secretary

Secretary of Commerce	Secretary of Labor	Secretary of Health, Education and Welfare	Secretary of Housing and Urban Development	Secretary of Transportation	Secretary of Energy	Secretary of Veterans Affairs
Maurice H. Stans 1969–1972 Peter G. Peterson 1972 Frederick B. Dent 1972–1974	George P. Shultz 1969–1970 James D. Hodgson 1970–1973 Peter J. Brennan 1973–1974	Robert H. Finch 1969–1970 Elliot L. Richardson 1970–1973 Caspar W. Weinberger 1973–1974	George W. Romney 1969–1973 James T. Lynn 1973–1974	John A. Volpe 1969–1973 Claude S. Brinegar 1973–1974		
Frederick B. Dent 1974–1975 Rogers C. B. Morton 1975 Elliot L. Richardson 1975–1977	Peter J. Brennan 1974–1975 John T. Dunlop 1975–1976 W. J. Usery 1976–1977	Caspar W. Weinberger 1974–1975 Forrest D. Matthews 1975–1977	James T. Lynn 1974–1975 Carla A. Hills 1975–1977	Claude S. Brinegar 1974–1975 William T. Coleman 1975–1977		
Juanita Kreps 1977–1981	F. Ray Marshall 1977–1981	Joseph Califano 1977–1979 Patricia Roberts Harris 1979–1980	Patricia Roberts Harris 1977–1979 Moon Landrieu 1979–1981	Brock Adams 1977–1979 Neil E. Goldschmidt 1979–1981	James R. Schlesinger 1977–1979 Charles W. Duncan, Jr. 1979–1981	

Secretary of Health and Human Services	Secretary of Education
Patricia Roberts Harris 1980–1981	Shirley M. Hufstedler 1980–1981

Secretary of Commerce	Secretary of Labor	Secretary of Health and Human Services	Secretary of Education	Secretary of Housing and Urban Development	Secretary of Transportation	Secretary of Energy	Secretary of Veterans Affairs
Malcolm Baldridge 1981–1987 C. William Verity, Jr. 1987–1989	Raymond J. Donovan 1981–1985 William E. Brock 1985–1987 Ann Dore McLaughlin 1987–1989	Richard S. Schweiker 1981–1983 Margaret M. Heckler 1983–1985 Otis R. Bowen 1985–1989	Terrell H. Bell 1981–1985 William J. Bennett 1985–1988 Lauro Fred Cavazos 1988–1989	Samuel R. Pierce, Jr. 1981–1989	Drew Lewis 1981–1983 Elizabeth H. Dole 1983–1987 James H. Burnley 1987–1989	James B. Edwards 1981–1982 Donald P. Hodel 1982–1985 John S. Harrington 1985–1989	
Robert Mosbacher 1989–1991 Barbara Franklin 1991–1992	Elizabeth Dole 1989–19 Lynn Martin 1992	Louis Sullivan 1989–1992	Lamar Alexander 1990–1992	Jack Kemp 1989–1992	Samuel Skinner 1989–1990 Andrew Card 1990–1992	James Watkins 1989–1992	Edward J. Derwinski 1989–1992
Ronald H. Brown 1993–1996 William M. Daley 1997–	Robert B. Reich 1993–1996 Alexis M. Herman 1997–	Donna E. Shalala 1993–	Richard W. Riley 1993–	Henry G. Cisneros 1993–1996 Andrew M. Cuomo 1997–	Federico F. Peña 1993–1996 Rodney E. Slater 1997–	Hazel O'Leary 1993–1996 Federico F. Peña 1997–1998 Bill Richardson 1998–	Jesse Brown 1993–1997 Togo D. West, Jr.[2] 1998–

JUSTICES OF THE U.S. SUPREME COURT

Name	Term of Service	Years of Service	Appointed By	Name	Term of Service	Years of Service	Appointed By
John Jay	1789–1795	5	Washington	Rufus W. Peckham	1895–1909	14	Cleveland
John Rutledge	1789–1791	1	Washington	Joseph McKenna	1898–1925	26	McKinley
William Cushing	1789–1810	20	Washington	Oliver W. Holmes, Jr.	1902–1932	30	T. Roosevelt
James Wilson	1789–1798	8	Washington	William R. Day	1903–1922	19	T. Roosevelt
John Blair	1789–1796	6	Washington	William H. Moody	1906–1910	3	T. Roosevelt
Robert H. Harrison	1789–1790	—	Washington	Horace H. Lurton	1910–1914	4	Taft
James Iredell	1790–1799	9	Washington	Charles E. Hughes	1910–1916	5	Taft
Thomas Johnson	1791–1793	1	Washington	Willis Van Devanter	1911–1937	26	Taft
William Paterson	1793–1806	13	Washington	Joseph R. Lamar	1911–1916	5	Taft
John Rutledge[1]	1795	—	Washington	**Edward D. White**	1910–1921	11	Taft
Samuel Chase	1796–1811	15	Washington	Mahlon Pitney	1912–1922	10	Taft
Oliver Ellsworth	1796–1800	4	Washington	James C. McReynolds	1914–1941	26	Wilson
Bushrod Washington	1798–1829	31	J. Adams	Louis D. Brandeis	1916–1939	22	Wilson
Alfred Moore	1799–1804	4	J. Adams	John H. Clarke	1916–1922	6	Wilson
John Marshall	1801–1835	34	J. Adams	**William H. Taft**	1921–1930	8	Harding
William Johnson	1804–1834	30	Jefferson	George Sutherland	1922–1938	15	Harding
H. Brockholst Livingston	1806–1823	16	Jefferson	Pierce Butler	1922–1939	16	Harding
Thomas Todd	1807–1826	18	Jefferson	Edward T. Sanford	1923–1930	7	Harding
Joseph Story	1811–1845	33	Madison	Harlan F. Stone	1925–1941	16	Coolidge
Gabriel Duval	1811–1835	24	Madison	**Charles E. Hughes**	1930–1941	11	Hoover
Smith Thompson	1823–1843	20	Monroe	Owen J. Roberts	1930–1945	15	Hoover
Robert Trimble	1826–1828	2	J. Q. Adams	Benjamin N. Cardozo	1932–1938	6	Hoover
John McLean	1829–1861	32	Jackson	Hugo L. Black	1937–1971	34	F. Roosevelt
Henry Baldwin	1830–1844	14	Jackson	Stanley F. Reed	1938–1957	19	F. Roosevelt
James M. Wayne	1835–1867	32	Jackson	Felix Frankfurter	1939–1962	23	F. Roosevelt
Roger B. Taney	1836–1864	28	Jackson	William O. Douglas	1939–1975	36	F. Roosevelt
Philip P. Barbour	1836–1841	4	Jackson	Frank Murphy	1940–1949	9	F. Roosevelt
John Catron	1837–1865	28	Van Buren	**Harlan F. Stone**	1941–1946	5	F. Roosevelt
John McKinley	1837–1852	15	Van Buren	James F. Byrnes	1941–1942	1	F. Roosevelt
Peter V. Daniel	1841–1860	19	Van Buren	Robert H. Jackson	1941–1954	13	F. Roosevelt
Samuel Nelson	1845–1872	27	Tyler	Wiley B. Rutledge	1943–1949	6	F. Roosevelt
Levi Woodbury	1845–1851	5	Polk	Harold H. Burton	1945–1958	13	Truman
Robert C. Grier	1846–1870	23	Polk	**Fred M. Vinson**	1946–1953	7	Truman
Benjamin R. Curtis	1851–1857	6	Fillmore	Tom C. Clark	1949–1967	18	Truman
John A. Campbell	1853–1861	8	Pierce	Sherman Minton	1949–1956	7	Truman
Nathan Clifford	1858–1881	23	Buchanan	**Earl Warren**	1953–1969	16	Eisenhower
Noah H. Swayne	1862–1881	18	Lincoln	John Marshall Harlan	1955–1971	16	Eisenhower
Samuel F. Miller	1862–1890	28	Lincoln	William J. Brennan, Jr.	1956–1990	34	Eisenhower
David Davis	1862–1877	14	Lincoln	Charles E. Whittaker	1957–1962	5	Eisenhower
Stephen J. Field	1863–1897	34	Lincoln	Potter Stewart	1958–1981	23	Eisenhower
Salmon P. Chase	1864–1873	8	Lincoln	Byron R. White	1962–1993	31	Kennedy
William Strong	1870–1880	10	Grant	Arthur J. Goldberg	1962–1965	3	Kennedy
Joseph P. Bradley	1870–1892	22	Grant	Abe Fortas	1965–1969	4	Johnson
Ward Hunt	1873–1882	9	Grant	Thurgood Marshall	1967–1994	24	Johnson
Morrison R. Waite	1874–1888	14	Grant	**Warren E. Burger**	1969–1986	18	Nixon
John M. Harlan	1877–1911	34	Hayes	Harry A. Blackmun	1970–1994	24	Nixon
William B. Woods	1880–1887	7	Hayes	Lewis F. Powell, Jr.	1971–1987	15	Nixon
Stanley Matthews	1881–1889	7	Garfield	**William H. Rehnquist**[2]	1971–	—	Nixon
Horace Gray	1882–1902	20	Arthur	John P. Stevens III	1975–	—	Ford
Samuel Blatchford	1882–1893	11	Arthur	Sandra Day O'Connor	1981–	—	Reagan
Lucius Q. C. Lamar	1888–1893	5	Cleveland	Antonin Scalia	1986–	—	Reagan
Melville W. Fuller	1888–1910	21	Cleveland	Anthony M. Kennedy	1988–	—	Reagan
David J. Brewer	1890–1910	20	B. Harrison	David Souter	1990–	—	Bush
Henry B. Brown	1890–1906	16	B. Harrison	Clarence Thomas	1991–	—	Bush
George Shiras, Jr.	1892–1903	10	B. Harrison	Ruth Bader Ginsburg	1993–	—	Clinton
Howell E. Jackson	1893–1895	2	B. Harrison	Stephen G. Breyer	1994–	—	Clinton
Edward D. White	1894–1910	16	Cleveland				

Note: Chief Justices appear in bold type.

[1]Acting Chief Justice; Senate refused to confirm appointment.

[2]Chief Justice from 1986 on (Reagan administration).

CHAPTER 16

p. 534 Reproduced from the Collections of the Library of Congress. **p. 539 (left)** The Granger Collection, New York. **p. 539 (right)** Corbis - Bettmann. **p. 540 (left)** The Granger Collection, New York. **p. 540 (right)** California History Section, California State Library. **p. 542** The Granger Collection, New York. **p. 543** The Granger Collection, New York. **p. 544** The Granger Collection, New York. **p. 545** Corbis-Bettmann. **p. 546** The Granger Collection, New York. **p. 549** The Granger Collection, New York. **p. 550** no credit necessary. **p. 552** Reproduced from the Collections of the Library of Congress. **p. 557 (left)** The Granger Collection, New York. **p. 557 (right)** The Granger Collection, New York. **p. 561** Kansas State Historical Society. **p. 562** The Granger Collection, New York. **p. 564** The Granger Collection, New York.

PASSAGES 1

p. xxxii (center) © Texas Inprint / David Sams. **p. xxxii (left)** North Wind Picture Archives. **p. xxxii (right)** Photo courtesy of the James Ford Bell Library, University of Minnesota. **p. 1 (right)** Colonial Williamsburg Foundation. **p. 2 (bottom)** Colonial Williamsburg Foundation. **p. 2 (top)** Rare Books Division, The New York Public Library. Astor, Lenox and Tilden Foundations. **p. 3 (left)** no credit necessary. **p. 3 (right)** Abby Aldrich Rockefeller Folk Art Center, Williamsburg, VA.

PASSAGES 2

p. 144 © Jonathan Nourok / PhotoEdit. **p. 145 (left)** The Granger Collection, New York. **p. 145 (right)** Reproduced from the Collections of the Library of Congress. **p. 146** New Haven Colony Historical Society. **p. 146 (left)** By permission of Yale University Press. **p. 147 (right)** Maryland Historical Society, Baltimore, Maryland.

PASSAGES 3

p. 284 (left) The Granger Collection. **p. 284 (right)** Eno Collection. Miriam and Ira D. Wallach Division of Art, Prints and Photographs. The New York Public Library. Astor, Lenox and Tilden Foundations. **p. 285 (bottom)** Collection of the Oakland Museum of California, Kahn Collection. **p. 285 (left)** The J. Paul Getty Museum, Los Angeles. **p. 285 (top)** Skillman Library, Lafayette College. **p. 287** The Granger Collection, New York.

PASSAGES 4

p. 420 (bottom) West Point Museum Collection, United States Military Academy. **p. 420 (top)** Reproduced from the Collections of the Library of Congress. **p. 421** © Stock Montage, Inc. **p. 422** From the Collections of the Library of Congress. **p. 423** Winslow Homer, *Sunday Morning in Virginia* 1877 Cincinnati Art Museum, John M. Emerey Fund. Acc.#1924.247.

INDEX

Abolition and abolitionism, 102, 126, 334, 340–342, 370–372
  Brown, John, and, 447–448
  in Civil War, 487
  Garrison and, 340–341
  Kansas and, 428
  Kansas-Nebraska Act and, 416
  Lincoln and, 445
  in Pennsylvania, 194
  after revolution, 193–195
  Thirteenth Amendment and, 515–516
  in Virginia, 259
Abortion, 557
Absolute Right to an Education (Mann), 364–365
Acadia and Acadians, 97. *See also* Nova Scotia
  Louisiana and, 153–154
Acculturation, Native Americans and, 255, 256
Ácoma, 43, *43*
"Act Concerning Religion" (1649) (Maryland), 68
Activism. *See also* Protest(s); Reform and reformers
  reform and, 320
  utopian communities and, 399–400
  women's rights and, 400–403
Act of Supremacy (England), 35
Act of Uniformity (England), 35
Adams, Abigail, 166
Adams, Charles Francis, 547
Adams, John, 163, *172, 184*
  on Bank of the United States, 232
  Boston Massacre and, 161
  Constitution and, 209
  election of 1800 and, 260
  France and, 260
  midnight appointments and, 264
  peace settlement and, 184–185
  presidency of, 244–248
  as vice president, 146, 223
  on voting rights, 191
  War of 1812 and, 278
Adams, John Quincy, 299, *315*
  Amistad case and, 370
  election of 1824 and, 316–317
  National Republicans of, 343
  as president, 325–327
  Treaty of Ghent and, 281
  War of 1812 and, 278
Adams, Samuel, 162, *162,* 163, 165
  Constitution and, 209
Adams-Onís Treaty, 299
Africa. *See also* West Africa
  Atlantic slave trade and, 18–21
  European map of, 19
African Americans. *See also* Abolition and abolitionism; Ku Klux Klan; Race and racism; Rights; Slaves and slavery; Voting rights
  abolitionism and, 193–195, 334
  casualties in Civil War, 517
  census of 1790 and, 228
  citizenship and, 527
  as Civil War soldiers, *500,* 501, 506
  in Civil War South, 474–475
  in colonial British America (1760), 126–129
  Dred Scott case and, 432–434
  emancipation in South and, 518–521, *520*
  free blacks in North, 256–259
  frontier robbers and, 158
  Gold Rush and, 395
  importance to Union of, *510,* 512–513
  Johnson, Andrew, and, 526, *526*
  lifestyle of, 100
  Lincoln on rights of, 446–447

  migration to Africa by, 312
  mobilization after Civil War, 521–524
  Native Americans and, 295
  in North, 409–410
  number enslaved (1800, 1810), 256
  population of, 101
  protests by, 156
  during Reconstruction, 529–531, *530,* 558
  religion and, 253
  revolution and, 147, 168–169, 179, 182
  South and, 373–374
  Special Field Order 15 and, 515–517
  Truth, Sojourner, and, 401–402, *401*
  Vesey's revolt and, 313–314
  violence against, 558–559
  voting rights and, 191
  women workers and, 555
African Methodist Episcopal church, 257, *257*
African people. *See also* Slaves and slavery
  in British mainland colonies, 2
  European colonization and, 7
  numbers of, 110
  slavery and, 1, 34, 97–102
  in Virginia, 50–51
Agriculture. *See also* Crops; Farms and farming
  of Eastern Woodland Indians, 12–13
  labor, after Civil War, *545*
  land clearing and, 13
  Native Americans and, 9–10
  slaves and, 100–101
  women and, 13
Aix-la-Chapelle, Treaty of, 130
Akerman, Amos T., 544, 545
Alabama (ship), 543
Alamance Creek, 158
Alamo, 352, *352*
Alarcón, Hernando de, 27
Alaska, purchase of, 537
Albany Congress, 131
Albemarle Sound, 69
Alcaçovas, Treaty of, 21
Alcohol and alcoholism, 236. *See also* Prohibition; Temperance
  temperance movement and, 321, 553
  Washingtonians and, 369–370
Alcott, Bronson, 363, 365
Alcott, Louisa May, "Journal" of, 470–471
Alexander VI (Spain), Line of Demarcation and, 23
Algonquian languages, 54
Algonquian people, 12, *12,* 47, 54, 75
  men's roles and, 14, *14*
  Metacom's War and, 79–80
  women's roles and, 14
Alien Act, 247
Alien and Sedition acts, 246–247, 248
Alien Enemies Act, 247
Aliens. *See* Immigrants and immigration
Allen, Charles, 399
Allen, Ethan, 166
Allen, Richard, 257, *257*
Alliance, Treaty of, 176
Alliances
  with France, 176, 260
  French-Spanish, 96
  with Native Americans, 105
Alphabet, Cherokee, 298
Alton, Illinois, 370–371
Amendments
  Bill of Rights as, 224–226
  procedures for, 213
America(s). *See also* North America; South America
  African slaves in, 34

  colonization of, 2, 3, 30
  before Columbus, 9
  exploration of, xxxii
  forced labor in, 33–34
  Native Americans in, 8–14
  Protestant and, 34–37
  settlement of, xxxii
  Spanish colonial societies in, 31–33
  Spanish exploration of, 25–34
American Anti-Slavery Society, 341, 370
  abolitionist differences and, 371
American Bible Society, 321
American Board of Customs Commissioners, 158
American Colonization Society, 312
American Indians. *See* Native Americans
American Museum, of Barnum, P.T., 369
American party. *See* Know-Nothings
American Red Cross, 470
American Revolution. *See* Revolutionary War
"American Scholar, The" (Emerson), 364
American Sunday School Union, 320
American System, 293
American Temperance society, 321
American Universalist Church, 254
American Woman's Home, The (Stowe), 556
American Woman Suffrage Association (AWSA), 539
America Triumphant and Britannia in Distress, 201
Ames, Adelbert, 559
Amherst, Jeffery, 133
Amish, 122
Amistad (ship), 370
Amity and Commerce, Treaty of, 176
Amnesty program, of Johnson, Andrew, 525–526
Amsterdam, 55
Anabaptists, 35
Anaconda Plan, 463, 466, 475
Anasazi people, 11
Anderson, Robert, Fort Sumter and, 453, 454
Andersonville, Georgia, prisoner of war camp in, 509–510, *509*
Andros, Edmund, 90, *90*
Anglican Church, after revolution, 195–196
Anglicans, 35, 58, 117
  church membership and, 117
  English Civil War and, 67
Anglo-America. *See also* Colonies and colonization; England (Britain)
  impressment in, 130
Anglo-Dutch War
  first, 68
  second, 70
  third, 70
Animals, Native Americans and, 8–9
Annapolis convention, 208
Anne (ship), 124
Annexation
  Dominican Republic and, 543
  of Texas, 353, 384
Antarctica, 382
Antebellum period. *See also* North; South
  culture in, 361–370
  race, slavery, and politics in, 405–417
Anthony, Susan B., 538, *539,* 552, 563
Antietam Creek, battle at, 489–490
Antifederalists, 213–217
  Bill of Rights and, 226
  Lee, Richard Henry, as, 213
Antigua (slave), 182
Anti-Itinerancy Act (Connecticut), 120
Anti-Masons, 328